THE ROUTLEDGE HANDBOOK
OF GLOBAL ETHICS

Global ethics focuses on the most pressing contemporary ethical issues – poverty, global trade, terrorism, torture, pollution, climate change and the management of scarce resources. It draws on moral and political philosophy, political and social science, empirical research, and real world policy and activism. *The Routledge Handbook of Global Ethics* brings together leading international scholars to present concise and authoritative overviews of the most significant issues and ideas in global ethics. The chapters are structured into six key parts:

- normative theory
- conflict and violence
- poverty and development
- economic justice
- bioethics and health justice
- environment and climate ethics.

Covering the theoretical and practical aspects of global ethics as well as policy, the *Handbook* provides a benchmark for the study of global ethics to date, as well as outlining future developments. It will prove an invaluable reference for policy-makers and for students and scholars in philosophy, international relations, political science, environmental and development studies and human rights law.

Darrel Moellendorf is Professor of International Political Theory at Goethe University, Frankfurt.

Heather Widdows is Professor of Global Ethics and Director of the Centre for the Study of Global Ethics at the University of Birmingham.

Routledge Handbooks in Applied Ethics

Applied ethics is one of the largest and most diverse fields in philosophy and is closely related to many other disciplines across the humanities, sciences and social sciences. *Routledge Handbooks in Applied Ethics* are state-of-the-art surveys of important and emerging topics in applied ethics, providing accessible yet thorough assessments of key fields, themes, thinkers and recent developments in research.

All chapters for each volume are specially commissioned, and written by leading scholars in the field. Carefully edited and organized, *Routledge Handbooks in Applied Ethics* provide indispensable reference tools for students and researchers seeking a comprehensive overview of new and exciting topics in applied ethics and related disciplines. They are also valuable teaching resources as accompaniments to textbooks, anthologies, and research-oriented publications.

The Routledge Handbook of Global Ethics
Edited by Darrel Moellendorf and Heather Widdows

Forthcoming:

The Routledge Handbook of Food Ethics
Edited by Mary Rawlinson

THE ROUTLEDGE
HANDBOOK OF
GLOBAL ETHICS

Edited by Darrel Moellendorf and Heather Widdows

Routledge
Taylor & Francis Group

LONDON AND NEW YORK

First published 2015
by Routledge
2 Park Square, Milton Park, Abingdon, Oxon OX14 4RN

and by Routledge
711 Third Avenue, New York, NY 10017
Routledge is an imprint of the Taylor & Francis Group, an informa business

© 2015 Darrel Moellendorf and Heather Widdows, selection and editorial
matter; individual chapters, the contributors

The right of Darrel Moellendorf and Heather Widdows to be identified as
the authors of the editorial matter, and of the individual authors for their
contributions, has been asserted in accordance with sections 77 and 78 of
the Copyright, Designs and Patents Act 1988.

Trademark notice: Product or corporate names may be trademarks or
registered trademarks, and are used only for identification and explanation
without intent to infringe.

British Library Cataloguing in Publication Data
A catalogue record for this book is available from the British Library

Library of Congress Cataloguing-in-Publication Data
A catalog record for this title has been applied for

ISBN: 978-1-844-65637-0 (hbk)
ISBN: 978-1-315-74452-0 (ebk)

Typeset in Bembo
by Taylor & Francis books

Printed and bound in the United States of America by Publishers Graphics,
LLC on sustainably sourced paper.

CONTENTS

Contents

CONTRIBUTORS

Chris Armstrong is Professor of Political Theory at the University of Southampton, where his current work focuses on issues of global justice, especially as regards natural resources. He is the author of *Global Distributive Justice* (2012), and is working on a book defending a global egalitarian theory of natural resource justice.

Richard J. Arneson holds the Valtz Family Chair in Philosophy at University of California, San Diego, where he teaches moral and political philosophy, and he has an affiliation with the Center for the Philosophy of Freedom at the University of Arizona. He is the author of "Discrimination, Disparate Impact, and Theories of Justice", in *Philosophical Foundations of Discrimination Law* (ed. Moreau & Hellman, 2014), "Paternalism and the Principle of Fairness", in *Paternalism: Theory and Practice* (ed. Coons & Weber, 2013) and "Rethinking Luck Egalitarianism and Unacceptable Inequalities", *Philosophical Topics* (2012).

Barrie Axford is Professor of Politics and Director of the Centre for Global Politics, Economy and Society at Oxford Brookes University UK. He is a member of the Executive Board of the Global Studies Association and serves on the editorial boards of the journals *Globalizations, Telematics and Informatics, International Journal of Electronic Governance* and *Reinvention* and *Journal of Undergraduate Research*. His books include *The Global System: Politics, Economics and Culture* (1996), *Cultures and/of Globalization* (2011) and most recently *Theories of Globalization* (2013).

Christian Barry is the Director of the Centre for Moral, Social, and Political Theory. His recent work includes *International Trade and Labour Standards: A Proposal for Linkage* (with Sanjay Reddy, 2008) and essays in *Philosophy and Public Affairs, Journal of Political Philosophy, Review of International Studies, International Affairs, Cornell International Law Journal* and the *Journal of Applied Philosophy*.

Alex J. Bellamy is Professor of International Security at Griffith University, Australia, Non-Resident Senior Adviser at the International Peace Institute, New York and Honorary Professor of International Relations at the University of Queensland, where he serves as Director (International) of the Asia Pacific Centre for the Responsibility to Protect. His most recent book is

Massacres and Morality: Mass Atrocities in an Age on Civilian Immunity (2012) and he will shortly publish *The Responsibility to Protect: A Defence* (forthcoming).

Andrew Brennan is Professor of Philosophy at La Trobe University. He is the author of many papers and book chapters, the most recent of which are "Globalisation and the Environment: Endgame or New Renaissance?", in *Reconceiving Environmental Values* (Paavola & Lowe [eds], 2005) and "Poverty, Puritanism and Environmental Conflict", in *Environmental Philosophy: Critical Concepts in the Environment*, vol. 4 (ed. Callicott & Palmer, 2004).

Gillian Brock is Associate Professor of Philosophy at the University of Aukland, New Zealand. She is the author or editor of many books, including *Global Justice: A Cosmopolitan Account* (2009).

Roger Brownsword has appointments at King's College London and Bournemouth University and is an Honorary Professor at the University of Sheffield, and a Visiting Professor at Singapore Management University. His many books include *Human Dignity in Bioethics and Biolaw* (with Deryck Beyleveld, 2001) and *Rights, Regulation and the Technological Revolution* (2008), and he is currently co-editing both the *Cambridge Handbook on Human Dignity* (2014) and the *Oxford Handbook on Law, Regulation and Technology* (forthcoming).

Alastair V. Campbell is Professor of Medical Ethics and the Director of the Centre for Biomedical Ethics in the Yong Loo Lin School of Medicine of the National University of Singapore. His recent books include *Medical Ethics* (with D. G. Jones & G. Gillet, 3rd edn, 2005), *The Body in Bioethics* (2009) and *Bioethics: The Basics* (2013).

Simon Caney is Professor in Political Theory at the University of Oxford and Fellow and Tutor at Magdalen College. He is the author of *Justice Beyond Borders* (2005), *Global Justice and Climate Change* (with Derek Bell, forthcoming) and *On Cosmopolitanism* (forthcoming), and a co-editor of *Climate Ethics* (with Stephen Gardiner, Dale Jamieson & Henry Shue, 2010).

Ruth Chadwick directed the ESRC Centre for Economic and Social Aspects of Genomics (Cesagen) (2002–13). She is editor in chief of *Encyclopedia of Applied Ethics* (2012), and author of "Epigenetics and Personalized Medicine: Prospects and Ethical Issues", *Personalized Medicine* (with Alan O'Connor, 2013) and "The Communitarian Turn: Myth or Reality?", *Cambridge Quarterly of Health Care Ethics* (2011). She also co-edits *Bioethics* and *Life Sciences, Society and Policy*.

Julian Culp is a postdoctoral fellow in the Leibniz research group "Transnational Justice" at the Goethe University of Frankfurt. He is a co-editor of the journal *Global Justice: Theory Practice Rhetoric* and the author of *Global Justice and Development* (forthcoming).

Nigel Dower is Honorary Senior Lecturer in Philosophy at the University of Aberdeen. He is the author of *World Ethics: The New Agenda* (1998).

Sarah Fine is a Lecturer in Philosophy at King's College London. She is the author of *Immigration and the Right to Exclude* (2014) and co-editor of *Migration in Political Theory: The Ethics of Movement and Membership* (with Lea Ypi, 2014).

Rainer Forst is Professor of Political Theory and Philosophy at the Goethe University Frankfurt am Main, Co-Director of the Research Cluster on the "Formation of Normative Orders" at the Centre for Advanced Studies "Justitia Amplificata" and Member of the Directorate of the Institute for Advanced Study in the Humanities in Bad Homburg. He is the author of *Contexts of Justice* (1994), *Toleration in Conflict* (2003), *The Right to Justification* (2007) and *Justification and Critique* (2011).

Hille Haker holds the Richard McCormick S. J. Endowed Chair of Catholic Moral Theology at Loyola University Chicago. She is co-editor of the international journal *Concilium*, the author of *Ethik der genetischen Frühdiagnostik* (2002) and *Hauptsache gesund* (2011), and co-editor of *The Ethics of Genetics in Human Procreation* (2000) and *Medical Ethics in Health Care Chaplaincy* (2009).

Benjamin S. Hale is Associate Professor in the Philosophy Department and the Environmental Studies Program at the University of Colorado, Boulder and Vice President of the International Society for Environmental Ethics. He is the author of "Clowning Around with Conservatism: Adaptation, Reparation, and the New Substitution Problem", *Environmental Values* (with Adam Hermans & Alexander Lee, 2014), "What is the Future of Conservatism?", *Trends in Ecology and Evolution* (with Daniel F. Doak, Victoria Bakker & Bruce Evan Goldstein, 2014), and "Can We Remediate Wrongs", in *Consequentialism and Environmental Ethics* (ed. Hillier, Ilea & Kahn, 2013), and is also the co-editor of the journal *Ethics, Policy and Environment* (with Andrew Light).

Nicole Hassoun is Associate Professor in Philosophy at Binghamton University. She is the author of *Globalization and Global Justice: Shrinking Distance, Expanding Obligations* (2012).

Virginia Held is Distinguished Professor of Philosophy at the City University of New York, Graduate School, and Professor Emerita at Hunter College. She is the author of *The Ethics of Care: Personal, Political, and Global* (2006), *The Public Interest and Individual Interests* (1970) and *Rights and Goods: Justifying Social Action* (1984).

Nien-hê Hsieh is an Associate Professor of Business Administration in the General Management Unit at Harvard Business School. His work has been published in a variety of journals, including *Business Ethics Quarterly*, *Economics and Philosophy*, *Journal of Political Philosophy*, *Philosophy and Public Affairs*, *Social Theory and Practice* and *Utilitas*.

Peter Jones is Emeritus Professor of Political Philosophy at Newcastle University, UK. He is the author of *Rights* (1994) and editor of *Human Rights and Global Diversity* (with Simon Caney, 2001) and of *Group Rights* (2009). As well as examining various aspects of rights, his published work has ranged over a number of subjects, including toleration, recognition, cultural diversity, discrimination law, democracy, freedom of expression, neutrality, international justice and the nature of liberalism.

Meena Krishnamurthy is Assistant Professor in the Department of Philosophy and an Associate Director of the Centre for Professional and Applied Ethics at the University of Manitoba. Her publications include "Completing Rawls's Arguments for Equal Political Liberty and its Fair Value: The Argument from Self-Respect", *Canadian Journal of Philosophy* (2013); "Reconceiving Rawls's Arguments for Equal Political Liberty and its Fair Value: On our Higher-Order Interests", *Social Theory and Practice* (2012); and "Justice in Global Pandemic

Influenza Preparedness: An Analysis Based on the Values of Contribution, Ownership, and Reciprocity", *Public Health Ethics* (with Matthew Herder, 2013).

Douglas P. Lackey is Professor of Philosophy at Baruch College and the Graduate Center, City University of New York. He is the author of *Moral Principles and Nuclear Weapons* (1984), *The Ethics of War and Peace* (1989) and *Ethics and Strategic Defense* (1989).

Norva Y. S. Lo is a Lecturer in the Philosophy Department of La Trobe University. Recent publications include *Understanding Environmental Philosophy* (Acumen, 2010), and essays in *Hume on Is and Ought* (ed. C. R. Pigden, 2010) and *The Routledge Companion to Ethics* (ed. J. Skorupski, 2010).

Graham Long is Senior Lecturer in Politics at Newcastle University, UK. He is currently writing *Global Justice and Global Diversity*, for publication in early 2015.

Hennie Lötter is Professor of Philosophy at the University of Johannesburg, South Africa. Among his books are *Justice for an Unjust Society* (1993), *Injustice, Violence and Peace: The Case of South Africa* (1997) and *Poverty, Ethics and Justice* (2011).

Darrel Moellendorf is Professor of International Political Theory and Professor of Philosophy at Johann Wolfgang Universität Frankfurt am Main. He is the author of *Cosmopolitan Justice* (2002), *Global Inequality Matters* (2009) and *The Moral Challenge of Dangerous Climate Change: Values, Poverty, and Policy* (2014).

Tim Mulgan is Professor of Philosophy at the University of Auckland, and Professor of Moral and Political Philosophy at the University of St Andrews. He is the author of *Future People* (2006), *Understanding Utilitarianism* (2007) and *Ethics for a Broken World* (Acumen, 2011).

Julia O'Connell Davidson is Professor of Sociology at the University of Nottingham, UK. Her most recent published paper is "Troubling Freedom: Migration, Debt, and Modern Slavery", *Migration Studies* (2013). She is also the author of *Children in the Global Sex Trade* (2005) and "New Slavery, Old Binaries: Human Trafficking and the Borders of 'Freedom'", *Global Networks* (2010).

Alan O'Connor is a barrister practising in Ireland. He worked as a research assistant at the ESRC Centre for Economic and Social Aspects of Genomics (Cesagen – now Cesagene) at Cardiff University from 2011 to 2013. He is the author of "Epigenetics and Personalized Medicine: Prospects and Ethical Issues", *Personalized Medicine* (with Ruth Chadwick, 2013).

John O'Neill is Director of the Political Economy Institute. He is on the editorial boards of a number of journals including *New Political Economy*, *Journal of Applied Philosophy* and *Historical Materialism*. His publications include *Ecology, Policy and Politics: Human Well-Being and the Natural World* (1993), *The Market: Ethics, Knowledge and Politics* (1998) and *Markets, Deliberation and Environment* (2007).

Brian Orend is the Director of International Studies and Professor of Philosophy at the University of Waterloo in Canada. He is the author of *The Morality of War* (2nd edn, 2013) and *Introduction to International Studies* (2013).

Andrea Sangiovanni is Senior Lecturer in the Department of Philosophy, King's College London. Recent publications include "The Irrelevance of Coercion, Imposition and Framing to Distributive Justice", *Philosophy and Public Affairs* (2012) and "Solidarity in the European Union", *Oxford Journal of Legal Studies* (2013). He is the author of *Domains of Justice* (forthcoming).

Udo Schüklenk holds the Ontario Research Chair in Bioethics and Public Policy at Queen's University in Canada. He is a joint editor-in-chief of *Bioethics*, the official publication of the International Association of Bioethics. His most recent book is *50 Great Myths About Atheism* (with Russell Blackford, 2013).

Henry Shue is Senior Research Fellow of the Centre for International Studies of the Department of Politics and International Relations, University of Oxford, and Professor Emeritus of International Relations and Senior Research Fellow Emeritus of Merton College, Oxford. He is the author of *Basic Rights: Subsistence, Affluence, and US Foreign Policy* (2nd edn, 1996) and *Climate Justice: Vulnerability and Protection* (2014). He previously discussed torture in "Torture", *Philosophy and Public Affairs* (1978) and "Torture in Dreamland: Disposing of the Ticking Bomb", *Case Western Reserve Journal of International Law* (2006).

Ricardo Smalling is a PhD candidate at Queen's University in Kingston Ontario. He is the co-author of "Queer Patients and the Health Care Professional – Regulatory Arrangements Matter", *Journal of Medical Humanities* (with Udo Schüklenk, 2013).

Teck Chuan Voo is Research Associate at the National University of Singapore, Centre for Biomedical Ethics. He has published in various bioethical areas including organ transplantation, medical ethics education, research ethics, and public health. His recent works include "Altruism and Reward: Motivational Compatibility in Deceased Organ Donation", *Bioethics* (2014), "Organs as Inheritable Property?", *Journal of Medical Ethics* (with S. Holm, 2014) and "The Social Rationale of the Gift Relationship", *Journal of Medical Ethics* (2011).

Florian Wettstein is Professor and Chair in Business Ethics and Director of the Institute for Business Ethics at University of St Gallen in Switzerland. He is the author of *Multinational Corporations and Global Justice: Human Rights Obligations of a Quasi-Governmental Institution* (2009).

Heather Widdows is John Ferguson Professor of Global Ethics. She is the author of *Global Ethics: An Introduction* (Acumen, 2011) and *The Connected Self: The Ethics and Governance of the Genetic Individual* (2013), and co-editor of *Global Social Justice* (with Nicola Smith, 2011) and *Women's Reproductive Rights* (with Itziar Alkorta Idiakez & Aitziber Emaldi Cirión, 2006).

Scott Wisor is Lecturer in the Department of Philosophy and Deputy Director of the Centre for the Study of Global Ethics at the University of Birmingham. He has published on international trade, the resource curse, social valuation, feminist methodology, and other topics in global ethics. He is the author of *Measuring Global Poverty: Toward a Pro-Poor Approach* (2012), "Property Rights and the Resource Curse: A Reply to Wenar", *Journal of Philosophical Research* (2012) and "The Moral Problem of Worse Actors", *Ethics and Global Politics* (forthcoming).

1

INTRODUCTION

Darrel Moellendorf and Heather Widdows

The *Handbook* is the first volume to attempt comprehensively to map the current state of play of global ethics and to say something about possible futures, academically and in terms of policy and practice.

Global ethics is a discipline, field, area of study or approach that responds to the most pressing contemporary global challenges. These challenges are many and varied, and include the challenges of climate change; pressure on scarce resources (including food, clean water and aid, land and drugs); conflict, war and terrorism; health threats, such as pandemics and the depletion of effective drugs; the movement of people, goods, services and information; and, perhaps most importantly, continued poverty of the majority of the world's population and extreme poverty of significant numbers. Global ethicists seek to respond to such challenges comprehensively and at all levels: from theory to policy to practice. Global ethicists engage in theoretical discussion about the nature of global justice and the good life, conceptions of which are necessary if we are to know what it would be for people to flourish and be respected, and for us to know when justice has, in fact, been done. In addition to developing overarching theory, global ethicists also seek to engage theoretically with the topical issues and responses, for instance, providing theories about ethical responses to particular challenges and assessing, ethically and politically, possible solutions. In this manner global ethicists are concerned directly with policy assessment, development and promotion. Likewise, global ethicists are eager to connect theory and policy to real-world practice and to impact and affect the lives of real individuals.

Given the breadth of global ethics, in terms of the topics it covers and the levels at which it works (theory, policy and practice), global ethics is necessarily multidisciplinary. It draws on moral and political philosophy, political and social science, empirical research, and real-world policy and activism. For global ethicists to engage with contemporary dilemmas they must understand the nature of the topics involved, and this requires expertise beyond the typical moral and political philosophical training of most ethicists. Accordingly, global ethicists cannot be "armchair" philosophers but must engage with experts of other disciplines – including economists, lawyers, development experts, sociologists – and be empirically informed, which means that, as well as knowing the relevant scientific and social-scientific data and theories, they often also work with practitioners, activists and policy-makers. This is demanding, as it requires far more knowledge and engagement than is standardly required of ethicists. But those who fail to do this will produce irrelevant or misguided theories, proposals and analysis. It is for this reason that the commitment of global ethics to multidisciplinarity has been termed fundamental and substantial, and not merely a contingent commitment, and it is methodologically defining of global ethics and one of its distinctive features.[1]

To address contemporary global challenges *The Handbook of Global Ethics* brings together leading international scholars to present concise and authoritative overviews of the most significant issues and ideas in global ethics. Among the scholars who have contributed to this volume are those who have shaped, dominated and developed the areas of their specialties, as well as those who have spearheaded changes to policy and practice in response to their theories. Individually and collectively, the contributors of this volume are impressive and show just how engaged global ethicists are across the extensive field which constitutes global ethics. The contribution that these thinkers have had should not be underestimated. The hope is that global ethicists will continue to develop theories which are academically robust and discipline shaping, but which are also of policy and practice import.

The volume begins with an empirical account of globalization by Barrie Axford. This introduces the reader to the context, which gives rise to the normative discussion in the subsequent six parts. Each of these parts represents a core area of global ethics. The first part focuses on the theoretical structures within which global ethics is done and on theories from which global ethics draws. Included in this part are discussions of ethical theory, theories of justice, human rights, universalism, cosmopolitanism and gender justice. Each of the following five sections addresses a key area of global ethics. Part II is devoted to conflict and violence. It has chapters on the ethics of war, torture, humanitarian intervention and finally on nuclear proliferation and containment. Part III, concerning poverty and development, has four chapters, on poverty, development, aid and charity, and immigration. Part IV addresses economic justice, with chapters on international trade, international finance, multinational corporations, consumption, trafficking and distributive institutions. The fifth part focuses on bioethics and health justice, with four chapters on research, body part trade, reproductive rights and patenting. The sixth part of the volume addresses climate ethics, with five chapters on climate change, pollution, sustainability, biodiversity and population ethics. Each of these sections begins with an introduction, which serves to map the topic, to explore how the topic connects to wider global ethics theorizing and how it is interconnected with other topics, as well as to introduce the particular chapters in the section.

We turn now to a brief summary of Axford's chapter. Axford begins by describing the two main understandings of globalization – globalization as interconnectivity and globalization as institutionalization – and the problems and criticisms of these positions. He suggests that whatever one's view of the extent of globalization or the most important features of it (economic, social, cultural or political), "current signs all seem to suggest a world at once more interconnected and independent and yet in woeful turmoil." Yet he also argues that historically there are stable long-term tendencies towards integration. To examine this complex picture Axford explores eight trends in turn, the first being that of "closer integration of the world economy." Economic globalization is often taken as the most obvious and least contested aspect of globalization; for instance, at state level it is virtually impossible to avoid participation in the global economic system. However, as Axford points out, this is not a linear process; power has shifted over the past millennium and may well shift again. Currently notable is the significance of emerging economies to the extent that "it may not be too far-fetched to claim that for the next couple of decades emerging and developing economies will constitute the main driver of global integration and global growth".

The second trend is the "crisis of the liberal global order." The recent and ongoing financial crisis brings into question previous assumptions about the stability of global economic liberalism.

Uncertainty surrounds not just the macroeconomic system, but also the sustainability of natural resources (addressed in detail in Chapter 29). The third trend is the current move to more flexible models for labour and production. These changes are responses both to the changing requirements of the global market, as outsourcing of production and labour becomes standard, and to the development of new technologies. The fourth trend Axford describes as the "cultural economy of speed," by which he means the growth and reliance on global information and communication systems; systems that transform understandings of borders, time and connectivity. The fifth (and connected) trend concerns media and consumption, which is transformative of cultural connections and identities, although Axford cautions against asserting globally shared cultures. The sixth concerns the relationship between democracy and globalization. Axford suggests that, despite its ideological baggage, democracy is an index of globalization and one which is significant in considering the changes of the last few years. The penultimate trend is towards global governance. Global governance institutions, while in some ways thin institutions, are now established to the extent that it is almost impossible to imagine many actions by states without a global element (for explicit examples see Chapter 12 on nuclear proliferation; Chapter 17 on international trade; Chapter 18 on financial institutions; Chapter 26 on patents; and Chapter 27 on climate change; and most chapters demonstrate this implicitly). The final trend Axford maps concerns world society. He suggests three sub-trends that suggest a global consciousness is emerging.

In closing we would like to thank Daniel Callies for the great help that he provided in preparing the manuscript and Herjeet Marway for her stirling work in editing and proof reading the final drafts. Their efforts are very much appreciated.

Note

1 Elsewhere the key features of global ethics have been defined as being (a) global in scope, (b) multi-disciplinary and (c) connecting theory and practice (Widdows 2011).

2

THE TRENDS AND TENDENCIES OF GLOBAL INTEGRATION

Barrie Axford

At one remove globalization is a simple concept embracing two processes that are sometimes, but not always, related. These processes are interconnectivity and institutionalization. Of course, there is also the little matter of consciousness: the awareness by actors of global constraints and, as Roland Robertson (1992) rather delicately puts it, their propensity to "identify with" the global condition in one way or another. For the most part other literature concurs. Thus, John Tomlinson talks about the "complex, accelerating, integrating process of global connectivity ... (a) rapidly developing and ever densening [*sic*] network of inter-connections and interdependencies" (2003: 270). He later uses the telling phrase that global flows and structures have become "ubiquitous in everyday experience" (2007: 30). These words carry a powerful charge, reminding us of the importance of the quotidian in making contested globality.

The sense of globalization as intensive and extensive connectivity abounds and can be found in work with quite different theoretical and ideological pretensions (Held *et al.* 1999). Jan–Aart Scholte's anthem to globalization as supra-territoriality is a prominent example (2005; see also Held *et al.* 1999), while Hardt and Negri's treatise on *Empire* (2000) and Manuel Castells's monumental trilogy on *The Information Age* ([1996] 2000, [1998] 2000, [1997] 2004) both traffic the image of a networked, de-centred and de-territorialized world of capitalism as a rejection of orthodox Marxism and state-centric models of international political economy. In all these accounts globalization appears as a form of intensified and increasingly extensive exchange, and or a process involving the diffusion of worldwide institutional rules and standards or cultural scripts. George Modelski and his colleagues (2008) underscore the sense of globalization as the emergence of institutions and networks of planetary scope and, crucially, point to its multi-dimensional character. This insight also directs us to treat globalization in all facets of social life, within and across the realms of economics, politics and culture, and not just as an exogenous force sufficient to meld all identities.

All of this is at a rather high level of generality and couched thus is quite anodyne. So too is the notion of globalization as the process by which the world is being compressed through new constructions of space and time, in David Harvey's neat encapsulation (Harvey 1989). Yet the real charge in Harvey's idea is that social relations and identities are being reconfigured on a world scale and that such changes result in the growth of a modal global consciousness. In light of the subject matter of this volume, it is worth noting that consciousness may breed discontent, including ethical objections and/or physical opposition to particular facets of globalization, or to the process in general.

The very idea of globalization presumes integration, and this motif is especially visible in so-called hyper-globalist accounts and in some of those conveniently summarized as trans-formationalist (see Held *et al.* 1999). To be sure, sceptical opinion remains doubtful about the world-integrative power of globalizing forces, even in the economic realm (Hirst *et al.* 2009), and there is now much talk of de-globalization, as global capitalism is buffeted by the extended financial and trading crisis. These days no one takes too seriously the idea that the process of global integration constitutes a neat teleology whereby borders and the identities tied to them have become nugatory, and territoriality as the organizational basis for much political and economic life is in demise. At the same time students of globalization still have trouble with the intuitively implausible notion that it is a contradictory process, one that does not even imply, let alone require, "uniformization", in Francois Bayart's inelegant, but still expressive description (Bayart 2007).

Caricatured and otherwise jaundiced accounts of globalization cavil at the idea of globalization as in some way indeterminate, because of the need to demonstrate homogeneity as a necessary outcome of the process. For in its absence, runs the sceptical argument, any globalization hypothesis must fail. To be sure, some critics of globalization do see an unremitting and explicitly regressive pattern of homogenization, damaging to diversity and locality, as well as being morally reprehensible when linked to patterns of deepening inequality and the failure of beyond-the-state governance to realize a more benign world order. But the balance of research findings tends to the counterintuitive and vaguely unsatisfactory conclusion that globalization implies and delivers the simultaneous production of sameness and difference.

All of which makes the notion of global integration central to the narrative about to unfold, but also one that is very difficult for the social-scientific observer. Difficult in that while it should muster as a purely empirical concept that is readable from a set of measurable indicators, it also carries a heavy normative burden. Moreover, the latter may be of greater weight in any reckoning of the impacts of globalization; especially in judgements about its progressive or regressive character. In this respect, it is not just a matter of weighing the consequences of variably intensive and extensive forms of global integration; it is also a judgement about how, or whether, globalization disrupts what Nancy Fraser (2008) calls "hegemonic frames" and, of especial interest in a book on global ethics, whether such changes alter both the quality of justice available to diverse actors and the sites at which it is meted out.

Fraser is exercised mainly by the question of how and for whom justice is served. Is another, better world of global justice possible, and is it being forged? She contends that in a period of intensive global integration, at the very least, the mapping of political space is more contested than ever and the hegemonic frame of the international system of states and national economies in some disarray. With this in mind, her own interests lie in the framing of social justice, where the issue of which mapping of political space is truly just and who counts as a *bona fide* subject of justice – citizens of territories or transnational "communities of risk", as she has it – are the key questions for analysts (*ibid.*: 4).

These are indeed important questions, even if one does not support a transformationalist position on globalization. Current signs all seem to suggest a world at once more interconnected and interdependent and yet in woeful turmoil. We are living through a crisis that is certainly economic and increasingly one of legitimation. The United States seems trapped in political deadlock and its position as the guarantor of liberal internationalism and Western modernity feels distinctly shaky. Europe (at least the EU) is in parlous financial health and in some danger of fragmentation. China and the other BRICs are on the rise, and the balance of world economic power is undergoing a seismic shift.

The crisis, however construed, is itself a measure of the trammels of interdependence; of risks without boundaries, and thus of globalization (Beck & Sznaider 2006). Beck and Sznaider write quite convincingly about the raft of "interdependency crises" that both threaten and are the product of a more integrated world. They include the aforementioned crisis in the global financial economy, and also global warming, terrorism, pandemics and over-population. Because of these hazards – though still counterintuitively – crisis phenomena may reinforce the sense of unremitting global integration, or else highlight its effects, albeit in pathological guise. The very speed of contagion heightens the awareness of risks incurred through globalization (World Economic Forum 2011).

But in historical perspective, is the real narrative of the era actually the reverse; not epochal change and dislocation, but stability; in other words is there a secular integrative tendency, and what does that mean? To address these and other issues we need to interrogate the currents and trends in global integration more fully and begin to identify some of their normative implications. Implicit in what follows is a set of antinomies that make up the dialectic of globalization. These include the tension between networks and borders that lies at the heart of globalization as an integrative process; the playing out of convergence and divergence as forces shaping world (dis)order; the extent of stability or continuity versus evidence of dislocation; and finally, the matter of consciousness – whether the global is now the primary frame of reference for both situated and mobile actors.

The extent and intensity of global integration will be examined by way of eight trends, each of which is no more than a catch-all for a set of cognate issues and themes. The trends – each contestable – are:

- closer integration of the world economy;
- crisis in the liberal global order;
- the transformation of production systems and labour markets;
- the cultural economy of speed;
- the media revolution and consumerism;
- the spread of democracy as a global script;
- the changing quality of global governance; and finally,
- the making of world society and global consciousness.

Before we commence, a word of caution is necessary. If globalization is a contradictory process, it is also non-linear. Periods of intense globalization have been followed by disruptions to the pattern of global integration; current globalization is unlike earlier manifestations and, as George Ritzer (2010) says, globalization is always a variable process; in some respects it flows, while in others it does little more than hop. If it is planetary in scope, parts of the globe are significantly less integrated, and less beneficially enjoined, than others. It is also a process mediated by actors of various hues, who "identify" with the global condition out of different traditions, identities and interests. We will start with, and spend more time on, the economy, because for many commentators it remains the touchstone for globalizing trends.

Closer integration of the world economy

A World Bank report published in 2011 makes the hardly contentious point that, in the second decade of the twenty-first century, sweeping changes are in train. Not all of these changes are driven by crisis conditions, nor do they all constitute hazards in the way Beck and Sznaider describe. At the same time they underline our previous observation that the pattern of global integration is certainly non-linear and may not be cyclical either, if by that is meant the unfolding of a hegemonic cycle or the reproduction of a simple core–periphery model of global political economy. Although it is certainly tempting to interpret what is happening as the playing out of a cycle of global economic integration, wherein one preponderant power is being replaced by another – with the US giving way to China – as we shall see, the reality is somewhat more complex. This is not to say that the global map of economic power has not shifted over the previous millennium, or that it will not shift again in the coming decades. Before the rise and spread of Western modernity, China and India were the world's dominant growth poles. Western European – principally British – and then American commercial and industrial capitalisms succeeded them. Germany and Japan played the role of at least regional hegemons from the mid-1960s to the early 1990s.

There is, however, another trend increasingly apparent over these post-war decades, and that is the growing multi-polarity of the global economy. The distribution of economic growth is becoming more dispersed, and because of this trend, no one country or region now dominates, or is likely to in the foreseeable future (World Bank 2011). As we know, the world economic and security order from the 1960s to the turn of the millennium was a product of the American worldview and, for much of that period, subsisted in a geo-economic environment framed by the Cold War. Spheres of influence politics extended to the ways in which regional allies of the US underwrote economic arrangements beneficial to American interests. These included maintaining the position of the dollar as the most widely used international reserve currency and ensuring its centrality in the world monetary system. But even during this period of American preponderance, there were signs of fragmentation. Ending the gold exchange standard in 1971 was the catalyst for many countries to float their currencies, the launch and the early success of the Euro provided an alternative haven for foreign exchange holdings, and there was a partial reversal of the north–south pattern of capital flows. These are all indicators of the longer-term rebalancing of the world economy.

The current driver in this rebalancing is the relative success of emerging economies in terms of production for international markets, trade and finance. Emerging and developing countries' share of international trade flows has risen from about 26 per cent in the mid-1990s to about 46 per cent in 2010 (*ibid.*). More than a third of foreign direct investment (FDI) in developing countries actually originates in other developing nations, not from northern or western sources. Where previously, advanced economies held over two-thirds of all foreign exchange reserves, the situation now is that some three-quarters of such reserves are to be found in emerging and developing economies. Sovereign wealth funds held by these countries have become a crucial source of international investment and, of course, it was Chinese investment capital that provided the wherewithal for the reckless sub-prime mortgage boom, first in the US, then elsewhere. These changes put a particular gloss on the notion and pattern of global economic integration. Indeed, it may not be too far-fetched to claim that for the next couple of decades emerging and developing economies will constitute the main driver of global integration and global growth. It is estimated that by 2030, at the latest, the total real output of six key emerging economies, the so-called BRIICKs (Brazil, Russia, India, Indonesia, China and South Korea), will at least match that of the Eurozone, and given the latter's short-term prospects for any sort of growth, this state of affairs may occur even earlier (*ibid.*).

Should they be realized, such changes would testify to a pattern of marked convergence. For example, in the same time-span the share of global trade accounted for by emerging economies and their more advanced counterparts will converge. By the middle of the 2020s this is likely to result in a roughly 50–50 balance, a considerable change from the current situation wherein advanced economies account for the majority of imports and exports. Moreover, sustained growth in the BRIICKs and probably also the CIVETS economies (Colombia, Indonesia again, Vietnam, Egypt, Turkey and South Africa; see Geoghegan 2010) will entrench global economic multi-polarity. Of course, none of this is certain. Dynamic emerging economies will still need to undergo quite dramatic structural changes to underpin modernization and, as always, that will be a fraught process, which may have adverse, as well as galvanizing, effects on those societies. Even the pace-setters in the race for economic growth are beset by huge internal inequalities and disparities in the quality of practical citizenship available to their people. The future of the Eurozone as a growth pole is in doubt, and signs of legitimation crisis are apparent in the response of domestic populations to austerity measures designed to stave off financial ruin, most obviously in Greece. Egypt might still not consolidate the early freedoms of the Arab Spring to take its place as a dynamic and modernized regional economy.

Crisis in the liberal global order

That said, evidence of rebalancing and convergence still goes some way to challenge, if not overturn, older models of world economic integration. These include theories of a systematic underdevelopment of countries in the global South; rigid core–periphery models of the world economic division of labour; and, as we have noted, those accounts that depict a world economic order comprised of an economic hegemon and sundry others. Instead, as Giovanni Arrighi (2007) suggests, in the first quarter of the new millennium, the world economy is increasingly characterized by the interaction of world markets, some organized on a regional basis, others spilling over into truly global networks involving technological and financial transfers, often specialized forms of migration and, of course, trade. All of which would seem to suggest a period of continued economic dynamism for the liberal global order. But are things that assured?

Inevitably, they are not. For one thing, the health of global economic liberalism and also its geopolitical stability cannot be assumed. Yet, writing in the journal *Millennium* in 2010, John Ikenberry was still reasonably sanguine, not just about its durability, but on the prospects for expansion. By this he meant an expanded "open, rule-based relations system organized around expanding forms of institutionalized cooperation" (2010: 6). His prediction rests on four claims. First, the contemporary liberal order is not dependent on US hegemony, but on cooperation between liberal democracies over the conditions of open trade and collective security. Second, the very openness and rule-driven nature of the liberal regime makes it easy to join, and this openness means that it is less reliant on the good offices of any one actor to make it work. Third, new powers, even proto-hegemonic ones, want to be part of the arrangement, rather than seeking to destroy it. Finally, for all the doom-laden talk about nuclear proliferation and the unpredictability of rogue states, it is clear that nuclear weapons and the dominance of democracies as possessors of these have made the past fifty years unparalleled as a period of "great power peace". He concedes that while American preponderance is diminishing, this is discommoding rather than terminal for the liberal global order.

In the wrack of the financial crisis and in light of what looks like the chronic parlous condition of global governance, these claims might appear a little sanguine. Using data for 2008–9, the KOF Index of Globalization (KOF Swiss Economic Institute 2011) notes that the pace of economic integration actually decelerated during 2008.[1] It is hard to judge whether this constitutes a seminal moment in the narrative of global economic integration since the early 1970s, or whether it is just another fluctuation in the fortunes of global capitalism, falling well within its tolerances. Certainly, previous events and interludes have had both galvanizing and debilitating consequences for economic convergence. The ending of the Cold War provided a fillip to more emphatic integration, while the bursting of the dot-com bubble and the fall-out from 9/11 both had deleterious consequences in the short term. A report on *Cross-Cutting Global Risks* produced for the World Economic Forum (WEF 2011) opines that the financial crisis has reduced global economic resilience and that geopolitical tensions and traumas are now making it increasingly difficult for governments and citizens to meet global challenges. Whether construed from a neo-Marxist standpoint (Callinicos 2010, Gills 2010) or couched in language more sympathetic to market liberalization (WEF 2011), the perceived risks are surprisingly similar.[2] They describe an interlocking set of crisis phenomena that are truly multidimensional. The indicators comprise a cluster of economic imbalances that have plagued the liberal economic order at least for the past half-decade. These imbalances include currency and fiscal crises, along with asset wealth disintegration caused by the tension between the growing clout of emerging economies and the high levels of debt troubling many advanced countries. Furthermore, savings and trade imbalances, both within and between countries, look increasingly fraught and unsustainable, as large parts of the world struggle with recession or the imminent threat of it.

Alongside these macroeconomic imbalances is growing evidence of risk to continuity of supply in key natural resources, notably energy, water and food. Demand for all of these essential commodities is likely to rise by 30–50 per cent in the first quarter of the century (WEF 2011). In themselves shortages and price rises in each of these sectors may precipitate periodic outbursts of civil unrest and possibly both intra- and inter-state conflicts. The impact of fiscal crisis, low growth and the deepening of economic disparities within and between countries, including some in the global North, have already triggered populist responses to the perceived ills of globalization and may produce further attempts at national retrenchment from global or regional integration. Without doing too much violence to the particularity of different national cases, we can interpret much of this as the playing out of risks associated with globalization. Clearly, some of the risks are linked to the process of rebalancing of the global economy, while others extend far beyond the current moment and the tendency to equate all dislocating phenomena as part of a crisis of capitalism or neo-liberalism (Gills 2010). In this respect the proliferation of capability in nuclear arms is a signal threat, especially where it is palpable, as in the current stand-off between Iran and Israel. Ikenberry's upbeat take on the stability of the geonuclear order looks somewhat less credible in this light. But taken together, do these risks constitute a crisis of the global order, sufficient to reverse secular integrative (and pacific) trends? To address that question, we need to address factors that are or may be less susceptible to the short-term vicissitudes of economic life.

The transformation of production systems and labour markets

The longer-term effect of globalization on the organization of industrial production has been to introduce smaller and more flexible production systems, where flexibility means rapid production cycles, along with computer-based design and accounting systems. Other changes involve new patterns of working, including part-time contracts, multi-skilling and de-unionization of the workforce. Some of these changes derive from the immediate impact of new technologies on the workplace, while the globalization of systems and practices owes much to the movement of investment capital around the world as foreign direct investment (FDI). Innovations in the ways in which firms conduct business have been made easier by the liberalization of controls on FDI and on the movement of capital in general, making it less costly to invest in other countries. Since the 1970s there has been a significant expansion in international production driven by multinational companies and dispersed across a growing number of countries. The present crisis has undoubtedly impacted on the pattern of FDI, so that by 2010 FDI flows were running some 15 per cent lower than pre-crisis levels (UNCTAD 2011).[3] However, trends suggest a return to pre-crisis levels of investment by 2013–14.

Fluctuations in international investment aside, two further globalization effects, each having systemic consequences, are worthy of comment. The first is not immune to the ravages of the present crisis, while the second may be vulnerable only contingently. The first effect is the impact of globalization on labour markets. In a globalized world where there is increased competition, labour markets need to be flexible. Flexibility is promoted best where there is a framework of rules that allows it to proceed while securing income and social and employment protection for workers (International Labour Office 2012). In advanced economies protection still remains at the heart of the employment system, but policy and practice have been pushed towards more flexibility by the ability to move investment capital – and thus jobs – around the world, by the shift from employment protection at company level towards collective social protection, and through the exigencies of the crisis. The result seems to be a chronic trade-off between employment and protection. Taken as a whole, the consequences for workers affected by recession/crisis will be long-term unemployment in a climate of opinion increasingly hostile to different kinds of welfare "feather-bedding". Moreover, people with poor education and weak job skills may face permanent/semi-permanent unemployment. The flip side of this picture is that those with skills in strong demand by employers in high-growth, high-tech industries will again become objects of the "global war for talent", just as they were before the present crisis hit home.[4]

The second globalization effect is also linked to the footloose nature of contemporary capital and business. This rootlessness takes many forms, including collaborative business models in activities such as trans-border outsourcing ("around-sourcing" as it is increasingly known) and supply chains. The latter constitute secular changes in the spatial organization of the global economy and the scalar processes at work there. In the past twenty years important shifts have taken place in the global economy and in its spatialization, such that it is now more clearly global than international. These shifts in the organization of economic activity turn on production processes largely, though by no means entirely, structured at the level of the firm, in relations between firms as producers and suppliers, and in the ways in which production is connected to processes of distribution and consumption through increasingly reflexive circuitry. The changes involve first, and at the most general level, *transnational production networks* (TPNs) and, second, the growing significance of *global value chains* (GVCs) (Dicken *et al.* 2001, Gereffi *et al.* 2005).[5]

Through networking, transnational firms increasingly show a single face to the world as they "around-source" supply and coordinate functions, often with competitor firms. Transnational companies have changed quite dramatically in the past few decades, outsourcing or around-sourcing many activities and developing strategic alliances with competitors. As a result, they have become less vertically integrated and more network-oriented. Better global standards in the realms of business processes and product specification, and the modal application of information technology in areas such as design, manufacturing, service provision, supply-chain coordination, and materials management, have enabled increased outsourcing in producer-driven chains and made it possible, even necessary, for firms to forge linkages between buyers and suppliers in both producer- and buyer-driven chains. All of which brings us nicely to our fourth indicator.

The cultural economy of speed

These developments can be seen as increments in the emergence of a world economy increasingly reliant on information systems and the opportunities they afford to construct global structures and "microstructures" built through various forms of scopic media (Knorr-Cetina 2007). Economic globalization entails a set of practices that de-constitute the national frame of action and reference and in this process the creation of digital architectures is of paramount importance (Sassen [2005] 2008). These architectures are modifying, possibly transforming, the routines and structures of economic and social life, as well as those of governance. The key point to bear in mind is the long-term significance for social practice that resides in the use of technologies whose key property challenges the very idea of place and of boundaries.[6] The whole cultural economy of speed, driven by advances in information and communication technologies, is one of the prime drivers of the global cultural economy.

Here we should advert Manuel Castells' notion of *timeless time*, which suggests that under conditions of globalization there has been a proliferation of social times (Castells 1991, [1997] 2004; Holton 2005). "Social" (rather than "natural", or singular) because, over history, different conceptions of time have been dominant depending on the prevailing social dynamics. Thus the advent of "clock time" heralded the birth of industrial modernity and both underpins and legitimates many of its social practices: the obsession with timetables, rule-governed workplace behaviour, positivist and linear assumptions about causation, and so on. The social character of time is altered markedly under globalization. Both cyclical and linear temporalities (features of the medieval and modern eras respectively) assumed a relatively predictable, sequential unfolding of events mediated, of course, by context, conditions and motivation. But "timeless time" introduces a new kind of temporality. Not only is time stretched and compressed, but it is "experienced disjunctively" (A. Jones 2010: 60), that is, through events or instances which may not have a sequential structure – or in other words, are unpredictable. Processes of globalization are at least closely linked with a "sense of virtually simultaneous or instantaneous time" (Holton 2005: 99), especially where they are driven by information technologies.

John Tomlinson makes much the same point in his discussion of the "culture of speed" (2007) and the changing social construction of speed, such that we have to distinguish between the "machine" speed of industrial modernity, the "unruly" speed of "living life in the fast lane" (which has such iconic status in the annals of cultural modernity) and the cultures of immediacy which so characterize the new millennium. Indeed, the main charge carried by the "culture of speed" motif is that information technologies and formats, especially those still labelled "new" media may actually frame how we engage with them and each other by promoting and embodying the value of speed, immediacy, interactivity and bespoke consumption as cultural aesthetics and almost as lifestyle imperatives.

The media revolution and consumerism

Of course, none of these developments can be read as implying a simple technological logic wherein the various attributes of digital media simply spill over into the transformation of social and cultural forms and practices. The increasingly widespread use of fast technologies and their status as avatars of an active life of consumption and communication are indicators of the growing mediatization of culture across the world. Indeed, there may be other, more profound, cultural consequences, in that the trend may also underscore the shift towards "networked individualism" as a trope for received models of society and how disembodied forms of interaction and integration contribute to its reproduction (Quan-Haase & Wellman 2004). Tomlinson also writes about the complete sense in which new media technologies and the aesthetics they express have been "domesticated" (2007: 81), absorbed into the fabric of living and thus made integral to how we conduct most aspects of social intercourse. In this respect, because they are so resolutely quotidian, their transformative impact on social intercourse and cultural production may be obscured.

The shift from "old" media culture to "new" media culture is an important but somewhat anodyne description of how these technologies and forms have been embraced in everyday lives.[7] Cell phones, DVDs, camcorders, digital TV and radio, TiVo and MP3 players, broadband, email, search engines, blogs and social media sites are not just means of communication and sources of information, but investments in culturally sanctioned lifestyle choices, and thus the stuff of mediatized and consumerized cultural economy. Moreover, media cultures frame consumer cultures that are rooted in the knowledge and information economies and delivered through creative industries.

Such cultures rely increasingly on "visual images, stylistic connotations and symbolic associations" (Knorr-Cetina 2007: 68) to promote product, while consumerization targets emotions and feelings of affect more than any other decisional or motivational factor. Much of this is cognate with the depiction of cultural media-scapes as part of global cultural flows that are fluid and irregular as they cross national and local boundaries. In such mediatized cultures the Web is only one facet of the systematic mediatization of culture now observed – variably – across the world. It is, of course, an increasingly important facet when assessing the impact of digitized connectivity on the conjoint globalization and individualization or personalization of communication and consumption. John Tomlinson's larger project concerns the ways in which the modern culture of speed – an eminently modern construct – is being superseded, at least in the global West, by a culture of immediacy wherein consumerism becomes modal through the "enticements" of marketing and branding and by the interaction of producers, advertisers, marketers, citizens, consumers and fans through ever faster and interactive media. What he labels "impatient and immoderate media" (Tomlinson 2007: 47) facilitate consumer immediacy and offer instant and increasingly bespoke delivery.

Lest all this smacks of unreconstructed globalism, or rather naïve transformationalism, more cautious science argues that the impact of what might be called cosmopolitan communication (Inglehart & Norris 2009) should be judged with a sceptical eye. The inventiveness and routine availability of border-erasing communication technology suggests that as interconnection between people separated by time and space becomes more extensive and intensive, its cultural impacts are very likely to grow. But we should be wary of attributing too many cultural consequences to cosmopolitan media because cultural *firewalls* exist which "preserve the imprint of distinctive national cultures, especially in poorer societies" (*ibid.*: 83). In this cautious take on the prospects for global culture, the enduring weight of distinctive historical conditions and traditions vitiates the power of border-crossing technologies and media formats, even where, as in the case of Google, they can appear as modal.

In like vein, and despite the protestations of social commentators like George Ritzer (2004, [1993] 2008) and Ben Barber (2007), there is only limited evidence that we are moving towards a shared global consumer culture. Rather, local values and habits remain important, whether we are talking about a tradition of particularly demanding customers in China, or differences in how and where people drink cappuccino in the UK, Italy and the US. But notions such as hybridity or creolization, as well as cultural syncretization, can still be used without too much violence to actual conditions in many societies. Entrenched differences, along with the spread of various "in-between" identities, provide continued evidence of a cultural tapestry that subsists quite easily in what might otherwise look like an increasingly and irrevocably uniform world. Differences are not always benign and even in a globalized world – perhaps most poignantly in a globalized world – the charge of being thought of or seen as different, "inauthentic" or alien remains a very powerful one. And in a globalized world, as James Clifford notes, "one is always to varying degrees 'inauthentic', caught between some cultures, implicated in others" (1988: 123).

The spread of democracy as a global script

The relationships between globalization and democracy are difficult to unravel. Of course, there is always the simplistic interpretation found in some commentaries. In such accounts globalization, seen as liberalization, Westernization or Americanization, musters as either a progressive or a regressive force. Liberal democracy as a global cultural script is applauded in some accounts with a strong normative inflection, or given short shrift where its extension is seen as an adjunct to or ideological justification for perceived Western expansionism or capitalist interests. For all that, it may be unwise to link the robustness or otherwise of democracy and democratization solely to globalization, especially where their relative health owes much to local or regional factors and only contingently to shifts in the global political economy. At the same time, democratization must stand as a signifier of global integration because of its universalist pretensions. The globalization of *liberal* democracy carries a good deal of ideological baggage, but it is also an index of global convergence. And as an index it shows some important changes in the past few years that provide evidence of volatility and both progressive and regressive tendencies. Sovereign debt crises, rising social unrest, endemic lack of confidence in political institutions and political leadership feature alongside unlooked-for demo-cratization in the Middle East and North Africa (Economist Intelligence Unit 2011). Tunisia and, initially, Egypt were heralded as the start of a new wave of democratization.

At the time of writing, this judgement remains premature given the uneasy state of politics in Egypt, sectarian conflict in Syria and the willingness of embattled rulers in authoritarian states to resort to repression, cosmetic changes, or a mixture of both to shore up their power. Over the same period in Europe, regressive tendencies seem to have followed from the effects of and responses to the Eurozone crisis. The deleterious consequences of that crisis again point up the paradoxical nature of globalization. On the one hand the pressures on governments in Greece, Italy, Portugal, Spain and Ireland to conform to EU and IMF prescriptions for economic crisis management underscore the interdependent character of the global economy. Yet in addition to imposed austerity measures, in Greece and Italy, the resort to government by technocrats has also damaged democratic accountability. On the other hand, the trammels of interdependency crises still threaten to derail the EU as a paradigm case of ever-closer integration, or else precipitate it into a purely defensive and instrumental, though deeper, fiscal union.

Longer-term trends actually reveal a more sanguine picture, at least in the two decades or so after the start of the "third wave" of democratization in 1974 (Diamond 2008). But since about 2007 the successes of the third wave process have been somewhat eroded across many of the democracies or proto-democracies that emerged then. In addition, there has been some retrenchment even in established or "full" democracies such as the UK and the US, where civil rights have been curtailed partly as a result of the "global" War on Terror and the growing securitization of everyday life. In 2008, Larry Diamond wrote about the beginnings of a "democratic recession", and the picture over the past four years reveals, at the least, some stagnation (Economist Intelligence Unit 2011). The present global economic crisis both undermines the status of authoritarian regimes and at the same time erodes democratic practices and rights in countries with stronger democratic traditions, as well as increasing the prospects for social unrest and inter-community conflicts. Do the MENA (Middle East and North Africa) uprisings signal a renewed wave of democratization or a false dawn?

The changing quality of global governance

Which brings us to our penultimate indicator of global integration, the condition of and pro-spects for global governance. The dispiritingly uniform "end of History" envisaged by Francis

Fukuyama (1992) in the early 1990s was, perhaps, the paradigm expression of a post-ideological world. In many ways it was predicated on the continued health and expansion of the liberal global order we canvassed above. Fukuyama is not generally viewed as a hyper-globalist, but the world order he prescribed and predicted is, in many ways, the apotheosis of global liberalism. Fukuyama's world order relies on forms of instrumental and advanced multilateralism, generally mustered under the banner of global governance. In fact, the idea of global governance comprises many variants of governmentality: from the multilateral arrangements associated with the *Pax Americana* – NATO, the World Bank and the IMF – all forms of complex interdependence, through varieties of governance without government, to the fragile, but still audacious experiment in de-bordered polity-making seen in the EU.

At root the notion of global governance refers to the attempts to build institutions that order some common aspects of world affairs without state control, or, more accurately, without direct and routine control. Perhaps more significantly, and certainly more contentiously, it is also a powerful normative concept, both in terms of the implied prescription to transcend, if not to entirely abrogate, sovereign power, and because it invests in a world order built around the idea of universals. Despite the raft of scholarship devoted to it, cosmopolitanism as a prescription for much thicker forms of global governance and world society is still seen as implausible. This is so even where the reforms bruited look a lot more like liberal conceptions of international society (a belief in the rule of law extended across nations and a robust set of multilateral institutions to uphold it) than the whole package of trans-cultural authority that is the hallmark of Kantian ethics. It may also qualify the claim that in a globalized world, people are impelled towards and more willing to enter into what Andrew Dobson (2006: 173) calls "relationships of justice" or "causal responsibility" with those who are "at a distance", such that ties of obligation invest mere cognitive awareness and connectivity with thicker and longer-term affinities.

The very idea of global governance expresses the immanent tension between the universal particularity of sovereignty and that universalism exemplified most clearly in the doctrine and politics of human rights (C. Brown 2007a: 177–78). Through such doctrines or global scripts, more or less state-centred models of international society have been under greater challenge since the 1990s. Pressures on states have arisen because of the growing scope and influence of different kinds of transnational connection, including capital-driven forms of geopolitics (which is the basis of much hyper-globalist rhetoric). Pressures also result from a greater willingness to countenance what are still very selective multilateral interventions in states where the oppression of domestic minorities (and some majorities) is deemed a violation of the universal human rights regime, a threat to international order and security, and inimical to the well-being of particular third party states.

But herein lies the continuing rub, since all the world knows that the status and force of global society as a moral order, at least when applied to the limiting condition of humanitarian intervention in the affairs of a sovereign power, is vitiated by the absence of a fully institutionalized and legitimate body of law and the institutions and will to enforce it. The upshot is that the temper of much commentary about global governance emphasizes its shortcomings, rather than applauding its successes or the fact that it is now institutionalized to such an extent that it is almost impossible to conceive of governance in some areas – environmental policy springs to mind – without a global dimension.

The weaknesses of global institutions, regimes, agreements and networks are in large measure the result of the gap between risks that are increasingly globalized and interconnected and governance capacity that is less than effective in marshalling disparate interests (national and otherwise) whose support or compliance is crucial. Evidence of signal and perhaps endemic incapacity can be found in the area of climate change, where UN-brokered negotiations always promise much and deliver less; the uncompleted Doha Round of trade negotiations; the failure to prevent the spread of nuclear capability in weaponry; and the chronic inability of the UN Security Council to reform itself and thus better reflect changing balances in world politics and economics. Arguably, the institutional framework that presently comprises global governance is unsuited to the challenges posed by risks of global extent and intensity.

And yet, a more modest, or less apocalyptic, interpretation of current trends in political globalization is available, although it relies on state-centric evidence of incipient globality. It seems that even if the process of economic globalization has faltered over the past few years, the graph of political globalization continues on an upward path, at least as reflected in data gathered for the KOF Index of Globalization (KOF Swiss Economic Institute 2011). Measures invoked to substantiate this claim may appear somewhat anodyne – number of embassies in other countries, membership in international organizations, participation in international organizations and international treaties; and of a certainty they do not allow us to assess the quality of integration, what motivated it and how it actually modifies behaviour. Nor do they say very much about the matter of consciousness, about how globalization is experienced by diverse actors. For this, we need to turn to our final indicator.

The making of world society and global consciousness

A plethora of complex trends, events and contingencies have all weakened and even de-legitimated a world order built around territorial states. But plausible alternatives muster only as a set of relatively weak intergovernmental associations or in the prescriptively more robust guise of the European Union, or some looked-for cosmopolis. In the absence of a world, or supra-national state, the prospects for anything resembling a world society may appear tenuous, unless the designation is simply a description of things as they are. Of course, this is a problem for all commentary on globalization, especially where it has normative – globalizing – intent.

When examining trends in word society formation, and especially with regard to the existence and/or health of global civil society, it is subaltern forces and sometimes rank outsiders who are increasingly cited, their "unusual" interventions bruited as new forms of practical democracy, from below. The language of potential transformation is rife in such observation, with the prospect of progressive globalization residing in the ability to challenge, subvert, bypass or reform the institutions of usual politics and the interests tied to them. The difficulty lies in how to interpret the evidence, what transformative weight to put on anti-regime movements spreading across the Middle East and the anti-police politics of youth protest in the UK, France, Chile and Spain. Is what is happening in Greece a reactive kicking against the pricks, rebellion, the voice of democracy, or some populist response to the threats of globalization, maybe a yearning for *dirigisme*? Is Occupy Wall Street dystopic or liberating, or both?

For the observer, if not the activist, this is just a matter of careful typology. A cautious social science of globalization distinguishes between global or transnational social movements, international non-governmental organizations, transnational advocacy networks, epistemic communities and publics constituted only through virtual networks. Some movements and groups consciously address the world scale and may revel in the sense that they are articulating new visions of world order, perhaps alter-globalizations. Others are resolute in their defence of purely local interests and see the global instrumentally, as an arena in which to raise visibility and mobilize support for local causes.

Yet in the longer term and certainly going forward it is probably useful to identify three secular trends that suggest a consciousness and a practical orientation beyond state and society to hint at what John Meyer calls "a supra-societal or transcendental cosmos" (2010: 11). The first is the global script of the individual as social actor and the global legitimation of general principles and highly valued collective goods, such as the environment, human rights and poverty reduction. A surprisingly large number of international non-governmental organizations extant in the last fifty years or so have been dedicated to sustaining and improving these global public goods (Boli & Thomas 1999). Second, and instrumental in the empowerment of the individual as a social actor, is the modern process of rationalization, and especially of scientization. As Meyer (2010) notes, in recent decades, the scientization of everyday life has underpinned the growing sense that the world can be ordered rationally and for the betterment of humankind. This too has become a global script, despite challenges to it in the heartlands of some Enlightenment cultures and resistance from true believers in other orthodoxies. Finally, the sense of the world as being ontologically ordered in a particular way – through national states and societies, unified cultures and immutable identities–is giving way to the idea that all social constitution is conducted by individuals through their choices as actors, even if action takes place in the context of structures and rules that remain ontologically thick and meaningful.

Conclusion

In this brief excursion we have challenged the very concept of global integration, not to offer a resolutely sceptical view of globalization, but to point up the vagaries in an ineffably contested process. It is possible to identify retrenchment from globalization, especially some forms of economic globalization, along with the risks to integration revealed in global recession, welfare austerity and growing poverty. Global institutions of governance often appear as weak and vacillating over serious and chronic issues; perhaps less so in the routines of day-to-day governance in areas such as famine relief and human reproduction. At the same time, evidence for longer-term integrative trends is available, notably with regard to widening acceptance of global cultural imperatives such as human rights and the affordances that enable a growing number of individual actors to mobilize in defence and pursuit of them. Integration is not a linear or monolithic process and the weight of the evidence we have cited underlines that judgement. The idea of globalization as contradictory and indeterminate, as well as elementally troubling and exhilarating, is conceptually imprecise, but probably an accurate depiction of the global condition.

Notes

1 The KOF Index of Globalization uses a set of indicators covering economic, social and political aspects of globalization. Critical commentary on such exercises (see Caselli 2012) laments the utility of at least some of the measures employed and their reliance on largely national-level data.

2 Of course, the endgame for these positions is quite different.

3 According to the UNCTAD report, global foreign direct investment (FDI) inflows rose modestly by 5 per cent, to reach $1.24 trillion in 2010. While global industrial output and world trade are already back to their pre-crisis levels, FDI flows in 2010 remained some 15 per cent below their pre-crisis average, and nearly 37 per cent below their 2007 peak.

4 Increasingly for workers in developing countries, the impacts are not realized just through loss of income or even jobs, but in the deleterious effects of being put aside after a working lifetime in relatively secure employment. Furthermore, what is apparent from the riots against austerity measures in Greece during 2011–12 is the growing sense of helplessness and hopelessness that seems to affect participants.

5 A *production network* may be defined as "the nexus of interconnected functions and operations through which goods and services are produced, distributed and consumed". A *transnational* production network is one whose interconnected nodes and links extend spatially across national boundaries and, in so doing, "integrate parts of disparate national and sub-national territories" (Dicken *et al.* 2001: 93).

6 Of course, the same technologies also enable actors to refurbish or reinvent a sense of locality and community, sometimes tied to territory, and this is very much in line with the sense that globalization is a contradictory process.

7 The distinction between notionally "old" and "new" media is often overstated, since old forms, for example print media, are often remediated by the use of digital technologies and formats. The "cutting edge" of new media now would lie in the application of Web 2.0 formats, including so-called cloud technologies and varieties of social media.

PART I
Normative theory

Introduction

This part provides an introduction to several important abstract normative considerations that are in the background of the discussions of subsequent issues. For instance, the first chapter of this part, Chapter 3, considers the ethical theories used to address all of the topics, which come up repeatedly as contributors either use one ethical approach or another to address the topics of global ethics, or question the adequacy of these approaches for actually doing global ethics and generating solutions to global challenges. Likewise Chapters 4 and 6 consider justice theorizing and cosmopolitan theory and so provide the framework for thinking about the scope of justice, the aims of justice and the actors of justice (states, institutions and individuals). Chapter 8 addresses the breadth of global ethics as it questions claims of universalization, and Chapter 7 on human rights considers the closest currently available universally recognized form of global ethics. The remaining chapter in the section, Chapter 5 on gender justice, raises issues which are pertinent to each and every topic of global ethics and, as discussed in detail below, the reasons for highlighting this in this first section in a separate chapter is to ensure that gender always features as a category in global ethics theorizing.

Having argued in the introduction that global ethics is multidisciplinary, a challenge at this point might be that the framework for global ethics set out in this first part is essentially that of moral and political philosophy and theory broadly conceived. This is undeniably the case and it might be that a word of explanation is required. It is indeed the case that global ethics is, and we have argued must be, multidisciplinary: arguments about climate change which neglect the scientific data or social science research on how to change behaviour will be at best naïve and at worst dangerously wrongheaded, just as claims about what contributes to human well-being and development are flawed if philosophers simply assert things without proper empirical support. However, this does not mean that there is no distinctive ethical voice for the philosopher in the debate. Global ethicists come to these discussions about contemporary global challenges with all the expertise and methodologies of philosophy, and this allows for a distinctive and valuable contribution to the debates. A final word on this is that such an approach does not simply mean that ethicists take the evidence of others and "apply" their fully formed theories. Rather, the ethicist's voice (and their theories) need to be informed and reformed by other disciplines, as well as, we hope, these informing and reforming the knowledge of others. In these collective ways we aim to address the challenges set out in this volume, from climate change, to extreme poverty, to the erosion of shared public goods such as effective treatments, clean water and adequate food.

In Chapter 3 Ruth Chadwick and Alan O'Connor consider traditional ethical theory and the extent to which it has changed, or needs to change, to address global concerns. This is no minor issue for global ethics, as many have claimed that ethical theory is Western, in its tradition, its focus on the individual, and its privileging of some concepts over others (such as autonomy). Chadwick and O'Connor begin by considering the nature of a global ethical issue. An issue may be one of global ethics either because it raises the question of the extent to which local principles can be used globally or because of the scope of involvement or risk it presents. If it is the former then the authors suggest it may be possible to expand previous theories to meet global challenges by seeking to expand the scope of moral concern. If they are to do this then a theory must explain who counts morally, and it must also provide a method for "determining the *content* of moral obligation in particular circumstances." Chadwick and O'Connor take a prominent proponent of each dominant tradition of ethics to explore how this is done and how successful it is: first, Peter Singer for utilitarianism; second, Onora O'Neill for Kantianism; and third, Amartya Sen and Martha Nussbaum for virtue theory. The authors argue that all of these approaches have accounts of moral standing that are applicable to recognizing all persons globally. However, understanding how obligations are to be discharged – who should do what and when – is more complex; for instance, "while all three theories recognize that the individual has duties towards distant strangers, it is only Singer that places the primary responsibility to give on the individual," while O'Neill and Nussbaum adopt institutional approaches.

The authors then consider the challenge that theorizing across different cultures poses (a problem which will return in many chapters and most prominently in Chapter 8 on universalism and difference). They conclude, at the end of the chapter, that there are Western tendencies still evident but that these are being challenged and change is visible. The chapter then moves on to whether such theories could ever be global in terms of their acceptability and whether this is required if global challenges are to be addressed. Here the authors focus on the changes to and transformations of theories that have occurred as the need for explicitly global theories has emerged. In particular, the turn from the individual to the collective and the prioritization of social and communal values such as solidarity and the growing prominence of cosmopolitanism (addressed in detail in Chapter 6).

In Chapter 4 Richard J. Arneson considers theories of justice. Arneson argues that there are two broad divisions in global justice theorizing: between extreme cosmopolitanism and others, and between those who accept a strong general principle of justice and others. These divisions concern whether or not justice is global in scope and whether it is justified to favour certain groups over others (this chapter can be read in conjunction with Chapter 6 on cosmopolitanism and Chapter 8 on universalism, topics which are introduced in this chapter). Having very briefly outlined a number of types of cosmopolitan theories, Arneson returns to the question of duties to distant others. Here he introduces Peter Singer's and Thomas Pogge's arguments. After outlining these theories he then looks at those who claim that national borders have moral significance and the reasons that can be given in support of the argument that co-nationals are owed more than distant others: first, that states enforce duties within their borders; second, and similarly, that states legislate; third, duties within states are more demanding because of the greater interaction within states; fourth, duties of reciprocity and fairness are stronger within states; fifth, that states institute cooperative schemes which trigger special duties of justice; and, sixth, that special relationships apply in nations understood as communities, as they do within families. Various types of cosmopolitans reject these "bounded" theories of justice for different reasons (again see Chapter 6 for more details on cosmopolitan theorizing). Arneson focuses on those who argue that duties beyond borders require at least a moral minimum of respect. This threshold requirement Arneson discusses as the "moral minimum," a concept which is understood in different ways in different theories and with various criticisms.

Chapter 5 on gender, care and global values is by Virginia Held. A chapter dedicated to gender is controversial. Many argue that gender should be "mainstreamed," by which is meant that gender is scrutinized in all discussions. Clearly gender should be overtly recognized in all aspects of global ethics (as was highlighted in Chapter 1 of this collection), and arguably to date gender has not been discussed enough by global justice and ethics theorists, who have been criticized for gender blindness. Too often women are treated as a group with minority interests, despite the fact that women are numerically not a minority, which in itself is testament to just how disadvantaged women continue to be. A separate chapter on gender is not an effort not to mainstream gender. Rather it is based on a concern that too often in mainstreaming attempts gender disappears even further, and is subsumed under other supposedly more pressing concerns, such as global poverty and climate change, as if it were not the case that women are likely to suffer disproportionally from these injustices as they do from others. Gender as a feature of injustice is just as pressing in global ethical issues as it is in other ethical issues and this should be remembered throughout all the global challenges which global ethics seeks to address.

In this chapter Held begins by noting how gradually philosophy and the social sciences have come to recognize the importance of gender and how it matters. This is true from political science to international relations, and transformations have resulted across moral and political philosophy as theories of global justice begin to recognize gender, and as moral theory begins to recognize concepts of caring and empathy. Held focuses on the emergence of the ethics of care, and the way that this ethic is expanding from its original concern for close relationships to a theory which can speak to "our most distant relations in political, social and global society." Held spends much of the first part of the chapter exploring the ethics of care and detailing its key features and what care can offer our moral and political assessment of current situations and how these can be developed. The second half of the chapter works through a number of examples and shows how adopting an ethics of care encourages new perspectives on global problems and challenges. Held argues that the ethics of care leads to more pervasive arguments for overcoming global poverty, for appropriate development, and also for addressing issues of violence and conflict.

With traditional feminist concerns in mind, Held argues that the realities of power are essential to addressing issues of migration, poverty and the prospects for international law. Considering these issues globally is crucial. For example, with increasing numbers of women entering the workforce in the developed world, migrants are being employed to provide care. So, advances in gender equality in one region may come at various cost in other regions. When it comes to poverty Held suggests that "dealing with world poverty in terms of individual rights has had limited success," and that again care offers a better approach. The final issue she addresses is that of international law, arguing that care highlights the destructiveness of violence and conflict. International law fits with care principles as it "expresses care for vulnerable populations, and provides for acting on the values of care." The potential for care, and care-compatible international law, to develop further constitutes the discussion of the final section of the chapter, as Held reflects on possible futures, including the gradual reduction of the need for law enforcement as caring cooperation and trust increase.

Chapter 6, by Gillian Brock, considers cosmopolitan theories of global ethics and justice. In this chapter she outlines different types of cosmopolitan theories, distinguishing between moral and institutional cosmopolitanism and weak and strong versions. She maps the varieties of starting points from which cosmopolitan theories can be developed – utilitarian, rights-based, Kantian, virtue ethical, contractarian or a combination of two or more – and different characteristics of types of approach, for instance humanist and associativist. Having mapped the terrain, Brock then considers the work of Rawls, because of his importance in revitalizing the global justice debate. Even though Rawls was not a cosmopolitan theorist, many cosmopolitans have taken his work as a starting point from which to develop global justice theories. For instance, Pogge has developed Rawls's theory and emphasized that global connections falsify Rawls's assumption that bounded political communities are effectively self-sufficient. Thus, Pogge defends expanding a broadly Rawlsian theory into a global theory.

In the second half of the chapter Brock moves to exploring four key issues of cosmopolitan theorizing. The first is whether cosmopolitans should prioritize sufficiency or equality, in other words, whether the primary aim should be meeting basic needs or achieving equality. In short, does inequality matter or is it just as important that – at least globally – some minimum standards are met? The second is the extent to which non-cosmopolitan commitments and duties can be accommodated. Brock argues that it is a misconception to think that no particularism – for instance commitments to family members or compatriots – is permitted by cosmopolitanism. The stronger the form of egalitarianism the less scope will be allowed – but this does not mean that no such obligations are respected. Third, Brock considers the claim that there can be no global obligations because there is no effective global enforcer. Fourth, she considers policy recommendations and the increasing engagement and concern of global ethicists to create policy impact, and this commitment to practice as a key feature of global ethics. Brock finishes by setting out some questions about the future of cosmopolitanism and the questions still to be addressed.

Chapter 7 is by Rainer Forst, and is devoted to human rights. Human rights are perhaps the most widely recognized and endorsed global values and perhaps the nearest thing to a global ethic that currently exists. However, while at one level there is at least some global consensus that human rights should be endorsed and respected, what this actually means on the ground, and who is required to ensure human rights are respected, is far from clear. Forst begins by recognizing these difficulties, stating that the nature of rights is a "topic of constant disagreement" and that "human rights comprise several dimensions that are difficult to reconcile." Human rights are moral, political and legal, and emerge from earlier historical conceptions of rights; all of these conceptions of rights have been developed, defended and critiqued in recent decades as the debate on global ethics and justice has emerged and intensified. In this chapter Forst introduces and evaluates the four most dominant approaches, the ethical, the political-legal/functionalist, the political/moral and the discourse-theoretical.

The ethical approach of James Griffin "identifies basic interests of persons in pursuing the good and transforms them into rights claims in accordance with their weight or value." Griffin claims not to attach rights to any particular version of the good life, but only to values such as autonomy. However, those with different views would reject the claim that the ascendancy of autonomy is not in fact a particular understanding of the good life. The political–legal view denies that there is a universal normative foundation for human rights, or that one is needed. The aim here is broadly practical: to derive certain standards by which human beings are to be treated, and which must not be violated. The political/moral approach seeks an overlapping consensus of what is the minimal threshold of rights, a threshold that human beings must not fall below. The final discourse-theoretical approach focuses on the conceptions and/or implications that underlie the assumptions of human rights, namely that human beings are worthy of respect as beings of autonomy, dignity or some other shared justification. In the final section Forst reflects on human rights as global ethics and so on the relationship between human rights and global justice. Human rights he presents as a part of global justice, as the means for delivering some aspects of global justice, or as a "subset of transnational norms of justice." In addition, and significantly, human rights are currently primarily connected to states: the state is the main, though not the only, institution for protecting, securing and maintaining human rights; at the very least this would need to be addressed to ensure that there are not, as there currently are, rights-less people.

In Chapter 8, Peter Jones and Graham Long return to an issue introduced by Chadwick and O'Connor at the beginning of this part, that of universalism and cultural difference, a key discussion for those wishing to endorse any global conception of ethics and justice. Jones and Long traverse this difficult and complex territory comprehensively, defining and explaining key definitions and points of contention, by structuring their discussion around four types of universalism.

First they consider the "universalism of application": that the correct morality – whatever that may be – is universal in its application. The recognition of human rights is one example of such universalism. Moreover, most ethical theories – such as utilitarianism and Kantianism (considered in Chapter 3) can be, and usually are, universal, and always are if a global approach is adopted. But they are not necessarily applied universally, for instance, if the application differentiates between different types or classes of people or is bounded to particular communities. The denial of universalism is relativism, which is often presented as offering a challenge to global ethics. So Jones and Long discuss cultural relativism and how it is derived and presented.

Jones and Long then consider a second form of universalism, "universalism of structure," which concerns the range of cases over which a morality might apply. At issue is whether or when it is possible to recognize context and case-specificity, moral particularism, and thus difference, without moving to a form of cultural relativism. The third form of universalism the authors consider is "universalism of content": whether universalism requires the exact same duties and rights to all or recognizes some differences. The fourth type of universalism is "universality of justification", whether all could accept the morality and find it justified. The extent to which this matters is crucial, for if this is essential to global ethics, then disagreement would threaten any global claims. Jones and Long finish the chapter with a discussion of anti-universalism and difference. They conclude that what is often presented as "universalism versus relativism" is often an argument "about what sort of combination of universal principle and difference sensitivity is right or appropriate."

3

ETHICAL THEORY AND GLOBAL CHALLENGES

Ruth Chadwick and Alan O'Connor

The branch of ethics that is known as "applied ethics" has a number of challenges to face. One of the most difficult is what exactly is meant by "applied." While there is a view that for ethics to be applied, there must be a theory to apply, there are opposing arguments supporting an anti-theory position. It is not part of our remit here, however, to examine the rival merits of these two views. If one *does* take the view that theory has a role to play, there still remain issues about how flexible existing theories are, at a time of rapid change. Here there are several different *types* of change that pose challenges for ethical theory, including scientific advance, global financial crisis and its effects on values, and threats to security in a post-9/11 world. In this chapter, however, we are concerned specifically with the challenge for ethical theory because of the very fact that issues now tend to arise on a global, rather than a local scale. How might ethical theory need to adapt to meet this challenge?

Applied ethics has been most prominent in the field of biomedicine: medical ethics, nursing ethics, bioethics and public health are all aspects of this. In this field, in particular, some academics have deployed theories such as utilitarianism and Kantianism, but another very influential approach has been that of the "mid-level principles" or "principlism" of Tom Beauchamp and James Childress: autonomy, beneficence, non-maleficence and justice (Beauchamp & Childress 2009). One of the advantages of these mid-level principles is that they can be grounded in different ethical theories. Autonomy, for example, can be supported by a Kantian or by a utilitarian theoretical position, although its role and justification will differ accordingly. The principles have been proposed as a focus around which agreement can be achieved, even across different cultures (J. S. Gordon 2011). On the other hand, it has been argued that bioethics (along with the ethical theories here mentioned) is itself a Western phenomenon (Gbadagesin 2009), and that the principles of biomedical ethics do not travel well, that they reflect a Western, even an American perspective, in relation to the importance typically accorded to autonomy in particular (Holm 1995). This may be perceived as an overemphasis on the individual at the expense of such considerations as relatedness, community and solidarity, among others. Specifically, the requirement of informed consent, which is one practical form that can be taken by respect for autonomy, has been expected, arguably, to do too much ethical work in contexts for which it is ill-suited.

A prominent example of this has been the reconsideration of informed consent in relation to the development of population genomic research and biobanking, first nationally, and now internationally. It has become clear in this debate, at least, that ethics change, in time as well as in space. The grand theories of Kantianism and utilitarianism, although both still influential today, were both products of an earlier age. Principlism was a twentieth-century development, but technological developments towards the end of the twentieth century required new input into our ethical thinking, as human beings confronted new ways of communicating and scientific developments made some ways of thinking no longer tenable. In the twenty-first century, the interdependence of societies around the globe is increasingly obvious, and is a major factor giving rise to global ethics as a distinct field of study, going beyond applied ethics to include insights from political philosophy.

What counts as global?

Before proceeding further, however, it is necessary to explore what exactly is meant by "global." There are at least two ways in which an ethical challenge can be global. One is where an issue that has arisen or continues to arise in one cultural or national context has global dimensions. For example, there is an ongoing issue about how healthcare resources should be distributed in a given society. But as Robin Attfield pointed out in "The Global Distribution of Health Care Resources" (1990), there are also serious questions about how resources should be distributed globally. Are there criteria for just *local* distribution which can also be applied *globally*, or does justice between nations require a different approach?

Historically there has long been a strand of discussion about the extent of our moral obligations, for example, first to *care* about the welfare of people we do not know on the other side of the globe, and second, actually to *do* something about it – by sending aid, for instance. These ethical issues are of course inextricably linked with political ones, in relation to policies on foreign aid and intervening in other countries. Hence global ethics is connected with global *justice*. Nevertheless, while some of these matters are in the domain of international relations, there remain issues for the individual citizen and moral agent to consider, as well as those facing institutions and governments. What is the individual's obligation to contribute to overseas famine relief, for example? There are, then, questions about the extent to which principles that might work *within* a society can be used in a global context. The issue of global *reach* of certain approaches is one thing: another, however, arises from the *logic* of the approaches themselves. In other words, the internal logic of an approach may set limits to its usefulness in some contexts.

There is a second sense in which an ethical challenge can be global in character, however, and this is where the issue is global in character *per se*; it is not a question of a local issue writ large. That may be because the whole globe is inevitably involved, perhaps at risk, certainly at least potentially affected, by the actions of human beings. Issues which fall into this category most clearly include environmental issues such as climate change; matters that affect the ways in which societies are inextricably connected, such as financial collapse; and also possibly issues related to security, including food security. The Human Genome Project and research into human genetic diversity have also been global issues; even without the rhetoric of the genome as the "common heritage of humanity," the results of this research have implications for all, and have given rise to questions concerning sharing the benefits of research.

Ethical theory: what is the problem and what is required?

Corresponding to the two senses in which global ethics *is* global, there are different types of response. The first is that traditional ethical theories "expand" to meet the challenges that are global in scope, or at least, that they examine the implications of their own premises for global issues. In other words, they seek ways to provide answers to those issues "writ large" with which they have dealt at a local level. A difficulty with this approach is that if the theories in question continue to be regarded as originating in one part of the globe, perhaps characterized as typically Western, they may reinforce a conceptual divide between the agents and recipients of moral practice. Nigel Dower's distinction between an ethic that is global in scope and an ethic that is global in acceptance is relevant here (Dower 2012). It may be that what is needed is a global ethic in the latter sense, which would require more than "expansion."

Second, it may be that the demands of global challenges require not just applying theories or principles in a new way, but reconfiguration of the conceptual scheme at work. Discussions about developments in ethics have turned to a perceived shift towards an emphasis on principles such as solidarity, leading to consideration of the possibility of solidarity across borders (Prainsack & Buyx 2011). Arguably, such rethinking is what is required for the issues that are global in the second sense outlined above.

We shall begin by examining the possibilities for "expansion" and then look at ongoing attempts to view the issues in different ways.

Ethical theories expanding

We will begin by examining how traditional ethical theories have addressed the first type of challenge, seeking to expand the scope of moral concern.

What is the work that we need ethical theory to do in addressing global challenges? Why should the global context pose a problem? First, the theory must explain who comes into the scope of moral concern, or who has moral standing. To some extent this issue forms part of the longstanding debate about the rival claims of partiality and impartiality in defining the moral point of view. These include familiar questions such as "Does charity begin at home?" or "Does suffering require a response wherever and whenever it occurs?"

Second, a theory must provide a means of determining the *content* of moral obligation in particular circumstances. Here, cultural differences arguably pose one of the greatest challenges in expanding ethical theory beyond national borders (Gbadegesin 2009).

Third, it must explain who has obligations to those who are within the scope of moral concern: individuals, institutions and/or governments. Some have argued that global citizenship or global governance may be required to impose global duties on governments (Falk 1994, Attfield 1999), or that international enforcement of conduct requires a specially created body (Harmon 2006: 233).

In examining attempts of ethical theories to meet global challenges it is necessary to be selective. We shall begin by considering the attempts of thinkers in different traditions – utilitarianism, Kantianism and virtue ethics – to address these challenges, focusing on the arguments presented by Peter Singer, Onora O'Neill, and the capabilities approach (CA) of Amartya Sen and Martha Nussbaum. We have chosen these because they all, in different ways, explicitly take on the issue of global moral obligation and/or justice.

As regards theories explicitly categorized as theories of justice, many writers have noted that the social contract has been the predominant framework in theoretical discussion in the past half-century, particularly post-Rawls (e.g. Venkatapuram & Marmot 2011: 216). As has also been remarked, however, its translation to international justice is not without problems. For example, Rawls's account of the "difference principle," whereby differences should only be permitted where they are to the advantage of the worst-off person (Rawls 1971), is not easy to apply in the international context. Onora O'Neill (2000b: 133–36) highlights the difficulties in determining the effect of the principle on a transnational scale. Although some have tried to apply it transnationally, others conclude that justice *is* a national matter (Nagel 2005, Deaton 2011).

We shall begin with the issue of who has moral standing and proceed to discuss who has global obligations and what they might be.

Moral standing

From a utilitarian perspective, although there are different versions of utilitarianism, including preference utilitarianism, the central issue is the ability to experience pain and suffering. Although Bentham famously applied this criterion to non-human species, and Peter Singer (2011a) has written eloquently about the "expanding circle" of morality, for present purposes the issue is confined to the geographical distribution of humans.

At first sight utilitarianism might appear to be the ethical theory which is most obviously suited to global application. Clearly, humans may experience pain and suffering wherever they are located; this very point, however, also leads to the fact that a key challenge of applying utilitarianism arises from the maximization principle. As John Mackie pointed out in *Ethics: Inventing Right and Wrong* (1990), if I am thinking of maximizing across the globe, there is a very large number of interested parties to take into account. For this reason he dubbed utilitarianism the "ethics of fantasy": how could such a calculation be carried out with any degree of confidence? Analogous issues arise with regard to the interests of future generations, and it is common practice to apply a "discount" principle when trying to calculate for the future. Where differences in space rather than time are concerned, however, it is not just the physical distance that may lead to some uncertainty about a calculation, but the degree to which cultural differences affect experience – although swift global communication has to some extent mitigated the problem of distance.

Onora O'Neill has argued that a Kantian-inspired approach can be developed to meet the demands of what she calls transnational justice.[1] In past times, and in Kant's own day, it would have been possible only in limited circumstances for people in one part of the world to help those in another part of it. Those outside one's national borders were often not attributed moral standing. In line with the spirit of Kantianism, those with moral standing are those we regard as moral agents or subjects, when considering particular actions: "Wherever activity is based on the assumption of others who can act and react, the standing of those others cannot coherently be denied" (O. O'Neill 1996: 103). It is not, then, a matter of how our actions affect the well-being of people in other parts of the globe, but a question of their own status as moral agents: at the heart of a Kantian approach is the value accorded to rationality.

The CA rejects both well-being and rationality as candidates for the exclusive basis of moral standing (Nussbaum 2003: 51–52). Instead it focuses on what people can *do* – human abilities give rise to a moral claim that they be developed. For Amartya Sen, well-being and agency are not to be regarded as independent. He argued that:

> to judge the well-being of a person exclusively in the metric of happiness or desire-fulfilment has some obvious limitations … It can be argued that advantage may be better represented by the freedom the person has, and not by … what the person achieves – in well-being or in terms of agency – on the basis of that freedom. This type of consideration will take us in the direction of rights, liberties and opportunities.
>
> *(Sen [1988] 2008: 46)*

Like Sen, Martha Nussbaum used the notion of capabilities, central human functions, as the basis of moral standing (Nussbaum 2002: 129–31).

The content of obligation: what are those with moral standing entitled to?

Each approach, then, has an account of moral standing which is independent of geographical location and ultimately leads to applications that are global in scope. There are also implications for what those who have moral standing are entitled to. In short, for utilitarianism, humans are entitled to be taken into account in the felicific calculus, however that is carried out in practice. For Peter Singer, in "Famine, Affluence, and Morality" (1972), it is clear that there is an obligation to minimize suffering wherever it occurs. There are two versions of the implications of this for action in relation to famine relief: one "hard" and one "soft". In the hard version, an individual ought to give towards famine relief until they would suffer more harm by their donation than the recipient would gain. In the soft version, an individual ought to give what they can until giving would mean sacrificing something of "comparative moral importance" to the bad which is likely to be avoided by the giving.

Any view such as this which suggests there is an obligation to give aid to people in other parts of the globe might appear to need a mechanism for determining what is needed. There is a weakness in a utilitarian reliance on desires or preferences to establish what people need: the consequence of this is that those who are unaware of what they lack cannot be said to have needs (see e.g. O. O'Neill 2000b: 124). O'Neill does, however, think that needs are important, arguing that it is possible to start with the bare necessities for survival: it is possible to base a concept of basic rights on these needs (*ibid.*: 118–19). Although the concept of needs is unclear and contested, it is widely agreed that there are some basic needs, without which one is quite likely to die prematurely: food, shelter and clothing appropriate to climate; clean water, sanitation, and some parental and health care.

When we turn to the CA, the important question is what are the capabilities that require development. There are two types of approach to this: one is to try to determine a list by philosophical argument; the second is to leave it up to democratic decision. While the latter has been defended by Sen, the former has been supported by Nussbaum. The problem with the democratic approach is similar to that identified by O'Neill (and others) in utilitarianism: majority preferences may support oppression of minorities. On the other hand, to try to define a list by argument alone runs the risk of being perceived as a top-down paternalistic approach which overlooks real cultural differences and local priorities. However, both Sen and Nussbaum wanted to use the notion of capabilities to develop a space of comparison in which to compare nations, as a rival to other types of measurement such as *per capita* GDP,[2] and wanted to go further and use the approach as the philosophical basis for fundamental constitutional principles establishing a social minimum or threshold.

Who has global obligations?

O'Neill has pointed to the "messiness" of trying to develop principles in transnational justice: to whom are they to be addressed? Who are the agents of change? It is impossible to avoid asking the question. Many writers assume that the only relevant agents are individuals; others include states. Philosophical discourse has arguably not kept up with economics in accepting the roles of collectives and corporations.

While all three theories recognize that the individual has duties towards distant strangers, it is only Singer who places the primary responsibility to give on the individual. O'Neill and Nussbaum try to find an institutional framework to improve the lot of those suffering in other parts of the world. For Singer, global obligations apply to everyone. While he acknowledges the importance of governmental donations, he rejects the notion that an individual's duties could be discharged merely by paying taxes (P. Singer 2011b: 209–10). He also argues that individuals should take political action to encourage state-level aid. Relatively high levels of private foreign aid could encourage governments to give from the public purse as well.

O'Neill argues for an institutional approach, pointing out that the needs are too great to be met by individuals. The establishment of these institutions is also more effective than the establishment of "rights", which could, in the absence of an effective corresponding duty, be illusory. Specifically, on the right to food, she says that "if the claimants of supposed 'rights' to food or development cannot find anywhere to lodge their claims, these are empty 'manifesto' rights" (O. O'Neill 2000b: 126). She rejects the profit motive as the sole motivation for companies and points to the potential for transnational companies to fight injustice globally (O. O'Neill 2001).

Like O'Neill, Nussbaum's is an institutional approach. While at one level it might be true to say that we all have duties, it cannot be the case that individuals in wealthier countries are under an obligation to spend all their efforts in the relief of suffering: they too should be able to flourish.

Cultural issues

The fact that theory with global pretensions has to grapple with cultural difference has already been alluded to. This may seem to be less of a problem for a utilitarian approach, which can take account of different preferences, but it is certainly relevant with reference to the idea of "sacrificing anything of comparable moral importance". What is regarded as of comparable moral importance is susceptible to different interpretations – can it, for example, be deployed to justify linking foreign aid to implementation of Western ideas, such as gay rights?

O'Neill (2000b: 122–24) describes as a "massive defect" of utilitarianism that it is inherently subjective: two utilitarians can analyse a given situation and come to completely different answers, often depending on their worldview, and this also makes it difficult to objectively choose between options. On the other hand, she does recognize a strength in that it takes account of the real world.

It is a challenge for O'Neill to address real world issues (and thus cultural difference) without sacrificing the universalizing spirit of a Kantian-inspired approach. O'Neill suggests two "moves" to ensure that a theory of transnational justice works in multiple cultures (O. O'Neill 1990, 1996, 2000b). The first is abstraction without idealization. While we need a system of abstract reasoning, this does not need to be based on the notion of idealized autonomous agents, but humans with "limited capacities and varied vulnerabilities" who interact. The second move is the taking into account of local context without building cultural ideals into the principles of justice, taking into account the real conditions of oppression in which people find themselves. She argues for a picture of transnational justice that does not depend on the agreement of ideal abstract agents as in the Rawlsian original position, nor upon what people actually would consent to in the real world, which ignores power relations, but on what people *could* consent to.

Both of O'Neill's moves seek to empower women (O. O'Neill 1990). Ideals have traditionally been based on men (and therefore biased in favour of men). In seeking to recognize only arrangements which could be rejected or renegotiated by the actor concerned, O'Neill's second move rejects structures which constrain women, or deny them justice by excluding justice from the realm of the home.

Martha Nussbaum's CA has also been particularly focused on the position of women and the recognition that a person's subjective assessment of their position will be affected by cultural norms. Nussbaum gives the example of a hypothetical woman who does not think herself to be lacking in economic power because women in her society do not have any significant economic power (Nussbaum 2002: 127). Using an objective framework provides a better chance of achieving meaningful gender equality as opposed to notional equality which might be pursued through preference-based approaches. Hence, as mentioned above, she supports a philosophically rather than democratically derived list of human capabilities which are of central importance to being human, fit for all purposes, and enabling these capabilities to be achieved. Such enablement has a number of elements, political, material, institutional, psychological, in order to facilitate opportunities. According to Nussbaum, specifying capabilities with a high degree of generality is not inimical to the recognition of cultural concerns: her example is that of the different free speech rights available in the US and Germany, the latter prohibiting certain forms of anti-Semitic expression (Nussbaum 2002).

In the next section we will briefly examine an example to show the differences, in practice, between the considerations prominent in the three approaches.

An example: food security

Singer took an important step in making actions to help those in need a moral requirement rather than an act of charity. It is also significant that he focused on the issue of famine. Food security is one of the most prominent challenges in global ethics. The concept changes but requires at least freedom from hunger and fear of starvation (see e.g. Food and Agriculture Organization 2006: 1). Food security is considered by the United Nations Development Programme to be a global public good, defined as a good that is enjoyable by all without detriment to others; it is non-rivalrous and non-exclusive. Food security is a wider concept than the individual *right* to food, as it is good for society as a whole. There has been considerable discussion over a number of years about the merits of agri-biotech as a (not necessarily the only) means to achieving security, but the discussion between proponents and opponents is not one that can be settled as a matter of empirical fact: there are deeper disagreements about values, which reflect the framing assumptions being used, as was recognized in the report of the UK Food Ethics Council (2003), *Engineering Nutrition*. That report was in disagreement with the Nuffield report, which made the following claim:

> Poverty has many causes … Poor efficiency of agriculture is one of them. It is also clear that the efficiency of agriculture has considerable impact on the standard of living of people involved in work on small-scale farms in developing countries. This is most notable in Africa, where the majority of the population lives and works in small farms in rural areas … Moreover, it is particularly true with respect to improving the situation of women, who make up the majority of the world's resource-poor farmers … In many instances, the improvements that can be achieved through GM crops may reduce much of the effort required in subsistence agriculture.
>
> *(Nuffield Council on Bioethics 2003: 49)*

This quotation appears to represent a consequentialist approach, if not a utilitarian one. It is looking at the effect on well-being, especially of women. *Engineering Nutrition* was concerned about the primacy of utilitarian considerations in the debate and the fact that consumer "choice" comes in too late in the research and development process. Moreover, the "choice" has been largely construed as that of the consumer to buy the product, which is not only a very limited but a very Westernized interpretation. The relevant choices are about styles of life and not just choices of products.

For O'Neill, as outlined above, a picture of justice has to take account not of idealized autonomous agents, but of real social and power relations. This is abstraction without idealization. In thinking about how this would work in practice, we might "ask to what extent the variable aspects of any arrangements that structure vulnerable lives can be refused or renegotiated by those whom they actually constrain" (O. O'Neill 2000b: 163). She argued that, in fact, the poor cannot refuse or renegotiate their role in economic structures: debtors who need further loans for survival cannot make much fuss about the terms creditors offer for purchasing their crops; the most dependent women are acutely vulnerable both to market factors and to more powerful kin.

This account of transnational justice appears to be at odds, then, with arguments about justice in the agri-biotech debate that emphasize the moral urgency of trying to help poor farmers through agri-biotech. Such arguments, which focus on well-being or even use the rhetoric of choice, frequently fail to take account of the real conditions of choice and in particular leave the entry of "choice" – in other words, areas over which people *have* a choice – to a late stage.

What about the CA in this debate? Improvements in well-being are not sufficient. Quality of life, which is distinguishable from "standard of living", cannot be reduced to discussions of wealth and poverty. In the context of GM crops much more than this is at stake. The relevant question is how technology will impact upon human capabilities, and the extent to which interventions will facilitate the pursuit of the human telos, the life of opportunity. Some of them, even if apparently "chosen", may in fact reinforce dependency and reduce opportunities, and thus not be facilitative of developing capabilities.

Thinking globally

We have examined ways in which theoretical approaches from utilitarian, Kantian and virtue ethics traditions can be deployed to address global challenges. The outcome of this is that all of them can have global application, in different ways. It might be thought that this is what should be expected – surely ethics is by its very nature universal.

However, this is not the end of the story. There are at least two issues to confront. First, it is still necessary to deal with the potential problem that what we have seen so far is the global *application* of Western theories, with the identity and nature of the agent being conceived in Western terms. This may be perhaps understandable when the topic of application is something like foreign aid, but Dower's distinction between ethics that is global in scope and ethics that is global in acceptance is important, whether or not foreign aid is at stake.

Is an ethic that is global in acceptance a realistic possibility? In our increasingly interdependent world there are also calls for harmonization in ethics, as well as in regulation. The question arises, however, as to what extent harmonization is possible in ethics. Although the four principles of biomedical ethics, as mentioned at the beginning, have been proposed as a candidate for global agreement, from another point of view they are a Western export. What other possibilities are there?

Harmonization

The drivers of calls for harmonization emanate from the practical demands of specific contexts such as international biobanking and healthcare tourism. A key example is the perceived need for data to flow across borders, which has led to thinking not only about regulation in the area of data protection, but also about ethics. The purpose behind the European Data Protection Directive, for example, was to remove obstacles to such free flow: the achievement of this goal required thinking about rights, and approximately fifteen years after the 1995 Directive (Directive 95/46/ EC) it was recognized that technological and social developments required a rethink.[3]

Where transfer of data becomes an issue, global recognition of ethical considerations is important, because problems may occur where the data and thus the interests of the data subject are treated differently in different jurisdictions. One option is for partners to enter into contractual agreements with each other (Goebel *et al.* 2009), but harmonization between the approaches of different parties would be preferable if it could be achieved, as less cumbersome than contracts if on a global scale.

Chadwick and Strange (2009) examined different possible approaches to harmonization, following Samuel Fleischacker's distinction between the (universal) human rights approach, the necessary conditions approach (what ethics is required as a condition for transnational coopera- tion?) and the cultural dialogue approach (the search for agreement through dialogue – where this is not conceived as an inter-state political activity). While all these have advantages as well as drawbacks, they are all "end-point" approaches, where the achievement of acceptance is the end point. Using a musical analogy, Chadwick and Strange argued that harmonization requires, not unison, but voices singing different vocal lines. From this perspective a prerequisite for a global ethics is not a finalized set of principles which gain acceptance as an end point, and the prospect of which may be distant, but a process of ongoing dialogue. The existence of the "score", however, is important. The process of setting international guidelines is a familiar one, as also is the variance in interpretation that exists in different parts of the world. The question then arises: what are the limits to variation?

The discussions about the possibility of global acceptance are ongoing, but there is another issue to address, corresponding to the second sense of "global" identified at the beginning of this chapter.

Ethics global in scope and acceptance

What about the arena of the common threat such as climate change or the global pandemic? Of course, it is frequently argued that foreign aid, discussed earlier, *does* raise issues of common threats, such as the fostering of terrorism in its absence, but what we are thinking of here is something more. It is here that the explicit search for new ways of looking at issues has to be addressed.

The shift that has occurred in bioethical thinking, at least since the mid-1990s, away from the primacy of individualism and towards emphasis on more communitarian approaches (for reasons which are beyond the scope of this chapter to address in detail), brings with it its own chal- lenges for global ethics, but is also arguably, at least in part, a *response* to global challenges. What has to be considered here is that the logic of the problems themselves makes some approaches inapplicable and demands others: the possibility of an ethics that has the potential to be global in both scope *and* acceptance, precisely because it is needed to address the issues in question.

Debates that are relevant here include those dealing with the concepts of communitarianism, cosmopolitanism and solidarity, and we shall now briefly address the relevance of these to the question of ethics meeting global challenges.

Communitarianism and cosmopolitanism

Whether or not it is appropriate to talk of a communitarian turn (Chadwick 2011), there has been considerable discussion, as already indicated, about the limits of an individual-centred approach in ethics. Communitarian thinking reflects an important space between individual-level autonomy and state-level interests. However, on the face of it communitarianism might seem to be at odds with a global ethic in so far as it links ethical thinking with the flourishing of particular communities. The implications for moral standing of people on the other side of the globe look distinctly unpromising: people from different communities limited in standing against one another. Perhaps what is needed, then, is not a communitarian but a cosmopolitan outlook (see e.g. van Hooft 2012). Cosmopolitanism reconceptualizes the agent as a citizen of the world rather than as a member of a particular community.

Communitarianism and cosmopolitanism do appear to be very different ways of looking at the world. Even though they agree that ethical principles should apply to all those in a certain domain, they disagree about where to set the boundaries. Cosmopolitanism is not necessarily indifferent to geography: it may recognize the importance of identification with a particular region or country, but such identification does not justify giving its members priority from an ethical point of view.

The question arises, however, as to whether cosmopolitanism is itself a product of a certain part of the globe. It is said to go back as far as Diogenes the Cynic (Hadas 1943). That fact does appear to suggest that cosmopolitanism is, at heart, rooted in a Western ethical tradition. However, Qiu Ren-Zonghas suggested that an appeal to the Confucian principle that "the sage sees the world as one family, one country as one person, this is not his illusion" (Qiu 2011: 11) may be helpful in this context.

Solidarity

Solidarity is increasingly appealed to as an ethical principle not only in bioethics but in ethics more generally (Prainsack & Buyx 2011). An appeal to solidarity suggests a communitarian approach, because solidarity is associated with group interests. An obvious example is the solidarity associated with protecting the interests of the members of a trade union. However, there are different kinds of communities. While members of a society or a union have interests *in common*, beyond that they have *common interests* in virtue of being human beings with shared vulnerabilities. Hence the statement of the HUGO Ethics Committee (2007: 45) that "because of shared vulnerabilities people have common interests and moral responsibilities to each other".

With such an expanded notion of community, solidarity can apply beyond the group of geographical borders and there is then reduced tension, in principle, between communitarianism and cosmopolitanism. Qiu Ren-Zong has taken up the suggestion that solidarity can be appealed to on an international level, but others take the view that global ethics needs to be based, not on a sense of international community, but on enforceable rights. Rights have been associated with both notable successes and failures at international level, and it has to be asked whether it is feasible to base a global ethics on rights in the absence of a sense of international community, if what is aspired to is an approach that is global both in scope and acceptance.

Conclusions

Our examination of ethical theories, selective as it has to be, suggests that while Western ethical theories have expanded somewhat, they are still essentially Western in several respects. First, they evolved in a Western context. Second, their starting point is that of the Western *agent*. The discussion about the obligation to give foreign aid is perhaps the clearest example of this. Third, they still set minimum standards that appear to be very much Western. Although some theorists have tried to make the theories more adaptable to non-Western cultural norms (as in O'Neill's second "move" of applying abstract theory to local context; Sen's argument for the democratic selection of capabilities), they still reject any ideas that are fundamentally opposed to Western ideals (for example, regarding the oppression of women).

A concerted effort to shift outlook so that we see ourselves as citizens of the world, with common vulnerabilities, addressing the same global challenges, may be required, along with consideration over whether principles such as solidarity, rather than the autonomy which has been dominant in Western approaches, can provide a meeting point. If not, the default position may be some agreement through international instruments, from a pragmatic point of view, without any convergence on underlying values. Nevertheless, the process of harmonization in relation to such texts needs to go on.

In his book *On What Matters* Derek Parfit suggested that the various branches of Western ethical theory are "climbing the same mountain on different sides" (Parfit 2011: 419). Perhaps different branches of world philosophy might also be construed as climbing the mountain, working towards convergence on the same answers to the difficult questions thrown up by our increasingly globalized world? This is an alternative metaphor but makes a point analogous to that of the interplay of voices in harmony with different but interdependent vocal lines, with variations on a theme. The extent to which harmonization is possible, and the summit of the mountain attainable, will be an ongoing but crucial question in the coming decades.

Notes

1 O'Neill refers to "transnational" justice and duties, rather than "international" or "global". This is to reflect the fact that the duties do not exist purely between nations or nation states, but between individual actors, irrespective of international borders (O. O'Neill 2000b: 115). "Global justice" is said to beg the question, assuming that a single regime of justice may prevail the world over.
2 The United Nations Development Programme's Human Development Index (HDI), based on the CA, has had minor success in filling the role of a non-economic metric for development.
3 At the time of writing, proposals have been made for the replacement of the 1995 Directive to take account of such developments.

4

THEORIES, TYPES AND BOUNDS OF JUSTICE

Richard J. Arneson

What do we owe to people in other countries around the globe? What do others owe to us? What does morality require of nation states in their policies towards other nation states and towards people other than co-nationals? (On the latter, see Buchanan 2004 and Rawls 1999c). These questions define the subject matter of global justice theory.

Philosophical thought on these issues goes back a long way, but the field is currently in an unsettled state. This may not be bad. New ideas are in the wind, old assumptions are being questioned, and different lines of thought are being explored. This chapter surveys the current state of theoretical discussion, and offers some assessments of arguments and some indication of where the most promising lines of thought are going. In the end the reader will have to decide for herself or himself which ideas are worth further consideration and which should be discarded.

"Justice" can mean many things. For the purposes of this chapter, the term will be used to pick out fundamental moral duties or obligations that are, at least in principle, apt for coercive enforcement. There may well be moral duties, such as the duty to be loyal to friends, that are ineligible for enforcement: it would be morally wrong to try to force or compel people to fulfil these duties. Such duties would not qualify as justice requirements. In the absence of a global state or the equivalent, enforcement of global justice obligations is bound to be sporadic and uneven. Not only is actual enforcement hit or miss, but it can be unclear on what parties responsibility for enforcement ought to lie. Nonetheless, global justice duties, if such there be, ought to be enforced, and a theory of such duties should specify what the duties are and who is responsible for enforcing them. (Perhaps if some important global justice duties cannot be enforced in the absence of a global state, and they morally must be enforced, then we morally must establish a global state, contrary to common current views.)

Global justice encompasses many types of issues. Some concern what is morally required in international relations between states. Nation states fight wars, build empires, develop trade relations, and the question arises as to in what conditions such policies and acts are morally acceptable. Some global justice issues have to do with what individuals are morally required to do when their actions might have effects on people in other lands. These issues perhaps become more salient as global trade increases: when (for example) Canadians purchase electronics made in China, is a special tie to the producers thereby established? Global problems such as climate change affect people across the globe, and appear to call for cooperation among nations and people on an enormous scale; one supposes a global justice theory should guide us in thinking about what would constitute a fair division of burdens and benefits of global cooperation. Especially in the decades since the Second World War, international bodies and non-governmental agencies and lawyers and theorists have proclaimed human rights that are thought to be possessed by all people on Earth. Egregious violations of human rights warrant intervention, even armed intervention, on behalf of the victims, many claim, and how to balance the imperative of humanitarian intervention against traditional doctrines of state sovereignty and autonomy is currently unsettled.

In this chapter the discussion focuses on a single (but widely ramifying) contentious issue. At the level of fundamental moral principle, is it morally acceptable to favour members of one's own nation over outsiders? If so, in what ways? And what might justify this moral tilt? Is partiality to co-nationals better regarded as allowed by justice principles or as morally mandatory? If justice dictates a set of moral requirements owed to co-nationals and another set owed to people generally, in each case, what are the shape and strength of the requirements?

Varieties of cosmopolitanism

In recent years global justice theorists have identified each other as cosmopolitans or non-cosmopolitans, but this term is used in many different ways and may be ceasing to be a useful label. Below I present a taxonomy of possible cosmopolitanisms, but the reader should be warned that usage varies.

A cosmopolitan moral theory might be one that posits universal moral norms that are claimed to hold everywhere and at all times and to apply even-handedly to all persons. Call this *universalism*. Notice that as stated, a moral doctrine that claims that white people are superior and should rule the world could qualify as cosmopolitan, so we might add a further requirement that a universal theory posits (a) that all persons have equal basic worth and (b) that everyone owes equal due concern to all persons (see Sangiovanni 2007).

"Due concern" admits of very different construals. At one extreme, a universal view might take the form of relativism, the idea that what is morally right in a particular society at a particular time is fixed by the norms accepted in that culture and time. The universal principle is then encapsulated in the slogan "When in Rome, do as the Romans do." At the other extreme, a universal moral theory might posit a single invariant set of fundamental principles that determines what anyone should do anywhere and everywhere. Utilitarianism along with other varieties of act consequentialism and Lockean libertarianism are the best-known examples of this type of view.[1] The term "cosmopolitan" sometimes singles out this class of views; call it cosmopolitanism as *invariant universalism* (an example is P. Singer 2004).

There are further wrinkles. As so far characterized, a moral theory that is cosmopolitan in the sense of invariant and universal could consist in the single injunction to be loyal to your family and friends. But sometimes the label "cosmopolitan" is used in a more restrictive way. In this spirit one might say the cosmopolitan identifies herself as a citizen of the world; the idea is that one has liberated oneself from parochial prejudices and loyalties, and takes the appropriate moral perspective to be that of one person among other persons, each of whom must figure appropriately in the determination of what one ought to do. In particular, the cosmopolitan is contrasted with the patriot, who puts loyalty to the nation above extranational ties (Nussbaum 1996).

Again, there are different contrasts marked in this general area (Scheffler 2001: 111–30). One contrast is between views that do and those that do not deny that facts about nations and states and membership in these entities have any intrinsic moral significance that registers at the level of fundamental moral principles that determine what acts and policies should be chosen. For the cosmopolitan denier, facts about nations and states, like any empirical facts, can have instrumental significance, but that is all. Call the denier an *extreme cosmopolitan*. Another contrast is between those who do and those who do not deny that, in addition to moral principles whose content depends on people's membership in nations and states, there are fundamental moral principles that generate significant moral obligations that people owe to one another merely as people independently of their national identities and ties. Call the non-denier on this issue a *moderate cosmopolitan*. Scheffler (2001), Moellendorf (2002) and Tan (2004) all defend moderate cosmopolitanism.

Another contrast in this area is between those who do, and those who do not, deny that different moral principles that play a role in fixing what we fundamentally owe to one another become applicable to people depending on the social relationships they have with others or the interactions in which they engage. Embracing this associationist position is neither necessary nor sufficient for becoming committed to the denial of extreme cosmopolitanism, but associationist doctrines are one source of purported justification for this denial.

Helping and harming those in other lands

In 1972 Peter Singer raised the question, when there are disasters around the world, and distant strangers are in grave peril, what are the grounds and limits of the obligation of better-off people to help? He proposed the principle that "if it is in our power to prevent something bad from happening, without thereby sacrificing anything of comparable moral importance, we ought, morally, to do it" (Singer 1972: 231). "Sacrificing anything of comparable moral importance" encompasses bringing about something equally bad and doing something intrinsically wrong. He insists that we ought to count everyone's interests the same in deciding what the principle implies, and not amplify the moral importance of preventing bads and gaining goods for ourselves and those near and dear to us. We are not to give extra weight to helping those to whom we have special ties, when we could instead help needier strangers. He makes the assumption that we can effectively reduce grave evils by contributing to aid agencies such as Oxfam. Even if we gave a lot, we could still give more, and the cost to us would continue to be less than the gain to others our transfers of resources would provide, down to the point where further giving would thrust us into abject, desperate poverty. His proposed principle sounds moderate but has extremely demanding implications (see also Murphy 1993). He urges that it is not merely nice, but morally required, to make huge sacrifices as demanded by this principle.

Singer's discussion stimulated a large literature of critical response. One line of response insists that it is at least morally permissible, and sometimes morally required, to give extra weight to ourselves and those near and dear to us, and not strive always to minimize the aggregate sum of worldwide bads (so far as we can doing so without violating rights or committing other serious wrongs) (R. W. Miller 1998, 2004, 2010). Going further, Jean Hampton (1993) asserted that each person has a strong duty to respect herself, which for all practical purposes requires giving a nearly absolute priority to satisfying one's own needs when helping others would interfere with self-fulfilment.

Many would balk at accepting the claim that we have moral obligations of beneficence that are as demanding as Singer claims. However, many of those who resist strong positive duties to aid accept strong negative duties not to harm others. On this view, if I made the mess, and especially if I made the mess by faulty conduct, and most especially if I am blameworthy for this faulty conduct, I should clean up the mess. Thomas Pogge (2002) maintains that under current conditions, affluent people in prosperous nations are not bystanders with respect to the disasters of extreme poverty and widespread misery occasioned by political turmoil. We are involved in wrongfully causing the disasters. If so, we may be under strong obligations to improve the condition of people around the globe even if there is no positive duty of beneficence at all of the sort Singer was seeking to characterize. The duty not to inflict wrongful harm is paired with a duty to repair wrongful harms we perpetrate.

Pogge maintains that by supporting and benefiting from an international institutional order that wrongfully causes harm especially to impoverished people around the globe, ordinary members of developed prosperous societies are wrongfully causing harm. Pogge strikingly claims that if we ceased wrongfully harming the global poor and repaired the damage to them we have recently caused, global poverty would be eliminated. People everywhere would have access to enough resources to live at least a minimally decent life. If this argument succeeds, the claim that we should eliminate global poverty is not hostage to controversial moral claims to the effect that we are all under very strong duties of beneficence of the sort that Singer endorses.

Attention should then turn to the arguments for the claim that by supporting the present international order and benefiting from its ordinary operation people in affluent nations are wrongfully harming the global poor. One claim Pogge makes is that the normal rules of respecting the sovereignty of independent nations play a malign role by encouraging and enabling takeovers of poor countries with rich natural resources by armed thugs. If they succeed in gaining state power they can use it to seize resources and appropriate the profits and also unjustly siphon tax revenues to their private coffers. The international order of states is complicit in the plundering that results, because this order generally calls for states to respect the property rights maintained by independent sovereign nations, even if the distribution of property stems from plunder by those who control state power. Another claim Pogge makes is that the international order via treaties and the work of international agencies imposes a grossly unfair set of rules for international trade, an imposition that bears especially heavily on poor societies with marginal economies.

Whether the global order harms the global poor and, if so, what responsibility individuals bear in this regard, are complex and controversial issues (Risse 2005a). Some would say that there are moral duties, resting on the right of individuals to live in self-determining states, to extend legal recognition to whatever state has power in a given independent nation, and not to interfere in its internal affairs (Walzer 1977). Some would hold that if a rich nation and its members have legitimate title to their wealth, and are not obligated to use it for the benefit of others, they are at liberty to trade or not, and to trade on any mutually acceptable terms, even if they drive hard bargains (Nozick 1974, Narveson 2003b).

Do national borders have moral significance?

A crucial divide in global justice theorizing separates theorists who hold that being a member of one rather than another country or nation or state is in itself a significant moral factor that contributes to the determination of what we owe one another and theorists who reject this claim. Do national borders have per se moral significance? Those who answer yes typically maintain that those who are fellow members of a nation state are under special justice obligations towards one another. Moreover, they are under no comparable obligations to outsiders.

A closely related divide separates those who affirm and those who deny that when people interact with others in certain ways, this interaction brings it about that their moral relationship changes in fundamental ways, such that new principles of justice apply to their mutual dealings. A variant version of this idea is that when people are bound together in close social relationships, their interactions are governed by different and more demanding principles of justice than apply to relations among strangers. When an adherent of this viewpoint adds that fellow members of a nation state usually or always interact densely or sustain important social relationships that trigger special justice duties, we get again the result that co-nationals owe more to each other than to outsiders.

In terms of the practical implications of the rival views, the dispute as to the per se moral importance of national borders has momentous significance. Suppose there are egalitarian duties of justice to act effectively to bring it about that the well-being of the people who are disadvantaged in their well-being prospects improves. If these duties are amplified by a standing duty to give extra weight to fellow members of one's own society, then an affluent citizen of an affluent society may well have greater, more stringent duties to bring about improvements in the lives of slightly less affluent fellow citizens than to bring about comparable improvements for the wretched of the earth. How much extra weight we should give to insiders over outsiders will vary with details of the various views, but it is immediately obvious that this is a big issue.

In the discussion to come, the idea that national borders are intrinsically morally important will be interpreted loosely. If one holds that dense interaction gives rise to special justice duties, and engaging in dense social interaction reliably correlates with being fellow residents of the same state, one falls on the "borders do matter" side of the line.

The idea that we owe more to fellow countrymen than to distant needy strangers will have an immediate appeal for many. However, we might wonder if this idea can be backed up by sound arguments, and fits coherently with other convictions we should hold. Below, some prominent arguments that claim to offer support for the idea that we owe more to fellow co-nationals than others, and that some fundamental justice principles apply only intra-nationally, are canvassed. In each case, I suggest some criticism.

States coerce

An obvious feature of states is that they massively coerce those within their territory but not so much those people who are outside their borders. States establish a vast apparatus of laws and public regulations and compel obedience by credible threats of fines, hassles with police, arrest, imprisonment and the gallows in the event of noncompliance. Some see state coercion as the key to the justification of the claim that fundamental justice requirements have intra-national scope (Blake 2001).

Perhaps the strongest version of the claim that justice duties apply primarily to those who are subject to the same state regime is the claim that the concept of justice only applies when conditions for reliable enforcement of claimed justice duties are present, and in the absence of a functioning state, there is no prospect of reliable enforcement. In a slogan: no state, no justice (Nagel 2005). The idea can be put this way: you only have a right to X if a sufficient number of people actually accept the duties corresponding to your claimed right to X, such that they are disposed to accord you X and you can standardly expect them to behave in ways that assure you X.

So stated, the advocate of the claim that asserted justice requirements apply only to members who are subject to the same state power may disagree only verbally with someone who affirms that justice requirements hold independently of the existence of states. The latter view can acknowledge that actual justice norms require state proclamation and enforcement but insist that there is also aspirational justice: the rights that people ought to accord us. From the standpoint of aspirational justice, injustice can occur when people fail to bring about enforcement of the rights that ought to be secured.

Theorists insist on the significance of state coercion for other reasons. One prominent view is that states massively coerce insiders but not outsiders, and in particular states coercively impose one or another particular set of property, contract and tort laws, which establish terms of exchange and cooperation among inhabitants. The particular set of such laws that a particular state imposes will channel advantages to some members of society and away from others. Someone disadvantaged by the coercive scheme in place can reasonably ask for justification of the particular scheme given that she would be better off if an alternative scheme were put in its place instead (R. W. Miller 1998, Blake 2001). The claim is then made that in response to such a query, only a scheme that either (a) is egalitarian and provides basically equal benefits for all or (b) conforms to maximin (and thus makes the person who is least advantaged under the scheme as well off as possible) can be justified.

A complementary idea is that the massive coercion that states by their nature impose on residents is a *prima facie* violation of their autonomy. The individual has the right to rule herself and set her own will, but state coercion subordinates the will of the coerced. The presumption that state coercion violates the autonomy of those subject to it is removed if the coercion is justified.

In response, the claims made above appear to exaggerate the presumptive moral badness of coercion, which we may suppose to involve issuing credible commands or threats that successfully induce those addressed to change their behaviour to compliance with the behaviour the coercer seeks. Coercing someone to refrain from doing what she has a right to do or to engage in conduct that she is morally at liberty to refrain from doing is normally morally odious. In these cases, the coercion should not take place. But there are other cases. Acts of coercion need a justification, but so does any act or omission. If you are coerced to prevent you from wrongfully harming another in a way that would count as a serious violation of that person's moral rights, that very characterization of what is going on provided a justification. So it is hard to see why the fact that the state massively coerces people might be thought to trigger the application of special higher requirements of social justice holding among coercers and coerced. The coercion is either justified on independent grounds, so no special justice principles come to apply, or the coercion is unjustified, and should not be done at all.

There may be intermediate cases, when coercing someone is not necessarily wrong, but is impermissible unless one supplies a special justification to that person or compensates the person for the burdens coercion impose on her. But it would beg the question at issue simply to assume that the coercion that the state imposes on those within its territory counts as such an intermediate case. The coercion that the state imposes must be justifiable, but it is a further step to suppose the justification must be specially addressed to those coerced, and must take the form of showing that the coercion works specially in their interests. For all that has been said, the state might justify the basic property rights and redistributive scheme it imposes on the ground that it is fulfilling a duty we all have to improve the lives of people generally, not just the people in our society, and this duty is particularly a duty to help those around the globe who are especially disadvantaged. The state then does not violate its citizens' rights to individual autonomy if it coerces them to fulfil their global justice duties.

The state claims to act in the name of all who are subject to its laws

At any rate, the state has a duty to make this claim, to maintain that those subject to the coercive power of the state can sensibly regard themselves as authorizing these state actions. For this claim to be met, the state must be justifiable in a special way to each person subject to its coercion.

The problem with this rationale for special distributive justice obligations that apply country by country is that the idea that the state must act in the name of its members on its most plausible interpretation applies more broadly and in fact is latently in play whenever anyone acts or refrains from action. When I act, I should have a justification for what I do, that all those who are affected or might be affected by what I do can endorse as rational and moral agents. In fact, whenever I act, I implicitly commit myself to having a justification that any rational and moral person can endorse. In this sense claiming to act in the name of other people is not a unique feature of state action but belongs to the action of any person whatsoever. Hence the fact that the state must claim to act in the name of those it coerces does not impose any special moral requirement on state action that does not hold of any action. Acting commits us to being able to satisfy a demand that might be posed by any agent, to the effect that our action should be supported by a sound moral justification.

One might claim that it is the combination of the facts that the state coerces its members and must claim to act in the name of the coerced that produces a special requirement of justification uniquely to the coerced, a requirement that only conformity to egalitarian principles can satisfy (Dworkin 1986, Nagel 2005). However, no one has advanced an argument that the combination has special normative properties, and in the absence of argument one may doubt there is any normative power in this combination.

As density of interaction and social relationships increase, more demanding justice requirements apply

Nozick (1974) once posed the question: If people lived on isolated lands, and did not interact with each other or cause harm or benefit to each other, and if one held that in these circumstances no one is under an enforceable obligation to extend benefits to those on other islands, why would stringent egalitarian principles of justice become applicable if some people engage in mutually beneficial trade with others? This is intended to be a rhetorical question; the intended answer is supposed to be that no new principles of justice kick in when interaction occurs. One might respond that Nozick is looking for a big discontinuity that is not to be found. Instead one finds a gradual shift. A bit of interaction triggers a bit of extra duties to give consideration to one's interaction partners, and as interaction and association become more frequent and various and dense, these extra duties gradually ramify and increase. According to this model, our justice duties to others around the world vary along several dimensions according to the degree and scale of interaction and association with them. A classic expression of this view is Beitz (1979). In that work Beitz maintains that global trade and other relations among nations constitute a global scheme of cooperation, so Rawlsian principles of justice apply on a global scale. Julius (2006; see also Cohen & Sabel 2006) sees cooperative relationships and with them, justice ties, varying by degree across different nation states.

In response, both the extreme cosmopolitan who accepts a strong beneficence component in what we owe to one another and the Lockean libertarian such as Nozick who altogether rejects general beneficence duties regarded as part of justice will remain puzzled as to how, if trading once with strangers does not trigger any obligations to them beyond what is specified in the particular deal we make, trading more than once somehow does give birth to new enforceable duties.

Reciprocity and fairness

Members of a functioning state cooperate together to provide basic goods of public order and security that fall on all inhabitants of the territory and are necessary for having a decent chance of being able to form and pursue a plan of life. This being so, all inhabitants of a state owe special obligations of reciprocity to one another, according to the terms of the Hart–Rawls principle of fairness, which holds that:

> when a number of persons engage in a just, mutually advantageous, cooperative ven-
> ture according to rules and thus restrain their liberty in ways necessary to yield
> advantages for all, those who have submitted to these restrictions have a right to
> similar acquiescence on the part of those who have benefited from their submission.
>
> *(cited from Nozick 1974: 90)*

These obligations are owed to insiders and not to those who live in other lands. The best interpretation of these obligations of reciprocity is that they involve a justice obligation to bring it about that the overall system of cooperation that is built on this foundation of public order brings about equal benefits for all or perhaps works to make the least advantaged members as well off as they can be made sustainably over the long run. In other words, egalitarian justice requirements, having to do with how well off one person is compared to others, arise only within schemes of cooperation that in the modern world take the form of independent nation states. These egalitarian justice requirements then hold country by country and not across national borders (Sangiovanni 2007).

The extreme cosmopolitan can raise several objections to this national cooperation account of the significance of nation states and the borders of nation states for global justice. The sim-plest objection is that conceding for the sake of argument all the rest of the premises of this argument, the cooperation that is necessary for basic order and security involves overlapping networks of mutual dependence that do not match up with national borders. Living in San Diego, California, I am very dependent for my security on the law-abiding goodwill of those who live near me, especially my rich neighbours in my affluent neighbourhood. I depend also on a wider circle of those who live near by, which includes millions of residents of Mexico living in the border region near San Diego. In contrast, the law abidingness of millions of US citizens who live at a distance makes little difference to my security, and my law abidingness is similarly a "don't care" from their standpoint. With other US citizens I pay taxes to support national defence, but my physical security depends as much or more on the forbearance and toleration that inhibit armed groups and states around the world from attacking San Diego. The duties of reciprocity that cooperation to provide public order generates do not coincide at all with national borders.

Other objections loom. The principle of fairness plausibly generates a duty not to be a free-rider and to pay one's fair share for goods that cooperation provides. The duty is not unlike the duty to pay a fair price for vegetables one buys, although because of the special nature of public goods, transaction by mutual voluntary consent is not in play. So it seems a huge stretch to claim that reciprocity in response to receipt of security and good order triggers a general requirement to establish an egalitarian social order or one that satisfies the difference principle. Moreover, the principle of fairness itself, regarded as a generator of enforceable duties, has been subject to widespread attack (see Nozick 1974; Simmons 1979, 2000; C. H. Wellman 1996). The attacks tend to challenge the idea that one can acquire enforceable obligations of reciproci-ty in the absence of either voluntary consent to the arrangements that are claimed to trigger these obligations or voluntary acceptance of the benefits that flow from these schemes. These attacks may be answerable, but they need to be answered if the national cooperation approach to justifying requirements of justice to favour co-nationals over others is to be vindicated.

A stiff-arm response to the reciprocity argument is that at the level of fundamental moral principles that determine what we should do, reciprocity is a purely formal notion. No substantive duties are implied by it. On this view, if I behave towards you in a certain way, your duty to reciprocate is to behave towards me in the ways that are specified in correct moral principles of conduct. If I do you wrong, reciprocity in this sense requires not necessarily that you do me wrong in return, but that you behave as morality dictates. If I am rich and you are poor and I help you, reciprocity may not involve pay-back, but again, is constituted by behaving as one morally ought to behave.

Being involved in a mutually advantageous cooperative scheme, the terms of which are nonvoluntary, triggers special justice requirements

The arguments surveyed so far might be regarded as purporting to support the claim, central to the thinking of John Rawls (1998, 1999c) that the principles of social justice are principles that regulate the basic structure of each single society regarded independently. Justice is in this sense a national not an international virtue. When free and equal people cooperate together in a democratic society, principles of justice regulate their interaction. This is the point of justice, what justice is for. When people cooperate together in small voluntary associations and clubs within a state, principles of justice do not regulate how they carry out their enterprise. When people simply inhabit a common globe and have at most thin ties of interaction to one another, different, less demanding principles regulate their interaction.

There is a special feature that marks the cooperative scheme that makes a nation state and is part of the background from which distributive justice requirements emerge. The cooperation is not voluntary in a strong sense: no one has any real choice but to accept the going terms of social cooperation (or exit the country, but even if legally permitted, migration out might be too onerous and costly for the choice to remain where one is to count as voluntary).

So far this is just assertion. One can regard all of the five arguments above as supports for the view, so the position collects the objections to those arguments. Another possible support is the idea that each person has a fundamental moral right to belong to a national community that is self-determining and not subject to outside interference. Strong global justice duties will diminish this right, since with the duties in place, nation A's economic policies that will be bad for nation A will also cause harm to other nations that will be required to come to A's assistance when these policies turn sour. But the extreme cosmopolitan who affirms strong beneficence duties will doubt that there is such a right of national belonging as just characterized. This takes us to a sixth consideration.

Nations are communities bound together, like friends, by special ties

The first five purported justifications of special justice requirements owed to compatriots do not rely on claims about special shared values or affective bonds uniting members of a functioning nation state. The proposed justification to be discussed now takes the justification to rely on just such claims. The idea is that if there is a genuine well-functioning nation, there will be a national community, whose members share a culture, an identity, a sense of a common history, a language, and more. Members of a nation take pride in the nation's accomplishments, and tend to be disposed specially to favour fellow co-nationals even if they altogether lack personal acquaintance with most of them. This national community gives rise to special justice obligations, owed by Canadians to fellow Canadians, Nigerians to fellow Nigerians, and so on.

Consider the claim that if a relationship in which one is involved is valuable for its own sake, not just as a means to something else, then one ought to acknowledge special obligations to those people who are participants in that relationship. The type of obligation generated in this way varies depending on the type of relationship in question (Scheffler 2001: 82–96; also 2010). Given the nature of family ties, family members have certain obligations to each other, and given the nature of friendship, friends have certain obligations to each other. Invoking this view, David Miller adds that being a member of a national community is participating in a noninstrumentally valuable relationship, so special obligations arise between fellow countrymen. He rounds out the account by interpreting some of these obligations as basic high-priority moral requirements, requirements of justice and so legitimately enforceable (D. Miller 2007).

An initial concern about this account is that it may appear to romanticize the nation state. National states in the modern world tend to corral together disparate groups under common borders. The unity the account prizes may be absent. The defender of the position can respond that it is a good thing, good per se and usually also instrumentally, for the members of states to constitute a national community, and where national community exists, special justice requirements hold among members. Whether a nation does constitute a nation state can vary by degree.

The claim that being a member of a national community is engaging in a valuable relationship likens fellow citizens to friends. How close is this likeness? Thomas Hurka (1997) notes that unlike friends and close family members, co-nationals do not share personal relations; one has no acquaintance at all with the vast bulk of fellow co-nationals. But just as a valuable friendship is founded on a shared history of doing good or suffering hardship together, a national community can also involve a similar shared history, and on a grander scale (ibid.).

That a shared history of doing good or suffering hardship together is necessary for genuine friendship is open to doubt. But the idea that shared history can constitute a valuable relationship that gives rise to special duties of favouring is also doubtful. As a man, I can reasonably take pride in the special contribution that men through the ages have made to reproduction (namely, providing semen). The claim under review is that a shared history of doing good, to qualify as a basis for a relationship that generates special ties, need not be a specially wonderful shared history. So one need not deny the obvious truth that women also share a history of even greater contribution to reproduction, in order to acknowledge the special shared history of men. But it seems wildly implausible to maintain that on this basis men have a special relationship that gives rise to special justice duties among men to favour men over women.

Perhaps national community is *sui generis*, so its failure to resemble friendship may not indicate any problem for the claim that sharing nationality is a basis for special-tie obligations. After all, family ties are very different from friendship ties, yet family relations are widely deemed to generate special obligations. But the claim that shared nationality generates unique special ties will be the target of cosmopolitan scepticism. The sheer fact that people share values and tastes is not a plausible basis of agent-relative duties. Nor is the fact that you and I share a history automatically a duty-establishing bond between us. Shared commitment to a valuable project might be thought to establish a bond, but whether shared commitment to a nation-sustaining project is commitment to anything specially valuable is what is here at issue. No doubt patriots have sentiments of affection and loyalty to fellow countrymen and the fatherland, but racists have similar sentiments of affection and loyalty to those who share the common lineage, and the mere existence of such sentiments does not establish agent-relative moral duties of partiality.

Perhaps the best line for the defender of nationalism to advance would be to adapt a suggestion by Niko Kolodny (2010). He proposes that the fact that one has a personal tie to an independently valuable form of association amplifies the value of the relationship from one's personal perspective. If sharing skin colour is not a valuable relationship, then there is nothing for personal involvement to amplify. But given that friendship is impersonally valuable, the fact that Alessandra is your friend gives you special agent-relative reasons to be a good friend to her. One might defend the idea that one has agent-relative duties to one's own nation and to co-nationals along this same line.

But once again this line of thought offers no bulwark against cosmopolitan scepticism. The sceptic might deny either that impersonally valuable relationships ever give rise to special-tie moral duties or that national community per se constitutes an intrinsically valuable relationship. A sceptic of the latter type might even allow that participating with others in a valuable project generates special ties and allow that building a just society is a valuable project but insist that building a just society is a project of global scope, not a parochial local undertaking.

Kolodny's amplification account resembles a suggestion by Samuel Scheffler already mentioned in this discussion seven paragraphs back. The suggestion was that to recognize a social relationship one has with another person as noninstrumentally valuable all things considered commits one to accepting this relationship as a source of agent-relative duties to favour the relationship partner. Consider friendship. One would misunderstand what it is to be a friend if one did not accept that being a friend, one has special duties to favour one's friend over others on appropriate occasions. Up to this point, we have noted that it is far from obvious that national community is noninstrumentally valuable. Also, the consequentialist cosmopolitan (who holds that we should always do what would produce the best outcome and that upholding national favouritism is not in itself bringing about any good outcome) can recognize that friendship is noninstrumentally valuable and that friendship includes a norm of agent-relative partiality. She can treat this norm as housed within the realm of good, and deny that it has a place within norms of right, where the duty to bring about best consequences rules the roost. The idea that noninstrumentally valuable social relationships are conceptually linked to agent-relative duties is ambiguous, and one can accept the link while denying that the duties in question show up at the level of fundamental duties of moral right. One might also deny the link: why think it is true in general that noninstrumentally valuable social relationships generate special-tie duties? The general point here is that the cosmopolitan who rejects special-tie moral duties of nationalist partiality has several options for objecting at her disposal, and if any succeeds, the nationalist special-tie advocate is defeated.

The moral minimum

For those theorists of global justice who hold that stringent egalitarian principles hold only among people who are related to each other in some special way, the question arises, what do we owe to people to whom we stand in no such special relationship? Suppose you and I are bound together by no social ties except our common humanity or (more plausibly perhaps) our common possession of qualities that qualify us for personhood status. What then do we owe one another? Call this set of moral requirements "the moral minimum".

The moral minimum so understood may include duties to nonpersons as well as duties to persons. It may include duties not to torture animals just for fun, to treat with a certain respect and consideration beings that possess some rational agency capacities but do not cross the threshold of personhood, and so on. The discussion to come focuses on what persons owe to persons as such.

Again, the overall character of a global justice account along this line will depend to a significant extent on its view of the moral minimum. If the requirements of the moral minimum owed to all are set high, the issue as to whether fellow countrymen have special justice obligations to one another becomes less pressing. At least, this is so if the moral minimum requirements are thought to have priority over any special obligations there might be in determining what one ought to do, all things considered.

The idea of a moral minimum might be interpreted variously. One might think of minimal justice requirements not as elements of fundamental theory, but as practical guidelines and aids to furthering other, fundamental goals. For example, one might endorse the use of a poverty line, a formula that determines an income level deemed sufficient, used to guide anti-poverty policy, without believing the formula reflects any deep fundamental moral requirements.

The idea being reviewed in this section is more ambitious. The aim is to identify, on fundamental grounds, minimal obligations that each person owes to every other person. Just for being a person, you are owed this much. We seek a nonarbitrary basis, grounded in first principles, for drawing the line that marks the moral minimum in one particular way. For different ways of grappling with this issue, see, for example, Rawls (1999c), Blake (2001) and G. Brock (2009).

There are reasons to be sceptical about this quest for a theoretically warranted specification of a moral minimum. However we define the minimum, the values and goods that the minimum so understood assures to people will vary by degree, and singling out any particular point or even range seems inevitably arbitrary. Why set the line here rather than somewhere else? If the minimum is specified in terms of resources or opportunities for resources, what determines the "good enough" line? The same point holds if the minimum is specified in terms of well-being or opportunities for well-being or happiness or desire satisfaction or whatever. The same point holds if the minimum singles out a set of basic human rights. If these rights include a right to education, how much is enough? A right to free speech can vary by degree along several dimensions of assessment. And so on.

From any maximizing consequentialist standpoint, the search for a theoretically warranted "moral minimum" must be an exercise in futility. For the welfarist (one who seeks to maximize welfare), it is better if one's life goes better rather than worse, and it can always go better. Moreover, wherever one (inevitably arbitrarily) sets the good enough line, if one makes it a moral priority to get as many people as possible across this line, one's morality will then recommend bad decisions if in fact there is no special moral importance that attaches to this line. One will discount excessively gains that could be obtained for people who are just over the line, and are not at risk of falling below it, and excessively discount significant welfare gains that could be obtained for people who are unavoidably not going to reach the good enough threshold no matter what one does. Moved by the imperative of getting people to the good enough line, one will not pay appropriate heed to the numbers of people above the line who might instead be helped, how well off they would be absent help, the costs and efficacy of helping those just below the good enough line compared to the costs and efficacy of helping others.

Theorists concerned to propose a moral minimum account have worked to locate a non-arbitrary line with clear moral significance that marks the threshold of sufficiency. One proposal is that each person ought to be provided what she needs to be able to lead an autonomous life, a life in which she exercises agency and is self-governing. If some people fall below that standard, then all the rest of us are together responsible for bringing it about that this situation is remedied, and all are able to live autonomously (Blake 2001). This proposal appears to set a very low bar for sufficiency. I can be living in dire poverty under conditions of squalor, heading towards an early death, but still possess and exercise capacities of agency. I can use my ingenuity to seek to hide from omnipresent local oppressors, or seek to find food that will stave off starvation. An autonomous life need not contain even minimal fulfilment.

One might identify the moral minimum with the conditions for a minimally decent life, this being understood as including some minimal level of fulfilment and achievement. Another possibility is to identify a list of basic moral rights, such as the right to free speech, freedom of movement, opportunity to participate in the economy of the society one inhabits, and so on. Against the complaint of arbitrary line-drawing, one might respond that it is frequently the case in moral reasoning that what one should do depends on how to weigh several conflicting considerations against each other, but there is no balance scale that allows precise weighing and measurement, and we use reflective equilibrium methods and seek a considered judgement after reflection. It is no objection against the assertion of a moral minimum that locating it requires considered moral judgement. So claims the defender of this approach.

Doubts remain. Suppose someone claims to have undergone reflective scrutiny and arrived at the intuitive judgement that what we owe to everyone, the moral minimum to be guaranteed to all, is X. This is supposed to represent an absolute threshold, above which the claim for help is optional, not a strict requirement. Now suppose lots of oil is discovered in Canada – really a lot. Or suppose there is a technological breakthrough, such that we can turn dirt into a kind of manna. We now could provide everyone on Earth with 2X, at no more necessary cost to anyone than would have been required to provide everyone with X, prior to the discovery. Is it still obvious that what we owe to all, the absolute moral minimum, is X and not 2X or something else entirely? The question is supposed to prompt the thought that our thinking about what is "good enough" reflects vague background assumptions about how much cost better-off people would have to sustain in order to provide worse-off people with this or that level of basic minimum. On reflection, this line of thought concludes, we see there is no absolute sufficiency line waiting to be discovered.

Another response to the various problems that beset the effort to identify the "good enough" line that constitutes the moral minimum is to set the line high. This is the approach of Martha Nussbaum (2006), who affirms that justice requires at least that each and every person be continuously enabled to achieve each and every one of an extensive list of basic human capabilities, at a good enough level, which Nussbaum seems to envisage will be rather high. (It should be noted that Nussbaum herself does not commit to the idea that we owe more to fellow countrymen than to those beyond the borders of our national state.) One might immediately wonder why my below-par endowment for one capability cannot be compensated by my above-par endowment for some other basic capability or for that matter for some nonbasic capability that greatly enhances my well-being. Leaving that issue aside, one still faces the problem that the justice duty asserted is entirely insensitive to the costs and benefits that would issue from efforts to fulfil it. Such a duty is too unyieldingly stringent. Further problems arise when we specify more precisely the asserted duty to provide capabilities for all. If the idea is that we ought to get as many people as possible to the sufficiency line, and the line is set very high, this will have the drawback that the sufficiency doctrine will insist that we ought to channel resources to getting a person who is just below the line to just past it, even at large cost, when the resources could alternatively be used to provide great improvements in the lives of many people who are unavoidably below the threshold and cannot be brought to it.

Rival principles of global justice

Suppose there are significant cosmopolitan justice requirements on institutions and individual actions that apply with global scope. What might be their content? Issues familiar from the study of social justice in a single society now reappear in a wider setting (for surveys see Roemer 1996, Kymlicka 2002). One class of views holds that justice requires equality or equality of opportunity in people's condition. What this comes to depends on what is the morally appropriate measure of people's condition for determining what we owe them; the range of contending views includes welfare or well-being, resources or general-purpose means to ends one might have, and capabilities or real freedoms to do or be what one has reason to value. Some deny that it is morally desirable in any respect that all people have the same or achieve the same. Instead one might propose that justice requires that we make the condition of the worst-off people as well off as possible, or maximize a function of benefits for people that gives greater moral weight to gaining a benefit for a person, the worse off in absolute terms she would otherwise be, or ensure that everyone is sustained at a good enough condition (this last view is described and queried in the previous section). Of course, some deny that we have any positive duties to improve the condition of others and assert that we owe others only negative duties not to harm.

Conclusion

This survey reveals two broad divides along with many lesser fissures and divisions in current global justice thinking. One divide is between extreme cosmopolitanism and its opponents. Extreme cosmopolitanism appears to many to be counterintuitive, but the main arguments so far offered against it are weak. A second divide is between those who accept, and those who deny, a strong general beneficence component in fundamental moral principles. The stronger this requirement, the stronger the gravitational pull of the claims of distant needy strangers on the overall constellation of forces that determines what we owe to one another all things considered.

Note

1 Utilitarianism holds that one morally ought always to do that act, among those available for choice, that would bring about the greatest aggregate amount of utility (human good). Lockean libertarianism holds that (a) each person has a moral right to do whatever she chooses with whatever she legitimately owns provided she does not thereby wrongfully harm others in certain ways (force, violence, fraud, theft of property, causing physical damage to the person or property of another, or threatening to do any of these things) that qualify as violations of their rights, (b) each person legitimately owns herself, and (c) each person has a moral right not to be harmed wrongfully in any of the certain ways just noted. Act consequentialism holds that one morally ought always to do that act, among those available for choice, that would bring about an outcome no worse than the outcome that would have been brought about by anything else she might have done. Utilitarianism is one possible version of act consequentialism; there are many others.

5

GENDER, CARE AND GLOBAL VALUES

Virginia Held

This chapter looks at changes in the social sciences and in the field of international relations as a result of an awareness of how gender matters. It looks also at changes in moral theorizing brought about by feminist perspectives, especially the development of the ethics of care. The chapter suggests changes in global political and social institutions that the ethics of care would recommend. It explores how feminists are rethinking global issues such as care and migration, global poverty and economic development, and the prospects for international law. It concludes with suggestions for how the ethics of care might lead us to rearrange global relations.

Gender and the social sciences

In recent decades, an awareness and acknowledgment of how gender matters has affected one field of enquiry after another. Previously, the experience and lives of women had been largely overlooked in many fields. The women's movement and feminist scholarship of the last quarter of the twentieth century succeeded in making it commonplace to consider the experiences and concerns of women along with the traditional approaches and problems of the various social sciences.

Where, for instance, political scientists had ignored the different voting patterns of women, or the low numbers of women representatives in legislatures or of women in positions of power, these aspects of political life became topics of study. Or where economists had paid scant attention to matters of women's employment and to pay differentials between men and women, again, there began to be sustained investigation into gender issues.

Not only were new topics and problems studied, however, but there also developed an awareness that paying attention to gender often changed the basic concepts and assumptions of whole fields of enquiry. What had been taken to be impartial social-scientific knowledge could now be questioned as perhaps, instead, reflecting a male rather than a neutral or universal point of view (Zalk & Gordon-Kelter 1992).

For instance, if the situations of women were given comparable attention in studies of economic development, what had counted as progress or success might look very different. As men were accorded rights to land, women might become more powerless and disadvantaged than before (Peterson & Runyon 1993, Jaggar 2009). As agriculture became more mechanized and commercialized, female farming systems might be undermined and the status of women worsened (Peterson & Runyon 1993, Jaggar 2009).

If the value of women's care of children would be included in estimates of a country's economic activity, the picture of its economy and of who contributed how much to it would need to be fundamentally revised. And if awareness of women's experience would be given equal weight in thinking about society, the picture of society as composed of individuals all pursuing their own interests and contracting with one another to establish rules and exchange goods would be seen to be highly questionable (Zalk & Gordon-Kelter 1992; V. Held 1993: 192–214).

With attention to women came awareness that women are not a single group, and that realities are often different for women of different races and classes, and for lesbian women. It became standard to investigate the factors of race, class and sexual orientation in the various issues studied. And an increased effort to explore non-Western as well as Western points of view developed.

The field of international relations was one of the last to undergo this kind of change (Halliday 1996). Examining the way the field had reflected a male rather than a gender-neutral point of view, J. Ann Tickner wrote,

> with its focus on the "high" politics of war and Realpolitik, the traditional Western academic discipline of international relations privileges issues that grow out of men's experiences; we are socialized into believing that war and power politics are spheres of activity with which men have a special affinity [and to which women are irrelevant].
>
> *(Tickner 1992: 4)*

The traditional focus of international relations was gradually challenged, and it was shown how "the values and assumptions that drive our international system are intrinsically related to concepts of masculinity" (*ibid.*: 17).

Images of masculinity and macho emotions shape what leaders and voters aim at. The fear of not being sufficiently "tough", and the idea that cooperation is for the "weak", lead to an overemphasis on states' military security and economic preeminence, and to the neglect of the security that can be cultivated through environmental restraints, legal processes, and habits of working together.

Realists and neorealists in international relations and politics have transferred the Hobbesian view of man in the state of nature to the international arena, advocating preparation for war and avoiding dependence on others as the means to their states' security and success. Feminists have shown the gender bias in Hobbes's view of the political world. As Spike Peterson and Anne Runyon write, it is revealed "when we ask how helpless infants ever become adults if human nature is universally competitive and hostile ... [W]ithout the cooperation that is required to nurture children, there would be no men or women" (Peterson & Runyon 1993: 34). Fiona Robinson has demonstrated how both mainstream international relations theory and mainstream normative theory about international relations have "resulted in the creation of a global 'culture of neglect' through a systematic devaluing of notions of interdependence, relatedness, and positive involvement in the lives of distant others" (Robinson 1999: 7). Feminist scholars conclude that "gender shapes our identification of global actors, characterization of state and nonstate actions, framing of global problems, and consideration of possible alternatives" (Peterson & Runyan 1993: 10).

New thinking and research are changing the way global problems are conceptualized. Philosophers are examining what global gender justice would require, as global processes so often result in disparate burdens on women (Jaggar 2009). Scholars are calling attention to such neglected issues as security for women against domestic violence and the threat of rape, the use of rape as a weapon in wartime, and human trafficking. Reflection on how to conceptualize the global arena and marketplace is leading to new ideas about meeting the needs of women, children and men, and bringing about the security of being cared for when in need, and being able to care for one's family. "Security" itself is being reconceptualized (Robinson 2011a).

Writing of recent developments in international relations, feminist scholars agree that matters of war and peace and the military security of states have "traditionally held pride of place in [international relations] theory and practice" (Peterson & Runyon 2010: 151). But some change has occurred. "Relatively new conceptions", some find, "of human security and environmental security, and even more recently, food, water, energy, and health security, have brought welcome international attention to sources of structural violence that undermine the well-being of people and the planet" (*ibid*.). On the other hand, there is a tendency once again to reduce these concerns to matters of the security of states, so the future is unclear.

Moral theorizing

There have been transformations also in theorizing about morality and how global actors ought to behave. Feminist attention to the experience and lives of women brought a focus on the enormous amount of labour that women do caring for children, the ill, the elderly, and often men. It was observed that traditional moral theories had paid almost no attention whatsoever to this entire region of human activity. Although persons engaged in the endeavours of mothering think a great deal about what they ought to do, and often discuss it with others, this sphere of human practice was often conceptualized as belonging to "nature" rather than to what is specifically human such as political or economic activity (V. Held 1993: 44–57). It was imagined by many to be governed by natural instinct rather than guided by morality, or it was simply overlooked and ignored. In any case, it was largely thought to be morally irrelevant.

Paying attention to the practices of mothering and other caring activities raises such questions as whether it is fair that women do such a large proportion of this work, that so much of it is unpaid, and that when it is paid it is so poorly paid. It can also lead to rethinking moral theory itself. When we pay attention to care work, we can become aware of the values incorporated into practices of care, values such as responsiveness to need, sensitivity and trust. These values are rather different from the rational consent to duty, or maximum utility, emphasized by other moral theories, but they are clearly compelling.

Care appreciates the moral value of emotions such as empathy and concern for others in enabling us to understand what we ought to do. Traditional moral theories such as Kantian ethics and utilitarianism, in contrast, fearing such threatening emotions as aggressiveness, anger, hatred and selfishness, base morality entirely on reason. Although utilitarianism's conception of reason as instrumental and calculative is different from Kantian conceptions of reason as demonstrating the universally valid norms for inherently right actions, both are rationalistic moral theories.

Attention to caring activities also leads us to understand persons as relational and interdependent, rather than as the self-sufficient individuals pursuing their own interests of so much other theory. What are central are caring relations. To the extent that virtue theory focuses on individuals and their dispositions, it resembles other traditional moral theories in conceptualizing persons as primarily separate and discrete rather than relational and interdependent. Caring relations, in contrast, need to be evaluated as much from the point of view of recipients of care as of providers. What constitutes *good* care depends as much on how it is experienced as how it is intended.

The moral considerations reflected in practices of care are different from those of traditional moral theories (Ruddick 1980, 1989; Gilligan 1982; Noddings 1986). Gradually, a moral approach or theory has developed to make explicit this alternative: the ethics of care (Tronto

1993, Bubeck 1995, Bowden 1997, V. Held 2006, Engster 2007, Slote 2007). Although its values are most evident in the contexts of family and friendship, in familiar practices such as caring for children and others who are dependent, its values of empathetic concern, of meeting people's needs with sensitivity, and of cultivating trust, can be seen as relevant to human activity outside the household as well. The implications are important for human activity in general and everywhere, and are being explored. The rigid separation of public and private that has rendered what happens in the household irrelevant to politics and law is superceded. We need to recognize how care is central to human well-being, to citizenship and to security, and how this recognition should change our theories and our practices (Sevenhuijsen 1998, Kittay 1999, V. Held 2006). We need to consider, for instance, what a caring society would recommend (M. Harrington 1999, Noddings 2002) and what the implications would be of a care approach for international relations and global concerns (Robinson 1999, 2011a; Mahon & Robinson 2011).

The ethics of care

The ethics of care is only a few decades old, a moment in the history of moral theorizing, yet it has affected the thinking of many feminist and other theorists, women and men. Starting with the work of Sara Ruddick, Carol Gilligan and Nel Noddings in the 1980s, it has been developed into a widely discussed and influential new approach to moral issues. This new moral outlook has the potential of becoming a comprehensive moral theory that could be an alternative to Kantian ethics, utilitarian consequentialism and traditional virtue theory, applied to global issues.

This new approach to moral theorizing, when further developed, will be able to provide guidance for the full range of human relations, from our closest relations in contexts of families, friendship and small groups to our most distant relations in political, civil and global society.

From the perspective of care, caring relations between persons are especially of value. In its earliest formulations, its focus was on the face-to-face interactions of those who give and receive care, especially in such activities as mothering, and some thought it was limited to such contexts. By now, however, it has moved far beyond this. It may be easiest to recognize the values in caring relations in the case of personal relations between members of families or of friends or small groups. But this understanding can be extended to valuing caring relations between all persons in any number of contexts. It can also encompass the moral considerations of justice. Although the emotions so central to care, of empathy, caring and concern for others, may be felt most strongly for those close to us, they can also be felt for distant others. As Hume argued persuasively, we are not indifferent to the pain of those we do not know (Hume [1752] 1957: section V, part II).

Instead of building ethics on the model of the independent, self-sufficient liberal individual contracting with his equals, the ethics of care understands persons as inherently relational and interdependent. Instead of assuming that morally relevant social relations are entered into voluntarily, it understands the moral significance of the unchosen relations in which we find ourselves. These are frequently between persons of very unequal power. The ethics of care fosters such practices as responding effectively and with sensitivity to actual needs of embodied persons, and dealing with conflict non-violently. It builds the trust that can only exist *between* persons, since being trusting when others are untrustworthy may be naïve and ill-advised. It attends as closely to the experience of recipients of care as of care providers, offering guidance for avoiding paternalism and the tendency of the strong to dominate.

To the ethics of care, effectiveness is of major importance. To care well and to provide good care it is not enough to intend to meet needs or to feel concern for others. This does not mean that the ethics of care is a form of utilitarianism, judging actions by their consequences alone.

Caring actions can have the intrinsic moral worth that deontological moral theories recognize. Caring actions should be evaluated in terms of the intentions they express as well as by their effects. And although the appropriate character is important for caring well, the ethics of care is not a form of virtue ethics because its focus is on caring relations between interdependent persons, not on the virtues of individuals. The ethics of care evaluates practices on many grounds: it fosters care that responds successfully, with empathy and sensitivity, to actual needs and does so in ways conducive to trust and mutual consideration.

Early critics of the ethics of care sometimes interpreted it as an affirmation of women's traditional caring roles and hence, to feminists, as unjustifiably conservative. But this view is mistaken. It is only plausible when applied to the earliest formulations of this alternative moral approach, and even then was based on a misunderstanding. By now, the ethics of care is clearly a feminist ethic that calls for the transformation of the most fundamental domination, that of gender. It advocates an end to domination itself and the overhaul of caring practices oppressive to women and paternalistic to recipients of care. The ethics of care appreciates women's experience, but it calls for a vast and fundamental transformation of the social structures and practices constituting and surrounding care. It builds on understanding the values of care and extends them to all persons, promoting caring practices for men as well as for women.

Care includes the practices of providing care and being cared for and the values that are reflected in such practices and by which they are evaluated. It is thus both value and practice. Existing practices of care need continual improvement, and the social structures in which care takes place need to be radically transformed so that all persons can be adequately cared for in non-exploitative ways.

To the ethics of care, care is a value at least as important as justice, and more fundamental. Its practices incorporate caring values and should be progressively improved. Practices of justice, such as the enforcement of law and distribution of goods, should reflect the values of justice, as practices of care reflect the values of care. Those of care are more essential. One can survive without justice, but no one can survive without having received a great deal of care.

The ethics of care is based on experience. One of its strengths is that the experience on which it is built is truly universal, the experience of having been cared for. Every single person everywhere and at any time in history has access to this experience, and most persons also have experience of providing care. The ethics of care thus has no need to appeal to religious views that are divisive. Nor does it rest on the individualistic outlook of theories that only claim to be universal.

Care does not assume, as many moral theories do, a context of individuals all seeking their own interests in competition with others doing the same. Nor does it assume that morality typically requires self-sacrifice. It reflects neither the egoistic pursuit of self-interest nor the altruistic denial of self. It promotes the cooperative pursuit of the mutual good of, and caring relation between, care recipients and care providers. Parents characteristically want their children to develop well and children usually want their aged parents to be well cared for. They can aim for what is good for both or all held together by care.

This is not to say that care always opposes competition. Much competition between members of a civil community is acceptable to an ethics of care: sports teams compete and persons can, within limits, seek to promote their economic interests. Sometimes such competition represents a lowering of deadly or violent competition between rival groups. However, if there is nothing else than competition in the interactions of persons and groups, persons will not be genuine friends and groups will not form a civil community. There must be some social glue to keep persons and communities together, and this can best be thought of as mutual concern within caring relations. The caring concern we have for strangers and those rather distant from us can be relatively weak. But without any underlying concern for the persons involved, assemblages of persons can easily disintegrate or descend into violence.

Within the weaker relations of care that can be formed with relatively distant others, we can well develop legal and political ways to interact. For these particular contexts, more traditional moral theories in which justice is primary can often be suitable. But care and its values should remain fundamental, with caring relations forming the wider and more fundamental context in which particular legal or political interactions occur.

We ought to extend caring relations to everyone, enough to care what happens to them and to care that their needs will be met. We can recognize, at the same time, that people are divided into separate societies, and we can seek the norms that should govern their relations with one another within these societies. For their governing institutions, traditional liberal norms may well be suitable. We do not need, however, to wait until the norms recommended within states are universally accepted as valid to accept the restraints of international law. Caring concern for all persons, though weak, should lead us to strongly promote the avoidance of violence between states, as between persons, and the furtherance of the human rights of all persons.

Once societies have coherence and can maintain legal and political systems, traditional theories such as Kantian ethics and utilitarianism may be appropriate for problems that can be treated as internal to them. However, legal and political ways of interacting should be seen as embedded within a wider network of caring human relations, for which the ethics of care is a more promising guide. The moral theories appropriate for legal and political interactions have been offered to us as comprehensive moral theories, but they are seriously unsatisfactory beyond legal and political contexts, as attention to care makes clear.

For the fundamental evaluation of legal and political practices and the laws and institutions they embody, and for understanding how they ought to be changed and their place in society modified, the ethics of care can offer guidance. And for recommendations on how groups and states ought to behave, and how persons ought to act as members of a global community, and not only citizens of given states, the ethics of care shows promise. We need to care sufficiently for persons distant from us to work for their rights to be respected. We need actually to care for and meet the needs of persons around the globe so that they can survive and improve their lives.

Rethinking global issues

Feminism leads us to rethink global realities and the ethics of care suggests new perspectives on global problems. Fiona Robinson has fundamentally reconceptualized human security, bringing in factors of race and class as well as gender. "Relations of care", she writes,

> are a central axis around which the security of all people, in the context of webs of relations, revolves … The ways we think about, describe and act in relation to care must be interrogated. In addition, we must consider the obstacles and inequities which currently serve to hinder the ability of many individuals and institutions (including states) to be attentive to care needs, and which obstruct and prevent the equitable and adequate delivery of care in many contexts around the world.
>
> *(F. Robinson 2011a: 6)*

Feminist scholars have turned their attention to various global problems that have been neglected, such as the migrations of care workers from developing countries to developed ones, leaving a serious deficit of care workers in the developing world (Ehrenreich & Hochschild 2003, Mahon & Robinson 2011). Such scholars are examining the way the neo-liberal restructuring of many economies are leaving many women unable to find jobs and unable to care for their families (Jaggar 2009, Peterson & Runyon 2010).

The ethics of care is more suitable than ethical views centred on justice and rights for dealing with many of these issues because of its focus on care work, its attention to gender, and more recently race and class, and its conception of persons as relational (Abu-Laban 2012, F. Robinson 2011a). It "may allow us to move from consideration of a 'world of strangers' to a 'world of relationships'" in ways more attuned to the realities and moral issues involved (Abu-Laban 2012: 157).

The ethics of care leads to different and potentially more persuasive arguments than previous theories for overcoming global poverty and achieving the kind of economic development that will enable people to provide the care all children need, and to improve the health of all (F. Robinson 2011a, 2011b). And it provides guidance for dealing with violence and accepting the restraints of international law as it has developed (V. Held 2011). The following sections will examine some of these developments.

Care and migration

Migration is standardly thought of in terms of male workers traveling to foreign countries to find work, sometimes bringing wives and children (Abu-Laban 2012). In fact, women increasingly migrate, often independently of men (Ehrenreich & Hochschild 2003). "Overall," two researchers write, "half of the world's 120 million legal and illegal migrants are now believed to be women" (*ibid.*: 5).

How needs are met and care provided reflect the realities of power: who has the resources and influence to bring it about that their children are well cared for and the health needs of their families taken care of, for instance. More and more, these issues must be thought of in a global context. As Rianne Mahon and Fiona Robinson write, "In the past, the politics of needs was played out largely within national contexts and reflected the existing balance of power therein" (Mahon & Robinson 2011: 2). More recently, "care needs in the richer countries are being increasingly met by the prodigious flow of female labour from poorer countries" (*ibid.*). They write about the "transnationalisation" instead of "globalization" of care work because, although states are increasingly unable to control the flow of migrants of all kinds, "the state remains a crucial actor in the regulation and promotion" of care, as care work in the global economy becomes "increasingly commodified" (*ibid.*: 2–3).

How care is provided varies with state policy. Commodification occurs when care work is not only paid but when access to it is made through the market. Without public support, most families cannot afford adequate care. Mahon and Robinson write:

> In social democratic welfare regimes, the state finances and often provides social-care services; in liberal regimes, tax incentives can be used to cheapen the cost of commercial care for some while others rely on low-wage informal (non-regulated) care; and in conservative continental regimes, the growth of monetized care is stunted.
>
> *(Ibid.: 8)*

Arrangements for elder care and for healthcare, as for childcare, differ with state policies, politics and ideology, and not necessarily in the same ways. However, the borders of states are increasingly permeable to flows of people. We need to recognize "an international division of reproductive labour" that is structured by social class, race and ethnicity, and gender inequalities (Yeates 2005: 232; see also Mahon & Robinson 2011: 15).

The flow of caregivers, mostly women, from poorer countries allows greater gender equality for women in developed countries as they enter the labour market and pursue careers, "solving" their problems of reconciling work with family responsibilities by hiring help. Their children are well cared for, but at the expense of families and societies in poorer countries as the women hired leave their own children behind for years at a time. As Arlie Hochschild writes, "the new emotional imperialism does not issue from the barrel of a gun. Women choose to migrate for domestic work. But they choose it because economic pressures all but coerce them to" (Hochschild 2003: 27).

In many cases, the women who migrate are trained as teachers or nurses, but can earn far more as domestic workers in rich countries (Mahon & Robinson 2011: 12). Trained women and men from poor countries are also hired in large numbers in health and elder care institutions, where even the ill-paid positions pay more than such workers can earn in their home countries. This migration brings about shortages of teachers and nurses in the poor countries most in need of them. Yet some governments, such as that of the Philippines, actively promote such migration as a source of income through remittances. An additional problem is that in the countries in which such migrants live and work, they are reduced to "partial citizenship".

To understand these realities and problems it is helpful to think in terms of transnational "care chains" (Ehrenreich & Hochschild 2003). And for evaluating the relevant practices and policies and proposals, the ethics of care has much to offer. As Mahon and Robinson argue:

> traditional concepts of rights, justice, and citizenship may be inadequate to address the contemporary challenges of care and well-being at the transnational scale … [A]n ethics of care is best suited to illuminate these issues … The ethical language of care can speak to the relationality … of care work … Ad hoc, exploitative, and excessively privatized solutions to the question of how we will care for each other are woefully inadequate in the current social, economic and demographic context. Care ethics can serve as a lens through which to focus and organize our thinking about the ways in which care is delivered.
>
> *(2011: 13–16)*

Fiona Williams argues that "we need to turn to those whose approach to global social justice embeds, theoretically and empirically, everyday social relations of care within macro understandings of inequality … The ethics of care is useful both as a method of analysis and as a normative framework" (Williams 2011: 35). Care ethics will maintain our awareness that progress in attaining gender, racial and economic justice will be possible only if we understand the context of caring relations in which this must be sought and which we must strive to improve.

Poverty and economic development

Nothing could be more of an affront to the values of care than the fact that still, in the twenty-first century, millions of children are dying from hunger and poverty. When the already huge gap between the rich countries of the global North and the poor countries of the global South grows even wider, as has happened, this is outrageous. And when the poverty of many developing countries grows even worse, as has occurred, this is inexcusable (see Part III of this volume).

Dealing with world poverty in terms of individual rights has had limited success. Arguments for global justice are important and often persuasive, but the claims of care are more powerful. In a world that can well afford it, all persons ought to have enough food to live. Elementary recognition of the values of care makes this compelling. Many of those who are unwilling to recognize the rights of distant others to a share of the wealth of their own countries are willing to acknowledge the moral call of humanitarian assistance.

Overcoming extreme global poverty has been a goal to which the states of the world have committed themselves through the United Nations Millennium Development Goals adopted in 2000. But clearly not enough is being done. The extremely modest goal of cutting in half the proportion of people with incomes of less than one US dollar per day by 2015 still leaves over a billion people in extreme poverty. Some genuine disagreement about which policies work combines with unwillingness to do what is needed. This has had particularly damaging effects for women and children.

Based on available data, the UN Development Fund for Women concluded in 2008 that "women are still more likely than men to be poor and at risk of hunger because of the systematic discrimination they face in access to education, healthcare, and control of assets" (United Nations Development Fund for Women 2008: 119). Progress has been made in awareness of how development policies affect men and women differently, and in calling attention to the gendered division of labour. But there is disagreement about how to address these problems (see Part III of this book).

Too often, purported interests in women's equality serve mainly to promote the ideology of economic neo-liberalism that privatizes social welfare and marketizes political and social life (Peterson & Runyon 2010: 135–36). This ideology turns women into versions of the "economic man" of economic theory, competing with others to promote his own interests with minimal interference from government. Where problems ought to be solved cooperatively, with those in a position to do so meeting the needs of the developing world, neo-liberalism promotes the advantages of those already advantaged in global economic structures. These developments undermine the values of care and community and the building of caring relations.

Meanwhile, the focus on security in the militarized sense continues to pull resources away from progress in development. "Human development", two feminist scholars write, "continues to be feminized and deprioritized as 'low' or 'soft' politics in relation to the masculinized 'high' and 'hard' politics of state security" (*ibid*.: 134). A focus on care and the ethics of care shows why this needs to change.

The prospects for international law

The concerns of care abhor the destructions wreaked by violent conflict. On most moral theories, arguments can be marshalled against violence. The ethics of care, all the same, is more reliable at reminding us of the damages of violence. It should never be far from our thinking and our emotions that violence destroys what care creates, and that there are almost always better ways of defending against violence than employing it.

Concerns to avoid violent conflict lead us to look to law to deal with conflict in ways that do not deteriorate into violence, and to international law to avoid the supreme destruction of war. The moral case for international law has usually rested on idealized versions of a hypothetical social contract that states could be imagined to have entered into. The case is unnecessarily weak, as states in the absence of law are imagined to be in a Hobbesian state of nature, and the Hobbesian conclusion follows: in the absence of a world government to enforce the law, states have no obligations to obey it because "covenants without the sword are but words" (Hobbes [1651] 1971: chapter XVII).

The argument for international law that the ethics of care can offer looks not to an ideal of international law but to international law as it has actually developed. This law already has considerable force, it is often effective, and its "normative pull" could be enhanced by the understanding of how much international law can contribute to the goals and practices of care (V. Held 2011).

For many in the United States, the standing of international law is in doubt. It is disparaged by critics on the left as merely supporting the interests of powerful states, and by those on the right as illegitimately interfering with the aims of US policy. From the perspective of care, however, there would be appreciation of what international law has already accomplished and could achieve with greater support.

In addition to promoting consequences sought by care, international law both expresses care for vulnerable populations, and provides for acting on the values of care. Such law enables at least enough cooperation to avoid violent international conflict, and allows the practices that foster care to develop among states. In place of constructing an abstract rational ideal of justice for independent individuals, the ethics of care and international law as so far developed seek to safeguard the lives and promote the well-being of actual, interdependent persons and groups.

Much of the philosophical literature on military intervention on moral grounds dismisses the arguments against intervention as "prudential considerations" or "considerations of international stability" not relevant to the moral argument (Laberge 1995). These would be at the centre of attention for and appropriately valued by the ethics of care, concerned as it is with the needs of actual, vulnerable people in distinct historical contexts. In contrast with theories focused on abstract justice for all, for which the case for military intervention is theoretically so easy (Beitz, Rawls), the ethics of care would be highly respectful of the need to keep the peace and avoid violent conflict. International law, out of caution, is respectful of sovereignty and hesitant to allow military intervention except in exceptional circumstances such as genocide or large-scale ethnic cleansing. Its respect for sovereignty is limited by such recently recognized norms as the Responsibility to Protect (Bellamy 2010b), but it still favours peace and stability over the use of intervening force to promote abstract rights (Hehir 1995). To the ethics of care, and within its guidelines, this would be approved. The US invasion of Iraq, with the turmoil to which it led and the hundreds of thousands of deaths and millions of refugees it caused, was a clear violation of international law and opposed by the guidelines of the ethics of care.

To the ideal theorists influenced by Kant, states with illegitimate regimes have no claim to the protections of international law. They remain in the Hobbesian wilderness and are morally and legally subject to intervention. In contrast, international law as so far developed would, within limits, accord some protection to states and the persons who would be harmed by such intervention.

Developing states seek, first of all, respect, interpreted as respect for their sovereignty. This is fundamental to establishing that imperial domination is unacceptable. International law as so far developed provides such respect, and the ethics of care, able to comprehend the strength of such sentiments, would value international law as expressive of the values of care and concern for actual, fragile, interrelated persons and groups.

The ethics of care asks us to develop its insights as much from the perspectives of the recipients of care as of care's providers. This gives it the resources to counter the tendencies of powerful states to impose their will on developing states. Good care avoids paternalism. It promotes dialogue with others and listening to those whose cultures, experiences and points of view are very different from one's own.

Trust is among the primary values of an ethics of care. Trust between potentially contentious states would be promoted by greater reliance on international law to handle conflicts and disputes. Such reliance would help the members of states to understand the points of view of their competitors. The ethics of care would encourage them to empathize with the aims and concerns of those with whom they are in conflict. It would promote cooperation between states that might otherwise become dangerously competitive.

The ethics of care inherently enlists the emotions. It builds on what Hume called "fellow-feeling". It cultivates what it sees as the moral and not only instrumental value of such emotions as empathy and responsiveness to need. Such emotions will support respect for international law and will increase law's ability to gain acceptance and to prevail. The rule of law and thus international law can be recommended on many moral grounds, such as Kantian ethics and utilitarianism, but it can be demanded even more effectively by the ethics of care.

The future of care

Given the realities of the current international situation, the ethics of care would recommend, for the present and near future, respect for international law. However, if one looks further ahead to the world to be aimed at, the view changes significantly. From the perspective of care, law is less of an answer to world conflicts and problems than many legal theorists suppose. Law is at best a limited approach for a limited domain of human activity. Legal approaches may be the best way in the short run to handle the conflicts of imperialist pretentions, religious aggression, environmental irresponsibility and ethnic hatred. Looking further ahead, however, we can try to envision how the world should progress towards something better than an aggregate of states and groups all primarily pursuing their own interests, restrained only by law and ever in danger of resorting to violence. We can hope for a more satisfactory global society. The ethics of care offers ways to move towards it.

Rather than emphasizing, as does the law, rules to be followed and violations to be punished, the ethics of care would focus on the social, political and economic problems that make the rules so often inadequate. To protect and promote the well-being of actual persons and groups, law is of very limited use. And rather than rely on military intervention to punish violators of the norms of international law, the ethics of care would promote dealing cooperatively with the underlying problems that lead to conflict (Robinson 1999, 2006, 2011a; V. Held 2006, 2011; Tronto 2008). It would foster the development of civil society groups and interactions of governmental officials that would press for solutions to specific problems (V. Held 2006: 125–37, 154–68). It would especially call for the restructuring of economic arrangements.

The ethics of care calls on persons and groups to take responsibility for meeting the needs of actual persons and groups. This would include promoting the peaceful resolutions of conflicts before they become violent. Negotiating disputes in non-coercive ways and confronting the problems of those who are exploited or politically disenfranchised can be developed as practices of care. With such practices in effect, the use of force to prevent wider violence and to uphold the restraints of law can become progressively less needed.

Some enforcement of law, within states and between them, may always remain necessary. The use of violence as a last resort is not ruled out by the ethics of care. Care would, however, hold that enforcement should be carried out in accordance with law and with international law, not unilaterally (see Doyle & Sambanis 2006). The ethics of care does not idealize human interactions. It recognizes and is able to handle tendencies towards violence, from domestic violence to international conflict (V. Held 2010). However, when caring relations within a state are developed to a sufficient degree and when caring practices are adequate, the need for enforcement can decrease as persons and groups grow accustomed to complying with reasonable rules and requirements. The same can be expected in interactions between states and groups.

The ethics of care, then, would support international law as it has developed but it would even more strongly promote the caring cooperation that decreases the need for law and its enforcements. And if the legal and political bounds that seek to contain violence fail, the ethics of care can offer insights on how to handle the situation. Many similar moral considerations apply in dealing with violence, whether in families or between states and groups: one ought to deter and restrain rather than obliterate and destroy; one ought to keep open the chances for reconciliation; in handling violence, one ought not cause any more harm to all concerned than is actually needed (V. Held 2008). In Sara Ruddick's words, "Many mothers know what many military enthusiasts forget – the ability to destroy can shock and awe but compelling the will is subtle, ultimately cooperative work" (Ruddick 2009: 307).

The ethics of care requires transformations of given domains within a society – the legal, the political, the economic, the cultural, and so on – but also transformations of the relations between such domains (V. Held 2006). Some would become more and others less influential, and this would also happen at the global level.

The transformation of economic activity would be demanded. Of *primary* importance would be the assurance of the kinds of economic development that actually would meet human needs and enable the care required by all to be provided. The ethics of care would call for very significant limits on markets (*ibid.*: 107–24). Such thinking is highly compatible with the inter-dependence between states and other groups increasingly understood by many persons thinking in global terms. Recognizing that caring relations exist and can be extended opens important new possibilities for rethinking the transformations needed to deal with global poverty and deprivation, in restructuring economic activity, and safeguarding the environment.

Fiona Robinson and others consider how care work can be justifiably apportioned on a global scale (Robinson 2011b). Unlike the current global marketplace that results in vast migrations of care workers who leave behind their own families in poor countries to do care work in developed countries, caring for children or the ill and elderly or becoming sex workers, the ethics of care asks that all persons have the ability to provide and to receive care. We need to develop the institutions and practices to reflect this concern.

6

COSMOPOLITANISM AND ITS CRITICS

Gillian Brock

What is cosmopolitanism? On one widely used account of the term, cosmopolitanism rests on the idea that every person has global stature as the *ultimate* unit of moral concern, and is therefore entitled to equal respect and consideration no matter what her citizenship status or other affiliations happen to be (Pogge 1992). Appealing to this premise of moral equality, cosmopolitanism guides the individual outwards from local obligations, and prohibits those obligations from crowding out responsibilities to distant others. The borders of states and other boundaries considered to restrict the *scope* of justice should not function as roadblocks in appreciating our responsibilities to all in the global community (Brock & Brighouse 2005).[1] But if this is what cosmopolitanism is, surely all ethically defensible views must be cosmopolitan in flavour? In order to locate the points of tension between cosmopolitans and those resistant to such approaches, we need to cover more ground.

In this chapter we begin by surveying some distinctions typically drawn among kinds of cosmopolitanisms, before surveying the diverse accounts of cosmopolitan justice. As much discussion between cosmopolitans and critics is still heavily influenced by John Rawls's views on international justice, we cover some of that disagreement next. We then explore views about the content of cosmopolitan duties of justice, especially whether the duties should focus on eliminating inequality or some other standard central to a decent life. Here we also examine the prominent debate between cosmopolitans and defenders of statist accounts of global justice, especially the position of egalitarian statists who believe that state borders do mark off some relevant boundary which affects what we owe one another. We examine such arguments and some important cosmopolitan responses to them. We then explore some common fears concerning cosmopolitanism and how they can be addressed, such as whether or not cosmopolitan commitments are necessarily in tension with other affiliations people typically have and how we should deal with issues concerning a perceived lack of authority in the global domain. Finally, we look briefly at how the concern with feasibility has led some to take up the challenge of devising public policy that is cosmopolitan in outlook.

Some types of cosmopolitanism: introduction to key terms and distinctions

Several distinctions are in use in the literature and it may be useful to review these.

Identity and responsibility cosmopolitanism

Early proponents of cosmopolitanism included the cynic Diogenes, and Stoics such as Cicero. These cosmopolitans rejected the idea that one should be importantly defined by one's city of origin, maintaining instead that they were "citizens of the world". The idea of being a citizen of the world captures the two central aspects of cosmopolitanism, as it is frequently understood today. These are: a thesis about identity and one about responsibility. As a thesis about identity, being a cosmopolitan indicates that one is a person who is influenced by various cultures.[2] Cosmopolitanism as a thesis about identity also maintains that belonging to a *particular* culture is not an *essential* ingredient for personal identity or living a flourishing life: one can select elements from diverse cultures, or reject all in favour of non-cultural options that are perceived as yet more important to particular people in living a flourishing life, as Jeremy Waldron (1992) maintains.

Cosmopolitanism as a thesis about responsibility generates much debate, as discussed below. Roughly, the idea is that as a cosmopolitan, one should appreciate that one is a member of a global community of human beings. As such, one has responsibilities to other members of the global community. As Martha Nussbaum elaborates, one owes allegiance "to the worldwide community of human beings" and this affiliation should constitute a primary allegiance (Nussbaum 1996: 4). We discuss responsibility cosmopolitanism in more detail in several sections below.

Moral and institutional cosmopolitanism

The core idea with moral cosmopolitanism is that every person has global stature as the ultimate unit of moral concern and is therefore entitled to equal consideration no matter what her citizenship or nationality status. Thomas Pogge gives a widely cited synopsis of what are thought to be the key ideas:

> Three elements are shared by all cosmopolitan positions. First, individualism: the ultimate units of concern are human beings, or persons – rather than, say, family lines, tribes, ethnic, cultural, or religious communities, nations, or states. The latter may be units of concern only indirectly, in virtue of their individual members or citizens. Second, universality: the status of ultimate unit of concern attaches to every living human being equally – not merely to some sub-set, such as men, aristocrats, Aryans, whites, or Muslims. Third, generality: this special status has global force. Persons are ultimate units of concern for everyone – not only for their compatriots, fellow religionists, or such like.
>
> *(Pogge 1992: 48)*

There is considerable debate about what the cosmopolitan commitment *requires*. Indeed, cosmopolitanism's force is best appreciated by considering what it rules out. For instance, it rules out positions that attach no moral value to some people, or weights the moral value some people have differentially according to their race, ethnicity or nationality. Furthermore, assigning ultimate rather than derivative value to collective entities such as nations or states is prohibited. If such groups matter, they matter because of their importance to individual human persons rather than because they have some independent, ultimate (say, ontological) value.

A common misconception is that cosmopolitanism requires a world state or government. A distinction is sometimes drawn between moral and institutional cosmopolitanism (also referred to in the literature variously as "legal" or "political" cosmopolitanism). Institutional cosmopolitans maintain that fairly deep institutional changes are needed to the global system in order to realize the cosmopolitan vision adequately. Moral cosmopolitans need not endorse that view, in fact many are against radical institutional transformations. Cosmopolitan justice requires that our global obligations (such as protecting everyone's basic human rights or ensuring everyone's capabilities are met to the required threshold) are effectively discharged. However, a number of suitable arrangements might do this effectively. There are various possibilities for global governance that would not amount to a world state. These include mixtures of delegating responsibilities for particular domains to various institutions, with multiple agencies able to hold each other accountable, and other ways of reconfiguring the structure of governance bodies at the global level (such as the United Nations) so they are brought into line better with cosmopolitan goals.

Weak versus strong cosmopolitanism

The way in which this distinction is typically drawn (e.g. D. Miller 2000: 174) is that weak cosmopolitanism underwrites, as requirements of justice, only the conditions that are universally necessary for human beings to lead minimally decent lives, whereas strong cosmopolitans are committed to a more demanding form of global distributive equality that will aim to eliminate inequalities between persons beyond some account of what is sufficient to live a minimally decent life. What is weak or strong, on this account, is the extent of one's commitments to redistribution.[3]

Cosmopolitan justice: an orientation to some central distinctions

Cosmopolitan justice can be argued for from a number of theoretical perspectives. After all, there are different conceptions of how to treat people equally, especially with respect to issues of distributive justice, and this is often reflected in these different accounts. Cosmopolitan justice could be argued for along various lines, including: utilitarian (prominently, P. Singer 1972); rights-based accounts (Shue [1980] 1996b, C. Jones 1999, Pogge 2002, Caney 2005b); Kantian (O. O'Neill 2000b); Aristotelian or capabilities-based (Nussbaum 2000, 2006); contractarian (Beitz 1979, Pogge 1989, Moellendorf 2002, G. Brock 2009); and sometimes using more than one approach (Beitz 1979, 2009; Pogge 1989, 2002). In recent years, one popular way of arguing for cosmopolitan justice has taken contractarian forms, following a highly influential debate between John Rawls and his critics. Because of its influence in current debates on cosmopolitan justice in political philosophy, we discuss this in the next section.

There are several different ways of arguing for cosmopolitan justice widely used in the literature. One common divide in accounts of cosmopolitan justice exists between those who argue for "humanist" and "associativist" approaches. Humanists, such as Simon Caney, believe that our duties of justice track our shared humanity. We have duties of justice towards all human beings in virtue of our humanity. Associativists, by contrast, believe duties of justice track co-membership in some association, such as political or economic association. Unless we are members of some important association, we have no duties towards persons. On such accounts, if we happen to come across persons existing on some distant planet, with whom we have no prior interactions, we could not have any duties of justice towards such people (though there might be some more minimal humanitarian obligations that we have towards them). Associativists, such as Darrel Moellendorf, tend to emphasize that all persons are part of at least one relevant association, namely a global economic association, and this is especially salient in our current era of economic globalization.

Cosmopolitan approaches to justice are often contrasted with "statist" accounts. For statists, the primary focus of our duties of justice is states rather than individuals. Cosmopolitans tend to place individuals front and centre of their theorizing about justice, though there might well be derivative implications concerning duties for states that flow from their analyses (Moellendorf 2009). There is a prominent debate between John Rawls and his critics that nicely follows these tracks and will provide a good illustration of the differences between the two approaches. Because of its enormous dominance in current debates on cosmopolitan justice, we discuss this next.

Rawls's *The Law of Peoples* and some of his prominent cosmopolitan critics

In *A Theory of Justice* (1971), John Rawls sets out to derive the principles of justice that should govern liberal societies. Because one's position in society can distort one's judgements about justice in profound but unrealized ways, Rawls sets out to shield us from this source of bias in constructing a powerful normative thought experiment. The idea is that you are to imagine yourself in a hypothetical choosing situation (the "original position") in which you are to select the principles of justice that will govern your society. In this choosing situation you are behind a "veil of ignorance" in which you are deprived of all knowledge of who you are in society. The veil of ignorance coupled with the facts that you are going to have to choose the basic principles to govern the society (a weighty matter) and you will have to live with these choices (you will be bound by the "strains of commitment") act as powerful constraints on your choices. You would not, for instance, choose principles that support a slave society, he argues, as you may end up being in the position of a slave or someone else who is badly off. Rather you would seek to ensure that the worst-off position is as good as possible, given the knowledge that you may end up having to occupy it. More positively, he famously argues for two principles: namely, one protecting equal basic liberties and a second permitting social and economic inequalities when (and only when) they are both to the greatest benefit of the least advantaged (the difference principle) and attached to positions that are open to all under conditions of fair equality of opportunity (the fair equality of opportunity principle). In *A Theory of Justice*, Rawls's focus is on the principles that should govern closed communities – paradigmatically, nation states. Cosmopolitans such as Charles Beitz (1979) and then Thomas Pogge (1989) argued that these two principles should apply globally. After all, if the point of the veil of ignorance is to shield us from knowledge of factors that are distorting yet arbitrary from a moral point of view, surely where one happens to have been born (or citizenship) qualifies as one of those quintessentially arbitrary factors from a moral perspective?

Cosmopolitans were then understandably disappointed when Rawls later explicitly argued against the global extension. He argued that, though the two principles should apply within liberal societies, they should not apply across them. Rather, in the international arena, Rawls argues that different principles would be chosen (in a second original position occupied by representatives of different, well-ordered peoples) and these would include principles acknowledging peoples' independence, their equality, that they have a right to self-defence, that they have duties of non-intervention, to observe treaties, to honour a limited set of rights, to conduct themselves appropriately in war, and to assist other peoples living in unfavourable conditions. A crucial factor for this apparently quite different position is the fact that in the global context it is *peoples* rather than *individual persons* that must make decisions about justice. Our membership in a "people" makes for a very different justice context for Rawls. We should aim for equality among peoples rather than individual persons in the international context, and so goods such as self-determination and political autonomy are prominent in this account. In the space provided, I cannot do justice to all the complexities of Rawls's sophisticated account, but for more detailed exposition of the views and critical discussion of these see Moellendorf (2002), Tan (2004), Martin and Reidy (2006) and G. Brock (2009). Here I focus on just a few commonly identified points of tension between Rawls and some of his prominent cosmopolitan critics.

In *The Law of Peoples* (1999c), Rawls engages directly with central claims made by some cosmopolitans, namely those who argue that the difference principle should apply globally. He takes up Charles Beitz's claim that, since a global system of cooperation already exists among states, a global difference principle should apply among them as well. Rawls argues against this, for a couple of reasons, but notably, because he believes that wealth owes its origin and maintenance to the political culture of the society rather than (say) to its stock of resources. Furthermore, any global principle of distributive justice we endorse must have a target and a cut-off point. Rawls believes we have a duty "to assist burdened societies to become full members of the Society of Peoples and to be able to determine the path of their own future for themselves" (*ibid.*: 118). Unlike his understanding of cosmopolitan commitments to a global difference principle, Rawls believes his principles have a target, which is to ensure the essentials of political autonomy and self-determination.

One of the most frequently raised objections critics make to Rawls's Law of Peoples is that the background picture Rawls assumes incorporates outdated views concerning the relations between states, peoples and individuals of the world. Rawls presupposes that states are sufficiently independent of one another so that each society can be held largely responsible for the well-being of its citizens. Furthermore, according to Rawls, differences in levels of wealth and prosperity are largely attributable to differences in political culture and the virtuous nature of its citizens. Critics point out, however, that Rawls ignores both the extent to which unfavourable conditions may result from factors external to the society and that there are all sorts of morally relevant connections between states, notably that they are situated in a global economic order that perpetuates the interests of wealthy developed states with little regard for the interests of poor, developing ones. We who live in the affluent, developed world cannot thus defensibly insulate ourselves from the misery of the worst off in the world, because we are complicit in keeping them in a state of poverty.

Thomas Pogge has done much to show the nature and extent of these connections (1994, 2001, 2002, *inter alia*). Two international institutions are particularly worrisome: the international borrowing privilege and the international resource privilege. Any group that exercises effective power in a state is recognized internationally as the legitimate government of that territory, and the international community is not concerned with how the group came to power or what it does with that power. Oppressive governments may borrow freely on behalf of the country (the international borrowing privilege) or dispose of its natural resources (the international resource privilege), and these actions are legally recognized internationally. These two privileges can have disastrous implications for the prosperity of poor countries (for instance) because these privileges provide incentives for coup attempts, they often influence what sorts of people are motivated to seek power, they facilitate oppressive governments being able to stay in office, and, should more democratic governments get to be in power, they are saddled with the debts incurred by their oppressive predecessors, thus draining the country of resources needed to firm up new democracies. Because foreigners benefit so greatly from the international resource privilege, they have an incentive to refrain from challenging the situation (or even to support oppressive governments). For these sorts of reasons, the current world order largely reflects the interests of wealthy and powerful states. Local governments have little incentive to attend to the needs of the poor, since their being able to continue in power depends more on the local elite, foreign governments, and corporations. Those in affluent developed countries have a responsibility to stop imposing this unjust global order and to mitigate the harms already inflicted on the world's most vulnerable people. As an initial proposal to begin to make some progress in the right direction, Pogge suggests that we impose a global resources tax of roughly 1 per cent to fund improvements to the lives of the worst off in developing societies (Pogge 1994).

One important feature of Pogge's argument is that it harnesses the firmly established negative duty not to harm and thereby arrives at powerful conclusions, rather than relying on the more controversial arguments concerning positive duties to assist. Whatever the merits of the case for a positive duty to assist, we should also harm less than we currently do. People have human rights not to suffer from deprivation and poverty and to the extent that we fail to make perfectly feasible reforms to the global institutional order we uphold, we violate their rights.

We see, then, how critics argue that Rawls ignores the extent to which societies suffering unfavourable conditions frequently result from factors external to that society, and that national policies are often heavily shaped by international factors. Rawls assumes we can talk coherently of bounded political communities that can constitute self-sufficient schemes of political cooperation. However, critics argue that this is an untenable assumption (Hurrell 2001). Some authors concentrate on showing that we actually have a system of global cooperation between societies and how this would give rise to obligations to the worst off (Hinsch 2001). Others believe that the relations among states of the world are more accurately described as ones of domination and coercion (Forst 2001, R. W. Miller 2010). Several critics, then, argue that the basic global structure is a scheme of coercive institutions that importantly affects individuals' life prospects. It should be transformed so that it becomes a fair scheme of cooperation among all citizens of the world. For some of these critics, this is best modelled by considering a global original position in which decision-makers have no knowledge of any morally arbitrary features, including country of citizenship. Using this kind of strategy, popular claims are that we should endorse a global difference principle (permitting economic inequalities just in case they work to improve the situation of the worst off in the world) or global equality of opportunity (Moellendorf 2002, Tan 2004, Caney 2005b), though other options, such as arguing for what is needed for a decent life (a "sufficientarian" account of global distributive justice) are also found in the literature (Nussbaum 2006, D. Miller 2007, G. Brock 2009).

Rawls aims at a realistic utopia, but critics charge that the result is neither sufficiently realistic nor utopian (e.g. Kuper 2000). It is not sufficiently realistic because, critics claim, he has not taken account of all the relevant realities; for instance, of interdependence or domination in the global arena. To the extent that he has not captured all the salient realities, his Law of Peoples is not as "workable" and likely to sustain ongoing cooperative political arrangements and relations between peoples. Furthermore, critics contend that the view is not very utopian in that the ideals embodied in the principles do not constitute much of an advance over the status quo. In his bow to realism, Rawls has tried to ensure that the Law of Peoples results in stability, yet the Law of Peoples he endorses is potentially very unstable because, arguably, stability is only achieved when just arrangements are in place, and Rawls has offered us nothing more than a *modus vivendi* with oppressor states. Some, such as Samuel Freeman (2006) and David Reidy (2006), continue to defend Rawls's views against these charges.

The content of cosmopolitan accounts of justice: should we aim for sufficiency or equality?

While cosmopolitans agree that justice has wide scope, they disagree among themselves as to what the *content* of these global justice obligations are: just what are we obligated to do for all in showing the necessary equal respect and consideration?

There is considerable debate about the content of our global distributive justice obligations among cosmopolitans. Much discussion centres around a particular question: should the focus of our obligations of global justice be on eliminating global poverty, especially ensuring people's basic human needs are met? Or, should we be concerned about eliminating inequalities more generally, even if people are above the poverty line? So, should we care about alleviating global poverty or inequality? In the language commonly used, should we care about sufficiency – whether people have enough for a decent life – or equality? Sufficientarians in the global context typically focus on meeting needs, sustaining capabilities, protecting basic human rights or securing self-determination, while egalitarians typically believe that there are more demanding duties than those advocated by sufficientarians.[4] Global egalitarians endorse various positions including a commitment to global equality of opportunity or distribution according to a global difference principle, equal positive freedom, or an equal share of the value of global resources, though many new options are also emerging, including the commitment to relational equality.[5]

Egalitarians often take as their point of departure a so-called luck egalitarian intuition. Consider how it is a matter of luck whether one is born into an affluent, developed country or a poor, developing nation. Yet where one happens to have been born tends to have such an important bearing on how one's life will go. The current distribution of global wealth and opportunities does not track persons' choices and efforts, but rather is greatly influenced and distorted by luck. What is thought to be objectionable here is that existing social and political institutions have converted contingent brute facts about people's lives into significant social disadvantages for some and advantages for others. Persons as moral equals can demand that any common order that they impose on one another start from a default assumption of equality and departures from this be justified to those who stand to be adversely affected. Many cosmopolitans are persuaded by the luck egalitarian view.

Should "the moral arbitrariness of birthplace" be a factor in determining the nature of our duties to one another? According to several contemporary egalitarians, membership in particular states can indeed be relevant to what we owe one another. We examine their views next.

A current debate rages between those who believe that full egalitarian justice applies within the state but not outside it, and those who believe the state does not and cannot make this kind of difference to one's commitment to egalitarian distributive justice. There are several forms of the argument. One kind emphasizes the fact that states are legally able to coerce whereas the lack of a global legal coercive authority rules out the need for global equality (R. W. Miller 1998, Blake 2001). The idea here is that legal coercion must be justifiable to those who will find their autonomy restricted, if it is to be legitimate. This coercion would be justifiable if no arbitrary inequalities are permissible in the society, hence we get a strong commitment to traditional egalitarian conceptions of distributive justice. This form of argument has been criticized from several directions. One line of attack is to dispute the idea that coercion is necessary for a concern with egalitarian distributive justice. There may be other reasons to care about equality in the absence of coercion. Another way to criticize this argument is to emphasize that even if we agree that coercion triggers egalitarian duties of justice, coercion in the global sphere being rampant, the necessary ingredient for egalitarian duties of justice is present at the global level (Cohen & Sabel 2006, Abizadeh 2007).

A second version of the "equality among compatriots but not among non-compatriots" position argues that when we make laws within a state, we become "joint authors" of the laws of our society (Nagel 2005). As joint authors, citizens live under a shared coercive system, the legitimacy of which relies on their consent. In order to give their consent, members can demand that no arbitrary inequalities are permissible. So their shared involvement in authoring and sustaining a coercive system triggers egalitarian duties among compatriots. But there is no relevant analogue in the global context: there is no global law-making process, and so no global legislation of which all persons are similarly joint authors. This argument has been challenged in several ways, including questioning whether joint authorship of legislation is necessary for the requisite concern (Caney 2008b) and also arguing that even if it is, similar processes can be found in the global context (Cohen & Sabel 2006). Furthermore, others contend that the argument is somewhat perverse in that I owe justification for coercion only to joint authors of a coercive scheme, whereas those who are not similarly placed are owed none. This thereby removes protection to some of the most vulnerable people: those affected by my coercion but uninvited to the joint authorship process in virtue of their status as non-members (Julius 2006, Abizadeh 2007).

Another attempt to justify the difference proceeds from an awareness that social cooperation grounds special duties. A democratic society is one in which there is fair social cooperation and arrangements that people can reasonably endorse. Members of a state owe egalitarian duties of justice to one another because each member plays a part in upholding and sustaining the collective goods of the society, such as maintaining a stable system of property rights or doing their part to uphold the good of security. Reasonable endorsement requires that there be no arbitrary inequalities within a society. Since there is no scheme of global social cooperation of the same type or scale, there is no similar requirement at the global level (Freeman 2006, Sangiovanni 2007). Several cosmopolitans have challenged the view that there is no set of global institutions based on social cooperation (Beitz 1979, Buchanan 2000). Others contest the normative argument that egalitarian justice only arises when there is social cooperation and maintain rather that justice can require the very establishment of such institutions of social cooperation (Abizadeh 2007, Caney 2008b). Sufficient interaction among agents may obligate agents to ensure that the interactions proceed on fair terms, which might require the establishment of institutional arrangements that can secure or protect such fair terms.

What role is there for partiality in accounts of global justice, according to cosmopolitans? Reconciling cosmopolitanism with other commitments

Do cosmopolitans make room in their theorizing for the special attachments and commitments that fill most ordinary human beings' lives with value and meaning? Do these affiliations conflict with our commitments to global justice?

A common misconception about cosmopolitanism concerns how a cosmopolitan must view her relations to those in local or particular communities, namely, that she must eschew such attachments in favour of some notion of impartial justice that the individual must apply directly to all, no matter where they are situated on the globe. But this is by no means entailed by several of the sophisticated accounts of cosmopolitanism on offer today.[6] Indeed, most contemporary cosmopolitans recognize that for many people, some of their most meaningful attachments in life derive from their allegiances to particular communities, be they national, ethnic, religious or cultural. Their accounts often seek to define the legitimate scope for such partiality, by situating these in a context which clarifies our obligations to one another. Cosmopolitan justice provides the basic framework or structure and thereby the constraints within which legitimate patriotism may operate (see, for instance, Tan 2004, 2005). Cosmopolitan principles should govern the global institutions, such that these treat people as equals in terms of their entitlements (regardless of nationality and power, say). However, once the background global institutional structure is just, persons may defensibly favour the interests of their compatriots (or co-nationals, or members of other more particular groups), so long as such partiality does not conflict with their other obligations, for instance, to support global institutions. So cosmopolitan principles should govern the global institutions, but need not directly regulate what choices people may make within the rules of the institutions. One of the strengths of Kok-Chor Tan's view (e.g. 2004) is that even though cosmopolitan justice provides the justification for the limits of partiality towards group members, the value of those attachments is not reduced to cosmopolitan considerations, which is arguably a flaw with other attempts (e.g. Nussbaum 1996).

A simple way to show how there is a gap between the cosmopolitan's position and what anti-cosmopolitans fear is this. Cosmopolitanism is essentially committed to these two central ideas: first, the equal moral worth of all individuals, no matter where they happen to be situated on the planet and what borders separate them from one another. Second, there are some obligations that are binding on all of us, no matter where we are situated. But acknowledging these two ideas still leaves plenty of room to endorse additional obligations, which derive from more particular commitments, and the preference some may have to spend discretionary resources and time on particular communities or attachments important to one's life plans and projects. In order to know just what constitutes our discretionary resources, and what our basic obligations to one another are, we need the input of cosmopolitan justice. So long as we act in ways consistent with those commitments, there are no residual ethical concerns. Whether or not there is still room for conflict depends on how much is packed into cosmopolitan justice. Very strong forms of egalitarian duties might leave little room; weaker ones might leave more. And yet we can appreciate that conceptually, at least, there is a gap and therefore no tension here, as feared.

Authority in the global domain

There are some who are sceptical of the cosmopolitan idea of obligations of justice that extend globally, at least given our current circumstances. Grounds for such scepticism include the fact that since there is no way to enforce obligations of justice at the global level, there can be no such obligations (Nagel 2005). Another concern revolves around fears that often accompany undesirable results which can ensue when there is a concentration of power (Kukathas 2006). An assumption is often made that obligations concerning cosmopolitan justice must entail a world state, and we have reason to fear the potential for world government to lead to oppressive consequences. Many resist this assumption and differentiate between global government and global governance. Though we may need some ways to coordinate management of our transnational affairs, this need not amount to world government. Supra-state organizations need not replace state-level ones, such as we see is the case with the European Union or the United Nations. Such institutions complement rather than replace states. Different models are available for thinking through a "post-sovereign" political world order, which incorporate scope for state-level institutions, as well as ones at sub-state and supra-state level (Pogge 1992, D. Held 1995).

A frequently raised issue concerns how divided authority and sovereignty arrangements might work in practice. In fact, we have examples of divided and delegated authority that work reasonably well in practice. States in a federation (such as in the US), local and regional authorities within a state, and the European Union all involve divided authority and often function effectively on a day-to-day basis. Forms of global governance can be diffuse and overlapping, so long as they have clear sites of accountability.

So to sceptics who wonder how well this is likely to work in practice, it is worth drawing attention to the fact that, whether we like it or not, we already have a system of global governance that is just like this, given all the international bodies (such as the United Nations, World Trade Organization, World Health Organization, World Bank or International Monetary Fund) that have authority over various domains that govern our lives. The question, then, is more one about how to reform this system to make it more responsive to the goals of global justice.

As Thomas Nagel (2005) notes, we have transitioned to more just arrangements in the past by demanding that the existing concentration of power be exercised more justly, that is, by working on what is already there. It is likely that there will be a similar path to global justice. How will people come to demand more legitimacy of the institutions that dominate their lives? Moves to promote global solidarity and community are often helpful in the struggle to ensure each person really is accorded the dignity and equal moral worth to which they are entitled. To that end, Nussbaum's suggestion (1996) that we educate for world citizenship is important. School curricula should be revised to promote more understanding of our global problems, and more opportunity to understand and create empathy with others no matter where they are situated. It is worth noting that there is a flourishing movement in the world to do exactly that.

The public policy turn and concern with feasibility

Philosophers have increasingly turned their attention to making recommendations for improvements in global policies, arrangements and institutions, often, in the process, advocating for important changes. Some of this concern is driven by a concern with feasibility and implementing change from where we are now, that is, quite a long way from the kind of situation of global justice to which cosmopolitans aspire. I have already noted some of the proposals Thomas Pogge has made concerning reforms to international borrowing and resource privileges in the section on Rawls's Law of Peoples and his cosmopolitan critics.

Other philosophers who discuss reforming current arrangements so that they better promote global justice include Leif Wenar (2008), who discusses how governments should block corporations from being able to purchase resources from repressive regimes. Christian Barry and Sanjay Reddy's work (2008) also provides a noteworthy attempt to outline detailed proposals for how Just Linkage arrangements can promote fair trade, creating desirable trading opportunities for those who offer improved employment conditions. Thomas Pogge's work on changing the incentives pharmaceutical companies face to better promote global justice is another example (Pogge 2011). And several philosophers are now concerned with reforming our accounting and taxation arrangements in areas governing transparency, accountability and less opportunity to evade tax, and also in the domain of introducing global taxes, such as Tobin taxes (G. Brock 2009, Moellendorf 2009).

In many ways the widespread and growing commitment to the importance of human rights in regulating our international affairs is something of a cosmopolitan achievement in the struggle for global justice. The fact that we have a document that clearly specifies the entitlements that all human beings have is quite remarkable, given the diversity of worldviews and perspectives represented among the world's people. Furthermore, we have an international legal order that has certain commitments to uphold these entitlements. All those states that are members of the United Nations have signed up to being committed to respecting human rights. And there is wide proliferation of treaties and agreements based on these commitments to human rights. The cosmopolitan idea that each person has equal moral worth and deserves some fundamental protections and entitlements is not just a theoretical position but has made some significant inroads in international law and global policy-making, though this is not to deny that we still have far to go before the cosmopolitan vision is adequately instantiated in the world.

Future directions

In each of the preceding sections, I have highlighted current points of tension in debates and shown how one might navigate a range of issues and challenges that are presented for cosmopolitanism. However, by offering possible ways cosmopolitans could resolve issues or respond to challenges, this should not mask the fact that *all* these matters are still the subject of lively debate.

Indeed, none of the debates raised here are settled and all are still the subject of vigorous analysis and further argument. Every aspect of cosmopolitanism treated here is still the subject of critical engagement: from the very ways in which one ought to define cosmopolitanism to what cosmopolitan commitment entails (see for instance, *Monist* 2011, G. Brock 2013).

In addressing the main issues identified as salient to various kinds of cosmopolitans and their critics, more work is needed on a range of central questions, including these: What significance, if any, does the moral arbitrariness of birthplace have to accounts of global distributive justice? How does membership in global and national associations influence our duties to one another in the global context? To what extent are cosmopolitan and special duties reconcilable? Do forms of coercion matter to the nature of our duties to one another and if they do, how and why does coercion matter? How, if at all, does equality matter at the global level? Is relational egalitarianism a promising global ideal? What kinds of reforms to our global and local institutions do cosmopolitan concerns require? Are these reforms feasible, even if normatively desirable? What account of feasibility ought we to embrace in discussing which cosmopolitan proposals could feasibly be implemented in our world? What might the cosmopolitan recommend as just policy in specific domains such as climate change, immigration, fair trade, healthcare, taxation, and the like? These kinds of questions emphasize how much work is still left to be done.

Notes

1 These standard accounts of the distinctive features of cosmopolitanism seem to be under some pressure in light of many recent arguments. See for instance, *Monist* 94(2), October 2011.
2 Depending on attitudes to the various influences, the word "cosmopolitanism" could have negative or positive connotations. It has had positive connotations when, for instance, it has been thought to mean that a person is worldly and well-travelled rather than narrow-minded or provincial. It has had more negative connotations, for instance in the case of Jews and Bolsheviks who, at one time, some considered to be a threat to the community. See Sypnowich (2005).
3 Samuel Scheffler also distinguishes between extreme and moderate cosmopolitanism. Using this terminology, Scheffler actually distinguishes at least two forms of cosmopolitanisms, giving rise to two distinctions. One concerns the *justificatory basis* of cosmopolitanism and the other concerns the content of what cosmopolitan justice consists in. An extreme cosmopolitan with respect to *justification* considers the underlying source of value to be cosmopolitan and it is with respect to cosmopolitan principles, goals or values that all other principles of morality must be justified. A moderate cosmopolitan can take a more pluralistic line on the source of value, admitting that some non-cosmopolitan principles, goals or values may have ultimate value as well. In particular, moderate cosmopolitans need not reduce our special obligations to principles of cosmopolitan value, which might be construed as devaluing and distorting the meaning of the special attachments that people have. We can best appreciate the force of the second kind of cosmopolitanism, cosmopolitanism about the *content of justice*, by considering the question: are there any norms of justice that apply within an individual society and not to the global population at large? The extreme cosmopolitan denies that there are *at the level of fundamental principle*, whereas the moderate cosmopolitan believes that this is possible – there might be some things we owe members of our own society that are not owed as matters of justice also to non-members.
4 Prominent sufficientarians include D. Miller (2007), R. W. Miller (2010), Nussbaum (2006) and Rawls (1999c).
5 Prominent global egalitarians include Caney (2005b), Moellendorf (2009) and Tan (2004). For the idea of relational equality see G. Brock (2009: 298–321).
6 See, for instance, the essays in Brock and Brighouse (2005).

7

HUMAN RIGHTS

Rainer Forst

Human rights may be the most generally recognized expression of global norms today, yet their content and even their nature is a topic of constant disagreement. One reason for this is that human rights comprise several dimensions that are difficult to reconcile. They have a *moral* nature, expressing urgent human concerns and claims that must not be violated anywhere in the world. Thus they have to be acceptable from many cultural perspectives. They are also *legal* rights, enshrined in national constitutions as well as in international declarations, covenants and treaties. Furthermore, they have a *political* meaning, expressing standards of basic political legitimacy. Thus, both nationally and internationally, questions are raised as to whether they are being fulfilled and about how violations could be sanctioned. Apart from these aspects, human rights also have a *historical* existence, although it is a matter of dispute as to when they actually came into existence. Some scholars date the beginning of the discourse of human rights back to early modern conceptions of natural rights (Tuck 1979), some to late-eighteenth-century "inventions" of human rights (Hunt 2007), while others believe that the Universal Declaration of Human Rights in 1948 marks a definitively new era and understanding of human rights as a task for the international community (Eide 1998, Beitz 2009). Others argue that it was only after the 1970s that human rights attained a central global political significance (Moyn 2010).

In philosophical debates, we encounter a plurality of perspectives on human rights that accord priority to one of the above-mentioned aspects.[1]

The first perspective is primarily an *ethical* justification of human rights, focused on the human interests they are meant to protect. There are some, like James Griffin (2008) in his *On Human Rights*, who argue that the value of personal autonomy is essential to what it means to be a "functioning human agent", and that human rights can be derived from the basic interests persons have in being such agents. Others, like James Nickel (2006) and John Tasioulas (2007, 2010), defend a more pluralist conception of essential human interests that ground human rights. William Talbott (2005, 2010) presents a consequentialist justification for human rights based on a conception of the relation between well-being and autonomy. Such ethical justifications of human rights share a focus on substantive notions of well-being or the "good life", and they view human rights as a means of securing essential conditions for such forms of life.

Amartya Sen (2004, 2009) and Martha Nussbaum (1997, 2011a) have developed a particular ethical approach to human rights based on the idea of human capabilities. For Sen, a qualitative account of human freedoms or functionings grounds human rights claims as universal ethical demands, whereas in Nussbaum's view a substantive conception of the human good (in the Aristotelian tradition) and the necessary capabilities to lead a good human life justify basic human rights.

The second approach, an alternative to ethical views, avoids grounding assumptions about the good life and rather stresses the *political–legal* aspect of human rights. According to these accounts, the main role or function of human rights is the one that they play in the area of international law or politics. And that role is, in John Rawls's formulations, "to provide a suitable definition of, and limits on, a government's internal sovereignty" and "to restrict the justifying reasons for war and its conduct" (Rawls 1999c: 27, 79). Favouring a "practical" conception of human rights over an "orthodox" ethical one, Charles Beitz's (2004: 197) view "takes the doctrine and discourse of human rights as we find them in international political practice as basic". Whereas Rawls relies on a philosophical "political" conception of the law of peoples, Beitz assumes current international law doctrine as well as practice to be authoritative. He follows Rawls, however, in defining the function of human rights as "justifying grounds of interference by the international community in the internal affairs of states" (*ibid.*: 202–3; also Beitz 2009: 41–42, 65). According to Joseph Raz, political reflections about the possibility and desirability of external intervention play a major role in judgements about human rights violations, with the consequence that human rights "lack a foundation in not being grounded in a fundamental moral concern but depending on the contingencies of the current system of international relations" (Raz 2010: 336).

A third group of approaches looks for *political–moral* justifications for human rights that also avoid strong ethical assumptions about the good life. Taking its lead from Rawlsian concerns about liberal parochialism and the search for justifications which can be the focus of an international "overlapping consensus" (C. Taylor 1999), several "minimalist" accounts of human rights have been suggested. An early view of such a kind has been developed by Henry Shue ([1980] 1996b) in his notion of basic rights as the precondition for the enjoyment of other personal rights. Michael Ignatieff (2001a) focuses on a more narrow set of rights that protect bodily security and personal liberty as the minimal core of human rights. Others fear that such a "lowest common denominator" approach (Vincent 1986: 48–49) runs the risk of mixing, in Joshua Cohen's (2004: 192) words, "justificatory minimalism" with "substantive minimalism". While the former is seen as a justified "acknowledgement of pluralism and embrace of toleration" in the international realm, the latter is to be avoided, for, according to Cohen, "human rights norms are best thought of as norms associated with an idea of *membership* or *inclusion* in an organized political society" (*ibid.*: 197). The latter requires, first and foremost, having the right "to be treated as a member", that is, to "have one's interests given due consideration" (*ibid.*) politically. The hope is that such a conception of rights can win support "from a range of ethical and religious outlooks" in "global public reason" (*ibid.*: 210).

Allen Buchanan, who defends an ethical justification for human rights in *Justice, Legitimacy, and Self-Determination* (2004: 118–90) that he believes can be supported by different ethical worldviews, also stresses the right to political membership and self-determination. Further developing that view, Buchanan (2010b) stresses the importance of the idea of equal legal and political status – a status that human rights exist to secure and protect.

Equality of status is also a major concern of a fourth approach, one that presents a *discourse-theoretical* argument for human rights (Habermas 1996, 2001a; Forst 1999, 2010; Benhabib 2004, 2011).[2] The main idea here is to ground human rights in a reflection on the status and rights of persons as autonomous agents of justification in norm-generating discourses, both morally and politically. The major differences among these approaches concern the moral status of the argument from either a discursive principle of rational argumentation (Habermas,

Benhabib) or from a moral principle of justification and autonomy implying a basic "right to justification" (Forst 2012). What they have in common is the emphasis on the *social* aspect of human rights in a historical perspective, namely that when and where they have been claimed, it has been because the individuals concerned suffered from and protested against forms of oppression and/or exploitation that they believed disregarded their dignity as human persons to whom a justification is owed for the norms and institutions to which they are subject. Human rights thus not only protect the autonomy and agency of persons; they also express their autonomy politically.

The above four approaches will be discussed in more detail in what follows, with a focus on their respective strengths and differences.

Ethical justifications

As noted above, James Griffin (2008) advocates an ethical justification for human rights that we can see as exemplary for such approaches. He sees them as "protections of our normative agency" (*ibid.*: 4) and he defines this kind of agency as a precondition for "deliberating, assessing, choosing, and acting to make what we see as a good life for ourselves" (*ibid.*: 32). Hence, a substantive notion of the good informs this view, one which breaks down into the three components of "autonomy" (i.e. choosing one's own path through life), the "minimum provision" (i.e. having adequate resources for choosing the good and acting on it) and the component of "liberty" (i.e. having the freedom to pursue the good) (*ibid.*: 33, 51). Human rights are derived from the value attached to the individual personhood of beings who have a higher-order interest in choosing and pursuing the good.

The fundamental philosophical issue for any theory of human rights is undoubtedly where its normative foundations lie. A teleological view such as Griffin's identifies basic interests of persons in pursuing the good and transforms them into rights claims in accordance with their weight or value, while other interests (such as being loved) do not qualify. The interests in autonomy and liberty that ground human rights are seen as morally fundamental, including an interpretation of what this means with respect to mutually binding rights "with enough content for them to be an effective, socially manageable claim on others" (*ibid.*: 38).

An important consideration in that respect stressed by rival approaches is that conceptions of the good – and corresponding interests – are considered to be reasonably contestable, even if they are as formal and general as the ones to which Griffin refers. He is careful to attach human rights not to a particular notion of the good or flourishing life but to the general idea of being a "functioning human agent" (*ibid.*: 35). Still, the main function to be realized is the "capacity to choose and to pursue our conception of a worthwhile life" (*ibid.*: 45), so it is for the pursuit of the good life that we value autonomy, in our capacity as "self-deciders" about our lives. This depends on the belief that the good life can only be thus called when it has been autonomously chosen and pursued. Speaking from a particular cultural perspective, this might be a reasonable belief, but it might also be reasonably doubted by someone who believes the good to consist in following a higher religious calling, or in one's duties as a member of a particular community in a traditional sense. Especially in an intercultural context, Griffin's seems to be a partial, non-universalizable conception of the good and of a basic human interest in pursuing it. Hence, it is questionable whether such a conception can ground universal human rights.

In addition, there is the question of how and why one's prudential insight into the value of autonomy for *oneself* translates into a moral insight that one owes it to every *other* person to respect their autonomy. With respect to this, Griffin argues for the independent normative reason-generating force of the value of autonomy: "To try to deny 'autonomy' its status as a reason for action unless it is attached to 'my' would mean giving up our grasp on how 'autonomy' works as a reason for action" (*ibid.*: 135). That argument, however, requires a notion of autonomy that is truly universalizable and thus detached from a reasonably contestable conception of the good, as alternative approaches would argue. From a discourse-theoretical perspective in particular, Griffin's position presupposes a prior insight that in the realm of morality, and especially of human rights, reasons for action must be reciprocally and generally justifiable and shareable. That implies, reflexively speaking, respect for every other person as an equal authority in the space of reasons where reciprocally valid justifications are being sought. If such a form of respect for others' normative agency is presupposed as the basis for human rights, then respecting such rights cannot depend on one's view that doing so contributes to one's own good life or that doing so contributes to the good life of others. For one might also reasonably think that pursuing one's self-interest in other ways would contribute more to one's good. One might also – from within a religious doctrine, for example – think that respecting another's right to the free exercise of religion leads this person to damnation. Still, given the grammar of human rights, one has to respect his or her basic rights unconditionally. To ground that claim to validity, it is doubtful whether it will suffice to employ a notion of respecting other's agency and autonomy attached to a reasonably contestable notion of the good or one that requires a translation of a prudential ethical value "for me" into a moral reason "for all".

This is also relevant for the important question of whether there is a human right to democratic political participation. Since Griffin's notion of autonomy as "deciding one's own conception of a worthwhile life" is, as he says, at a distance from political self-legislation, there is "no inferential route from human rights to democracy without adding some non-universal empirical premises" which would link democracy and human rights in an instrumental way, given the circumstances of modern societies (*ibid.*: 247). From the perspective of rival approaches, however, it is an important methodological demand for a theory of human rights to be able to reconstruct the internal perspective of those who fought or fight for such rights. Given the nature of such struggles, these rights should be seen as putting an end to political oppression and the imposition of political and social statuses which deprive one of one's freedom and of access to the social means necessary to be a person of equal standing. What is at stake in this context is being regarded as an agent worthy of effective political justification.

Political–legal approaches

Proponents of the political–legal or "functionalist" accounts of human rights mentioned above object to ethical approaches because they see them as being at odds with current human rights doctrine and practice. In the contemporary world, the huge plurality of ethical worldviews does not allow for a universal normative justification; but more than that, there is no need to look for such a justification. If one reconstructs human rights based on the current political practice that has coined these rights, one finds that they have a particular normative shape, but not a single or universal ground. What matters is the function that human rights have, namely to fix certain standards of treatment of persons by their own states, the violations of which justify "remedial or preventive action by the world community or those acting as its agents" (Beitz 2009: 13). In this way, a "practical" idea and doctrine of human rights can be developed on the basis of the best and most coherent reconstruction of current human rights practice.

Yet from the point of view of the rival approaches, to focus on the role of human rights as that of limiting sovereignty in the *international* realm neglects the important *intra-national* purpose of human rights. These approaches see it as misleading to prioritize the political–legal function (providing reasons for a politics of legitimate intervention) of human rights within international law or political practice. They insist that the first task is to find (or construct) a justifiable set of human rights which a legitimate political authority must respect and guarantee and then to ask what kinds of legal structures are required at the international level to help ensure that political authority is exercised in that way. Only after that step will it become necessary to think about and set up legitimate institutions of possible intervention (as measures of last resort). The first question of human rights according to these views is not how to limit sovereignty from the outside; it is about the essential conditions of the possibility of establishing legitimate political authority. International law and a politics of intervention have to *follow* a particular logic of human rights, not the reverse. Such a logic is not a simple one, one must add, for several additional factors need be taken into account when it comes to the issue of legitimate intervention (see Buchanan 2004 and Jean Cohen 2012).

Human rights, according to these approaches, do not serve primarily to limit internal "autonomy" or "sovereignty" but to ground internal legitimacy. The claim to external respect depends on internal respect based on justified acceptance; however, that does not mean that one can infer the legitimacy of intervention – or the lack of international "recognitional legitimacy" (Buchanan 2004: 261–88) – from a lack of internal acceptance. Violations of human rights place the *internal legitimacy* of a social and political structure in question, but they do not necessarily dissolve the independent *standing* of that state in the international arena. To be sure, violations of human rights can provide a strong reason for taking external action. Beitz (2009: 203) is right to point out that this can take several forms, but this does not mean that the point of human rights can be defined as that of generating interference-justifying reasons.

Furthermore, since one important goal that drives functionalist views of human rights is avoiding a broad list of human rights which could serve to justify a wide range of interventions, reducing the list of core human rights accordingly is problematic. Rather, the correct conclusion is to devise legitimate international institutions with justifiable procedures for assessing and deciding cases of necessary external action.

Political–moral perspectives

Similar critiques have been made of "minimalist" justifications for human rights. A "lowest common denominator" approach would run the risk of drastically reducing the content of human rights. In looking for a possible universal consensus on these rights, one opts for a minimal justification and, all too often, for a reduced conception of human rights. Even if Rawls in *The Law of Peoples* did not locate the justification of human rights in a presumably existing or possible "overlapping consensus", he was willing to restrict the list of human rights so that certain important rights, such as equal liberties for persons of different faiths or a right to equal political participation, were not included (Rawls 1999c: 65, 71). One reason for this was the aim to respect non-liberal but "decent" peoples as full members in a common law of peoples (thereby seeking to avoid Western ethnocentrism). But the question of whether "decent hierarchical peoples" can or should be expected to conform to a "liberal" conception of human rights which is foreign to their cultural self-understanding – if asked from the perspective of the "ideals and principles of the *foreign policy* of a reasonably just *liberal* people" (*ibid.*: 10, original emphasis) – gives a one-sided political answer to a normative philosophical question. Rather, the essential question from a perspective that puts human rights first would be whether such peoples (or their governments) had legitimate reasons to *deny their members* equal liberties or the claim to political participation.

Rawls presupposes that a "decent" society is characterized by a "common good conception of justice" and by a "decent consultation hierarchy" (*ibid.*: 61) and the presumption is that no further claims to human rights are raised since there is a high degree of internal acceptance in that society. However, if disunity and conflict were to appear in such a society and some members raised the claim to more demanding rights such as human rights, would the internal authorities then have good reasons to deny these claims and would outsiders have good reasons to say that the claims raised are not really human rights claims? That seems questionable. From a "Western" point of view, one must remember that this was historically the context in which human rights were "invented" in feudal or monarchical societies; therein lies their original and still important meaning. Furthermore, there is no reason to assume that what those who engage in such struggles want is to transform their societies into "liberal" ones, following certain established examples. Human rights do not prescribe a concrete specification of the arrangements of a society.

Joshua Cohen suggests a notion of human rights that addresses this worry. He views human rights norms as securing individual membership or inclusion in a political society,

> and the central feature of the normative notion of membership is that a person's interests are taken into account by the political society's basic institutions: to be treated as a member is to have one's interests given due consideration, both in the process of authoritative decision-making and in the content of those decisions.
>
> *(Cohen 2004: 197)*

Cohen argues that there is a difference between a basic, universalizable account of such membership rights and a full-blown, say, liberal conception of social and political justice (*ibid*.: 210–13). Regarding the question as to whether there is a human right to democracy, Cohen holds that a notion of democracy based on a strict version of political equality is too demanding; rather, a conception of human rights should call for forms of collective self-determination that need not be democratic in an egalitarian sense of the term (Cohen 2006: 233). From the perspective of "global public reason", he believes, it is reasonable to insist on human rights that ensure membership and inclusion, even if that does not mean full political equality, but it is not reasonable to insist on a liberal idea of free and equal persons (*ibid*.: 244).

Cohen's argument for the toleration of non-democratic societies in the international sphere (so long as they exhibit a certain level of political self-determination) attempts to do justice to the problem of pluralism in a global society and to avoid overly strict standards for "external reproach", which may take the form of sanctions and intervention (*ibid*.: 234). But it shares the problems of Rawls's view as seen from an ethical or moral perspective on human rights. Cohen stresses that the primary reason to argue against a narrow-minded "liberal" way of judging the legitimacy of a society's basic structure and possibly to infer external permission to intervene is the respect for the collective self-determination of such a society. But then to express that respect by narrowing the human right to political self-determination (as included, for example, in the Universal Declaration) runs the danger of contradiction. It is appropriate to "resist the idea that the political society should be held to a standard of justice that is rejected by its own members" (Cohen 2004: 211), if that rejection is not the result of political pressure and domination, but to infer from this that these members do not have a human *right* to resist unequal and undemocratic forms of organizing political government seems unwarranted. A political community can decide to settle for different forms of political organization, but the point of human rights is to strengthen those who dissent from "decisions" which have not been and cannot be reciprocally justified. One cannot limit the right to democracy by appealing to the principle of collective self-determination, for that is a recursive principle with a built-in dynamic of justification which favours those who criticize exclusions and asymmetries. Whether the members of a society interpret and use the right to democracy in such a way that it realizes a form of liberal or egalitarian democracy is up to them (as long as these decisions are not made under pressure and indoctrination), but given the nature of human rights as protecting and expressing the right to codetermine one's polity in an autonomous manner, there seems no reason to doubt that there is a human right to democracy.

Discourse-theoretical views

The importance of the right to democracy is stressed by discourse-theoretical approaches. They start from the following recursive consideration: human rights are meant to ensure that no human being is treated in a way that could not be justified to him or her as a person equal to others. This implies that one claim underlies all human rights, namely human beings' claim to be respected as autonomous agents who have the right not to be subjected to certain actions or institutional norms that cannot be adequately justified to them. Different discourse-theoretical approaches spell this idea out in different ways, stressing the "equiprimordiality" of personal and political autonomy and of the rights that secure these dimensions of autonomy (Habermas 1996: 118–31) or the "communicative freedom" that is the basis of human rights as well as protected by them (Günther 1992, 2011; Benhabib 2011, 2013) or arguing that human rights have a common ground in a basic moral right, the *right to justification* (Forst 1999, 2010). Contrary to the latter approach, Habermas (2001a) denies an independent moral ground for human rights, stressing their juridical character in legally securing private and discursive political autonomy.

In comparison to the theories of human rights discussed thus far, a moral justification for human rights as suggested in a discourse-theoretical framework is of a reflexive nature, not relying on an ethical notion of the good life, on a reconstruction of given political practice or on minimalist justificatory considerations. "Reflexive" means that the very idea of *justification* itself is reconstructed with respect to its normative and practical implications (Forst 2010). The argument states that since a moral justification of human rights must be able to discursively redeem the claim to general and reciprocal validity raised by such rights, then such a justification presupposes the right to justification of those whose rights are in question. They have a qualified "veto right" against any justification that fails the criteria of reciprocity and generality and which can be criticized as one-sided, narrow or paternalistic, as the case may be. Reciprocity means that no one may make a normative claim he or she denies to others (call that reciprocity of content) and that no one may simply project one's own perspective, values, interests or needs onto others such that one claims to speak in their "true" interests or in the name of some truth beyond mutual justification (reciprocity of reasons). Generality means that the reasons that are to ground general normative validity have to be shareable by all affected persons, given their (reciprocally) legitimate interests and claims.

The notion of "dignity" that lies at the heart of such a conception of human rights is not a metaphysical or ethical one, combined with a doctrine about the good life. Rather, dignity means that a person is to be respected as someone who is worthy of being given adequate reasons for actions or norms that affect him or her in a relevant way. This kind of respect requires us to regard others as autonomous sources of normative claims within a justificatory practice. Hence, all content of human rights is to be justified discursively, yet one must be aware of the twofold nature of human rights as general *moral* rights and as concrete *legal* rights. At the moral level, a discursive "construction" leads to a list of those basic rights which persons who respect one another as equals with rights to justification cannot properly deny one another. That list is to some extent general and subject to further elaboration, but it expresses basic standards of respect that must be secured in the form of legal basic rights. It is important to emphasize that the basic right to justification is not only conducive to rights that secure the political standing of persons as citizens and agents of the political-legal construction of a rights regime in processes of democratic "iterations" (Benhabib 2011). It is also the basis of rights to bodily security, personal liberties and secure equal social status. That implies rights against the violation of physical or psychological integrity as well as rights against social discrimination. The right to justification is a right to be respected as an independent social agent who at the same time codetermines the social structure of which he or she is a part.

From the perspective of an ethical view of human rights, such a justification is too narrow to cover the whole range of human rights just mentioned. A discourse-theoretical approach, these critics suspect, stresses the political and procedural aspects of human rights but neglects the substance of rights that protect personal autonomy. Defenders of a practice-immanent view of human rights might likewise point out that current practice puts less emphasis on the political agency of human rights and stresses more fundamental rights to bodily security, the protection of which is the main task of the international community. Finally, those who think that a more minimal justification is needed doubt that the idea of a right to justification is a universally valid ground for human rights.

Universalism and cultural contexts

To further enquire into the debate between these four approaches, one might take up the question as to which of them best fulfils the basic requirement for any justification of human rights to be universally valid without importing culturally biased ethical, moral or political ideas. Does, for example, the argument for human rights based on the notion of an individual right to justification of free and equal persons violate the claim to justificatory ethical impartiality, given the plurality of cultural understandings of the ethical good? Discourse theorists reply that their approach does not rely on any assumption about the good life, but only on a conception of what we owe to each other in terms of equal respect. One might hold a deeply religious view that the "tutored life" in accordance with God's will is the correct path in life; yet one would still have the duty to respect others as reason-giving and reason-deserving beings according to the principle of reciprocal and general justification. Thus it is denied that the notion of moral autonomy is internally connected to a liberal notion of the good.

Let us suppose that we are confronted with a position which holds that such an understanding of justification and autonomy is foreign to a particular social context and cultural tradition (see Bauer & Bell 1999). Therefore, respect for that particular social order is demanded which is not to be measured via human rights. Such a position claims to defend the integrity of a certain social order as an integrated unity. The whole is supposed to constitute the identity of its members and vice versa. Thus, violating the integrity of the whole also violates the integrity of the members of that society and an imperative to respect human rights is seen as such a violation. Yet that seems unfounded, for the claim raised implies that a defence of communal integrity cannot come at the cost of the integrity of its members, be they a majority or a minority. The culturalist position is not meant to be a majoritarian one which only addresses the interests of dominant social groups. Thus, there is an internal criterion of legitimacy built into the argument, namely, that of unforced acceptance, for any forced acceptance of social or legal norms would be incompatible with the claim for communal integrity. That claim is suspended when internal dissent arises concerning the acceptability of the dominant social idea of order or its realization. If a society denies criticism of its dominant justifications and of the ways in which justifications can be questioned and formed, its social integrity is placed in question *from the inside*. In any justifiable social order, internal critique cannot be legitimately answered by force or domination; whatever substantive demands those who protest raise, they demand in the first place that their dissent should be heard, taken seriously, and channelled in such a way that it could lead to a reform of the social structure. Hence, human rights play a double role here: in one sense, they are basic claims for justificatory standing as a full member and, in another sense, they can also be means of addressing particular shortcomings of a social structure, such as a lack of religious liberties, the resources necessary for education, or a decent income. Still, such substantive claims must also be fed into the justification procedures of a society since the common political structure is the first addressee of these claims.

This insight is captured in a reflection of Uma Narayan concerning the difficulties encountered by feminists in non-Western societies in finding a critical language that avoids the pitfall of being seen as an "outsider" who speaks the "alien" language of human rights and betrays local traditions:

> We all need to recognize that critical postures do not necessarily render one an "outsider" to what one criticizes, and that it is often precisely one's status as one "inside" the culture one criticizes, and deeply affected by it, that gives one's criticisms their motivation and urgency.
>
> *(U. Narayan 1997: 412)*

Social criticism of patriarchal structures and of certain forms of brutality and violence associated with it is always context-related and specific. However, there is no reason to assume that one cannot identify certain basic standards of respect and equality which are implied in these many criticisms and which, first and foremost, imply the basic claim not to be subjected to actions, norms or institutions that cannot be adequately defended towards those affected. According to Narayan, to assert that human rights express "Western values" represents a highly problematic form of cultural essentialism and Western ethnocentrism, which denies the place of human rights in other socio-cultural contexts and struggles (U. Narayan 2000: 91). Those who use the language of these rights are not "aliens" in their societies and should not be declared as such by a theory of human rights. The discourse-theoretical account of human rights seems to best capture this insight.

Human rights as norms of justice

To fully understand the notion of human rights as "global ethics", it is necessary to reflect on the relation between human rights and global justice (Pogge 2002; Moellendorf 2002, 2009; Caney 2005b; Forst 2012). Undoubtedly, human rights norms do constitute an important part of global justice claims, yet they do not predetermine whether the institutions that secure these rights are to be those of single states or those of a global political and legal order. Moreover, a full-blown conception of transnational justice is more comprehensive than a conception of human rights can be, and it entails many additional aspects of political and economic, as well as historical, justice. Although conceptions of human rights imply rights to the necessary means for an adequate standard of living, which cannot be denied to any person to whom reasons are owed for the social structures to which they belong, this might not satisfy the demands of justice, either nationally or transnationally. Human rights are only a subset of transnational norms of justice.

What is important, however, is that the primary addressee of human rights claims is a political and legal basic structure with the form of a state. In that respect, a conception of human rights needs to combine moral-universalist and contextual institutional aspects. Still, an institutional view which not only argues that the state is the central institution for securing human rights but also contends that it is only violations perpetrated by official actors that count as human rights violations (Pogge 2002: 58–60) would draw too narrow a connection. It is the task of a state to secure human rights and to protect citizens from human rights violations by private actors, such as large companies. Failure to do so, either because the state decides not to act or because it is too weak, constitutes insufficient protection of human rights, although their violation is not the work of the state but of other agents.

Human rights, once again, have a transnational moral as well as a political–legal meaning. Their moral meaning is that a violation of human rights is a breach of standards which the human community in general believes should be respected; thus, in case states either prove to be the perpetrators of such crimes or prove unable to stop them, the "world community" is called upon to react not just morally but also politically. That, however, calls for a "mediation" (Shue 1988) of such duties to avoid or put a stop to violations of human rights in the form of proper institutions, not only because it needs to be determined who has what kind of duty to assist those in need, but also because a structure of justification needs to be established to avoid arbitrary judgements concerning cases of aid or of intervention. Hence, the moral meaning must again be transformed on a legal and political level in order to establish credible international institutions to prevent, judge, stop or sanction human rights violations.

There are further aspects of the legal existence of human rights in international declarations and covenants that cannot be discussed here at length. There are duties to establish institutions for those who must flee their states because of human rights violations or for other reasons, such as economic deprivation. The "right to have rights" (Arendt 1979, Benhabib 2004) and to belong to a political community where one is protected from rightlessness is an important issue in a world of forced migration. So too is the duty to avoid the creation of zones of lawlessness, such as extraterritorial detention camps, in international conflicts.

Notes

1 In the following, I partly rely on Forst (2010).
2 See also Erman (2005), Bohman (2007), Günther (2011).

8

UNIVERSALISM, RELATIVISM AND DIFFERENCE

Peter Jones and Graham Long

Moral universalism and global ethics would seem a natural pairing. A universal morality must be global in scope and a global ethic must be universal in range. In fact, the adjective "universal" is not necessarily synonymous with "global". Something is or is not universal with respect to a given unit. A society that enfranchises all of its adult citizens would be said to have a "universal franchise" even though its franchise is universal only to its own citizens. A regulation might govern all and only member states of the European Union and so apply universally within the EU but not beyond it. The doctrine of human rights is typically conceived as a universalist doctrine, but a proponent of animal rights will ascribe rights universally to a larger set of beings than the set that possesses uniquely human rights. Global universality is therefore only one of many possible sorts of universality. Even so, in what follows we shall use "universal" synonymously with "global" unless we indicate otherwise.

"Universal" describes the scope or range of whatever is said to be universal. However, the claim that a morality or ethic is universal can take different forms depending upon the respect in which its scope is alleged to be universal. Use of the term "universalism" in moral philosophy most commonly describes the view that the morality that should govern people's conduct is the same morality for all mankind. It refers to the scope of a morality's *application*: it claims that there is one morality that applies universally to humanity and accordingly rejects any form of relativism that holds that different moralities properly govern different groups or societies. It need not, and usually does not, make the claim that all humanity actually complies with a single morality or recognizes it as the correct morality; rather the claim is only that there is one morality that should govern the conduct of all. That form of universalism is often associated with, but is distinct from, another which concerns the *structure* of morality. A morality may be alleged to be universal in that its action-guiding principles can cover all human situations and circumstances; it is allegedly universal in competence. This sort of universalism opposes the claim that the particularity of situations and circumstances requires moral thinking and moral conduct that is fundamentally particular in nature. Universality can also be a feature of the *content* of morality as a quality that relates to the status a morality gives to human individuals and to the proper scope of their moral relationships. Cosmopolitan moralities, for example, generally emphasize the rights, duties and responsibilities that human beings possess in relation to one another just as human beings; in that way, they take a strongly universalist view of the proper nexus of moral relationships. More communitarian moralities, on the other hand, give greater emphasis to local attachments and consequently conceive communities of right-holders and duty-bearers in more circumscribed ways. Finally, universality can relate to the issue of *justification* – the issue of whether a morality can be justified and should be justifiable to all human individuals so that they have compelling reason to accept it.

These different forms of universalism can be held together, or not, in various combinations. It is possible to embrace, or to reject, all four. Alternatively, we might embrace one form while rejecting another. For example, we can consistently take a communitarian (non-universalist) view of our moral relationships while embracing a universalist view of the morality that applies to those relationships. It is also possible to subscribe to universalist positions partially rather than wholly and without qualification. We might, for example, think that, in providing for moral relationships, a morality should give weight to both universal obligations and local attachments rather than only to one or the other. And we might think that, while some moral principles are rightly universal in application, others can reasonably vary from society to society, or that, while a morality structured in terms of universal principles can often guide our conduct, it cannot provide fully for every circumstance we may confront.

Universalism of application

Universalism of application holds that the morality that should govern human conduct applies to humanity universally. Universalists may disagree over what that morality is but nevertheless agree that the correct morality, whatever it is, is universal in application. A doctrine that conspicuously embodies this form of universalism is the doctrine of human rights. Generally, those who embrace that doctrine hold that, while human rights may not, as a matter of fact, be recognized or respected by everyone everywhere, they *ought* to be recognized and respected by everyone everywhere. That is only one of several international doctrines that exhibit this form of universalism. Other examples are the doctrines of just war, responsibility to protect, national or popular self-determination, and state sovereignty.

When we move away from doctrines addressed specifically to the international world to more general moral theories, universalism of application is commonly their default position. Utilitarianism and other consequentialist moralities conceive themselves in universalist terms. Utilitarians do not understand the principle of utility to be merely local in application; rather they conceive it as properly governing all human conduct, ultimately if not always immediately. The same is generally true of Kantian and deontological moralities. Religions such as Christianity and Islam are similarly universalist in conception, including in their prescriptions for human conduct. Political ideologies, such as liberalism, socialism, Marxism, anarchism, libertarianism and fascism commonly, though not invariably, claim universal application even if their adherents sometimes, for practical reasons, adopt less universal aspirations.

The doctrine of human rights adopts human beings *qua* human beings as its moral subjects and it ascribes rights to all human individuals equally. Utilitarian and Kantian moralities are similarly human-centred and egalitarian in the status they ascribe to human individuals. But these are not necessary features of universality of application. A moral doctrine can accord different statuses and prescribe different codes of conduct for different categories of human being – different genders or races or classes or castes for example – and still be, in its self-conception, universal in application. It will exhibit that universality if it understands itself properly to apply across the human world, rather than only within some communities or societies.

A morality can remain universal in application even though it recognizes a great variety of specific acts as rightful. Utilitarianism provides a good example. Realizing the principle of utility can require very different acts of different people simply because different people are differently situated and acts that are best calculated to maximize utility in one set of circumstances may not be so in others. Rather than presenting us with a rigid set of universal principles, utilitarianism presents us with one basic principle that can require diverse and flexible conduct for its realization. But utilitarianism remains universal in application; it applies to all mankind and the diversity it sanctions is not one that assigns different people to different moralities.

We noted earlier that moralities can claim universality partially rather than wholly. Utilitarian moralities generally, and Kantian moralities often, claim an unlimited universality of application. But the doctrine of human rights might form part of a larger moral position that exemplifies a partial claim of universality of application. It would be unusual for a doctrine of human rights not to claim universality of application for itself, but it does not normally aim to provide comprehensively for human living. More commonly, it aims to set out norms governing only some aspects of human life while remaining silent on the norms that might govern many others. It is therefore possible to make the doctrine part of position that does not claim university of application outside the domain of human rights. Indeed, it is quite common for people to subscribe to a doctrine of human rights while also holding that, within the limits set by that doctrine, societies rightly have discretion over the norms that should govern the lives of their members.

Very often moral positions are universalist by implication rather than by avowal. A moral position is often conceived as simply "true" or "correct" or "right" such that it follows by implication that it is universally true or correct or right and therefore universal in application. If Boyle's law or the law of the conservation of matter is true, it is universally true. It is not true in Europe or Brazil but untrue in Asia or the US; it is true anywhere and everywhere. If Islam or Christianity is true, it is universally true rather than true only within the existing Muslim or Christian world. Similarly, if we conceive a moral position as true or correct − true or correct without qualification − we shall conceive it as universally true or correct, that is, as true or correct for anyone and anywhere and irrespective of whether people recognize its truth or correctness. Of course, whether moralities can, like scientific laws or mathematical theorems, be true or correct is moot. But very often universality of application is the offspring of a morality's being conceived in those terms. Indeed, we might subscribe to universality of application as a conditional truth: we may be unsure what the correct morality is or even if it exists but hold that, if there is a correct morality, it must be universal in application simply in virtue of being correct.

Perhaps the greatest challenge faced by universality of application is its apparent failure to match the reality of the human world. Our world is, and has long been, one in which people subscribe to a great variety of moralities. Logically, that is not fatal to universality of application. The universalist can continue to claim that one morality properly applies to all mankind and dismiss the diversity of moral beliefs exhibited by humanity as so many manifestations of error. On the other hand, if there really is one morality that is properly universal in application, it is surprising that so many people have so sincerely and for so long failed to agree on what it is. Moreover, there seems no obvious way of resolving that disagreement. Scientific hypotheses are open to empirical testing and mathematical truths are capable of proof, but no similarly robust and decisive test is available that we can use to resolve conflicting claims about the right or the good.

The notion of universalism of application is also sometimes associated with self-deception, arrogance and imperialism. Its critics complain that it invites people to mistake moralities that are merely local in origin and relative in foundation for truths that should govern the lives of all. In doing so, it licenses those who conceive themselves as the bearers of truth to impose their "truth" on benighted others who think differently. The doctrine of human rights, for example, is sometimes alleged to be no more than a cover that enables the West to impose its culture upon other parts of the world and to do so in a way that disguises its local provenance.

Relativism

If we deny universalism of application, what is the alternative? One common answer is relativism. To say that a morality is relative is to hold that it pertains only to a particular group or community and is therefore local or particular in application. Morality can also be deemed relative to the individual person, in which form it is also known as "ethical subjectivism". The doctrine that each individual should be governed by the voice of his or her conscience, even though conscience speaks differently to different individuals, is an example of that form of relativism.

The most commonly discussed form of relativism is *cultural relativism* (henceforth CR), and we shall concentrate on that form here, particularly because of the prominence of CR in arguments about global ethics. CR holds that morality is a cultural phenomenon: each society evolves a culture and its morality will be part of the culture it evolves. Different societies evolve different cultures and therefore embrace different moralities. CR goes on to claim that there is no territory external to cultures upon which we can stand in apprehending or assessing what is morally right. Morality is therefore irredeemably relative to culture. A culture may not perceive its morality in that way; it may perceive its morality as non-relative to itself and universal in application, but that perception will be an illusion.

Three kinds of relativism need to be distinguished, even though they are often run together in affirmation and critique of CR. *Descriptive moral relativism* (DMR) is empirical in content: it observes that if we survey humanity, both now and in the past, we discover that different people subscribe to different and conflicting moralities. The findings of anthropologists have been especially influential in substantiating the claims of DMR. The popular, if unreflective, appeal of CR as an ethical and metaethical position probably owes more to the apparent truth of DMR than to anything else. Yet critics of CR often argue that DMR is exaggerated. For example, the Eskimo practices of exposing unwanted babies to the elements and abandoning the elderly to die may seem wholly at odds with the mores of many other cultures but, when we take account of the harsh conditions in which the Eskimos have to survive, the values driving those practices can appear less alien.

Normative moral relativism (NMR) constitutes a first-order moral position. Whereas DMR comments only on the empirical matter of what people *believe* to be right and remains agnostic on the question of what is actually right, NMR is an ethical position and affirms that right conduct for a person is compliance with whatever morality relates to that particular person, either as an individual or as a member of a particular society. *Metaethical relativism* (MER) is not similarly prescriptive. It holds only that morality is relative in nature and, as long as it remains strictly metaethical, takes no view on the morality with which people ought to comply.

CR as an ethical position is often inspired by DMR and makes both normative (NMR) and metaethical (MER) claims. As a guide to ethical conduct, it holds that a person should act, and be judged, according to the morality of the appropriate culture (though there are disputes over whether this should be the culture of the *agent* or *appraiser*). It holds that right conduct for a person is whatever that person's culture identifies as right. Thus, if A and B belong to different cultures, *x* can be right and *not-x* wrong for A, while *not-x* can be right and *x* wrong for B. When CR takes the form of NMR, we might think of it as a social form of ethical subjectivism. In this form, CR denies universality of application. Rather than action being appraised or judged according to a single morality that applies to all, it should be judged against the particular standards of the relevant culture.

One set of objections to CR focuses on the way that it contradicts our normal thinking about morality. The most obvious of these is that CR tells us that there can be no judgement on practices that we would normally find abominable, such as slavery, racial and religious persecution, the subordination of women, human sacrifice and cruelty, beyond that afforded by the cultures in which they occur. We can distinguish between good and bad cultural practices only from the standpoint of a particular culture; we cannot hold that slavery, racial persecution and the like are intrinsically (i.e. non-relatively) wrong.

CR also requires us to rethink the nature of moral disagreement between societies. We might imagine two societies that hold different views on, say, gender equality or the treatment of non-human animals, debating with one another over whose view is right. But their debate will be misguided if it supposes that a right answer is available that is independent of either society's culture. For the cultural relativist, the debaters will differ rather than disagree; what is right for one (really right, not merely believed to be right) is wrong (really wrong) for the other.

The obvious riposte to these kinds of criticism is that they are question-begging (Levy 2002: 45–49; Caney 2005b: 32–33), and indeed they are. They presuppose that there exists a culturally neutral or independent perspective from which we can assess the moral merit of different cultures. This is what *metaethical cultural relativism* denies and what *universalism of justification* affirms. Both the relativist and the universalist, in taking stands on this issue, are going rather further than claiming or denying bare universality of application. The universalist's claim is a richer one: that the morality that applies universally to mankind is also universally valid or justified for all mankind. We shall consider this debate over the nature of morality – the question of whether there is a single universally valid morality – when we examine universality of justification.

Even for those inclined to defend NMR or MER, cultures are significantly problematic as sources of moral authority. If culture determines the morality with which each person is to comply, he or she and we need to know clearly what that culture is. Cultures are still sometimes talked about as though they mimicked a patchwork quilt, with each culture being homogeneous and clearly distinguished from those around it. That way of conceiving cultures has long been discredited. First, in so far as cultures can be individuated, they are typically internally diverse and contested so that it will often be unclear what a person's culture requires. Second, it is increasingly difficult to assign each person to a single culture given movements of populations, the impact of globalization, and the diversity of influences to which people are now subject. Third, and for the same reasons, it is increasingly difficult to individuate cultures. Our world is intercultural rather than merely multicultural. People's "culture" is supposed to describe not just inheritances from their forebears that appear quaint and exotic to outsiders but also the real "life-world" in which they live and function – the internet and global media as much as folk-dance and national costume. The reality of that world is not easily squared with the picture of culture that CR seems to presuppose.

Additionally, if a culture determines what is right for a society, relativists invoking culture face a problem of how to understand and judge criticism arising within a culture. A society's culture may contain incoherencies or anomalies that enable critics to use some of its aspects to criticize others. But those opportunities for criticism may be extremely limited and there is no straightforward reason to suppose more evil or unjust societies are especially internally incoherent.

A final question is what, if anything, CR might say about the nature and character of a global ethic. That is not a simple question, since CR eschews specifying the substance of a morality: that is the business of particular cultures. CR directs its attention to the morality internal to each culture and so cannot easily provide for relations between different cultures. Indeed, the very idea of an ethic that is global in range runs counter to CR as normally conceived. Yet CR is often thought to provide reason for mutual toleration among cultures. If we embrace CR, so the argument goes, we shall cease to condemn cultures whose moralities differ from our own and, in ceasing to condemn them, we shall lose our reason to be intolerant of them. While there is force in that claim, the relationship between CR and toleration is not quite that simple.

Suppose it is part of a society's culture that it should displace and replace the cultures of others (a common enough phenomenon in human history). It is difficult to see how CR can condemn that culture's imperialism since its condemnation would contradict its fundamental claim that what is right for a society is only what that society's culture deems right. More generally, CR is unable to hold either that cultures should tolerate one another or that cultural communities have a right to be self-determining without making the very kind of claim whose possibility it rejects: a moral claim that should govern all cultures and that is independent of any them. (For critical discussions of cultural and other forms of relativism, see Wong 1984, 2006; J. W. Cook 1999; Levy 2002; Baghramian 2004; Long 2004; Lukes 2008.)

Universalism of structure

The opposition between universality of application and cultural relativism concerns the scope of the agents and patients over whom a morality ranges. A different kind of universality, sometimes described as "generalism", relates to the scope of circumstances and cases for which a morality provides. A morality might conceive itself as being "structurally" universal in that it understands itself to provide for all of the various situations and circumstances in which people might find themselves. It might do so by providing general principles that range over particular cases and that indicate what should be done in those cases. Utilitarianism, for example, instructs us always to maximize utility. Utilitarians accept that discerning what that injunction requires in particular cases may not be easy and that we shall often need the assistance of the lower-level maxims of "common sense" morality if our conduct is to be successful in promoting utility (e.g. R. M. Hare 1981). Even so, "maximize utility" remains the principle that ultimately governs right conduct in any particular case. Structurally, universal moralities can take more complex forms. They might, for example, consist of a plurality of principles that might weigh differently in different cases and admit of qualification and exception (e.g. W. D. Ross 1930).

Moral particularism rejects this sort of universalism. Its best-known contemporary exponent is Jonathan Dancy (1993, 2004). One reason for doubting the universal competence of a morality is the sheer diversity and complexity of human circumstances for which it has to provide. While Dancy sympathizes with that doubt (2004: 2), his moral particularism is a thesis about the nature of moral judgement rather than a claim about the messy character of human circumstances. Sound moral judgement consists, he argues, in identifying and taking appropriate account of all of the reasons, moral and non-moral, that bear upon a particular case rather than in subsuming the particular case under general moral principles. But will not those reasons themselves assume a universal character? Dancy argues not, since reasons are context-sensitive: "a feature that is a reason in one case may be no reason at all, or an opposite reason, in another" (*ibid.*: 73). For example, if an action is fun, that will often provide reason to do it; but, if we derive fun from a sadistic act, fun so derived is reason not to do it. Dancy describes his context-sensitive conception of reasons as "holism", since it understands reasons to depend for their character upon the context in which they function. Holism contrasts with "atomism", which supposes (mistakenly, for Dancy) that a feature that is a reason in one case must remain the same reason and have the same import in any other case (*ibid.*: 73–74).

Particularism is not relativism. It is particular not to different individuals or groups but to morally relevant differences in circumstances, contexts and cases. The right thing to do in a particular case will be the same for any individual who confronts it, unless a feature of that individual is itself genuinely salient to the case and provides reason to handle it differently. Dancy's particularism, for example, forms part of a larger moral theory that is both cognitivist and objectivist (Dancy 1993).

The defenders of structural universalism do not suppose that moral decision-making can consist in the mechanical application of general principles. Working out how principles apply and what they require in a particular case can require a good deal of skill and judgement; think analogously of the skill and judgement required of judges when they apply general laws to particular cases. But the universalist can accept the reality of complexity and the need for context-sensitivity while still holding that moral judgement requires some form of general guidance. He may also think in terms of reasons rather than principles, but still hold that reasons cannot be irredeemably particular.

Even though particularism is a metaethical doctrine, Dancy believes its acceptance would make a considerable difference to moral practice (*ibid.*: ix). "Generalism", he holds, "is the cause of many bad moral decisions, made in the ill-judged and unnecessary attempt to fit what we are to say here to what we have said on another occasion" (*ibid.*: 64). But the practical effect of particularism has also been called into question; it might undermine the trust and reliability among people that a shared morality is supposed to provide (Hooker 2000). Structural universalism would certainly seem more in sympathy with the aspirations of a global ethic, yet the particularist need not hold that a global effort to regulate human affairs must be misplaced. He can recognize that a society needs laws, even though he will differ from the universalist over the kind of reasoning that makes the case for law in general and for any particular law. He might present a similarly particularist case for rules at the international or global level. However, a context-sensitive view of good decision-making would seem to argue for modesty in our efforts to order human affairs through general rules, and for rules whose content is alive to particularity. The particularist might, for instance, recognize the case for securing international safeguards through the institution of human rights, but he is likely to scorn the efforts of philosophers to derive the content of human rights from a single moral foundation (e.g. Gewirth 1978, 1982; J. Griffin 2008) and to hold instead that different rights will be grounded in different reasons.

Universalism of content

We have considered universalism as a thesis about the scope of people to whom a morality applies and as a thesis about the range of cases over which it is competent. Universalism can also be a feature of a morality's content; it might, that is, be a view of the moral status of individuals and the way in which they relate morally to one another. For example, an ethic that gives identical rights and responsibilities to everyone and in respect of everyone, and so places everyone on an equal footing and in an identical moral relationship with everyone else, will be universal in this sense. An ethic that was fully universal in content would demand the same of all and accord the same to all. It would stand comprehensively opposed to moralities that ascribed any difference in role, obligation or entitlement to different individuals. However, universalism of content, like other forms of universalism, can admit of degree; a morality might be universalist in some of its content, while also giving moral significance to some human differences and some special relationships.

Universalism of content in its more full-blooded forms is closely associated with moral cosmopolitanism. Cosmopolitanism can take different forms and embody different claims (see Chapter 6 on cosmopolitanism). Nevertheless, there is an identifiable core to contemporary moral cosmopolitanism as advanced, for example, by Thomas Pogge (2002), Simon Caney (2005b) and Martha Nussbaum (2006). An element of that core is that features of our identity, such as our gender, ethnicity or nationality, and of our social situation, such as our citizenship of a particular state, are not morally salient to our basic rights and duties. Moral cosmopolitanism is commonly conceived as a position that rejects the moral relevance of national or state membership, but its rejection of the moral salience of that membership is really part of its rejection of the moral relevance of a much larger set of human differences. However, the universalism of cosmopolitanism is consistent with its taking account of differences, such as disability or the capacity to bear children, and cosmopolitans do not generally dismiss the moral salience of family ties.

Pogge's account of moral universalism illustrates universalism of content and some of the issues it raises. According to his account, an ethic will be universalistic only if (a) it "subjects all persons to the same system of fundamental moral principles", (b) these principles assign the same fundamental moral benefits and burdens to all, and (c) those benefits and burdens "are formulated in general terms so as not to privilege or disadvantage certain persons or groups arbitrarily" (Pogge 2002: 92). Pogge's cosmopolitanism combines univeralism of application and of structure with a strong universalism of content. A religion that ascribed different rights and responsibilities to men and women, or a political order that allowed differences in wealth to translate into differences in political power, would fall foul of his universalistic ethic.

An ethic that is universal in content must apply equally to all human beings and must challenge the moral relevance of many particular attachments that are commonly deemed morally relevant. Both elements of this universalism might be disputed. Against the first, a critic might hold that different groups, such as men and women, are properly subject to different ethics and might subsume those different ethics within a single higher-level ethic, such as a principle that "people ought to act appropriately to their status". Against the second, the critic might dispute the claim that particular attachments, such as shared national or cultural attachments, are morally irrelevant. These disputes will turn on which benefits and burdens are "fundamental", and what constitutes benefiting and burdening persons or groups "arbitrarily". The philosophical nationalist, for example, will reject the cosmopolitan's view that ties of nationality or citizenship are morally "arbitrary" and properly of no consequence for the fundamental benefits people should enjoy and the burdens they should bear (e.g. D. Miller 1995).

A detailed discussion of these issues would take us far beyond the scope of this chapter. Here, we note only that a "thick" account of universalism of content is not self-justifying. It has no force beyond the reasons adduced for requiring a certain scope of application from universality, or for rejecting the moral salience of the attributes in question. Our brief discussion here shows, at least, that the ambiguous connection between claims about the form and scope of an ethic, and its normative content, is an important area for further investigation.

Universality of justification

A final species of universalism claims that a given ethic is *justified* or *true* with respect to all human beings. This is a claim – or rather a family of claims, since these terms need not be coextensive – that is distinct from universalism of application. To claim that a morality should apply to all is not necessarily to claim that it is justifiable to all. Richard Rorty (1993), for example, holds that the morality of human rights should be apply to all even though it is not justifiable to all. Something like this distinction, though couched in different terms, is common to many analyses of universalism (e.g. Rawls 1993; Larmore 1996: 57–59; Tan 2000; Caney 2005b: 26–28), and has been employed to different ends by universalists (e.g. Caney 2005b) and anti-universalists (e.g. Rorty 1993). As we have already noted, universalism of justification may seem a natural foundation for universality of application, and a claim of universality of justification or truth may be implicit in an assertion of universal application. If one morality is universally true, that provides good reason, at least *pro tanto*, for its being the only morality that should apply to humanity. Conversely, it would seem odd to apply to others a standard that they had no reason to accept, or that we doubted was true. What is at stake, in asserting universalism of justification, is the power and meaning of the moral "ought" central to the formulation of moral universalism.

The practical import of a claim about justification or truth for a global ethic in a diverse world is obvious. The claim to universal application is one that is made by starkly conflicting moralities: consequentialism and deontology; radical political Islam and universal human rights; libertarianism and socialism. Each of these, according to its adherents, ought to govern the conduct of all. In such a divided world, the account we give of universalism of justification marks the line between legitimate difference and indefensible error. If there is reason to prefer the terminology of justification over truth here, it might be that justification points us towards the interpersonal reason-giving that would be necessary to make good on a claim to a morality's being uniquely true in the midst of such dispute.

The question posed by this kind of universalism – what precisely is required of a morality if it is to be universally morally compelling? – is itself a divisive one, the answer to which will depend on the answers we give to a range of larger issues in moral philosophy. For some scholars, a focus on justification misleads in suggesting too great a reliance on what other people currently think. What is important, they would insist, is establishing the evident truth of an ethic. This would yield, as a by-product, a justification that should prove convincing for all. For a different set of scholars, a morality should be justifiable to all reasonable agents, and so debate turns to the nature of reasonableness and the idea of justifiability. A further complexity is that justification itself can be understood in stronger or weaker terms. It is one thing to give reasons for a view, such that all *must* accept it on pain of irrationality; it is quite another to give reasons that are accessible to all and that *could* prompt their assent. A major challenge for theorists wanting to underpin universal application with universal justification is to specify this test in a satisfactory way.

Universalism of justification conflicts with views that deny there is a single uniquely justified ethic. Metaethical relativism, as we noted earlier, is one such view. Indeed, MER might be identified precisely as the rejection of this claim about moral justification or truth (Wong 1984, Long 2004). Metaethical relativists claim that the content and structure of morality is sufficiently interrelated with issues of culture, framework or worldview that no single ethic can claim to be uniquely true or immune to reasonable rejection. Like the universalist, they too must provide an account of the nature of morality. We cannot attempt to resolve the disagreement between these conflicting accounts here. Some universalists of justification address the relativist challenge head on, arguing that there is indeed a uniquely compelling ethic grounded *a priori* either in rationality itself or on a deeper and unchallengable ethical foundation. A different strategy is to defuse the relativist objection by recognizing and taking account of the role of specific cultures or contexts: for example, Nussbaum's capabilities approach is deliberately designed to respect pluralism, in part by offering only "general" and "abstract" universal values that are "subject to ongoing revision and rethinking" (Nussbaum 2006: 78–80).

Debate over universal justification matters for a global ethic since it tells us how we should regard global disagreement over moral questions. If a single ethic – for example, an ethic of human rights – is evidently true or compellingly justified, disagreement with that ethic will indicate error. Such a view implies that there is a body of immensely powerful reasons (those that constitute its truth or justification) available (a) to convince those who disagree with it and (b) to underpin forms of intolerance in the event of disagreement. By contrast, those who doubt the existence of such compelling reasons might respond by offering a humbler global ethic and by appealing to more contingent, local or sentimental reasons to support it.

Universalisms and anti-universalisms

We have seen, then, that accounts of morality that are anti-universalistic in one or more of the senses we have identified can be universalistic in others. Some who deny universality of justification affirm universality of application. A particularist might, at a suitable level of abstraction, propose a morality that applies to all agents. Some moralities will claim to be universal in their application and justification, but not in their content.

Conversely, there are approaches to morality that embrace all four types of universalism. For example, universalizability is central to Kantian approaches to ethics. This notion functions as a test of the validity and justification of potential ethical principles, but it is also designed to determine their content. And it reinforces a conception of a morality as composed of principles that range over all cases. Universalizability therefore brings together all four types of universality. We can also see why interconnections between universalisms, though sometimes difficult to investigate and unpick, seem intuitively correct. Embracing one sort of universalism will often induce us to embrace another; it is difficult, for example, to insist that an ethic should apply universally if we do not also believe it to be correct.

Universalism and difference

The idea of universality is sometimes regarded with suspicion and disfavour in contemporary thinking because it is thought to be at odds with "difference" (e.g. Young 1990). "Difference" as the term is used in this context denotes differences among people that are thought to be especially salient for them in the contemporary world. It encompasses differences such as race, ethnicity, culture, nationality, religion, gender, sexual orientation, disability and language. There is no final or finite list; what makes a difference part of "difference" is its salience for its bearers' identities, for their forms of life, and for the status they enjoy in relation to others, especially their fellow citizens or fellow human beings.

Universalism has been mobilized against claims that differences of race, gender and nationality are morally significant and that they justify the superior or inferior treatment of their bearers. Contemporary calls for the recognition of difference do not, by and large, seek to reinstate the inequalities that universalism has sought to erode. Rather they stem from the belief that ignoring differences can result in rules and policies that are, in reality, biased in favour of some identities and against others and that fail to treat different groups in a genuinely equal fashion. For example, if we merely universalize rules and arrangements that have developed to suit a male-dominated world, we shall not secure genuine equality between the sexes.

What sort of universalism is at stake in argument over the relevance of difference? It is not universalism of application since, as we have seen, that form of universalism can encompass moralities that provide differently for different sorts of human being. Nor, for the same reason, is it universalism of justification. Universalism of structure is also quite consistent with moralities that give significance to differences among people. It is universalism of content that is often charged with being committed to treating all human beings identically or uniformly and with ignoring the moral salience of difference. Universalism of content will normally be accompanied by universalism of application and frequently by universalism of structure, although those other forms of universalism need not themselves entail universalism of content.

The apparent tension between universality and difference in global ethics is illustrated by the different pulls of human rights and national self-determination. The doctrine of human rights ascribes its rights universally to human beings. The doctrine of national self-determination ascribes to each nation (however we understand that term) the right to determine its own future and, in so doing, provides for difference since it entitles different nations to take different paths in providing for their collective futures. If we put these two doctrines together, the norms embodied in human rights will impose universal constraints upon the extent to which nations can differ in their collective lives. The two doctrines may therefore seem emblematic of the competing claims of universality and difference. Indeed, an enduring theme in debate over these doctrines is the extent to which the uniformity of human rights should constrain differences among nations or peoples. Some (e.g. Walzer 1994) argue for a "thin" set of human rights so that societies will have as much freedom as is reasonable to conserve or to fashion their collective characters. Others (e.g. Donnelly 2003) are less impressed by the claims of national difference and more alive to the common needs and vulnerabilities of human beings, and so argue for a "thicker" catalogue of human rights.

However, a moment's reflection on this debate reveals that juxtaposing the claims of human rights and national self-determination as those of the universal and the different is altogether too simple. For one thing, the doctrine of national self-determination is itself a universalist doctrine: it ascribes a right of collective self-determination universally to humanity conceived as nations or peoples. For another, the attribution of rights of self-determination to nations creates the possibility for new sites of uniformity, albeit in more circumscribed forms. Nations may have the collective freedom to differ from one another but they also have the power to establish uniform arrangements within their own borders, arrangements that will apply to all of their citizens. So it can be uniformity within nation states that competes with difference and it can be human rights that protect and provide for difference. Some human rights do demand universally uniform conduct, such as abstention from torture or enslavement, but others provide universally for difference. Consider the right to freedom of religion. That right entitles people to decide for themselves whether to embrace a religious faith and which faith if any they should embrace. Universal individual rights, like universal collective rights, need not make for uniform lives. In general, human rights seek to secure for people some of the basic conditions necessary for living any sort of decent human life rather than to prescribe the living of a particular sort of life.

Even so, the idea of human rights may still seem inhospitable to difference. For the most part, human rights are conceived as rights held by individual persons, yet "difference" typically describes group differences – characteristics that people share with others. In fact, individual human rights frequently can and do provide for group differences. If we return to the example of religion, people commonly share their religious beliefs with others and much religious practice takes a collective form, but shared religious belief and practice are still protected by individually held rights to freedom of belief and the freedom to manifest belief. The Universal Declaration of Human Rights states expressly that everyone has the right to manifest his beliefs "either alone or in community with others" (United Nations 1948: article 18; Brownlie & Goodwin-Gill 2010: 39–44). Similarly the International Covenant on Civil and Political Rights provides that persons belonging to ethnic, religious or linguistic minorities shall not be denied the right "in community with other members of their group" to enjoy their culture, to profess and practise their religion, or to use their language (United Nations 1966: article 27; Brownlie & Goodwin-Gill 2010: 388–404).

There are, however, some group differences that need to be recognized and provided for collectively rather than individually. Indigenous peoples, such as the Inuit of Canada, the Native Americans of the US and the Aborigines of Australia, provide clear examples. Those peoples possess their own collective forms of life, incorporating their distinctive political, legal, economic, social and cultural institutions, and they usually possess historical claims to particular lands or territories. They nevertheless find themselves encompassed within states that claim ultimate authority over the entire population and territory that fall within their borders. They also commonly find themselves in a minority position and heirs to a legacy of mistreatment by the majority population. Consequently, they are vulnerable as groups and they seek protection as groups. Nowadays they are commonly granted a degree of collective autonomy so that they can function as separate communities in lands or territories that are recognized as theirs, although the division of authority between themselves and their encompassing states and the extent of their land rights often remain hotly contested matters.

Provision for sub-state group differences can be made through universal instruments. The UN has, for example, provided for the different treatment to which indigenous peoples are entitled through its Declaration of the Rights of Indigenous Peoples (United Nations 2007; Brownlie & Goodwin-Gill 2010: 293–303). However, many of the rights in the UN's Declaration are special to indigenous peoples. They are, in Will Kymlicka's terminology (1989, 1995), "group-differentiated rights". They may be universal to indigenous peoples but they are also unique to those peoples. Do they therefore constitute a rejection of universality? Not according to Kymlicka, who conceives group-differentiated rights as necessary to provide for the special circumstances, peculiar vulnerability and relative disadvantage that typically characterize indigenous peoples. The rights may be special to indigenous peoples but they are justified by a general principle of equality that applies across both minority and majority populations.

The more general point implicit in the idea of group-differentiated rights is that some differences may need to be treated differently if their bearers are to be treated equally or fairly with others. Law or public policy may need to be "difference-sensitive" rather than "difference-blind" if it is to be genuinely just. There are some differences, such as disability, for which this claim is largely uncontroversial. If planning regulations, for example, fail to take account of the special mobility needs of the disabled, we can hardly claim that the regulations' "blindness" to differences in people's physical abilities ensures that they provide even-handedly for the able-bodied and the disabled. Similarly, if employment legislation takes no account of the fact that women give birth and men do not, it can hardly claim to provide equally for the genders, although that is a more contentious matter since some hold that if women or couples choose to have children, they rather than others should bear the consequences of that choice. This sort of argument for the relevance of difference is opposed to universalism only at the most superficial level; typically it appeals to a fundamental principle of just treatment that is universal in scope and content but that, for its realization, requires sensitivity rather than blindness to difference.

Two related areas in which the claims of difference have been especially significant are culture and religion. Cultural and religious differences have an especial propensity to generate demands for difference-sensitivity, since they normally include codes of conduct with which their members feel obliged to comply. The legal systems of some societies accord a degree of recognition to religious difference. India, for example, allows differences in the family law that applies to Hindus and Muslims, so that each community can be governed by the demands of its own faith. Many Western societies have had to confront issues of cultural and religious difference as they have become increasingly multicultural and multi-faith, largely as a consequence of immigration. In some cases, they have resolutely resisted the demands for different treatment, as France did in refusing to modify its commitment to *laïcité* to allow Muslim girls to wear hijabs while attending state schools. But, in other cases, societies have been more accommodating. In Britain, for example, turban-wearing Sikhs who ride motorcycles have been exempted from the legal requirement to wear a crash-helmet and Muslims and Jews have been exempted from animal welfare legislation so that they can practise ritual slaughter as their faiths require. The issue of whether a society should accord special treatment to different cultural or religious groups has evoked sharp differences of view. Some commentators (e.g. B. Barry 2001) regard it as an unacceptable derogation from the principle that a society's laws should apply equally to all of its citizens. Others (e.g. Parekh 2006, Quong 2006) regard special accommodation as essential if a society is not unfairly to disadvantage cultural and religious minorities. Here again, however, the issue is not merely one of universalism versus difference. Typically both sides in the debate appeal to principles of justice or equality that are universal in content; they differ only over what those principles require.

Universalism of content and recognition of difference begin to part company when a cultural or religious group demands either that others should recognize, or that it should be itself able to recognize, differences in a way that accords different statuses or different opportunity sets to different members of its group. Universalism of content can embrace recognition of difference only as long as that recognition is consistent with the equal moral status of human beings and is needed to provide, in Pogge's phrase, "the same fundamental moral benefits and burdens to all". But if the demands made for difference are demands that some should count for more than others and be privileged in relation to them, those demands cease to be compatible with universalism of content. Demands of that sort can arise within societies, or within sub-state groups, that have cultures or beliefs that sanction social hierarchies and justify differential treatment. They are especially likely to confront a global ethic that wishes to extend recognition to groups, including groups distinguished by their cultures or faiths, by according them a significant measure of autonomy. If those groups wish to mete out different and unequal treatment to their members, universality of content might still obtain among groups but it will not survive within them. Even in these cases, however, opposition between universality of content and recognition of difference may not always be straightforward and unambiguous. For example, societies and cultures that assign different roles to men and women often insist that those roles are merely different rather than unequal and imply no fundamental difference in the moral status of men and women. Moreover, even if a culture or religion does treat its adherents unequally, the defender of difference might still insist that treating people equally as the adherents of a culture or religion entails allowing their lives to be governed by their culture or religion, even when it accords them fundamentally different statuses.

Conclusion

In the argument over universalism and difference, then, closer inspection reveals that frequently the dispute is not really about whether we should embrace universalism or difference; rather, it is about what sort of combination of universal principle and difference-sensitivity is right or appropriate. The possibility of effecting some form of reconciliation between a universalism and its opposite (real or apparent) is one that might be explored for each of the four types of universalism identified in this chapter. We might, for example, claim universality of application for a particular set of norms while consigning others to the realm of cultural relativity. Or we might commit to a universal set of values but allow that there is legitimate scope for plurality in the way those values are understood and realized. Similarly, we might espouse one form of universalism while fighting shy of another. We might, for example, insist that a core of principles is properly applied universally while abstaining from a universalist stance on the controversial issue of how those principles are properly justified. Internationally recognized human rights can in practice (and, on some accounts, can in theory) exemplify this possibility: while they set minimum standards that apply across all societies, each society can sign up to human rights charters for its own socially or culturally relative reasons.

Efforts to combine the universal with the non-universal can be more or less extensive and each will encounter its own difficulties. The motivation for seeking to reconcile the universal with the non-universal can also differ. It some cases it may be philosophical; it may be driven by the belief that a particular combination of the universal and the non-universal is simply the right or the most rationally defensible position. In other cases it may be more pragmatic or political, in which case combination is more likely to assume the form of compromise. Many people in contemporary global circumstances clearly feel the force of one or both of these motivations. Thus, while there will continue to be argument about whether we should subscribe to a particular form of universalism or to its opposite, future debate is also likely to focus on whether and how we might reconcile the competing claims of each.

PART II
Conflict and violence

Introduction

War, conflict and violence are central concerns of global ethics, and indeed to moral and political philosophy in general. Violence and killing are *prima facie* unethical acts – they always harm individuals – and therefore war and conflict, which require violence and killing on a large scale, should always be deemed unethical. Surely, if anything is morally wrong, then killing people on a massive scale must be. However, the question is not whether these are good acts, but whether they can ever be justified, or indeed even morally required. For example, is violence permissible or obligatory if it prevents worse violence? Many think that there are times when war is morally sanctioned, for example, in self-defence, to prevent atrocity or to protect the vulnerable. In global governance this is now a major discussion. For instance, is war acceptable to prevent "rogue states" from acquiring nuclear weapons or other weapons of mass destruction, to punish unacceptable behaviour (such as the use of chemical weapons or treatment of certain groups), or to prevent mass starvation or ethnic conflict? These are pressing issues. Examples of such issues that come to mind at the time of writing include possible intervention in Syria (to deter the additional use of chemical weapons and to protect civilians), possible intervention in Iran (to prevent the development of nuclear weapons), possible intervention in East Africa (to prevent the spread of terrorism), and possible intervention in the Central African Republic (to protect innocent people). And, of course, as a result of practices during the War on Terror concerns about torture have become increasingly serious.

If and how war and conflict can be justified have traditionally been determined using just war theory; a tradition going back to St Augustine (fifth century) and St Thomas (thirteenth century). Traditional just war theory distinguishes two doctrines: one concerns the reasons for going to war (*jus ad bellum*), the other the conduct of war (*jus in bello*). According to this traditional distinction a war might be just but its means unjust, for instance by bombing civilians, laying landmines and using chemical weapons.

The nature and limits of just war theory are considered in detail in Chapter 9 by Brian Orend. He begins by outlining the three traditional approaches to the ethics of war and peace. The first is realism, which assumes essentially that there are no ethical constraints to war and conflict; the only requirement is one of doing what is in one's own best interests. What matters is power not ethics. The second is pacifism, which opposes all war, and regards the ethics of war

95

as problematic from the outset. The third approach is that of just war theory and international law (which often assumes "just war" premises), which is where the theoretical debate influences and overlaps with actual political decision-making. For instance, questions mentioned above about legitimacy and proportionality, questions which pepper the debate about current acts of war, are pressing concerns in just war theory. Orend then discusses the possible principles of just war theory in more detail using recent conflicts of Afghanistan and Iraq to explore these. In the final section Orend considers terrorism.

Chapter 10 by Henry Shue explores torture. He considers the types of torture, practices of torture and arguments surrounding torture in recent decades. Shue begins by documenting the development of torture and torture techniques in the US; a place that he had thought, when he began writing on the topic in the 1970s, had forsworn the practice. This serves to remind the reader that torture is not rare practice, but planned and systematic. He then proceeds to consider arguments and justifications for the practice of torture (practices that would at first glance appear wholly unethical) and to this end he considers the "ticking-bomb scenario". He argues that this is not an adequate justification for torture. In the second half of the chapter he turns to substantive arguments and looks at claims about "sophisticated interrogation." Here he considers whether by prohibiting torture we might at some point fail to attain some crucial information which will result in terrifying consequences. In response to this Shue emphasizes two key points upon which he finishes his chapter: first that there is no evidence to believe that torture is the most effective form of interrogation; and second, that abandoning restraints on torture bequeaths an even more barbarous world to our children.

Chapter 11 by Alex J. Bellamy considers humanitarian intervention – which for some is the most ethical of all wars and for others is a contradiction in terms. In this chapter Bellamy considers the ethics of the practice of humanitarian intervention, taking examples from Liberia in 1990, through Haiti, Rwanda and Kosovo, among others, to Libya in 2011. In order to explain and evaluate humanitarian intervention Bellamy suggests "a way of thinking about different perspectives on humanitarian intervention in relation to two critical questions, one about the nature of world politics … and the other about which type of actor should be privileged." In other words what do we think the aim of world politics should be, and who matters – individuals or states?

Bellamy then proceeds to use these two questions throughout the rest of the chapter to frame the debate, which he divides into five sections. In the first, he uses his two questions as axes to plot different possible positions; this results in four main clusters of views (optimistic/state-centred, tragic/state-centred, optimistic/people-centred and tragic/people-centred). The next four sections then go on to explore each of these clusters and their likely acceptance of and commitment to humanitarian intervention. He concludes by noting a general trend away from a state privileged view; at least he claims that the assumption that states should always be privileged no longer dominates and that there is some coherence, evidenced in the emerging commitment (at least in theory) to the doctrine of Responsibility to Protect. He finishes by emphasizing uncertainty with regard to the future of humanitarian intervention.

In Chapter 12 Douglas P. Lackey addresses the nuclear threat. As with many of the other topics discussed in the chapters of this section, particularly terrorism and torture, it is hard to see how the nuclear threat can even be justified using the traditional framework of just war theory. For instance, the use of nuclear weapons would seem never to be proportionate. However, even though their use is arguably always prohibitive this does not exhaust the discussion, as significant ethical discussion surrounds the ethics of amassing nuclear weapons even if they are not used. Lackey focuses the chapter on the usefulness and the justice of the non-proliferation treaty.

Lackey begins the discussion with the global aims of non-proliferation and the assumptions which lie behind the aim to reduce the proliferation of nuclear weapons (both in terms of the counties which have such weapons and the number of weapons which countries have). He then evaluates considerations of utility in the first half of the chapter and considerations of justice in the second half of the chapter. In considering utility he asks whether the assumptions about non-proliferation are correct. Did the non-proliferation treaty in fact reduce both the number of countries with weapons and the size of the arsenals of those who have the weapons? He then considers the arguments connected to justice, most particularly whether the non-proliferation treaty is unjust. There are a number of reasons one might consider, including that the treaty is exclusive, benefiting only the previously imperialist powers, that it carries increased risks for those who do not have nuclear weapons, and that the possession of such weapons is neither general-izable nor equitable. Lackey's conclusion is that on balance the non-proliferation treaty has benefited humanity, but that this benefit is not huge, is questionable and needs to be qualified.

9

WAR AND TERRORISM

Brian Orend

War is well defined as an actual, intentional and widespread armed conflict between groups of people (Orend 2013). This is true whether these groups are *within* one country (civil war) or in *different* countries (classic international warfare). "Armed conflict" means the use of weapons and physical violence with the intention of inflicting harm upon people, trying to coerce them into doing whatever one wants. As Clausewitz said, war is "an act of violence, intended to compel our opponent to fulfil our will". War is like a duel, he concluded, "only on an extensive scale" (Clausewitz 1995: 10–11). There have been over two hundred wars (thus defined, and with a minimum of a thousand battlefield deaths) in the last hundred years alone. So, on average, there are *two new wars every year*. As of writing, there seem to be, around the world, about twelve armed conflicts ongoing (Harrison & Wolf 2009).

Armed conflict has a massive impact on all our lives. It shapes the fate of nations, alters the course of history, consumes enormous resources, determines who is in control and, obviously, causes much death and destruction (Keegan 1994). How should we think about "the ethics of armed conflict"? Or is this an oxymoron (like "deafening silence")? The purpose of this chapter is to explain what dominant traditions of thought have had to say about the morality of war (and terrorism), using current and historical case references to illustrate the relevant ideas and values.

There are three basic, and influential, perspectives on the ethics of war and peace. They can be diagrammed, crudely, on the following continuum:

Extreme	*Middle*	*Extreme*
Realism	**International law/just war theory**	**Pacifism**

Each of these traditions has something very important and influential to say about the ethics of war and peace. Let us begin by looking at the extremes, to get a better fix on the middle, which tends to be the more commonplace, or majority, understanding (if not always the prevailing practice).

Realism

Realism is the view that, as a country, your goal should be *to advance your own country's national interests*. National interests are those things that improve, benefit or enhance the position of one's country in the world. Realism is like a form of national egoism or selfishness. When dealing with the outside world, or "the international community", one ought to (as they say) "look out for number one!" Do the best you can for your own society, especially in terms of national security and defence, growing your economy, population and access to natural resources, and augmenting your cultural and political influence around the world. At minimum, realism insists that *you've got to protect what you've already got*; and, at most, you should get as much as you can and, in fact (if it is possible), *try to re-make the world in your own image*. In terms of war, realism adheres to the doctrine of "anything goes". Realists usually believe that there is no such thing as "the ethics of war and peace": it is all about power and protecting one's country. And, since history teaches us that few things are worse for a people than losing a war, it follows that people are going to feel free to, and should feel free to, use whatever means at their disposal to try to win. As the old saying goes, "all's fair in love and war". (Note that some realists are risk-favouring, whereas others are risk-averse, when it comes to debating the most advantageous thing to do in terms of using armed force on behalf of one's country. Some are quite aggressive, others quite cautious.) Prominent realist thinkers would include Machiavelli and Hans Morgenthau. Prominent realist politicians would include Henry Kissinger and former US President Richard Nixon (Morgenthau 1970, Kissinger 1995, Machiavelli 1998).

Strengths and weaknesses

In terms of strengths and weaknesses, one need only look at history to realize that realists paint a plausible picture of how states and peoples *actually tend to behave* during wartime: "looking out for number one" even seems to put it mildly. Also, smart governments need to fear the risk of "being suckered" by less scrupulous players on the international stage: soft-mindedness and kind-heartedness can sometimes lead to harmful results. Finally, few people can deny that one of the most basic purposes of a national government is to protect its own people, especially from the kinds of suffering, and foreign attack, which war typically involves.

At the same time, many view realism as unbearably cynical: if everything is indeed this ultra-competitive struggle over power and resources, how is the world supposed to get any better? In other words, *there's not enough idealism in realism*. Others have noted how realism's obsession with power props up the status quo, and is biased in favour of the most powerful. More bitingly, in terms of war, many have pointed out that realism actually seems a recipe for escalation in war-fighting: the lack of trust and jostling for power lead to war; and then one belligerent tries a controversial tactic, and then the other replies. Not to be outdone, the first does something even stronger, and then it is a "race to the gutter" in terms of tactics and measures. This, critics say, is the true, ugly face of the "anything goes" attitude: total warfare. Indeed, some have noted that the "anything goes" permissibility offered by realism may be a seductive psychological motive in favour of its belief: it is not so much that it is true, or that it is good advice but, rather, that people *want to be free of moral constraints*, especially in such stressful circumstances as armed conflict. But constraints nevertheless prevent a spill-over into total warfare, and serve plausible, and laudable, goals of reigning in war's destructiveness (Forde 1992, Mapel 1996, McMahan 1996).

Pacifism

At the other extreme is pacifism. Different pacifists define pacifism differently, and offer various kinds of justification for their beliefs. But it seems that what unites all forms of pacifism – the basic proposition, or lowest common denominator – is opposition to warfare. The logical core of pacifism, as Jenny Teichman says, is "anti-war-ism" (Teichman 1986). No matter what kind of pacifist you are, you believe that *war is always wrong*; there is always some better approach to the problem than warfare. So, unlike realists, pacifists believe that it *is* possible and meaningful to apply moral judgement to international affairs. In this, they agree with just war theorists (more below). But they disagree with just war theorists regarding the application of moral judgement to warfare. Just war theorists say war is *sometimes* morally permissible, whereas pacifists say war is *never* morally permissible. If realism asserts that, during wartime, "anything goes", pacifists rejoin: "nothing goes": *there is always some morally superior option to war-fighting, such as non-violent resistance.* The most relevant (secular) pro-pacifist arguments here include the following: (a) a more "teleological" form of pacifism (or TP), which asserts that war and killing are at odds with human excellence and flourishing; (b) a more "consequentialist" form of pacifism (or CP), which maintains that the benefits accruing from war can never outweigh the costs of fighting it; and (c) a more "deontological" form of pacifism (or DP), which contends that the very activity of war is intrinsically unjust, since it violates foremost duties of morality and justice, such as not killing other human beings. Most common and compelling among contemporary secular pacifists, such as Robert Holmes and Richard Norman, is a mixed doctrine that combines, in some way, all three (Holmes 1989, Norman 1995).

Strengths and weaknesses

The obvious strength of pacifism is that it very much desires to secure a more peaceful world. No lack of idealism here. And it is hard to disagree with the claim that war brings enormous costs and casualties in its train, and is steeped in tragedy. And pacifism's discussion of non-violent resistance does open people's minds to alternative, and additional, tactics to use when resisting nasty regimes. Consider the following list of tactics offered by Gene Sharp:

> general strike, sit-down strike, industry strike, go-slow and work to rule … economic boycotts, consumers' boycott, traders boycott, rent refusal, international economic embargo and social boycott … boycott of government employment, boycott of elections, revenue refusal, civil disobedience and mutiny … sit-ins, reverse strikes, non-violent obstruction, non-violent invasion and parallel government.
>
> *(Sharp 2005: 254)*

But what are some of the weaknesses? Michael Walzer, the just war theorist, contends that pacifism's idealism is excessively optimistic. In other words, pacifism lacks realism. More precisely, the non-violent world imagined by the pacifist is not actually attainable, at least for the foreseeable future. Since "ought implies can", the set of "oughts" we are committed to must express a moral outlook on war less utopian in nature. While we *are* committed to morality in wartime, we are forced to concede that, sometimes in the real world against especially brutal regimes, resorting to war can be morally justified (Walzer 1977).

Another objection to pacifism is that, by failing to resist international aggression with effective means, it actually ends up: (a) rewarding aggression; and (b) failing to protect people who need it. Pacifists reply to this argument by contending that we do not need to resort to war in order to protect people and punish aggression effectively. In the event of an armed invasion by an aggressor state, an organized and committed campaign of non-violent civil disobedience – perhaps combined with international diplomatic and economic sanctions – would be just as effective as war in expelling the aggressor, with much less destruction of lives and property.

After all, the pacifist might say, no invader could possibly maintain its grip on the conquered nation in light of such systematic isolation, non-cooperation and non-violent resistance. How could it work the factories, harvest the fields, or run the stores, when everyone would be striking? How could it maintain the will to keep the country in the face of crippling economic sanctions and diplomatic censure from the international community? And so on, perhaps citing further from Sharp's list above (Ackerman & DuVall 2000).

Though one cannot exactly disprove this pacifist proposition – since it is a counter-factual thesis – there are reasons to agree with John Rawls (1971) that such is "an unworldly view" to hold. For, as Walzer (1977) points out, the effectiveness of this proposed campaign of civil disobedience relies on the moral scruples of the invading aggressor. But what if the aggressor is brutal, ruthless? What if, faced with civil disobedience, the invader "cleanses" the area of the native population, and then imports its own people from back home? What if, faced with economic sanctions and diplomatic censure from a neighbouring country, the invader decides to invade it, too? We have some indication from history, particularly that of Nazi Germany, that such pitiless tactics are quite effective at breaking the will of people to resist. The defence of our lives and rights may well, against such invaders, require the use of political violence. Under such conditions, Walzer says, adherence to pacifism would amount to "a disguised form of surrender" (*ibid.*: 334–35).

Pacifists respond to this accusation of "unworldliness" by citing what they believe are real-world examples of effective non-violent resistance to aggression. Examples mentioned include Mahatma Ghandi's campaign to drive the British Imperial regime out of India in the late 1940s and Martin Luther King Jr's civil rights crusade in the 1960s on behalf of African-Americans. Walzer replies curtly that there is no evidence that non-violent resistance has ever, of itself, succeeded. This may be rash on his part, though it is clear that Britain's own exhaustion after the Second World War, for example, had much to do with the evaporation of its Empire. Walzer's main counter-argument against these pacifist counter-examples is that they only underline his main point: that effective non-violent resistance depends upon the scruples of those it is aimed against. It was only because the British and the Americans had some scruples, and were moved by the determined idealism of the non-violent protesters, that they acquiesced to their demands. But aggressors will not always be so moved. A tyrant like Hitler, for example, might interpret non-violent resistance as weakness, deserving contemptuous crushing. "Non-violent defense", Walzer suggests, "is no defense at all against tyrants or conquerors ready to adopt such measures" (*ibid.*: 335).

International law and just war theory

In between the extreme views of realism and pacifism resides just war theory. Like pacifism (and unlike realism), just war theory believes that there *is* both sense and value in applying ethics and moral values to issues of international relations. But unlike pacifism (and like realism), just war theory believes that there *can sometimes* be instances where resorting to war is justified, if only as "the least-worst" option. Thus, if pacifism says "nothing goes" with regard to the ethics of war, and realism declares that "anything goes", just war theory opines that "something, sometimes, goes". While war *can* be morally permissible, just war theory nevertheless views war dimly and dangerously, and insists that it is too risky and lacking in restraint to allow for "anything goes". Just war theory seeks to substitute, for that realist permissiveness, a set of sensible rules to restrain and guide those considering warfare as a tool for solving some serious foreign policy problem. The just war approach has been deeply influential on the international laws of armed conflict, for instance as contained in the Hague and Geneva Conventions, as well as in the United Nations (UN) Charter and the various resolutions of the UN Security Council (UNSC) (Reisman & Antoniou 1994). To be crystal clear: just war theory refers to the prior moral tradition, with a pedigree stretching all the way back (at least) to the ancient Greco-Romans, whereas international law refers to agreed-upon contractual treaties between national governments (and most such treaties regulating warfare date only from about 1850 forwards). They are thus separate things; but the point here is that the content of the laws, and even their general structure, has been heavily influenced by just war theory, and so we can put just war theory and the laws of armed conflict together, for our purposes, as a tightly related bundle of concepts and values, sporting a shared outlook on how countries and peoples ought to behave during armed conflict.

Jus ad bellum

Jus ad bellum is Latin for "the justice of war". When, if ever, may states fight? The just war answer is that states may fight *only if* they satisfy *all* of the following rules: just cause; right intention; public declaration of war by a proper authority; last resort; probability of success; and proportionality. (Like the other traditions above, there is pluralism and some interpretive dispute as to the exact and best meaning of these rules within just war theory.) Those with "the war power" (usually the executive branch in non-democratic societies, and the legislative branch in democratic ones) are to ensure they satisfy these principles before embarking on war.

Just cause

The way international law renders just war theory in this regard is very clear and quite helpful. Most experts agree that, when it comes to a just cause for war, three general principles are at play:

- All countries have the inherent, or "natural", right to go to war in *self-defence* from aggression. (Aggression is defined as any unjustified first use of armed force against another country. Any armed attack which crosses an international border constitutes aggression and is a *casus belli*, that is, "a cause for war".)
- All countries have the further natural, or inherent, right of *other-defence* – otherwise known as "collective security" – to go to war as an act of aid, or assistance, to *any* country victimized by aggression.
- Any other use of force – for example a pre-emptive strike, or armed humanitarian intervention (AHI) – is *not* an inherent, or natural, right of states. Any country wishing to engage in such is supposed to get *the prior approval* of the UNSC. Failing to receive such prior authorization renders any such use of force illegal, itself an act of aggression (Roberts & Guelff 1999, Orend 2012).

So, if country A commits an armed attack against country B, then B (and any other country C) is entitled to go to war against A as an act of *defence from, resistance to* and *punishment of* aggression. Aggression is seen as a wrong so severe that war is a fitting response because it violates the most basic rights of groups, and individuals, to life and security, and to freedom and well-being: that is, to go about their lives peacefully, on a territory where their people reside. Classic examples of international aggression include: Imperial Germany's invasion of Belgium in 1914, sparking the First World War; Nazi Germany's invasion of Poland in 1939, sparking the Second World War; Japan's invasion of China in 1937, and its attack on the US at Pearl Harbor in 1941, sparking the Pacific part of the Second World War; the USSR's invasion of Afghanistan in 1979; and Iraq's invasion of Kuwait in 1990, sparking the Persian Gulf War. There are actually thousands of historical examples of international aggression (R. K. Grant 2008).

Proportionality

In every kind of law or rule, there is supposed to be a proportion, or balance, between problem and solution (or between violation and response). What, if anything, might be a problem truly so severe that war is a proportionate response? The answer of international law and just war theory (for reasons stated above) is: aggression. When confronted with an aggressive invader – like Nazi Germany, Imperial Japan or the Soviet Union – who is intent on conquering and enslaving other nations, it is deemed reasonable to stand up to such a dark threat to life and liberty and to resist it, and beat it back, with force if need be. Just as dangerous criminals must be resisted and not be allowed to get away with their crimes, countries are entitled to stand up to aggressors, and to resist and defeat them (Orend 2006: 59–61).[1]

Public declaration of war by a proper authority

War is supposed to be declared out in the open, officially and honestly, by the proper authority for doing so. In every country, some branch of government has "the war power": that is, the authority to order the use of force and warfare. In Canada and Britain, the war power rests with Parliament; in America, the war power likewise rests with the legislature: that is, Congress. But the American President, as Commander-in-Chief of the Armed Forces, has enormous *de facto* power to order the American military into action. As a result, many experts argue that the war power in the US is actually split – in classic American "checks-and-balances" style – between the legislative and executive branches of government.[2] We have seen, further, how in all cases where non-defensive armed force is being considered, the UNSC must also approve of the action, and beforehand. This is to say that, with non-defensive war, *both domestic and international* authorization must be satisfied (Orend 2006: 50–57).

Last resort

State governments are only supposed to go to war as a last resort, after all other reasonable means of problem-solving have been tried, and failed. It is said that countries have four basic tools in their foreign policy tool-box: diplomacy, positive economic incentives, sanctions and force. Obviously, you want to exhaust all other means of problem-solving before engaging in something as expensive, bloody and risky as war. A nice illustration of this rule in action happened during the run-up to the Persian Gulf War of 1991. In August 1990, Saddam Hussein's Iraq invaded its tiny neighbour, Kuwait. International allies, as led by the US and UK, tried to talk to Saddam and threaten him, to no avail. They offered him financial incentives, but he refused, preferring to hold on to Kuwait's oil fields. They then slapped sweeping sanctions on him, and got most of his neighbours to agree and also put pressure on Iraq. Still nothing. As a result, the international community felt it was the last resort to go to war to push Saddam out of Kuwait, and back into his own borders. This they did, within two months, in early 1991 (Johnson & Weigel 1991).

The above *jus ad bellum* rules are all part of the international laws of armed conflict (Best 1994). Just war theory, as a theory of ethics, levies two additional moral requirements.

Right intention

The notion here is that one's motives need to be ethically proper. It is not enough merely that one's *actions* comply with the above rules but that, furthermore, one acts with *the right frame of mind* and, in particular, that seedy, ulterior motives, such as greed, play no role. In the case of a just war, then, the idea would be that one's intentions in acting are to resist, repulse and punish aggression, and nothing more. Though this rule is *not* part of international law – largely owing to the difficulty involved discerning the true intentions of a complex, multi-part actor like a state government – it is, nevertheless, very frequently invoked in common moral discussion of warfare. It was, for example, a popular criticism of the Bush Administration's decision to invade Iraq in 2003 to suggest that the decision had as much, or more, to do with the desire to gain secure access to oil as it did with, say, ensuring that Iraq was not about to deploy weapons of mass destruction (WMD) against the US (Orend 2006: 46–48).[3]

Probability of success

The rule here is that one should not begin a war one knows in advance is going to be futile. The point is *to prohibit pointless killing and suffering*: one should have some probability of success before resorting to war. At the same time, this can be very difficult to predict at the start of war, and history has shown that, sometimes, long-shots can actually win. Moreover, this rule seems biased in favour of powerful states, who (for that very reason) have better chance of winning their wars. This probably explains the absence of this rule from international law, which is based around theoretical ideals regarding the equality of sovereign states: if a country – any country, big or small – has been victimized by aggression, who are we to say that they should not go to war, because at the outset it looks like such a risky venture (Orend 2006: 58–59)?[4]

Two quick recent applications of *jus ad bellum*

Many experts felt that the recent war on Afghanistan was justified, according to the above criteria, whereas the war on Iraq was not. The war in Afghanistan was justified because it was a response to America being attacked by the terrorist group al-Qaeda on 11 September ("9/11") 2001. It was quickly determined that the then-government of Afghanistan, the Taliban, was offering state sponsorship – safe harbour, protection and resources – to al-Qaeda, and as a result was complicit in the 9/11 act of aggression. America was thus seen as exercising its right of self-defence when it went to war in late 2001, and overthrew the Taliban regime in early 2002. The twenty-eight other countries who joined in were seen as offering other-defence, or collective security (Corbin 2002, Barfield 2009).

By contrast, in March 2003, America launched an anticipatory attack, aimed at changing the regime in Iraq. We have seen above that, when it comes to cases other than self- or other-defence, a country is supposed to get prior permission from the UNSC. America failed to secure such, and thus most international law experts view the resulting war as having lacked legitimacy. America tried to argue instead that the attack was needed as an act of "pre-emptive self-defence", alleging that Saddam was plotting with remnants of al-Qaeda to give them WMD and have them strike the US. Most countries did not believe this argument (as the secular dictator Saddam and the religious fanatics al-Qaeda would have made very strange bedfellows), and the fact that Iraqi WMD were never found only called into deep further question the justice of the start of this war (McGoldlick 2004). Now, there is a range of opinion as how best to interpret the law and just war theory on these points and cases. Though the above may be a common view, not all agree. But what does seem almost entirely agreed to – among those within this tradition – is how just war theory and international law provide a rich and appropriate moral framework for having these kinds of discussions intelligently and usefully.

Jus in bello

Whereas we saw above that the rules of *jus ad bellum* are aimed at those with the war power, the rules of *jus in bello* are aimed at soldiers and officers: those who actually do the fighting. If they violate these rules, they can find themselves – after the conflict – facing war crime charges, either domestically through their own military justice system or internationally through The Hague (Walzer 1977: 40–156). And by far and away the most important, strongly worded and repeatedly mentioned and codified principle in this regard is that of discrimination and non-combatant immunity.

Discrimination and non-combatant immunity

"Discrimination" here means the need for fighters to distinguish, or discriminate, between legit-imate and illegitimate targets, and to take aim only at the former. A legitimate target is anyone, or anything, which is part of the war machine of the enemy society. "The war machine" refers to the military–industrial–political complex that guides the war and fights it. Loosely speaking, it is anything which is a source of potential physical harm, or armed force, directed against oneself. More specifically, legitimate targets include: soldiers, sailors, marines, pilots and their officers; their weapons and equipment; their barracks and training areas; their means of transportation; their supply and communications lines; and the industrial sites which produce their supply. Core political and bureaucratic institutions are also legitimate objects of attack, in particular things like the Defence Ministry. Illegitimate targets include residential areas, schools, hospitals, farms, churches, cultural institutions and non-military industrial sites. *In general, anyone or anything not demonstrably engaged in military supply, or military activity, is immune from direct, intentional attack.* Thus, non-combatants – that is, civilians – are "immune" from intentional attack. This is seen as probably the worst war crime: the intentional killing of civilians (Orend 2006: 105–40).

Strange as it may sound, the non-combatant immunity principle does *not* mean that it is illegal for civilians to die in wartime. What is illegal is *taking deliberate and intentional aim* at civilians with armed force. If a fighting side has taken every reasonable effort to avoid and minimize civilian casualties, but some civilians still die accidentally, or in the indirect way just noted, then that is *not* a war crime. Such civilians are viewed as "collateral damage": accidental, unintended casualties of the fighting. An example would be an air-bombing raid on an enemy's industrial sites, during which a few bombs accidentally go astray and hit a close-by residential area, wounding and killing some civilians.[5]

So, civilians are *only* entitled to "due care" from fighters; they are *not* entitled to absolute and failsafe immunity from warfare.[6] What does "due care" include? It includes all serious and sus-tained efforts, from the top of the military chain of command down to the bottom, to protect civilian lives as best as possible amid the difficult circumstances of war. So, for example, strate-gists must make their plans with an eye to minimizing civilian casualties; intelligence needs to be gathered and analysed regarding which are the permissible targets; soldiers need to be trained exhaustively in proper – that is, restrained and discriminating – ways of fighting; any rough treatment of civilians needs to be investigated and punished; and so on (Walzer 1977: 40–156).

What about so-called "dual-use" targets? The question arises: what about things used *both* by the military and civilians during war, such as roads, bridges, radio and TV networks and trans-mitters, railway lines, harbours and airports? International law forbids targeting them but, in rea-lity, they often are, as they are so useful in helping military planners communicate with their troops and to move them around to where they are needed to fight. More controversial, and thus more criticized, is targeting basic infrastructure, like farms, food supply, sewers, water treatment plants, irrigation systems, water pipelines, oil and gas pipelines, electricity generators, and power and telephone lines. The civilian population pays a huge price for any damage inflicted on such vital social infrastructure, and so it seems to violate civilian immunity to go after them. America did this twice recently. During the opening days of both the 1999 Kosovo War and the 2003 Iraq attack, America launched a so-called "shock and awe" campaign – relying on air power, bombing raids and cruise missiles – to inflict heavy damage on basic infrastructure (especially communications and electricity) in Serbia and Baghdad, respectively. The military goal of such a strike is to hit the enemy as fast and furiously as possible, dazing them, and "softening them up" for a subsequent ground invasion by army soldiers. It is also to shock the civilians in that society into putting pressure on their regime to give up and surrender quickly (Ignatieff 2001b, Clark 2002).

Prisoners of war and benevolent quarantine

It follows from the idea of non-combatant immunity that, should enemy soldiers themselves cease to be a source of harm during war – for example, by laying down their weapons and surrendering – then they cannot be targeted with lethal force after that point. In fact, they are to become prisoners of war (or POWs) offered "benevolent quarantine" for the duration of the war. "Benevolent quarantine" means that captured enemy soldiers can be stripped of their weapons, incarcerated with their fellows and questioned verbally for information. But they cannot, for example, be tortured during questioning. Nor can they be beaten, starved or somehow medically experimented on. They cannot be used as shields between oneself and the opposing side; the understanding is that captured enemy soldiers are to be incarcerated far away from the front lines. And very basic medical and hygienic treatment is supposed to be offered: things like aspirin, soap, water and toothbrushes. When it is all over, they are then usually freed in exchange for POWs on the other side (Orend 2006: 105–59).

Proportionality

The *jus in bello* version of proportionality mandates that soldiers deploy only proportionate force against legitimate targets. The rule is *not* about the war as a whole; it is about tactics *within* the war. Make sure, the rule commands, that the destruction needed to fulfil the military objective is proportional to the good of achieving it. The crude version of this rule is: don't squash a squirrel with a tank, or shoot a fly with cannon; use force appropriate to securing the target (Walzer 1977: 129).

Prohibited weapons

There is a vast number of relevant conventions and legal treaties on this issue, aside from the canonical Hague and Geneva Conventions, such as those banning the use of chemical (1925 and second protocol 1996), biological (1972) and "excessively injurious weapons" (1980). Also relevant are the conventions against genocide (1948), against "methods of warfare which alter the natural environment" (1977) and banning land mines (1999). Prohibiting certain weapons puts an added restriction upon belligerents and, as such, is consistent with the deepest aim of *jus in bello*, namely, to limit war's destruction (Reisman & Antoniou 1994).

Means mala in se

There is a traditional ban on "means *mala in se*", or "methods evil in themselves". The imprecise yet interesting idea here is that some weapons and means of war are forbidden not so much because of the badness of the consequences they inflict but, more importantly, because they themselves are intrinsically awful. Using rape as a tool of warfare, for instance, to drive a population off a territory, or to reward one's troops after battle, is a clear example. Rape is ruled out not so much because of all the pain it produces, or because it is aimed at civilians, but because the act itself is rights-violating, a disgusting disregard for the humanity of the woman raped: a coercive violation of her bodily integrity and her entitlement to choose her own sex partner(s). Rape was used as a tool of war both in the Bosnian Civil War (1992–95) and in the presently ongoing war in the Congo in Africa. Methods like campaigns of genocide, ethnic cleansing, use of child soldiers and torture probably also fall under this category of means *mala in se* (Allen 1996, Orend 2002b, Danner 2004, P. Singer 2006).

Reprisals

Reprisals are not permitted in the laws of armed conflict. At the same time, they have happened in history, and are rather frequently threatened during wartime. The reprisal doctrine permits a violation of *jus in bello* rules – but *only* in response to a *prior* violation by the opposing side. Walzer offers an example of what he labels a justified reprisal, and it focuses on proportionality and prohibited weapons. He claims that Winston Churchill was "entirely justified when he warned the German government, early in World War II, that the use of [poison] gas by its army would bring an immediate Allied reprisal". International law, for its part, disallows any reprisals, on grounds that, more often than not, they will lead to a serious escalation in violence. One is supposed to win well, so to speak: the pursuit of victory, but within the rules (Walzer 1977: 207; Regan 1996: 172–78).

Emerging military technologies

There is a new category of weapons and methods of warfare, which have come to be known under the umbrella term "emerging military technologies" (EMTs). These include: *soldier enhancements* (notably drugs designed to augment one's biological energy); *incapacitating agents* (designed to knock out, but not kill, enemy soldiers); *unmanned weapons systems* (notably, drones); and *cyber-warfare* (the use of advanced computer, and Internet, technologies to substantially harm the interests of a target community). Since these are freshly emerging, international law is racing to keep up, and no clear, agreed-upon rules have yet been structured. For instance, in 2011, America, China and Russia met to try to craft a treaty regulating the means of cyber-warfare, only to have the talks fall apart amid bitter mutual accusations. The ongoing, future development of *jus in bello* will include rules regulating the use of these new technologies (Dockery 2007; P. Singer 2009; Orend 2012: 186–245).

Interconnections

Traditionally, the categories of just war theory and international law, like *jus ad bellum* and *jus in bello*, have been treated as separate, demanding the attention of different groups of people (e.g. politicians the former, soldiers the latter). But, starting perhaps with Kant, and recently gaining momentum with the works of David Rodin, Jeff McMahan and others, there is a definite body of thought which calls this traditional separation into question, preferring to stress instead the robust linkages which must exist between the categories. A notable point here is how the justice of the start of the war in question seems to affect our judgements of everything else: how to describe a *jus in bello* tactic, for example, as "proportionate", unless one knows the overall justice of the war whose objective it advances (Rodin 2005, McMahan 2011)?

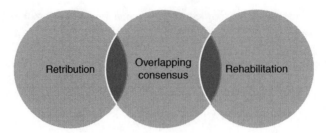

Figure 9.1 Overlapping consensus: theories of post-war justice.

Jus post bellum: *aftermath*

Substantially (and sadly) unregulated by international law (Orend 2000), we can only speak of different theories of post-war justice. There are two major rival theories in this regard – retribution and rehabilitation – though they do share some common ground.

Most people agree this common ground (or "overlapping consensus") posits that the basic goal of post-war justice is *to vindicate the rights whose violation triggered the war to begin with*, forcing the defeated aggressor[7] to accept a proportionate policy on surrender which includes:

- public (as opposed to secret) terms of settlement;
- mutual exchange of POWs at war's end;
- aggressor to apologize (for committing aggression);
- aggressor to give up any unjust gains;
- aggressor to de-militarize (so no short-term repeat of aggression is possible);
- war crimes trials (*jus ad bellum* trials for the aggressor; *jus in bello* trials for all sides).

(Orend 2002a: 43–56)

Thick Theory 1: Retribution

So much for the thin theory of post-war justice and its general, and rather familiar, principles. What of the more rebust, and controversial, thick theories, as depicted in Figure 9.1. Historically, we tend to see two major rivals. The first one is that of retribution. Defenders of this model of post-war justice have, as their goal, to make the defeated aggressor *worse off* than prior to the war (as backward-looking punishment). The means to be used to achieve this include all elements of the thin theory above, plus:

- compensation payments from aggressor to victim, and possibly to the international community more broadly;
- sanctions put on the aggressor, to hamper its future economic growth;
- no aid, or assistance, with post-war reconstruction. Such is left up to the locals, with no forcible regime change imposed on the aggressor.

Prime historical examples of the retribution model in action would be the Treaty of Versailles, ending the First World War in 1918–19, and the terms ending the Persian Gulf War in 1991 (Orend 2000: 217–67).

Now, why does the aggressor need to be made worse off than it was prior to the war? The defenders of this model suggest several reasons. First, it is thought that justice itself demands retribution of this nature: the aggressor must be made to feel the wrongness, and sting, of the war which it unjustly began. Second, consider an analogy to an individual criminal: in domestic society, when a thief has stolen a diamond ring, we do not just make him give the ring back, say he is sorry, and take away his thieving tools. We also make him pay a fine, or send him to jail, to impress upon him the wrongness of his conduct. And this ties into the third reason: by punishing the aggressor, we hope *to deter or prevent* future aggression, both by him (so to speak) and by any others who might be having similar ideas (Orend 2006: 160–90).

Thick Theory 2: Rehabilitation

The goal of this model, by contrast, is to make the defeated aggressor *better off* than prior to the war (as forward-looking reconstruction). The means to be employed include all of the elements of the thin theory above, plus:

- no compensation payments;
- no sanctions;
- aid and assistance with post-war reconstruction, including forcible regime change imposed on defeated aggressor.

Prime historical examples of the rehabilitation model in action would be the post-Second-World-War (1945–55) reconstruction of West Germany and Japan, and today's cases of Afghanistan and Iraq (early 2002 and mid-2003, respectively, until 2013 or even, arguably, the present) (Orend 2013: 215–50).

Where the two models of post-war justice differ is over three major issues. First, the rehabilitation model *rejects sanctions*, especially on grounds that they have been shown, historically, to harm civilians and thus to violate discrimination. Second, the rehabilitation model *rejects compensation payments*, for the same reason. In fact, the model favours *investing in* a defeated aggressor, to help it re-build and to help smooth over the wounds of war. Finally, the rehabilitation model *favours forcing regime change* whereas the retribution model views that as too risky and costly. That it may be, but those who favour the rehabilitative model suggest that it can be worth it over the long term, leading to the creation of a new, better, non-aggressive, and even progressive, member of the international community.[8]

Strengths and weaknesses

Just war theory and international law (JWT/IL) clearly carve out a more detailed and comprehensive account of the ethics of war and peace than either realism or pacifism. As such, they enable a more finely grained and thorough analysis. While realists and pacifists might counter that JWT/IL is thus rendered more complex, the JWT/IL reply would be that the subject matter itself is quite complex and difficult, and hence simplicity in this regard is no virtue.

Realism views JWT/IL as actually being likely to create more wars than necessary, what with its moral "crusading" and insistence on justice being done. Moreover, realists will assert that it is just plain silly to prosecute a war "with one arm tied behind one's back", as it were, in adherence to *jus in bello*. Modern JWT/IL, in reply, disavows any association with strident crusading and insists that it only makes sense to limit war-fighting with sensible rules of restraint. The realist alternative – unrestrained, total warfare – seems a recipe for humanitarian disaster (Welch 1993).

Pacifism, for its part, almost has more respect for realism, for at least the realist does not pretend to be serving morality with his/her views on war, whereas the just war theorist does. For the pacifist, the only morally acceptable opinion on these matters is pacifism, and thus the just war theorist appears morally distasteful. We have already seen the JWT/IL reply above: the pacifist's excess optimism about non-violence in our world – the real world – is what is the true moral mistake, as it can quite predictably lead to: (a) the failure to protect those who need it; and (b) rewarding aggression by default.

JWT/IL views itself as being more moderate and sensible, more detailed and less sweeping, more rational and less extreme, than either of its rivals. It prides itself on being more realistic than pacifism, yet not so "realistic" as to give in to the cynicism and ruthlessness of the realist world-view. JWT/IL still insists upon moral rules and ideals, yet tries to responsibly tailor such to the rough-and-tumble circumstances of actual geopolitics. It thus sees itself as having the best of both worlds. Quite literally: JWT/IL borrows content from realism (especially regarding rules like proportionality and probability of success) as well as from pacifism: for example, as witnessed through the rule of last resort and the rehabilitation model of post-war justice (which is obviously concerned with structural changes in favour of creating a less violent world). Critics view JWT/IL as thus being "messy", maybe even a grab-bag jumble of concepts and values, squished into the "cramped quarters" between the two coherent options of realism and pacifism. But JWT/IL prefers to see itself as occupying the big middle – the expansive, commonsense middle ground – with the other two doctrines residing at the extreme fringes of opinion on these issues.

Application to terrorism

Terrorism is defined as the use of violence – especially killing force – against civilians with the intent of spreading fear throughout a population, hoping that this fear will advance a political objective. Crucial to terrorism is not just the deed itself but also what some have called "the propaganda of the deed". Since terrorists want to spread fear, it is vital that their deed not only be terrible but be so terrible that it gets covered by media, and word/image about the threat become disseminated throughout the population. The 9/11 attacks, for example, were clearly motivated not just by the desire to kill civilians but also by the drive to maximize the propaganda value of the high-profile attacks (*Der Spiegel* 2002, Sterba 2003).

Terrorism also gets used as a tool of authoritarian regimes to crush their own populations into submission: for example, the dictatorship under Robespierre, during the French Revolution, established the "Reign of Terror" (which I believe is the root source of the word "terrorism" in Western vocabularies). The Reign of Terror, 1793–94, was when "Enemies of the Revolution" were rounded up and, in a very deliberate, public, propagandistic way, given their own special "close shave" by Mme La Guillotine. At the Terror's peak, Robespierre had forty thousand people guillotined in just one month.[9] And terrorism gets used as a tool of extremist outsiders against representative regimes. In this context, which is obviously where the 9/11 attacks fit, terrorism is a violent attempt to circumvent such democratic processes as rational persuasion, coalition- and consensus-building, the rule of law, and the will of the majority expressed in free elections. The terrorist seeks to short-circuit all these things and simply inflict his will on a population, probably because he knows his extreme beliefs would have no chance of achieving mainstream success. He cannot persuade people, so he seeks to coerce them. The terrorist, in this sense, is actually much like a tyrant, but without the power and control the tyrant already has. The terrorist is a tyrant-in-waiting, and he dreams of becoming someone like Robespierre, who is able to radically re-fashion all of society from the top down through what he views as the cleansing power of violence. The personnel of al-Qaeda seem to fit this mould precisely (Corbin 2002, Berman 2003).

Whether terrorism, as a tactic, is consistent with any "-ism" or "-ocracy" is a difficult and delicate debate. Fortunately, I do not have to resolve it here. From the point of view of both pacifism and JWT/IL, *terrorism is always an impermissible tactic*, since it involves the deliberate killing of innocent civilians: which right-thinking people view as murder. Realists would not frame the issue in moral terms, but would probably note how, historically, terrorism has not proven massively successful in achieving its objective. And the reason is obvious: while it may spread fear in the short term, over the longer term, people feel outrage at acts of terrorism, and discover a new-found resolve in dealing with terrorists and not letting them have their way through the use of such decrepit measures. For instance, 9/11 did not force America out of the Middle East and North Africa: indeed, it began the War on Terror and has led to the direct fall of at least two regional governments, and some even credit the War on Terror for indirectly inspiring some of the popular, pro-democracy uprisings now known as the Arab Spring (Falk 2002, Eshtain 2003, Noueihad & Warren 2012).

It is important to note that *either state- or non-state actors can commit aggression*, which we have seen is what roots, from the perspective of JWT/IL, a morally justified resort to war. Consider the 9/11 attacks, which were clear instances of aggression. They involved the use of armed force, first to hijack the planes and then to use the planes themselves as high-powered missiles. They violated America's right to territorial integrity, in so far as they were lethal attacks on American soil, having penetrated American airspace. And they violated America's right of political sovereignty, by attempting to force serious foreign policy changes upon a freely choosing population. So 9/11 was an act of aggression, very reminiscent of Pearl Harbor, just as it was obviously designed to be ("propaganda of the deed" and all). And aggression, we explained above, justifies a defensive war in response.

But, likewise, the rules of JWT/IL remain relevant when it comes to permissible tactics used in the War on Terror. We have seen, notably, that these include a ban on torture, and may raise questions about the use of drone-strikes and extra-judicial killing. Thus, even though the beginning of the War on Terror, in Afghanistan, seemed to be well founded, numerous questions can be raised about certain weapons and methods which have since been employed in its name, and further questions need to be raised sharply about the endgame: what would be a satisfying and acceptable "victory", or end, in the War on Terror? Would the democratization of the Middle East, through the Arab Spring, be the ultimate goal – or is the war seen instead as a longer-term, Cold-War-style protracted conflict, decades in length, which demands ultimately the eventual destruction of the opposing ideology and social system, in this case radical Islamic extremism? The tools of JWT/IL, more than their rivals, can help decision-makers think through their options in this regard (Orend 2013: 297–98).

Notes

1 Aquinas is often credited with bringing proportionality into just war theory: see Tooke (1975).

2 This became an issue of struggle between the branches during both the Korean War (1950–53) and especially the Vietnam War (1954–74), when Congress felt successive presidents were running a *de facto* war without actually publicly declaring it and getting *de jure* authority for doing so: that is, getting a clear vote of support from Congress: see Regan 1996.

3 Augustine is seen as the inventor of right intention in just war: see Deane (1963). On Iraq, see, e.g., Murray & Scales (2003), B. Woodward (2004).

4 Grotius is considered the first proponent of probability of success: see Tuck (1999).

5 This raises the complex issue of the Doctrine of Double Effect. The core moral problem is this: even if soldiers intentionally aim *only* at legitimate targets, they can often *foresee* that taking out some of these targets will still involve *collateral* civilian casualties. And if civilians do nothing to lose their human rights, does it not follow that such acts will be unjust, since civilians will predictably suffer some harm or even death? The DDE stipulates that an agent A may perform an action X, even though A foresees that X will result in *both* good (G) and bad (B) effects, *provided all* of the following criteria are met: (a) X is an otherwise morally permissible action; (b) A only intends G and not B; (c) B is not a means

to G; and (d) the goodness of G is worth, or is proportionately greater than, the badness of B. For more, consult P. Woodward (2001).

6 Pacifists object loudly to this, and argue that, since modern war-fighting always involves civilian casualties, this shows it to be an intrinsically corrupt practice.

7 The assumption is that the Aggressor who began the war is defeated. This does not always happen in the real world, of course, but, in those cases where Aggressors win, post-war justice does not get realized; and thus the idealizing assumption. See Orend (2002a).

8 To those who scoff that such deep-rooted transformation simply cannot be done, supporters of the rehabilitative model reply that, not only *can* it be done, it *has* been done. The two leading examples are West Germany and Japan after World War Two. But difficulties with imposing this model on the more recent cases of Afghanistan and Iraq give ammunition to supporters of the retribution model, who view attempts at rehabilitation as too costly, lengthy, and even questionable in principle, as such involves the imposition of such values as human rights. Defenders of rehabilitation reply that such values are genuinely universal, and bound over the long term to result in a more peaceful world (Orend 2006: 190–220; Kant [1795] 1983).

9 Mind you, in the end things turned out badly for Robespierre, getting the guillotine himself (Laqueur 1987, 1999).

10

TORTURE

Henry Shue

The practice

Torture has torn through additional restraints since I first tried to get a grip on it (Shue 1978). Then I began by apologizing for raising an issue that I thought most Americans considered closed. The worst torturers seemed to be in such places as the Shah's Iran, Marcos's Philippines, South Korea and various Latin American dictatorships, including Chile, Argentina, Brazil and Guatemala.[1] Courageous US Congress members like Don Fraser of Minnesota and Vietnam war veteran Tom Harkin of Iowa led an outcry against torture in the early 1970s, a protest that provoked my own interest and was later embraced by the presidency of Jimmy Carter after 1976. Many of us thought that torture was practised in the Third World but condemned by Americans and Europeans, reminiscent of the author of the 1911 entry on "Torture" for the *Encyclopaedia Britannica*, who claimed "[t]he whole subject is now one of only historical interest as far as Europe is concerned" (Waldron 2005b: 1683–84; 2010: 187). How far, and how sadly, wrong can one be!

It emerged that a number of the Latin American torturers had been trained at Fort Benning, Georgia, in the School of the Americas in techniques developed by the Central Intelligence Agency (CIA) (Gill 2004; McCoy 2006: 60–107; Rejali 2007). Unknown to me and most other US citizens whose taxes were funding it in 1978, CIA had already for decades been funding a massive academic research programme designed to create a new paradigm of torture, which is now in operation and has to a considerable degree corrupted the US military (Wolfendale 2007, Forsythe 2011). The most penetrating account of this secretly funded research is Wisconsin historian Alfred W. McCoy's *A Question of Torture: CIA Interrogation, from the Cold War to the War on Terror*: "From 1950 to 1962, the CIA became involved in torture through a massive mind-control effort, with psychological warfare and secret research into human consciousness that reached a cost of a billion dollars annually – a veritable Manhattan Project of the mind" (McCoy 2006: 7).

In April 1953 the CIA organized its various research grants "under the umbrella of a unified project, MKUltra" (*ibid.*: 28). Much of the research on human consciousness involved human experimentation: "[f]rom 1953 to 1963, MKUltra and allied projects dispensed $25 million for human experiments by 185 nongovernmental researchers at eighty institutions, including forty-four universities and twelve hospitals" (*ibid.*: 29). Direct and indirect CIA contracts went to universities including, for instance, McGill, where pioneering research had been done by the great psychologist Donald O. Hebb (*ibid.*: 32); also Yale, with Irving L. Janis and Stanley Milgram (*ibid.*: 32–33); and Cornell Medical Center's Lawrence Hinkle and Harold Wolff (*ibid.*: 41, 45).[2] Further research was done during the war in Vietnam as part of the Phoenix programme (and others) where, in McCoy's ironic words, there was "a limitless supply of human subjects" (*ibid.*: 65).

> In 1963, the CIA distilled its findings in its seminal *Kubark Counterintelligence Interrogation* handbook. For the next forty years, the *Kubark* manual would define the agency's interrogation methods and training programs throughout the Third World. Synthesizing the behavioral research done by contract academics, the manual spelled out a revolutionary two-phase form of torture that relied on sensory deprivation and "self-inflicted" pain for an effect that, for the first time in the two millenia of this cruel science, was more psychological than physical.
>
> *(Ibid.: 50)[3]*

The "Manhattan Project of the mind" paid off for the CIA with "the first real revolution in the cruel science of pain in more than three centuries" (*ibid.*: 8). McCoy thinks the revolutionary method is "best described as 'no-touch torture'" (*ibid.*: 7); I will refer to it as the CIA paradigm of psychological torture or, sometimes, the American way of torture, funded as it was by receipts from US taxpayers provided to CIA by a somnolent Congress. As McCoy indicated, the CIA paradigm of psychological torture has two central elements: sensory deprivation and "self-inflicted" pain.

First, "sensory deprivation became the conceptual core of the agency's paradigm" (*ibid.*: 32). What to an ordinary layperson are the amazingly powerful effects of sensory deprivation were summarized in the *Kubark Manual*, relying on human experimentation done at Harvard, as follows:

> Drs. Wexler, Mendelson, Leiderman, and Solomon conducted a somewhat similar experiment on seventeen paid volunteers … The results confirmed earlier findings that (1) the deprivation of sensory stimuli induces stress; (2) the stress becomes unbearable for most subjects; (3) the subject has a growing need for physical and social stimuli; and (4) some subjects progressively lose touch with reality, focus inwardly, and produce delusions, hallucinations, and other pathological effects.
>
> *(CIA 1963: 89)*

Kubark goes on to quote another researcher as having said: "Three studies suggest that the more well-adjusted or 'normal' the subject is, the more he is affected by deprivation of sensory stimuli" (*ibid.*). And this section of the manual concludes:

> The deprivation of stimuli induces regression by depriving the subject's mind of contact with an outer world and thus forcing it in upon itself. At the same time, the calculated provision of stimuli during interrogation tends to make the regressed subject view the interrogator as a father-figure. The result, normally, is a strengthening of the subject's tendencies toward compliance.
>
> *(Ibid.: 90)*

The CIA's hope that sensory deprivation will produce regression to the state of a compliant infant appears frequently in the manual: "all coercive techniques are designed to induce regression" (*ibid.*: 83).[4]

"Self-induced" pain is of course not actually self-induced, but the interrogators contrive to make the person being tortured feel that he is causing his own pain, thereby greatly enhancing the unbearability of the stress mentioned above by the Harvard experimenters.[5] For example, a victim is told to stand up against a wall in a certain specific position and not move, lest something else very distressing be done to her. After a relatively short period, this rigid stance becomes quite painful. On the one hand, the subject is likely to feel that the pain is her own fault because she is obeying the order not to move. But if, on the other hand, she moves and the other distressing thing is done to her, she is also likely to feel that that distress is her own fault because she disobeyed the order not to move. Obviously she cannot win but is in fact likely nevertheless to feel that she is responsible for whichever bad outcome she suffers, although of course the torturers are responsible for having created the inescapable Catch-22. According to McCoy, the discovery of how profoundly stressful "self-inflicted" pain is "emerged from a series of studies by two respected neurologists at Cornell Medical Center, Lawrence Hinkle and Harold Wolff, who founded the Human Ecology Society in 1953–54, soon making it the most important CIA conduit for legitimate scientific research" (McCoy 2006: 45).

Secretary of Defense Donald Rumsfeld demonstrated the depth of his ignorance about the very CIA techniques he was authorizing for use by the Bush Administration on its prisoners at Guantanamo and elsewhere with his notorious mocking marginal comment on one of the torture-authorizing memos from the Pentagon's chief lawyer, William J. Haynes, II: "However, I stand for 8–10 hours a day. Why is standing limited to 4 hours? D. R." (Haynes 2002: 236 [photocopy] and 237 [transcription]). Presumably Rumsfeld shifts position at will when he chooses to stand. Here is one experienced insider's interpretation of the Rumsfeld scribble: "It said, 'Carte blanche, guys'. That's what started them down the slope. You'll have My Lais then" (Mayer 2008: 223).

If discussion of torture is to have any semblance of a connection with torture as actually practised, it is essential to remember at least that torture is not some rare and exceptional one-time ad hoc emergency measure, but a carefully researched and tested practice adopted as a matter of policy for a general category of suspects whose psychological equilibrium is, if possible, shattered (Constitution Project 2013, Singh 2013). As indicated by the subject line of the above-mentioned Haynes memorandum that Rumsfeld annotated, torture is conceived by its proponents as consisting of "counter-resistance techniques", where the resistance to be overcome is constituted by what one would normally consider to be a person's identity, self or personality, embodying her commitments and values. One's identity as a person is the "resistance" that must be broken! *You* are the resistance. Whether, once broken, you will ever mend is an open question. Space does not permit also taking up the damaging effects on torturers here, but we have good reason to think that "the toxic dividends of torture are shared by victims and victimizers" (Phillips 2010: xi).

Methodological arguments

When one reflects on what torture typically consists of – specially trained government agents holding a person captive and assaulting the structure of his personality by the most effective means known to modern psychology – one is strongly inclined to think that torture ought indeed to be absolutely prohibited, precisely as it has been by international law (Waldron 2005b: 1688–91; 2010: 191–94). The first step in the contemporary justification for torture is to attack the absoluteness of the moral and legal prohibitions with "a single mesmerizing example: the ticking time bomb" (Luban 2005: 1440; 2006: 44). The ticking-bomb scenario has appeared in many guises, at least as far back as Bentham's frequently quoted bomb-less version (Ginbar 2010: 379–86); for the origins of the modern "imaginary of torture" with the ticking bomb, Rejali emphasizes novels and films about the Franco-Algerian War, especially fiction by Jean Lartéguy (Rejali 2007: 545–46), commenting "too often fantasy sells better than reality" (*ibid.*: 547).

The gist of the scenario is that "we" manage to capture someone who is known to have planted in some unknown location a ticking bomb that will surely cause a catastrophe if not defused, who refuses to disclose the location, but whom "we" quickly and successfully torture, only as much as necessary and in time for the information gained to enable us to keep the bomb from exploding. Different variants deal with the various implausibilities here in alternative ways with various degrees of success, and toying with different versions seems to provide endless fascination for analytic philosophers who think hypothetical examples can teach us more than we can learn from studying what actually happens and what is likely to happen (Shue 2009).

David Luban analyses the general function of the reasoning focused on ticking bombs, whatever the details of the hypotheticals. Someone who begins by believing that torture ought to be subject to the kind of absolute prohibition found in international law is made to confront what is presented as an undoubted case of torture that is, all things considered, justified. Yes, she is told, torturing anyone is not just wrong but terribly wrong; however, the preventable catastrophe would be an even more terrible wrong, and so – surely! – it would be irrational to allow a much more terrible wrong to occur rather than being willing to commit a less terrible one oneself in order to bring about a rescue by torture. The defender of the absolute prohibition may grant the exception and thus qualify the absolutism of her original position. "Now that the prohibitionist has admitted that her moral principles can be breached," Luban observes, "all that is left is haggling about the price" (Luban 2005: 1440; 2006: 44): that is, haggling about how catastrophic the preventable catastrophe needs to be in order to make the torture the better choice, all things considered.

All that one really needs to see, on the contrary, is that the ticking-bomb scenario is not an example of torture as it is practised on planet Earth. First, it might be that one can imagine a possible world in which, although torture is almost never used, it somehow can virtually instantly be employed successfully to deal exclusively with rare emergencies. But, in Luban's words, "the real world is a world of policies, guidelines, and directives. It is a world of *practices*, not of ad hoc emergency measures" (Luban 2005: 1445; 2006: 47). The scenario is at best irrelevant in focusing on one-off or rare instances rather than on routine bureaucratic policies and general directives.

Second,

> in a world of uncertainty and imperfect knowledge, the ticking-bomb scenario should not form the point of reference … The real debate is not between one guilty man's pain and hundreds of innocent lives. It is the debate between the certainty of anguish and the mere possibility of learning something vital and saving lives.
>
> *(Luban 2005: 1444; 2006: 46–47)*

The scenario is positively misleading in transferring intuitions about certain success to cases of possible success. So, as Bob Brecher has put it in one of the most thorough and persuasive critiques of the use of ticking-bomb scenarios:

> your position therefore has to be that torture is justified by even the possibility of catastrophe – not [only] by its certainty … [W]hat we are actually being invited to accept is that interrogational torture is morally justifiable because it *might* – and, if my arguments so far are right, *only just might* – avoid the catastrophe.
>
> *(Brecher 2007: 29, 35)*

Third, once mere possibility seems to be enough, torture easily becomes a "general fishing expedition", merely hoping to turn up something useful sooner or later (Luban 2005: 1443; 2006: 46):

> The torture at Abu Ghraib had nothing to do with "ticking bomb" terrorism. It was intended to "soften up" detainees so that U.S. military intelligence could get information from them about likely attacks by Iraqi insurgents against American occupiers. The important point is that the use of torture is not an area in which human motives are trustworthy.
>
> *(Waldron 2005b: 1717; 2010: 221)*

But for those eager to believe in short cuts as a substitute for patient investigative work, the scenario may now seem to provide a rationale for practices that are much more different from it than similar to it.

"Ticking-bomb stories are built on a set of assumptions that amount to intellectual fraud … Ticking-bomb stories depict torture as an emergency exception, but use intuitions based on the exceptional case to justify institutionalized practice and procedures of torture" (Luban 2005: 1427; 2006: 36). That these ticking-bomb scenarios have harmful effects is not speculation. The Schlesinger Report, provoked by Abu Ghraib, noted: "[f]or the U.S., most cases for permitting harsh treatment of detainees on moral grounds begin with variants of the 'ticking time bomb' scenario" (Independent Panel to Review Department of Defense Detention Operations 2004: 974). One repeatedly finds politicians, journalists, and talk-show participants moving from premises based on the ticking-bomb scenario to conclusions about, for example, treatment of prisoners at the U.S. prison in Guantanamo, even though the cases are worlds apart (Sands 2008: 117, 135, 158, 170, 191, 200–210). One cannot entirely prevent others from misinterpreting what one writes, but in an area like torture one should take every possible measure to discourage it.

Empirical work on state torture bureaucracies provides explanations of why the practice of torture has the features it has (Bufacchi & Arrigo 2006), not the features built into ticking-bomb scenarios. For empirical reasons – psychological, political, sociological and bureaucratic – the carefully limited use of torture is impossible: "history does not present us with a government that used torture selectively and judiciously … One can imagine rare torture, but one cannot institutionalize rare torture … It is an optimistic thought with no social embodiment" (Shue 2006: 234, 238). In Brecher's words, "the institutionalization of the profession of torturer is a necessary condition of the example's even getting off the ground" (Brecher 2007: 24).

However, a hard-nosed consequentialist willing to bite any necessary bullet can respond by abandoning such fantasies of isolated instances of successful torture in rare emergencies and embracing torture bureaucracies for "permanent" emergencies. "The general point is simple: any finite costs to torture can be outweighed by sufficient expected benefits. The worse the anticipated evil, the more horrible the things we can do to ward it off" (Luban 2009: 201). Now, one might well judge that if this is the direction in which consequentialism is taking us, it is time to bail out. In a recent essay that breaks new ground, David Luban suggests two different ways to think about such an exit, one turning on the limits of moral theories in general and one turning on a category of the morally "unthinkable" (*ibid.*: 202–6).

In my 1978 essay "Torture" I had proposed the methodological principle that "artificial cases make bad ethics" (Shue 1978: 141). Rightly observing that this dictum was left rather enigmatic, Luban notes that in so far as I elaborated it at all, the point seemed to be that it is fallacious to reason from extraordinary cases to ordinary cases with different features from the extraordinary ones (Luban 2009: 196–98). We both still think that this is an important point. It has been the guiding principle here so far and is the reason I have emphasized that real-world torture is done by entrenched (secret) professional bureaucracies with a far lower threshold for using it than any almost certain, imminent catastrophe. Luban formulates this first reading of my methodological principle as:

> By focusing on improbable artificial cases, theorists misdirect readers' attention from genuine issues in the real world to specious issues. They illicitly change the subject from important and authentic questions about the limits of legitimate interrogation in non-TBS [ticking-bomb scenario] cases to intuition-mongering about a tendentious hypothetical.
>
> *(Ibid.: 197)*

I agree that this still matters very much.

However, employing extremely generous principles of interpretation, Luban also finds the seeds of three other readings buried in "artificial cases make bad ethics". Ignoring the second reading here, I shall briefly consider the other two closely related readings, which probe considerably deeper than I had done at the time and which draw on subsequent insights by Bernard Williams. The next reading to which we turn says:

> Ordinary practices of moral rationality fail in cases where all courses of action are monstrous. The artificial cases ethicists cook up to control for monstrosity by isolating the right- and wrong-making characteristics of action are misleading. That is precisely because they cover over the monstrousness with a veneer of rationality.
>
> *(Ibid.: 203)*

Luban is thinking of a philosopher's conundrum like "would you be justified in torturing one person in order to find out a secret location where ten other persons were being tortured so that you could rescue them? How could you not?" But Williams had proposed: "there are certain situations so monstrous that the idea that the processes of moral rationality could yield an answer in them is insane", and "to spend time thinking about what one would decide if one were in such a situation is also insane, if not frivolous" (Williams 1973: 92).

Luban offers an explanation of why moral rationality might be limited in the way Williams suggested:

> Moral systems ... arise by generalizing and abstracting from prototypical cases in which they make intuitive sense and yield intuitively satisfying answers ... But completeness claims are illusory ... This should not surprise us: the origin of moral systems suggests that they are good only over certain domains, those in the neighborhoods of their prototypical cases.
>
> *(Luban 2009: 203, 204)*

If one finds it disgusting even to consider torturing a person in order possibly to rescue ten others from torture, but one is told that it would be morally irrational not to do so, one has no particular reason to trust the judgement about moral rationality to be one's guide rather than trusting one's strong feeling of disgust. This bizarre case may well fall completely outside the range of cases in which the moral theory is a reliable guide.

Williams had also suggested that "the *unthinkable* was itself a moral category" (Williams 1973: 92). Insightful analysts have suggested that the other assault to which torture is most similar is rape (Sussman 2005: 4–5). A column in the *New York Times* had said:

A clear sign of progress in Western society is that one does not need to argue against rape: it is "dogmatically" clear to everyone that rape is wrong. If someone were to advocate the legitimacy of rape, he would appear so ridiculous as to disqualify himself from any further consideration.

(Žižek 2007)

Luban comments:

Suppose that the only way Jack Bauer [of Fox's torture-romanticizing *24*] can prevent ten women from being raped is to rape one woman. You will never see that plot-line on television, for obvious reasons: the audience, which is meant to root for Jack Bauer [when he tortures], would find Jack the rapist viscerally revolting. That's the mark of the unthinkable. Conversely, if we insist on arguing the costs and benefits of rape with an unblinking accountant's eye, as if it is just one option among others, we run the risk of normalizing it, moving it out of the category of the unthinkable.

(Luban 2009: 205)

So, Luban proposes, a final reading of my principle is: "Artificial cases make bad ethics because their very artificiality makes the unthinkable thinkable" (*ibid.*: 206).

Luban's two points, about limits of moral rationality and about unthinkability, are closely connected, if not two facets of a single one. If our moral theories generalize from cases where they can be brought into equilibrium with our intuitions, then when they confront a case with radically different features from the original cases and suggest a response that seems intuitively wrong, we may do better to trust our intuition instead of the response that follows from the theory. If the action seems disgusting or revolting and the only reason to do it is that a permission flows out of a moral theory, we may simply have crossed outside the range of reliability of that theory. Perhaps we could construct a better theory that adequately accounts for the horror that torture instinctively arouses. Meanwhile, perhaps we should "stop thinking" in the following very specific sense: avoid following the guidance of a theory the reliability of which is dubious in the range that includes the case at hand. We have good intuitive grounds in our revulsion and disgust to believe that a moral theory that suggests one rape to prevent ten, or one torture to prevent ten, has blundered beyond its competence. Leave the rape and the torture morally "unthinkable" until such time as we have a moral theory that we can be confident is robust enough reliably to guide any thinking we do in this disorienting territory.

Substantive arguments

Mercilessness

Space here does not permit discussing the features of the contemporary American way of torture, which are the empirical basis for the arguments, in any detail. David Luban and I elaborated a number of features in the course of showing that McCoy's "no-touch torture" can easily slip through the crude net of badly drafted US statutes that purport to prohibit torture, revealing a desperately urgent need for re-writing US law on torture if anyone is to be protected against the new American way (Luban & Shue 2012). We emphasized the mercilessness of all torture:

part of the special wrongfulness of torture lies, then, in the limitlessness of the extent to which the victim is at the mercy of the torturer, who never relents until he himself, for his own reasons, chooses to end the terror which this implants in the victim. The victim can attempt to end the torture by trying to give the torturer what the victim thinks the torturer wants, but the torturer decides entirely for himself what he wants at any given time and whether he believes he has it all. The victim may well guess wrong about what the torturer wants, and often the victim does not have what the torturer wants in any case, especially of course if the victim is not who the torturer thinks he is or has not done what the torturer suspects he has done. All power remains with the torturer, who may move the goal posts as often and as far as he wishes. The victim is utterly at his mercy. Unlike even war, torture has no natural end. It ends when the torturer chooses to end it.

(Ibid.: 859)

Psychological torture in accord with the CIA paradigm, in particular,

undermines the structure of the personality – it literally breaks apart the self, unhinging its parts from each other. The victim is reduced to a quivering bundle of fears, driven to try to please, that is, to try to fulfil the wishes of others, with few wishes of her own, except release from the awful psychological stresses that are being systematically and relentlessly imposed by all-powerful others. This goes far beyond what slavery involved and gives new meaning to being at the mercy of someone else.

(Ibid.: 856)

Writing decades later about the psychological effects of his crude old-fashioned physical torture by the SS, much less devilishly fine-tuned than the state-of-the-art CIA paradigm, Jean Améry wrote:

Whoever was tortured, stays tortured … The tortured person never ceases to be amazed that all those things one may, according to inclination, call his soul, or his mind, or his consciousness, or his identity, are destroyed when there is that cracking and splintering in the shoulder joints … Whoever has succumbed to torture can no longer feel at home in the world … Trust in the world, which already collapsed in part at the first blow, but in the end, under torture, fully, will not be regained. That one's fellow man was experienced as the antiman remains in the tortured person as accumulated horror. It blocks the view into a world in which the principle of hope rules.

(Améry [1966] 1980: 34, 40)[6]

Lest anyone think that Améry's loss of what he movingly calls "trust in the world" is a melodramatic exaggeration by a powerful writer, a typical report by a group of empirical researchers finds:

Although the psychological impact of torture on the individual is determined by his/her personality and personal history, in most cases the survivor undergoes irrevocable change. Torture often unleashes a traumatic neurosis with symptoms of recurrent dreams of the traumatic event, anxiety, fear, crying, panic and feelings of helplessness.

(Kordon et al. [1992] 2007: 444)

Tyranny

The best very brief characterization of the American way of torture is law professor Seth Kreimer's phrase, "government occupation of the self" (Kreimer 2003–4: 299).[7] The CIA paradigm for torture constitutes the most intrusive imaginable assertion of state tyranny over the individual: the elimination of personal autonomy by means of intentionally undermining the structure of that individual's personality and producing a psychological regression to a less differentiated, compliant servant to the torturer's master. The new twist in contemporary justifications for the use of torture is that they are forward-looking: the torture is part of the intelligence gathering that will keep us safe from, this time around, terrorists. Torture's "sole purpose is preventing future harms ... It becomes possible to think of torture as a last resort of men and women who are profoundly reluctant to torture ... Torture to gather intelligence and save lives seems almost heroic" (Luban 2005: 1436; 2006: 42).

Luban observes, however, that such a "protective" state practice is an extreme instance of the kind of political tyranny that Western political philosophers, for centuries, and the global human rights movement, especially since the Second World War, have strenuously condemned: "torture is tyranny in microcosm, at its highest level of intensity" (Luban 2005: 1438; 2006: 43). And Luban's latest, penetrating, "communicative" formulation is: "Torture of someone in the torturer's custody or physical control is the assertion of unlimited power over absolute helplessness, communicated through the infliction of severe pain or suffering on the victim that the victim is meant to understand as the display of the torturer's limitless power and the victim's absolute helplessness" (Luban 2014: 128).

Legal archetypes

Jeremy Waldron has presented an entirely independent case for the absolute prohibition against torture already found in international law, including the International Covenant on Civil and Political Rights, Articles 4 and 7 and the Convention Against Torture and Other Cruel, Inhuman or Degrading Treatment, both of which apply to absolutely everyone, and the *Geneva Conventions*, which apply to the persons they protect, including prisoners of war. Waldron notes that "[n]o one denies that law has to be forceful and final ... But forcefulness can take many forms ... [L]aw can be forceful without compromising the dignity of those whom it constrains and punishes" (Waldron 2005b: 1727; 2010: 233–34). What he calls "an important underlying policy of law" is:

> Law is not brutal in its operation. Law is not savage. Law does not rule through abject fear and terror, or by breaking the will of those whom it confronts. If law is forceful or coercive, it gets its way by nonbrutal methods which respect rather than mutilate the dignity and agency of those who are its subjects.
>
> *(Waldron 2005b: 1726; 2010: 232)*

The legal prohibition against torture, besides its importance in its own right, serves as an archetype of the policy that legal force is not brutal or savage. The prohibition against torture has a kind of iconic significance as a symbolic anchor of the intransgressible requirement that law respect dignity by avoiding brutality. Legal archetypes

> do foreground work as rules or precedents, but *in doing that work* they sum up the spirit of a whole body of law that goes beyond what they might be thought to require on their own terms. The idea of an archetype, then, is the idea of a rule or positive law provision that operates not just on its own account ... but ... also operates in a way

that expresses or epitomizes the spirit of a whole structured area of doctrine, and does so vividly, effectively, publicly …

(Waldron 2005b: 1723; 2010: 228)

The archetype is a functioning symbol. Waldron explains the working of the archetype as follows:

[T]he archetype idea is the reverse of a slippery slope argument … Starting at the bottom of the so-called slippery slope, I am arguing that if we mess with the prohibition on torture, we may find it harder to defend some arguably less important requirements that … are perched above torture on the slippery slope. The idea is that our confidence that what lies at the bottom of the slope (torture) is wrong informs and supports our confidence that the lesser evils that lie above torture are wrong too … The confidence we have in them depends partly on analogies we have constructed between them and torture.

(Waldron 2005b: 1735; 2010: 243)

If Waldron is correct in his partly empirical hypothesis about the torture prohibition's anchoring role in legal argument, it is not surprising that the upsurge in the use of torture by American authorities in the twenty-first century has been accompanied by other governmental assaults – all in the name of national security against terrorists – on fundamental civil liberties, including Congressional legislation authorizing indefinite detention without trial, thereby assaulting even the ancient principle of *habeas corpus*. The maintenance of the prohibition on torture may in fact have been the vital protection of a crucial anchor for the general rule of law, which is now shakier in America than it was in 2000 (McKeown 2009, R. Gordon 2014).

The arguments made by Waldron and Luban in 2005 are strongly complementary. Luban, as we saw earlier, focused in 2005 on the evil of state tyranny; Waldron focused at the same time on the evil of state brutality. Contemporary state-of-the-art torture, as we saw at the beginning, is a form of psychological brutality in which the state invades and at least temporarily occupies the mind, removing the "resistance" consisting of the person's personality structure. A government that uses torture is both tyrannical and brutal: the CIA paradigm uses brutal assault on the individual's identity to exercise its tyranny over her. Torture is Kreimer's "government occupation of the self". An absolute prohibition on torture is a wall against brutal state tyranny, a wall that, as Waldron emphasizes with the idea of a legal archetype, is also part of the larger structure of the rule of law. The rule of law is protection against tyranny and brutality.

Moral archetypes

David Rodin has suggested that the absolute moral prohibition on torture may play an archetypical role within our system of moral norms somewhat analogous to the archetypical role of the absolute legal prohibition (Rodin forthcoming). If, Rodin observes, one thinks of the Quinean image of a web of belief such that beliefs near the centre of the web can be changed only if substantial portions of surrounding beliefs are also changed, the absolute prohibition on torture serves as one of those key central beliefs. My version of this would be that, as Waldron says of the legal case, the absolute moral prohibition is vital in its own right but is also a symbol of the fundamental point that morality demands limits. A person who will stop at nothing is a person without morality. That no one may ever torture is both an instantiation of a firm moral limit and a radiant emblem of intransgressible moral limitation.

In my account of basic rights, I noted that the enjoyment of every right can potentially be thwarted by any of a multiplicity of "standard threats" (Shue [1980] 1996b: 29–34). A basic right in my sense directly protects one vital interest but in doing so it also blocks a standard threat to other vital interests. For example, a right against CIA-style psychological torture protects the integrity of one's personal identity, which is intrinsically valuable in the case of every person, but the right against torture also blocks a standard threat against many other rights, such as freedom of assembly and freedom of speech. If I know that if I go to the square and say what I think, I will be whisked away by government agents and tortured in order to find out who my friends are and what I read, the threatened assault against my psychological stability is also a coercive threat against my free speech. A right that protects me against torture partially protects my free speech as well as my mental balance. In this respect this right helps to anchor other rights.

Rodin (forthcoming) makes the significant additional point, however, that one can embrace an absolute prohibition against torture even if one does not believe that the right not to be tortured is absolute: the absolute prohibition does not presuppose an absolute right. Suppose, for example, that just as many people believe that the right not to be killed is not absolute and that one can forfeit it in at least some cases by killing someone else, the right not to be tortured might also be thought not absolute and one could forfeit it by, say, torturing others. Suppose, that is, that one believed that torturing a torturer is not a violation of any right. Because they have forfeited that right, we are assuming for the sake of argument, we would not wrong *them* by torturing them (especially, perhaps, if in accord with the usual narrative of the ticking-bomb scenario, we might possibly thereby obtain the information that would enable us to destroy a secret site where many other torturers are operating, thereby producing a net reduction in torture, etc.).

Even so, Rodin points out, one might still judge that although it would not wrong the guilty torturer, it would still be wrong – perhaps disastrously wrong – to engage in the torture because it is supremely important to maintain the moral firewall against torture. The function of the absolute moral prohibition against torture as an archetype of the fact that there are some activities in which civilized people do not engage is too important to allow a breach of the prohibition even if the degree of the wrongfulness of torturing the person in question were not reason enough in itself. One is tempted to ask: how bad does it have to be before we torture? Rodin's point is: nothing compels us to open any discussion of "how bad it needs to be". We can perfectly well simply say: no torture. As Waldron put it, "*there are some scales one really should not be on*" (Waldron 2005b: 1701; 2010: 205, emphasis original).

Sophisticated interrogation

But, someone is bound to ask, is all this not too confident? Is it not conceivable that if we never torture anyone, we will some day pay a terrible price because we will fail to obtain the only information that would have enabled us to avoid a catastrophe: some monumental act of terrorism, for example? This is of course simply one more variant of the ticking-bomb scenario: this time there really is a bomb, and it is a really bad one, and we really will get the information in time, but only if we torture, and so on. Yes, if it is conceivable that if we torture enough people, we will find out something very important, then if we torture no one, we may not find it out, and we may suffer the consequences. Of course, there are all the usual questions about ticking bombs, such as whether we are simply to assume that our intelligence agencies – which did not foresee even monumental developments like the collapse of the Soviet Union and the rise of the Arab Spring, for example – are so good that they immediately have the person who knows most, or, if they have to blunder their way through a sequence of torture victims, each of whom leads them to the next, they will have time to reach the end of the trail. But I want to underline two quite different considerations.

First, we have no empirical basis on which to believe that interrogational torture is the most effective form of interrogation (Kleinman 2006: 130 and n.93). If we torture no one, we may not find out something important – unless we have a better method than torture for finding it out! Space here does not allow a thorough discussion of issues about effectiveness, and I obviously do not believe that torture would be justified *if* it were effective. But it surely could be justified *only if* it were the most effective alternative, given how wrong everyone on all sides admits torture is. *A priori* it is difficult to understand how the CIA paradigm in particular can be a good method of gathering accurate information. The person whose personality structure is undermined and who is made to regress to an infantile state of wanting to please certainly will be inclined to give the interrogator what the torture victim thinks the interrogator wants. But is this a reliable method of quickly gathering accurate information? It partly depends on how often a person tortured simply does not have the information that he thinks the interrogator wants; in those cases the victim is likely to manufacture something in order to try to please the interrogator. Améry, under SS torture, tried hard to comply but could not because, like any member of a moderately well-run underground, he had been allowed to know only the aliases of his colleagues:

> What they wanted to hear from me in Breendonk [Prison], I simply did not know myself. If instead of the aliases I had been able to name the real names, perhaps, or probably, a calamity would have occurred, and I would be standing here now as the weakling I most likely am, and as the traitor I potentially already was. Yet it was not at all that I opposed them with the heroically maintained silence that befits a real man in such a situation … I talked. I accused myself of invented absurd political crimes, and even now I don't know at all how they could have occurred to me, dangling bundle that I was.
>
> *(Améry [1966] 1980: 36)*

And even if torture does obtain correct information at some stage, it may well be less efficient than other approaches to interrogation. This is certainly the view of a number of experienced American interrogators. For example, Matthew Alexander (a pseudonym) was a US Air Force interrogator who was instrumental in locating the rural safe house in which Abu Musab al Zarqawi, the leader of al-Qaeda in Iraq, was hiding so that he could be killed by an air strike on 7 June 2006 (Alexander & Bruning 2008). The choice of verb in the title of his account, *How to Break A Terrorist*, is unfortunate because it does not mean what "break" means in the CIA torture paradigm: there is no assault on the personality structure of the person being interrogated. "Break is the jargon we use to signify getting a prisoner to open up a little – like cracking an egg" (*ibid.*: 108). Alexander has only contempt for the American torturers with whom he had to serve in Iraq, mainly because of their incompetence, which may involve trying to tear down the prisoner's self-respect (*ibid.*: 185). Alexander gives his prisoners the opposite treatment: "Still, I have given him hope, and hope is the most powerful weapon" (*ibid.*: 257).

So, is Alexander interrogating with kindness? Far from it: the hope he gives is false hope. He pretends, and tricks, and lies to his prisoners, treating them in ways that in almost any other circumstances would be clearly immoral:

The best interrogators are outstanding actors. Once they hit that booth, their personalities are transformed. They ... allow a doppelgänger to emerge. What doppelgänger
is most likely to elicit information from a detainee changes from prisoner to prisoner.
Sometimes I must have a wife or children so I can swap stories with the prisoner,
though I have neither.

(Ibid.: 91)

The interrogation that Alexander practises does not make a pretty picture. He coercively
manipulates his prisoners. They are not treated as ends: they are used instrumentally to obtain
information. Some people will certainly feel that it is morally wrong ever to treat people like this.

But it is not torture. Alexander's technique is unrelenting until he obtains the information he
wants, but it is not mercilessly cruel and destructive. No severe pain or suffering, physical or
mental, is inflicted on prisoners. The struggle is a battle of wits. The prisoner's values and beliefs
are not respected: he is, if he can be, tricked into betraying them. He is treated as an enemy and
outwitted if possible. But the soundness of neither his body nor his mind is undermined. He is
not shamed and humiliated like the men at Guantanamo who were forced to wear women's
underwear and made to learn dog commands like "stay" and "bark" in order to mock their
values and undermine their dignity. Alexander's prisoner may well ultimately regret that
his interrogator outsmarted him and obtained the wanted information, but his regret will be
possible because his mind will have remained sound, unlike the minds of those assaulted by the
CIA torture method. "We don't have to become our enemies to defeat them" (*ibid.*: 284).

Of course, the testimony of a single interrogator does not settle which interrogation technique is more effective, torture or something else. I claim only to have illustrated through anec-
dotal evidence that a serious, smart and successful American interrogator, who personally has
conducted three hundred interrogations and supervised more than a thousand, and who was
awarded the Bronze Star for service in Iraq, believes that alternatives to torture are more
effective. On the other hand, supporters of torture also have only anecdotes at best and –
mostly – fictional accounts (written and film/TV) to support their claims. All the fabulously
expensive CIA research established that people can be broken and made to regress, not that
they can be made to reveal timely information, even when they know something relevant.

The second point is this. Suppose Alexander is mistaken and was just lucky with Abu Musab al
Zarqawi and others, but we have believed him and returned to the legally required refusal to use
torture. Consequently, we fail to find out about a danger that we cannot otherwise prevent, and
some of us die as a result. I still say: "What kind of world would these children live in if I added
torture to the terrorism while imagining that I was saving their lives? Conceivably they would
live, not die, but they would live in a world in which even the strong had abandoned restraint
and sunk further into barbarism ... Let's risk it ... and live in civilized countries" (Shue 2003: 91).

Notes

1 Even then it was clear that the hands of the US Government were not entirely clean; for example, the
  Shah had been restored to power by CIA and was receiving massive US security assistance, as was the
  South Korean dictator viewed as a bulwark against North Korean communism.
2 One Milgram experiment has of course become infamous: see Milgram (1974).
3 The *Kubark Manual* is now available (but was not then, of course: it was classified as "Secret") at www.
  gwu.edu/~nsarchiv/NSAEBB/NSAEBB122 (accessed April 2014).
4 Also see CIA (1963: 41), which observes "regression is basically a loss of autonomy", and *ibid.*: 50.
  Cornell's Hinkle is quoted as assuring CIA: "most people who are exposed to coercive procedures will
  talk and usually reveal some information that they might not have revealed otherwise" (*ibid.*: 83).

5 David Sussman is therefore absolutely correct to observe that "it is perhaps not accidental that many of the most common forms of torture involve somehow pitting the victim against himself, making him an active participant in his own abuse" (Sussman 2005: 22). This not only is not accidental, it is firm policy, in the case of the CIA paradigm. Sussman's philosophical analysis is one of the most faithful to the actual practices.

6 Having physically survived until 1978, Améry committed suicide.

7 In his note 73, Kreimer quotes the Supreme Court decision in *Stanley v Georgia*, 394 U.S. 557 (1969), at 565: "Our whole constitutional heritage rebels at the thought of giving government the power to control men's minds".

11

HUMANITARIAN INTERVENTION

Alex J. Bellamy

Despite pronouncements that the age of humanitarian intervention was over (e.g. Cottey 2008), the 2011 NATO-led intervention in Libya has reignited debate about when, if ever, it is legitimate to use force to protect populations from mass killing, rape, forced displacement and other crimes which, as Michael Walzer (1977) put it, "shock the conscience of humanity". The practice of "humanitarian intervention" refers to the use of military force by external actors for primarily humanitarian purposes, usually against the wishes of the host government. Indeed, it is often governments themselves that attack sections of their own populations, raising difficult dilemmas about how the world should respond. Should we privilege peace over justice in such cases, or vice versa? Do the rights of peoples trump those of sovereigns? What is more, the use of force always provokes difficult moral questions about whose lives to protect and sacrifice in order to "save strangers" (Wheeler 2000) in grave peril. And, if we accept that there is a right to intervene in some cases, there are questions about what sort of right it is. Do we have a moral duty to intervene to save strangers or a more limited right to do so if we choose?

These are urgent moral questions, matters of life and death on a terrible scale. There have been several humanitarian interventions since the end of the Cold War (see Table 11.1), typically responding to the most massive and grievous of crimes. In the 1990s, genocide in Rwanda (1994) killed at least 800,000, and war in the former Yugoslavia (1992–95) left at least 100,000 dead and forced thousands more to flee their homes. Protracted conflicts in Sierra Leone, Sudan, Haiti, Somalia, Liberia, Ethiopia, East Timor, the Democratic Republic of Congo (DRC) and elsewhere killed millions more. The catalogue of misery has continued into the new century: conflict in the Darfur region of Sudan cost the lives of around 250,000 people and forced more than three million people from their homes; protracted conflict and natural disasters in Somalia caused an untold number of civilian deaths, with a single refugee camp in Kenya housing some 400,000 refugees in squalid conditions; during the "Arab Spring" which began in 2011, governments in Egypt, Bahrain, Yemen, Libya and Syria turned their guns on unarmed protestors, killing thousands between them. These deaths were a product of violence aimed directly against unarmed civilians, not an unfortunate by-product of war (see Slim 2008).

Recent episodes of mass killing perpetrated by states against sections of their own populations have typically ended in one of two ways: either the perpetrators succeed in destroying or seriously weakening their target group or they are removed from power (Bellamy 2010a). Facts

Table 11.1 Humanitarian intervention in the post-Cold War era.

Place	Date	Intervener	Type of intervention	Outcome
Liberia	1990–1997	ECOWAS – Nigeria	Active combat against anti-government rebels	ECOMOG defeat Taylor in 1992, but Taylor elected president in 1997 elections
Iraqi Kurdistan	1991	US, UK, France	Establish safe area and no-fly zone	Kurds protected from Iraqi army
Somalia	1992–3	US/UN	Secure delivery of humanitarian relief, disarm warlords	Humanitarian relief delivered but warlords resist disarmament, prompting withdrawal after US sustains casualties
Bosnia-Herzegovina	1993–5	NATO	Limited airstrikes followed by deployment of rapid reaction force; large-scale air operations in 1995	Bosnian Serbs and Yugoslav government accept Dayton peace accord
Haiti	1994	US	Deployment to restore elected government	Peacekeepers deployed to maintain order and disarm rebels
Rwanda	1994	France	Creation of safe areas at the end of genocide	Safe areas save some lives but allow the perpetrators of the genocide to flee to safety in Zaire (DRC), destabilizing that country
Kosovo	1999	NATO	Aerial bombardment to coerce compliance with the Rambouillet accords	After 78 days, Yugoslavia concedes and permits deployment of KFOR
East Timor	1999	Australian-led coalition	Deployment of peacekeepers to deter and end militia violence	Militia withdraw or lay down arms, INTERFET hands over to UN transitional administration
Liberia	2002	ECOWAS – Nigeria	Deployment of peacekeepers in support of new government	Hand over to UN Mission in Liberia (UNMIL)
DRC	2003	EU – France	Deployment of forces to prevent genocide in the town of Bunia after Ugandan withdrawal	Atrocities in Bunia deterred but pushed into countryside in Ituri province; hand over to UN Mission (MONUC)
Libya	2011	NATO-led	Aerial bombardment to maintain no-fly zone and protect civilians	With NATO-led support the National Transitional Council overthrow the Qaddafi regime

like this pose major dilemmas because they pit different moral principles and ways of under-standing and practising world politics against one another. They also raise hard questions about how to interpret agreed moral principles. One of the most basic of those principles is the "right to life" – the idea that humans ought not to be killed without good reason. The use of force itself is always morally problematic from a right to life perspective because no matter how carefully it is employed, the innocent will always be caught in the crossfire. Does this mean that fidelity to the right to life demands a policy of non-intervention in the face of mass atrocities? Or, should external actors be prepared to get "dirty hands" and intervene, gambling that the unintentional endangering of some innocent lives will be compensated for by the saving of a far greater number of innocent lives?

Given the importance and complexity of the questions involved and the pronounced differences between individual cases it is not surprising that there are dozens of perspectives, each of which offers its own account of whether force might or should be used for humanitarian purposes and, if so, in what circumstances. To further confuse the matter, proponents of similar moral theories can, and often do, hold different positions on humanitarian intervention in general as well as on specific cases (Holzgrefe 2003: 51). For example, some communitarians defend intervention in some circumstances, others reject it outright. Likewise, whereas cosmopolitans are more generally inclined towards supporting a duty to intervene, one of the theory's progenitors, Immanuel Kant, defended the rule of non-intervention. These complexities partly stem from the centrality of consequentialist reasoning in debates about humanitarian intervention, which requires us to make empirical judgements to weigh up the relative value of actions and inactions, and the anticipated utility of different courses of action – all of which is a highly imprecise science. A further complicating factor is that it is impossible to separate out ethics and law without losing an important part of the picture (*ibid.*).

In order to explain and evaluate different ways of thinking ethically about humanitarian intervention, this chapter suggests a way of thinking about different perspectives on humanitarian intervention in relation to two critical questions, one about the nature of world politics (is it unendingly tragic or potentially progressive?) and the other about which type of actor should be privileged (the state or the individual?) (see Table 11.2). How we answer these two questions shapes the way we think about the ethical possibilities of using military force for humanitarian purposes. The chapter proceeds in five parts. The first clarifies the relevance and scope of these two questions in a little more detail and the remaining sections examine the four basic perspectives made possible by this heuristic framework.

Possibilities and actors: the fundamentals of debate

This section sets out a way of understanding different ethical perspectives on humanitarian intervention. As a heuristic tool, it suggests that different positions can be plotted along two axes, the first relating to our conception of what is possible in world politics and the other relating to which actors should be privileged (see Table 11.2).

Table 11.2 Contending values and perspectives.

	State-centred	People-centred
Optimist	rule utilitarian	liberal internationalist
	legal positivist	social contractualist
	pluralist (English school)	cosmopolitan
	communitarian (?)	solidarist (English school)
		natural law
Tragic	realist	post-structuralist
	post-colonialist (?)	feminist (critical)
	Marxist	post-colonialist (?)
	communitarian (?)	classical humanitarian

The first axis on Table 11.2 refers to the way we understand the potentiality and limits of world politics. Some theories of international ethics are prefaced on an essentially optimistic vision which holds that because dialogue and therefore moral consensus and the development of shared purposes are possible across diverse communities, so too is human progress. As a result, dialogue can foster shared visions of the good, and determined and ethical collective action can move humanity in a positive direction towards it. Immanuel Kant's vision of a perpetual peace brought about incrementally through the regulation of war and then by the establishment of a community of nations is a good example of an optimistic account (Kant [1795] 1903). The alternative is a basically fatalistic or "tragic" conception of world politics. This perspective is based on the view that the world comprises culturally distinct units with different values that pursue their own, distinct, goals, with limited possibility for cooperation (e.g. Niebuhr 1938, Morgenthau 1970; see also Lebow 2003). Those that try to impose their own particular beliefs on others will meet only resistance, often producing tragic effects that leave everyone worse off. This account is sceptical about the chances for progress, doubts that morality does (or should) play a role in world affairs, and predicts that efforts to spread moral values will prove costly and counterproductive. Simply put, the tragic conception suggests that "it would be wrong to think that were people to act ethically, humankind's condition would progress or improve" (Frost 2003: 484).

The second axis in Table 11.2 relates to an ontological question about what sort of actor should be privileged. For our purposes we can boil this down to the question of whether states or people should be awarded priority. It is common for theories of international relations to privilege the state on the grounds that it is the principal actor in world affairs, the main source of order, and the bearer of international rights and responsibilities. This perspective also suggests that communities or nations have value in themselves – a view associated with "communitarianism". Nations enjoy a "common life" and culture and should be free to determine their own forms of governance. There is a "fit", communitarians argue, between the political community and the state, and the latter enables the former to develop and protect its own values and ideas about how its members ought to live (Walzer 1977: 87; 1994). According to Walzer,

> justice is relative to social meanings: there are an infinite number of possible lives, shaped by an infinite number of possible cultures, religions, political arrangements, geographic conditions and so on. A given society is just if its substantive life is lived in a certain way – that is, in a way faithful to the shared understandings of its members.
> *(Walzer 1983: 312–13)*

An alternative perspective privileges individuals as the only irreducible ontological entity. From this perspective, statehood and its attendant sovereignty should be understood as instrumental values – not as ends in themselves – because they derive their moral value from the state's capacity to protect the welfare of its citizens. After all, humans invented states to fulfil certain purposes, not the other way around. When states fail in their duty, they lose their sovereign rights (Téson 2003: 93). There are a variety of ways of arriving at this conclusion. Some draw on Kant's concept of the rational individual to insist that all individuals have certain pre-political rights (Caney 1997: 34). Others use Augustine's insistence that force be used to defend public order to argue that intervention to end injustice was "among the rights and duties of states until and unless supplanted by superior government" (Ramsey 2002: 20, 35–36). Alternatively, historical accounts show that in both theory and practice sovereign rights have always been associated with responsibilities of one form or another (Glanville 2011).

As Table 11.2 illustrates, and remembering that this is only a heuristic exercise, thinking of ethical positions on humanitarian intervention in terms of these two axes gives us four main clusters – optimistic/state-centred, tragic/state-centred, optimistic/people-centred and tragic/people-centred – which offer different accounts of the morality of intervention, different ways of evaluating specific interventions, and different ways of responding appropriately to the problem of mass killing and human suffering. The following sections examine these four perspectives in a little more detail.

Optimistic and state-centred: a rule-governed international society

The first perspective accepts that progress in international affairs is possible, but that in a world characterized by radical difference the basis for progress should be voluntary cooperation between states in a rule-governed international society of states. As Table 11.2 suggests, this perspective is associated with moral theories that privilege mutual recognition and shared rules as a basis for co-existence and cooperation between dissimilar actors. This perspective shares the belief, associated here with more tragic accounts, that international society comprises a plurality of diverse communities each with different ideas about the best way to live (Rengger 2000: 105) but is essentially optimistic because it holds that relations between these diverse communities can be regulated by shared rules that promote co-existence and allow each of the units to develop and progress. Indeed, Immanuel Kant, a theorist closely associated with an optimistic vision of human potential, argued that states ought to scrupulously obey the rule of non-interference in each other's domestic affairs. One of the core principles of his *Perpetual Peace* was that "no state shall violently interfere with the constitution and administration of another" (Kant [1795] 1983: 10). This, he argued, was a basic principle of international order derived from the individual duty to respect one another's autonomy. For Kant, this mutual respect was itself a prerequisite for the world community he ultimately envisaged.

From this perspective, international society is based on rules that permit communities to pursue their own conceptions of the good without infringing on others' right to do likewise (see Linklater 1998: 59). Sitting at the heart of this system of rules of co-existence is positive international law, and particularly the UN Charter, which is founded on the principle of sovereign equality, prohibits the use of force in international affairs (Article 2(4)) and forbids interference by the UN in the domestic affairs of states (Article 2(7)). The various theories housed in this quadrant hold that that the common good is best preserved by maintaining these rules of co-existence and especially the legal ban on the use force. What is more, the two permissible exceptions to this legal ban – the inherent right of self-defence (Article 51) and the right of the UN Security Council to authorize collective enforcement (Article 39) – should be narrowly interpreted to protect the integrity of the underlying rule.

From this perspective, in a world characterized by radical disagreements about how societies should govern themselves, humanitarian intervention amounts to the forcible imposition of one state's values on another. To permit such intervention would be to create disorder by allowing states to wage wars to protect and impose their own values on others (Jackson 2000: 291). Disorder would weaken the rules-based system itself, undermine human development, make cooperation between states more difficult, and weaken any progress that might be made towards a moral consensus. This is demonstrated by the fact that states have shown a predilection towards "abusing" humanitarian justifications to legitimize wars that were anything but. Most notoriously, Hitler insisted that the 1939 invasion of Czechoslovakia was inspired by a desire to protect Czechoslovak citizens whose "life and liberty" were threatened by their own government (Brownlie 1963: 217–21). The general ban on the use of force is an essential barrier against such abuse. Without it, there would be *more war* in international society but not necessarily more genuine humanitarian interventions (Chesterman 2001: 231).

At least four theories that have offered perspectives on humanitarian intervention fall into this category. First is a pluralist conception of world politics as a society of independent units (states) bound together by constitutive and regulatory rules which guide their mutual relations but do not place demands on their *internal* characteristics. Second is rule utilitarianism, which holds that actions are judged good or bad on the basis of their compliance with shared rules which, if followed by everyone would produce the best consequences for all. Writers coming from a rule utilitarian perspective argue that the greatest good is served by the preservation of international order, which would be jeopardized by any relaxing of the rules on the use of force (e.g. Henkin 1979: 145). The third is legal positivism, which is founded on pluralist and rule utilitarian assumptions and finds the substance of shared rules in positive international law. From this perspective, positive law is the glue that holds units with very different sets of moral belief together. As one lawyer put it, if humanitarian intervention were legally permissible, powerful states would receive "an almost unlimited right to overthrow [other] governments" (Schachter 1984: 649). Finally, all of these perspectives rest on basic communitarian assumptions about the irreconcilable diversity of the values and goals of different communities. All four privilege rules of co-existence, though individual writers differ on what this means for specific practices of humanitarian intervention. Although all are cautious and sceptical, believing intervention itself to be a challenge to precious international rules, some such as Michael Walzer believe that there is a duty to intervene when atrocities are so bad that they "shock the conscience of mankind" whereas others take a more absolutist approach to non-intervention. Robert Jackson (2000: 291) bluntly remarked that "in my view, the stability of international society, especially the unity of the great powers, is more important, indeed far more important, than minority rights and humanitarian protections in Yugoslavia or an other country – if we have to choose between these two sets of values".

There are two principal critiques of this way of thinking. First, it is unnecessarily pessimistic about the capacity of states to reach consensus about moral principles and ways of protecting them. Despite its optimism about the potential for cooperation between states in developing shared rules of co-existence, this way of thinking tends to assume that states are unable to forge consensus on the use of force to defend shared principles because any relaxing of the rules governing force would lead to greater disorder. However, there is little solid evidence on which to base the claim that permitting humanitarian intervention would undermine rules of co-existence or produce more overall harm than good to international order (see Mason & Wheeler 1996: 106). Indeed, recent research suggests that the deployment of international peace operations to troubled regions can significantly reduce the likelihood of future war, strengthening international peace (Fortna 2008). Moreover, past interventions have not eroded the international legal order and there is little evidence to suggest that the law itself has actually inhibited willing interveners (Chesterman 2001). Although there are a few notorious historical cases, it is sometimes claimed that the fear of "abuse" is exaggerated (Weiss 2004: 135). It is highly unlikely that in 1939 Adolf Hitler would have been deterred from invading Czechoslovakia by the absence of a humanitarian justification. Finally, critics complain that international society has – in fact – established a mechanism for collectively authorizing the use of force for purposes that could include the protection of populations from grave crimes: Article 39 of the UN Charter, which gives the UN Security Council the authority to impose enforcement (including military) measures on states.

Second, some critics question the idea that there is a neat overlap between the community, the nation and the state and the assumption that states protect their citizens' rights and reflect the community's common values. Given the litany of murderous states described at the beginning of the chapter, it is clearly not the case that states always protect the best interests of their peoples – in fact, more people are threatened by their own state than by other peoples'. This point challenges the assumptions that states should be treated as goods in themselves, that people consent to be governed by particular regimes and that the preservation of order between states is always in the best interests of the peoples within those states (see Lepard 2002, Tesón 1997). Additionally, in reality very few states are culturally homogeneous and most house a variety of groups with different moral values and preferences, making the claim that states protect certain common cultural values a shaky proposition on which to base their claims to legitimacy.

Tragic and state-centred: the realities of life in an international state of nature

The perspectives in the second quadrant share the communitarian view about the diversity of communities and the relativity of values and conceptions of justice, but reject the optimistic view that such diverse communities can reach meaningful accord on rules of co-existence, let alone substantive rules. That is primarily because they are *materialist* theories of politics which hold that material forces and interests drive political behaviour. At their most basic, these theories agree that ideas, rules and norms are insubstantial when set against material forces. Theorists who hold these perspectives are generally sceptical that states will commit resources to enterprises, such as humanitarianism, that do not advance their material interest. The exception is the communitarians who fall into this category. They do so largely because they are more sceptical than their optimistic colleagues about the extent to which communities can bind themselves to mutual rules of co-existence and substantive or purposive rules about life inside communities. Although this perspective allows for the possibility of law, morality and the pursuit of common goals, it is commonly argued that these can only flourish *within* communities and never between them, except at the most superficial level. In the world beyond the community, there is only the perpetual competition of interests and values, and relative power rather than relative merit or fidelity to shared rules is the foremost means for resolving disputes. As such, whenever there is a clash between apparent self-interest and shared rules, self-interest will prevail every time. As the British realist and some-time communist sympathizer E. H. Carr argued in 1939, what may appear to be "common morality" is in fact nothing other than the interests and preferences of the powerful masquerading as universal moral truth (Carr 1939). From this perspective, the *raison d'etat* is the provision of security to a state's citizens, which can only be achieved if the state itself survives. The survival of the state and prosperity of those within it can only be guaranteed through strict adherence to the logics of self-help and power maximization (Morgenthau 1970). As a result, states cannot be expected to use force to protect non-citizens.

The post-colonial and Marxist theorists who join political realists in this category would go so far as to argue that this latter point is why states cannot be trusted with a right of intervention let alone a duty. Because they only ever act in their own interest, states only use humanitarian justifications to legitimize the coercive use of force for purposes that are anything but humanitarian. In fact, when states interfere in each other's affairs they do so primarily because it serves their material interests (Chomsky 1999). What might appear humanitarian is therefore really an act of imposition and colonial domination, which is why from this perspective the results are almost always negative. Writers like Tariq Ali (2000), Noam Chomsky (1999) and Mahmood Mamdani (2011) believe that humanitarian discourses cast a veil over Western attempts to protect and extend its neo-liberal order, which enriches the already powerful while impoverishing the weak. Mahmood Mamdani (2011), for example, argued that the 2011 NATO-led intervention in Libya was driven by the West's self-interest – in particular an interest in grabbing Libyan financial assets, testing new weapons for urban warfare and eroding the sovereignty of the Libyan people.

The realist tradition, which sits squarely in this quadrant, also opposes humanitarian intervention. As noted earlier, political realism tells us that a state's primary responsibility is to its own citizens. It cannot therefore be legitimate for states to risk the lives of citizens (in the armed forces) on humanitarian crusades to "save strangers" in foreign lands (Wheeler & Morris 1996). Realism generates instrumentalist objections to humanitarian intervention. North American realists have argued that humanitarian intervention never helps to strengthen power or prosperity and does not usually further the national interest of the intervening state. It makes no difference to the US, they argue, if Hutus and Tutsis, Libyans or the Sudanese want to kill each other. The tragic vision of politics tells realists that intervening cannot resolve these complex problems and will only drag external actors further into the mire (Van Evera 1991, Kissinger 1992).

The realist tradition has been subjected to widespread critique – indeed, much more critique than the post-colonial and Marxist theories that it shares so much in common with on this question. In addition to the critiques levelled against more optimistic state-centred accounts – that they underestimate the potential for consensus and cooperation and assume a neat fit between the community, nation and states – which apply equally to these tragic state-centred theories, there are two additional problems.

First, and perhaps most fundamentally, the empirical basis for the claim that states use humanitarian intervention to cloak the violent pursuit of their own interests is shaky at best. To take just one example, there is little evidence to support Mamdani's claims (above) that NATO states wanted to use Libyan financial assets for their own purposes, test urban warfare weapons, or erode the Libyan people's sovereignty, let alone any evidence that any of this was a factor in decision-making. Similarly, it is unclear what Western material interests were served by the intervention in Kosovo in 1999 or by the US-led intervention in Somalia in the early 1990s.

Second, accepting that states tend to do what they perceive to be in their interests does not get us very far in terms of explaining their behaviour, let alone in providing moral guidance for how they ought to act. All it does is rule out the possibility that they will intentionally act contrary to their perceived interests. This begs, rather than answers, questions about how states define their interests and how interests shape action. As constructivist theorists have shown, social actors – whether individuals or states – do not have pre-given interests. Alexander Wendt (1999: 169–70) commented that "to assume *a priori* that interests are never socially constructed is to assume that people are *born* with or make up entirely on their own all their interests ... clearly this is not the case". Interests are socially constructed and shaped by a range of ideational factors such as identity (we cannot know what we want until we know who we are), normative values (we cannot know what we want until we know what we cherish), and shared local, regional and global norms (we cannot know what we want until we know what it is appropriate for an actor with a given identity to want) as well as material conditions (see Finnemore 1996: 2). To understand *why* states act in certain ways we need to be able to understand variation in the way that states (even similar states) construct their interests and this, in turn, requires a deeper understanding of the factors that guide national decision-making.

Optimistic and people-centred: defending humanity and our common values

The third quadrant – optimistic and people-centred – is the one that is most positively disposed to humanitarian intervention. Usually associated with various forms of liberalism and cosmopolitanism, theories in this quadrant argue that states have a *duty* as well as a *right* to intervene on behalf of the victims of egregious human rights violations. Theories in this quadrant agree that there are universal values, basic rights that ought to be defended. Natural law theorists, for example, hold that human beings have *prima facie* moral worth, whether derived from their capacity to reason (for secular theorists) or from God (for theological naturalists), and that this, in turn, imposes common moral obligations by virtue of our shared humanity; in this vein, Terry Nardin speaks of a "common morality" (Nardin 2002, also Finnis 1980, R. P. George 1998). From this, we arrive at the social contractualist view that the rights which sovereigns enjoy are conditional on the consent of the governed and that this is based on the fulfilment of the state's responsibility to protect populations under its care and satisfy their basic human rights (Buchanan 2010a). When states fail in their duties, they lose their sovereign right to non-interference (Caney 1997: 32; Tesón 1998, 2003: 93). What is more, some liberals and cosmopolitans argue that when populations are persecuted others have a moral responsibility to step in to protect them. Theorists articulate different grounds for this obligation including the principle that all humans have a duty to defend basic natural rights and the idea that human interconnectedness creates moral obligations (respectively, Caney 1997, Pogge 2008).

According to theorists in this tradition, states have agreed certain minimum standards of behaviour. As such, humanitarian intervention is not about imposing the will of a few Western states upon the many but about protecting and enforcing the shared values and collective will of international society (Wheeler 2000: 14). They argue that there is agreement in international society that cases of genocide, mass killing and ethnic cleansing constitute grave humanitarian crises warranting intervention (see Evans 2009, Bellamy 2010c). This consensus was given meaning in 2005 when world leaders unanimously adopted the responsibility to protect (RtoP) principle in paragraphs 138–40 of the UN World Summit Outcome Document (United Nations 2005). As agreed by member states, the RtoP rests on three pillars. The first is the responsibility of each state to use appropriate and necessary means to protect its own populations from genocide, war crimes, ethnic cleansing and crimes against humanity, and from their incitement. The second pillar refers to the commitment of the international community to encourage and help states to exercise this responsibility. The third pillar refers to the international responsibility to respond through the UN in a timely and decisive manner when national authorities are manifestly failing to protect their populations from the four crimes identified above. The principle has become part of the working language of international engagement with crises involving the commission or potential commission of mass atrocities, and has been specifically invoked by the UN Security Council in relation to crises in Darfur, Libya, Yemen and South Sudan.

In addition to RtoP, advocates of these positions typically point to three other clear signs of international consensus on core moral principles and processes for enforcing compliance. First is the emergence of international humanitarian law (IHL). The global effort to strengthen IHL – as well as the concomitant development of international criminal law – has become the legal and moral foundation for arguments about intervention for human protection purposes. As is well known, IHL had its origins in the mid- to late nineteenth century with the development of the US Government's "General Orders No. 100" (better known as the Lieber code) and the emergence of the Red Cross movement inspired by Henry Dunant (Hartigan 1983, Moorhead 1998, Forsythe 2005). After the Second World War, IHL was developed and codified in the four Geneva Conventions (1949), two additional protocols (1977), and in a range of protocols covering the use of Certain Conventional Weapons (1980, 1995, 1996, 2008). Of particular importance were Common Article 3 of the 1949 Geneva Conventions, which committed parties in non-international conflicts to respect the human rights of all those placed *hors de combat*, and the Convention on the Protection of Civilian Persons (Convention IV), which – among other things – offered legal protection to non-combatants in occupied territories. The first Geneva Protocol (1977) extended the protection afforded to non-combatants by insisting that armed attacks be strictly limited to military objectives (Article 52, Protocol I).

Second is the customary practice of the UN Security Council. Since 1998, the UN Security Council has explicitly considered a civilian protection agenda focused on ensuring compliance with IHL (see Wills 2009). In 1999, the Council unanimously adopted Resolution 1265, which expressed the Council's "willingness" to consider "appropriate measures" in response "to situations of armed conflict where civilians are being targeted or where humanitarian assistance to civilians is being deliberately obstructed" (United Nations Security Council 1999). The Security Council issued a further landmark resolution (number 1674) on the protection of civilians in April 2006. This reiterated its demand for access to be granted to humanitarian agencies, stated the Council's willingness to take action in cases where civilians are deliberately targeted and reaffirmed the RtoP (see above).

Third, the UN Security Council has given meaning to its consideration of civilian protection through the mandates it has crafted for peace operations. Starting in 1999 with the UN mission in Sierra Leone (UNAMSIL), the Security Council has regularly invoked Chapter VII of the UN Charter to create civilian protection mandates, albeit while inserting some important geographical, temporal and capabilities-based caveats (Holt & Berkman 2006).

Optimistic people-centred accounts tend to hold that not only is there shared agreement about universal rights and ways of protecting populations from grave breaches of them, but that collective action produces more good than harm overall. Earlier, I mentioned studies showing that foreign intervention reduces the chances of conflicts recurring. Other studies have also shown that collective efforts have reduced the incidence of armed conflict and mass atrocities overall and that armed intervention in the face of mass atrocities tends to save many lives when compared with estimates of what would have happened absent intervention (Goldstein 2011, Pinker 2011).

Understandably, this optimistic and people-centred account has been subjected to criticism from those who prioritize the state or whose conception of political life is more inclined towards tragedy. First, some critics are simply not persuaded by the evidence of agreement across diverse communities on fundamental moral principles. They argue that it is not self-evident that individuals *do* have universal and fundamental human rights. From a communitarian perspective, Parekh (1997: 54–55) argues that liberal rights – the basis for much of what was discussed above – cannot provide a convincing basis for a theory of humanitarian intervention because liberalism itself is rejected in many parts of the world. Other arguments from this perspective suggest that rights are only meaningful if they are backed up with the power to enforce them. For example, America's Bill of Rights is hard law supported by the full coercive power of the American state. Given that there is no world government or police force with the capacity to enforce human rights globally, there are no meaningful international human rights. Such accounts are typically sceptical about the capacity of the UN Security Council to play this role.

Second, as I noted earlier, state-centred minded theorists – and especially those with a tragic bent – worry that any permissive norm endorsing the use of force to protect individual rights would be abused by powerful states, making armed conflict more frequent by relaxing the rules prohibiting it but without making humanitarian intervention any more likely (Chesterman 2001).

Third, this perspective exaggerates the extent of global consensus about the use of force to protect human rights. There is a gap between what theorists would like to be the norm and what the norm actually is. Not only is there little agreement in international society about the idea of a right or duty to intervene, there is little evidence that states act *as if* such a right or duty exists. More often than not, states have stood aside in the face of mass killing. The putative "golden era" of humanitarian intervention in the 1990s included the world's failure to halt the Rwandan genocide, failure to protect civilians sheltering in the "safe areas" in Bosnia and the failure to act as Zaire/Democratic Republic of Congo destroyed itself, taking millions of lives, and the more recent failure to halt mass killing in Darfur. This dismal record encourages sceptics to argue that when intervention does occur it does so because the interveners have some other interests at stake. If they were primarily driven by humanitarian concern, goes the logic, they would have acted more decisively in these cases.

Moreover, world leaders have been more hesitant about advocating a permissive right of humanitarian intervention than implied by this optimistic account. Most notably, the Security Council authorized intervention against the wishes of a fully functioning sovereign state for the first time only in 2011, in relation to the situation in Libya. When it did, it imposed restrictions on the intervention, demanding, for example, that no "occupying force" be deployed (see Bellamy & Williams 2011). The only other instance of humanitarian intervention against a fully functioning sovereign state in recent times was the highly contentious NATO intervention in Kosovo in 1999. We should therefore avoid the temptation of thinking that there has been a "rash" of humanitarian interventions since the end of the Cold War era (Finnemore 2008: 197), which the optimistic and people-centred account seems to imply.

Tragic and people-centred: the distinctiveness of humanitarian action

The theories in the final quadrant – tragic and people-centred – tend to privilege the offering of assistance to individuals in dire need irrespective of what their host state might think but are deeply sceptical about military intervention on the grounds that they tend to make situations worse for those most in need and/or because they reinforce Western militarism, neo-colonialism and economic neo-liberalism, which in their view are among the chief underlying causes of humanitarian crises in the first place. From this perspective, military intervention fails to offer protection to populations because it does not address why mass killing happens. At very best, all it can offer is a short-term palliative but often even this comes at great cost. Theories that address the question from this perspective insist that we not allow a preoccupation with intervention to obscure the manner in which hegemonic powers, conceptions of statehood, and neo-liberal economics sustain the preconditions for mass atrocities (Levene 2004: 156). They point out that the idea that intervention is a discrete event creates the mistaken impression that the intervening states are not already implicated in the crises they are ostensibly trying to "resolve".

Military intervention, it is argued, is but one aspect of wider relations of interference by the powerful in the domestic affairs of the weak. It is the very policies of Western states and financial institutions such as the World Bank and IMF that exacerbate the grinding poverty and patrimonial politics that are often identified as the root causes of supreme humanitarian emergencies (e.g. Abrahamsen 2000).

This position is related to what might be described as classic humanitarianism based on the principles that underlie the Red Cross movement: a group of organizations almost universally accepted as unambiguously humanitarian. Four principles are particularly important here: (a) *humanity*: humanitarianism aims to prevent and alleviate human suffering wherever it may be found; (b) *impartiality*: humanitarianism does not distinguish between people according to race, sex, religion, nationality, class, whether they live in a powerful state or strategic ally, or whether "we" have interests there–it distinguishes only according to need; (c) *neutrality*: humanitarianism does not take sides in a conflict and is only interested in ensuring that people have access to food, shelter, clothing and medical care; (d) *universality*: humanitarianism is universally applicable and all humans have identical humanitarian rights.

Clearly, even in the best of cases, armed humanitarian intervention has difficulty satisfying these moral principles: interventions are *selective* and do not target suffering wherever it is found or even discriminate on the basis of greatest need; partial in that they assist some groups more than others, and by their very nature are never neutral. Because it involves the use of force, humanitarian intervention is also likely to privilege some people's rights over that of others. As a result, to advocates of an approach to humanitarianism based on these principles, no military intervention qualifies as genuinely humanitarian. As Donald Bloxham (2007: 48) has argued, "humanitarian intervention tends to occur only when the cause overlaps with the material interests of those intervening". Decisions about using force are never "disinterested" or "other-regarding" and neither do they focus on the areas of greatest need. Instead, they are always tainted by power politics and are therefore not properly "humanitarian" (Parekh 1997, B. Williams 2005). Armed interventions in East Pakistan (Bangladesh), Cambodia, Uganda, northern Iraq, Somalia, Rwanda, Bosnia and Kosovo were all partial and selective. They were political and military acts, not humanitarian. Even if we accept the prudential argument that humanitarian assistance needs to be rationed and therefore cannot in practice satisfy the Red Cross principles, we are left with the problem that the financial cost of military intervention massively outweighs the value of humanitarian assistance. Far more lives would be saved each year by diverting what is spent on military intervention to vaccination programmes and natural disaster risk reduction (Valentino 2011).

Some aspects of the way in which the Red Cross interprets humanitarianism have been challenged. Most notably, the principle of neutrality has been questioned on both moral and practical grounds. Critics question how suffering can be "alleviated" let alone "prevented" without taking a political stance. Other humanitarian organizations, most famously Médecins Sans Frontières (MSF), argue that although impartiality in terms of treating and judging everyone on an equal basis is important, it is not possible to tackle major humanitarian crises without making a political stand (see e.g. Groenewold 1996). Indeed, throughout its history, the Red Cross's stance on neutrality has provoked fierce criticism, particularly when it caused the organization to refuse to condemn the Holocaust or the more recent genocide in Bosnia (Favez 1999).

But despite its criticism of the Red Cross principles, MSF is also hostile to military intervention for humanitarian purposes. It argues that humanitarianism must involve a commitment to pacifism. Thus, it maintains that "if the purpose of humanitarian action is to limit the devastation of war, it cannot be used as a justification for new wars" (Weissman 2010: 199). From this perspective, the aim of humanitarianism is to "civilize war" by distinguishing soldiers from civilians and protecting the latter from the former; "it is not to conduct 'wars of civilization' that split the world into civilized people and barbarians, thus paving the way to unbridled violence". Armed intervention, MSF holds, imposes its own "standard of humanity" and drives whatever resists it "beyond the boundaries of what is human". This, MSF holds, is nothing short of a "tyrannical principle of integration: the inevitable eradication of anything that obeys other standards and resists inclusion" (*ibid.*: 200). Additionally, MSF opposes humanitarian intervention on consequentialist grounds, arguing that "deploying troops and protecting civilians are two different things" and that intervention "is naturally a perilous undertaking which is subject to the hazards of war and runs the risks of failure, escalation and the massacre of civilians" (*ibid.*: 197). According to MSF, even when humanitarian intervention has "succeeded", such success has come at a high price in terms of civilian casualties and human rights abuse.

These concerns are echoed by some critical theorists, post-structuralists and feminists. In the study of international politics, critical theory usually starts from Robert Cox's view that theory is always *for* someone and *for* some purpose and that it frames issues and actors that are considered to be important, while marginalizing others (Cox 1981). Its defining feature is often a commitment to the concept of "emancipation", by which it means "freeing people from those constraints that stop them carrying out what freely they would choose to do". From this perspective, "true security can only be achieved by people or groups if they do not deprive others of it" (Booth 1991). Such constraints include war and conflict, but also poverty, curable disease, political oppression, poor healthcare and the lack of education. Following Cox, critical approaches problematize the focus on military matters and state-centrism and self-consciously highlight perspectives that are often ignored, such as the daily atrocity of the tens of thousands of children who die of preventable illnesses as a result of grinding poverty (estimates of the daily death toll of children from preventable disease vary from 30,000 to 50,000, or *at least* eleven million children each year).

Besides demonstrating that the debate about military intervention privileges certain kinds of unnatural or early deaths (those caused by conflict) over others (those caused by politics) – and perhaps reminding us of Valentino's (2011) point that in terms of lives saved, the money spent on military intervention would be much better spent on vaccinations – critical approaches to intervention have highlighted several important points. First, some writers point out that threats to individual security in the global South come from local sources, are almost always exacerbated by armed conflict, and that foreign intervention is not well suited to helping communities resolve their problems (e.g. Autessere 2010). Second, in asking who the moral theories of intervention serve, some feminist-minded writers have suggested that humanitarian intervention helped re-legitimize the use of armed force – and protect defence budgets from the Cold War "peace dividend" – by providing Western armed forces with an acceptable, even prestigious new role. Sandra Whitworth (2004: 25) goes as far as suggesting that intervention "provides the rationale for a number of militaries that otherwise have no raison d'être". In such cases "peacekeeping serves as a form of insurance for post-Cold War militarism". Third, some historical accounts have argued that the humanitarian crises to which interventions respond were attributable to Western colonialism in the nineteenth century and that the interventions themselves imposed (or re-imposed) Western neo-liberal capitalism, undermining local self-determination and preventing the resolution of underlying conflict (e.g. Orford 2003).

This tragic and people-centred approach is vulnerable to many of the criticisms of the tragic approach mentioned earlier. Most notably, it maintains consequentialist scepticism in the face of empirical evidence that humanitarian intervention saves lives and reduces the chances of a conflict recurring. It also views armed humanitarian intervention to protect fundamental human rights as an essentially Western and hegemonic enterprise in the face of evidence of moral consensus on basic rights and agreement outside the West that in some cases it might be necessary to use force to protect those rights. The conceit that humanitarian intervention is a Western enterprise is exposed partly by the fact that the most recent intervention, the NATO-led operation in Libya, was authorized by the UN Security Council with no negative votes and with the support of all three of the Council's African members (South Africa, Gabon, Nigeria), Lebanon and Colombia, and partly by the fact that past humanitarian interveners include Nigeria (see Table 11.1), Tanzania (in Uganda 1979), Vietnam (in Cambodia 1978–79) and India (in East Pakistan/Bangladesh 1975). An additional criticism is that the notion that politics and humanitarianism are separable – and that one can be, indeed should be, humanitarian without being political – is deeply flawed. Humanitarianism is an essentially political activity and the humanitarian principles are not moral "truths" but are rather a set of political and moral choices made as much on the basis of pragmatism as of principle (see Forsythe 1977, Barnett & Weiss 2008).

Conclusion

This chapter has attempted to map contemporary debate about the ethics of humanitarian intervention by identifying four basic perspectives into which are clustered many different theories. My basic claim in setting out the debates in this way was that how one thinks about humanitarian intervention is very much related to how one thinks about two basic theoretical questions: is progress possible in world politics and should the state or the individual be privileged? In relation to the first question, debate revolves around the extent to which diverse communities are able to agree common values and methods for enforcing their shared standards and the extent to which past practices have reflected genuinely common values. How and by whom interventions are authorized, the degree of international support they receive and the long-term effects of intervention will play a crucial role in shaping this debate in the future. In relation to the second question, although there has been a clear move away from the straightforward privileging of states' rights over people's rights, to the extent that only diehard realists and Marxists would continue to argue that the former should always be privileged and that international society is incapable of agreeing any shared rules or mechanisms for enforcing them, state-centred accounts, with their connection to communitarianism, continue to provide a powerful rationale for protecting states from outside intervention. Here again, though, a premium is placed on international consensus, with optimistic statists holding out the possibility of a deeper moral consensus between states on fundamental human rights. With the emergence of RtoP, championed by liberals but embraced by states of most stripes and from every continent, that consensus might be tantalizingly close and should be watched carefully. Among those that adopt a people-centred account, the key schism is over whether military intervention can open spaces for humanitarianism and long-term development or whether it is antithetical to them. Again, this is a difficult consequentialist question and the evidence is mixed. Going forward, much hinges on the extent to which consensus can be found both on the general principles of armed humanitarian intervention and their application in specific cases and on whether interventions prove an effective way of "saving strangers" and laying the foundations for human progress in troubled lands.

12

NUCLEAR WEAPONS
AND CONTAINMENT

Douglas P. Lackey

In the forty or so years since the Non-Proliferation Treaty (NPT) went into effect a large literature has developed in which two persistent themes resonate. One theme, perhaps dominant, is that the Treaty is good thing, a boon to mankind. The other is that the Treaty is inequitable, creating an invidious division between nations that have nuclear privileges and those that do not. The Treaty seems to pit utility against justice; that remains the ongoing issue.

The general problem of policies that maximize utility but distribute utility inequitably, or of policies that maximize utility but violate the rights of individuals, or of policies that maximize utility but require intuitively repugnant acts, has been intensely studied by philosophers over the last 250 years. Utilitarians like Bentham, Godwin, Mill and Russell have pressed the claims of utility, while anti-utilitarians like Kant, Whewell, Bradley, Ross and Rawls have asserted opposing claims of rights and justice. The considerations raised in these disputes have not been systematically applied to international affairs, in which moral debates have typically been dominated either by realists who hold ethics in contempt or by idealists who prize utopian futures over contemporary moral details. What follows is an attempt to adjudicate the balance of utility and justice in the NPT, in hopes that political scientists and international affairs theorists can learn something from intellectual struggles inside moral philosophy.

The NPT utility claim

Let us begin with the *prima facie* claims of utility in the NPT. Here is the Preamble: "Believing that the proliferation of nuclear weapons would seriously enhance the danger of nuclear war … considering the danger that would be visited on all mankind by a nuclear war … The states concluding this treaty … have agreed … " (International Atomic Energy Agency 1970: 1).

The dangers of proliferation are worth rehearsing. Suppose you have only one nation with nuclear weapons, and a 10 per cent chance of that nation using them over the course of a century. Then you have a 10 per cent chance of nuclear use in one hundred years. Now suppose you have ten nations with nuclear weapons, each with the same 10 per cent chance of use over a century. You now have a 65 per cent chance of nuclear weapons use in the same time period. At these percentages, if you have one nation with nuclear weapons, it is likely that there will not be nuclear war in a hundred years; if you have ten nations with nuclear weapons, it is likely that there will be.

Each new nation that acquires nuclear weapons raises new risks that domestic terrorists will steal and use these weapons. Each new nation that acquires nuclear weapons raises new risks of accidental or unintentional nuclear war. Furthermore, one can expect, as a pretty general rule, that each new nation that acquires nuclear weapons will be less technologically developed than the preceding, with more haphazard command and control procedures. The percentage risk of nuclear theft, and of accidental or unintentional nuclear war, goes up exponentially as more nations acquire nuclear weapons.

Furthermore, the newest nuclear states are on average less politically developed than the preceding, in the sense of having little or no history of the rule of law and no system of checks and balances in their governments. Prospective nuclear states also are smaller on average than incumbent nuclear states; each has less to lose economically and more to gain ideologically from nuclear war, the *terminus ad quem* of this imbalance being the nuclear terrorist who has nothing to lose economically and everything to gain ideologically from nuclear threats or nuclear use. It is one thing to think of Gorbachev controlling nuclear weapons, and another thing to think of Kim Jong Il controlling them. It is disturbing to think of what might have happened, in early 2011, if Qaddafi had not abandoned his nuclear weapons programme in 2003. Certainly Obama and Sarkozy would have thought twice about rescuing Benghazi had they been faced with credible nuclear threats against Paris.

Finally, each new nuclear nation is on average less economically developed than the preceding. So the newer nuclear nations will be more tempted to sell nuclear weapons and weapons material to non-nuclear states. The United States has no economic need to sell nuclear materials, and never sells them, but the newest members of the nuclear club, underdeveloped Pakistan and impoverished North Korea, have done just that. Proliferation has many bad results, but one of the most troubling is that proliferation breeds proliferation.

Evaluating the utility claim

The premise of the NPT preamble is that the more nuclear states there are, the higher the risk of nuclear war. The presumption that the relation between nuclear possession and nuclear war is linear, however, needs to be thought through. The single, still agonizing, case of nuclear use was a case where nuclear weapons were used without fear of nuclear reprisal. Many nuclear war theorists believe that nuclear weapons possession is an effective deterrent against nuclear weapon use. The chance that the United States would use nuclear weapons against the Soviet Union probably diminished when the Soviets acquired nuclear weapons in 1949; the chance that the Chinese would use nuclear weapons against India probably diminished when India acquired nuclear weapons in 1974; the chance that India would use nuclear weapons against Pakistan probably diminished when Pakistan tested nuclear weapons in 1998, and so forth. It stands to reason that if the chance of nuclear war against one's principal adversary goes down, the chance of nuclear war in general goes down. A set of pairs of mutually deterring nations might be less dangerous than a set of nuclear nations existing separately but undeterred.

The idea that the newest nuclear states will be less responsible in their nuclear weapon policies than the older members of the nuclear club, and that old possession is therefore less dangerous than new possession, is also questionable. It is true that the older states have more advanced technology, and therefore better systems of command and control. But is also true that the older nuclear states have much larger nuclear arsenals than the newest ones, so that they have much more to control, a larger beast to tame. There are different levels of nuclear war: only the American and Russian arsenals are large enough to generate a catastrophic nuclear winter if used. The divide between the older nuclear states and the newer ones is the divide between older states that pose a smaller risk of a larger war and newer states that pose a larger risk of a smaller war. From the standpoint of utility, the increase in disutility with proliferation is probably not linear and very probably does not increase exponentially with newer nuclear states.

The NPT and proliferation, arsenals and use

Suppose that the preceding qualifications are wrong and that nuclear proliferation is as bad as is usually supposed. We must consider whether the NPT has in fact had the desired effect of curbing nuclear proliferation. The fact that it intends to prevent proliferation is no guarantee that it does, no more than the peace intentions of the Versailles Treaty freed the world from war.

For many authors, the success of the non-proliferation treaty is obvious. In the early 1960s, President Kennedy and his advisors believed that there would be fifty or so nuclear states at the end of the century; in fact, by the century's end only nine had emerged: the United States, Russia, UK, France, China, Israel, India, Pakistan and North Korea, and so the number remains. Between Kennedy in 1963 and the century's end in 2000 looms the NPT. To what degree is the NPT responsible for the present small size of the nuclear club? How much good has the treaty done in this regard?

Some philosophers find the question "How much good was done?" incomplete. They want to know how much good was done compared to all the alternatives. So they would ask about all the logically possible nuclear alternatives in the late 1960s. The five nuclear powers, for example, could have, in some sense of "could", accepted a treaty in which they destroyed their nuclear weapons, set up a system of inspections to detect any attempt at reconstruction, and created an international agency that would control all future production and storage of fissile materials. (Lest this suggestion be dismissed as completely crazy, the reader should recall that the United States presented just such a proposal to the United Nations in the spring of 1946.) Certainly general nuclear disarmament at the end of the 1960s, reducing the nuclear club to zero, would have diminished the risk of nuclear war more than the NPT did. But here the philosophers' sense of "possible" diverges from the ordinary sense of "possible". In the ordinary sense of "possible", general nuclear disarmament was not possible in 1969. The Soviet Union would not permit inspections, and the newly elected American President was seriously considering nuclear threats against North Vietnam as his preferred "secret plan" to win the war. Every nuclear power in 1969 believed that it was very unlikely that the other nuclear powers would disarm even if it did, and absent any first unilateral step there seemed no way to get an upward cascade of confidence-building probabilities in favour of general nuclear disarmament. So perhaps it is not fair to compare the actual effects of the NPT with the hypothetical effects of a more comprehensive treaty.

What is legitimate in estimating utilities, however, is to compare the NPT with no treaty at all: doing nothing is always a real political possibility. Suppose there had been no NPT, what would the nuclear club have looked like in 2000? The development of nuclear weapons by Israel was well under way when NPT negotiations began in the late 1960s; there is little sign that the treaty in any way slowed Israeli nuclear development. Given that China had nuclear weapons, it was highly probable that India would develop them; given that India got them (in 1974) it was highly probable that Pakistan would develop them. The two non-nuclear nations that could have most easily developed nuclear weapons in the last half-century are Germany and Japan, but these states, given their experiences with obliteration bombing and nuclear attack, very probably would not have developed nuclear weapons, NPT or no NPT.

In general nuclear weapons are expensive to build, expensive to maintain, require frequent updating, and are more obstructive than useful in military operations. These factors by themselves keep the nuclear club small, regardless of the NPT. By and large, nations that intend to build do not sign, and nations that sign do not intend to build.[1]

There are, however, some special cases that should be considered.

Iraq and Iran

Article III.2 of the NPT specifies that signing states shall refrain from providing "special fissionable material", that is, upgradable uranium or plutonium, to any state, whether a signatory of the NPT or not. The treaty blocks the development of a "white market" in upgradable materials, and requires states that seek to develop nuclear weapons to obtain weapons grade material on the black market or to develop homegrown sources of their own. These requirements slowed down the development of nuclear weapons in non-nuclear nations, though it did not stop resolute states, like North Korea, from developing nuclear weapons. Difficulty in obtaining upgradable fissile material slowed down the Iraqi nuclear weapons programme in the late 1970s, and the same difficulty has slowed down the current Iranian nuclear weapons programme. But in neither case did the NPT alone prevent the acquisition of nuclear weapons. Iraq was prevented from obtaining nuclear weapons not by the NPT alone but by the Israeli attack on the Osirak reactor in 1981. Iran is being prevented from acquiring nuclear weapons by the Israeli/US Stuxnet cyber attack in late 2010. Now, suppose there had been no NPT. Would any present signatory have sold weapons grade material to Saddam's Iraq or Khameni's Iran? Furthermore, if Iraq or Iran did more speedily arrive at nuclear weapons, the Israelis would even more speedily have acted to take them out. (Having studied philosophy, the Israelis call such strikes "existential".) For these reasons, it cannot be said that the NPT kept Iraq and Iran out of the nuclear club.

Former Soviet republics

Another special case involves states formerly in the USSR. It is a remarkable fact that these states chose to forgo nuclear weapons after the dissolution of the Soviet Union on 26 December 1991. Since that momentous date, Estonia, Latvia, Lithuania, Ukraine, Belarus, Kazakhstan, Uzbekistan, Turkmenistan, Tajikistan and Kyrgyzstan have all signed the NPT. The states, to be sure, had little reason to acquire nuclear weapons, as their main foreign policy objective, leaving the Soviet Union, had been achieved without them.[2] As there was plenty of weapons grade or upgradable fissile materials in these states, the decision not to sell these materials on the world market has slowed their dissemination, and the NPT provided a part of the framework in which this decision could be made. Nevertheless, the primary credit for the denuclearization of Kazakhstan, Belarus and the Ukraine must go to the Nunn–Lugar agreement to pay Kazakhstan, Ukraine and Belarus to transfer weapons out. Under Nunn–Lugar, Kazakhstan transferred its weapons in 1993, and signed the NPT in 1995. Certainly the Nunn–Lugar arrangements did not presuppose the NPT or lean on it in any a particular way.

The NPT and nuclear arsenals

We should also consider what effect the NPT has had on the nuclear arsenals of the nuclear signatories, who are committed under Article VI to negotiate "effective measures relating to the cessation of the nuclear arms race at an early date and to nuclear disarmament".

The nuclear arsenals of the nation states have waxed and waned since the NPT went into effect, very much up in the 1980s, somewhat down in the 1990s. The process of nuclear arms reduction is sporadic, responding to world events, the moods of the leadership, technological innovation and the obsolescence of weapons systems. Though the various START treaties dutifully recognize the NPT in their preambles, the treaties are obviously so much in the interest of the contracting parties that they would have proceeded even in the absence of the NPT. Certainly the START process has its own cycle, not at all connected to the five-year schedule of NPT renewals. What is notable is the continued maintenance of large nuclear arsenals in a world in which there are no military tasks those arsenals could facilitate. There seems to be a lingering belief among some world leaders that a capacity for nuclear explosions is a necessary condition of world power: that nuclear weapons are "the winning weapon" even though little has ever been won by them.[3] In dealing with such deep irrationalities, Article VI has been a weak reed.

The NPT and nuclear use

History presents a paradox about nuclear weapons: nation states have an intense desire to keep them, and an intense repugnance about using them. Eisenhower rejected the nuclear option in Korea and again at Dienbienphu; Nixon eventually rejected it against North Vietnam; Israel considered and rejected the nuclear option in October 1973, when only six Israeli tanks on the Golan Heights stood between the Syrian army and all of Galilee. If the Israelis did not use them in 1973, it is hard to imagine they will ever use them. So for the other nuclear states. When the first atomic bomb went off at Alamogordo, Oppenheimer said, "I am Shiva, destroyer of worlds." Ever since then, everyone believes, everyone knows, that nuclear weapons are different. Eisenhower *said* you could treat them like bullets, but he did not *think* that they were bullets. That was, in the jargon of the trade, only "declaratory policy".

The term "proliferation" refers to the proliferation in nuclear weapons *possession*. Fortunately for us all, there is no immediate connection between nuclear weapons possession and nuclear weapons use.

The bottom line on utility

These considerations yield the result that nuclear proliferation, though a bad thing, may not be an absolutely terrible thing. They also yield the result that the NPT, though having some effect on proliferation, has not had a decisive effect on the rate of proliferation. Multiplying the two results, I conclude that the NPT does generate positive utility, but its benefit to mankind is not huge. The phrase "boon to mankind" may be too generous.

The injustice claim

The claim that the NPT is unjust was pressed by its early critics, most notably, Red China. The Chinese argued that the treaty was an attempt by the imperialist powers to preserve imperialism and its injustices.[4] This historical entanglement of injustice claims against the NPT with Communist propaganda has confused the critique and blunted its effect. Nevertheless, there are at least three non-ideological lines of attack: first, that the Treaty is discriminatory, favouring incumbents over new arrivals in the nuclear game; second, that the nuclear states have unfairly exploited the NPT, enforcing obligations on non-nuclear states while not honouring their own; and third, that the NPT prolongs nuclear weapons possession, inflicting unreciprocated risks on the non-nuclear states.

The charge of discrimination, via a parable

Suppose that the knowledge that greenhouse gases produce global warming had been available in the late 1960s, and that in the 1960s highways and private cars existed only in the US, Russia,

UK, France and China. Suppose that the five "automobile possessing" states devised a treaty that would ban the transfer of automobiles and automobile-producing technology to non-automobile states, and would permit international inspectors to enter construction facilities in non-automobile states to verify that private cars are not being produced. The automobile states commit themselves to "pursue negotiations in good faith" (as per NPT Article VI) for reductions in automobile use, in order to reduce greenhouse gas emissions. All signatories will check in every five years to see how things are going, but there is no enforcement mechanism to penalize automobile states should their automobile use increase.

It is easy to imagine how non-automobile states would react to this proposal. Why should I agree, an Indian diplomat might argue, that the people of India should not have cars while the people in United States have them? If the use of a car is a risk to the atmosphere, then the continued use of cars in the United States puts the atmosphere everywhere at risk. Why should the people of India forgo private cars to protect the atmosphere over the United States, when the people in the United States do not forgo private cars to protect the atmosphere over India? To have a world divided between automobile states and non-automobile states would be simply unfair. If the automobile non-proliferation treaty models the nuclear non-proliferation treaty, the nuclear non-proliferation treaty is similarly unfair.

Undergraduates in ethics courses are often instructed that an act is immoral if it cannot pass the "generalization test". Ask, they are told, how you would feel if everyone did what you are contemplating to do. If the results of everyone doing X would be very bad, from your point of view, then X is immoral for you to do. In the case of nuclear weapons, the US, Russia, France, UK and China clearly think it would be very bad if all states had nuclear weapons: that is why they developed and signed the NPT. But if it is bad for all, then it is bad for each. It is unjustly discriminatory to condemn nuclear possession by others while permitting it for oneself.

The argument from inequity

The NPT does not name which of its signatories are nuclear states and which are not. The directive of Article VI imposes an obligation on all parties to work towards the elimination of nuclear weapons from the world. But it is common sense that the obligation to work towards nuclear disarmament falls more heavily on nuclear states than on non-nuclear states. After all, a nuclear state can "work towards" the elimination of nuclear weapons by eliminating its own. Nevertheless, the nuclear states that have signed the NPT have not charted a viable course towards nuclear abolition, and have continued to maintain arsenals at higher levels than when they first signed the NPT. In addition, the United States has since 1983 invested in an anti-missile programme (ABM) that proved to be the stumbling block to nuclear disarmament. Indeed, at the one moment since the NPT was signed that the two nuclear superpowers might have taken the required steps to nuclear disarmament (11 October 1986), the ABM fouled the works. To a non-nuclear signatory, the NPT is classic "bait and switch". They entered into the regime thinking that it would produce a world without nuclear weapons but ended up with a world in nuclear states enjoy nuclear weapons for the foreseeable future.

The argument from rights violation

Surely one of the unintended effects of the NPT is that it has prolonged nuclear weapons possession by the nuclear states. If there had been no NPT, the end of the Cold War might have produced substantial steps towards the general abolition of nuclear weapons. Indeed, figures like Henry Kissinger and George Schultz, not noted for utopian thinking, made serious suggestions along these lines, and the alleged success of "smart bombs" during Desert Storm, with their fancy video ops, made nuclear weapons look clumsy and obsolete. One reason that nuclear abolition did not move forward in the 1990s is that world leaders generally believed that the NPT had kept proliferation tolerably controlled, and the NPT requires nuclear disarmament only tomorrow, always a day away.

The possession of nuclear weapons imposes risks on all other states. Developing an arsenal of nuclear weapons, even just for deterrence, is like loading up the basement of one's house with dynamite, and posting a warning "beware of dynamite" in order to deter burglars. Unfortunately, if some burglar does not heed the sign, the entire neighbourhood will be blown up. My local neighbours are at risk from the dynamite in my basement, and my global neighbours are at risk from my nuclear weapons.

Is this imposition of nuclear risks, risks ensuing from the mere possession of nuclear weapons, a violation of the rights of my neighbours? Most authorities find mere possession morally clean. It is generally assumed that nations have the right to defend themselves, at least, as Article 51 of the UN charter concedes, "in the event of armed attack". From this it follows that they have a right to develop and store weapons for their own defence. True, these weapons, all weapons, impose risks on innocent parties, since they might end up killing innocent parties. But the right to defend oneself implies a right to impose such risks. And surely there is no moral rule that says I cannot impose risks on others at all: that would make me wicked every time I drive my car.

Nevertheless, there is something special, something exceptional, about nuclear weapons, which is that they cannot be used without injuring third parties, through the effects of radiation released by their use. The explosion of nuclear weapons use poisons the earth, for this generation and for future generations. So does nuclear weapons production and nuclear testing, including underground testing. This makes nuclear weapons different from ordinary weapons, which might or might not, when used, harm innocent parties.[5] This is why the International Court of Justice declared, in 1996, that almost any use of nuclear weapons is contrary to "international humanitarian law", which forbids the use of weapons that cause "indiscriminate damage". It is a short step to the conclusion (though the Court did not venture to take this step) that it is immoral to possess a weapon that cannot be morally used.

If nuclear weapon possession is an injustice, and the NPT preserves nuclear weapons possession, then the NPT is a source of injustice, whatever its good effects.

Evaluating the injustice claim

The issue of consent

We noted earlier that very little pressure was exerted on nation states to sign the non-proliferation treaty. And certainly states knew what they were getting into when they signed the NPT. The decision to sign the treaty was free and informed. How, then, can those who signed it complain of the injustice of it? If there are no speed limits, then I can drive as fast as I like, but if I agree to let the government set a speed limit, I waive my right to drive as I like, and I cannot complain even if I dislike the chosen speed limit. All three of the "injustice" arguments directed at the NPT seem to be knocked down by the free consent of the signing parties. By signing, they accept the status assigned them by the treaty; by signing, they agree to meet treaty obligations, regardless of the behaviour of other signatories; by signing they waive their right not to be exposed to risks permitted by the treaty. Furthermore, signatories that find the treaty discriminatory, or the conduct of other parties inequitable, can simply abrogate, like the United States did with the 1972 ABM treaty. There is no Abe Lincoln on hand to declare that secession means war.

On the other side, one might argue that there was coercion, of a strange sort, that pressured states into the NPT. If your state does not sign the NPT, then other states will not, and the world may fill up with nuclear states with nuclear weapons that threaten everyone, including you. One enters the NPT regime, then, for fear that things may get much worse for you if you do not, which is a coercive threat, if not a threat coming from any particular state. And one might also argue that states signing the NPT, at least at the outset, signed in ignorance, since they were ignorant of the fact that the nuclear states would not keep their part of the bargain. Had states that signed the treaty in the 1970s known that the United States in the 1980s would engage in the greatest nuclear build-up in history, they might not have signed in the first place. For these reasons, then, signing the NPT was not a fully free or fully informed decision.

Finally, it is not in general true that free and informed entry into a contract implies that the contract is just. In the Roman Empire in the third century AD, unstable economic conditions pushed many Roman citizens into extreme poverty, and many petitioned affluent Roman families to take them on as slaves. It does not follow from this that slavery is just. Consent to the NPT may not wipe the stain of injustice out of it.

Generality and equity

The argument against the NPT based on the generalization test is weak because the generalization test is weak. There are many permissible acts which are not generalizable. I teach philosophy, but I would be unhappy to see everyone teaching philosophy: someone has to grow the vegetables. That does not prove that teaching philosophy is immoral. Perhaps one might say that what the test shows is that it is immoral for me to seek to stop others from teaching philosophy, just as the nuclear states in the NPT try to prevent other states going nuclear. But even here the test fails. It is not immoral for a murderer to attempt to prevent others committing murders.

There is a problem that the non-nuclear states have met their obligations by the NPT, while the nuclear states have been lagging in fulfilling their obligations under Article VI. But there is no timetable set for general nuclear disarmament, and no international court has found the nuclear states to be in violation of the treaty because of their continued possession of nuclear weapons. Let us suppose, however, that the nuclear states have exploited the cooperation of the non-nuclear states. Such exploitation would not show that there is anything wrong with the NPT. It would show that there is something wrong with the conduct of the nuclear signatories. The fact that an agreement has been abused does not show that there is anything wrong with the basic structure of the agreement.

Evaluating risk imposition

The nuclear states are not apologetic about retaining their nuclear arsenals. They believe that they have a right to their nuclear weapons, and they believe that the treaty, broadly construed, confirms them in that right. They believe that their right to possess is serious; they believe that their duty to disarm, in conformity with the treaty, is vague. They agree that there are risks imposed on others by nuclear possession, but they feel that nuclear disarmament imposes equally weighty risks on their own populations. So to determine whether or not the NPT is unjust, we have to move to the more general question of whether states have a duty to forgo nuclear weapons or a right to possess them. This discussion applies to all states, including those outside the NPT regime, like Iran.

The right to possess: the Iranian problem

The Iranian case for nuclear weapons possession

Let us focus on the case that has most alarmed the world community: the acquisition of nuclear weapons by Iran. The Iranians have consistently denied that they intend to produce nuclear weapons, but they *are* trying, and if they spoke honestly in defence of what they are actually doing, the argument might go like this:

> The nuclear states that signed the NPT have retained their nuclear weapons despite the requirement to end the nuclear arms race "at an early date": The continued possession of those weapons creates a risk to other states, who would suffer the side-effects of an intentional or unintentional use of these weapons. The nuclear states consider it morally right to inflict such risks, that is why they have not disarmed. But it is *right* to do something that is risky for others only if one has *a right* to do that thing.[6] So the nuclear states must consider themselves to have a right to nuclear weapons. But if they have a right to nuclear weapons, then so do we.

The Iranian speaker continues

> The nuclear states must believe that they have a legitimate interest in retaining nuclear weapons, allegedly for purposes of defence. Indeed, it is universally presumed that nation states have a right to take steps in their own defence. But if the nuclear states have a right to defend themselves with nuclear weapons, based on an argument from self-defence, then so do we. We do not intend to use these weapons for aggressive purposes, but only to deter aggression.

Indeed, from the beginning of the nuclear era, the main function assigned to nuclear weapons has been deterrence. Bernard Brodie remarked in 1946, "they can have no other purpose" (Brodie 1946: 76). Their first US assignment was to deter a Soviet attack on West Germany, next to deter a Soviet nuclear air attack on Europe, then to deter a Red Chinese invasion of Taiwan, then to deter a Soviet missile strike on the US. In each case, the argument for deterrence has force only if there is some probability that these aggressive acts will occur, and only if some reduction in this probability is produced by deterrence. What might the Iranians be deterring?

The Iranian answer, never stated but always thought, is that they intend to deter attacks by the United States and attacks by Israel. The reader should consider these possibilities from the Iranian point of view. The United States overthrew the democratic government of Iran in 1953, backed Saddam's aggression against Iran in the Iran–Iraq war in the 1980s, and shot down an Iranian passenger jet in 1988. Is the Iranian fear of further American aggression *less* rational than American fears of Soviet attack during the Cold War, when the Soviets had no comparable record of aggressive acts against the United States? As for Israel, Israel attacked an Islamic neighbour in 1956, attacked three Islamic neighbours in 1967, and launched an air attack on an Islamic state adjoining Iran in 1981. Further, Israel possesses nuclear weapons which it can use against Iran without fear of an Iranian nuclear reprisal. If it was unthinkable for the United States to give up nuclear weapons while the Soviets kept theirs, symmetry requires us to consider it unthinkable for the Iranians to forgo nuclear weapons while the Israelis keep theirs.

Consider the following scenario. Suppose that the Palestinians develop a non-violent movement for statehood, the Israeli army responds, and Hezbollah in Lebanon launches missile attacks on Israel in response. The new Hezbollah missiles prove to be much more accurate than those used in 2006, and are used against the Israeli military forces in plausible support of the pro-democracy movement, enforcing a no-fly over the West Bank and Gaza. The Israelis discover that the new guidance systems are produced in Iran. The factory producing the guidance systems can be taken out with an Israeli air attack. Now, consider the probability of an Israeli attack on present-day Iran, and the probability of an Israeli attack on nuclear Iran. If the Iranians do not have nuclear weapons, Israel attacks, and then Iran counterattacks against the Israel raid on their factory, they run the risk of an Israeli nuclear reprisal. If the Iranians do have nuclear weapons, and launch a non-nuclear counterattack, then the Israelis cannot take the next escalatory step for fear of an Iranian nuclear reprisal. The presence of a capacity for assured destruction on both sides diminishes the probability of nuclear and non-nuclear strikes against Iran.

Nevertheless, the possession of nuclear weapons by Iran poses threats to the whole world: the risk of intentional nuclear attack, accidental nuclear war, theft of materials by terrorists. But exactly the same risks are imposed by every nuclear state on every other state. And it cannot be argued that the Iranians would necessarily be less responsible in their handling of nuclear weapons than the United States, given what we now know about the numerous "near misses" that again and again during the Cold War brought the United States to the verge of nuclear use.

What must be inferred from all this is that the Iranians have at least as much right to possess nuclear weapons as the Americans do. The Iranian case in a nutshell is this: "if you Americans believe that it is permissible for you to practise nuclear deterrence, fairness requires you to believe that it is equally permissible for Iran to practise nuclear deterrence. Therefore it is moral for us to practise deterrence." That is the logic of the Iranian case. *The dangers of nuclear possession are exactly the same as the dangers of nuclear proliferation.* Why should Israel be permitted to possess while Iran is not?

Evaluating the right to possess

There is a subtle fallacy in the Iranian argument. It shifts from demanding consistency of judgement regarding the justice of policies to conclusions about the policies themselves. True, if I believe that it is permissible for me to tell lies, then I should, on pain of inconsistency, believe that it is permissible for you to tell lies. It by no means follows from this that it is okay to tell lies. Likewise, if I believe that it is permissible for the United States to practise nuclear deterrence, then I should believe that it is permissible for Iran to practise nuclear deterrence. But it by no means follows that it is morally permissible for either state to practise nuclear deterrence. It might be immoral for both of them.

The fact that most Americans believe that American nuclear deterrence is moral does not make it moral. It may in fact be immoral, regardless of what Americans believe, and if it is immoral, then if Iranian nuclear deterrence is a parallel case, it is immoral too. And if it is immoral, one cannot have a right to do it.

It is not possible here to rehearse all arguments for or against the morality of nuclear deterrence. Many philosophers, over the centuries, have argued that it is immoral to make threats when it is immoral to carry out those threats. This particularly goes for nuclear threats. Some have argued that the risks posed to innocent parties by my possessing the nuclear weapons are not at all outweighed by the advantages to me of possession (Lackey 1984). Let me press this case in more detail. Since 1945, the United States has fought four wars with three non-nuclear states – North Korea, North Vietnam, Iraq and Afghanistan – without finding a single plausible use of a nuclear weapon. In 1991, the Soviet Union fell apart, and the entire Russian nuclear arsenal was incapable of holding it together. To find the usefulness of nuclear weapons, one must imagine a dialectic of escalation in which the nuclear state credibly commands the top step of the escalatory ladder. This credibility is ephemeral and has never proved effective. The bluff is too easily called. North Vietnam called it and proceeded to win its war with conventional weapons. Saddam surely must have thought that the nuclear bluff could be called when he invaded Kuwait in 1991, and it was not nuclear reprisals that stopped him in the end. Against all this, one must consider that nuclear weapons are expensive to build, expensive to maintain, not saleable as exports, and do little to help the domestic economy.

The case that nuclear weapons are as much a burden as a benefit has a strange effect on the injustice argument against the NPT. The argument is that the nuclear states have reserved great advantages to themselves while denying these advantages to the non-nuclear states. But if there are hardly any advantages that come from possessing nuclear weapons, then hardly any injustice follows from denying them to anyone. This is where the analogy between the automobile non-proliferation treaty and the nuclear non-proliferation treaty break down. The advantages in each nation, and to each individual, of owning a car are manifest. The advantages in each nation, and to each individual, of nuclear weapons possession are subject to debate. Suppose that Americans were presented with the following two scenarios. In the first, Americans are plausibly told that they must each pay $500, or their highways will fall apart. In the second, Americans are plausibly told that they must each pay $500, or American nuclear weapons systems will fall apart. I suggest that Americans, and people of any nation, would put up the $500 for the highways, but would not put up $500 to maintain nuclear weapons. They would tote up the advantages of nuclear weapons, and find them a bad buy.

Conclusion

The non-proliferation treaty has, in the last half-century, probably done more good than harm, at the cost of some inequity to the non-nuclear states. The inequity can only be removed by the renunciation of nuclear weapons by the non-nuclear states. If the nuclear states renounce nuclear weapons, the main moral argument *for* nuclear weapons possession, the argument from deterrence and self-defence, is substantially weakened (Shultz *et al.* 2007). There is no need for nuclear deterrence if there are no other nuclear states. On the other hand, the main argument against nuclear weapons possession, the argument from risk imposed on third parties, remains even if the present nuclear states renounce nuclear weapons. The best case against proliferation, then, is the case against possession. If the NPT has unwittingly prolonged possession, it undercuts its own goal of non-proliferation. On the other hand, the treaty itself provides an ongoing international framework for a nuclear-free world. In a world of nuclear abolition in which the distinction between nuclear powers and non-nuclear powers no longer exists, the utility of the NPT treaty will remain; its injustices will have been resolved.

Notes

1 It is interesting that the nuclear nation states have not made serious efforts to force allies to sign the NPT. When Golda Meir walked in the White House garden with President Nixon in April 1969, she confirmed to Nixon that Israel had developed nuclear weapons. The conversation was Shakespearian. According to James Adams in *The Unnatural Alliance* (1984), Nixon asked Meir if Israel had any "dangerous toys". Meir said, "We do." Nixon said "Be careful." Nixon never mentioned the NPT. Similarly Red China, before and after joining the NPT, does not seem to have ever pressured North Korea to sign, despite the immense sacrifices made by the Chinese on behalf of North Korea during the Korean War.

2 In the summer of 1989, I had lunch with an Estonian physicist in Tallin, a scientist active in anti-nuclear weapons movements for decades. After a few drinks, he burst out, "I know how to handle the Russians – one small nuclear bomb, hidden in my desk!" Fortunately, except for Russians living in Estonia, history took a better turn.

3 Yes, there was the Second World War, the Pacific theatre and Hiroshima. But "X won the war" implies that X was a *sine qua non* of winning. Against an already defeated Japan, nuclear weapons were no such *sine qua non*.

4 Now that China has entered into the NPT regime we may conclude either that imperialism has ended or that the Chinese have become imperialists.

5 There is immense confusion about this in discussion of nuclear ethics. It is true that we have two similar looking claims: "ordinary weapons might harm innocent parties", and "nuclear weapons might harm innocent parties", which seem to put the two sorts of weapons on a moral level. But there is a difference between nuclear weapons, which *will* harm innocent parties, *if* used, and ordinary weapons, which *might* harm innocent parties *if* used.

6 Though this seems odd to nonphilosophical readers, there are indeed some rights that are rights to inflict harm on others, even innocent others. I have a right to reject a marriage proposal, even if I know my rejection will cause psychological havoc on the other side.

PART III
Poverty and development

Introduction

Poverty is perhaps the most pressing issue of global justice. Arguably much of the early impetus for global ethics came from the wish to address what many saw as the evil of extreme global poverty. As discussed in Chapter 2, many of the early thinkers, such as Peter Singer and Onora O'Neill, who led the turn to *global* ethics and justice, were overtly concerned with issues of famine and extreme poverty. This concern with addressing poverty remains core to the global ethics agenda, and even when ethicists are focusing on other issues the need to address global poverty, to consider the effects of other interventions on the poor, is essential.

The problem of global poverty, like other issues addressed in this volume, such as climate change, can seem overwhelming. The facts and figures showing the extent of the number of those who live in global poverty are stunning. Thomas Pogge draws on UNICEF figures to state that, "roughly one third of all human deaths, some 18 million annually, are due to poverty-related causes, easily preventable through better nutrition, safe drinking water, mosquito nets, re-hydration packs, vaccines and other medicines" (Pogge 2012: 1).

In light of global integration and interdependence, discussed in Chapter 1, it is surprising that poverty has not yet been addressed. On any reading, extreme poverty is morally unacceptable as it is debilitating and dehumanizing, to the point that individuals are unable to pursue their own ends, flourish or enjoy basic rights. That poverty is still so globally dominant is even more shocking if one considers that according to at least some global thinkers it could be addressed with relative ease. For instance, Pogge states that:

> never has poverty been so easily avoidable. The collective annual consumption of the 2,735 million people reportedly living (on average 42%) below the World Bank's $2/day poverty line is about $440 billion and their collective shortfall from that poverty line roughly $330 billion per year. This poverty gap is less than one per cent of the gross national incomes of high-income countries.
>
> *(Ibid.)*

This part of the book discusses why poverty is not yet addressed and how it can be, and other important issues related to global poverty.

In addition to being a primary topic of global ethics poverty also contributes to, exacerbates or complicates all of the other issues addressed in this volume. For instance, poverty increases the likelihood of conflict and terrorism as desperation often renders persons more willing to engage in violence. Conversely, conflicts increase the number of poor by destroying land and crops, and, as civilians are driven off their land, result in increased numbers of migrants and refugees. Poverty also drives out other long-term concerns, such as concern for the environment, and leads to practices, such as deforestation (done in order to gain land and resources to survive), which compound other problems. Likewise environmental degradation increases poverty, as adverse weather events and processes connected to climate change, such as desertification, destroy crops, result in less available fertile land, and contribute to famine and once again to migration and even trafficking (discussed in Chapters 15 and 21). In health terms the poor are particularly vulnerable, with poverty greatly exacerbating health threats. This vulnerability is clearly shown in the "90–10 disequilibrium," that is, that 10 per cent of total health-related research and development is devoted to 90 per cent of the global disease burden. In other words, 90 per cent of the global disease burden is made up of diseases that affect the global poor, such as malaria, but only 10 per cent of the total money spent on researching and developing drugs is dedicated to combating these illnesses. It is this type of disparity that has led key global ethicists, such as Pogge, to address the patent system (discussed in Chapter 26) and to advocate the Health Impact Fund. Those who are poor also lack access to essential medicine, again partly through the global patenting system (Chapter 26); it is estimated that a third of the world's population has *no access* to essential drugs and more than half of this group of people live in the poorest regions of Africa and Asia. Conversely, poverty increases global health threats; for instance, when drugs are difficult to access and expensive then they are likely to be hoarded rather than shared. Such behaviour contributes significantly to the emergence of drug-resistant strains of disease and makes the emergence of devastating pandemics much more likely. For example, the WHO states that "Modern healthcare depends substantially on antibiotics and other antimicrobial medicines to treat conditions that would previously have proved fatal. Today, there is more resistance – and there are fewer new antimicrobial medicines in the pipeline – than ever before" (World Health Organization 2011a). Such threats are not idle, but real and already manifesting, and like the threat of climate change (discussed in Chapter 27), such threats are global and threaten not only human flourishing but perhaps human survival.

Gender justice is also relevant when it comes to poverty, as it is when it comes to every other issue of global ethics. Women make up 70 per cent of the world's one billion poorest people (Global Poverty Project 2013). Although it may be the case that the most extreme differences are between rich and poor, UNDP Human Development Reports (http://hdr.undp.org/en) show that in all countries women do not average the same income as men. That the dangers to women are exacerbated by poverty is quickly demonstrated by a few statistics, for instance, "of the 500,000 women who die in childbirth every year, 99% live in developing countries. In other words, in developing countries, a girl or woman dies every minute in giving birth" (Global Poverty Project 2013). The inequality between men and women globally is dramatic. "Women work two-thirds of the world's working hours, produce half of the world's food, but earn only 10% of the world's income and own less than one per cent of the world's property. On average, women earn half what men earn" (*ibid.*).

Therefore, although this section is dedicated to poverty, it needs to be remembered that poverty is not a separate issue to be addressed alone, but fundamentally connected to the other issues raised in the volume. In this part, we are concerned explicitly and directly with poverty, who causes it, who is responsible and how it should be addressed; for instance, by development (Chapter 14) or aid (Chapter 15). We are also concerned with its consequences (Chapter 16).

Chapter 13 by Hennie Lötter outlines the challenges of and responses to global poverty and inequality. As Brock discussed in Chapter 6, addressing global inequality and poverty are not the same and there is currently an important debate ongoing about whether inequality itself is problematic and in exactly what ways, or whether what matters most for global ethics and justice is addressing basic needs and a minimum threshold. Lötter begins with Peter Singer's shallow pond example (which states that if we can prevent something very bad from happening without sacrificing anything morally significant, we ought to do it), introduced in Chapter 3, which leads to a utilitarian claim for strong global obligations between individuals. Singer's analogy has been widely critiqued, but Lötter advises us not to underestimate the power of the example and the important questions it raises. He then moves to Rawls, discussed in Chapters 4 and 6, and his importance in returning us to justice theorizing, but his failure to provide a theory of global justice and to address global poverty. In the following sections he introduces the approaches of Thomas Pogge, Amartya Sen and Martha Nussbaum as thinkers who drove the debate forward and raised issues of global poverty directly.

Having set out these approaches and thinkers, so core to current global ethics theorizing, Lötter then considers practical concerns about whether and to what extent we have addressed, or failed to address, global poverty and inequality. He notes the international consensus, which suggests progress towards poverty reduction: a claim which his next section seems to belie as it recounts the facts and figures of global poverty, bringing him to perhaps the core discussion of his chapter, on the nature of poverty. Here he considers poverty indexes, measurements and definitions, and briefly also levels of aid and charity (the subject of Chapter 15). Lötter concludes by returning to Singer and Rawls and arguing that many of the core questions of justice they raised are still the ones that challenge us.

Julian Culp discusses theories of development and their intellectual history in Chapter 14. As he notes, it is vitally important to think critically about the morality of development because although development is a major international priority, to which a great deal of attention and institutional resources are directed, development efforts are guided almost exclusively by economists, political scientists and lawyers. If there were broad moral agreement about the aims of development this might seem less problematic. But in fact there is no such agreement. The concept of development is generally understood to mean social progress. But there are several different understandings, or conceptions, of development, each of which takes its aims very differently.

Culp discusses four main conceptions of development. The first is economic development, or development as economic growth. For several decades in the twentieth century this conception of development enjoyed wide support, even as its adherents disagreed with one another about the means by which to achieve economic growth. It still has plenty of influence in policy circles. Critics of economic development contend that it is based upon a moral mistake. The second conception discussed by Culp is human development. Influential advocates of human development, such as Amartya Sen and Martha Nussbaum, maintain that economic growth cannot command our moral allegiance. On the contrary, development should pursue enhancing people's effective freedoms or "capabilities." Economic growth confuses a means for an end. Economic growth is valuable only to the extent that it serves the goal of capability expansion. Advocates of human development disagree about which human capabilities should properly guide development. Nussbaum defends a list of ten core capabilities, whereas Sen eschews such efforts, preferring to leave the task of capability identification to political and moral debate.

The third conception of development discussed by Culp is sustainable development. One concern that is characteristic of theorists of sustainable development is that present development not undermine the moral claims of future generations. There are a variety of accounts of what those claims might be. Hence, conceptions of sustainable development vary. Another way in which such accounts differ from one another is the extent to which they take into consideration the non-human natural world. Some accounts of sustainable development are explicitly anthropocentric, concerned only about the moral entitlements of humans, whereas others take into consideration members of some or all other species and even abiotic aspects of the environment. The fourth conception that Culp summarizes is not considered a conception of development at all by its advocates. Adherents of post-development contend that conceptions of development are inherently biased towards a Western or developed world agenda. The rest of the world would do well to free itself from such aims. Culp points out that, in so far as these accounts advocate that policies that would free countries from the developed world agenda would constitute an improvement for such countries, they advocate a conception of development and not a rejection of the concept of development. Culp closes with an important discussion of responsibility for development, which is informed by the changing world of development in which we live. Culp's discussion of development aid provides a natural segue to the discussion in Chapter 15.

Chapter 15 by Nigel Dower addresses the ethics of aid and charity. For those who accept that there are obligations to distant others (see Chapters 3, 4 and 6), the next question is how such obligations can be fulfilled. One answer is to give charity and aid, either as individuals, NGOs or states. However, Dower discusses several alleged problems with this solution. First, despite a long history of aid giving, empirically it does not appear to have addressed the poverty it sought to address; second, aid creates dependency and thus fuels future poverty; third, aid is ecologically problematic (see Chapter 31 on population ethics); fourth, aid often has undesirable political effects, for instance, as a resource which leads to conflict; fifth, aid is often undesirably conditional; and sixth, a focus on aid is always reactive and fails to address underlying problems. Dower responds to these criticisms in turn, and finally to the claim that arises from all of these, namely that as a result of the problems with aid, it should be rejected as a method of remedying poverty.

Key to Dower's counter-arguments is recognizing that all aid is not the same, and that some aid is problematic does not entail that all aid is. Dower argues that aid should be long-term development aid and not simply short-term emergency aid, and should be focused on the empowerment of the poor. He argues that many of the problems currently attributed to aid can be addressed by more attention to context, to whether conditions of aid contribute to long-term development, and to structural and institutional changes. He cautions that we are not justified in abdicating the responsibility to help the poor simply because not all negative consequences cannot be avoided.

In Chapter 16 Sarah Fine and Andrea Sangiovanni consider immigration. Like so many chapters in this volume, this chapter could have gone in other sections, for instance in Part II because so often migration is a result of conflict or in Part IV on economic justice. However, the immigration chapter is placed here because poverty is perhaps the primary push-factor in migration. Many global ethicists are cosmopolitans and to some degree or another deny the legitimacy (at least over the long term) of state borders; however, currently states control their borders and have a right to prevent immigration. In this chapter Fine and Sangiovanni consider the arguments that support the current state of affairs and that are used to justify the moral "right to exclude."

Fine and Sangiovanni consider four arguments. The first is that states' right to self-determination includes the freedom to associate and therefore the right to exclude outsiders. They question the extent of this right and whether it obviously belongs to states. Second, they discuss the liberal nationalist argument to the effect that there are special rights and obligations between co-nationals and these rights and that obligations permit excluding non-compatriots. Again the

authors consider the arguments for this view and possible responses. Third, Fine and Sangiovanni address a Kantian argument which is based on the assumption that states can regulate the
territory over which they have jurisdiction and within which they promote public good.
The authors consider this to be one of the most promising arguments for those seeking to
defend the right to exclude, and accordingly the discussion of this justification is significantly
longer than the others. The final argument is the special obligations argument, that immigration
can be resisted if it harms the worst off within the state. The authors' conclusion, having
reflected on what they consider to be the strongest arguments in favour of the right to exclude,
is that it is exceedingly difficult to defend an all-things-considered right to exclude.

13

POVERTY

Hennie Lötter

The main champions of the cause of the poor

Pioneering Peter Singer

In November 1971 Peter Singer added a global twist to the centuries-old debate about rich and poor (see Vaughn 2008) when he asked: What are the moral obligations of rich people in developed countries to relieve the hardship of poor people suffering from hunger in developing countries? He proposed a principle that "if it is in our power to prevent something very bad from happening, without thereby sacrificing anything morally significant, we ought, morally, to do it". As justification Singer used this analogy:

> An application of this principle would be as follows: if I am walking past a shallow pond and see a child drowning in it, I ought to wade in and pull the child out. This will mean getting my clothes muddy, but this is insignificant, while the death of the child would presumably be a very bad thing.
>
> *(Singer 1972: 231)*

Singer argues that letting someone die by doing nothing is as morally wrong as killing a person, especially if the death can be prevented with little cost to oneself. Is Singer's analogy appropriate? Frances Kamm (2004), for instance, points out that this analogy is not perfectly equalized with the moral situation it intends addressing. She observes differences such as that in Singer's analogy the child had an accident, whereas in the case of children dying of hunger they are suffering as a result of injustice or a natural disaster (*ibid*.: 61–62), and the poor far-away children are not fellow citizens, or members of the passer-by's community, but complete strangers. Kamm thus claims Singer's analogy is ill-suited to address the issue of aiding hungry, poor people in foreign countries.

For Balakrishnan and Narayan (1996: 232–35) the analogy suggests there are no poor people in the First World, and First World people stand as aid donors in relation to Third World people as aid recipients. This, they say, creates a "false picture of a uniformly affluent Western world and a uniformly poor and hungry Third World" whose citizens do not relate to one another as equals (*ibid*.: 233). Shue (1996a: 125) complains that it "would be silly" to think that any analysis that takes "the form of random individuals relating directly to other random individuals" could be adequate for problems as "engrained and persistent" as poverty and global inequality. Jamieson (2005b: 154) objects that both Singer's conception of the problem and his proposed solution "de-contextualises, depoliticises, and dehistoricises famine, as well as masks the victims' agency".

Whatever the shortcomings of Singer's analogy, don't underestimate its power (see Cullity 2004: 2). He confronts us with a fundamental issue: millions of people, including young children, are dying premature deaths, while millions more people have the power to prevent those deaths without significant inconvenience. Singer appeals to our emotions: how horrifying that people could let a child die for the simple reason of not wanting their clothes dirty. The premature death of a child is deeply upsetting, especially one that could have been easily prevented.

The analogy raises illuminating questions (see also Jamieson 2005b: 156–58):

- Who had responsibility to take care of the child?
- Who had to ensure the safety of the pond?
- Who had to teach the child about safety when swimming?
- Who has the means or competence to prevent this specific premature death?
- Who allows her death through neglect or failure to step in?
- What reasons can a person offer that stand up to critical scrutiny when refusing to save the child?
- How are similar occurrences of children drowning in ponds to be prevented in future?

We can transpose these questions into the humanitarian disasters caused by poverty in many parts of the world that create emergencies crying out for immediate response. If done, core ethical issues confront everyone to give reasonable answers about their own chosen conduct in the face of so many premature deaths. Also, what initially looks like an individual ethical issue of charity turns into complex collective issues of justice (see LaFollette 2003), suggesting that appropriate dealings with poor people require doing them justice, as Rawls's work indicates. Singer's analogy stood as proxy for the comprehensive neglect of these issues in 1971, as the parable of the Good Samaritan stood for similar obligations to help those in need for almost 2,000 years (see Lötter 2008: 1–2).

Ground-breaking John Rawls

Also in 1971, John Rawls published his now famous book, *A Theory of Justice* (1971; see also Rawls 1993, 2001). He gave new life to twentieth-century Anglo-American political philosophy by rehabilitating the significance of the concept of justice as tool for thinking about proper cooperative relations between citizens sharing a country to ensure mutual benefit for everyone. He offered an imaginative hypothetical situation, "the original position", where individuals are deprived of any identifying information and thus, as equals, can deliberate on behalf of all citizens about appropriate principles of justice. These principles are to determine the basic structure of their society so as to be fair to everyone. Through this ground-breaking work Rawls defended the choice by participants in the original position: liberty, equality and solidarity must be implemented by means of both equal political rights and approval of only those inequalities serving the best interests of the least advantaged persons. The latter implied a social minimum of all-purpose means for everyone to have a decent life, while retaining incentives for those more advantaged. Justice functions as a "pact of reconciliation" between citizens that protects the basic interests of everyone sufficiently.

Many political philosophers expressed disappointment when Rawls (1999c) extrapolated his theory of justice to the global context (see Wenar 2001: 85–88). He had no single original position to determine what is just for everyone everywhere. In addition to his original position to determine what is just for a country, he presented a second one for representatives of peoples to discuss justice between states (Rawls 1999c: 17). Rawls offered no full global, cosmopolitan theory of justice, although he allowed for complex relations between states and global institutions, recognizing that states might prefer to cooperate with the international community in a diversity of ways, sovereignly decided.

His extrapolation offered no obvious solution for the grinding global inequality that hundreds of millions of poor people endure. To his considerable credit he argued for competitive, free and fair trade and made provision for mutual assistance to enable "burdened societies" to be able "to manage their own affairs" and thus "to determine the path of their own future for themselves" (Rawls 1999c: 111, 118). Rawls thus leaves room for countries to set their own priorities after they have achieved basic justice. Once those societies have escaped the worst burdens, they must deal with any further economic inequalities on their own, even if they remain "relatively poor" (*ibid.*: 118), in part because Rawls judged "the crucial element in how a country fares" to be "its political culture" (*ibid.*: 117). Poverty thus seems to be their "own fault" as the developed countries of the First World seemingly have – or had – no part in it. Pogge accuses Rawls (and some economists) of obscuring the negative impact of the global economic order imposed by powerful developed countries that harms millions of people in poor developing states (Pogge 2001: 17; see also Pogge 2004).

The great political philosopher who inspired two generations of successors seemingly failed to develop his own theory for the global context according to the expectations of his students, peers and followers. Is the state the primary agent of justice where most of our obligations of justice ought to be discharged to our fellow citizens only, as Rawls seems to suggest? Should we develop Rawls's theory into a cosmopolitan one that advocates global governance structures that dispense justice equally to everyone, as Moellendorf (2002) has so challengingly done? Must we design a global theory of justice that will ensure all children – the ones in Switzerland and those in Mozambique, Mali and Burkina Faso too – have equal opportunities to reach similarly coveted positions in their societies (see Caney 2001, Moellendorf 2009)? And, most challengingly of all, do First World countries have to accept a major part of the responsibility for causing the destructive poverty that leads to so many deaths each day? Or is Rawls correct in absolving them of such blame?

Low impact and high frustration for Thomas Pogge ...

After more than forty years a second generation of philosophers are debating these issues more intensely than ever before. A troubling question arises: did the debates about Singer's arguments and Rawls's theory have an impact on reducing the negative consequences of global poverty and inequality on millions of suffering poor people? Or is all philosophical thinking about these matters in vain?

The frustrations expressed by Thomas Pogge suggest philosophical contributions might be in vain. While people are suffering and dying, and human potential being wasted, those with means and responsibility still just do not seem to care. Pogge alerts us to the heart of the matter: as a result of the consequences of our actions and the impact of our neglect millions of people are dying every year and millions more live stunted lives. Pogge talks in language steeped in moral outrage matching the dire consequences of abject poverty for millions worldwide. This is clear in his expression of the two main themes of a recent book: "the

monumental crime we are committing against the world's poor and the monumental deception we are visiting upon ourselves and our children to cover up this crime" (Pogge 2010: 3).
The consequences of abject poverty are in some ways worse than the horrors of the Nazi
Holocaust, in other ways less. The "worse" part is that some eighteen million people die
prematurely every year from poverty-related causes, three times the number killed in the
Holocaust during the Second World War. The "less" part is that millions of people do not
intend the death of poor people, although they act "with wilful indifference to the enormous
harms they cause" (*ibid.*: 51). Pogge warns that millions of people today are making the same
fundamental moral mistake the Nazis did, that is, not to determine for themselves their moral
responsibilities in their specific circumstances (*ibid.*: 73).

Pogge goes to great lengths to argue that developed countries are at least partially responsible
for poverty and global inequality through imposing global institutional arrangements on developing countries and allowing unjust rulers in those countries to commit major injustices (Pogge
2002: 23; for critique see Reitberger 2008, Barry & Øverland 2012). For these reasons people
suffering from poverty in developing countries have legitimate moral claims on people in
developed countries based on universally accepted ideas on human rights. The developed
countries violate the negative duty human rights impose on them not to cause harm to others
(see Pogge 2002: 22–24, 197; 2010: 51–52).

Pogge's impatience with the lack of progress in eradicating poverty shows in the ways he is
mobilizing academics across the world to stand against poverty. He is also willing to do philosophy in interdisciplinary ways – often judged not to be "philosophy" by his colleagues,
although he believes his work is "closer to the historical roots of philosophy than much of what
is done today" (Pogge 2010: 8–9). Pogge's philosophy, undergirded by collaborative work with
other experts (*ibid.*: 9), is dictated by the perceived urgency to present ethical guidelines as calls
to action to convince politicians and citizens across the globe to immediately start acting in
defence of suffering poor people, as eighteen million lives are at stake every year.

Despite Pogge's understandable frustration, can one reasonably expect philosophy to have a
direct short-term impact on the world of politics and public policies? Philosophers do not have
the glamorous appeal of pop star celebrities like Bono and Bob Geldof, whose anti-poverty
campaigns have had major impact in recent decades. Their impact results from their large
audiences, open and receptive to their message and their exclusive access to political leaders of
the global community of states. Philosophers help to prepare the ground for such campaigns by
offering justified theories. They clarify conceptual issues, develop and evaluate arguments,
examine the quality of the lives we live, and propose ideals for betterment. Convincing proposals for changing our collective self-understanding that require revising principles guiding our
joint actions take time to have effect, sometimes decades or even centuries.

Take, for example, the cosmopolitan political ideas formulated by Immanuel Kant more than
two hundred years ago. Based on his defence that each person has a dignity to be respected by
everyone else, Kant ([1795] 1983) proposed a league of nations to regulate relations between
states to prevent the horrific wars his fellow Europeans fought. More than 150 years later, after
two devastating world wars that cost the lives of, *inter alia*, millions of Europeans, the idea of a
league of nations came into being as the United Nations in 1948, based on respect for the
human dignity of all individuals as specified in an internationally accepted, comprehensive
charter of human rights. The league of European nations that joined forces on so many different
levels over the past few decades secured a flourishing peace for Europe. For this reason the
European Union was awarded the Nobel Peace Prize in 2012 for the ways the EU contributed
to "the advancement of peace and reconciliation, democracy and human rights in Europe"
(Norwegian Nobel Committee 2012). Kant would have been proud!

... and pointed satisfaction for Sen (and Nussbaum)?

Amartya Sen, the economist–philosopher, might not feel frustrated to the same extent as Thomas Pogge. Sen and Mahbub ul-Haq from Pakistan are credited for the Human Development Reports, produced annually by the United Nations Development Programme (UNDP) (see United Nations Development Programme 2010: iv). Their vision at the outset in 1990 was that development should not be measured only by how money determines people's well-being. Measurements must also gauge "whether people can lead long and healthy lives, whether they have the opportunity to be educated and whether they are free to use their knowledge and talents to shape their own destinies" (*ibid.*). Helen Clark, administrator of the UNDP, claims that this "human development approach has profoundly affected an entire generation of policy-makers and development specialists around the world" (*ibid.*). Clark's claims are confirmed by Sen's Nobel Prize in Economic Sciences in 1998, awarded for similar reasons.

In his theories developed over decades, Sen suggests we look at the kinds of lives people actually live and the freedom they have "to live the kind of lives they have reason to value" (Sen 2009: 244; see also 18–19, 231–32). He calls the kinds of lives individuals manage to craft for themselves their functioning. Their capabilities are the opportunities they have freedom to choose from, combined with their individual personal characteristics. These capabilities and functionings form the lens through which Sen gathers information to judge the level of advantage individuals possess in their lives compared to those of others (see Sen 1992: 39–41, 73, 81; for critical discussion see Dowding 2006, Brighouse & Robeyns 2010).

Poverty is deprivation of basic capabilities (Sen 1992: 109). Poor individuals have less freedom than others to choose the kind of lives they value. Therefore their lives are selected from far fewer alternatives compared to those available to others. In addition they have access to far less resources. The role of our "conversion capacity", that is, our capacities to utilize resources efficiently or not, affects poor people more because they have so much less economic resources (*ibid.*: 82). Poverty as deprivation of basic capabilities requires us to question the efficiency and equity of a country's policies that are supposed to work in the best interests of justice for every citizen. Information on the actual lives people live and their freedom to choose a life they have reason to value from alternatives provides the basis for evaluating the justice a society offers its citizens.

Note the significance Sen assigns to freedom. In his book *Development as Freedom* (1999) he argues for the reciprocal influence that different kind of rights – including liberty rights – have on one another and for the mutual support that the acknowledgement of one kind of rights gives to the successful implementation of others. This emphasis has now been adopted by both the UNDP (see United Nations Development Programme 2013: 21–37) and the Organisation for Economic Co-operation and Development (OECD), who says "recognition and implementation of universal human rights can be seen both as a goal and a driver of human development" (OECD Insights 2012: 131; see also 127–31).

Between 1987 and 1989 Sen worked with Martha Nussbaum to refine the capabilities approach. Their cooperation eventually led to an international organization with its own journal devoted to this approach. According to Nussbaum's version of the capability approach (see Nussbaum 2006, 2011a), people must have opportunities to develop their internal capabilities (talents, etc.) and have freedom to choose where and how they might want to exercise them. The exercise of capabilities turns into valuable functionings that fulfil what they want to be and do. Nussbaum sets out a list of ten such capabilities: things like life; bodily health; bodily integrity; senses, imagination and thought; emotions; practical reason; affiliation; other species; play; and control over one's environment (for critique on her list, see Dowding 2006). Nussbaum argues that a society is minimally just if every person can choose to exercise those capabilities above a minimum threshold (Nussbaum 2011a: 42), set by what human dignity requires. As poverty violates the human dignity of persons, the level of economic well-being that lifts someone above accepted poverty lines indicates the threshold. Dorsey's judgement that Nussbaum's list of capabilities is "simply too expansive to be required for a life of human dignity" (2008: 431) shows the issues still to be resolved.

Nussbaum judges that two capabilities, affiliation and practical reason, play an "architectonic role" in people's lives as they "organise and pervade" the other capabilities and thus become "woven into" them (Nussbaum 2011a: 39). To develop and maintain them intact is crucial for well-being and for understanding why poverty sometimes stubbornly persists. Some capabilities provide the "best intervention points for public policy" aimed at eradicating poverty (*ibid*.: 45), because they exhibit "fertile functioning", that is, they enable other capabilities to function, or they have a "corrosive disadvantage", that is, their unfulfilled status has a negative impact on some other capabilities too. What they are must be determined in context, but they could be education, landownership, access to credit, and so on. Nussbaum's notion of capability security is important for full eradication of poverty (*ibid*.: 43). The idea implies that poor people must be able to count on aid and its resultant self-empowerment to transform their lives sufficiently so that they can continue their chosen functionings in the foreseeable future. Only reliable aid will ensure that such a transformation does not become something that ends abruptly with discretionary withdrawal of aid.

Sen's major impact (combined with Nussbaum's) gives reason for hope about the value of intellectual contributions to eradicate poverty and reduce inequality worldwide, despite critique that their approach is "radically underspecified" as it contains a "number of theoretical lacunae that can be filled in a variety of ways" (Robeyns 2006: 353). Nevertheless, Robeyns (2005: 41) judges Sen's approach superior to the "income metrics or resource approach" for its ability to "pick up … morally relevant information that is overlooked" by the others.

Have we made progress in dealing with poverty and global inequality?

Aid transformed into development cooperation

Maybe the tide is turning in the struggle against poverty and global inequality? The complex, crowded and almost hyperactive world of development cooperation suggests that many states, organizations and individuals have become involved with issues of poverty and global inequality.

The global community of states has committed themselves to eradicate poverty and reduce inequality. Official development assistance (ODA, aid given by governments) offered by donor countries (development partners) to recipient countries (developing countries) was $105,292 million in 2006 (see OECD 2008b). This amount excludes money given by all other aid donors, such as philanthropists and non-governmental organizations (NGOs). Miller controversially judges this aid as "meager", because "it amounted to $115 per person in donor countries, 0.31% of their total Gross National Income, and $21 per person in recipient countries" (R. W. Miller 2010: 218).

The international community of states, as organized by the United Nations, committed themselves to implement the Millennium Development Goals (MDGs). These goals were set after 189 countries adopted the Millennium Declaration at the UN Millennium Summit in September 2000 (United Nations Development Programme 2003: v). These specific, measurable, time-bound targets aim to halve the incidence of serious poverty by 2015. They are based on the best possible scientific understanding and wisdom about how political institutions can deal with poverty eradication and inequality reduction. The matters they address together form proxies for the comprehensive, multidimensional aspects of the phenomenon of poverty. The MDGs are:

- eradicate extreme poverty and hunger;
- achieve universal primary education;
- promote gender equality and empower women;
- reduce child mortality;
- improve maternal health;
- combat HIV/AIDS, malaria and other diseases;
- ensure environmental sustainability;
- develop a global partnership for development.

Their implementation is a priority on national, international and global agendas and progress is monitored, reported, discussed and evaluated to revise and adapt where necessary for successful implementation (United Nations 2012a). The MDGs express improved ways of eradicating poverty however flawed the plans to implement them, or the execution and monitoring thereof, might be (see Pogge 2009, 2010). Researchers are already presenting proposals for new multi-dimensional poverty measures on which so-called post-2015 MDGs can be based. They claim these measures indicate better the incidence and intensity of poverty based on expert views and participatory discussions (Alkire & Sumner 2013).

Note the changing emphasis from "aid" to "development cooperation", where relations between donors and recipients are redefined into partnerships between equals with mutual accountability to enhance aid effectiveness (see MDG Gap Task Force 2012; OECD 2008b, 2008c, 2009a, 2009b, 2012a; OECD Insights 2012). As a result many international organizations now focus on ensuring adequate aid works effectively and many international meetings develop policies and practices national governments are expected to implement (see OECD 2008b, 2008c, 2009a, 2009b, 2012a). To what extent aid has worked is in dispute, as some argue that aid has been detrimental exactly to those people who needed it most (see Collier 2008: 99–123; Moyo 2009).

We now have a comprehensive focus on a social-scientific understanding, monitoring and evaluation of the complex phenomena of poverty and global inequality, as well as on their complex interplay with aid and development cooperation. These long-term efforts to understand all dimensions of poverty and global inequality combine with attempts to design feasible solutions based on scientific research done by major international organizations (UNDP, OECD, World Bank, etc.), research institutes and academics. Such research offers hope that finding the correct understanding of the causes of poverty and global inequality assists in developing tailor-made solutions and figuring out best practice to reduce their incidence. Note the quality of scientific reporting by World Bank researchers already achieved in 1980 (World Bank 1980).

For reasons mentioned thus far, the "donor fatigue" of earlier decades (see Pogge 2010: 55) has faded in the light of many successes achieved. National, international and global agendas have made many remaining intractable problems priority issues. Of course, major work remains to be done as poverty and global inequality still have devastating consequences on the lives of more than a billion people. Nevertheless, massive amounts of human energy go into organiza-tion, research, funding and partnerships that are slowly getting more priority – and becoming more effective.

If philosophers are having some kind of impact in conjunction with the efforts of others, and progress towards poverty eradication and inequality reduction is real, maybe we can believe that the world is in the midst of a transitional period of several decades towards full eradication of poverty worldwide (see also Gilabert 2008). In the meantime the frustrations for philosophers like Pogge, who so clearly see the immorality of our inaction and the injustice of our unfair rules of international cooperation, are understandable as many people and politicians are still stuck in modes of thinking that allow millions of deaths annually. Although the global human community *has* made progress in dealing with poverty and global inequality since 1971, some voices dispute its efficacy (see Wenar 2001: 81; Jamieson 2005b: 160; Moyo 2009; Hanlon *et al.* 2010: 8–11). The progress yet to be achieved remains a Herculean challenge. The good work done thus far simply is not yet good enough.

How many people are still poor?

Despite all the positive developments, the numbers of poor people in the world are still overwhelmingly staggering. Scientific measures expressed in statistics help us understand poverty through local snapshots to global landscapes that show us the nature, incidence and depth of poverty and global inequality. Data on a global scale are provided by the World Bank, the UNDP, the OECD and UNICEF (see OECD 2009b, UNICEF 2012, World Bank 2012, United Nations Development Programme 2013). These statistics for measuring the incidence and dimensions of poverty across all countries in the world as well as trends over decades are under intense scrutiny (see Gasper 2004: 36–45; Collier 2008: 9; Klasen 2009; Ward 2009; Esposito & Lambert 2011; Hassoun 2011). Robeyns, for example, claims that "global income inequality statistics remain vital" but they "will not tell us the full story, perhaps not even half the story, of the current trends in local and global inequalities" (2005: 44). There are nonmaterial dimensions of poverty, like democratic agency, that the "purely income-based indicators of poverty and inequality are unable to capture" (*ibid.*: 46). Researchers providing these statistics are well aware of this scrutiny, as they caution readers to take into account the shortcomings in methodology of what essentially remains work-in-progress (see United Nations Development Programme 2011: 123).

A well-known poverty statistic is the number of people in the world living on less than one dollar per day, the so-called international poverty line, now raised to $1.25 PPP (purchasing power parity) per day. The measure, expressed in US dollars, thus requires converting all non-US currencies into US dollars. A second adjustment to this criterion requires converting the prices of consumer goods usually bought by people in their own countries (referred to as "available consumption") to the prices paid for similar goods in other countries. As poor people "face the prices where they live", this conversion is justified to eliminate the fact that "the price level is lower in one country than another". In these two ways statisticians calculate the so-called purchasing power parity exchange rates, expressed as PPP US dollars (see Milanovic 2005: 12–15).

In 1990 2 billion people (47% of the world population) had less than $1.25 PPP per day. In 2008 1.4 billion people (24% of world population) had less than $1.25 per day, while the UNDP estimates that in 2015 more than 1 billion people will still have to cope with so little income. A different indicator of extreme poverty is the number of people who are undernourished. In 1990/92 about 848 million (19.8% of the world population) were undernourished, while in 2006/8 about 850 million people (15.5% of the world population) suffered a similar plight.

A different poverty line for individuals is the level where poor citizens of European countries become eligible for welfare benefits, which is an income level of $4,000 PPP (the European standard used by Milanovic 2005: 130). In these terms 77.4% of the world's population is poor and 95% of all poor people in the world (3,879 million) live in so-called poor countries. Also, 2% of poor people (92 million) live in rich countries, while 83% of all rich people (707 million) live in rich countries, and 11% of rich people (96 million) live in poor countries (*ibid.*: 129–33). Milanovic finds the "scarcity of the middle class" most interesting, as less than 14% of the world population live in middle-income countries and only 6.7% of individuals in the world fall into the global middle class (*ibid.*: 131).

The UNDP provides other statistics for comparing people's poverty across countries. The Human Development Index (HDI) combines measures dealing with "average achievement in three basic dimensions of human development – a long and healthy life, knowledge and a decent standard of living" (United Nations Development Programme 2011: 130). The value for every country is expressed as a number (decimal fraction) between 0 and 1. A ranking of 187 countries in the world is given based on this indexical number (*ibid.*: 127–30). The UNDP also provides an inequality-adjusted HDI (IHDI), the gender HDI that reflects "inequalities in achievements between men and women" (*ibid.*: 142). The Multidimensional Poverty Index (MPI) reflects the subjective aspect of the "percentage of deprivation experienced" and the objective side of those numbers of people living in "severe multidimensional poverty" (*ibid.*: 5, 6, 45–47).

The OECD is developing an even more refined measure that focuses on "many aspects of people's lives" and endeavours to understand "their relative importance" (OECD 2011a: 18–19), based on the recommendations of a commission appointed by President Nicholas Sarkozy of France (with Amartya Sen in an expert role; *ibid.*). The commission recommended a more nuanced, refined and accurate set of measures to provide deeper insight into the nature of poverty and well-being. The measurements will reflect various dimensions of both material living conditions (income and wealth; jobs and earnings; housing) and the quality of human life (health status; work and life balance; education and skills; civic engagement and governance; social connections; environmental quality; personal security; subjective well-being) to provide more precise, wider-spectrum profiles of poverty.

Do we know what poverty is and how it works?

Debates about the adequacy of these statistical measures raise two further issues: what exactly we are measuring, and the relevance of statistical profiles and social-scientific explanations of poverty for moral reasoning. These two factors are neglected in the philosophical debates (see Dieterlen 2005: 6). For example, very little discussion is devoted to definitions of poverty, as is common in the empirically driven human science of sociology. Many sociologists have attempted to measure the incidence and depth of poverty by qualitative or quantitative means with measuring instruments based on exact definitions, illuminating explanatory theories, and best practice in research methodology (see Townsend 1979, Alcock 1993).

To know that we measure the phenomenon of poverty and nothing else, we need a definition of what poverty is. Note the following definition and ask if it assists us to deal with poverty better (see Lötter 2011). Poverty's core meaning is that human beings suffer as a result of the consequences of not having enough economic capacities. Poverty as lack of economic capacities makes it impossible for people to develop and deploy their abilities to engage in valued life projects as rich people do. Extreme poverty articulates the "irreducible absolutist core in the idea of poverty" (Sen 1983: 159) that states that a person does not have enough economic capacities to provide adequate food, clothing, shelter, security and medical care to maintain their physical health. They do not have enough means to procure even the necessaries of life and are often dependent on others for help. Intermediate poverty means that although people have sufficient economic capacities to provide adequate food, clothing, shelter, security and medical care to maintain their physical health, they cannot participate in many other activities regarded as indicative of being human in that society. They can merely afford the barest necessities to keep themselves physically alive and well. Poverty thus harms a core aspect of being human: our human dignity (see J. D. Jones 1990).

If poverty is fully eradicated so that each person has sufficient economic capacities to enable a life of human dignity, substantial inequalities of different kinds might still exist. For example, even in a society with no poverty at all, levels of income and wealth can still range widely. Numerous other kinds of inequality might also exist, based on personal characteristics, gender, office, political power or group membership (see Sen 1992).

The measures of the extent and incidence of poverty expressed in statistical profiles of single or multiple dimensions of poverty tell us only part of the truth. Although somewhat more attention is devoted by philosophers to theories that explain the working and causes of poverty than the definition of poverty itself, even these issues are not sufficiently taken up. Significant work, for example, is done by Pogge (2002, 2010) on the global institutional order and Moellendorf (2005) on the World Trade Organization, but it is not yet enough.

Note the direction an explanation of poverty can go (see Lötter 2011). Poverty is a multi-dimensional complex human phenomenon that in each case consists of a complex interweaving of contingent circumstances and factors. Poverty is caused by a configuration of factors complexly assembled that jointly play a causal role in any specific case. Normal human activities can be derailed by myriad human actions to produce poverty. The complex series of human activities consisting of the location, conversion, exchange and distribution of resources can be short-circuited and thwarted in a diversity of ways, some of natural and others of human origin. Humans can directly or indirectly influence these activities through the use and abuse of any kind of power. Thus, thousands of things can go wrong with the activities that humans engage in to ensure survival and flourishing through social cooperation.

Poverty is thus the result of the choices humans make about the structures of their society, about the social forces they allow space to operate. Therefore the levels of poverty and riches in society are the collective responsibility of its citizens. Poverty is entirely remediable, if the appropriate suite of actions are taken from a wide range of possible interventions based on a careful consideration of the configuration of factors that are involved, their weight and interplay that determine the dynamics of a particular case (see also J. D. Sachs 2005: 73; Banerjee & Duflo 2011: 15).

But is this view correct that statistical profiles, definitions and explanations of poverty are needed for trustworthy moral reasoning (see Risse 2005b: 86)? Is it not enough just to say that poverty often causes destructive harm and lots of suffering and that we must therefore work out what our moral response ought to be? Such an answer is profoundly mistaken. If we ignore detailed information about the diverse manifestations of poverty in widely differing contexts, how will our ethical responses be different from those responses to people suffering other kinds of traumatic life experiences, like divorce, loss of a loved one, or physical injury? How will we be guided to determine what exactly are appropriate responses to poor people's specific challenges? How will we know whom to hold responsible, for what reasons, and in what ways? How will we determine obligations of justice, fittingly assigned?

Balakrishnan and Narayan (1996: 245) claim that philosophers are "often profoundly ignorant of economic realities and theories, and thus liable to misunderstand the causes of world poverty and hunger, and misconstrue the nature of moral obligations such problems generate" (see also Shue 2004: 226). Note how the empirical analyses presented by Pogge (2002, 2010) of the global institutional arrangements, and the analysis offered by Moellendorf (2005) of how the World Trade Organization functions, enable them to develop more focused moral evaluations, make more specific suggestions for change and improvement, and offer more precise assignments of responsibility to rectify what is wrong.

Thus, are we listening to what all the diverse, unique "voices" are trying to tell us about poverty and global inequality? Do we determine the truth about poverty to figure out how best to deal with it? To do so we must first listen to what the human sciences claim to know about poverty and global inequality, knowledge that is often not adequately taken into account in philosophical debates (see also Shue 1996a: 126). These studies rest on a range of social science research methods that offer in-depth profiles of the effects of poverty on the lives of people in specific regions or countries. Do we note the narratives and personal testimonies of people suffering from poverty and global inequality, like those in the books *Voices of the Poor* (Narayan *et al.* 2000a, Narayan *et al.* 2000b, Narayan & Petesch 2002)? Do we listen to people who break down from poverty and those who fight back, refusing to be overcome, as reported by Wilson and Ramphele (1989) in *Uprooting Poverty: The South African Challenge*? Do we know how developed countries experience poverty in the midst of their wealth (see Sen 1992: 114–16)?

A related issue is particularly sensitive: voices from First World philosophers (from the UK, the US, and a few countries in Europe) dominate these philosophical debates. So, are they the only intellectual voices heard and listened to? Often the viewpoints of intellectuals from developing countries are not taken into account. For example, how often has Mukherjee's book on hunger (2004) been quoted? Alison Jaggar (2006: 321) cautions participants in debates on global justice to "reason philosophically across cultures in ways that are inclusive, respectful of difference, and sensitive to inequality". We must therefore trace how any form of bias or prejudice influence what evidence and modes of reasoning are excluded or overemphasized so as to skew our depictions of poverty or distort our proposed solutions.

Listening to, engaging and evaluating all these voices speaking in such different keys is the only way to get a sure grip that reflects the truth about poverty in all its myriad manifestations.

Is justice or charity the route to the eradication of poverty?

Some people suggest the idea of charity as preferred framework to guide the eradication of poverty. For example, Fuller seeks to assign more accountability to international aid organizations to enable them to deliver aid more effectively. They can do so as they "are the least affected by considerations of national interest and profit" (Fuller 2005: 286, 297). Hanlon *et al* argue: "Give the money directly to those who have the least of it, but who know how to make the best use of it." They plead for aid as "investments that enable poor people to take control of their own development and end their own poverty" (Hanlon *et al*, 2010: 9).

Others propose a comprehensive framework built on a theory of justice to incorporate all the issues that affect the eradication of poverty (see N. Fraser 2008; United Nations Development Programme 2013: 4–9, 36–37). Such a framework will enable a multi-pronged series of strategies at all levels by everyone involved, giving priority to the voices of poor people to guide a multi-faceted global struggle (see also Collier 2008: xi; O. O'Neill 2008: 152–53; for a similar argument, see Sobhan 2010: 1–12). Ideas like these underlie the global perspectives from the major international organizations working in this field, like the World Bank, UNDP and the OECD.

If justice functions as the core concept for dealing with the eradication of poverty, does it deal with institutions only, or also with individual action? A strong assumption in debates on poverty, drawn from the work of John Rawls, is that justice deals with normative issues regarding institutions, and ethics deals with normative issues faced by individuals and groups. Moellendorf (2009: 19–20) regards social justice as "a property of social and political institutions" and Pogge refers to this distinction as one between "institutional and interactional moral analysis" (Pogge 2010: 16); the one kind focuses on "individual and collective agents" and the other on "institutions" (see also Nagel 2005: 140). This divide is so strong that Pogge, Moellendorf and Horton use this distinction to divide the contents of their selection of the most important readings on global moral issues into two books, one entitled *Global Justice* (Pogge & Moellendorf 2008) and the other *Global Ethics* (Pogge& Horton 2008). Is this distinction correct?

Judge for yourself in this alternative reading of Rawls's *A Theory of Justice* whether he agrees. Although Rawls acknowledges that his concern with social justice is a focus on the "basic structure of society" (its main institutions and their combined effects), he insists that "we also call the attitudes and dispositions of persons, and persons themselves, just and unjust" (Rawls 1971: 7).

Is Rawls the only one thinking that justice is a property that applies to individual human actions as well? No, Plato, Aristotle and John Stuart Mill thought so too. Mill argues for justice as a more intense form of ethics. Obligations of justice have greater weight than those of ethics, different contents, and more urgent meaning. Mill thus talks of the "superior binding force" of justice that forms the "chief part" of all morality that has "more absolute and imperative requirements" than any other part of our morality (Mill 2003: 217, 231, 235). Justice, for Mill, thus deals with the "central core" of morality (Riley 2010: 84).

Why the challenges posed by Rawls and Singer persist

Rawls's challenge has always faced *Homo sapiens* throughout our history: to act justly in all relationships towards every other human being. This challenge now requires us to spell out obligations of justice at multiple levels of human organization in our twenty-first-century global context, "partly globalised, characterised by 'complex interdependence' among states – and suffering a major governance gap" (Follesdal 2011: 62). The challenge that stretches from local family relationships to global relations of all kinds is to carefully develop and conscientiously implement a comprehensive theory of justice to protect the core interests of every human being anywhere.

Once we have assigned obligations of justice for eradicating the existing miserable conditions of so many suffering people who are withering away or dying from poverty, scenes of deprivation from some countries will still starkly confront us. Some suffering caused by poverty will seemingly always fall through the cracks. Gasper (2004: 4) reminds us: "Large-scale, extreme, remediable, undeserved suffering demands a response."

If we still confront human beings who face "maximally urgent" threats to their well-being when all else had been said or done, we ought to act, Charles Beitz (2009: 167) argues. We ought to act as Singer suggests, provided the cost is slight or moderate. We ought to act if we are one of the "set of eligible agents with the resources, position, and capacity to act so as to alleviate the threat or to mitigate its consequences" (*ibid.*). We ought to act, guided by triage, Arneson (2005: 141) argues, so that the "comparative moral urgency of channelling aid to one person rather than another depends only on how badly off one is and to what extent one's condition would improve with an infusion of resources".

Rawls and Singer are inextricably linked (see Reitberger 2008): as we can never alienate ourselves from our fundamental obligations of justice towards other human beings, the arguments of Singer, as refined by other philosophers, will thus continue to challenge and even haunt us. If you have the means, once you have fulfilled all your other obligations of justice, why are you not acting on your most fundamental, inalienable obligations of justice towards other human beings? Why are you not saving those you can when it does not cost you falling victim to suffering yourself?

Elizabeth Anderson (1999: 307) argues that compassion simply "aims to relieve suffering wherever it exists, without passing moral judgement on those who suffer". If we do not experience compassion towards suffering members of our global moral community, what does that betray about the ways we honour our own human dignity in our choices about how we live?

14

DEVELOPMENT

Julian Culp

Many international development organizations, like the World Bank and the Development Assistance Committee (DAC) of the Organisation of Economic Co-operation and Development (OECD) tend to be populated mostly by economists, political scientists and lawyers. Moral and political philosophers represent at most a small minority in such institutions. Arguably, this is because most of the members of such international development organizations believe that their work consists mainly in identifying and implementing the most effective means for realizing given ends.

They may think this because development constitutes the overarching goal that their work must realize. They may point out that to put into question the desirability of development involves a contradiction in terms, because development simply stands for change that is socially desirable. Therefore there is no need for normative reflections and justifications of the philosophical kind. This kind of reasoning apparently explains why such organizations rely almost exclusively on personnel of the above-mentioned sort who are capable of responding to the instrumental, or technical, questions as to how one achieves development.

This chapter will show that – contrary to this reasoning – the work of international development organizations requires a constant reflection of the moral and political philosophical kind. A major reason for this is that while people agree that the abstract concept of development, in its normative usage, indeed, simply means social progress or good, or desirable, social change, they disagree profoundly about what social progress consists in exactly. There exists a normative disagreement about the conception of development that expresses best how social progress ought to be defined in concrete terms.[1] For example, should we really think of social progress only in terms of economic growth, that is, in the accumulation of goods and services? Or should we instead, for example, think of it in terms of the eradication of extreme poverty? Or in terms of yet something else, like the expansion of options for human choice?

The next section begins by articulating more clearly how to define a normative conception of development and in which way such a normative conception relates to what this chapter refers to as the "development practice". The three following sections go on to differentiate the very influential normative conceptions of economic development, human development and sustainable development. The subsequent section exposes them to the radical critique of post-development theorists who argue that any normative conception of development is parochial. The final section concludes by explaining why the normative debate about who is responsible for achieving development is likely to receive a lot of scholarly attention in the near future – owing mainly to the nascent multi-polarity in the global economy.

Normative development conceptions

When we use the concept of development descriptively, such as when we speak about how this month's weather has been developing, then we simply utilize the ideas of "transition", "changeover", "trend" or "change." Thereby – that is, only in virtue of the usage of the concept of development – we do not make an evaluative statement about the recent changes in weather. However, when we use the concept of development normatively, then we make the evaluative statement that something has changed in a desirable manner. For example, we may say that a company made a significant development in order to express our positive assessment of the changes that a company has undergone. In particular, when we talk in a normative sense about the development of a social arrangement, we usually refer to the idea of human or social progress (Lebret 1960: 1, in Goulet 1995: 6; Chambers 1997: vi; Dower 2000: 44; Nuscheler 2006: 225; Hopper 2012: 3). Consider, for instance, that the Human Development Report 2010 of the United Nations Development Programme (UNDP) states explicitly that its approach to assessing development "is the best way of thinking about human progress" (United Nations Development Programme 2010: 11). Normative conceptions of the development of social arrangements thereby determine how one ought to conceive of human or social progress by arguing for a particular set of conditions whose fulfilment amounts to the realization of such progress.[2]

This chapter differentiates three distinct normative conceptions of development that claim to have universal validity and which are therefore able to guide policy-makers of a global development practice. As further explained below, international development organizations like the World Bank as well as governments and non-governmental organizations that aspire to promote development constitute a development practice of global scope. Normative development conceptions are of great practical importance, because it is in light of such a conception that the members of the development practice orient their policies and decision-making processes.

The development practice emerged as a distinct field of world politics together with the creation of the United Nations in the aftermath of the Second World War (United Nations 1945: articles 1 (3), 55, 73, 75). In hindsight, Harry Truman's inaugural address as President of the United States in 1949 represents the kick-off to the development practice's project of realizing development everywhere. In the fourth point of his "Four Point Speech", Truman (1949) emphasizes the global dimension of a necessary international effort to promote development:

> [W]e must embark on a bold new program for making the benefits of our scientific advances and industrial progress available for the improvement and growth of under-developed areas. This should be a cooperative enterprise in which all nations work together through the United Nations and its specialized agencies wherever practicable.

Before 1945, by contrast, border-transcending development policies were restricted to some of the colonial powers' endeavours within their colonies and were mainly directed at securing the economic exploitation of natural resources (Arndt 1981: 462–63; Fischer *et al.* 2008: 15; Lepenies 2009). Nevertheless, it would be obviously false to hold that the development practice would be disconnected from the colonial endeavours.[3] The fact alone that many governmental development bureaucracies often originated from their former colonial administrative offices is very telling indeed.

The institutions that are assumed to be involved in the development practice today are, first of all, the actors that participate in the practice to give and receive official development assistance (ODA). The DAC (OECD 2011c) defined ODA in 1969 as follows:

> [ODA consists of] those flows to states and territories on the DAC List of ODA Recipients and to multilateral development institutions which are: i. *provided by official agencies*, including state and local governments, or by their executive agencies; and ii. each transaction of which: a) is administered with the promotion of the *economic development and welfare of developing countries* as its main objective; and b) is *concessional in character* and conveys a grant element of at least 25 per cent (calculated at a rate of discount of 10 per cent).[4]

The inter-state provision of ODA is the aspect of the development practice that is usually referred to as "bilateral aid". In 2011, the donors belonging to the DAC provided a total of US$134 billion ODA. ODA includes humanitarian aid, which amounted to nearly US$10 billion in 2011 (OECD 2012b). In addition, there are further donors who do not belong to the DAC. These include emerging donors who have close relationships to the DAC (e.g. the Czech Republic), providers of South–South cooperation like Brazil, and Arab donors like Kuwait. These non-DAC donors provided between $12 billion and $14 billion ODA in 2008 (Smith *et al.* 2010).

The second pillar of the development practice consists of the international organizations that have the primary purpose of promoting development. These institutions include most prominently the World Bank Group, the European Development Fund, the Asian and the African Development Banks, the United Nations Funds and Programmes and the Global Fund to fight Aids, Tuberculosis and Malaria. This part of the development practice that promotes development via international institutions is commonly labelled the system of "multilateral aid". In 2011, the multilateral aid amounted to almost $55 billion, roughly 40 per cent of total ODA (OECD 2013a). The third pillar of the development practice is "private aid" provided by philanthropic foundations and non-governmental organizations like *ActionAid*, *Eurodad* or the *Bill and Melinda Gates Foundation*. Estimates range between $32 and $58 billion for the total volume of private aid in 2011 (OECD 2013b; Center for Global Prosperity 2013: 12).

Economic development

For nearly half a century after the inception of the development practice, *economic development* has been the most influential normative conception.[5] Its central thesis is that the increase in a country's production of goods and services, which is measured by the country's growth of its gross domestic product (GDP), expresses a country's development.

The fact that this particular conception of development has been so influential for so long may be easily overlooked because scholars of different sorts have disagreed profoundly about the proper means for achieving economic development. Structural economists, dependency theorists, modernization theorists and adherents of the Washington Consensus argued fiercely about how to bring economic development about. Nevertheless, they have never put into question what development in the normative sense actually means. They all accepted that development consists simply of economic growth. The reason why these scholars were considered development scholars – and not just economists of different sorts – is that they all assumed that countries with a very small GDP need to adopt a set of developmental policies distinct from that of countries with greater GDPs (Sen [1988] 2008: 159).

Along these lines *structuralist economists* like Rodan-Rosenstein, for example, argue that economic development in poorer countries requires a "big push" in the form of heavy investments in the productive capacities.[6] Other structuralist economists emphasize that international economic structures constitute obstacles to the progress of the poorer countries. Most prominently Singer and Prebisch predicted in 1950 that under existing arrangements the terms of trade for poorer countries would worsen (Prebisch 1950, H. Singer 1950). This is because in a global environment of economic growth, the sellers of manufactured products benefit over-proportionally from trade compared with the sellers of natural resources. This results from the discrepancy in the income-elasticity of the demand for manufactured goods relative to that for natural resources. As countries become richer, the more prone their inhabitants become to consume manufactured products rather than natural resources. This, of course, is to the detriment of those who sell only natural resources. One central conclusion of the analysis of these structuralist economists is that poorer countries have to rely on a so-called import substitution strategy. This strategy consists in erecting barriers to imports of manufactured goods and in subsidizing domestic companies in order to stimulate the internal production of such goods.

Dependency theory is an offspring of structural economics but adopts several elements of Marxist economic theory. It claims that the global capitalist order serves to exploit the labour of poorer countries in the periphery in ways that provide the richer countries in the centre with economic surpluses (Baran 1957, Frank 1967, Amin 1976, Cardoso & Faletto 1979). Thereby the global capitalist order is said to engender the "development of underdevelopment". Later, in a less deterministic fashion, some dependency theorists stressed that although the global capitalist order strongly influences the shape and pace of domestic economic development, there are alternative ways for countries to deal with the exploitation by the global capitalist order that includes the possibility of "dependent development". Cardoso and Faletto (1979: xi), for instance, claim that while dependency does not hinder economic development, it conditions and constrains it.

It is easy to mistakenly believe that dependency theory views development as the ceasing of the domination occurring at the global level. Its major concern, in fact, is to overcome the dependency of the world's poorer countries – especially their dependency on the international markets' demand for natural resources. But one must note that dependency theory emphasizes that halting domination at the global level is simply a very effective *means* to facilitate economic growth on the domestic level (Greig *et al.* 2007: 73).

Like the dependency theories, modernization theories attribute to the state the role of organizing and directing the structure of the domestic economy and society (Rostow 1960, Inkeles 1966). Unlike dependency theory, however, modernization theory strongly emphasizes *endogenous* prerequisites for development, such as certain sociocultural characteristics of the population and the availability and quality of infrastructure. Paradigmatic for modernization theory, Rostow's *Stages of Economic Growth* (1960) describes economic development with a linear five-phase model through which societies would have to pass in order to develop and become modern before industrialization eventually permits a high level of output. Non-modern, traditional societies need to gradually overcome deficiencies of several kinds: their lack of technological knowledge, of a scientific understanding of the world, of entrepreneurial individuals, of a centralized administrative political power and of decentralized, market-based financial institutions.

Like modernization theory, the "Washington Consensus" (Williamson 1990) holds that development has its way when societies transform internally. Hence the genuine novelty of the Washington Consensus consists in its reliance on the market mechanism to effectuate development. *Market-led* development is meant to reduce the government's role in society, promising to increase economic efficiency. Accordingly, the Washington Consensus belongs to the influential "neo-classical" paradigm of economic thinking.

Human development

The so-called capabilities approach to human development formulates a normative development conception that is fundamentally different from the conception of economic development. Its core claim is that people's effective freedoms or "capabilities" and not the economy must be at the centre of development.[7] This normative development conception arose in the 1980s and soon gained considerable influence on the development practice. From 1990 onwards, the UNDP has published an annual report on human development in all countries. The first Human Development Report in 1990 expressed the transition from an economic to a human development conception as follows: "People are the real wealth of a nation" (United Nations Development Programme 1990: 9).

The conception of human development calls into question the conception of economic development for merely concentrating on the amount of goods people hold rather than their effective freedoms to do things and to experience certain states of being that they have reason to value (Sen 1999; Nussbaum 2000, 2006, 2011a). Therefore this conception is also referred to as "development as freedom". Goods can count only as a means of development, not as an end in and of themselves, because goods can only be valued instrumentally in enabling people to choose among certain options (Sen 1984: 510).

Thereby this conception places people's *capabilities* onto the centre stage of development and argues that capabilities are the only appropriate metric, or "informational base" (Sen 1999: 55) for assessing development. "Capabilities" refer to the effective freedoms to realize so-called *functionings*, which represent the various "beings" and "doings" that an individual may experience or exercise. So the real opportunity of being healthy or riding a bicycle is a capability. And the various combinations of functionings that an individual has the effective opportunity to choose constitute her capability set (Sen 1992: 39–54).

Nussbaum and Sen also make clear that goods are very poor proxies with regard to the capabilities that people actually enjoy (Sen 1992: 28–30, 36–38; [1980] 1997: 364–67; 1999: 70–71; Nussbaum 2000: 60–61; 2011a: 47–50, 56–58). This is because the possibilities of individuals to convert goods into capabilities vary greatly depending on their internal characteristics – such as their metabolic rates or cognitive capacities – and their external circumstances – such as the social, political and natural environment in which they live. So even if economic conceptions of development are considered as accounts of the means rather than of the ends of development, they are still deficient, because they neglect that the heterogeneity of people and their social and environmental contexts render goods an unhelpful and misleading indicator of the capabilities that people actually enjoy.

Despite Nussbaum and Sen's agreement on the inappropriateness of economic growth as a measure of development, their conceptions of human development are very distinct. The first difference is that Sen is reluctant to determine which particular capabilities should enjoy priority in cases of conflict between alternative realizations of different sets of capabilities (Sen 1999: 33–34). Nussbaum's conception, by contrast, argues that some capabilities are of special moral importance. She defends a list of *ten central capabilities* that, she argues, are necessary elements of a life worthy of human dignity[8] (Nussbaum 2000: 70–86; 2003; 2006: 69–81; 2011a: 31). These central capabilities are viewed as constituting an account of a "minimally flourishing life" (Nussbaum 2011a: 33) and enjoy priority over other capabilities.

The second major contrast between Nussbaum and Sen is that Sen refers to his approach as a "perspective of freedom" and sometimes appears to endorse freedom as a meta-good that can be instantiated in various ways by different sorts of capabilities (Sen 1999: 13–34, *passim*; cf. also Nussbaum 2003: 44; 2006: 297; 2011a: 70–74). For example, he argues that development should be "seen as a process of removing unfreedoms and of extending the substantive freedoms of different types that people have reason to value" (Sen 1999: 86). Accordingly, the goal of development, according to Sen's version of human development, appears to consist in the extension of people's capability sets.[9] Nussbaum, by contrast, clearly rejects the view that any expansion of people's capability sets will count as development. She emphasizes that what matters above all is that every single one of the ten central capabilities on her list is realized.

Arguably, the reason for this difference is that Nussbaum, but not Sen, explicitly follows the basic ideas of Rawls's *Political Liberalism* (2005) and offers a "political" rather than a "comprehensive" justification of the measure of development (Nussbaum 2000: 76–77; 2003: 42–43; 2006: 79, 297; 2011a: 19; 2011b). A *political* conception is different from a *comprehensive* conception in two ways: first, the scope of validity of a political conception is restricted to normative questions about the fundamental justice of a social order. A comprehensive conception is broader and may include normative questions about personal relationships or relations within a narrower association as its subject matter. Second, the validity claim of a political conception is that of public justifiability, which is to say that a political conception is meant to be acceptable for everyone, regardless of which particular, reasonable view about the good life one may hold. A reasonable comprehensive conception does not claim to be publicly justifiable because it accepts that the world is characterized by a plurality of reasonable but incompatible comprehensive views about the good. This is because, as Rawls puts it, "the burdens of judgment" (2005: esp. 56–57) make it the case that within free institutions, the free exercise of reason makes such a plurality a permanent feature of the social world. These burdens of judgement include that people undergo different experiences throughout their life, differ on which empirical information they deem relevant for practical judgement, and have to rely on interpretations of moral and political concepts that are necessarily underspecified.

Following these basic ideas of political liberalism means to recognize, however, that it is inappropriate to base a conception of development in a "perspective of freedom" that endorses a particular, comprehensive and not publicly justifiable view regarding what constitutes the good life. A person may reasonably reject the idea that her conception of the good ought to consist in an expansion of effective freedoms. However, a development conception should be able to orient public decision-making and, consequently, ought to be based on a justification that aims at redeeming the claim of public justifiability.

Given the fundamental importance of political liberalism, Nussbaum's version of human development appears more compelling than that of Sen. However, one may question, of course, whether or not there may be a way of substantiating development through the lenses of a political conception that is more democratic and less fixed than Nussbaum's list of ten central capabilities (cf. Crocker 2008: 297–337).

Sustainable development

The conception of human development is compelling because it does not confound means with ends. It places human beings' effective freedoms at the centre of the assessment of development and ascribes only derivative importance to economic growth. However, this conception seems to have two blind spots that the conception of sustainable development promises to avoid. The first one is that the conception of human development apparently fails to take into consideration future generations; the second one is that it has an anthropocentric bias because it neglects the moral importance of non-human animals as well as non-animal nature.

The United Nations World Commission on Environment and Development (WCED) articulated the politically most influential conception of sustainable development in *Our*

Common Future, the so-called Brundtland Report, published in 1987. The Brundtland Report defines that development is sustainable if "it meets the needs of the present without compromising the ability of future generations to meet their own needs" (WCED 1987: ch. 2 (1)). It further specifies that it understands needs as "essential needs ... for food, clothing, shelter, [and] jobs" (*ibid*.: ch. 2 (4)). Hence this conception of sustainable development is concerned with some of the standard needs of human beings in modern times.

This conception of sustainable development aligns itself to the human development conception and its critique of the economic development conception. As the Brundtland Report clarifies: "[S]ustainable development clearly requires economic growth in places where such needs are not being met. ... But growth by itself is not enough. High levels of productive activity and widespread poverty can co-exist, and can endanger the environment" (*ibid*.: ch. 2 (6)). In addition, the first principle of the Rio Declaration, which resulted from the United Nations Conference on Environment and Development in 1992, emphasizes: "Human beings are at the center of concern for sustainable development" (principle 1).

Nevertheless, sustainable development envisions a distinctively novel development conception, because it emphasizes the importance of being able to satisfy human needs in the future. It thereby adds the further normative dimension of sustainability to development, which according to Brian Barry means "that there is some X whose value should be maintained, in as far as it lies within our power to do so, into the indefinite future" (Barry 1997: 50).

But of course one can also argue that the conception of sustainable development only makes explicit what is implicit in the conception of human development. To the extent that scholars of the capabilities approach like Nussbaum and Sen ascribe fundamental moral importance to effective human freedoms, it seems natural to think that such freedoms possess moral value whether they exist now or in the future.

The second blind spot of the conception of human development mentioned above is that it only ascribes moral value to the effective freedoms of human beings, and neglects the potential moral importance of non-human animals as well as nature as such (Dower 2000: 41–42). However, it is also distinctive of the conception of sustainable development, at least in the way in which it is defined in the Brundtland Report, that it contains an anthropocentric bias. The preservation of non-animal nature and of non-human animals is not viewed as something that is intrinsically valuable and constitutive of sustainable development. As the report makes clear:

> Every ecosystem everywhere cannot be preserved intact. A forest may be depleted in one part of a watershed and extended elsewhere, which is not a bad thing if the exploitation has been planned and the effects on soil erosion rates, water regimes and genetic losses have been taken into account.
>
> *(WCED 1987: ch. 2 (11))*

The preservation of non-animal nature and of non-human animals is only valuable conditional on its contribution to enabling the fulfilment of essential human needs.

Therefore some theorists, for instance Dower, argue that a novel meaning of sustainable development is needed that also ascribes moral importance to non-animal nature and to non-human animals. Dower argues that there is no clear divide between human animals, non-human animals and non-animal nature. Rather, human animals are part of nature and historically evolved from other animals. Therefore, so the argument goes, it seems plausible to consider not only human animals as constitutive elements of development but also non-human animals and non-animal nature, that is, the "biotic community" (Dower 2000: 48), as a whole.

It is questionable, however, whether Dower is proposing at all a re-formulation of a *conception of development* because such a conception is meant to substantiate the idea of human or social progress – and not the idea of progress in non-animal nature and the non-human animal world. Therefore Dower's proposal of widening our understanding of development may be viewed simply as a suggestion about how to concretize the demands of sustainability but not as a suggestion about how to conceive of sustainable development.

Furthermore, one needs to resist the temptation to argue that whatever protects the current state of non-animal nature and non-human animals is desirable. This is because it is flawed to believe that this current state represents a scientifically explainable inherent harmony or balance that requires protection. After all, evolution is characterized by constant change and the extinction of species. And therefore measures that simply protect the environment in its current state cannot be viewed at all as the conservation of some inherent harmony or balance. In addition, the very idea that one could gain insights into moral requirements solely by scientifically explaining the functioning of non-animal nature and of non-human animals commits a naturalist fallacy. Just because non-animal nature and non-human animals function in a certain way does not justify that human beings are responsible for ensuring that they continue to function in that particular way.

Hence the best way to incorporate concerns about the environment into a conception of development may be by acknowledging an anthropocentric bias while at the same time urging that human beings have morally important interests in the preservation of certain natural resources. Indeed, one may even argue that the enjoyment of preserved natural resources constitutes an essential human need. Thereby one can ascribe moral importance to certain parts of the environment on the basis of the conception of sustainable development articulated in the Brundtland Report.

Post-development

After this survey of three prominent normative conceptions of development, this section will present the challenge that post-development theory poses for all of them despite their diversity. Post-development theorists argue – quite radically indeed – that it is necessary to avoid expounding any normative conception of development (cf. Sachs [1992] 2010, Rahnema & Bawtree 1997, Ziai 2007). They hold that every normative conception of development is parochial and thereby undermines societies' political autonomy. Therefore they search for an *alternative to development* rather than justifying further, as they put it, "development alternatives" (Escobar 2012: xiii).

Post-development theorists come to the view that any given normative conception of development is parochial by analysing how the discourse about development emerged in the decade after the Second World War and has been maintained thereafter. They assume that certain norms are constitutive of the development discourse and that the interests of the more powerful actors in world politics have created and shaped these norms in the discourse's formative period. The norms of the development discourse are, for instance, that economic poverty, that is, a lack of material goods, must be viewed as an international political problem and that only a capitalist mode of economic organization is apt in order to solve it (Escobar 2012: 21–55; Rahnema 1991, [1992] 2010; Rist 2008: 8–24). The formulation and recognition of such norms, for instance by Harry Truman in his Four Point Speech cited above, is said to serve the interests of powerful actors like the United States. Such interests include the expansion of export markets for goods and services, the access to natural resources in the so-called Third World, the possibility of making foreign investments there, and the possibility of exerting political influence in order to win the

Cold War (Escobar 2012: 31–34). Thus post-development theorists view the notions of a Third World and of underdevelopment as a "regime of representation" (*ibid.*: 6) and as conceptual "inventions" (*ibid.*: 31) that enable the more powerful actors to exert power through, and to benefit from, a certain kind of discursive practice: "The production of discourse under conditions of unequal power … entails specific constructions of the … Third World subject in/through discourse in ways that allow the exercise of power over it" (*ibid.*: 9).

The parochialism of the discourse about development and, consequently, of any normative conception of development belonging to it, traces back to the fact that the norms which characterize development are Western norms that are part of a "Western epistemological order" (*ibid.*: 7). After all, the development discourse "is the process by which, in the history of the modern West, non-European areas have been systematically organized into, and transformed according to, European constructs" (*ibid.*).

In a similar vein, Esteva holds that any normative conception of development is necessarily parochial, because the very usage of the *concept* of development goes along with a flawed, deterministic – or teleological – philosophy of history of the kind propagated by Hegel and Marx. This philosophy of history has it that all societies must pass through the same, predetermined stages of development (cf. Esteva [1992] 2010: 3–6).

The fact that the concept of development is associated with a deterministic philosophy of history is no coincidence, of course, given that this concept has its origins in biology. In biology development describes the sequence that an organism follows in its unfolding of its inherent potential. So some social theorists have simply transposed the necessity that natural laws impose upon the biological sequential unfolding of an organism to their conceptualization of social development. The upshot is that they regard certain social changes as unavoidable and ascribe to social science the task of identifying the "laws" governing these changes.

The effect of this conceptualization of development is that whenever some societies are further ahead in development and, correspondingly, others are further behind, then those societies that are further behind *must and will* move forward to the stage in which other societies already are. Post-development theorists like Esteva hold that all normative conceptions of development are therefore necessarily parochial because they all claim that the norms of some developed societies are *ipso facto* valid for all of the other societies (*ibid.*: 5). Thereby development creates "an image of the future that is a mere continuation of the past: that is development, a conservative, if not reactionary, myth" (*ibid.*: 21).

Some development scholars attack post-development theorists for solely criticizing the status quo (Pieterse 2000: 188). However, post-development theorists also contribute in several ways to the formulation of action-guiding alternatives to development. Their recognition of the moral importance of the political autonomy of societies is accompanied by a great appreciation of grassroots social movements, decentralized, local decision-making and a sweeping scepticism regarding the claims of "Western" science and of experts of all sorts. Therefore they advocate a form of radical democracy, of the kind that Laclau and Mouffe (2001) propose, which is incompatible with representative forms of democracy and which foresees the democratization of all spheres of social life to be realized on a small scale through direct democracy (cf. Ziai 2004: 1056–57).

This raises the question, however, whether post-development theorists actually formulate an alternative to development rather than simply another normative conception of development. It seems obvious that the ideal of radical democracy cherished by many post-development theorists could be viewed as a substantiation of the abstract notion of development understood as social or human progress. Thus, post-development theorists seem to propose a way of assessing social or human progress based on the perspective of radical democracy.

If post-development theorists are plausibly understood in this way, then their critique of the *concept* and the discourse of development that constructs it is flawed, because it confounds a normative conception of development with the concept of development. This implies that these critiques question merely the normative conceptions of development which subscribe to a teleological philosophy of history and which endorse a conception of economic development that benefits predominantly the more powerful actors in world politics by enabling them to exercise power in certain ways. After all, a normative idea of human or social progress is conceivable without endorsing such a philosophy of history and without committing oneself to an economic development conception. In fact, the conceptions of human and of sustainable development have already transcended the alleged conceptual boundaries that the post-development theorists claim that the development discourse imposes.

In sum, while the post-development perspective helps to keep in mind the decisive challenge to avoid a parochial formulation of what development means, its radical imperative to avoid the usage of the concept of development is ill-founded. This is because the abstract meaning of the concept of development, namely in the sense of human or social progress, is more narrow than the post-development theorists assume and thereby avoids the problems that these theorists associate with it.

Who is responsible for development?

In conclusion, I would like to draw attention to a question that is gaining more and more importance: "Who is responsible for development?" We are now living in an increasingly multipolar world with several economically very powerful countries in the global South. As a result, it is no longer possible – if it ever was – to provide only an account about what development means and then go on to assume that the more powerful countries of the global North possess the major responsibility for realizing it.

To elaborate, consider that in the second half of the previous century the question as to who is responsible for development, for instance along the lines of the conception of sustainable development, which requires the satisfaction of essential human needs in the present, seemed to be answerable rather easily. The rich countries were much richer than the poor countries[10] and almost all of the world's poor people (in terms of income per day below US$1.25) were living in poor countries. In 1990, for example, 93 per cent of the global poor were living in low-income countries (Sumner 2010: 1). Because of the small size of the economies of the poor countries and the large degree of poor people among their population (52 per cent in 1981: Chen & Ravallion 2012: 2), it probably seemed evident that these countries could not possess the major responsibility for realizing essential human needs, because this would burden them too heavily.

By contrast, in light of the rich economies' prowess it was widely believed that a relatively small effort of the rich countries would be sufficient to facilitate development elsewhere.[11] Consequently, the widely shared principle of mutual aid (or of humanity or of beneficence) alone – according to which one is obligated to avoid the suffering of someone else if one is capable of doing so at a relatively low cost to oneself – was thought to be sufficient to morally justify the richer countries' moral obligation to promote development.[12] Consider, for instance, that the former World Bank president McNamara affirmed in 1973 that "The whole of human history has recognized the principle – at least in the abstract – that the rich and the powerful have a moral obligation to assist the poor and the weak" (McNamara 1973: 8). The argument of some moral and political philosophers to the effect that promoting development was a *duty of justice* of the rich countries, thus, simply over-determined the moral justification of the duty to satisfy the essential human needs (Beitz 1999a: 172–73; Pogge 1989: 256 n.18, 264–65; Moellendorf 2002: 61).

In the early twenty-first century the situation looks very different (cf. United Nations Development Programme 2013). Although global interpersonal inequality is rising, inter-country inequality has decreased significantly (Milanovic 2012: 12–13) and nearly three-quarters of the world's poor lived in middle-income countries in 2008 (Sumner 2012: 7). There are also a relatively low number of "aid-dependent" countries, that is, countries who heavily rely on ODA (Klingebiel 2012). In addition, the absolute number of poor people living on less than US $1.25 per day has decreased from 1.94 billion in 1981 to 1.29 billion in 2008, and the share of poor people in low-income countries decreased from 52 to 22 per cent in the same period (Chen & Ravallion 2012: 2). Furthermore, development economists like William Easterly argue compellingly that there is little empirical evidence that ODA contributes significantly to the economic growth of the poorer countries (Easterly 2006; see also Moyo 2009). This may also put into question that ODA is effective in supporting the satisfaction of essential human needs.

The upshot of the increasing multi-polarity of the global economy and the problem of the apparent ineffectiveness of the development practice is that it has become very questionable that the high-income countries, that is, the donors belonging to the DAC, are responsible for development beyond their borders. Middle-income countries that oftentimes provide develop-ment funds themselves, like Brazil, China and South Africa, can no longer be viewed as overly burdened by this task of achieving certain kinds of development at home. Moreover, given the problem of the development practice's apparent ineffectiveness, the high-income countries probably would have to invest much more than they have so far in order to contribute to the realization of development. Hence the provision of ODA can only be justified, if at all, on the basis of the principle of mutual aid for the few cases of the low-income aid-dependent coun-tries. Consequently, the question as to whether the high-income countries have a *duty of justice* to promote development abroad, which would be binding on them even if its fulfilment would require incurring relatively high costs, is currently becoming practically very relevant. Therefore the question as to who is responsible for development in this increasingly multi-polar con-stellation is likely to arouse considerable scholarly interest.

Notes

1 For the distinction between concept and conception, see Rawls (1971: 5), who relies on Hart (1961: 156). Dower (2000: 44) also distinguishes between the concept and different conceptions of develop-ment.

2 Subsequently "normative conceptions of development" refers to normative conceptions of the development of social arrangements.

3 The Colonial Development Act was enacted 1929 in the UK and set up a Colonial Development Fund. Similiarly, the Fonds d'Investissement pour le Développement Economique et Social was created by France in 1946 (cf. Hopper 2012: 4).

4 For the DAC List of ODA Recipients of 2009 and 2010, see OECD 2011d. The DAC ascribes to countries the status as a developing country on the basis of its gross national income (GNI) per capita.

5 Greig *et al.* (2007: 73–99) and Rapley (2007: 13–34, 63–86) provide helpful overviews of this con-ception.

6 For a recent revival of the *big push model*, see J. D. Sachs (2005). Former World Bank chief economist Lin (2012) argues for "new structural economics" as a model for reconsidering development. For a similar, though more complex idea of a "cumulative causation model" that explains how processes can move in the direction of promoting or hindering development, see Myrdal (1957); and for the related idea of a vicious poverty circle or "poverty trap", see Nurske (1953).

7 Sen coined the term "capabilities" in his 1979 Tanner Lecture on Human Value that he delivered at Stanford University, titled "Equality of What?" (Sen [1980] 1997).

8 The ten central capabilities are: life; bodily health; bodily integrity; sense, imagination and thought; emotions; practical reason; affiliation; contact with other species; play; and control over one's environment.

9 Alkire (2005: 2, emphasis added) posits that the capabilities approach to development "argues that the goal of … human development … should be to *expand* the capability that people have to enjoy 'valuable beings and doings'".

10 Following Milanovic (2012: 13), inter-country inequality decreased from 65 Gini points to 55 Gini points in the period between the 1960s and 2006: that is, inter-country inequality has dropped by roughly one-sixth. Gini points range between 0 and 100, and indicate the level of inequality.

11 The 1970 United Nations General Assembly called for the provision of merely 0.7% of the GDP of the DAC donors for ODA and "recognized special importance of the role that can be fulfilled only by official development assistance" (UN General Assembly 1970: paragraph 43).

12 Scanlon (1998: 224) refers to this principle as the Rescue Principle. It is similar to what is often called the principle of "mutual aid", for instance by John Rawls (1971: 109).

15

AID AND CHARITY

Nigel Dower

The scope of this chapter

It is generally assumed, at least by people interested in global ethics, that individuals in rich countries in the "North" have obligations to help alleviate world poverty through supporting relevant charities, and that countries in the North likewise have obligations to provide aid, which, apart from helping with development more generally in poor countries, is focused on programmes that reduce extreme poverty. The arguments that in principle individuals have obligations to do this derive from a number of sources – philosophical theories, religious worldviews, and so on – and can generally be seen as "cosmopolitan" in conception (though the term will not always be used). The argument that countries should do the same, apart from similar cosmopolitan considerations in the background, depends on considerations such as the fact that international agreements have been made – notably the commitment by rich countries made in the 1970s to give 0.7 per cent of Gross National Product (GNP) in aid to poor countries – or the fact that the democratic electorates may mandate such aid policies.

The issues of aid came to be more prominent as global issues after the Second World War. The United Nations Charter (1945) and the Universal Declaration of Human Rights (1948) set out the goal of the progressive realization of human rights including the social and economic rights to the conditions of a decent human life. The United Nations Development Programme (UNDP), along with other specialist agencies such as the Food and Agriculture Organization (FAO), was set up, and set in train the "development decades" in which the twin goals of poverty reduction and reducing the gap between rich and poor countries were axiomatic. Meanwhile, philosophers, theologians and other thinkers were beginning to think hard about the ethical challenge of world poverty, given that a fifth of the world's population was living in extreme poverty in a world increasing in affluence overall in which there was increased capacity for those in some parts of the world to do something about what happened in other parts of the world.

This challenge is *par excellence* a challenge within the field we now call global ethics. If global ethics is about the ethical relations that people have across the globe, then the questions "What obligations do individuals in one country have towards individuals in other countries in respect to reducing their poverty?" and "Why do we have such obligations?" are global ethics questions – even if, earlier on, they would not have been described in this way.

Nevertheless, there are numerous difficulties and objections raised about aid programmes, whether those directed by charities which are non-governmental organizations (NGOs), national governments or international agencies, and whether the aid programmes are humanitarian responses to disasters such as famines or floods or forms of development assistance designed to enable poor people to be less poor on a sustainable basis. These difficulties arise from several different kinds of consideration. The objections to the ethical obligation to give aid fall into three broad categories. First, there is no general duty to give aid to help alleviate poverty in another country because there is no general duty to do this in one's own society: one's general "minimalist" conception of morality does not include this. Second, although it may be a feature of an ethical code that one does have general duties to help others needing help, this only applies to one's own society. We do not live, ethically speaking, in a global society or community (the challenge of relativism), or, if we do, it is in some attenuated sense, and the ethical claims are much weaker than those within our own community (the challenge of communitarianism). Third, the giving of trans-boundary aid is in one way or another inappropriate.

There are a number of reasons for this inappropriateness. First, aid does not generally work: the empirical record is a dismal catalogue of failures. This claim is often backed by more complex considerations which tend to explain not only why this is so but why it often has negative consequences. Second, aid cannot work because aid by its nature creates dependency whereas genuine development that really helps poor people reduces dependency and encourages autonomy. Third, from an ecological perspective it is disastrous since it keeps more people alive, and this puts strains on ecological carrying capacity and only stores up more suffering from absolute poverty in the future. Fourth, aid is often socially or politically counterproductive, for instance contributing to upsetting settled social orders, or contributing to the continuation of illegal regimes, or helping, no doubt inadvertently, to prolong armed conflict. Fifth, aid is generally ethically compromised because the means and further objectives involved are often ethically dubious; there may be, for instance, further foreign policy agendas in official aid and it comes with conditions (the "tied aid" or "conditionalities" problem), or, in the case of NGO charities, with further ethical, political or religious objectives. Sixth, focus on aid is an inappropriate distraction from the real challenges, because the real focus should be on reforming the whole international economic system. Seventh, even if some aid is satisfactory, most aid falls foul of one or more of the considerations given above, so the claim that people – or charities or governments – ought generally to give aid, given that it is based on their mistaken beliefs about appropriate means and ends, cannot be made.

A full discussion of the ethics of charity and aid would need to consider the positive arguments for aid, for instance examining different ethical theories such as utilitarianism, Kantianism and human rights theories and comparing them, as well as defending the whole global ethics approach against the alternative approaches of ethical minimalism, relativism and communitarianism (and related approaches in international relations theory). However, because these issues are all fully explored elsewhere in the handbook, they are not systematically discussed here (though some reference to them will be made in the course of replying to the criticisms later). What this chapter focuses on are the various types of criticism of aid that are made and the ethical discussions which they generate.

My strategy in this chapter is to consider each criticism of aid in turn. In each case I shall argue that the criticism certainly points up an issue relating to some forms of aid but that this does nothing to confirm a general conclusion that aid generally is not appropriate or that it ought not to be carried out. Sometimes the aid "sceptic", by availing himself of a number of the criticisms, may give the impression that generally aid is not appropriate and that the cumulative impact of these criticisms is that we can have no confidence that aid programmes we might support or advance are really appropriate. This scepticism is not warranted. Once we are aware of the problems, we can, duly informed and with reasonable diligence, distinguish what is and what is not appropriate and can support and advocate support for appropriate aid strategies.

Replies to various objections that aid is inappropriate

As indicated earlier, this chapter takes as its starting point the claim that we do have significant obligations to help alleviate poverty (and so *inter alia* we ought to support charities to do their work with donations of time and service, and at the level of political engagement get governments to adopt appropriate aid policies). However, even if these arguments – or at least one of them for any particular thinker – are seen as right or acceptable, we face a series of hurdles. Addressing these hurdles is important for both theoretical reasons and practical reasons. Theoretically, addressing them brings out the ethical complexity of thinking about aid (and adds, as it were, ethical colour to the main positive arguments). Practically, it helps to defuse many of the reasons, often unvoiced and below the surface, which give people pause in regard to supporting aid programmes. Thus the discussion should be of interest both to those who accept the claim that we have in practice significant obligations to give aid by making their defence of it more nuanced, but also to those who come to the issue from an initially sceptical point of view and might move from a position of negative criticism to one of constructive criticism and a greater willingness not to dismiss aid as such even if they have good reason to reject certain forms of aid. (For a balanced assessment of the successes and failures in aid see Riddell 2008.)

Aid does not work

It cannot be denied that many aid projects do not succeed either in achieving what, on their own terms, they set out to achieve – whether through incompetence or through corruption with the benefits ending up in the wrong hands – or in achieving what, from a third-person point of view, they ought to be achieving, because, for instance, they are going about the reduction of poverty in the wrong way. Four points need to be made about this commonly voiced objection.

First, unless the claim is that no aid works, then the conclusion cannot be drawn that we do not in practice have a duty to give aid. If we thought that no aid worked, then indeed, given the Kantian principle that "ought implies can", since we cannot effectively help, we have no duty to do so. But if one thinks that some kinds of aid do not work, then the argument must be that people ought to support those kinds of aid that do work. Generally speaking, people choose the charities they choose because of their track record.

Second, the claim that aid does not work, though it looks like an empirical claim, often conceals certain value assumptions which are different from those informing the project. What is success for one thinker is failure for another. For instance, a programme may well lead to more food being grown or a higher standard of health being achieved and it may well be judged successful by the agency promoting it, but if it fails really to empower local people or it undermines local cultural values by imposing "Western" assumptions about development, then from the point of view of the critic it may still not actually be successful. (I take this up again later.) So for any given thinker, no doubt some aid projects are bound to fail, even if others may be successful, given her criteria.

Third, it is an advantage for the advocate of aid-giving if she can show not merely that some aid projects work but that most work, precisely because a perception by those not already committed to aid that most aid does not work leads to inertia. For someone ill-informed about aid the thought "most aid does not work" may lead to the inference "therefore it is likely that this aid project will not work, so why risk my money on something uncertain?" This is a poor inference but to counter it, one has to show either that this project is not like most, or that most do not fail.

Fourth, the claim that aid does not work is actually generally shorthand for a more complex claim that in various ways aid actually causes harm or negative consequences. It is one thing to argue that the donors do not have a duty to give aid if it does no good, quite another to say that we ought not to give aid because it actually does harm – or, given that almost any complex human activity will have some negative but nevertheless acceptable consequences, because the amount of harm done is greater than the good done or the amount of harm done is sufficient to undermine the justification of doing it, whatever good may also be achieved through doing it. The later objections all focus on one or other negative consequence of aid or of certain forms of it.

Counterproductive: the creation of dependency

One particular objection often voiced, but with particular vigour by Peter Bauer, is that development assistance fails because those who are helped become dependent on the aid (Bauer 1984). Since the aim of a development project should be to enable the poor to take control of their lives and thus have autonomy, aid is almost by definition counterproductive. In a sense aid cannot work. The kind of example that is sometimes cited is a village which, given its inability to grow its own food, becomes dependent on the continuing arrival of food parcels. More recently, Dambiso Moyo has taken a similar line in regard to the systemic aid by governments or international agencies such as the World Bank and IMF, namely that the vast injections of aid into African economies have perpetuated relationships of dependency not at individual levels but at institutional levels (Moyo 2009). I shall make three observations about this kind of argument.

First, as a general objection to development aid, its real target has to be long-term development assistance rather than emergency assistance. Responding to floods, earthquakes and the like does not pretend to do more than provide, at least initially, short-term relief. Such actions in saving lives as such do not create dependency, any more than a Good Samaritan act in helping a wounded man in the street or a motorist to get his car going creates persons who are "dependent".

Second, although I happen to agree that a major part of the rationale for aid ought to be the empowerment of the poor (see e.g. O'Neill's Kantian approach in O. O'Neill 1986), it has to be accepted that if an aid agency saw its goal as enabling people to stay alive by providing them with food on a long-term basis or providing ongoing medical interventions to keep people alive, then, on their own terms, it would have succeeded if the people helped remained alive but also dependent.

Third, if it is the case that development projects can be so designed and delivered that they do precisely empower the poor, then it is by no means the case that aid as such creates dependency. If some does and some does not, we simply need to know the difference and choose accordingly. "Simply" is perhaps misleading, since it requires hard work to become properly informed about what aid projects achieve. What, however, are we to make of the large-scale condemnation of multilateral aid programmes by Moyo, her call for such aid to come to an end and for whatever takes its place to get rid of African institutional dependency and to be premised on African nations having equal status? A lot depends upon whether and to what extent one believes the mindsets of people on the World Bank, IMF or national departments of international development can be changed – an optimism/pessimism issue linked to the parallel question of whether and to what extent, realistically, models of development can be successfully advocated that are not dependent on economic growth and/or neo-liberal assumptions (see, e.g., the work of the International Development Ethics Association at http://developmentethics.org).

Counterproductive: ecological limits and human harm in the long run

In the 1970s a particular argument was made well known through Garrett Hardin's writings. He argued that keeping people alive with food aid merely compounded problems in the future because even more poor people being kept alive will put more pressure on the land beyond its "carrying capacity". The "case against aiding the poor" was therefore made (Hardin 1974). There are really two strands to this argument: first, a more general argument that we should only help if it does not hurt; second, a more specific justification for the claim that it does not help in terms of ecological limits. We could actually accept the first without the second.

The main argument is that if helping the poor now leads to other people later on suffering, we ought not to help them. An ethical objection to this might be that it is wrong to sacrifice the needs of the present in order to avoid harm to others in the future, since the suffering now is known and something we can do something about, whereas the suffering in the future is probable and its extent will be subject to various contingencies not as much in our control (including the possibility of solutions to the problems not now known). How we strike the ethical balance between present and future is a big topic in its own right, and central to the whole "future generations" issue in environmental ethics.

But still it is the empirical claim that is the main issue here. The argument that aid merely exacerbates problems later on in the future only makes sense if one focuses on emergency aid alone, such as food aid (or indeed medical intervention) that simply keeps people alive. Simply doing this without creating better life conditions in the future would indeed be likely to perpetuate extreme poverty. The ethical argument for alleviating poverty by providing emergence assistance and food handouts, although it makes sense in itself in humanitarian terms, is much strengthened in the context of long-term development projects through which the very poor people can escape their poverty.

What of Hardin's claim about populations growing and putting pressure on ecological carrying capacity? First, this is questionable on empirical grounds. If, as I suggested above, aid involves both emergency assistance and long-term development, then, as is commonly recognized, there is a positive correlation between genuine development for the poor and halting population growth. It is often called the "demographic transition" argument. On this view the main way to limit population growth is through creating access to reliable social/health services: this leads to smaller families, since it is no longer rational from the point of view of the poor to have large numbers of children as an insurance policy for old age or illness. This is not to overlook the significance, particularly for women, of the availability of birth control options. This option is controversial because of opposition in certain cultural traditions, just as the issue of population, of which the birth control issue is a part, is also controversial.

Hardin's claim that the poor are in danger of exceeding the carrying capacity of the land on which they live is itself highly controversial since it smacks of a certain moral arbitrariness. It all depends on what is meant by carrying capacity and what units should be seen as having it. Aiken, for example, takes issue with this claim (Aiken 1996). After all, cities or whole countries, such a densely populated country like the UK, can be said to dramatically exceed their carrying capacity, but this is not usually seen as a problem because of their economic power and relationships with what lies outside them – near and far. Still, the point needs to be acknowledged that at a global level, there are carrying capacity limits which increasing populations along with high levels – let alone increasing levels – of consumption will come up against, where the resultant heightened competition and conflict will *inter alia* make the poor even more vulnerable.

Counterproductive: unwelcome social consequences

Most aid programmes, certainly those that go beyond humanitarian assistance at times of disasters, have some consequences, sometimes considerable, for the society where the programme takes place: changes in social relations including power relations, changes in knowledge and understanding including various new kinds of knowledge and skills introduced, changes in technology used to sustain life, changes in worldviews including people's religious attitudes, and so on. These are often deliberate and positive, sometimes deliberate and negative, sometimes negative but not deliberate, occasionally positive but not deliberate or positive and both deliberate and not deliberate. The introduction of a well, done for good reasons and no doubt welcome to the village, may alter social relations, as women no longer have to walk miles to collect water (which would be positive), but it could alter power relations over who controls the use of the well (which may be negative). Certain styles of development based on economic entrepreneurship may displace or weaken more communitarian social relations. New forms of knowledge and technology may undermine traditional knowledge and technologies. Development paradigms based on secular models of human well-being may weaken traditional religious values.

If these effects are seen as unwelcome – for instance, more unequal social relations, lessening of communal values, disvaluing of older forms of knowledge, or weakening traditional religious values – then it is either the case that the aid agencies do not expect these consequences or they expect them and regard them as positive changes, whereas others criticize them from another standpoint. The criticisms may stem from two kinds of worry.

First, by not taking the traditional social and cognitive framework sufficiently into account, the programmes are less effective in delivering what they set out to do; local knowledge and the worldviews that go with it contain much sound wisdom that is lost in embracing the external epistemology introduced (see e.g. chapters in Lee *et al.* 2000). Schumacher's famous thesis "small is beautiful" (Schumacher 1974) was very much about stressing the value of "intermediate" or "appropriate" technologies that extended and developed from traditional technologies as opposed to high-tech solutions and the mindsets that went with them.

Second, the programmes fail to account sufficiently strongly for the *inherent* importance of these traditional frameworks quite apart from their effectiveness. Something significant is lost with Westernization or modernization, especially if it is introduced fast and insensitively. This point can be made whether one is inclined to relativism in regard to values, which denies the universality of values (and with it a coherent account of trans-boundary responsibility), or one is inclined to a broad "universalism with diversity" which acknowledges diverse ways in which human well-being can be authentically lived (while acknowledging a common framework including the idea of global responsibility which needs to underpin aid anyway).

It will be clear that often there can be no agreement over whether certain consequences are positive or negative – it largely depends on the values one thinks are appropriate to development or rather, since in turn the justification of any model of development lies in this, the very notion of human well-being.

Counterproductive: unwelcome political consequences

It is sometimes argued that aid delivered in countries where there is armed conflict has far more serious negative consequences than merely not delivering appropriate development programmes.

As Linda Polman argued, examples would be aid missions in war-torn countries, whether it is the UN in Bosnia (where much of aid supplies were taken by the military groups), or various independent aid agencies in camps in Goma in Zaire (now the Democratic Republic of Congo), where the militant Hutus in the camps derived financial support from aid and were able to carry on their attacks in Rwanda, or Sri Lanka where the Tamil Tigers would expect their cut (Polman 2010).

Clearly the objection to aid here is one directed to a very specific context in which aid is given – namely armed conflict – so it is not an objection to aid as such. However, in some respects this situation simply puts into sharper relief problems with many aid programmes. First, there is the diversion of aid meant for humanitarian assistance into the pockets of others who use it for other purposes – a problem certainly not restricted to war situations. Second, there is the fact that such aid has significant political impacts on how things go in the area where the aid is given. Aid is rarely neutral in its political impacts, whatever the intentions of the aid-givers.

But the peculiarly horrifying aspect of aid in these circumstances is that aid contributes to the prolongation of armed conflicts, and this is seen as being a powerful reason for objecting to it. Wars and armed conflicts are, if anything is, "anti-development". (Indeed, as I have argued elsewhere (Dower 2009), since war undermines human well-being for almost all those affected by it, any argument for aid must be an argument for minimizing the conditions of war and promoting the conditions of peace.)

There are, however, three different responses to such an objection. One would be to stop giving aid with all the implied callousness of simply abandoning poor people caught in conflict to their fate. Another would be to play down one's responsibility for the evils that, after all, other agents perform, and to focus on what humanitarian aid can achieve, acknowledging that in war situations a certain percentage of one's aid will get diverted one way or another. A third response is to take a middle route between the other two responses, and to see one's humanitarian efforts in the context of a wider political commitment by others – mediators and behind them the international community – to find negotiated solutions to such conflicts, and to advocate the latter as the framework within which their humanitarian efforts are made. (This is parallel to the point made earlier that short-term aid only really makes sense within the framework of longer-term development assistance.) A fourth response would be to abandon one's commitment to neutrality and see one's humanitarian efforts as contributing to one side in a struggle (consider the case of Médecins Sans Frontières, discussed again in the next section). It is one thing, however, not to mind if one's humanitarian efforts happen to help one side in a struggle (it is welcomed but that is not the reason for one's doing so), another actively to support a group where supporting it is part of one's intention. In the latter case it ceases to be aid in the commonly understood sense (in just the same way as military aid given by governments as part of their "aid" programmes is regarded with scepticism by many).

Wrong values and priorities: aid is generally ethically compromised

Critics of official aid may point to one or more of the following features of official aid. The conditionality of aid is often criticized as a problem in that either aid is tied to certain conditions such as the provision of goods and services from the donor country, or certain conditions need to be accepted by the recipient country as a condition of entering into a "partnership" agreement. Such conditions include respect for human rights, the need for transparency and non-corruption, democratic values, the value of the free market or environmental sustainability. These two aspects of conditionality reflect two more general worries: the fact that aid is seen an instrument of foreign policy so that the countries selected or the kinds of aid given (such as military assistance) reflect the geopolitical interests of the donor country, and the fact that aid is done in such a way that it projects inappropriate wider values: the accusation of cultural imperialism may have been associated in the past with the spread of Christian values, but now it is more often to do with, as noted above, things like promoting human rights standards.

Such criticisms may be made in two ways. It may be that conditionalities, pursuit of geopolitical interests and projection of certain values all shape or affect the way aid is generally delivered so that aid fails to deliver, or deliver as effectively as it might, the goals which, from the point of view of the critic, it ought to deliver. Such appropriate policies are ones that promoted development of people in general (rather than, say, bolstering rich elites) and in particular reduced extreme poverty (see e.g. Sen 1999, Pogge 2002). However, it may also be argued that the problem is with conditionality *per se* or with aid being an arm of foreign policy *per se* or with the projection of values *per se*. What is wrong is not the distorting *effects* of these features, but the features themselves. This would be a more radical critique.

The first point to note in response to the more modest critique about reduced effectiveness of aid in terms of what aid ought to achieve is that again it is not clear that all – or even most – aid does not do what aid is meant to do, given these circumstantial factors. Just because aid has conditionalities of various kinds does not prevent it from actually enabling appropriate development to occur. Furthermore, in so far as these factors are seen as negative, the argument can be made that this shows that multilateral aid channelled through UN agencies is to be preferred, as it is less likely to reflect conditionality, geopolitical interests of particular counties or inappropriate global values. We need to say "less likely" because there is always still the danger that these features will be present if these bodies are dominated by certain countries.

Second, we need to grasp the nettle of the more radical critique and say that not all values are inappropriate as universal values; not all forms of conditionality are bad, not all forms of foreign policy objective are in themselves unreasonable or unreasonably reflected in aid programmes. If we accept global ethics then the task is sorting out what is and what is not genuinely universal. As noted above, a "contextual universalism" is needed that provides a suitably "thin" account of human well-being along with a cosmopolitan account of trans-boundary responsibility or solidarity.

Not all conditionalities are bad. If, for instance, an aid programme is conditional on the recipients accepting a sustainability feature for projects, or on a focus on poverty reduction, such conditionalities seem appropriate. (If aid were given to a country to spend just as it will – for instance to bolster the elite and to neglect the rest of the country if the rulers so wanted – most people would be very quick to criticize such lack of reasonable safeguards.)

In regard to the issue of foreign policy there is a further consideration which shows that the way we handle the ethics of government aid is more complex than for private aid. There are two other factors, noted at the beginning, which determine the ethical satisfactoriness of a country's aid policy (sometimes pulling the same way, sometimes in the opposite direction): first the democratic mandate within a country, and second the framework of obligations a country has in relation to other countries in international relations.

Broadly speaking, the character of a country's aid policy – its levels, its general objectives and how it is done, whether or not it should further the national interest – ought to reflect what electorates want or regard as reasonable. A government that seriously stepped out of line with that would be criticized. (A corollary to this is that if we want a change in aid policy to, for instance, a more cosmopolitan approach, then we have to persuade fellow citizens to accept this and want their government to reflect it.)

Furthermore, countries enter into agreements with other countries, bilaterally and multilaterally, to deliver aid of certain kinds and at certain levels. The principle *pacta sunt servanda* ("treaties ought to be honoured") gives some moral weight to what countries have agreed to do; for instance, if rich countries agreed in the 1970s to give 0.7 per cent GNP in aid, then that itself indicates an obligation to do so.

The point here is not that democratic theory or international relations norms trump the ethical issue – far from it. For any cosmopolitan who thinks that generally we ought to be much more generous with aid, it remains appropriate to make the argument that countries ought to do so and do so in certain ways, where what is actually done falls short of this. Rather, these considerations make the picture more complex, and suggest that it is unreasonable to expect government aid to be entirely free from factors such as conditionalities, foreign policy implications or value projection – if these are what electorates want or what the international community has agreed upon. It remains the case, however, that often aid policy, like the rest of foreign policy, cannot be justified in these ways and is simply to be criticized as inappropriate or wrong.

When we turn to NGOs a parallel criticism can be made – namely that NGOs pursue a wide range of different objectives, pursue objectives in very different ways, and, given that most NGOs are based in the North, often project certain values which may be culturally biased. Curiously (since it is hardly mentioned), what NGOs do is always characterized by some form of conditionality, implied at the very least by the criteria they use to decide which projects to engage in and with whom. However, although it is inevitable that, for any given aid advocate, what some NGOs do will be unacceptable in relation to means, goals and/or underlying values, it is likely that at least some do things well and probably most NGOs will be regarded as tending in the right direction, so the argument that we ought to help alleviate world poverty will find practical expression in one or more charities to support. But this fact that NGOs vary considerably in their goals, means and values – and therefore understand appropriate aid in rather different ways – raises a more general question: "What is one's position vis-à-vis the range of different views?" I return to this question at the end of this chapter.

Wrong values and priorities: need for institutional reform

Focus on aid, it may be said, is an inappropriate distraction from the real challenge, because the real focus should be on reforming the whole international economic system. This argument is parallel to the argument that within a country the action of charities in trying to meet the needs of disadvantaged groups acts as a palliative and therefore, by making things a little better, dissipates the energy for serious reform of the social system that allows people to be in these disadvantaged situations. What is really needed in order to tackle world poverty is serious reform of the whole international system, both politically and economically. Focusing on aid and the ethical requirements of aid deflects from this.

In the domestic setting the debate is sometimes cast in terms of the serious requirements of justice as the implementation of social and economic rights through legislation and appropriate institutions as opposed to the merely voluntary and legally not enforceable expression of charity which is of limited effectiveness. (Such acts of charity may or may not be understood by volunteers as a kind of duty rather than as lying beyond duty (supererogatory), but they are of secondary importance.) Likewise, internationally, decisions to give aid by governments, and even more so what NGOs do, are simply palliative acts of benevolence, not requirements of global justice such as through the implementation of international human rights law.

This argument needs rebuttal in two ways, the one theoretical, the other practical. First, however, it needs to be conceded or even advocated that the solution to world poverty is not going to occur merely through the concerted actions of NGOs or the aid policies of governments, acting either bilaterally or multilaterally. Serious changes are also needed in the way the world economy functions and in how strengthened international law and institutions can give proper expression to everyone's social and economic rights. But it is a serious mistake to characterize the argument for the latter as a matter of justice and rights in contrast to the arguments for aid by NGOs and governments as not being a matter of justice and rights. Commonly the latter are seen as a matter of beneficence, reducing harm as an expression of doing good, where that beneficence is seen as either beyond duty or as another less demanding form of duty. It can be argued, however, as I would argue, that the ethical motivation for aid is identical to that for wider institutional reforms. They can both be grounded in concern for global justice or human rights as discussed above.

Second, at a more pragmatic level, there is no reason at all to think that vigorous "civil society" or voluntary sector commitment to social causes, either local or global, necessarily leads to the diminution of public commitment to institutional and political reform, or that arguments for better government aid undermine arguments for global economic reform. The very same people who are involved in voluntary sector working for social causes, local or global, may very well be concerned with trying to make laws and political institutions more effective in dealing with the same issues. There is no inconsistency in someone who with the one hand helps someone now in need and with the other hand campaigns for institutional changes that would meet those needs more effectively in the future (or even led to that kind of voluntary response to need no longer being required; see e.g. A. Wellman 2005). Even less is there any inconsistency in welcoming the fact that some put their efforts into a Third World charity and others campaign for reforming the international economic system. This leads to the next objection I wish to consider.

The prevalence of errors in aid thinking

I consider this objection last both because it is not a standard objection but rather one I have come to formulate in response to many informal discussions of aid issues, and because it is of a different kind from the others, a kind of meta-objection built on the claim that most aid falls foul of one or more of the considerations given above. Since aid is given and supported because, *inter alia*, those involved have certain beliefs about what goals should underlie aid, what means are effective and what means are ethically acceptable, and since there is a wide variety of beliefs about goals and means, it is bound to be the case that often what is done in the name of aid ought not to be done from the point of view of anyone thinking about aid who has her own view about appropriate goals and means. The point here is not that there is no ethically appropriate way of giving aid; someone may well believe that aid ought to be given in certain ways (and maybe supports a charity that has the same beliefs). However, given that such beliefs inform aid, most aid that is given ought not to be given.

We have already seen in the criticisms often made of official aid how there may be many kinds of objection made to what is actually done. So although theoretically government aid could be just fine, in practice it often (or almost always) is not. Here I want to reinforce the point by looking at a couple of examples of difference between NGOs. An organization like the International Planned Parenthood Federation promotes the use of contraception, whereas pro-life agencies are utterly opposed to that kind of aid. The International Red Cross goes into conflict situations with a strict observance of neutrality, whereas an organization like Médecins Sans Frontières enters a conflict zone and takes sides. Supporters of child sponsorship schemes are often criticized by others who prefer programmes that change the lives of whole communities.

The claim that most aid ought not to be given because it is based on false or inadequate empirical or ethical understandings is on the face of it bizarre – in much the same way as would be the view that, given the fact that there are many different views about justice or religion, people ought not to do what they do in order to practise justice or express their religious faith. But there is an interesting challenge here, which is both practical and theoretical.

Practically, it is rather important, if one makes the general claim that people ought to support aid, that one can show that most aid efforts, even if some are not so efficient or not as well thought out, or have goals that one is not entirely happy with, do *tend in the right direction*; that it is better that all these forms of aid happen than that they do not, even if it would be even better if they were not flawed in these ways. It is also practically important that one acknowledges that different situations require different responses (neutrality is right in some contexts but not in others) or that different skills in donors make different forms of aid appropriate (maybe child sponsorship is appropriate for some situations while most aid needs to be more broadly based).

Theoretically, we need to embrace a way of thinking about moral judgements which is less in terms of saying some forms of action, in this case in aid programmes, are either right or wrong, and more in terms of saying that they have gradations. We can on this view say that people should generally give aid – it is good that they do – even though what they do is not really what one advocates or would do in the circumstances. What I have just said takes us to the edge of a big field in metaethics about how we assess what others do generally in the light of their different ethical understandings of what they do, and how far we welcome actions that converge out of divergent worldviews and ethical theories. The willingness to be generally "for" aid despite its manifest pitfalls and to be energized and to encourage others to be energized to address world poverty partly depends on embracing this diversity of ethical starting points.

Conclusion

The last point leads to a more general claim about global ethics which the issue of aid well illustrates. Arguments for transboundary obligations are arguments for part of a certain normative content to an acceptable global ethic. If an argument for one of these positions coupled with further arguments about how to implement this in the world is then seen as the basis for taking issue with other arguments for different contents for a global ethic and different modes of implementation, then the arena of global ethics becomes yet another arena for much theoretical disputation (fun for some as that may be) but in a sense a lost opportunity for serious collective action to tackle urgent global problems such as world poverty (but also climate change, conflict and so on). But if the argument for a global ethic is part of an argument for the adoption of various global ethics with different thinkers formulating their principles, goals and means in somewhat different ways, and one welcomes most of these (though not all of them), then there is a greater hope that global problems are actually tackled in an adequate way.

16

IMMIGRATION

Sarah Fine and Andrea Sangiovanni

Across the world, large numbers of people who wish to move to another country are prevented or deterred from doing so by immigration controls, and many have moved or attempted to move *despite* such controls. To what extent should states have a right to exclude would-be immigrants from taking up residence (rather than merely from entering, e.g., as tourists)? Is the widely accepted belief that states have an expansive right to exclude would-be immigrants from settling[1] morally justifiable? In this chapter, we will explore four arguments in favour of the right to exclude: the *freedom of association argument*, the *liberal nationalist argument*, the *Kantian argument* and the *special obligations argument*. Our aim will be neither to provide a comprehensive survey of possible arguments for the right to exclude (there are, obviously, many more than four) nor a conclusive argument for or against any one of them. Rather, our aim is to canvass four of the arguments that we believe carry the most promise for establishing the right, and try to articulate their main strengths and weaknesses. Along the way, we will also make several distinctions that we believe require more attention than they have so far received, and that should help in bringing to light the main hurdles facing any argument for the right to exclude.

The "pure" case

We begin by discussing five assumptions that will help structure and limit our search for a viable right to exclude. While such assumptions may seem, at first glance, to assume away some of the most difficult problems at the root of current debates on immigration, they will enable us (as we will explain in more detail below) to focus on the normative core of arguments for the right to exclude. With that normative core in place, we will then be able to take a much clearer view of what the consequences of relaxing our assumptions might be.

First, we will not discuss refugees. We assume, for the sake of argument, that would-be immigrants are not suffering from severe forms of political, cultural, religious, personal or social persecution in their country of origin. Second, we assume that would-be immigrants are not suffering from severe economic deprivation. They are not so poor as to be in the kind of need that would trigger, at the very least, a duty of rescue or aid. Third, we assume that the number of those seeking entry is neither so large as to overwhelm the capacity of the receiving state to maintain the provision of central public goods (such as public security, education, access to healthcare, and so on) nor so small as to have a negligible impact on the host society. Fourth, we assume that would-be immigrants have a strong interest in residing in the host state – strong enough for the choice to take up residence to be at least more than a mere "whim". This interest could be based in the fact that would-be immigrants residing in the host state would have, for example, significantly better job opportunities, greater scope for religious or social association, or more wide-reaching political affinities with residents and citizens than they would in their country of origin. Fifth, we assume that would-be immigrants are not seeking to immigrate in order to reunite with their families.

Proceeding under this five-fold restriction is important for two reasons. First, it helps us to isolate the core of the normative case for the right to exclude. If the right to exclude has any weight at all in an all-things-considered calculation of whether it is morally permissible for a receiving state to restrict access, then focusing on this "pure" case – stripped as it is of further complicating factors – will aid us in assessing the grounds and force of the right with as clear a mind as possible. Put another way, to determine whether states have an *all-things-considered* right to exclude in a particular range of cases, we do best to begin our enquiry by asking: under what conditions, if any, do states even have a *pro tanto* right to exclude (a right determined by holding constant further complicating factors, such as the ones enumerated above)? If we are able to establish such a right, we can then wonder, in a second step: how weighty is this right? Is it weighty enough, for example, to override interests deriving from, for example, economic deprivation, family reunification, or political and religious persecution?

Second, and closely related, abstracting away (for the moment) from cases involving severe economic deprivation, political and religious persecution, and family reunification can help us to avoid confusing a *qualified* right to exclude and an *unqualified* one. Those who hold an *unqualified* right to exclude treat states' right to exclude as a "trump" over all (or almost all) competing interests. When confronted with such an unqualified claim, many find it much too strong. Surely, they will say, those who have nowhere else to go, who will starve if they are not let in, who have been separated from their families, have a claim to enter (and take up residence) that no state can rightfully deny. It becomes tempting to conclude that states do not have a right to exclude *simpliciter*, and that, indeed, a policy of open borders (or nearly open borders) is the only way to give due consideration to such weighty interests. The problem is that the conclusion does not follow. At most, the argument demonstrates that an *unqualified* right to exclude is unpalatable. What it does not establish is that a more *qualified* right to exclude does not exist – a right, that is, that outweighs or overrides a range of competing interests, but not all such interests. Focusing on the pure case thus will help us to determine more carefully the weight, nature and grounds of states' claimed right to exclude by establishing whether a more qualified right exists. If there is at least *some* right to exclude (however qualified), training our gaze on the core case will aid us in finding it.

It is also important to emphasize that the right to exclude which we focus on here is to be understood as a *moral* right. What *legal* rights might best promote or recognize or implement the moral right (if there is one) will not be discussed here. In this chapter, we do not discuss or defend any such legal rights, focusing only on the moral case.

We proceed as follows. In the next section, we discuss the *freedom of association argument*; in the following section, we turn to the *liberal nationalist argument*. The subsequent section focuses on the *Kantian argument*, and the final section on the *argument from special obligations*.

The freedom of association argument

One potentially promising line of argument in defence of the state's *pro tanto* right to exclude would-be immigrants from settling is that states enjoy a right to self-determination, which includes the freedom to associate, and, in turn, that the right to exclude outsiders is a constitutive element of the freedom to associate. This argument, which has been advanced by Christopher Heath Wellman, is potentially promising for a number of reasons (see Wellman 2008, Wellman & Cole 2011). First, as Wellman argues, the freedom to associate is a freedom that people take very seriously. What is more, it seems to include "the right not to associate and even, in many cases, the right to disassociate" (Wellman 2008: 109). Take the case of marriage. Marital freedom of association seems to include the right to marry a willing partner, the right not to marry a specific prospective partner, and the right to remain unmarried (but no right to marry unwilling potential partners) (Wellman 2008, Fine 2010).

Second, the connection between freedom of association and the right to exclude is already familiar to us. Within the context of civil society, associations of various shapes, sizes and purposes – sports clubs, youth groups, religious communities, and so on – often claim the right to exclude unwanted outsiders (and indeed even a right to exclude unwanted insiders). And they claim that right as part of their (and/or their members') freedom to associate. Is not the same sort of argument applicable to the context of the state and would-be immigrants? Wellman certainly thinks it is:

> just as an individual has a right to determine whom (if anyone) he or she would like to marry, a group of fellow-citizens has a right to determine whom (if anyone) it would like to invite into its political community. And just as an individual's freedom of association entitles him or her to remain single, a state's freedom of association entitles it to exclude all foreigners from its political community.
>
> *(Wellman 2008: 116)*

Third, one can defend an individual's or a group's freedom to associate, without condoning everything that they choose to do with that freedom, just as one can defend a person's right to freedom of speech without condoning what the person chooses to say. In a similar way, Wellman defends what he sees as the state's right to freedom of association, and its attendant right to exclude outsiders, while at the same time noting that, "if anything", he is "personally inclined toward more open borders" (*ibid.*: 116–17). This may seem an intuitively attractive position, then, because a state's decisions about who to exclude might not be to our liking, they might not be commendable, they might not be in the best interests of particular would-be immigrants – indeed, they might not even seem to reflect what is in the state's best interests – but we might still think that states are entitled to make those sorts of decisions for themselves.

Fourth, it looks as though we already grant that *states* have the right to freedom of association, in so far as we consider it impermissible to force them against their will to associate with other groups and institutions, or for one state forcibly to annex another or part of another. As Wellman writes,

> no one believes that it would be permissible to force Canada into NAFTA or to coerce Slovenia to join the EU. (Of course, nor may Canada or Slovenia unilaterally insert themselves into these associations!) And the reason it is wrong to forcibly include these countries is because Canada's and Slovenia's rights to self-determination entitle them to associate (or not) with other countries as they see fit.
>
> *(Ibid.: 112)*

In that case, is not the state's right to exclude would-be immigrants just another aspect of the state's right to freedom of association?

One possible line of response is to grant that states may have a *pro tanto* right to exclude would-be immigrants from settling within their territories, in virtue of states' rights to freedom of association, but then to emphasize that this does not get us very far, because the *pro tanto* right can be overridden by competing claims (*ibid.*: 19). The opponent might argue that the freedom to associate, important as it may be, is but one among a number of competing freedoms and other significant values. In the civil society context it does not always take precedence when it clashes with other values, goals and interests. For instance, sometimes states decide that it is legitimate to prohibit certain associations from excluding prospective members according to discriminatory criteria (e.g. on the basis of their sex or ethnicity).[2] Freedom of association is valuable, but it is not the only thing that is valuable. One might consider that, in the civil society context, non-members' interests in equality of opportunity and the state's interests in furthering the goals of sex equality are also important (Gutmann 1998). Similarly, in the context of states and would-be immigrants, we encounter a clash of values, goals and interests, and we should not just assume that the state's *pro tanto* right to exclude will override many or even most such competing considerations. Perhaps, for instance, one might think that individuals enjoy a right to freedom of movement, and that this is sufficiently weighty to override the state's interests in exclusion.[3]

Here, though, proponents of the freedom of association argument might respond that, while it is possible that the state's freedom to associate occasionally may be outweighed by *some* especially strong competing considerations, it is certainly not going to be outweighed in the "pure" case under discussion, with respect to would-be immigrants who are not in desperate need. In a conflict between the interests of someone wishing to immigrate in search of a better standard of living (for example) and the interests of the state in freedom of association, the interests of the state should take precedence. In fact, Wellman goes so far as to argue that, as long as states discharge their obligations towards outsiders, they are permitted to exclude even those would-be immigrants who *are* in desperate need (see e.g. Wellman 2008: 129–30). Think about the civil society context: if associations were not permitted to exclude would-be members whenever those individuals claimed to have a significant interest in being admitted, then there would be very limited room left for freedom of association. Or think of the example of marriage again. Antonio may have a substantial interest in marrying Beatrice, but that does not seem to be enough to outweigh Beatrice's own interests in freedom of marital association.

Yet, at this stage, we might start to wonder about whether enough has been done to establish the case for a *pro tanto* right to exclude on the grounds of the state's freedom to associate. After all, the opponent of the freedom of association argument could point out that the case of states is relevantly different from that of associations within civil society and from individual relationships in a number of significant ways. It is clear from the start that there are important differences. For instance, marriage is an intimate relationship in a way that sharing residence in and/or citizenship of a state is not. When it comes to an individual's life plan, lacking the liberty to reject an unwanted suitor seems to be in a different order of magnitude from lacking the liberty to reject unwanted prospective immigrants.[4] On the other side, though, exclusion from a state is ordinarily far more significant with respect to life plans than exclusion from, say, a sports club. First, we cannot really avoid living under the jurisdiction of some state, because states have claimed all or nearly all the habitable surfaces on the planet, and so we need to be allowed to settle in one, somewhere. There is no option not to live in a state, in the way that we have the option not to be a member of a golf club or not to get married. Furthermore, it may be possible to set up a club of one's own, but it is not usually an option to establish a state of one's own, because that would require some territory not under the jurisdiction of another state or ceded by another state, and territory is not normally up for grabs (see Carens 1987: 267–68; Cole 2000: 70–73; Fine 2010; Seglow 2005).

But what this shows, the proponent may reply, is that everyone needs to be permitted to reside *somewhere*. As long as an individual is allowed to settle in one state, the individual's interests in settlement are satisfied, and all other states still may enjoy the *pro tanto* right to exclude that individual (for this line of argument see e.g. D. Miller 2005b: 197; forthcoming). However, this neglects another distinctive aspect of states as compared to associations in civil society. Residence within a particular state is a necessary condition for the pursuit of the majority, if not all, of the extensive benefits and opportunities (social, economic, political, romantic, educational, and so forth) specific to *that* particular state.[5] Hence an individual who is excluded from settling in state A, even if allowed to reside within state B, is excluded from pursuing all the opportunities specific to state A. Generally, then, the stakes are likely to be far, far higher for excluded would-be immigrants (including in the pure case) than for excluded would-be members of associations within civil society. That does not necessarily undermine the freedom of association argument in defence of the state's right to exclude, but it does suggest that we should be very cautious when drawing analogies between the state's right to exclude outsiders and the rights of associations within civil society, especially when we think about how to weigh the state's interests against competing considerations.

But note that so far we have not directly questioned whether it is appropriate to assign the state, or to conceive of the state as having, a right to freedom of association. It is worth thinking about that in more detail, because it is not obvious that states do have a right to freedom of association. Even proponents of the freedom of association argument presumably would not wish to grant states the *full* rights of freedom of association. Whereas voluntary associations ordinarily claim the right to exclude *existing* members, would proponents wish to grant states the right to exclude existing citizens (from membership and/or residence) on the grounds of their right to freedom of association? This seems implausible: citizens should not normally be at liberty to deprive one of their number of the full rights of citizenship. But if this is true, then proponents of the freedom of association owe us an explanation for why we should not similarly restrict the right of states to exclude would-be immigrants. If we can curtail rights to full freedom of association in one case, why not in the other too?

Now, we are familiar with the idea of individual rights to freedom of association, and with collective rights to freedom of association – as when we discuss the associational rights of the Girl Scouts, for instance. The usual argument in favour of allowing voluntary associations to exclude unwanted outsiders (and, indeed, insiders) is that this respects the associational choices and rights of the individual members, without unduly burdening the interests of those excluded (who are usually free to join other similar associations should they want to). But, as Wellman recognizes, and most people seem to agree, states as we know them are not voluntary associations and "do not owe their membership to the autonomous choices of their constituents" (Wellman 2008: 112). And for some critics of this view, the simple fact that states are not properly conceived as voluntary associations and that membership within them is not ordinarily voluntary is reason enough to reject the freedom of association argument. Ryan Pevnick, for instance, contends that "it is a mistake to defend immigration restrictions by reference to the citizenry's claims of freedom of association when the relevant association is not freely entered into" (Pevnick 2011: 30).

In addition, the state's freedom of association and accompanying right to exclude appear to clash with the associational rights of its individual members, since the state may choose to exclude would-be immigrants with whom individual members wish to associate (see Steiner 2001: 79–88). So if we are taking freedom of association seriously, why should we conclude that the state's right to exclude should trump the right of individual citizens to associate freely with outsiders?

The defender of the freedom of association position might reply that these differences between states and voluntary associations are not actually significant in this context. What matters is just that states have a right to (or at least some of the rights involved in) freedom of association, and that this much is clear from Wellman's examples of forced association above: we do not usually think that it is permissible to force states into regional associations or for states to forcibly annex others. But it is not clear why we must accept that states have a right to freedom of association in order to believe that there are problems with forcing states to do things against their (and/or their citizens') will. We could believe that there are problems with forced annexation because forced annexation does not respect the rights of sovereign states to territorial integrity, for example. In short, there are other grounds for opposing these kinds of impositions (see Fine forthcoming: chapter 4).

At the same time, though, we should also note that it is possible to agree that states have *some* freedom of association rights, including the right not to be forced to associate with other states, without thinking that this commits us to the conclusion that states must also enjoy a right to exclude would-be immigrants as well (just as the proponents of the freedom of association argument seem to grant states some associational rights, but not the right to exclude current members).[6]

Lastly, the freedom of association argument is, in the first instance, an argument about access to *membership* in the form of citizenship, rather than residence. It is an argument about states (and their citizens) maintaining control over their membership rules, which in turn enables them to control the direction of policy and (to some extent) the future shape of the citizenry: to be in control of their own "association". And so, again, further work is needed to explain why (if at all) this argument, which is ostensibly about control over membership, should deliver something like a right to exclude would-be immigrants from settling within the state's borders. Freedom of association does not seem to do all the work on its own.

The liberal nationalist argument

The freedom of association argument in defence of the state's right to exclude does not depend on the state's members sharing a special, distinctive connection to each other or to the territory over which the state claims jurisdiction. But what happens when we consider the importance of just that kind of special, distinctive connection between fellow members and to a particular territory? So-called "liberal nationalists", for example, maintain that co-nationals share a special relationship with one another and with a particular territory, and this is a relationship which comes with a variety of special rights and obligations. Liberal nationalists generally conceive of national groups as sharing some combination of cultural features (such a common language, and historical points of reference), a national consciousness and subjective sense of their own distinctiveness, and a connection to a territory (see e.g. Tamir 1993, D. Miller 1995, M. Moore 2001, Gans 2003, Meisels 2005). How might a liberal nationalist approach the issue of immigration? Liberal nationalists appear to have at their disposal a powerful case in defence of the state's right to exclude would-be immigrants. There are four key arguments on which liberal nationalists draw (separately or in combination).

First, liberal nationalists point out that people have a strong interest in protecting and preserving the character of their national culture, and they argue that one of the legitimate roles of the state is to protect the national culture(s) within the state. While national cultures inevitably adapt over time in response to various internal and external forces, states should be entitled to control immigration and thus to exclude prospective entrants in the name of ensuring that the national culture is not put under too great a strain or forced to change at too fast a pace.[7]

Second, liberal nationalists argue that members of national groups have a special claim to the territory to which they have a particular attachment – which has been transformed by their presence, has become their "home", and has symbolic significance for them (see D. Miller 2007: 201–30; Meisels 2005: 25–42). This special national relationship to the territory in question may seem to lend support at least to *some* of the claims that states make with respect to the territory under their control. As David Miller explains, "the case for having rights over the relevant territory is then straightforward: it gives members of the nation continuing access to places that are especially significant to them, and it allows choices to be made over how these sites are to be protected and managed" (D. Miller 2007: 219).

Third, liberal nationalists often argue that sharing a national identity has important instrumental benefits, such as engendering a sense of solidarity and trust between fellow nationals, and even that it may be necessary for the maintenance of a well-functioning democracy and the pursuit of social justice (see Tamir 1993: 121; Canovan 2000; D. Miller 2000: 31–33). If immigration represents a danger to the national identity and the benefits that it brings, then this might be a strong reason in favour of states enjoying a right to exclude would-be immigrants.

Fourth, liberal nationalists tend to argue that fellow nationals have special obligations to one another in virtue of their membership of a national community: these obligations are part of what it means to be members of a national group (D. Miller 2005c; Tamir 1993: 95–116). And these special obligations are not owed to non-nationals. If, for instance, fellow nationals have an obligation to protect each other's interests over above those of non-nationals, then this might form the basis for an argument in defence of the state's right to exclude would-be immigrants (but we will not explore this fourth argument in this section: the final section will introduce and assess the special obligations argument in more detail).

In response to the first argument, even if we grant that immigration might have an impact on the national culture or at least on the pace of change, and agree that members of national communities may have a significant interest in maintaining some control over the character and pace of change of their national culture, nonetheless we might wonder why this interest should be considered more weighty than the interests of would-be immigrants in being allowed to settle within the state's borders. It looks as though we just have competing interests here, and so we need to know why one set of interests should take priority.

The liberal nationalist has a range of possible replies. The liberal nationalist might argue that one's national culture is of fundamental importance to one's individual identity, to one's sense of belonging and place in the world, and/or to one's individual autonomy, to the ability to make meaningful choices (see e.g. Margalit & Raz 1990; Kymlicka 1995: 75–106; and the discussion in Tamir 1993: 35–56). But, again, the opponent might just reply that following one's own plans, even if that requires migrating across borders, and even in the "pure" case, is of fundamental importance to individual lives. Why does the importance of the role of national culture take precedence?

The second, territorial argument appears to offer a stronger basis for the claim that the state should enjoy a *pro tanto* right to exclude, as it seeks to establish a special, morally significant connection between nationals and the territory in question, a connection not shared by non-nationals. Yet, how do we identify those who have the right sort of special connection to the territory? In the case of Scotland, for example, is it just those who reside within Scotland, or also those who reside in the rest of the United Kingdom, or also those within the European Union, or also those who were born in Scotland but now live elsewhere, or those who have some kind of ancestral connection to Scotland even though they have never lived there? And why should this special connection deliver a right to exclude others from residing there rather than just a right to reside there? (On this point see Fine forthcoming: chapter 6.) Moreover, given the complicated, conflict-ridden, contested histories of territorial borders, there are always going to be deep disagreements about which groups have the relevant connections to the relevant areas.

The strength of the third argument depends on whether the empirical evidence actually supports the claim that sharing a national identity brings with it the various alleged benefits, whether it is important or even necessary for the pursuit and achievement of a range of goals, and indeed whether immigration does represent a threat to the national identity such that these projects would be undermined in the absence of a right to exclude would-be immigrants. Even if the empirical evidence supports any of these claims, we would still have to think about how exactly a shared national identity is supposed to perform that important role. What kind of overarching national identity could unite the diverse residents of today's states, such that it would promote solidarity and trust among them? Do such identities exist? Consider the British case. British politicians are constantly struggling to define what it means to be British, in a way that is supposed to generate pride and a sense of unity, without alienating members of minority groups and historically disadvantaged groups. How might it avoid being divisive and parochial, rather than cohesive and broad? But note that once we start thinking about how the state might foster the *right kind* of national identity, we are moving away from the idea that the state should protect the actual national cultures (messy, exclusive, divisive and contentious as they may be) that exist within their borders. Furthermore, as we know, states and nations are not perfectly overlapping (Fine forthcoming: chapter 3). There are multinational states (such as Britain and Belgium) and there are nations without their own states (such as the Kurds). This, of course, complicates the relationship between nationality and the *state's* right to exclude. In summary, then, while the liberal nationalist argument may do a fine job of explaining some of what lies behind many a state's *desire* to exclude large numbers of would-be immigrants, it does not appear to deliver anything like a decisive defence of the state's *right* to exclude, even in the pared-down "pure" case.

The Kantian argument

Another promising argument for the state's right to exclude begins with the assumption that states have rights to control and regulate the territory over which they have jurisdiction, and then goes on to claim that this set of rights must also include the right to exclude. In this section, we focus on a specifically *Kantian* argument for the extension from territorial rights of jurisdiction and control to territorial rights to exclude. (See above for the argument departing from a specifically nationalist account of territorial rights.) The reason we focus on Kant is that, although often mentioned in both the literature on territorial rights and the literature on Kantian cosmopolitanism, the argument has not yet received sustained attention in the immigration debate (though see Benhabib 2004). We also believe it is one of the more promising among territory-based arguments for the right to exclude.[8]

How do we get from territorial rights to jurisdiction and control, which *inter alia* entitle states to make and enforce law within their borders, to a right to exclude? We believe the most promising Kantian argument begins with an account of the grounds for granting states jurisdictional rights over territory, and then claims that such grounds also support granting states a moral right to control their borders. Let us unpack the argument step by step.

The Kantian begins by asserting a universal, "innate" right to freedom, which guarantees our freedom understood as independence from subjection to others' choices. In the state of nature, this freedom is insecure. Because there is no political agent capable of coordinating our wills, and because we cannot know with any certainty others' intentions or designs, we are permitted, Kant says, to "do what seems right and good to us" (Kant [1781] 1991: 456; *Metaphysics of Morals* [hereinafter *MM*] Ak 6:312). Each one of us is permitted, that is, to protect our person and provisionally acquired property with violence if necessary. But for Kant there is a further problem in the state of nature, which creates an enforceable *moral* (rather than merely prudential) obligation to attempt exit from it. The problem is that, in each interpreting for ourselves what the protection of our innate freedom requires, we must *unilaterally* impose our will – our view regarding what right requires – on others. I sincerely believe that this particular piece of land is mine and your use of it counts as a trespass; you disagree. Because we are both authoritative interpreters of the rights that define the limits of our freedom, the actions we take under our own conception of freedom therefore necessarily subject the choices of others with whom we interact. This would be true even were we to agree with others what right (or a system of rights) requires of each of us. Because there is no mechanism available that can assure me that you will continue to comply with the currently agreed distribution of rights, there is an important sense in which I still remain subject to your choice to continue supporting the agreement. If you change your mind, and begin acting on a set of rights that I believe prejudices my freedom, then I have no recourse (Kant [1781] 1991: 408–10; *MM* Ak 6:255–57).

To emerge from this "lawless freedom", we must set up a public authority capable of coordinating our wills under a system of equal freedom. When properly constituted, such a public authority – a state – will guarantee and protect each person's right to freedom under "universal law", such that each person's sphere of freedom is defined by a set of rights equally enjoyed by everyone. The public will that coerces us into compliance with such a system of rights will not be *unilateral* but *omnilateral*: it will be the product of a united and coordinated will. When, in addition, (a) the public will rules in the name of the people, by protecting basic rights and giving everyone a say in its formation, (b) the people over whom it exercises authority have a (permission) right to occupy that territory (e.g. they did not acquire residence there unjustly), and (c) authority was not acquired via unjust annexation, the Kantian will say that the state's exercise of jurisdiction over a specific territory is *legitimate*.[9]

In summary, on the Kantian view states acquire legitimate jurisdiction over a territory when they effectively provide a central class of public goods (including, most importantly, the rule of law), which together serves to protect a system of equal freedom. Once a state is discharging its public role, it acquires a robust right to non-interference: all those who are not subject to its authority (including other states and foreigners) must respect its autonomy. They must not interfere in its internal affairs, or annex its territory, or otherwise undermine its capacity to govern. But must such a capacity to govern also include the right to exclude?

To answer this question, we must turn to Kant's argument for "cosmopolitan right", which governs the relations between states and the citizens and residents of other countries, that is, the permissible ways in which citizens, residents and public institutions can treat foreign visitors, and (as we will see in a moment, more importantly for Kant) the permissible ways in which foreign visitors can treat the citizens, public institutions and land of the state they are visiting. And here we find there is only one cosmopolitan right, namely "universal hospitality".[10] "Conditions of universal hospitality" include:

> the right of a foreigner not to be treated with hostility because he has arrived on the land of another. The other can turn him away, if this can be done without destroying him, but as long as he behaves peaceably where he is, he cannot be treated with hostility.
>
> *(Kant [1781] 1991: 329;* MM *Ak 8:358)*

The right to hospitality therefore establishes, according to Kant, a right to exclude foreigners from settlement and residence but also imposes an obligation to allow foreigners to establish contact and trade. On what basis do states have a right to exclude but lack a right to keep foreigners and other states from establishing contact and trade? Why can we not simply refuse, on whatever grounds we like, foreign visitors who want to trade and communicate with us (but who are not in mortal danger) in the same way as we might refuse to answer someone ringing our doorbell? Why would such a refusal undermine their right to be somewhere (given that they can, we are assuming, just return home)?

The best response from within the Kantian framework, we believe, begins by questioning the analogy between individual private ownership (of, say, a house) and collective jurisdiction over territory. States do not "own" territory in the same way as an individual "owns" a house. First, houseowners only have conclusive rights in their houses, according to Kant, under civil law. They do not at any point (including the state of nature) exercise a unilateral right to control what laws apply to their house, including the laws which govern how they may bequeath, transfer, rent or sell their property. These jurisdictional rights are held exclusively by states that govern via an *omnilateral* will (recall the argument about the instability of the state of nature). At the same time, however, Kantian states do not have full *private* ownership rights over any part of the territory. Although Kant says that a state's territory belongs to the state as "supreme pro-prietor" (or "lord of the land"), he denies both that the people *qua* state own the territory *col-lectively* and that the state can own any part of the land *individually* (as in a patrimonial kingdom). The upshot of this discussion is that the state's sole function as "lord of the land" is to *regulate* the division and use of territory (including taxation, public roads, public spaces, etc.). As Kant writes,

> one can say of the lord of the land that he owns nothing (of his own) except himself; for if he had something of his own alongside others in the state, a dispute could arise between them and there would be no judge to settle it. But one can also say that he possesses everything, since he has the right of command over the people, to whom all external things belong (*divisim*) (the right to assign to each what is his).
>
> *(Kant [1781] 1991: 466;* MM Ak 6:324)[11]

Jurisdiction is one thing, private property ownership, quite another. The direct inference from rights inherent in private ownership of, say, a house to the rights that a people exercises over a territory cannot, therefore, be made within a Kantian framework, and hence cannot be used to undermine cosmopolitan right.[12]

With this move blocked, the argument then points to the fact that the foreigner at our doorstep is, with respect to us and unlike the citizen ringing our doorbell, in a state of nature. There are no civil laws to which both we and he or she are a party; the omnilateral will does not speak in the name of the foreigner. This would not be a problem as long as none of our laws applies to the foreigner. But some of them do. In particular, laws which govern who and under what conditions foreigners can visit, traverse, settle, occupy and take up residence within our territory clearly apply to them as much as to us. From the point of view of the for-eigner, such laws must therefore count as *unilaterally* imposed. In enforcing them against the foreigner, we must then be wronging him or her, as Kant says, "in the highest degree" *unless such enforcement can be made compatible with the idea of a rightful condition.* Among *states,* the "law-less" character of the international state of nature can be (albeit always only partially) superseded by a voluntary congress of states which together can establish the definitive articles of perpetual peace. Such a congress makes the provisional control we claim over our territory conclusive with respect to other parties to the contract (since by joining the congress they consent to that control). But what about the state of nature still existing between states and *foreigners*? Can *its* inherent lawlessness be superseded? Under what conditions?

The key is Kant's assertion of our "common possession" of the earth, which gives each of us an innate right to be "where nature or chance has placed him" (Kant [1781] 1991: 414; *MM* Ak 6:262). Our right to be somewhere entails that if, say, a shipwrecked sailor were to wash up on the shores of our country, we would have a duty to allow him entry until he was in a position to return home. The original right to common possession of the earth also sets limits on rightful appropriation (Risse 2012). As we have seen, Kant argues that individuals and groups are permitted to take possession of a tract of land (for example, by hunting on it or using it to plant orchards or in some other way by which they signal possession). In such cases, all other individuals acquire a provisional obligation not to hinder them in that possession. (We could hinder them, recall, only in cases in which their possession was a threat to us.) Notice, however, that their local possession of a part of the earth, though not a conclusive property right (which could only fully emerge in a civil condition), limits our previous right, as individuals, in a truly common and universal possession. Kant argues that such local possession (and hence exclusion) can be justified *but only if we, as individuals, retain the right to interact and exchange goods with the appropriators*. Such interaction preserves the "commerce" on their territory that would have been possible under our original communal possession of the earth. As we have seen, however, cosmopolitan right does not extend to the right to *settle* or *reside* on their land (which, *nota bene*, we also would have had had the earth remained in common possession).

The reason, we believe, has to do with Kant's concerns with European imperialism. Sankar Muthu (2003) has shown convincingly that the "foreigners" Kant had in mind when discussing cosmopolitan right were European settlers in the New World and European trading organizations like the Dutch East India Company. The right to hospitality was meant to protect their right to establish contact and trade with distant lands, but not to enslave, conquer or sequester land from the original inhabitants (even in cases where the original inhabitants did not live in a fully rightful condition). As Kant writes:

> if the settlement is made so far from where that people resides that there is no encroachment on anyone's use of his land, the right to settle is not open to doubt. But if these peoples are shepherds or hunters (like the Hottentots, the Tungusi, or most of the American Indian nations) who depend for their sustenance on great open regions, this settlement may not take place by force but only by contract, and indeed by a contract that does not take advantage of the ignorance of those inhabitants with respect to ceding their lands.
>
> *(Kant [1781] 1991: 489; MM Ak 6:353)*

The argument seems to be this: to allow any individual or private association a right to settle or reside in a territory that has already been provisionally appropriated (either by a state or by less organized forms of land use) would undermine the security required for that very appropriation eventually to sustain different modes of peaceful and civil life. By constantly threatening to return us to the state of nature, such an expansive right of settlement would thereby undermine the very ability to act on our moral duty to exit the state of nature. Restrictions on settlement and residence are therefore necessary in order to make the creation and maintenance of a civil condition possible.

In view of Kant's concern for the injustice of European settlement and conquest of native peoples, his account of the right to hospitality is laudable. But notice further that if Kant's argument were successful, it would establish a state right to exclude in the pure case. Because no foreigner has a right to settle and reside, no wrong is done when the claims of those seeking to immigrate are rejected (as long as they are not in mortal danger). Is it successful? We want to argue that Kant's attempt to drive a wedge between the right to establish contact and trade, on one hand, and the right to settle and reside, on the other, fails *even if we grant his concern with imperialism and his concern that such a right would undermine the stability of the civil condition.* The argument is simple. Recall that the need for cosmopolitan right emerges because the state of nature still existing between states as moral persons and foreigners must be "wrong in the highest degree". It must be wrong in the highest degree because, as in the domestic case, such a state of nature allows the unilateral imposition of duties on others. The law of a state governing the legal rights of a foreigner to enter, visit, and so on, must count as a unilateral imposition because the foreigner plays no role in their formation. In the case of states, the wrongness inherent in remaining in an (international) state of nature can be superseded as long as states join together in a voluntary pact of mutual recognition and mutual non-aggression. While not fully omnilateral, this pact is sufficiently omnilateral to make what were previously only provisional rights to national control much more conclusive (at least with respect to other parties to the pact). In the case of relations between states and foreigners, we then saw that the wrongness of the unilateral imposition involved in the regulation of entry, visit, residency, trade, and so on, could be superseded as well, but only if states recognized a right to hospitality. Such a right would pay tribute to our original communal possession of the earth by granting every individual or private association a right to establish contact and trade *as long as they did so without hostility.* We then argued that this right did not extend to settlement or residence because such an extension, given the experience of European settlers in the New World, would threaten to undermine the capacity of peoples to create and maintain viable, self-governing states. But here is the thought: why not just say that states must grant a right to settle and reside to foreigners *as long as such residence or settlement does not threaten public peace or the stability of public institutions*? Why cannot we add, in other words, a rider similar to the one attached to the right to establish contact and trade? Such a rider would also serve as a bulwark against colonial imperialism, since settlement and residence that was established in order to subjugate or rob another people would be expressly prohibited.

More importantly, it also strikes us that such a qualified right to reside and settle follows directly from the original and motivating concern with unilateral imposition. Recall that the solution to the wrongness inherent in unilateral imposition within the original state of nature is to create a rightful condition. Indeed, Kant argues that our duty to exit the state of nature is enforceable: we can be forced to join a nascent state in order to establish (ideally) a system of equal freedom in which everyone's rights are equal, consistent and conclusive. But if that is true, then surely the solution to the unilateral imposition of our state laws on the foreigner must be *to give the foreigner the option of joining our state or return home* (i.e. to take up residence). By joining our state, the foreigner exits the state of nature that exists between him or her and us. To be sure, the foreigner may already be a citizen of another state, but *as long as he or she is within the scope of our coercive power* he or she remains subject to our unilateral will, and hence we do him "wrong in the highest degree". The conclusion is reinforced when we reintroduce the original right to communal possession of the earth. Just as Kant argued that the right to hospitality was necessary in order to compensate for the loss of our rights to travel freely and take up residence wherever we like across the globe, we can now argue that the right to settle and reside is also necessary *in exactly the same way.* While our right will now be circumscribed by the legitimate concerns for security and stability of the host state, the right would not be annihilated completely. Such a more expansive right of "hospitality" strikes us as much more consonant with the original universal right to communal possession than Kant's more truncated version.

Notice further that Kant's argument against imposing a duty on states to join a world state cannot be used in this instance to block the demand on a state to incorporate the would-be immigrant. Kant famously argues that states are not, like individuals, under an obligation to enter into a *world* state. He makes two main arguments. The first is that such a world state would be a "soulless despotism": the very freedom individuals had sought to protect by entering a (domestic) state would be annihilated once they entered into a world state with a truly global dominion. It is clear that such an argument cannot be made against our expanded cosmopolitan right: while an *unqualified* right to settle might warrant such a rejection (on the basis that truly open borders would undermine the capacity of a state to maintain a system of equal freedom), our cosmopolitan right is *qualified*, allowing states some (bounded) discretion in deciding when foreigners would constitute a threat to the security and stability of the civil condition. The second argument Kant makes against the requirement to join a world state is that, by joining, the domestic state must necessarily lose its political autonomy (to which it has a claim right given by its contribution to protecting the equal freedom of its subjects). Unlike individuals, internally states are already (ideally) domains of equal freedom. As Kant writes, "states already have an internal legal constitution, and hence have outgrown the coercion of others to subject them to a broader legal constitution according to their conceptions of right" (Kant [1781] 1991: 326; MM Ak 8:355–56). Once again, such an argument cannot be used against our expanded cosmopolitan right for the simple reason that our domestic state continues to exist even after the immigrant has joined it. Immigration does not require the dissolution of our political order in the same way as joining a world state would.

In sum, in this section, we have argued that the Kantian argument cannot be used to ground a right to exclude in our core case. According to our expanded version of cosmopolitan right, states have a moral duty to give immigrants who pose no threat to the stability or security of our public institutions the option of taking up residence (and hence, eventually, also citizenship). Even if states have some discretion in deciding whether immigrants pose a threat to the stability and security of public institutions,[13] there is, on our expanded argument, a presumption in favour of granting the right to settle: states have the burden of proof in showing that a given immigrant (or class of immigrants) will constitute a significant threat to public institutions (in the way, say, the *conquistadores* did). We have shown, furthermore, that this conclusion is in fact forced by premises that the Kantian already accepts. The case, that is, was prosecuted from an entirely internal perspective.

The special obligations argument

One of the most popular and politically volatile arguments on behalf of a qualified right to exclude claims that immigration can be restricted if it harms the domestic worse off.[14] The version of the argument that we will consider grounds the claim in a defence of special socio-economic obligations among fellow residents of a state.[15] More specifically, all special obligations arguments (SOAs) of the kind we are considering hold that broadly egalitarian[16] obligations of socio-economic justice apply among all and only residents of states. Although there may be significant, demanding and stringent humanitarian obligations to secure adequate access to sanitation, shelter and nourishment to all human beings, and also other socio-economic obligations arising from specific forms of international interaction among states (such as within, say, the World Trade Organization), demands of egalitarian justice among individuals only arise within states. There are three prominent versions of SOA, namely the *nationalist argument*, the *coercion argument* and the *reciprocity argument*. For reasons to be explained in a moment, we will treat them all under the same heading.

To fix ideas, we begin with a few general assumptions. First, although the claim is controversial, we assume for the sake of argument that the net effect of a given immigration policy would in fact make the domestic worse off even worse off than they otherwise would have been absent that policy. This assumption is required: if an immigration policy left the domestic worse off better off or equally as well off as they would have been without the policy, then they would lack a reasonable complaint, from the point of view of SOA. (We return to this point below.) Third, we assume, again for the sake of argument, that there are indeed special egalitarian obligations among residents. This is because we want to evaluate the *implications* of SOAs for immigration, rather than evaluate SOAs *tout court*. Of course, if SOAs fail to establish the existence of special obligations, then they must also fail to establish a qualified right to exclude. But addressing arguments for or against special obligations among citizens would require forays into the global justice debates, which would take us far away from our primary interest in this chapter. Instead we evaluate the following conditional: if there are special egalitarian obligations of justice among all and only residents, then states must also have a (qualified) right to exclude. Whatever the truth of the antecedent, does the consequent follow?

Coercion-based versions of the SOA contend that obligations of egalitarian justice are only triggered among individuals who are subject to a comprehensive web of legally backed mutual coercion. While would-be immigrants are also coerced by domestic laws governing rights of entry, residence, and so on, they are not subject to the full panoply of laws governing property rights, taxation, administration, and so on, typical of any modern state (see e.g. Blake 2001, Nagel 2005, Risse 2006). Nationalist versions of the SOA include those which hold that obligations of egalitarian justice are only triggered among individuals who share a comprehensive public culture (for more on the content and specific structure of nationalist views, see above and see e.g. D. Miller 1995). And reciprocity-based versions of the SOA contend that such obligations are only triggered among those who share in the mutual production of the central class of collective goods supplied by any well-functioning modern state, including defence against physical attack, protection of property rights and the rule of law (see e.g. Sangiovanni 2007). Because we are, in this chapter, assuming that at least one or more of these arguments succeeds in establishing a necessary condition for triggering egalitarian social obligations, we will not discuss further their grounds or their differences. We proceed as if there are special egalitarian obligations among all and only residents, and seek to determine whether a (qualified) right to exclude follows.

We unfold the argument via a dialogue between a representative of those would-be immigrants whose economic, social and cultural prospects would be greatly improved by moving, on one hand, and the state to which he wants to move, on the other.

> **STATE:** We can't let you in because, if we do, then we will harm the worse off in our society.

A brief but important interlude: If we are not to be led astray, we pause to consider the causal mechanism by which the domestic worse off are, *ex hypothesi*, harmed by immigration. Imagine, for example, that there is a feasible institutional scheme available to compensate the domestic worse off post-immigration. With this feasible policy, call it policy *a*, the worse off would do no worse or even better than they would have without immigration. But say that policy *a* is never enacted (though it could have been). In that case, the worse off of course still have a justice-based complaint *but it would no longer be a complaint against the more open immigration policy; rather it would be a complaint against the domestic failure to implement the policy a.* Though there is still injustice, the injustice is not a result, in the relevant sense, of the more open immigration policy. The only kind of harm that legitimately grounds a complaint against a more open immigration policy would be one that it was infeasible to prevent. So when the "state" says that the worse off will be harmed, they mean that there is no feasible policy option available post-immigration such that the harm would be prevented. We return to this important qualification below. With that interlude, we can now continue the discussion.

IMMIGRANT: Yes, but by not letting us in you harm us too, by making us worse off than we would have been had you let us in.

STATE: Let's grant that you are harmed in the sense you mention, but why would such harm be a violation of your rights, or otherwise impermissible? After all, by letting you in we also harm the worse off in our own society.

IMMIGRANT: Yes, it is true that by admitting us you would harm your domestic worse off, but we surely stand to gain much more than the domestic worse off stand to lose, so our interest in being let in is much stronger than the domestic worse off's interest in keeping us out. And, since your and our commitment to moral equality entails that all human interests are of equal importance, not letting us in is equivalent to treating our interests as having less worth than the domestic worse off. So you must let us in, or treat us as, in effect, subhuman.

STATE: You move too quickly. Your argument from moral equality elides the distinction between giving someone's interests special weight because of the morally relevant nature of a relationship, and giving someone's interests special weight because they are intrinsically of greater moral worth. Only the latter counts as a violation the ideal of moral equality. SOAs need not deny that all persons' interests are of equal worth. When proponents of SOA say that residents have special obligations of egalitarian justice to one another, this is not because their interests are somehow intrinsically more important or weighty than those of others. Rather, the argument is that the character and nature of the social relations in which such individuals stand gives them special moral reasons to reject inequalities that those not sharing in those relations lack. Consider a familiar analogy. When one claims that one has a special obligation to save one's daughter (rather than a stranger) from drowning, one does not believe this is because one's daughter's interests are intrinsically more morally weighty than those of others. One does not, for example, believe that others, unrelated to one's daughter, also have an obligation to save her rather than the stranger. The reasons stem from the moral significance of the relationship, rather than from her greater moral worth. So the reason we can deny your request to settle is not that your interests are somehow of lesser worth than the interests of the domestic worse off. Rather, the special relationship in which we stand to our domestic worse off gives us a special responsibility for their fate.[17]

So SOAs would seem to ground a (qualified) right to exclude. Here is a more schematic version of the argument we have just given, which is useful, among other things, for showing how heavily qualified an SOA-based *pro tanto* right to exclude must be.

Prove: If being a resident of the same state is a necessary condition for egalitarian obligations of type y to apply, then states have a (qualified) right to exclude would-be immigrants.

(1) Assume, arguendo, that being a resident of the same state is a necessary condition for egalitarian obligations to apply (but not a necessary condition for stringent humanitarian obligations to apply).

(2) Therefore, if, under some policy z, I have fewer resources, opportunities or welfare than I would have had under a feasible and optimal egalitarian policy z', then I am objectionably worse off, and hence have a claim in justice against z, and in favour of z'.

(3) Assume: A more open immigration policy x makes some in the host society worse off (in the sense defined by (2)) than they would have been under a more closed immigration policy x'.

(4) Assume: There is no feasible post-immigration scheme that could compensate those made worse off under (3), and that leaves no one else worse off (in the sense defined by (2)) than they would have been under x'. (If there were such a post-immigration scheme available, then there would be a justice-based complaint in failing to implement that further scheme, but none against x.)

(5) Assume: (a) would-be immigrants are not so badly off that they would be subject to starvation or severe forms of political, social or cultural persecution were they not granted a right to settle and (b) there is no question of family reunification.

(6) If (3), (4) and (5) are satisfied, those worse off in (3) have a claim in justice against x and in favour of x'.

(7) If states ought, as a matter of justice, to implement x', then this entails that they have a (*pro tanto*) moral right to exclude those immigrants that would have been accepted under x.

Conclusion: If being a resident of the same state is a necessary condition for egalitarian obligations to apply, then states have a qualified and *pro tanto* right to exclude would-be immigrants, namely a right to exclude immigrants when (3), (4) and (5) are satisfied. The argument implies that if any of (3), (4) or (5) are not satisfied, states do not have a right to exclude.

In bringing this section to a close, we note how important (3) (and hence (4)) is for the argument to succeed. The reason is this. It is sometimes assumed that SOAs ground an unqualified right to exclude, such that immigrants can be turned away *even if admitting them would harm no one domestically* (in the sense defined by (2)) (see e.g. Nagel 2005). If this were the case, then the argument would fail. To see the point, imagine the State in our dialogue responded to the Immigrant in this way:

> **STATE**: We can deny you entry because you do not share in the relations that ground egalitarian obligations of justice (you neither share public culture, nor engage in the mutual production of public goods, nor are subject to jointly authorized coercion).

The immigrant could easily respond:

> **IMMIGRANT**: Sure, but I would like to *join* your public culture, system of mutual production, system of authorized coercion. It is no argument against *that* claim to simply repeat that we do not belong to that scheme yet! Why shouldn't I be permitted to belong? After all, I have very strong interests in joining you, and hence we would be harmed – my interests would be set back – if you turned me down.[18]

The only reasonable response the proponent of an SOA can make here is to say, as the state said above, that a more open immigration policy would also *harm the domestic poor*. It is only if that is assumed (along with (4)) that the argument goes through. This crucial distinction is often overlooked.

It is also important to emphasize that the SOA-based (qualified) right to exclude is only *pro tanto*. For all we have said here, it might be true that some other independent considerations can rebut the presumption in favour of the right to exclude even when (3), (4) and (5) are satisfied. This would be the case, for example, if we also adopted the Kantian argument for territorial rights adumbrated above (which is compatible with all of the variants of the SOA discussed above). If we did, then we would need to consider whether the right to original communal possession was strong enough to override the *pro tanto* right to exclude grounded in the SOA.[19] Another independent consideration that might rebut the presumption in favour of the right to exclude would be the existence of a universal, human right to freedom of movement stronger than the rights of the domestic worse off.[20] Assessing the balance of rights in either case is obviously beyond the purview of the task we have set ourselves here. It is enough if we have clarified the issues that would be involved in any such attempt.

Conclusion

We have presented a selection of the most popular and powerful arguments in defence of the state's moral right to exclude would-be immigrations from entering and settling within their territories. We have illustrated some of the significant challenges faced by these arguments, and we have highlighted the empirical and normative conditions that are required for these arguments to succeed. In the case of the special obligations argument, for example, for it to support even a *pro tanto* right to exclude would-be immigrants we must assume: (a) that being a resident of the same state *is* a necessary condition for obligations of egalitarian justice to apply (and this is the subject of profound and enduring disagreement among political philosophers);[21] (b) that a more open immigration policy would make some existing residents in the receiving state worse off (note that economists, for example, are divided on this question, but the existing empirical evidence suggests that we should be extremely wary of assuming that more open immigration policies do or would have this effect, particularly in the long run);[22] (c) that there is no feasible post-immigration scheme which could compensate those made worse off under the more open immigration policy (and it seems reasonable to remain sceptical about that assumption); and, of course, (d) that we are discussing would-be immigrants in the "pure" case.

Once we relax the restrictions introduced for the "pure" case, though, each of the arguments in defence of the state's right to exclude would-be immigrants faces far more significant hurdles, as many proponents of these arguments acknowledge. Where the most basic interests of the would-be immigrants are at stake, the state's interests in, say, protecting its national culture(s) obviously pack less of a punch. Therefore, in the course of highlighting the challenges encountered by attempts to defend even something like a *pro tanto* right to exclude in the pared-down "pure" case, we have indicated just how difficult it would be for states to justify anything like an all things considered, and far less qualified, right to exclude would-be immigrants.

Notes

1 From now on, we will refer to the right to exclude would-be immigrants from settling or taking up residence as "the right to exclude" simpliciter. Note also that, in this chapter, we will not discuss under what conditions resident non-citizens should be granted full membership, i.e., citizenship (except in so far as it bears on argument for the right to settle).

2 An example often raised is the case of the Jaycees in the United States. See for example, White (1997: 376), Gutmann (1998: 8–9) and Fine (2010: 351).

3 See the discussion of this concern in C. H. Wellman (2008: 135). See also Phillip Cole's counter-argument (Wellman & Cole 2011, esp. chapter 15). While Wellman thinks that the state has a pre-sumptive right to exclude, Cole disagrees.

4 For more detailed discussion, see Fine (forthcoming: chapter 4). See also White (1997) and D. Miller (2007: 211).

5 Presumably this is exactly why enforced exile is and has been considered such a significant punishment.

6 For further discussion of freedom of association and its connection to the right to exclude, see Fine (forthcoming: chapter 4).

7 See D. Miller (2005: 128). For further discussion of the immigration-related questions faced by liberal nationalists, see Tamir (1993: 140–67, esp. 159–67).

8 Other territory-based arguments for the right to exclude might depart from Lockean premises, or nationalist ones. We discuss the nationalist argument above. On Locke and territory, see Nine (2008) and Steiner (2008).

9 For this list of conditions, we are indebted to discussion in Stilz (2011: 578); these conditions are not explicitly stated as such by Kant, but, as Stilz convincingly argues, there are implications of his view.

10 This is no doubt because "extensive" lists of enforceable natural rights were associated, in Kant's day, with justifications for conquest and appropriation of the New World, much of which Kant was opposed to. See Muthu (2003). See also Benhabib's (2004) helpful discussion.

11 Cf. also Kant ([1781] 1991: 318; [1795] 1983; *MM* AK 8: 344).

12 Stilz (2011) makes a similar point. Can it made be made within a Lockean framework? For some doubts, see Brilmayer (1989). See also Nine (2008).

13 For further discussion of stability and security concerns, see Fine (forthcoming: chapter 5).

14 See e.g. Macedo (2007). But of course this kind of argument is pervasive in the domestic politics of every advanced industrialized nation.

15 We assume, for present purposes, that the scope of SOAs extends to all long-term residents (rather than to all citizens); this expansion in scope is most evident in the case of coercion- and reciprocity-based argument; we note in the text that it might not apply to nationalist ones, since there are residents who are not "nationals" in the relevant cultural sense. On a nationalist view, they would therefore fall outside of the scope of socio-economic equality.

16 By "broadly egalitarian obligations", we mean to include obligations that require us either to narrow the gap between the well-off and those less well-off, or to give greater moral weight (but not lexical priority) to the well-being, opportunities or resources of the badly off in an overall calculation of how to distribute scarce resources, or to ensure that everyone has enough, where the threshold is set at a higher level than humanitarianism.

17 Think of another analogy: a student from another university (call him Jay) comes to your office and demands supervision for his dissertation (at the other university). You say you cannot give him super-vision because it would be unfair to your own students, who would have less time than they otherwise would have for supervision. Jay then responds, "Yes, but I surely stand to gain much more than your students stand to lose by your supervision of me, so my interest in getting your supervision is much stronger than your current students' interests in keeping me out." Surely the right answer is: "But I have a special responsibility to my own students that I don't have to you because of the nature of our (institutional) relationship."

18 Abizadeh (forthcoming) makes a similar argument against SOAs.

19 For an argument for the view that communal possession might ground (rather than be used to refute) a limited right to exclude, see Blake and Risse (2009) and Risse (2012).

20 We thank Darrel Moellendorf for raising this possibility. There are, of course, many others that might also serve this role. In defence of a human right to international freedom of movement, see Oberman (forthcoming), and for the case against, see D. Miller (forthcoming). See also the discussion in Carens (2013: 225–54).

21 For the opposing view, see Beitz (1979), Moellendorf (2002) and Caney (2005b: 102–47).

22 See the fascinating discussion in Pandey *et al.* (forthcoming). For concerns about the future impact of immigration, see Collier (2013).

PART IV

Economic justice

Introduction

Economic justice is another core area of global ethics. It provides the structure within which everything else, from aid and development to the delivery of healthcare, is mediated and accessed. This section considers the architecture of the global economic system and its key players, features, characteristics and consequences. Clearly this part on economic justice overlaps with the previous part on poverty, as addressing poverty could be understood as economic justice, and likewise, as a reading of Chapter 16 and Chapter 21 will show, migration and trafficking are not easily separable. We have distinguished these sections, however artificially, for the purpose of providing a detailed focus of poverty in the previous part, and enough attention to economic justice in total, given the importance of these topics for the global ethics debate.

In this section we consider, broadly speaking, aspects of international economic transactions. At the global level Chapter 17 focuses on the institutions of international trade, particularly the General Agreement on Tariffs and Trade (GATT) and the World Trade Organization (WTO), and Chapter 18 focuses on the International Monetary Fund (IMF) and World Bank, an issue returned to in Chapter 22. Chapter 19 considers multinational organizations, which are transnational, and sometimes truly global, actors, but not states, and thus traditionally fall outside the global infrastructure that is organized around states. Chapters 19 and 20 consider different aspects of how individuals function within the sphere of economic justice, considering consumption and trafficking respectively, both of which are ways in which individuals feed into global trade. The breadth of this section is representative of the complexity of the topic. The overarching theme that runs through this part, and is addressed by all of the chapters in one way or another, is whether the current structures of the economic system are appropriate to deliver justice. If they are not, can they be reformed in such a way as to deliver justice, and if not, then what are the alternatives?

The global institutions that govern economic justice, and indeed many other aspects of global ethics, fall primarily within the United Nations (UN) and its institutions and declarations, conventions and covenants, all of which taken together constitute the framework of global governance.

The UN funds and supports a number of dedicated organizations to address particular global concerns. A number of the key UN organizations crucial to economic justice are the UN Conference on Trade Development (UNCTAD), the UN Development Programme (UNDP), the UN High Commission for Refugees (UNHCR) and the World Food Programme (WFP). In addition there are also agencies which are not directly UN agencies, but nonetheless are coordinated by the UN's Economic and Social Council. The most important of these for economic justice are the International Labour Organization (ILO), IMF, WTO and the World Bank. For all of these organizations and agencies states remain primary and it is through states that these organizations seek to have an impact. However, the establishment of such organizations and associations has resulted in some shift towards global norms and has placed new expectations on states. It is no longer realistically possible for states simply to ignore the global nature of governance and those that do so to a significant extent are deemed to be "failed" or "rogue" states. States that fall short are subject to sanctions of some type or another, including international condemnation, ostracism from the global political community, exclusion from the funds of the World Bank or the IMF, economic sanctions, and in the extreme cases force will be used against them.

Some argue that such infrastructure leads to a political and economic association that is powerful enough to impose global duties. This idea will be considered in different ways in different chapters of this section. Economic ties are evident at every level, between individuals (as producers and consumers), between states in trade, between companies and individuals and states. In addition, international financial markets, considered in Chapter 18, are increasingly interconnected to the point where it makes little sense to see the financial market as anything but global. This is shown clearly in the current financial crisis.

Certainly it is almost impossible for countries to choose to flout the rules of the WTO, no matter how justified some might think it would be, on grounds that it is effectively biased towards rich countries. Claims of bias are, in fact, pervasive. A frequent criticism of the structural adjustment programmes implemented by the World Bank and the IMF was that the conditions of such programmes had disastrous results, including the destruction of local infrastructure, failure to improve living standards and increased corruption, as well as ultimately leaving countries servicing debt rather than spending on development. Likewise the Agreement on Trade-Related Aspects of Intellectual Property Rights (TRIPS) is criticized for favouring developed countries and their pharmaceutical companies, making it harder for poor and middle-income countries to access essential drugs (returned to in Part V).

All of these chapters make suggestions about how we can better deliver economic justice, either by revising the current institutions, or by bringing in institutions and concerns that are not considered within the present system, or by recognizing the failings of the current system for delivering justice to real individuals and changing the definitions, practices, policies and institutions accordingly. The part finishes with some practical proposals for reform that have received the attention of global ethicists, namely, the Global Resources Dividend (GRD), the Tobin Tax and the Birthright Levy.

Chapter 17 by Christian Barry and Scott Wisor is concerned with the ethics of international trade. The internationalization of trade is standardly viewed either positively, as the developing of an international infrastructure which can be used for the global good, or negatively, as exacerbating and embedding global inequality, sustaining global injustices and contributing to global poverty. Barry and Wisor consider the various possibilities, beginning first with the possible gains of international trade, turning after that to some of the critiques of such trade, and finishing with a discussion of normative ethical claims and how they might apply to natural resources.

Barry and Wisor begin by describing international trade as "the voluntary exchange of goods and services across state borders, whether by states, firms or individuals." They then list the types of benefit that such trade, and perhaps any trade, might bring, such as mutual gain, greater efficiency, specialization, and the resulting gains deriving from such comparative advantage.

The authors claim that the assumptions about the gains of free trade, which go back to Adam Smith, and the contributions to welfare from free trade inform the practice of the current institutions of international trade, such as GATT and the WTO. Current critics of international trade either object to these assumptions and the claims that free trade results in welfare enhancement, or they deny that such institutions do in fact support trade that is really globally free. Barry and Wisor consider several objections. First they examine objections about the content of trade, including the trading of goods and/or services which are not owned, or should not be owned, by those who trade them. Second, they consider objections to the process of trade, for instance, when some form of coercion, deception or injustice is evident in the process. Third, they discuss harmful trade, and fourth they take up complaints about the fairness of trade.

The final third of the chapter considers the real-world institutions of international trade and some current concerns about international trade. In this section they first outline the WTO, describe its history, rationale, aims and intentions, and then go on to consider what there is to commend in this system as well as the problems with it. From this discussion emerges the final consideration of the chapter, namely the ethical conundrum known as the "resource curse." Countries that are rich in natural resources have a tendency to authoritarian governments, which are unstable and beset with coups and civil war. Although the countries are rich in resources, their populations are often very poor. Barry and Wisor finish the chapter with the unresolved challenge of channelling international trade to contribute to the welfare of all.

In Chapter 18 Meena Krishnamurthy focuses on the international financial institutions of the IMF and the World Bank. Krishnamurthy argues that moral attention to international institutions is crucial, given their role in economic globalization and the effects of these institutions on the everyday lives of all in the global community. Krishnamurthy considers financial institutions in three sections. First she sets out the history, structure and intended functions of the institutions. Second, she discusses moral criticism of the institutions. She finishes with some proposals to address some of these moral concerns and produce better-functioning institutions.

In the second section Krishnamurthy considers some key moral criticisms. One criticism concerns the conditions that are attached to loans, which conditions have at times left developing countries in worse positions than before they were granted loans, and arguably have led to stunted growth among the poorest countries. A second charge is that granting loans increases debt, and thereby makes development harder to achieve, limits the capacity of countries to provide public goods and arguably promotes oppressive elites. A third criticism is that these institutions are not democratic or consistent with democratic values and in fact undermine both autonomy and self-respect. The last section of the chapter is dedicated to possible ways to overcome these problems. Krishnamurthy sets out ways to improve and reform the current systems, finishing with the place of social movements in such possible future reforms.

Chapter 19 by Nien-hê Hsieh and Florian Wettstein considers multinational corporations (MNCs) and corporate social responsibility (CSR). CSR has been increasingly important in a number of arenas, for instance, in business ethics and in social responsibility reports intended for shareholder consumption and for the wider public. While there has been some scepticism regarding CSR, with some regarding it as little more than "ethical window dressing", emerging international CSR standards are essential for global ethics, as MNCs are effectively beyond the law of any individual nation state, and yet often have wealth and power beyond that of many countries. Given this, as Hsieh and Wettstein begin, MNCs have a potential to do great good or great harm to developing countries. Hence, they focus on the standards that should apply to MNCs and how such standards can be enforced. To do this the chapter first provides some background on MNCs; second, it summarizes existing standards; third, it considers CSR and its critics; fourth, it considers the universality of ethical standards in this area; and in the fifth and sixth sections it moves to a discussion of standards for MNCs in general. Taken together this chapter provides a comprehensive overview of the current state of play regarding developing and enforcing ethical standards for MNCs, finishing with an in-depth analysis of CSR and a moral assessment of MNCs and their purposes.

Moving from companies to individuals, Chapter 20 by Nicole Hassoun considers the ethics of consumption in the context of global justice. Hassoun begins by considering the current state of the debate, suggesting that to date there is no general theory which can be used to access the moral status of consumption or types of consumption. On the one hand some consumption is necessary and the ability to consume at least some goods may be a human right, a right which many currently lack. On the other hand over-consumption is problematic in terms of using scarce resources and increasing inequality. Hassoun documents the complexity of the debate and the contested nature of virtually all its claims. It is the lack of simple solutions and easily applicable theories of justice that leads Hassoun to spend the rest of the chapter focusing on how to approach real cases, in order to figure out what kinds of consumption are permissible or required.

To answer this question Hassoun first defends the "argument for creative resolve." This has two premises. First, we should not justify actions simply because there are no good alternatives; and second, we should aim to avoid terrible choices and find alternatives to address the problems. Hassoun works through this argument using a number of cases, including buying tomatoes and products made with the use of child labour. Hassoun concludes by suggesting that such an argument not only helps to answer whether a particular instance of consumption is permissible, it is also a method which can be more broadly applied and so contribute to methodologies of global justice and global justice theorizing.

The rejection of terrible dilemmas fits well with Chapter 21 by Julia O'Connell Davidson, on prostitution and trafficking for sexual labour. O'Connell Davidson maps this controversial debate well, bringing out the complexity of the topics and presenting a position which seeks to respect the diversity of views that surround this issue. Her focus is particularly on those who are "trafficked" rather than on prostitution in general, noting that "migrants are often among those found at the most exploited and unfree pole of the prostitution spectrum" (although she is quick to note that this is not always and by no means necessarily the case). Unpacking the definitions of trafficking and the, often rhetorical, debate surrounding it, O'Connell Davidson moves to a focus on irregular migration, and suggests that that the extent and nature of abuse differs from case to case. O'Connell Davidson problematizes the discourses of trafficking; criticizing much of the "slave trade" rhetoric, she states "there is no universal, established, external referent against which cases can be measured and judged to be trafficking or not trafficking." Similarly, she argues that voluntariness or consent provides no clear boundary between free wage labour and slavery; the assumption that consent can do this in liberal society rests on a "belief that economic pressures are less coercive than physical force or the threat of imprisonment". In fact, she points out, being unable to feed or provide healthcare for one's family "may be experienced as just as irresistible a force as the threat of physical violence." O'Connell Davidson promotes a view that recognizes that there is a spectrum, with degrees of voluntariness and desirability and of exploitation, which avoids the polarization of current debates about trafficking.

In Chapter 22 Chris Armstrong focuses on future institutions, and in particular on proposals for distributive institutions, which would constitute central institutions of global justice. Armstrong's chapter is divided into three sections. First, he considers why institutions matter morally; second, he considers existing institutions and the aim of promoting of global justice; and, third, he considers possible new institutions. Of the existing institutions that might feature in attaining a more just world he considers the IMF, World Bank, ILO and WTO, with particular focus on the WTO and how to reform it. The last section discusses proposals for possible new institutions, which could supplement or replace existing institutions and global policies. Here he considers proposals for global taxation for the purposes of reducing poverty or addressing inequality, a GRD, the Tobin Tax and the Birthright Levy.

17

INTERNATIONAL TRADE

Christian Barry and Scott Wisor

Moral and political debates about globalization – the expansion of the flow of goods, capital, ideas and people within a market-oriented framework – have often concentrated on the governance and practice of international trade. For some, the evolving international trading system is indicative of all the benefits that globalization makes possible. For others, it is a sign of the hypocrisy and self-seeking orientation of wealthy people in affluent countries that, they allege, have crafted a global economic order that unduly benefits them at the expense of the poor countries (along with poorer workers in their own countries).

International trade has also begun to attract the attention of moral and political theorists. Here too there have been significant disagreements. For example, some elements of the World Trade Organization (WTO) – the treaty body that governs international trade relations between 155 member states – have been singled out by some as paradigmatic instances of the ways in which the affluent countries contribute substantially to poverty abroad (Pogge 2002). Others have welcomed its emergence as an (admittedly imperfect and still nascent) international institution oriented towards promoting welfare throughout the world (Risse 2005a). Controversies among moral theorists have in part been due to differences in their views on the effects of current international trade arrangements. But they are also due to different views about the evaluative and normative principles that are appropriate to assess and govern international trade. In this chapter we explore some of these controversies.

We begin by explaining some of the reasons why it might be supposed that there can be substantial gains from international trade. We then explore some distinct types of complaints about trade policies and arrangements for governing international trade, and conclude with a brief discussion of how these normative considerations apply to the international trade in natural resources.

International trade

As we shall understand it, international trade involves the voluntary exchange of goods and services across state borders, whether by states, firms or individuals. The voluntary exchanges may be regulated or unregulated. One country may expose other countries to a range of pollutants (dumping toxic waste, spewing particulates into the air, releasing excess carbon-dioxide emissions, and so on). This does not properly count as trade because the transfer is involuntary.

However, if two countries agree that one will accept the pollutants of another in exchange for something, then this transfer counts as (regulated) international trade. And if buyers in one country agree to purchase illegal narcotics that are produced in another country, this counts as (unregulated) international trade. We shall understand goods and services broadly, including not only familiar fare like agricultural produce, industrial manufactures and services, but also items such as intellectual property, financial derivatives or carbon permits.

In limited forms, international trade has existed for millennia. Most historians of trade date the emergence of substantial and sustained international trade volumes to the fifteenth century (Irwin 1996). The rise of mercantilist economies in the seventeenth century and the Industrial Revolution further contributed to the rise of international trade as a defining feature of economic activity and a central concern in foreign affairs.[1] Continued technological advancements in transportation and communication, and political and economic changes, have made possible further and deeper international economic integration. This is not to say that progress towards such integration has been unstinting. Indeed, some economic historians have pointed out that periods of globalization have sometimes been followed by periods of de-globalization (H. James 2002, Frieden 2007). To those with a longer historical understanding, globalization is not an inexorable process but a reversible and perhaps even fragile development. Conflict or sharp rises in the cost of oil could no doubt undermine international integration, at least to some degree (Robb 2008). Moreover, the extent of international economic integration should not be exaggerated: most goods and services today are still traded intra-nationally, not internationally. Nevertheless, far more goods and services are traded today internationally than at any other point in human history, and many of the goods we trade intra-nationally have been created through a process involving inputs in many different countries. The conduct of states engaging in trade, and the arrangements that are brought about to govern trade, are thus quite consequential for human welfare.

Gains from trade

Why might it make sense to engage in international trade? In one sense, the answer is quite straightforward: international trade is just a type of market exchange. As such, it can offer the characteristic benefits that such exchanges can bring. Mutual gain from market exchange is possible whenever one agent is able to provide a good or service that other agents value more than she does. How much any particular agent values a good will depend on their preferences, and how many goods of that type they already possess. Since people throughout the world have different preferences and different holdings, gains from trade are often possible. International trade also gains impetus because it connects with a familiar idea, championed by Adam Smith in his classic work *An Inquiry into the Wealth of Nations* (Smith 1776). Smith famously argued that goods could be produced more efficiently (e.g. at lower cost) through the division and specialization of labour. Just as markets in which labour is specialized within each country can increase the quantity and quality of goods produced while lowering their cost, so too can markets in which there is specialization across countries. Smith also argued that the extent of specialization that would be possible within any particular market is in large measure a function of the size of that market. The larger the market, the more room it can afford for specialization. Correspondingly, the larger the market, the greater the increases in productivity that further specialization can potentially yield.

What then drives the possibility of gains from trade? As Smith understood it, the main reason that international trade could yield gains for those participating in it resulted from differences between countries that made it possible for countries to produce some goods more cheaply than others could: a relation economists now typically refer to as "absolute advantage". Country A enjoys absolute advantage in the production of some good over country B if A can produce that good more cheaply than B can. Smith writes, "if a foreign country can supply us with the commodity cheaper than we ourselves can make it, better buy it of them with some part of the produce of our own industry, employed in a way in which we have some advantage" (*ibid.*: 424). On this account, the gains from international trade are driven by the ability of different countries to produce different goods at different levels of cost.

Contemporary economists have tended to downplay the role that absolute advantage plays in driving international trade. Instead, they have emphasized what is now called "comparative advantage", an idea that is usually attributed to David Ricardo (though James Mill and Robert Torrens seem to have entertained similar ideas at roughly the same time) (Irwin 1996, Maneschi 1998). Country A enjoys comparative advantage in the production of some good relative to country B if A is able to produce that good at a lower opportunity cost than B can. The "opportunity cost" here refers to the extent to which A's producing some good diminishes its capacity to produce some other good(s). The idea is that countries would do best to focus on producing what they are *relatively* most efficient at producing, even if there are other things that they can produce at lower absolute cost than others can.

Ricardo famously illustrated his idea through a simple example (Ricardo [1817] 1821: chapter 7). He invited us to imagine two countries (England and Portugal) in their capacities to produce two goods (wine and cloth) on the assumption that labour was the only input (factor of production) determining the cost of production. In his model, he posited that Portugal produces both cloth and wine more efficiently (i.e. at lower cost in terms of labour input) than England does. Portugal thus enjoys absolute advantage (in the sense defined above) over England with respect to the production of both goods. According to the principle of absolute advantage, it would appear that Portugal has little reason to trade with England in either of these goods. However, Ricardo demonstrated that in his model trade in both goods would be beneficial to *both* countries. In order to reap the largest gains from trade, Portugal should produce only that good (wine) which it is relatively most efficient at producing, while England should produce only that good (cloth) which it is relatively most efficient at producing. When countries produce the goods that they are relatively most efficient at producing, their so-called opportunity costs – the cost of not producing other things that they could otherwise produce – will be minimized. He showed that if each country bought their entire share of some good from the country that possessed the greatest comparative advantage at producing it, each would be better off than they would be in the absence of specialized production and trade. Ricardo's seemingly counterintuitive idea has radical implications. It suggests that even countries that lack absolute advantage in the production of any goods can still reap quite substantial gains from trade and benefit from integration with other countries.[2] On these grounds economists have typically argued that just as economic exchange between citizens within a country is an efficient means of allocating resources (and correspondingly increasing welfare) in that country, so too international trade can increase the welfare of countries independent of how economically developed those countries are (Krugman 1998).

Diversity and trade

Why would some countries enjoy comparative advantage in the production of some goods over others? This question has been the focus of much work in contemporary economics. One very influential response to this is the so-called Heckscher–Ohlin theorem (Heckscher [1919] 1991, Ohlin 1933). According to it, comparative advantage is determined by what are commonly referred to as a country's "factor endowments": the resources it possesses that can be marshalled to produce goods and services. These resources can be of various types, including labour, land and capital (resources are referred to simply as "inputs"). Thus, a country will enjoy comparative advantage with respect to the production of some good in so far as the inputs necessary for the production of that good are abundant, relative to its possession of the inputs necessary to produce other goods. On this model, it would be rational in a system of free international trade (given assumptions to be explained shortly) to specialize in the production of those goods for which they enjoy relatively abundant factor inputs. There are other factors that contribute to generating comparative advantage, including level of technological development, preferences, and economies of scale (Krugman 1998). These have been much studied by economists (Morrow 2010 provides a good overview). The basic message of these models remains the same: whenever there are differences between the rates at which one country can transform one commodity into another and the international rates of such transformation, increased production (and, correspondingly, gain from trade) is possible.

Smith himself devoted significant attention to arguing not only that international trade would bring benefits to the countries, but that any attempts to restrict trade would undermine the possibility of the gains made possible by such specialization (Smith 1776: book IV, chapter 2). They would therefore probably be harmful to the economy implementing them (along with others), rather than helpful to them. In addition to being inefficient, such market interventions would, he feared, typically be used to benefit particular interest groups, rather than society as a whole: a concern that is echoed today by many advocates of trade liberalization (Bhagwati 1998, Srinivasan 1998). Smith thus argued that countries ought to liberalize trade, freeing it from government interventions (e.g. tariffs, quotas and subsidies), and become more integrated with other countries economically. In his view countries not only had reasons to engage in trade and to engage in specialization, but also to avoid interposing obstacles to free trade. Connected with these explanations of why people would wish to engage in trade and why it could be beneficial to them is a clear and powerful justification for protecting such practice. Establishing practices of free international trade (whether within or across countries) enhances freedom to make agreements that are welfare enhancing.

Implications

The ideas of the classic political economists discussed in the previous section are of more than merely historical interest. They continue to enjoy a great deal of prestige today. These ideas have informed a great deal of economic thinking about trade. And they have also played a fundamental role in shaping institutional arrangements that have been developed to regulate trade. These institutions, including the General Agreement on Tariffs and Trade (GATT) and the WTO, along with other bilateral and multilateral agreements, have all been oriented towards liberalizing trade between their members.

We discuss these ideas also because many of the moral complaints against current arrangements for international trade depend on objections to these ideas. Few critics of such arrangements reject these ideas altogether, or deny that there can be substantial gains from international trade. Indeed, most accept that some of these models succeed admirably in their own terms. But many insist that, despite their power, these ideas stand in need of substantial qualification, and should not be interpreted as providing simple and unproblematic advice about how different countries should structure their trade policies, or how arrangements for governing international trade should be designed (Stiglitz & Charlton 2006, Rodrik 2011). The elegant models that have been developed to explain the possibility of gains from trade incorporate assumptions that do not hold in the real world. This is not problematic in itself, but it does suggest that we should be cautious in drawing direct policy implications from such models: a point to which we return below.

Moral complaints about trade

Trade involves voluntary exchange. There is ordinarily a presumption in favour of allowing agents to engage in voluntary exchange. How then could there be moral complaints about trade? Four types of moral complaints can be distinguished, which can apply to a particular trading activity, or to institutional arrangements governing trade. The first type of complaint focuses on the content of the trade. The second type of complaint focuses on the process by which the trade came about. The third type of complaint alleges that the trade causes unjustified harm. The fourth type of complaint alleges that the trade brings about an unfair distribution of benefits.

Content

Trade can trigger moral complaints whenever those engaging in trade do not rightfully possess the goods that they wish to exchange. There is nothing wrong with trading books for money, but there is something wrong when I trade a library book for money. Trade always assumes property rights over those things that are tradable, even if not all things over which people have property rights are tradable.

In so far as some goods and services simply should not be traded, there is obvious reason to complain about such trade, or about institutions that encourage or permit it. That is, most accept that there are some limits to markets, and any markets in goods that fall outside of such limits are problematic. The services of child prostitutes, to take an extreme example about which there is general consensus, are not thought to be tradable. But of course there is a great deal of disagreement over just which things are tradeable. Body parts, rare cultural artefacts, reproductive labour and various animal products are traded, but it is not clear whether they should be (Radin 1996, Satz 2011, Sandel 2012). Other goods and services are thought to be tradable, but only for certain things, or in narrowly circumscribed contexts. As Michael Walzer has put it, "citizens can't trade their votes for hats" (Walzer 1983: 23).

Even with respect to goods that are accepted as tradable, not every agent can permissibly engage in trading them. It seems plausible, for example, that children or mentally incapacitated persons cannot always engage in trades of goods over which they have property rights, even if they would do so voluntarily. And even those who affirm that there can be markets in sexual services typically demand that children be excluded from them as buyers and sellers.

We have been illustrating complaints about trade through simple examples involving individual agents. But these considerations apply also to collective agents such as governments. For example, Thomas Pogge and Leif Wenar have recently argued that certain types of governments should not be permitted to trade certain things that are ordinarily tradable (Pogge 2002, Wenar 2008). If the government of A is not even minimally representative of the interests of its people, for example, then it is not obvious that it can trade and thereby grant rightful title to the natural resources of the territories that it controls. Similarly, if a country sells away various cultural artefacts and relics (as the Chinese government did for a period), citizens may object to these sales because they were undertaken by a government that was not a legitimate seller (Hessler 2007: 444).

These types of considerations can apply in parallel to the making of trade agreements. The rules of international trade are decided or agreed to by particular governments. The decisions of these countries are treated as binding on all present and future people in that country. Because of that, we may wish to ask whether these governments ought to meet requirements in order to be deemed legitimate rule-making agents in international trade. And if the rules they agree on include as "tradable" things that should be excluded from markets, or permit agents who should be excluded from certain markets to enter them, they will be objectionable for these reasons.

Process

Complaints can also be made about the process through which trade is conducted. A might wrong B through bullying, coercion, or various forms of deception, either in making particular trades or in negotiation over standing and coercively enforced rules that will govern trade in the future. Some who would engage in trade in some market may lack crucial information that would provide them with decisive reason not to do so. And some are so vulnerable that it is easy to manipulate them into trades that may be contrary to their interests. These types of process considerations seem to be relevant not only to trading activity, but to rules governing trade. That is, whether international trading rules have been agreed to as a result of bullying, coercion, or various forms of deception may be deemed relevant to their legitimacy. And even if some rules have indeed been agreed to in a way that has not involved such interactions, it may nevertheless be maintained that the legitimacy of these rules is seriously called into question, if past interactions between countries making such agreements involved such conduct.

An additional process consideration focuses on the manner in which some good or service has been produced (Barry & Reddy 2008). For example, it can be complained that it is wrong to import goods and services that are produced through the use of slavery or the worst forms of child labour, or which arose from a process that caused grave harms to the environment or non-human animals. For example, WTO/GATT article XX explicitly permits the adoption of impediments to trade in goods produced with the use of prison labour (World Trade Organization 2011a).

Harm

In what sense could the trade policy adopted by Country A be harmful? It is easy to think of simple cases where this could happen. Through trading something – industrial products, say – it might initiate a continuous causal process that leads to environmental damage and health problems in the country that receives them. This would be a clear-cut instance of doing harm through trade. But many of the harms that people complain about in trade are not of this sort. They do not involve discrete causal processes that stretch from the conduct of one agent to injuries of another. They relate instead to the ways in which shifts in the allocation of resources as a consequence of trade policies can make people much worse off, whether in the countries adopting the policy or elsewhere. That is, they focus on the way agents can enable harms to occur through trade (Barry & Øverland 2012).

Now, the very idea that engaging in trade could enable harm by making people worse off may seem odd given what was said about the impetus to engage in trade the first place. Recognize, however, that the agents engaging in international trade, and deliberating over trading rules, are not only individuals acting alone, but are collective agents making these decisions in ways that have impacts on the welfare of a great many people.

Consider, first, complaints alleging harm that might be made against A by its citizens were it to adopt the policy of becoming more fully integrated into the global economy, say by removing its tariffs or by refraining from supporting domestic producers with subsidies. It may be that through such integration A gains on aggregate, while some people and groups within

A do not. It is important to bear in mind that in Ricardo's model discussed above, the only input into production was labour. Consequently, his model does not allow differences between the overall gains from trade and the gains from trade to particular groups. Typically, however, there are multiple factors that are inputs in the production of goods in an economy. Trade liberalization and specialization can consequently lead countries to shift their production in ways that will benefit some groups and harm others. For example, if as a result of its removal of tariffs A shifts from production that is labour intensive to production that is capital intensive, then ordinary workers (owners of labour) may be harmed even while owners of capital are benefited. The magnitude and duration of such harm may depend on how "mobile" the factors of production are: how easily those displaced can be redeployed in other production. That the gains of liberalization make it *possible* for A to compensate those who are harmed by this policy (whether through lump sum transfers or assistance in gaining access to new production opportunities) will be cold comfort for those who are made worse off if they have little assurance that such compensation will actually occur. The direct harmful impacts of trade might be mitigated by states with strong systems of social protection that are able to redistribute resources to support displaced workers, perhaps through unemployment programmes, and/or to place them in job retraining programmes. These redistributive efforts might be made possible by welfare gains elsewhere in the economy resulting from new trade arrangements. However, in the absence of such a redistributive programme, assessments of proposed or existing trade arrangements will depend upon whether harms to some groups can be justified by benefits to others – whether compatriots or foreigners.[3]

Just as such harm-based complaints can be made against a particular trade policy, so too can they be lodged against institutional arrangements for governing trade, for example those that require countries to respect the highly restrictive intellectual property rights of foreign firms, including rights over needed medicines and technologies. While countries may accrue net benefits by joining these trade arrangements, some of their constituents may be rendered worse off because they can no longer be provided with generic versions of new medicines and technologies at manageable cost. The question is then whether the benefits to some groups of citizens of increased trade opportunities outweigh the costs to others engendered by compliance with more stringent intellectual property rights (Moellendorf 2005, Pogge 2005a).

Another type of harm-based complaint against trade policies is rooted in doubts about how comparative advantage should be understood, and the policies and arrangements that would best enable countries to benefit from it. Recall that comparative advantage (in Ricardo's sense) is static and can identify the most advantageous forms of production for a country at a particular point in time. However, what is arguably more important is what steps a country can take to increase over time its productive capacities and to transform such growth into widespread benefits for its people. This is necessarily a dynamic, not a static, process of transformation. Some economists have tried to capture this idea by distinguishing between natural and acquired comparative advantage. But Roberto Unger has rightly noted that the more important distinction is between what might be called "established" comparative advantage – what a country can now produce most efficiently, whether for reasons of natural advantages or otherwise – and "constructed" comparative advantage – what comparative advantages can feasibly be developed (Unger 2007). One harm-based complaint, then, would be that by engaging in a process of liberalization the government is achieving short-term gains at the cost of significant medium- and long-term disadvantages (Rodrik 2011).[4]

So far we have been considering harm-based complaints that can be made by the citizens of a country against its government's policies. But the populations of other countries can also lodge harm-based complaints against some government. In recent years the complaint has often been raised that policies such as subsidies paid to domestic producers by affluent countries and tariffs on goods produced by foreign producers in poorer countries violate important moral require- ments because they do severe harm to poor people, even killing them. For example, *New York Times* columnist Nicholas Kristof argues that "[b]y inflating farm subsidies even more, Congress and the Bush administration are impoverishing and occasionally killing Africans whom we claim to be trying to help" (Kristof 2002).[5] And Pogge has frequently cited rich country tariffs on imports from poor countries and subsidies paid to their own domestic producers when suggesting that the leaders of affluent countries have become "hunger's willing executioners" in relation to the poor in the developing world (Pogge 2002: 24).

It is important to note that different harm-based complaints can pull in different directions. Import tariffs and domestic subsidies are likely to increase welfare for some while decreasing it for others. Consider, for example, the effects that A's removing an export subsidy, say for rice, will have. Such a policy may: harm some domestic rice producers (the recipients of the subsidy); benefit rice producers abroad, because the price their produce will fetch should increase as A is no longer forcing down its price; and harm consumers abroad, who will have to pay more for rice.

A further complication is that even if some countries benefit from this shift, many people in those countries may not benefit. These gains may instead be captured by powerful minority groups (who may agitate politically for policies that favour themselves at the expense of others).[6] Because trade is likely to have very different effects on different groups both at home and abroad, normative assessments of whether or not some policy ought to be adopted will necessarily depend on the appropriate way of balancing these competing claims.

Though we cannot provide here a comprehensive assessment of how these various claims should be weighed, a few preliminary notes are in order. First, the assessment of the justice of any shift in trading arrangements should arguably be sensitive to the background conditions of justice existing in the countries in question. For example, if a new trade arrangement may benefit women but harm some men (say, by increasing the amount of textile manufacturing in the country and reducing the amount of resource extraction), this may be more permissible, and perhaps obligatory, if the background conditions are such that women are systematically dis- advantaged relative to men. Second, adequate assessment of competing claims must take some position on the overall moral significance of the status quo. If, for example, government pro- nouncements and programmes gave workers reason to believe that a particular industry would flourish in the coming years, and then the government considers a new trade arrangement which would make it quite difficult for that industry to take hold, these workers arguably have a greater claim to government redress given the creation of reasonable expectations by government pronouncement.[7] Third, normative assessments of new trade arrangements have to take a position on the moral significance of non-economic benefits that are alleged to accrue from the persistence of certain industries. For example, European agricultural policy permits French subsidies for farmers (Kurjanska & Risse 2008). This move is defended in part by the perceived importance of the French farmer to the identity of those living in the French countryside, and the nation as a whole. In our view the claims to cultural protection that justify many market-distorting trade policies are probably exaggerated, and this cultural protection could arguably take place through redistributive mechanisms that would not affect international trade.

Fairness

Even if all of the citizens of A, or all of the citizens of its trading partners, do benefit from the liberalization of trade, there is a further moral complaint that may be made against A or its trading partners. Some trade arrangements, while mutually beneficial, may distribute those benefits in ways that seem unfair. For example, if A is a large and very wealthy country, and enters a bilateral trade agreement with B, which is a much smaller developing country, and B agrees to lower restrictions on foreign direct investment and strengthen legal protections for investors against expropriation, in exchange for lowered tariffs on goods exported to A, then citizens in both countries may on the whole gain. But if, ten years after making this agreement, it appears that gains in both employment and profit have accrued greatly to A's firms, although there have only been marginal benefits to exporting firms in B, B's citizens may object that too much was traded away for too little gained. That is, they have not got a fair share of the benefits of the liberalized trading relationship, particularly if some alternative feasible arrangement could have produced more gains for the developing country.[8]

One may arguably also do wrong by offering terms of exchange to trading partners that result in their receiving less than the *fair value* of what they provide to you. Fair trade activists, for example, demand that coffee producers in developing countries (and others) receive a fair price for the goods that they are exchanging, claiming that it is unfair that growers receive prices that barely allow them to maintain their basic needs while the firms that market such goods enjoy massive profits. Similarly, one complaint made against "land grabs" – the purchase by foreign investors of land in developing countries for the production of food and other goods – is that the sellers are not being paid the fair value of their land (made possible, in part, through limited knowledge and coordination among sellers, and the vulnerability of those who need to sell).

The governance of international trade

So far we have outlined the rationale for engaging in international trade and distinguished between different types of complaints that could be made against such trade. We turn now to discussing existing arrangements governing international trade.

The World Trade Organization

The WTO is a "treaty-based" organization: it was constituted through an agreed legally binding treaty made up of more than thirty articles, along with additional commitments by some members in specific areas.[9] At present, 155 states are members of the WTO. They collectively make up over 98 per cent of all trade worldwide (World Trade Organization 2011b). The WTO treaty specifies the rights and obligations of its member states. To become a member of the WTO, a state must treat the agreement as a "single undertaking". Members cannot choose *à la carte* which agreements – for example, regarding tariffs, or trade in services or intellectual property – they want to accede to and which they do not. Instead, they must take on the obligations of the agreement *in toto*.

The WTO came into existence in 1995 at the Marrakech Agreement, itself the culmination of the Uruguay Round trade negotiations, which lasted from 1986 to 1994 (World Trade Organization 1994). The Uruguay Round negotiations were, in turn, carried out against the framework for multilateral trade established in the 1947 GATT, which had been subject to some modifications through successive rounds of earlier negotiations. Indeed, a great many of the cornerstone articles of the WTO treaty and the principles animating it are inherited from the GATT. Yet although there are continuities between the GATT and the WTO, the Marrakech Agreement marked a very significant change in the governance of international trade.

First, the WTO represented the first truly international organization to be charged with regulating international trade. This organization allowed for greater juridification of trade norms and a greater capacity to enforce them. It thus represents a drive towards a much more ambitious sort of international economic integration. New arrangements incorporated into the WTO included a Dispute Settlement Body (DSB) that was charged with, among other things, making authoritative rulings on trade disputes between members, and a new mechanism for monitoring the trade policies of member states (the Trade Policy Review Mechanism). Second, the domain of economic activity covered by the WTO agreement is much larger than that of previous trade agreements. In particular, it includes areas that had not previously been regulated as matters of trade, such as rules governing investment (TRIMS), intellectual property (TRIPS) and services (GATS). Third, the WTO incorporated many countries into the multilateral trading order that had previously been at its margins. While the GATT was constituted by a relatively small group of similarly situated and like-minded countries (advanced industrialized countries), the membership of the WTO is far more diverse (a significant majority of its members are states from the developing world).

Although the WTO treaty is complex – over 30,000 pages of text in all – it is animated by a few core principles. The first principle is non-discrimination. This is expressed in its so-called Most Favoured Nation (MFN) and National Treatment clauses. The MFN requires that all benefits or advantages conferred by one member of the WTO onto another regarding trade be automatically extended to all other members (World Trade Organization 2011c). Effectively, this is a commitment to avoid preferential trading blocs, though such blocs have continued to play a significant role in international trade (Bhagwati 2008). National Treatment requires that goods and services traded by locals and foreigners be treated equally once they have entered the local market. The second principle is reciprocity: member states are expected to make concessions to each other in such a way as to balance out the exchange of benefits provided through trade. The third (as noted above) is liberalization: the aim of the trade policies of member states should be to remove barriers to free trade so as to enable them to capture potential gains from trade. A fourth principle, which is in some ways in tension with the first three, is that of special and differential treatment for developing countries. This principle calls for measures such as support for poorer countries so that they can participate more effectively in the WTO (enabling them to take better advantage of trading opportunities) and flexibility for poorer countries in implementing various accords (especially those requiring regulatory and administrative reforms) (Stiglitz & Charlton 2006).

Although the WTO is the dominant international organization governing international trade, it is far from the only game in town. Multilateral trade agreements (such as the North American Free Trade Agreement, between Canada, the United States and Mexico) and bilateral trade agreements (between any two countries, such as the United States and Peru) also govern much international trade. And of course international trade is also governed in large measure by policy-making undertaken at the level of states. Governments can decide whether to permit the production of goods or their export and import, and what types of economic activity to encourage and promote. The evolution of the governance of international trade and its increasing complexity is a response to the rapidly expanding size of international trade and the scope of goods and services subject to international exchange.

Commendable features

There are several features of current international trading arrangements that are morally commendable. First, such arrangements are voluntary. Countries must voluntarily accede to the terms of the WTO treaty. Domestic governments must approve accession to the WTO, and they must approve regional and bilateral trade agreements. They cannot be compelled to join it. And no member of the WTO is in any way prevented from engaging in trade with non-members. Further, existing trade arrangements aim at *democratic authorization*. By requiring domestic authorization, these processes in principle allow domestic constituencies to contest disagreeable aspects of any particular trade arrangement. Of course, some domestic efforts to change these agreements will be strictly driven by the narrow self-interest of a given sector. But in other cases genuinely moral concerns – for example concerning the distribution of benefits and burdens engendered by trade – may be introduced in the domestic context that lead to reforms in international trade agreements.

The WTO also creates more reliable conditions of mutual market access to countries engaged in international trade, through a transparent rule-based system with impartial adjudication of trade disputes. By binding of tariff rates (i.e. the placing of a ceiling on tariffs) it prevents countries from engaging in a damaging competition to maximize access to markets of their own producers, which typically will result in a collectively self-defeating outcome. A rule-based multilateral trading system in which countries' freedom to raise tariffs unilaterally is limited is in the interests of all.

Further, it aims at *non-discriminatory treatment*. Non-discrimination requires that trading benefits conferred upon any individual member of a trade agreement be conferred upon all members of the agreement. This is morally significant as it helps to prevent the use of trade as a coercive tool to promote an individual state's self-interest, at the expense of some trade partners and their citizens.

When trade disputes arise, existing trade arrangements aim at impartial adjudication according to transparent and previously agreed rules. At the WTO, the primary avenue for resolving a trade dispute is through the Dispute Settlement Mechanism (DSM). The DSM settles disputes between WTO members, and authorizes actions by those states after a verdict has been reached. It makes WTO agreements binding and enforceable, through an independent system which relies on (and develops) international trade law. Such mechanisms help to prevent the escalation of bilateral trade disputes into protectionist trade wars or, worse yet, disputes spilling out of the domain of trade and into political or military dispute more generally. While there have certainly been many cases in which the DSM has failed to settle disputes quickly, or satisfactorily, it has in other cases led member countries – including quite wealthy and powerful ones – to revise their policies.[10]

Many existing trade arrangements aim at *improving human welfare* by reducing inefficiencies in the exchange of goods and services. This improvement in welfare is both direct, in that two trading parties are made better off than they would have been if they had not traded, and indirect, in that trading parties are thought to be more likely to cooperate in other arenas and less likely to be in conflict, especially violent conflict. Human welfare may also improve in various indirect ways through regular trading relationships through the diffusion of progressive norms and ideas, such as the idea that disputes should be resolved through transparent, rule-based mechanisms in a forum in which the interests of diverse countries are well represented.

Most trade arrangements, notably regional trade agreements and the founding treaties of the WTO, aim at *multilateral agreement* on trade. This is morally commendable as the trade in goods and services between any two countries inevitably impacts third-party countries that are also trading partners or trade in similar goods and services. For example, if the United States agrees to reduce or eliminate tariffs on imports from Ghana, this will disadvantage producers in other countries if they do not receive the same treatment. Therefore, including all affected parties in a trade arrangement makes it less likely (though certainly still possible) that trade will be structured so as to benefit a few trading partners while ignoring the impacts on other trading partners.

The fact that the principle of special and differential treatment for developing countries has been incorporated into the agreement is also commendable. This commitment is reflected in particular articles of the agreement, including Article XVIII, which permits latitude to developing countries in imposing trade restrictions to reduce balance-of-payments problems or to promote economic development (World Trade Organization 2011a). Additionally, developing countries are required to make fewer tariff reduction commitments than rich countries.

Finally, it is morally commendable that, despite criticisms to the contrary, many existing trade arrangements permit individual states a significant amount of flexibility in balancing their obligations to trading partners with national prerogatives. Countries can, for example, act unilaterally to interfere with trade (within constraints) so as to protect public morals, or to protect human or animal health in international trade. We take this to be commendable in two senses. First, it is important that trading partners not be required to partake in trade that is morally objectionable. Second, it is important that trade arrangements take account of the reasonable pluralism of various participants. Given that international trading partners reasonably disagree about various questions of public morals, it is important that trade arrangements not impose values when said values could be reasonably disputed.

Concerns

There are other aspects of international trading arrangements that make them vulnerable to some of the moral complaints identified above. Consider, first, complaints about the process by which such agreements have come about. In negotiating trade agreements, it is clearly morally wrong to engage in outright bullying, coercion, deception and manipulation. Arguably, it is also morally wrong to conclude trade negotiations with partners that do not have the time, resources or expertise to fully understand the implications of a trade agreement. Many critics of the international trade regime argue, plausibly, that some of these features have characterized international trade negotiations (Ryan 1998, P. Singer 2002, Stiglitz & Charlton 2006). They object, rightly, that while countries are not forced to join the WTO, refusing membership comes at high economic costs. In many ways, the WTO represents an offer that developing countries cannot refuse (Valentini 2011, A. James 2012). Once members, developing countries have, in practice, much less influence over the direction of trade policy than wealthy countries, and this tends to be reflected in the content of the evolving rules of the system.

In our view it is also uncontroversially wrong to engage in deliberate or foreseeable promise-breaking in the negotiation of international trade. The Doha development round of trade negotiations at the WTO is supposed to deliver on a range of issues important to developing countries. But for the last ten years, rich countries have failed to make any progress on an agreement that would address subsidies, tariffs and intellectual property: at the time of writing, the Doha round is largely viewed as a failure that undermines the legitimacy of the WTO.

Most issues of international trade are very complex – empirically and normatively – and require a great deal of scrutiny to reach well-reasoned assessments. We conclude this chapter by examining one issue that has attracted the attention of political philosophers working on trade: natural resource exports. We suggest how the framework developed above can provide a basis for addressing this particular issue of international trade. In doing so, we will also draw attention to other areas of concern in current arrangements for governing international trade.

Natural resource exports

The current international trade system confers on all governments the power to authorize the trade in natural resources from that country. This resource right, in conjunction with a variety of other rights, is typically bestowed on a government regardless of how that government came to power or how it governs.[11] There is reason to believe that this right contributes to what some economists have called the resource curse – the propensity of resource-rich countries to be beset by civil war, authoritarianism, coups, economic mismanagement and high levels of gender inequality (Karl 1997; M. Ross 1999, 2012; Wantchekon 2002). Various explanations have been given for this correlation. Pogge and Wenar appeal to the incentive structure created by the resource right.[12] Because any group knows that they will be granted full control over the resources should they succeed in taking power, this provides them with powerful incentives to arm themselves and take power through illegitimate means (Pogge 2002: 112–15; Wenar 2010). The rulers who control the resources both recognize this threat and desire to stay in power. So they use the revenues from resource extraction to arm themselves, purchase support, and pay off potential spoilers. The revenues from resource extraction prevent the ruler from needing to rely on citizens as an important tax base, therefore undermining incentives to govern democratically or systematically respond to the interests of citizens (Wenar 2008, M. Ross 2012, Wisor 2012).

Citizens of resource-exporting countries can rightfully object to the sale of such natural resources. First, they may rightfully object that their governments ought not to authorize the sale of resources without democratic input, especially when the benefits of these sales should accrue to citizens rather than to a small group of elites. Second, they may object to trading partners that they should not be complicit in the theft of natural resources. Such sales not only fail to benefit them but also provide agents with the means to harm. The revenues received by their governments also make them relatively unaccountable to their people (Wiens forthcoming). Sudanese citizens may object, for example, that China and India extract large quantities of Sudanese oil knowing that the revenue from this oil is spent on armaments used to make war against Sudanese civilians, and to line the pockets of elites connected to the regime in Khartoum, while very few benefits trickle down to most citizens. Furthermore, Sudanese citizens may object not just to the immediate trading partners of Sudan, but to the participants in the world trade system more generally, which permits the continued trade in Sudanese oil.[13]

However, identifying justified reforms to the trade in Sudanese oil is not a simple task, because most proposals are vulnerable to at least some of the grounds for complaint that we have identified earlier. We have argued that when arrangements are designed, they ought to be brought about in a manner that is free from coercion, deception and bullying, and made by the legitimate (democratically authorized) representatives of the trading partners. We have argued that the agreement should permit the trade of only properly tradable goods; lead to increases in human welfare; distribute the benefits of trade fairly; and avoid unjustified harm. There are several possible reforms that resource importers might make regarding the importation of Sudanese oil. They may impose unilateral or multilateral sanctions on Sudanese oil exports. Or they may institute reforms, such as requiring companies involved in the Sudanese oil industry to be transparent with oil payments and to make efforts to ensure that benefits of the sale of Sudanese oil reach Sudanese citizens. In the first case, participants in Sudan's oil industry risk imposing (at least short-term) additional harm by departing from the trade relationship if it is foreseeable that they will be replaced by even less scrupulous trade participants. In the latter case, the risk of *additional* harm may be lower, but at the moral cost of participating in illegitimate trade that harms a great many people. Sudan's current and potential trading partners, and advocates concerned with Sudan, must assess difficult trade-offs between competing moral considerations in selecting the best feasible alternative to the status quo. While we will leave the particulars of this case unresolved, we hope that this chapter provides some guidance on the moral reasons that are relevant to prescribing reforms to the resource curse.

Notes

1 Mercantilists promoted international trade, but on condition that such trade would result in a balance of trade for their country whereby the value of its exports exceeded the value of its imports. That is, they were pro-trade conditional on surplus, and favoured intervention to forbid trade that could result in deficit (particularly when the goods in question were valued metals) (Ormrod 2003).

2 Of course, it is not typically countries that are engaged directly in trade (as in Ricardo's model), but private actors trading across national borders.

3 The domestic political economy of the liberalizing country may in fact make it less likely that compensatory actions are undertaken. For example, Joseph Stiglitz (2012: 58–62) argues that trade liberalization (and in particular financial and capital liberalization) in the United States has been promoted by wealthy special interest groups (especially those in the finance sector). These groups are exceedingly unlikely to then endorse progressive taxation and social spending to compensate those who are harmed by trade liberalization, and they actively oppose unionization and other measures that might allow labourers to bargain for a greater share of the social product that arises from international trade.

4 This is related to, but broader than, the so-called infant industries argument (Mill [1848] 2004, List 1841), according to which it would be harmful to the economy to refrain from protecting nascent industries, which can propel the economy in the future.

5 Both of these harm-based complaints rely on the idea that by adopting some trade policy, some people are made unjustifiably worse off than they otherwise would have been. Another type of harm-based complaint does not assert that people are made necessarily worse off under some trade arrangement than they would have been in the absence of the trade arrangement, but rather that they are made worse off by some trade arrangement than they would be under a fair or morally justified arrangement.

6 One further complication in real-world cases is that some small poor countries enjoy tariff-free access to some rich country markets (particularly, under the European Union's "Everything But Arms" Initiative), which enables them to receive a higher price for their exports than they would were the market to be more fully liberalized (Mattoo & Subramanian 2004).

7 This point is emphasized by Kurjanska & Risse (2008).

8 For an extended discussion of how the gains from trade should be divided among trading partners, see A. James (2012).

9 We draw in the next two paragraphs on Barry & Wisor (2013).

10 Notable examples include India's complaint about the EU's Generalized System of Preferences (GSP) scheme (DS246), and the Brazil-led complaint regarding the EU sugar programme (DS265).

11 The phrase "resource right" is due to Wenar (2010). Pogge himself refers to this right as a "resource privilege".

12 For an overview, see M. Ross (2012).

13 Iris Marion Young (2011) argues that participants in systems of trade can be held responsible for the harms that result from those systems, even if they are not directly causally responsible for the resulting harms. On this account of responsibility for injustice, even if a government, company or individual withdraws from the trade in Sudanese oil, they still bear some responsibility to those who are harmed by such trade if they remain active in the broader system of oil exploration that permits the harmful extraction of Sudanese oil.

18

INTERNATIONAL FINANCIAL INSTITUTIONS

Meena Krishnamurthy

In the era of increasing economic and financial globalization – the closer integration of the countries in the world economy through increased flow of goods and capital – international financial institutions have become of great importance. This is largely because economic globalization and its effects are managed in significant part by international financial institutions such as the International Monetary Fund (IMF) and the World Bank.

Few philosophical works have considered in detail the moral dimensions of international financial institutions. As Thomas Pogge notes, philosophical discussion of international ethics has focused on important questions relating to just war (particularly the rules governing the use of force) and individual duties to provide aid to needy non-compatriots (Pogge 2005b: 1). For the most part, it has not been concerned with questions about the design and conduct of existing international institutions such as the IMF and the World Bank. There is, however, good reason to engage in the moral assessment of international institutions such as the IMF and the World Bank.

Two points are important here. First, as John Rawls argues in his prominent work on domestic justice, "the basic structure is the primary subject of justice because its effects are so profound and present from the start" (Rawls 1999a: 7). On Rawls's view, from the perspective of justice, the social and political institutions that comprise the basic structure are of central importance because they inevitably have a significant impact on how people's lives proceed. Something similar can be argued of international financial institutions and their effects on economic globalization. People's life prospects and expectations are inevitably determined in significant part by the international economy and the benefits it produces and distributes. International financial institutions manage the economy and the benefits it produces and, as a result, inevitably have a profound effect on people's everyday lives and how well they proceed. In at least this sense, the IMF and the World Bank are the international analogue to those institutions that are part of the domestic basic structure. For this reason international financial institutions, such as the IMF and the World Bank, should be considered among the primary subjects of international justice.[1] Second, as Rawls argues, "justice is the first virtue of social institutions" (*ibid.*: 3). On his view, "laws and institutions no matter how efficient and well-arranged must be reformed or abolished if they are unjust" (*ibid.*). However, it can be argued that justice is not only a virtue of social institutions at the domestic level but is also the first virtue of institutions at the international level. If this is correct, then in so far as we ought to be concerned with justice in the domestic sphere, we ought also to be concerned with justice in the international sphere. We ought to be concerned with the extent to which international financial institutions are unjust and how they can be made more just. These are the fundamental reasons for engaging in moral assessment of international financial institutions such as the IMF and the World Bank.

In this chapter, the main aim is to explore some of the central moral critiques of international financial institutions as well as proposals to overcome the moral problems that they face. We begin with a brief discussion of the history, function and structure of the IMF and the World Bank. We then turn to the moral critique of these institutions, considering both outcome- and process-based concerns. We close by considering some initial proposals to overcome the moral problems that are discussed in the previous section.

The history, function and structure of the IMF and the World Bank

The creation and function of the international finance regime

The International Monetary Fund (IMF) and the World Bank are international financial institutions which were created in July 1944 at a conference – led by the United States and the United Kingdom – in Bretton Woods, New Hampshire.

The conference took place in the wake of the Great Depression of the 1930s and towards the end of the Second World War. The Great Depression was believed by many governments to be caused by countries' attempts "to shore up their failing economies by sharply raising barriers to foreign trade, devaluing their currencies to compete against each other for export markets, and curtailing their citizens' freedom to hold foreign exchange" (International Monetary Fund n.d. a). As a way of avoiding the economically disastrous policies that led to the Great Depression, governments sought international economic cooperation, where goods would move freely between countries and be regulated by institutions that would promote greater economic and financial stability and predictability (Peet 2009: 36). The IMF and the World Bank were created to meet these goals.

The IMF

The IMF is an organization that consists of 188 countries. It is part of the United Nations system and is the central institution of the international monetary system. Historically, its main aim was to prevent economic and financial crises and to ensure stability in the international payment system. However, over time, the IMF's aims have broadened and now include the promotion of economic growth and alleviation of poverty. The IMF has worked to achieve these goals in three primary ways: (a) by monitoring the international economy and the economies of member countries; (b) by providing member countries with macroeconomic and financial policy advice; (3) by lending money to member countries to help them overcome economic difficulties such as meeting their international payments (International Monetary Fund n.d. b).

The World Bank

The IMF works closely with the World Bank. The "World Bank" is an organization that is managed by 188 countries. It is composed of two institutions: (a) the International Bank for Reconstruction and Development (IBRD), and (b) the International Development Association

(IDA) (International Monetary Fund n.d. a).[2] "The IBRD aims to reduce poverty in middle-income and creditworthy poorer countries, while the IDA focuses exclusively on the world's poorest countries" (World Bank Group 2012). The World Bank aims to meet its goal of poverty reduction by providing policy advice, research and analysis, and technical assistance to member countries and by lending money to developing countries for projects aimed at development. The IBRD lends to governments of middle-income and creditworthy low-income countries (World Bank Group 2013b). The IDA "provides interest-free loans – called credits – and grants to governments of the poorest countries" (*ibid.*).

The structure of the IMF and the World Bank

The IMF and the World Bank have a similar structure of governance. The IMF and World Bank are managed by 188 member countries. These member countries, or shareholders, are represented by a board of governors.[3] Each member country appoints one governor and one alternate governor. Typically, the position is held by the "country's minister of finance, governor of its central bank, or a senior official of similar rank" (World Bank Group 2013a). The governors meet every twelve months at the annual meetings of the boards of governors of the IMF and World Bank Group. The board of governors is the highest decision-making body of the IMF and World Bank. However, while all powers are vested in the board of governors, with the exception of certain reserved matters, the board of governors delegates day-to-day decision-making to the executive board (International Monetary Fund 2013b).

The executive board is composed of a group of executive directors,[4] who are appointed by member countries or by groups of countries, and a managing director who acts as the group's Chair. Most countries are grouped in constituencies representing four or more countries, but large economies, such as the United States and Japan, have their own seat on the board. Members of the executive board typically meet two to three times a week to oversee the business of the IMF and the World Bank. The executive board manages day-to-day operations under the leadership and guidance of the president, vice-president, management and senior staff.

Quotas

The IMF's resources are provided by its member countries through the payment of quotas. Each member country of the IMF and World Bank is assigned a quota, based broadly on its relative position in the world economy (International Monetary Fund 2012a). This quota then serves as the basis for formal decision-making power within the IMF and World Bank. For example, the larger a country's quota in the IMF, the more votes the country has, in addition to its "basic votes" – of which each country has an equal number (cf. International Monetary Fund 2012b). So, each member of the board of governors has a weighted vote equivalent to its country's IMF quota plus the basic votes it is given, while each director belonging to the executive board has a weighted vote equivalent to its constituency's combined IMF quota plus the basic votes. Something similar holds true in the World Bank.

Conditionality

One of the main functions of both the IMF and the World Bank is to lend money to developing countries. The IMF typically lends money to countries specifically for addressing balance of payment problems[5] while the World Bank lends money to countries more generally for economic development. Typically, disbursement of money is contingent on implementing specific economic policies that are meant to address the economic problems that initiated the country's request for a loan. At the same time, these measures are meant to safeguard IMF and World Bank resources by ensuring that the country's balance of payments and/or economy are strong enough to permit it to repay the loan (International Monetary Fund 2012a). The conditions and policies that loans are contingent on "depend on country circumstances. But the overarching goal is always to restore or maintain balance of payments' viability and macroeconomic stability, while setting the stage for sustained, high-quality growth and, in low-income countries, for reducing poverty" (*ibid.*). Typically, conditions have tended to include privatization and liberalization of the economy.

Sometimes borrowing countries who are unable to repay the money they borrow are granted debt relief or reduction. Debt relief and reduction have also tended to be contingent on implementing specific economic policy conditions.

The moral critique of international financial institutions

In what follows, we will consider a variety of moral critiques of the IMF and World Bank. We begin by considering outcome-based critiques and then continue by considering more process-based critiques of these institutions.

Outcome-based worries

Some of the most common and most plausible criticisms of the IMF and the World Bank concern the poor outcomes that their policies are purported to lead to. In what follows, we will explore outcome-based critiques of (a) loan conditionality and (b) international debt.

A critique of conditionality

One of the central critiques of loan conditionality is that, even if well intentioned, the conditions attached to international loans granted by the IMF and World Bank have failed and sometimes have even had disastrous results, leaving countries less able to address the pressing problems that led to their economic instability in the first place and, as a result, left them less able to repay their loans.

Consider the example of capital mobility. Joseph Stiglitz writes, "for the past couple of decades, the United States and the EU have pressed, with considerable success, for the liberalization of capital markets which enables investment to flow more freely around the world, arguing that this is good for international efficiency" (Stiglitz 2006: 89) and "economic stability" (*ibid.*: 100). Stiglitz argues that free flow of capital is to the advantage of those in the developed world. It allows investors from developed countries to move money – which they have a significant amount of – around freely which in turn allows them to make high returns. However, he argues, the free flow of capital has not proved to be in the interests of developing countries who tend to lack capital. Unrestricted capital flows can have devastating effects on those who need capital. This is because capital tends to flow out of a country when a period of recession occurs, that is to say, precisely when a country needs it most (*ibid.*). Just as countries need outside funds, the investors ask for it back. Without foreign capital, developing countries are less able to recover from a recession. This is evident when we consider the East Asian financial crisis.

After the East Asian crisis, many countries, including Thailand, Korea and the Philippines, turned to the IMF for financial assistance. In order to spur recovery, the IMF had, as part of its loan package, required the removal of all capital restrictions: restrictions placed on the flow of money into and out of a country. This, however, only exacerbated problems as investors pulled their money out of investments (that is, as capital flowed out of the countries). In contrast, Malaysia did not take an IMF loan and imposed capital restrictions in the form of an exit tax that could be (and eventually was) gradually lowered. The tax discouraged investors from pulling their money out of the country. In comparison to Thailand, who followed IMF pre-scriptions closely, Malaysia, through use of capital restrictions, recovered "more quickly, with a smaller downturn, and with a far smaller legacy of national debt burdening future growth" (*ibid.*: 125). This is just one of many examples of how economic policy conditions have left countries with greater economic instability and lesser ability to pay back loans.[6]

Adam Przeworski and James Raymond Vreeland have reached similar conclusions, arguing that "if growth is the primary objective then IMF programs are badly designed" (Przeworski & Vreeland 2000: 402). Their research shows that the

> growth observed under IMF programs was lower regardless of the conditions under which countries participated … countries [that] remained under IMF programs even though they had decent reserves and low deficits … grew by 1.02% slower than countries which enjoyed the same conditions while not being subject to these pro-grams. But even countries with low reserves and high deficits did better if they did not participate: their growth was 1.79% faster. Thus, while countries facing bad conditions grew slower, participation in IMF programs lowered growth under all conditions.
>
> *(Ibid.: 395–97)*

In short, countries grow much slower when they follow IMF conditions.

An objection to this line of argument could be raised. Compliance with IMF loan conditions is often argued to be low.[7] If this is true, then in many cases, it could be argued that IMF loans are not the cause of bad outcomes such as low growth. It could potentially be argued that the poor outcomes are the result of the lack of compliance with IMF loan conditions. Countries have failed to grow and reduce poverty, not because they have followed IMF loan conditions, but rather, because they have failed to do so. In response to this worry, Axel Dreher (2006) has shown that acceptance of IMF programmes and conditions tend to lower growth by 1.5 percentage points under full compliance. Michael Hutchison and Ilan Noly reach similar conclusions, arguing that IMF programmes hurt growth, even after controlling for levels of compliance (Vreeland 2006: 109). This suggests that even when countries fully comply with IMF loan conditions, they grow less than they would otherwise.

International debt

When developing countries borrow from the IMF and the World Bank they are obliged to pay it back. A number of popular critics, including NGOs[8] and average citizens, have been critical of this requirement, arguing that the debt of the poorest countries ought to be forgiven. The central worry is that debt exacerbates poverty and worsens social conditions. This general worry takes two more specific forms.

The first worry is that repayment of debt prohibits economic and social progress among the poorest countries and, in turn, promotes the violation of human rights. Paying back debt requires funds that could be used for other important purposes such as provision of social and public goods such as healthcare or efforts to alleviate local poverty and to stimulate the economy.[9] Christian Barry argues that "high levels of debt can limit the capacities of countries' governments to provide social services necessary to ensure even a minimally adequate standard of living for their people"

(C. Barry 2011: 284). For example, Barry notes, "in 2000 Tanzania spent nine times more on debt service than on health, while 1.6 million lived with AIDS" (*ibid.*: 285). For this reason, Barry concludes that the negative consequences of debt are also a concern from a human rights perspective. Servicing debt can undermine efforts to promote human rights satisfaction.

One could object to this argument by noting that borrowing countries willingly entered into the loan with full knowledge of the terms of repayment. As result, it could be argued, borrowing countries owe repayment of the loan, even if it undermines human rights satisfaction within that country.

This objection may not be fully compelling. One could argue in response that we cannot rightly be held to terms that violate or undermine our human rights. For example, even if someone genuinely promises to be your slave, it would not be morally appropriate to hold that person to his commitment, if it violates his human right to freedom or liberty. Similarly, even though borrowing countries promised to pay back the loan (under all conditions), it may not be morally appropriate to hold them to this commitment, if it undermines human rights satisfaction within that country.

The second worry is that the current structure of debt promotes the incidence of oppressive and corrupt elites in the developing world (Pogge 2004: 271). Traditionally, the IMF and the World Bank have not considered whether they are lending money to a democratic government, a dictator or a corrupt government. They simply lend to the government that is in political power at the time.[10] Pogge has argued that this policy is problematic for, at least, two reasons. First, it promotes borrowing by destructive leaders who can then use the money "to maintain themselves in power even against near-universal popular discontent and opposition" without having to suffer the burden of paying the loan back (*ibid.*: 272). For example, the current South African government has, since it came to power, "been paying off a debt of $22 billion lent to the apartheid regime, money that helped to prop up that regime" (Jubilee Debt Campaign n.d. b). Second, the current process of debt "imposes upon democratic successor regimes the often huge debts of its predecessors"(Pogge 2004: 272). Even if the money was originally lent to a dictatorial regime, so long as debt still exists at the time of its implementation, a newly implemented democratic regime owes repayment of the loan to the IMF and the World Bank. These fledgling democratic regimes are saddled with significant debt payments, which in turn leaves them less able to implement the economic and political reforms that are needed for economic progress and stability, leaving the successor regimes less successful than they might otherwise be.

Against these claims, it is commonly argued that debt is not the sole or even among the most important factors that lead to destructive leaders or failed regimes.[11] Rather, it is argued, factors internal to the country itself, such as cultural or economic factors (such as poor economic policies), lead to such things. In response, one could acknowledge that internal factors often do play an important role in the creation of destructive leaders and failed regimes. Pogge's claim might simply be understood as the claim that internal factors are not the only factors that matter. External factors such as international debt can and often do play a role in the creation of destructive leaders and failed regimes. Moreover, it could be argued that external factors often shape internal factors. It is the internationally created incentive system, for example, that fosters a culture of corruption within a country and that, in turn, supports oppressive and dictatorial leadership within that country.

Moral significance of outcome-based worries

The sorts of poor outcomes – human rights violations, worsening of poverty, oppression and corruption – that have been associated with the IMF and the World Bank's policies can be argued to be morally problematic for at least two reasons. First, some thinkers, such as Jeremy Bentham and other utilitarians, have argued that political institutions and policies ought to be structured so that they maximize well-being. It seems clear that the well-being of the poor is negatively affected by poor outcomes such as increased poverty and oppression in poor countries. Second, others, such as Thomas Pogge, argue that these poor outcomes are indicative of a violation of a negative duty not to harm. In voting for politicians who, through their greater political influence in such institutions, support and encourage the harmful policies that are implemented by the IMF and World Bank, individuals in developed countries are contributing to the harm of the international poor and thus violating their (negative) duty not to harm others.

Process-based worries

Some of the most prevalent and compelling criticisms of the IMF and the World Bank concern the processes by which they are operated and structured. In what follows, we will consider the criticism that the IMF and the World Bank suffer from a deficit of democracy.

The deficit of democracy

A central criticism of international financial institutions is that they suffer from a deficit of democracy. Critics have often argued that these organizations do not operate in a way that is consistent with core democratic values. The clearest examples of the deficit of democracy within the IMF and the World Bank are weighted voting and conditionality of loans.

As already mentioned, in the IMF and the World Bank, votes are weighted by economic status. For example, in the IMF, the G-7 countries together have over 44 per cent of the votes, and the G-10 countries with Switzerland have just over 51 per cent, with the US holding just over 17 per cent of the total votes. In the IMF, this means that in a number of important categories of decisions such as financial policy revisions (including how its resources are used), constitutional revisions, and changes in quotas and membership that require special majorities of 85 per cent, the United States is the only single country to retain veto power.[12] Because of this voting structure, the United States and the ten most developed countries are able to sig-nificantly shape and restrict the agenda of policy-making in both the IMF and the World Bank. Because "little weight is given, for instance, to the voices and concerns of the developing countries", critics such as Stiglitz worry that weighted voting is not consistent with democratic values (Stiglitz 2003: 12).

There are a number of democratic values that are thwarted by the IMF and the World Bank's policies of weighted voting. The most fundamental value that weighted voting conflicts with is self-respect.[13] To see why this is the case, consider what is wrong with the following argument for weighted voting within a country. Imagine a country where how many votes you have is contingent on how much you pay in income taxes. In so far as you pay more in taxes you con-tribute more than others to the running of the country and, on this argument, this would justify your having more votes than others who paid less in income taxes. It is clear that in the domestic political case, this arrangement is morally objectionable. After all, as John Rawls has suggested, a country is not a monopolistic firm (Rawls 1993: 264). The operations of the government are important to the interests and life prospects of all its citizens, not just those who "contribute" more. This impact is broad in its scope: it shapes people's life prospects in many different areas. It is also, in a sense, inevitable: typically, one cannot just pick up and leave one's country. Although there is usually a right of exit in most countries, it is usually rather difficult to exercise this right. Given the large scale and the broadness in scope of the impact of the state on citizens' life prospects, it is important that each citizen's interests are taken into account equally. The scheme should distribute burdens and benefits as equally as possible. It would be disrespectful to ask some to bear great burdens while others benefit greatly, for it would suggest that some people's interests or prospects are not as important or worthy of consideration as others'. The only way to ensure that there is an opportunity for everyone's interests to receive genuinely equal consideration is to ensure that everyone has an equal say. Therefore, everyone ought to be given an equal say in the running and operations of the country that they are members of.

A similar argument can be made in relation to the IMF and the World Bank (Krishnamurthy n.d. b). The economic policies associated with loans, as chosen by the IMF and the World Bank, have a significant impact on people's life prospects. How well a person's life proceeds in a variety of spheres of life, economic, political, social and cultural, is shaped to a significant extent by such institutions. Moreover, typically, their policies are not something that can be opted out of, at least not without great cost. The IMF and the World Bank are essentially the only lenders that offer loans for such large amounts to poor countries with unstable economies. Most countries that receive financial assistance from the IMF and the World Bank are in desperate need of such loans. For this reason, while they can opt out of IMF and World Bank policy, it could only be done so at great cost (i.e. at the loss of the loan). In this sense, international financial institutions are analogous to governments. Their policies affect large spheres of life including economic, political, social and cultural spheres. So, for reasons analogous to those above, it can be argued that the IMF and World Bank should distribute the burdens and benefits associated with its policies as equally as possible. It would be disrespectful to ask some (say, the poor) to bear great burdens while others (say, the rich) benefit greatly, for it would suggest that some people's interests or prospects are not as important or worthy of consideration as others'. In turn, the IMF and World Bank ought to ensure that genuinely equal consideration is given to the interests of all individuals whether they are the interests of those in developing or developed countries. The only way to do this is to give all members and their citizens an equal say in the operations of the IMF and the World Bank.[14] Denying this would be inconsistent with foundational democratic values.

The deficit of democracy is apparent in the IMF and World Bank's policy of loan conditionality as well. The economic policies associated with the IMF and the World Bank's loans are not chosen by the borrowing countries' elected officials; they are usually determined by economists who work for the IMF and the World Bank, who, in turn, are greatly influenced by the United States and other developed countries who have the greatest power over decision-making. Critics worry that conditions make democratic processes difficult, for there is little opportunity for citizens of the borrowing countries (which tend to be developing countries) to influence which economic policies are pursued.

A fundamental democratic value that is thwarted by conditionality is the value of self-determination or autonomy.[15] Many philosophers have argued that individuals have a right to autonomy. This is to say, individuals have a right to a way of life where they can make choices in ways that are consistent with what they value and identify with. As Thomas Christiano suggests, democracy can be thought "to extend the idea that each ought to be master of his or her life to the domain of collective decision making" (Christiano 2006). The argument for democracy from the value of autonomy is twofold. First, each person's life is deeply affected by the larger social, legal and cultural environment in which he or she lives. Second, only when each person has an equal voice and vote in the process of collective decision-making will each individual have an opportunity to shape this larger environment in ways that are consistent with what she values and what she identifies with (*ibid.*). Therefore, an individual's right to autonomy can only be fully exercised when democracy is in place. Thus, in so far as individuals have a right to autonomy, they have a right to democracy.

So understood, the value of autonomy is not consistent with the practice of loan conditionality. In some countries, citizens have collectively decided, in the sense that there seems to
be enough of an agreement among citizens, on social conditions or programmes that require a
high level of public spending. For example, the citizens of a country, say, Greece, might
collectively decide on a system of healthcare and education (including higher-level education)
that is publicly funded. Any significant reduction of public spending would conflict with this
decision. To the extent that loan conditionality might require this type of significant reduction
in public spending, it would conflict with Greek citizens' interest in being able to choose and to
pursue ends and goals that are truly their own and that they identify with. As autonomous
agents, Greek citizens have a right to choose their own particular path of development. To
deny them this opportunity is to deny them the grounds for autonomy. So, for this reason, loan
conditionality can be argued to be inconsistent with foundational democratic values because it
thwarts citizens' right to autonomy (c.f. Krishnamurthy n.d. a).

It is important to note that the arguments from self-respect and autonomy probably apply
only in the case of sufficiently democratic countries. If a country is not sufficiently democratic,
then its citizens may already lack the grounds for self-respect. For example, an undemocratic
regime may not take the interests of its citizens into genuinely equal consideration, perhaps
ignoring the interests of the worst off or those of certain ethnicities or cultural backgrounds.
Similarly, if a country is not sufficiently democratic, then its citizens may already lack the ability
to exercise their right to autonomy. They may lack the ability to collectively choose and pursue
ends and goals that are truly their own such as public education.[16] For instance, in a dictatorial
regime, because they are the only ones who are able to influence the operations and structure of
political institutions and policies, only those who are part of the regime itself (and not the
people or citizens) may have such abilities. For these reasons, one could argue that the weighted
voting and loan conditions that are imposed by the IMF and the World Bank in the case of
insufficiently democratic countries would not conflict with citizens' sense of self-respect or
violate citizens' right to autonomy. The arguments from self-respect and autonomy simply may
not apply to insufficiently democratic countries.

Some might worry that this limitation poses a significant problem for the arguments from
self-respect and autonomy. After all, many of the countries that participate in the IMF and
World Bank and that do most of the borrowing might be considered insufficiently democratic.
If this is right, then these two arguments cannot explain why weighted voting and loan
conditionality are objectionable in relation to many of those countries that are participating in
the IMF and World Bank. The arguments from self-respect and autonomy seem extremely
limited in their relevance to the moral critique of the IMF and World Bank.

In response, it could be argued that the arguments from self-respect and autonomy do have
some implications for insufficiently democratic countries. First, it could be argued that allowing
insufficiently democratic countries to participate in such institutions would not be consistent
with citizens' sense of self-respect. If insufficiently democratic countries are permitted to participate and to make decisions in the IMF and the World Bank in ways that are not genuinely
representative of their citizens' interests, then such participation would be undermining of those
citizens' sense of self-respect. It would be undermining of their sense of self-respect because it
would not allow for equal consideration of their interests within the IMF and World Bank.
Second, it could be argued that granting loans of any kind to insufficiently democratic countries
is itself inconsistent with citizens' right to autonomy. If the funds are used in ways that go
against or are not consistent with the choices and aims of the people or are used to prevent
people from choosing and implementing their own collectively chosen ends, then it would be a
clear violation of individuals' autonomy-based right to democracy.[17] In short, the arguments

from self-respect and autonomy suggest useful limitations regarding who should be included as members of good standing in institutions such as the IMF and World Bank. They suggest that insufficiently democratic states should not be included as members of good standing; they should not have decision-making and borrowing privileges.

Weighted voting and loan conditionality are not the only areas where the lack of democracy is evident. As Richard Miller has aptly noted, the influence of the United States over the IMF and the World Bank is both more subtle and pernicious than our previous discussion of weighted voting and loan conditionality highlights. First, as Miller notes, there is a "quasi-official rule that the World Bank's President must be a U.S. citizen nominated by the U.S. government" (R. W. Miller 2010: 135). Second, there is routine interaction between the IMF and the World Bank and the United States Treasury. Quoting a recent study of the World Bank by Catherine Gwin, Miller writes,

> the United States is the only country that carries out detailed reviews of every bank proposal and the only one to maintain constant contact with the Bank through government officials, in addition to its representative to the board. The United States will question a prospective loan early in the preparation process, and during final deliberation of a loan proposal by the Bank's executive board, it will make comments designed to draw attention to general matters of concern in order to influence future lending.
>
> *(*Ibid.*)*

Miller writes of similar occurrences at the IMF. During the East Asian financial crisis in 1997, South Korea sent an envoy to work out an IMF loan. "'I didn't bother going to the IMF,' the envoy subsequently recalled, 'I called Mr. Summer's office at the Treasury from my home in Seoul, flew to Washington and went directly there. I knew this was how this would get it done'" (*ibid.*: 136).

What allows the United States to have such significant influence over the IMF and the World Bank? Miller argues that the United States uses its threat influence to shape the world trade regime through institutions such as the IMF and the World Bank. In particular, "fears due to the U.S. financial resources" (*ibid.*: 135) are most influential, since the US is the largest financial contributor to both the IMF and the World Bank. In addition to the United States's quota payments (which are the largest), the United States contributes in significant ways to both institutions. The IMF, for example, receives additional funding for its reserves from the United States when world liquidity requirements increase. The World Bank also gains access to capital markets within the United States upon its approval. For example, as Miller writes, when:

> the Bank sought to raise new capital in 1984, a U.S. Treasury official told the Bank's Vice President that failure to accommodate the U.S.'s emphasis on private funding of the energy sector in developing countries had led to the government's "reviewing whether the Bank should continue to have access to U.S. capital markets".
>
> *(*Ibid.: 135)*

The overarching power of the United States is an important concern for those who are committed to democratic values. First, a system which allows one country and its individuals to have more influence than any other country and its members is undermining of the self-respect of those who have less influence. Just as is the case with weighted voting, this arrangement is not consistent with their sense of self-respect because it fails to ensure equal consideration of their interests.

Second, a system in which the US is allowed to have superior influence in the IMF and World Bank is not consistent with autonomy. Through its superior influence, the United States is significantly more able than other member countries to shape the operations and the policies (e.g. the conditions that are part of loans) of the IMF and World Bank according to its own values and interests. This is not consistent with other countries' right to autonomy, since their ability to exercise their right to autonomy by influencing and shaping the policies and operations of the IMF and Bank would be significantly constrained.

Some might argue that, at least for instrumental reasons, American influence over and control of institutions such as the IMF and the World Bank are actually good things. It seems clear that we need economic stability – stability in growth rate, employment and prices – particularly because such instability is bad for the poor. Some, like Robert Gilpin and Charles P. Kindleberger, argue that countries are not likely to cooperate with one another in order to achieve stability. On their view, the creation of economic stability requires a powerful leader or a hegemon (Kindleberger 1973; Gilpin 2001, 2002). Through exercise of its power, the hegemon motivates countries to cooperate with one another, thereby imposing a stable and predictable economic order on the world.

In support of this thesis, Kindleberger points to the worldwide depression in 1929. On Kindleberger's view, the world depression lasted so long and was so pervasive because there was no dominant economic power to contain the damage that was done and to take on burdens in the way of extending credit (playing the role of "lender of the last resort"), creating and maintaining a liberal trade regime, and establishing an international monetary system. In short, Kindleberger argues that the depression was "so deep and so long because the international economic system was rendered unstable by British inability and United States unwillingness to assume responsibility for stabilizing it" (Kindleberger 1973: 292). This example is meant to show that in order for world economic stability to be achieved there must be a dominant economic power. So, in a similar vein, one might argue that in order to achieve the objective of economic stability, the United States must exercise its power through the IMF and the World Bank.

In response, one could argue, the United States, or any other dominant economic power for that matter, does not know what will lead to economic stability. Indeed, American involvement through the IMF and the World Bank in the economies of other countries has led, in many cases, to serious economic instability. Take the case of Latin America. In the years from 1950 to 1980 Latin America's per capita income grew at 2.8 per cent annually (Stiglitz 2006: 35–36). In the 1980s the United States dealt with its own inflation problems, causing it to raise its interest rates, which eventually passed 20 per cent (*ibid.*: 36). These increased interest rates affected loans made to Latin American countries and prompted the Latin American debt crisis of the early 1980s. Mexico, Argentina, Brazil and others defaulted on their loans. During this time, "Latin American economic policies changed dramatically, with most countries adopting Washington Consensus policies" (*ibid.*), a set of policies determined by Washington-based institutions – the IMF, the World Bank and the United States Treasury – to be the right policies for growth and development. Latin American countries needed to borrow money from the IMF and the World Bank, and the Washington Consensus became the basis of the policies upon which IMF and World Bank loans were conditional. Although countries such as Argentina, who thoroughly adopted the Washington Consensus policies, did resume growth and restore price stability, this was only for a short amount of time. Stiglitz writes, "growth was not sustainable ... Growth was to last only a short seven years, and was to be followed by recession and stagnation. Growth for the decade of the 1990s was only half what it had been in the decades prior to 1980" (*ibid.*). This example illustrates that the policies endorsed by the United States as part of the Washington Consensus did not lead to long-term economic stability and in fact seemed to elicit economic instability over the long run.

The East Asian crisis is another important example of how United States involvement seems to have precipitated economic instability. Stiglitz writes:

> the IMF and the US Treasury believed, or at least argued, that full capital liberalization would help the region [East Asia] grow even faster. The countries in East Asia had no need for additional capital, given their high savings rate, but still capital account liberalization was pushed on these countries in the late eighties and early nineties. I believe that capital account liberalization was *the single most important factor leading to the crisis.*
>
> *(Stiglitz 2003: 99, original emphasis)*

Typically, the IMF and the World Bank, led by the United States, have argued that capital liberalization promotes economic stability. As we have already discussed, Stiglitz is very sceptical of this claim because he believes that full capital liberalization leaves developing countries open to the whims of foreign investors, which does not support economic stability, since money often leaves countries just as they desperately need it. If Stiglitz is right and capital liberalization was a central cause of the East Asian crisis, then, in so far as the United States pushed full capital liberalization, it seems clear that actual United States dominance is at least partially responsible for the onset of the crisis.[18] This and the previous example are in direct contradiction to Gilpin and Kindleberger's claim that a dominant economic power will lead to economic stability.[19]

Moral significance of process-based worries

The previous discussion illustrates the complexity of the deficit of democracy within international financial institutions. The lack of democracy in international financial institutions is of particular significance for those who hold that being sufficiently democratic is a necessary requirement of just political institutions. For example, Meena Krishnamurthy (2012, forthcoming) argues that democratic decision-making processes are required by Rawls's theory of justice. If justice requires something similar at the international level, and the IMF and the World Bank fail to meet this requirement, then it follows that the IMF and the World Bank are unjust.

Proposals for correcting the moral flaws of the IMF and World Bank

Given that the IMF and the World Bank arguably suffer from a number of moral flaws, we must consider whether and how these can be overcome. There are three ways of responding to these moral failings: we can either (a) dismantle or eliminate the IMF and World Bank; (b) reform the IMF and the World Bank to deal with the specific problems that have been outlined; or (c) take up more general reforms that go beyond mere changes in IMF and World Bank policy and structure. In what follows, we will consider these options in more detail.

Elimination of the IMF and World Bank

Walden Bello argues that the crisis faced by the IMF and the World Bank is systemic and for this reason "is not one that can be addressed by mere adjustments in the system, for these would be merely marginal in their impact or they might postpone a bigger crisis" (Bello 2004: 107). Instead, Bello believes that we should work to eliminate or at least drastically scale back the power of the IMF and the World Bank. For example, he suggests that we could reduce the power of the IMF by turning it into a research agency, whose primary function would be to monitor the exchange rates of international capital flows. Alternatively, he also suggests that we could turn the IMF and the World Bank into a set of actors that co-exist with and are checked by other international institutions and agreements, and regional groupings. This option would require strengthening a diverse range of other actors, such as regional groups and the United Nations Conference on Trade and Development (UNCTAD).

In the end, dismantling the IMF and the World Bank may not be the best way of overcoming their moral failings. There is an important need for some coordination of multinational activity, since, in the modern world, there are deep and unavoidable economic and financial interdependencies among the world's people. For example, as Iris Marion Young notes, "a change in the value of currency or interest rates within one country often has ripple effects on the financial markets of the whole world. Commodity prices on the world market are determined by the interactions of many agents across borders" (2004: 247–48). Given their impact on individuals' life prospects, we will also need to establish and implement principles and standards of justice to govern international economic and financial interactions. These considerations support the conclusion that some kind of centralized decision-making in the areas of economics and finance through institutions such as the IMF and the World Bank is necessary.

Reform of the IMF and World Bank

If institutions such as the IMF and World Bank are necessary, then we must implement specific policy or structural changes within the IMF and World Bank to overcome the specific moral failings that have been identified. In what follows, we will consider some options.

Improving the effectiveness of loans

As discussed in the previous section, a central criticism of loan conditionality is that it leads to poor outcomes. Countries that tend to take up and to adhere to IMF and World Bank loans tend to experience less growth and greater poverty than those that do not.

Dani Rodrik has suggested that economic prosperity, growth and development are not things that can be imposed by developed countries, through policies such as conditionality, on developing countries. Rodrik argues while "market-based incentives ... competition and macroeconomic stability are essential everywhere", there is no one size fits all plan for development, since the actual policy content of these general principles must be determined in a country's specific settings (Rodrik 2001: 29; Birdsall *et al.* 2005: 9). Rodrik argues that to be successful, plans for economic reform must be tailored to "domestic realities" and be based on local knowledge and local expertise.

In support of these claims, Rodrik and Birdsall *et al.* point out that countries that adhered most strictly to orthodox reform agendas, under the authority of the IMF and the World Bank, for example, Latin American countries, have not done well, while almost all successful cases of development in the last fifty years have taken up more creative and unorthodox reforms, as in South Korea, Taiwan, China, India, Vietnam and Mauritius (Rodrik 2001; Birdsall *et al.* 2005: 9–10). For instance, China and Mauritius successfully combined their emphasis on state regulation with unique measures of market liberalization. Thus, Birdsall and colleagues conclude, "the secret of economic growth lies in institutional innovations that are country-specific, and that come out of local knowledge and experimentation" (Birdsall *et al.* 2005: 10).

All of this suggests that the G-7 is not (and has not been) in a position to determine which path to economic progress is best for developing countries to pursue. Thus, if economic progress is to be made and economic stability is to be guaranteed in developing countries, then the IMF and the World Bank must involve on-the-ground experts, that is, individuals from borrowing countries, in decisions and plans about which policies ought to be implemented as part of the borrowing country's loan packages.

Improving the structure of debt

One of the main criticisms of international debt raised by Pogge is that countries that receive loans often suffer from repeated cycles of oppression and corruption. One obvious solution is to simply stop lending to regimes that are known to be corrupt, oppressive or dictatorial. If there is no financial gain to be had by overthrowing a popular government, for example, then there will be less incentive to attempt a coup.

This still leaves open the question of what is to be done in the cases where loans have already been granted to such countries. Should newly instated democratic regimes be saddled with the debt of previously undemocratic regimes? It also leaves open the issue of how to deal with debt when its service might exacerbate conditions of poverty and economic instability.

In response to public criticism of international debt, the IMF and the World Bank launched the Heavily Indebted Poor Countries (HIPC) Initiative in 1996. The aim of this programme is to ensure that no poor country faces a debt burden that it cannot manage (International Monetary Fund 2013a). In 2007, the HIPC Initiative was supplemented by the Multilateral Debt Relief Initiative (MDRI). The MDRI allows for 100 per cent relief on eligible debts by the IMF and the World Bank for countries completing the HIPC Initiative process. The process is a two-step process. "Countries must meet certain criteria, commit to poverty reduction through policy changes and demonstrate a good track-record over time. The Fund and Bank provide interim debt relief in the initial stage, and when a country meets its commitments, full debt-relief is provided" (*ibid.*).

The response to this initiative is largely critical. Critics are concerned that debtor countries are required to meet a set of "conditions" selected by the IMF and the World Bank. They also point to the sorts of worries that we discussed in relation to the IMF and World Bank's more general policy of loan conditionality. In line with these worries, the Jubilee Debt Campaign, one of the most active NGOs on this issue, argues that there should be 100 per cent unconditional cancellation of "unpayable" debts, which a country cannot afford while meeting basic human needs, and "illegitimate" debts, which arose from unfair or irresponsible lending (Jubilee Debt Campaign n.d. a).

In contrast, Christian Barry suggests that imposing certain conditions on debt relief might be morally permissible. Recall, Barry suggests that international debt among the poorest countries can have negative consequences for human rights. He suggests that if the additional resources that are saved as a result of debt forgiveness are spent on restoring public services and infrastructure in health, for example, then debt relief may contribute significantly to human rights satisfaction within that country (Barry 2011: 291). However, there is no necessary connection between debt relief and the satisfaction of human rights. A country could easily choose to spend the additional resources on something other than what would contribute to human rights satisfaction. For example, a country could use the funds to repress the rights of minorities or support an undemocratic regime. So Barry argues that one way to ensure that forgiveness of debt works towards human rights satisfaction is to make it contingent on the debtor country having a specific human rights status. For example, he argues that it might be contingent on:

human rights *achievements* (for example, the extent to which the human rights of those living within its territory are fulfilled) and what might be called its human rights *efforts* (for example, the extent to which it implements, or shows evidence that it will implement in the future, a plan oriented towards fulfilling the human rights of those living in its territory).

(Ibid.: *292, original emphasis*)

Forgiveness of debt might also be continent on earmarking some of the additional resources for policies aimed at furthering the satisfaction of its citizens' human rights.

Reforming weighted voting

Weighted voting has been criticized for being insufficiently democratic. In response to this criticism, the World Bank and IMF have committed to increasing the votes of countries to more accurately represent the economies of the world. For example, under the new proposal, China would have the third most votes after the United States and the United Kingdom. However, in order to genuinely overcome the deficit of democracy within the IMF and World Bank, mere increases of votes to reflect economic progress are insufficient. Even if China is given more votes, there would still exist a system where some countries (namely, the economically strongest) have more of a say than other countries in significant matters of mutual concern. As suggested earlier, this sort of arrangement would not be consistent with the self-respect of all citizens. In particular, it would be undermining of the self-respect of citizens in countries with weak economies who have fewer votes.

Another solution to the problem of the democracy deficit is for each country to have a director, either directly elected by a country's citizens or appointed by an elected official, with each director having an equal amount of votes. This would ensure that all individuals in all member countries (rich or poor, economically strong or weak) play an equally influential role in IMF and World Bank decision-making and that their interests are given equal consideration.

One worry is that this proposal would give countries, such as the Maldives, with little population as much of a say over the operations of the IMF and World Bank as countries, such as India, with very large populations. One way to correct for this problem would be to grant countries extra votes in proportion to their population. This could be argued to be a means of ensuring that the interests of all individuals are genuinely given equal consideration and hence would be consistent with the value of self-respect.

One worry that arises in relation to this proposal concerns feasibility. If large contributors to the IMF and the World Bank such as the United States no longer (formally) have central control over these institutions, then they may not be willing to continue to fund the IMF and the World Bank. Without these funds, the IMF and the World Bank may not be able to continue to operate. Without these institutions, countries in need of finances for economic progress would have no option for borrowing. This would be a significant problem.

The solution to this matter is not obvious. One option is to compromise on democratic values and to allow countries such as the United States to continue to control and to have significant influence over the operations and policies of the IMF and World Bank. This is not a morally favourable option, however, since as we have already discussed, the current system, which is led by the United States, has led to continued impoverishment and inhibition of social and economic progress in poorer countries. Another option might be to follow Bello's suggestion and to dismantle international financial institutions and, in their place, to support the building of regional financial institutions that might be more hospitable to democratic values and, potentially, to poverty alleviation. This option is discussed below.

There are also questions about undemocratic countries and the weight their votes should be given. Given the arguments discussed earlier, one might conclude that weighted voting is permissible in the case of undemocratic countries. After all, as argued earlier, the arguments from self-respect only hold in the case of sufficiently democratic countries. In undemocratic countries, citizens do not play a distinct and meaningful role in politics. Consequently, one could argue that giving less weight to the votes of undemocratic countries would not thwart the citizens' interest in self-respect in the way that it would with democratic countries.

If this argument is right, then one might conclude, as was suggested earlier, that we should exclude such countries from participating in international financial institutions altogether. There is at least one reason against excluding insufficiently democratic countries from international financial institutions altogether: those who are most in need of being included and participating in international financial institutions (and perhaps in international decision-making in general) are those individuals who tend to live in undemocratic countries. The interests of these individuals are profoundly affected by decisions that take place at the international level. Moreover, excluding such countries altogether would punish the citizens of these countries, citizens who tend to be impoverished and are already disenfranchised, and not the leaders, who should probably be the targets of such punishment. In short, one could argue that it makes little sense to have a citizen barred from having her interests represented equally in international institutions because the leadership under which she lives is tyrannical or undemocratic.

Though Daniel Weinstock (2006) is concerned with international institutions in general, he makes a suggestion that is well worth considering in relation to undemocratic countries and their role in the IMF and the World Bank. Taking the domestic sphere as his starting point, Weinstock notes that democracies contain a number of disenfranchised people, such as children and others who are judged to be incompetent. "Though these people cannot vote, their interests are nonetheless represented by such institutions as youth protectors and public curators" (*ibid.*: 15). Weinstock suggests that something similar could be pursued at the international level. He suggests that there should be "a global democratic sphere in which people who cannot select their own representatives are appointed trustees who ensure that decisions made at the global level take proper account of their interests" (*ibid.*).

As Weinstock himself acknowledges, this proposal raises at least two further questions. First is the question of how these trustees should be chosen: on the basis of what procedure should trustees be appointed? Second, and related, there is the question of accountability: how can we ensure that those who are appointed will represent the interests of their people? These questions will have to be addressed before Weinstock's proposal can be appropriately instituted.

Moving beyond the IMF and the World Bank

One might argue that any measures to overcome the deficit of democracy are unlikely to be effective. As was suggested above, informal power dynamics play a significant and influential role in the operations and policies of the IMF and World Bank. As a result, mere changes in the formal procedures and policy, such as voting structures of the IMF and World Bank, might be unlikely to result in real change (that is, change towards being more genuinely democratic). If this is correct, then more general reforms that go beyond mere changes in IMF and World Bank policy and structure are necessary. In what follows, we will consider some possible routes for more general reform.

Economic equality as a means of genuine reform

As Miller's arguments work to illustrate, mere changes in the formal structures and policies in the IMF and World Bank may not work to overcome the deficit of democracy within such institutions. Even if all countries were given an equal share of votes, the United States could still influence policy through the informal mechanisms that are described by Miller. So, a further suggestion is that the deficit of democracy can be overcome in the IMF and the World Bank only after egalitarian measures in the international economy have been taken and there is greater economic equality among countries. Differences in economic wealth seem to result in differences in political influence: rich countries tend to have more power, formally and informally, within the IMF and the World Bank than poor countries.[20] For this reason, egalitarian measures in the economy may be necessary to fully overcome the deficit of democracy within the IMF and World Bank. If there were no longer a concentration of cash in certain groups, that is, if there were rough economic equality between countries participating in the IMF and the World Bank, then there would likely be rough equality in the use of political influence and power. For example, the United States would no longer possess the economic grounds for its threat-power. If participating countries have more equal political influence and power within international financial institutions and these countries are themselves sufficiently democratic, then the individuals within them will be ensured that their interests are given equal consideration and that they will be able to exercise their right to autonomy sufficiently. If this is correct, then these claims strongly support egalitarian measures in the international economy.[21]

Regional financial institutions

Even if egalitarian measures in the international economy are taken, it will take some time for countries to reach a level of international economic equality that is sufficient for the genuine expression of democratic values in international financial institutions. So, the question arises, what ought we do in the mean time? After all, poorer countries will still need to borrow money for economic progress and stability. One option is to establish regional financial institutions. For example, as an alternative to the IMF and the World Bank, Hugo Chavez, the President of Venezuela, tried to establish the Banco del Sur (the Bank of the South), a development bank for and funded by Latin American countries. On the one hand, even within regions, there are significant differences in the economic status of countries. In South Asia, India is a significant economic power in comparison to Bangladesh, for example. In Latin America, Mexico is of significantly greater economic status than Bolivia and Nicaragua. So one worry is that because of these significant differences in economic status, regional institutions are likely to face many of the problems relating to the democracy deficit that international financial institutions do. However, on the other hand, because countries within Latin America are more likely to have similar and joint interests – because of somewhat similar geographic locations, cultures, languages, economies, and so on – it seems that the interests of all Latin American countries are more likely to be met by regional institutions such as the Bank of the South than by international institutions such as the IMF and the World Bank. Moreover, economic inequalities within regions such as Latin America seem to be significantly less than across regions: less than, say, those between Latin America and North America or Europe. In turn, though regional institutions are likely to face some problems, they seem much more hospitable to democratic values than international financial institutions. Moreover, in so far as regional financial institutions would be aimed at fostering economic stability and growth within their particular region and would be more likely to possess local knowledge and expertise, it may be that such institutions will work better to foster growth and stability.

A central worry that arises in relation to regional banks is that in certain regional areas, such as sub-Saharan Africa, there may be insufficient capital to finance such institutions. It is perhaps for this reason that the current African Development Fund[22] is funded by both African and non-African countries, with the United States and Japan being among the largest financial contributors.[23] This problem, however, will not apply to all regions equally and so regional banking may still be workable in some specific regional cases.

When regional institutions are unworkable, another promising option may be for countries to borrow from commercial banks. This solution poses its own problems, however. Typically, the IMF and the World Bank give loans to developing countries at rates far below those available in the commercial market. This practice is of clear advantage to poor countries. Since the main goal of commercial banking is to make a profit, unlike the IMF and the World Bank, commercial banks will be unlikely to give loans at below market interest rates. This is problematic for borrowing countries that may not be able to make payments at higher interest rates and, in turn, may not be able to qualify for loans from commercial banks in the first place.

Reforming loan conditionality

Loan conditionality has been argued to be objectionable because it leads to poor outcomes and conflicts with individuals' interest in being autonomous. One way of reforming loan conditionality so that it avoids these worries is to implement outcome-based conditionality. This type of conditionality can ensure repayment of loans without requiring borrowing countries to take up specific policies.[24] Under this scheme, financing would be conditional on the borrowing country meeting certain desired objectives or outcomes rather than implementing specific policies. These outcomes would be negotiated with the IMF and the World Bank. They would be mutually decided upon by both lender and borrowing countries. Borrowing countries would play an equal role (equal to lender countries, that is) in deciding which outcomes should be aimed at. Moreover, policy content would be left up to borrowing countries to decide on their own (Khan & Sharma 2001: 25). Only the desired outcomes would have to be agreed upon by borrowing countries and the IMF and World Bank staff, not the mechanisms that lead to the outcomes. This would give countries greater room to design their own economic policies, while also providing countries with an incentive to implement appropriate policies, that is, policies which will lead to certain desired (and negotiated) outcomes. Examples of appropriate outcomes might include financial support being contingent on reaching certain levels of growth, inflation, or net international reserves, or reductions in balance of payments problems, and so on (Johnson 2005: 20). Outcome-based conditionality would be an appropriate means of overcoming the deficit of democracy within the IMF and World Bank because it is more consistent with individuals' right to autonomy. It allows citizens in developing countries to choose and implement their own paths to development (which may involve public funding of various industries, for example). It would also be more likely to successfully promote economic development because, following Rodrik's view about what leads to economic development, it would give local expertise and knowledge a central place in choosing the appropriate route to development.

This sort of approach could work in relation to Barry's suggestion about granting debt relief on the basis of human rights satisfaction. In this case, outcomes would consist of human rights related outcomes and countries could decide on their own about how to meet these. Outcome-based conditionality could potentially be compatible with lending to undemocratic countries as well, so long as the outcomes are also agreed to by trustees that are appointed to represent the country.

Such an approach is not without problems, however. For example, some difficulties may arise in implementing outcome-based conditions. First, outcomes such as an increase in growth (in GDP or purchasing power parity), or reduction of balance of payment problems, and so on, will take time to meet and will probably not be able to be assessed in periods of less than a year (Johnson 2005: 20). For this reason outcome-based conditions might be more difficult to implement in the case of short-term loans. Second, deciding when to disburse money may be difficult. As Khan and Sharma note, there can be some difficulties in assessing whether an outcome was not met because of a country's bad policies or exogenous factors not under their control (Khan & Sharma 2001: 26). So, evidence will need to be analysed carefully in order to determine whether outcome targets were missed because of exogenous factors or because the countries' policies came up short (*ibid.*). If it is the former, then there may be a case for a waiver and the country could continue to receive funding.

The role of social movements in reform

International social movements have an important part to play in the achievement of the various goals that have been described as part of reforming the IMF and World Bank. An international social movement is an informal group of individuals, from many countries (developed and developing countries), who work together to achieve certain multinational goals, political and/or social. The goals might mainly be goals within each country, so long as they are part of or are steps to achieving some predominant multinational goal. On Richard Miller's view, examples of international social movements include the:

> international bunch of people who bash Bush, have opposed the Iraq war and occu-
> pation, seek to relieve inequities and burdens of globalization, call for more action
> against international climate change, or are concerned that what governments do to
> relieve poverty is too little or the wrong sort of thing.
>
> *(R. W. Miller 2006: 511)*

Generally, governments are sensitive to and are often swayed by public opinion. For example, as Miller notes, in the Vietnam era, "in the *Pentagon Papers*, outraged public opinion ranks with the provocation of Chinese or Russian intervention as the only reasons not to kill lots more Vietnamese in pursuit of victory" (*ibid.*). This suggests that public opinion, as expressed through a social movement, can have significant influence over the actions of governments. International social movements can have a similar influence in relation to reforming the IMF and the World Bank.

Bello, for example, argues that the main aim of international social movements should be the derailment of any further actions by institutions such as the IMF and the World Bank.[25] They ought to focus their energies on preventing agreements from coming about in any areas now being negotiated or about to be negotiated in the IMF and the World Bank (Bello 2004: 110). Presumably this would include preventing agreement on new issues of governance within these institutions and the negotiation of loan packages.

Alternatively, for those who do not hold that international financial institutions should be dismantled, international social movements could work to encourage greater international eco-nomic equality. Members of international social movements within the most developed coun-tries can work together to encourage national economic powers to take up internationally egalitarian measures. Furthermore, members within these countries could encourage the cor-rection of the current institutional structure by supporting debt relief (perhaps contingent upon human rights conditions) for the poorest countries, and, once sufficient economic equality exists, reform of quotas/voting powers and loan conditionality more generally within the IMF and World Bank.

Notes

1 The upshot of this claim is that, even if there is not a "global basic structure" per se, the reasons that justify a focus on domestic political institutions justify a focus on international financial institutions.
2 These institutions are part of a larger institution known as the World Bank Group. For information about the other components of the World Bank Group see World Bank Group (2012).
3 If the country is a member of the IDA, then the appointed governor and alternate governor also serve on the board of governors of the IDA.
4 There are 24 directors in the IMF and 25 directors in the World Bank.
5 Balance of payment problems exist when a country's payments for imports are greater than the payments received for exports. IMF loans focus on problems of this sort.
6 On the failure of conditionality see Stiglitz (2006, especially 25–60).
7 For a brief discussion of this worry see Boughton (2003: 4).
8 The Jubilee Debt Campaign (www.jubileedebtcampaign.org.uk) is among the central NGOs that have been critical of international debt.
9 Christian Barry points out that "the negative social consequences, such as plummeting employment and impoverishment of the population, of financial crises in indebted middle-income countries such as Argentina and Turkey provide recent examples of this phenomenon" (2011: 284).
10 It is important to note that this practice is sanctioned under international law (Pogge 2010: 49).
11 See, for example, Risse's (2005a: 351) argument in favour of "the empirical thesis … that it is the quality of domestic institutions that primarily explains whether a country is rich or poor ('the institutional thesis')".
12 It has been suggested by the IMF that formal votes rarely take place at the executive board. Instead, decisions are made by consensus, where the IMF's managing director determines the consensus from his "sense of the meeting", taking into account support from the various executive directors and their respective voting shares, such that if an issue were to be put to vote there would indeed be the required majority. It seems, then, that, even if formal votes are not taken, the weighted voting system strongly influences the decisions that result from the consensus-formation process. Rapkin and Strand reach a similar conclusion (see 2006: 309). Moreover, when no consensus can be reached, decisions are made on the basis of a simple majority. Abbas Mirakhor, one of the longest-serving IMF board members, has suggested that, currently, this happens more and more because there has been a decline in consensus building (see Chowla *et al.* 2007).
13 For an argument regarding self-respect and its importance to the justification of democracy see Krishnamurthy (forthcoming).
14 There are real questions about how exactly to ensure that all participations have an equally influential say. We will consider this issue in the final section of this chapter.
15 For example, see Gould (1988). Another argument for democracy that focuses on autonomy (in the Rawlsian sense) is developed in Krishnamurthy (2012).
16 Note that Rawls's notion of a decent consultative assembly – which takes seriously and is responsive to the views and opinions of citizens – would probably be sufficiently democratic. For more on this see Krishnamurthy (2012).
17 This discussion leaves open the question of whether genuinely benevolent dictators (who are responsive to the views and choices of the people) are sufficiently democratic. At least in theory, they could be.
18 As Dani Rodrik's work suggests (for discussion of his work, see below), the reason for the United States' failure may be that they lacked local knowledge and local expertise of Argentina and East Asia, both of which, on Rodrik's view, are essential to short- and long-term growth and development.
19 Historically, there has been some scepticism regarding the value of democracy in the international sphere. There are different ways of cashing this argument out. Some might wish to argue that international financial institutions are not analogous to the institutions that are part of the domestic basic structure and, in turn, that the analogy between domestic arguments for democracy and global ones fails. But it is difficult to fill this worry out plausibly. The onus is on the sceptic to show where the analogy fails. Arash Abizadeh (2007) makes similar claims regarding the analogy between domestic and international distributive justice.
20 Gould (2004: 215) briefly makes a similar suggestion.
21 One option might be to implement an international difference principle, which would work to distribute wealth so that it maximizes the benefits of the worst off. Rawls himself is adamantly against an

international difference principle. See Rawls (2002: 116–18). In contrast, Kok-Chor Tan (2004) argues in favour of implementing a global difference principle.

22 The main goal of the African Development Fund is to reduce poverty in regional member countries by providing loans and grants.

23 Cf. African Development Bank Group (n.d.).

24 Others have advocated something similar. Birdsall *et al.* (2005: 11) makes brief mention of outcome-based conditionality. More detailed discussion of outcome-based conditionality can be found in Johnson (2005) and Khan and Sharma (2001: 2–8).

25 Bello makes this suggestion in relation to the WTO, but it is clear that such a suggestion can be extended to the IMF and the World Bank.

19

CORPORATE SOCIAL RESPONSIBILITY AND MULTINATIONAL CORPORATIONS

Nien-hê Hsieh and Florian Wettstein

Multinational corporations (MNCs) represent an influential class of actors in the global economy. By coordinating the production and consumption of goods and services across national boundaries, they facilitate the global movement of capital and the creation of new employment opportunities. For developing countries, the investment by MNCs represents a significant source of external finance (UNCTAD 2011: 21), and for many people in these countries, MNCs have the resources to help meet many of their unmet needs. At the same time, the activities of MNCs have the potential to harm persons and the natural environment, especially in countries that lack robust legal and political institutions. In addition, MNCs are able to avoid national regulations and policies by shifting the site of their activities, and because of the benefits they bring, commentators argue that MNCs possess bargaining power in the area of policy-making (Navaretti & Venables 2004: 1; Dine 2005: 222). In this light, a central question that arises from the perspective of global ethics is what standards ought to apply to the activities of MNCs.

This chapter surveys the contemporary theoretical literature on this question. The first section provides background on MNCs and their rise. The next section provides some grounding for the chapter by summarizing existing attempts to promulgate global standards for MNCs in relation to human rights, labour, bribery and the natural environment. In the light of the challenges associated with legally regulating MNCs at a global level, a good deal of scholarship has focused on the theory and practice of corporate social responsibility (CSR): those corporate activities and policies that are not legally mandated and are framed in terms of corporations' impact on society. The following section surveys some of this literature by summarizing different conceptions of CSR and criticism of both the theory and practice of CSR.

The chapter then turns to discuss attempts to specify and ground standards for the activities and policies of MNCs from the perspective of ethical theory. The fourth section of this chapter introduces this literature with a discussion of the debate surrounding the universality of moral standards in the context of business activity. The next section describes attempts to specify standards for MNCs that involve taking a position on two key debates in the broader literature: the debate over the purpose of the for-profit business corporation and debate about the moral agency of corporations. The sixth section of the chapter summarizes accounts that aim to specify standards for MNCs without having to take a position on the purpose of the corporation or the moral agency of corporations.

Multinational corporations

Put simply, MNCs are "firms that control income-generating assets in more than one country" (Chandler & Mazlish 2005: 3). In more formal terms, an MNC is a business enterprise chartered in one country (often referred to as the "parent enterprise") that controls the activities of one or more enterprises that are based in other countries (often referred to as "subsidiaries"). The creation, acquisition or expansion of a foreign subsidiary is achieved through foreign direct investment (FDI).[1] Control is usually exercised through the ownership of a significant share of equity capital in the subsidiary, which typically involves ownership that grants at least 50 per cent of voting power in the subsidiary (UNCTAD 2013). This control results in a decision-making structure that allows for a common strategy and a coherent set of policies across the parent and subsidiaries. Although the MNCs that capture the public attention are large publicly traded companies with thousands of employees and billions of dollars in revenue, the equity capital of the parent enterprise may also be privately held or controlled by a national government, and many MNCs are small and medium-sized enterprises (SMEs).[2]

The idea of an enterprise to facilitate the movement of labour, capital, goods and services across wide geographic areas is not new. Scholars have identified the operation of MNC-like entities as far back as the Old Assyrian kingdom shortly after 2000 BCE (Moore & Lewis 1999), and the British, Danish and Dutch East India Companies of the seventeenth century are considered examples of "proto-multinationals" (G. Jones 2005a: 17). It is in the rapid and unprecedented globalization of the late nineteenth century and early twentieth century (*ibid.*: 18), however, that we see the rise of the modern MNC that not only locates in one entity "transfers of goods, capital, people, ideas, and technology", but also the movement of "business culture, practices, perspectives, and information along with products, processes, and managers" (Wilkins 2005: 51). Areas in which MNCs had a substantial presence included transportation, telephone and radio communication, public utilities, oil, mining, banking, and plantation agriculture (*ibid.*: 53–70). The period also saw the rise of industrial manufacturing MNCs, producing goods such as sewing machines, baby food, soap and cars (Wilkins 2005: 73–77; G. Jones 2005a: 80–86).

After the Great Depression and the Second World War, the 1950s brought the start of the growth of a new global economy. Until the 1980s, however, MNCs played a relatively small role in economic activity around the world. Many sectors of national economies were closed to FDI. More generally, during this time, restrictions on trade and immigration meant that capital, labour and commodity markets were much less integrated relative to the late nineteenth century (G. Jones 2005a: 31–33). In 1913, the world FDI stock as a share of world output was estimated to be 9 per cent. In 1975, it was just half that at 4.5 per cent (UNCTAD 1994: 130; G. Jones 2005b: 90).

Starting in the 1980s, the rate of market integration grew, with MNCs playing a significant role. During the 1980s, the average annual growth rate for FDI outflows was 14 per cent. Between 1996 and 2000, the average annual growth rate was 40 per cent. During that time, the average annual growth of world output was 1.2 per cent. A number of factors contributed to the growth in MNC activity, including financial deregulation, the widespread adoption of market-based economic policies (e.g. China, Eastern Europe and Russia), declines in tariffs (e.g. the North American Free Trade Agreement and the growth of the European Union), and communication and transport technologies that decreased the costs of managing across large distances (e.g. personal computers and the internet). By early 2000, the stock of FDI as a share of world output approached levels before the First World War. During this time there was a shift in the composition of MNC activity, most notably a rise in service sector activities. Service sector activities now accounted for at least half of FDI, with trade-related activities and financial services comprising 85 per cent of service sector FDI (G. Jones 2005a: 34–40).

The period of 2000 onwards saw continued growth with respect to the activity of MNCs. By 2010, the production of MNCs accounted for about a quarter of global GDP, which was comparable to the contribution of the public sector (UNCTAD 2011: 25). Depending on the basis for comparison, MNCs comprised anywhere from twenty-nine to over fifty of the world's top one hundred economic entities.[3] At the same time, this period saw new trends with regard to the nature of MNCs. One was the increase in FDI from developing and transition economies. Although around 80 per cent of all MNCs are headquartered in developed economies (*ibid.*),[4] in 2010, capital from developing and transition economies accounted for 29 per cent of FDI outflows, and of the top twenty countries ranked by FDI outflows, six were developing and transition economies (*ibid.*: 7). Another trend was the rise of state-owned MNCs. In 2010, there were at least 650 state-owned MNCs. Although numbering less than 1 per cent of all MNCs, they accounted for roughly 11 per cent of global FDI flows in 2010, with nineteen of the world's hundred largest MNCs categorized as state-owned (*ibid.*: 28).

Global standards and areas of concern

From the perspective of global regulation, MNCs pose some complexities. International law takes its main subject to be states. The rights laid out in the Universal Declaration of Human Rights, for example, are given the form of law through subsequent covenants that aim to bind the states that ratify them. They are not claims made directly by persons against non-state actors, such as MNCs (T. Campbell 2006: 104).[5] MNCs, however, possess a decision-making structure that allows for a common strategy and a coherent set of policies across national boundaries. Furthermore, commentators have raised concerns about a "race to the bottom" in which "poor countries seek to attract foreign direct investment and are therefore unwilling to subject incoming companies to strict regulation" (Dine 2005: 222).

As alternatives to global regulation, there have been various initiatives to promulgate global standards of responsible business activity to serve as guidelines for MNCs and for their voluntary adoption by MNCs. Given their number, it is beyond the scope of this chapter to provide a comprehensive survey of these initiatives.[6] Rather, the aim of this section is to illustrate the range of initiatives, to distinguish among types of initiatives, and to highlight key areas of concern with regard to the activities of MNCs.

Among the most comprehensive of these initiatives are the OECD Guidelines for Multinational Enterprises. First adopted in 1976 and updated five times since then, the OECD Guidelines cover everything from labour and environmental considerations to areas of science, technology and taxation. A central aim of the Guidelines is to ensure that the operations of MNCs "are in harmony with government policies" (OECD 2011b). Although they are not legally binding and are presented as "recommendations" from OECD member governments to MNCs (*ibid.*), it has been argued that the OECD Guidelines are not strictly optional in the sense that MNCs need not opt in for the OECD Guidelines to apply to them (Ryder 2010: 47). The thought is that the Guidelines reflect the expectations of member governments for all MNCs that are based in OECD member countries.

In contrast, the United Nations Global Compact represents a strictly voluntary initiative. It also differs from the OECD Guidelines in promulgating a set of universal standards for MNCs. Launched in 2000, the Compact calls upon MNCs to enact and support ten principles in the areas of human rights, labour standards, the environment and anti-corruption. These principles are taken from the Universal Declaration of Human Rights, the International Labour Organization's Declaration on Fundamental Principles and Rights at Work, the Rio Declaration on Environment and Development, and the United Nations Convention Against Corruption (United Nations 2004). Since its inception, over ten thousand organizations have signed on to the Compact (United Nations Global Compact 2013). While the initiative has been praised for its prominence and ambitious scope, questions have been raised as to whether there should be restrictions on the kinds of companies that may sign up (e.g. tobacco companies) and the degree of enforcement involved to ensure adherence to the principles (Leipziger 2010: 75–77).[7]

A third set of guidelines aims to clarify the relationship of MNCs to the international human rights regime more generally. These are the Guiding Principles on Business and Human Rights as adopted by the United Nations Human Rights Council in 2011. Underlying the Principles is the United Nations "Protect, Respect, and Remedy" Framework, which was developed by John Ruggie in his role as Special Representative of the United Nations Secretary-General. According to the Framework, whereas states have a duty to protect against human rights abuses by third parties, business enterprises have a duty to respect human rights, which means they "should act with due diligence to avoid infringing on the rights of others and address adverse impacts with which they are involved" (Ruggie 2013: xx–xxi). Although the Guidelines do not attribute to MNCs the same duties as states under international law, they deny that MNCs have no responsibilities whatsoever with respect to human rights, a point that will be discussed in greater detail later in this chapter.[8]

The initiatives discussed thus far are quite broad in the scope of activity by MNCs that they cover. The majority of initiatives to promulgate standards for MNCs, however, are addressed to specific industries or issues of concern. One area that has received a great deal of public attention is labour, particularly in the apparel and footwear sectors. Most of the initiatives in this area take as their starting point the standards enumerated in the International Labour Organization Declaration on Fundamental Principles and Rights at Work and other ILO conventions. Adopted in 1998, the Declaration requires all member states of the ILO:

> to respect, to promote and to realize ... (a) freedom of association and the effective recognition of the right to collective bargaining; (b) the elimination of all forms of forced or compulsory labour; (c) the effective abolition of child labour; and (d) the elimination of discrimination in respect of employment and occupation.
>
> *(International Labour Organization 2010)*

What serves to distinguish these initiatives from other initiatives discussed thus far is their emphasis on monitoring and implementation of the standards through training, review processes and other management systems. Some of the ways in which these initiatives differ from one another are whether they require payment of a "living wage", the nature and stringency of monitoring, the audit process, their membership, and whether they provide accreditation and certification (Leipziger 2010: 182–84). The Fair Labour Association, for example, is a collaboration among colleges, universities, civil society organizations and businesses that works with companies to improve internal monitoring systems and also accredits independent, external parties to monitor participating companies. Their Workplace Code of Conduct requires companies to pay "at least the minimum wage or the appropriate prevailing wage, whichever is higher" (Fair Labor Association 2012). In contrast, the Clean Clothes Campaign is a coalition of European civil society organizations that aims to educate consumers and work with governments and companies to improve working conditions. Their Model Code requires companies to provide workers with living wages.[9]

Another area of concern is the impact of MNCs on the natural environment. An example of an initiative in this area is the Coalition for Environmentally Responsible Economies (Ceres). Founded in 1989, Ceres is a network of investors, companies and public interest groups that developed a set of ten principles covering areas such as energy conservation, waste disposal and risk reduction.[10] Commentators point out two distinguishing features of Ceres as an initiative. First, companies cannot unilaterally adopt the Ceres Principles. Companies that publically commit must report and respond to problems identified by the Ceres Board of Directors. Second, the investors in the Ceres network are able to exert pressure on companies to adopt the principles (Leipziger 2010: 316). Another initiative that recognizes the influence of capital providers is found in the Equator Principles. The Principles specify standards for a number of areas affected by large infrastructure and industrial projects, including the natural environment. Financial institutions that adopt the Principles commit to implementing the standards in their financing of projects, which includes withholding funds from clients that will not or are unable to comply with the standards (Equator Principles 2013). Other initiatives are industry-specific and involve industry self-regulation. Companies that are members of the International Council of Mining and Metals, for example, are required to meet a set of performance standards that cover a variety of areas including the natural environment and conservation of biodiversity (International Council of Mining and Metals 2013). In contrast, the Forest Stewardship Council (n.d.) represents an initiative that provides third-party certification for companies that meet standards relating to the production and processing of forest products through the supply chain.

A third issue of concern is bribery by MNCs in the course of business activity. In contrast to other issues, this is one area in which there are legally binding standards. Adopted in 2003, and with over 160 countries party to it, the United Nations Convention on Corruption requires countries to criminalize corruption in a variety of forms, including bribery of national and foreign public officials, the solicitation and acceptance of bribes by public officials, embezzlement of public funds, trading in influence, and the concealment and laundering of the proceeds of corruption.[11] In addition, the Convention calls upon governments to consider enacting legislation that criminalizes bribery and embezzlement of funds in the private sector. In this manner, the Convention extends the aims of prior initiatives, including the OECD Convention on Combating Bribery of Foreign Public Officials in International Business Transactions and the Business Principles Concerning Bribery.

In addition to initiatives focused on specifying standards of conduct for MNCs, there are two other kinds of initiatives that have been pursued. The first involve reporting initiatives. These initiatives aim to provide a framework and set of reporting standards for companies to report their activities and the impact of those activities across a wide range of economic, social and environmental areas. Examples of such initiatives are the Global Reporting Initiative (GRI) and the Global Impact Investing Rating System (GIIRS). One aim of these initiatives is to provide companies with information to measure their own activity as well as provide information to third parties that may hold them accountable. The second set of initiatives in this area can be understood as process-based initiatives. These initiatives provide companies with a set of standards and guidelines for achieving their objectives with less emphasis on specifying those objectives. An example is the International Organization for Standardization ISO 14000 standards for environmental management (ISO n.d.).[12] Another example is the AccountAbility 1000 Assurance Standard, which is "intended to give stakeholders assurance on the way an organisation manages sustainability performance, and how it communicates this in its sustainability reporting" (AccountAbility 2008: 9).

Corporate social responsibility

Given the complexities in legally regulating MNCs and the voluntary nature of existing standards, attention has been focused on the activities and policies undertaken by MNCs that are not legally required and that take into account, or have as their focus, the MNCs' broader impact on society (Dine 2005: 222). Commonly referred to as a company's corporate social responsibility activity, or CSR, the activities that for-profit business enterprises pursue under the heading of "CSR" can be categorized into six major types (Kotler & Lee 2005, Perrini 2005). These are:

> (1) cause promotion (increasing awareness and concern for social causes); (2) cause-related marketing (contributing to causes based on sales); (3) corporate social marketing (behavior change initiatives); (4) corporate philanthropy (contributing directly to social causes); (5) community volunteering (employees donating time and talents in the community); and (6) socially responsible business practices (discretionary practices and investment to support causes).
>
> *(Carroll 2008: 40–41)*

In practice, what qualifies as a "social cause" is understood broadly. What have been termed CSR initiatives include sponsorship of art museums, investments in public education, changes in manufacturing processes to reduce greenhouse emissions, and requirements on suppliers to improve wages and working conditions.

Contemporary scholarship on CSR traces back to the work of Harold Bowen, who has been called "the Father of Corporate Social Responsibility" (Carroll 1999). In his 1953 book, *The Social Responsibilities of the Businessman*, Bowen set out to address the question of "what responsibilities to society may businessmen reasonably be expected to assume?" (Carroll 1999: xi). In defining his subject matter, Bowen provides a definition of social responsibility. For Bowen, social responsibility "refers to the obligations of businessmen to pursue those policies, to make those decisions, or to follow those lines of action which are desirable in terms of the objectives and values of our society" (*ibid.*: 6).

Since Bowen's initial work, definitions of CSR have varied in three respects. The first concerns the extent to which activity is directly motivated by the intrinsic considerations that make the social cause in question worth respecting or promoting (Dunfee 2008: 347). In the management literature, it is argued that there are circumstances under which engaging in CSR can improve the enterprise's profitability and financial situation.[13] The benefits to business enterprises can be categorized into four types. CSR activities may (a) reduce costs and risks for an enterprise; (b) provide enterprises with a competitive advantage; (c) preserve or improve their legitimacy and reputation; and (d) enhance the economic position of other parties (e.g. consumers and workers) who then will be able to contribute more to the financial success of the enterprise (Kurucz *et al.* 2008). Lynn Paine (2000) has spoken of a positive or negative business case in this regard, depending on whether a company's social engagement provides positive benefits (e.g. recruitment of better employees) or rather prevents negative risks from materializing (e.g. reputational damage). Some scholars define CSR in a way that excludes activities undertaken for the sole reason of benefiting the business enterprise, even if they do result in substantial benefits for society (K. Davis 1960: 70; Frederick 1960: 60; Windsor 2001). Others allow for mixed motives, so that CSR activities include those with both instrumental and moral motives (Aguilera *et al.* 2007), whereas others distinguish among types of CSR on the basis of motive. Husted and Salazar (2006), for example, distinguish three types of CSR: strategic, altruistic and coerced. Similarly, Ulrich (2008) distinguishes between instrumental, charitable, corrective and integrative approaches to CSR. Another set of definitions includes economic considerations, such as profitability, as explicit criteria for responsible activity on grounds that the financial viability of business enterprises is beneficial to society (Carroll 1979, Schwartz & Carroll 2003).

Definitions of CSR also differ with respect to their treatment of policies and activities required by law. There are two points of divergence. The first is whether mere compliance with legal requirements is sufficient for an activity to qualify under the heading of CSR or whether CSR involves "going beyond what the letter and spirit of the law requires" (Baron 2001: 12; see also Paine 1994). The second is whether the policies or activities of a business enterprise qualify as instances of CSR when they go against what is legally required or mandated by regulators. Some definitions of CSR include compliance with legal requirements as a component of CSR (Carroll 1979, Schwartz & Carroll 2003), but this may exclude from consideration policies or activities that are seen as illegal, but ethically required (Schwartz 2011: 108–9).[14]

The third respect in which definitions of CSR vary relates to the intended beneficiaries of an initiative or to whom the responsibility is owed. Some definitions of CSR exclude policies and activities that are directed at specific parties with whom the business enterprise directly interacts or contracts (e.g. consumers or workers). CSR, on these definitions, is concerned with broader social goals (Frederick 1960: 60). Other definitions include activities and policies directed towards parties with which the enterprise directly interacts, adopting more of a "stakeholder" approach to the conception of CSR (T. Jones 1980: 59–60; Aguilera *et al.* 2007; Dunfee 2008).

The variety of conceptions of CSR has led some commentators to question its usefulness as a concept in academic scholarship. Van Oosterhout and Heugens (2008), for example, argue that CSR is "conceptually epiphenomenal", meaning that "what the notion of CSR typically means to capture is best seen as a by-product of the work of other more powerful conceptual schemes" (*ibid.*: 231). Other scholars have advanced concepts that are meant to complement or replace the concept of CSR. One example is the concept of corporate citizenship, which in its more robust versions adds a public dimension to the role of the corporation: one that involves administering individual citizenship rights (Matten & Crane 2005), for instance, or that conceives of wealth creation as "public work" (Post 2002).[15] As a matter of business practice, CSR has invited criticism as well. Some critics have raised concerns that CSR activities are used to divert attention from corporate misdeeds (O. Williams 2004, Palazzo & Richter 2005, Deva 2006) or that the sorts of social causes that attract corporate attention may not be the most beneficial to society (Doane 2005, Zorn & Colllins 2007) or that CSR activities fail to address the fundamental sources of societal problems (Cloud 2007, Fleming & Jones 2013). On the other hand, others have argued that CSR activities run counter to a manager's responsibilities to the extent that they divert resources from more profitable business activities (Friedman 2002).

Universal moral standards for global business

Implicit in many of the above debates about the appropriate conception of CSR and its desirability as a corporate practice is an account of the moral responsibilities of MNCs (Werhane 2007). These next sections turn to summarize philosophical accounts that have been advanced in the scholarly literature about the standards that ought to apply to MNCs independently of existing laws and regulations. As a starting point, this section briefly discusses the debate over the universality of moral standards in the context of global business activity.

As an illustration, consider the case of *guanxi* in China. Broadly defined as "relationships between or among individuals creating obligations for the continued exchange of favours", *guanxi* is seen as having an important role in Chinese society and as helping to facilitate the conduct of business. At the same time, many of the practices associated with *guanxi* are seen by some as involving bribery or corruption (Dunfee & Warren 2001: 192–93). The case of *guanxi* is one of many examples cited in the literature of standards for business practice that differ across countries.

In the light of examples such as these, one answer that has been given to the question of what standards ought to apply to MNCs is that MNCs ought simply to conform to prevailing norms and laws in the specific country of operation. This answer admits of a number of variations. The "when in Rome" version takes MNCs to be citizens or guests of the host countries in which they operate, arguing that MNCs ought to adhere to local law and custom. Following in the tradition of moral relativism, a variation of this answer holds that there are no universal moral standards that apply to the activities of MNCs (De George 1993: 9–10). Another variation is a cautionary one: namely, that because the question of standards is largely raised with respect to Western-based MNCs, in answering it, we need to ensure that the global ethical norms "do not merely reflect the dominant ideologies of the most economically powerful market actors" (Michaelson 2010: 237). One other approach has been to point to the different levels of economic development as justifying divergent standards (Donaldson 1989). Drawing on the realist tradition in international relations, it also has been argued that in the absence of an international enforcement agency, MNCs do not have responsibilities to contribute to the common good (Velasquez 1992).

Most commentators argue for some set of universal standards (De George 1993, Donaldson 1996). In doing so, commentators vary on the degree to which they aim to accommodate differences in business norms across countries. One of the more ambitious attempts to provide guidance in cases of difference is found in integrative social contracts theory (ISCT) advanced by Donaldson and Dunfee (1999). Drawing on the social contract tradition and making explicit considerations of economic efficiency, ISCT argues for "hypernorms" that apply across all contexts, while allowing for "moral free space" in which a range of certain business practices are morally permissible.[16] Other accounts have focused on specifying moral minimums (Donaldson 1996, Hsieh 2013) or appealing to theories that argue for universal applicability, such as human rights or global justice, as will be discussed below.

Corporate purpose and corporate agency

The chapter now turns to summarize accounts that have been advanced in the scholarly literature about the standards that ought to apply to MNCs independently of existing laws and regulations. The accounts are divided between those that involve taking a position on foundational debates in the business ethics literature about corporate purpose and corporate agency, and those that do not. This section outlines these two foundational debates and then summarizes accounts about the standards that ought to apply to MNCs that involve engaging in one or another of these foundational debates.

The first debate concerns the purpose of the for-profit business corporation. Although the question of purpose can be understood in a variety of ways, in the contemporary literature, the debate is framed in relation to "shareholder primacy": the view that corporate activity should be directed exclusively towards maximizing shareholder wealth (Stout 2012). This is a view most famously associated with Milton Friedman (2002, 1970). On Friedman's account:

> there is one and only one social responsibility of business – to use its resources and engage in activities designed to increase its profits so long as it stays within the rules of the game, which is to say, engages in open and free competition without deception or fraud.
>
> *(Friedman 2002: 133)*[17]

In the business and management literature, defences of shareholder primacy fall into three broad categories. The first is a broadly libertarian property-rights view according to which shareholders own the corporation and hire corporate managers as their agents, whose responsibility is to maximize their interests (Sternberg 2000). A second approach is welfarist. On this approach, shareholder primacy is justified on grounds that it maximizes social welfare (Jensen 2000).[18] The third approach invokes a social division of labour between market-based activities and government-based activities. Activities that belong to the market sphere are appropriately conducted according to market norms, which include the pursuit of self-interest and by extension the pursuit of shareholder wealth (Friedman 2002). A great deal of scholarship has been devoted to developing these lines of argument as well as arguments in response to them. What matters for philosophical accounts about the relevant standards for the policies and activities of MNCs is that in so far as these standards may not be to the benefit of shareholders, then a successful account needs to have some response to shareholder primacy and the question of corporate purpose.

A second foundational debate in the business and management literature concerns the question of whether corporations are entities to which moral responsibility can be attributed. Three sorts of arguments have been advanced that attribute some form of moral responsibility to corporations. The first is to argue that corporations possess attributes that are held to be necessary for morally responsible agents, such as the capacity for intentional action (French 1996, Arnold 2006), the attribution of a corporate conscience (Goodpaster 2007), or that they are proper objects of blame (Silver 2005). The objection to such an approach is that only natural persons display these qualities (Friedman 2002, 1970; Velasquez 2003). The second approach emphasizes the practical need to attribute to corporations some form of moral responsibility (Werhane 1985, Wolf 1985) and to invoke a less demanding requirement for responsibility, such as the capacity to act on reasons, rather than autonomy (Donaldson 1982). A recent example of this approach is found in Dubbink and Smith (2011).[19] A third approach is to relax the requirement that a corporation must be an agent if it is to be held morally responsible. Taking this approach, Dempsey (2013) argues that it is sufficient for a corporation to be a "morally significant system" to be held morally responsible.

Corporate purpose and responsibility

In the business ethics and management literature, the most prominent alternative to shareholder primacy is stakeholder theory, which holds that business enterprises ought to be managed in the interests of all stakeholders and not just shareholders.[20] Stakeholder theory, in this manner, provides one way to specify a set of standards for the activities and policies of MNCs that is independent of existing law and norms in the country of operation. Stakeholder theory, however, has been criticized on grounds that it lacks normative foundations and fails to specify standards of business conduct (see e.g. Orts & Strudler 2009). Many of the accounts that ground the responsibilities of MNCs in a positive account about the purpose of the corporation have been developed outside the realm of stakeholder theory.

Approaches that evoke this kind of argumentation can be classified in four categories, defined by the primary function one bestows on corporations. Thus, the following paragraphs will roughly distinguish between economic, social, legal and political approaches to MNC responsibility. Depending on what one perceives to be the purpose or nature of MNCs, one may argue for more or less extensive social responsibilities.

Some scholars have argued that even a narrow view on the economic function of corporations as advocated by Friedman must, by matter of contradiction, imply at least some social responsibilities for MNCs. For example, Arnold and Bowie (2003) have argued that the very achievement of efficiency as the primary function of MNCs implies, by matter of contradiction, the observance of labour rights along their supply chain, at least where such rights are stipulated, although not enforced, in local laws. Violating such rights weakens the rule of law on which companies depend to fulfil their primary function; after all, companies are able to operate efficiently only if contracts can be freely negotiated, if there is basic security that such contracts will be honoured and, if necessary, enforced, and if both physical and intellectual property is protected. Thus, violating the rule of law for the sake of efficiency amounts to a Kantian pragmatic contradiction: one cannot reasonably act upon a principle whose general observance by all other agents would promote actions that are inconsistent with one's very purpose.[21] Thus, while such a view rejects the libertarian assumption that corporations are mere expressions of the private interests underlying them (see Bilchitz 2010: 6), it shares its narrow understanding of corporate function or purpose. The question that necessarily arises when thinking about how MNCs ought to meet such supply chain responsibilities is that of influence and leverage over the conduct of their suppliers. This is one of the core question of agency-based interpretations of corporate responsibility, which will be addressed shortly.

As opposed to such narrow economic views on the company, some have argued that the purpose and function of business is an inherently social one (see e.g. Ulrich 2008: 377). "Defining business per se and its proper concern is a social question," as Richard De George (2010: 5) concurs, "one that must be answered in a social context." The social responsibility of companies, then, is not to be understood as merely referring to external effects of business activity, but as deriving from its very social function. To view companies as merely responsible for providing goods for payment is not a sufficient determination of their purpose, as Ulrich (2008: 410) asserts. Rather, business activity must be guided by "a vision of real-life practical values which ought to be created, be it on the level of fulfilling fundamental human needs or on the level of enlarging the abundance of human life." Thus, underlying business activity is an "idea of value creation which aims to make a genuine contribution to the quality of life in society" (Ulrich 2008: 410–11). Correspondingly, a focus on the social function of a global player, for example, in the food industry would suggest a responsibility to make meaningful contributions to the improvement of the general food supply in countries where a substantial part of the population suffers from undernourishment, rather than an exclusive focus on "selling luxury goods to the moneyed class" (*ibid.*: 411). Richard De George (2010: 173–74), too, perceives the responsibilities of MNCs to go beyond the avoidance of harm. MNCs ought to actively benefit the host countries in which they operate: this holds particularly for MNCs that operate in poor countries.

Others have chosen the legal nature of MNCs as a starting point for the contemplation of their social responsibilities. For example, Bilchitz (2010), a legal scholar, argues that, based on their legal nature, MNCs have positive duties to realize human rights. Corporations are legal structures. Legal structures, as he argues, cannot be justified with reference to the narrow interests of a particular group, but must benefit all members of society (*ibid.*: 22). A key criterion to assess the social benefit deriving from such a structure is how it affects the most basic rights of human beings (*ibid.*: 21). Thus, the purpose that underlies the legal nature of the corporation and thus justifies its existence and defines its obligations is inherently social. Furthermore, as Bilchitz argues with reference to the Lockean proviso on property rights, claims to property can never be unlimited; they are legitimate only to the extent that they do not deprive others of their fundamental needs and rights. Thus, property owners have positive duties to provide access to essential goods, where such access is restricted by their collective holdings.[22]

In addition to arguments that emphasize the economic, social or legal nature and purpose of MNCs, a new stream of research has recently proposed and advanced an "extended conceptualization" of MNCs' responsibilities (Matten & Crane 2005). It has done so based on an understanding of MNCs not merely as economic or social but as political actors (Scherer & Palazzo 2007, 2011). Because mere compliance is no longer sufficient to deal with pluralist and changing social demands and expectations in a global context, there is a need for MNCs to get actively involved in public processes of political will formation in order to discharge their social responsibilities. As such, they become inherently politicized (Scherer & Palazzo 2007: 1108). Thus, under the banner of "political CSR" such research has generally called for more thoroughly embedding MNCs in democratic processes and a more extensive responsibility in tackling global political challenges (*ibid.*: 1098). Such responsibility is no longer seen as genuinely social or moral, but as inherently political.

Corporate agency and responsibility

Agency-based approaches to define MNCs' responsibilities refer to MNCs' enlarged scope of action, which they commonly tie to similarly extensive, often positive responsibilities. Typically, such accounts deal with the question of to what extent MNCs ought to be held responsible for problems and issues beyond their actual involvement in bringing them about. That is, agency is seen to breed responsibility beyond a corporation's causal involvement in or contribution to a particular problem. Several approaches have been proposed for the framing of such non-causal responsibility and all of them have to answer two central questions. Those are the question about the moral foundation on the one hand and the question about the reasonable limits and thus of the proper extent of such responsibility on the other.

Iris Marion Young's (2003, 2004, 2006) "social connection model" of responsibility has become paradigmatic for this view. In her view, it is not merely one's involvement in bringing a problem about which gives rise to remedial responsibility, but similarly one's belonging to harmful or unjust structures. It is this belonging to such structures which creates a social connection between agents and the harm caused by the structural processes and forces. Such agents, then, bear a responsibility for the transformation of unjust structures. For Young, such responsibility is forward-looking and inherently political. Not surprisingly, it has inspired large parts of the above-described research on political CSR. Young's account hinges on one's position within such unjust structures and thus on one's power or influence to transform them. In other words, those who determine and control social structures to considerable extent ought to bear responsibility for the outcomes they produce. The extent of this responsibility increases further based on privilege. That is, those agents who benefit relatively from unjust structures have special responsibilities to help transform them, because they are best able to adapt to changed circumstances without suffering serious deprivation (Young 2006: 128). Additional increasing or limiting factors are an agent's interest in the perpetuation or transformation of injustice as well as his or her ability to engage in collective action.

A similar argument has been advanced by philosopher Onora O'Neill (2001). O'Neill argues that especially when states are weak, MNCs have the clout and capability to play an extended role in furthering justice: O'Neill writes, "Corporate power can be used to support and strengthen reasonably just states. Equally, TNCs can accept the status quo, fall in with local elites and with patterns of injustice, and use their powers to keep things as they are – or indeed to make them more unjust" (*ibid.*: 194). Precisely in the context of weak and unjust states, the common distinction between states as primary and non-state actors as secondary agents of justice falters. Justice, as O'Neill (*ibid.*) asserts, has to be built by a diversity of agents with varying ranges of capabilities which can contribute in ways that are commonly not acknowledged if ideological separations between state actors and non-state actors as primary and secondary agents of justice are upheld dogmatically.

Building on both Young and O'Neill, Wettstein (2009) advances an account of MNC responsibility grounded in an understanding of justice as human development. The idea of human development is conceptually based on Amartya Sen's (1999) capability-based notion of development as freedom and operationalized in the UNDP's human development index (see e.g. Haq 1995). As agents of global justice, it is a distinct responsibility of MNCs to use their power to proactively contribute to human development by providing essential goods and services as well as by promoting good social and economic policy. Such an account goes decisively beyond conventional connections between MNC activity and development, which are commonly based on the attempt to prove a positive correlation between the mere provision of FDI and positive economic development (see e.g. W. H. Meyer 1996, Lodge & Wilson 2006, Prahalad 2006).

Michael Santoro's (2000: 143–58; 2009: 14–17; 2010) "Fair Share Theory" is also concerned with the potential impact of MNCs to improve the protection and realization of human rights. Such responsibility, according to Santoro, increases (decreases) along an agent's increasing (decreasing) potential to have a positive impact on the situation, its strong (weak) relationship to the victims and its ease (difficulty) in withstanding potential retaliation by a perpetrator.

Thus, most of such agency-based accounts refer, in one way or the other, to MNCs' power and influence on outcomes or over other actors. As such, agency and thus the responsibility which derives from it is most commonly seen as a function of a MNC's unique and extensive capabilities (e.g. Wettstein 2009, 2012a), its leverage over other actors (Wood 2012), as well as its proximity to injustices taking place (Campbell 2006: 260) and thus of its position to intervene (D. Miller 2005a: 102).

Natural persons

This section turns to accounts about standards for the policies and activities of MNCs that, at least in the first instance, appear to avoid the need to take a position on the plausibility of holding corporations morally responsible or attributing agency to corporations.

Lane (2005) articulates two ways in which to set standards for the activities and policies of MNCs without attributing moral responsibility to corporations themselves by focusing on the actions taken by those that act on behalf of MNCs. First, using the example of slavery, Lane writes: "because all natural persons have the fundamental moral duty not to enslave others, no role can absolve them of that duty per se: Therefore, since no one could morally act for it to do so, no corporation can permissibly enslave people either" (*ibid.*: 238). On this view, not all moral duties that apply to natural persons attach to MNCs. Rather, the point is that certain duties – most notably those that place constraints on what persons may permissibly do to others – apply to natural persons across all contexts such that they represent constraints on the activities and policies of MNCs as well. Second, those who represent MNCs gain new responsibilities in virtue of their exercise of the new capabilities enabled by MNCs, especially those capabilities that enable the decisions taken by persons representing MNCs to "effect changes in the material world" that "may far exceed those of most ordinary people" (*ibid.*). These are role responsibilities of the representatives that attach to the corporation itself.

The focus on corporate representatives helps to provide normative foundations for accounts concerned with constraints that ought to apply to the activities and policies of MNCs (Hsieh 2013). Recall the United Nations "Protect, Respect, and Remedy" Framework developed by John Ruggie (2013). In contexts of weak governance and conflict, because economic activity may have negative impacts on the rights of people, Ruggie advocates for an unconditional responsibility to respect human rights in and through all economic activity. In response, Ruggie has been criticized for the lack of a firm normative foundation for his claims. Bilchitz (2010: 2), for example, argues that responsibilities cannot be established by mere reference to empirical facts, but calls for the support of genuinely normative arguments. Other scholars have criticized Ruggie on grounds that he relies heavily on instrumental and pragmatic argumentation (see, e.g., Arnold 2010, Cragg 2012, Wettstein 2012b), which may appeal more readily to corporations, but lack moral force.[23]

Part of the criticism is that human rights are normally understood as claims that citizens have to be protected by the state. However, some of the enumerated rights correspond to rights that, on most theories, all natural persons possess in virtue of their humanity. Two examples are liberty rights (e.g. a right to freedom of movement) and security rights (e.g. a right to bodily integrity), which are generally held to ground duties of forbearance that are perfect and general. In so far as it would be wrong for any individual to violate these duties, so would it be wrong for any individual to do so in the context of the MNC's activities. In addition, human rights violations may result in harm. Duties not to harm others are "about as well established as any moral duties could be" (Lichtenberg 2010), and their recognition places constraints on MNCs by way of corporate representatives who enact policies and set into motion the activities of MNCs.

The concern with rights violations and harm can be extended to include the business relations of MNCs to its suppliers, contractors and sub-contractors. The outsourcing and fragmentation of global supply chains has turned especially issues connected to labour conditions and sweatshops from a direct internal responsibility of MNCs into a predominantly indirect external responsibility (Wettstein 2012a: 747). The question connected to such indirect responsibility, then, is whether MNCs ought to be held responsible for the harm and rights violations caused by parties in their supply chain and to what extent they ought to use their leverage over suppliers to press for adequate treatment of workers.[24]

Another way that has been advanced to connect MNCs to human rights violations is to specify the conditions under which MNCs are complicit in human rights violations by states (Tripathi 2005, Hoffman & McNulty 2009, Brenkert 2009, Monge 2013). The thought is that it would be wrong for corporate representatives to undertake activities or to enact policies that would help states to violate their duties to citizens. One question that arises for this line of reasoning is whether it involves attributing to MNCs a direct responsibility in the protection of human rights.

As suggested in the previous section, the most direct way in which to attach positive responsibilities to MNCs is by way of attributing to them some sort of moral agency or a corporate purpose beyond that of maximizing shareholder value. There are, however, accounts that aim to ground positive responsibilities on the part of MNCs without attributing to them moral agency or specifying the nature of corporate purpose. In the case of weak institutions of the sort described by Ruggie, it has been argued that the nature of the harms caused by MNCs may require not only curtailing their activities and mitigating the harms that result, but also contributions of resources and expertise, on the part of MNCs, to strengthen existing institutional arrangements (Hsieh 2009).[25] Another approach has been to argue that a duty of rescue applies to corporate representatives (Wood 2012). It has been argued, for example, that pharmaceutical companies have a responsibility to provide medicines to persons suffering from HIV/AIDS who are not able to afford them (Dunfee 2005). Because rescue is required under specific, limited conditions, it has been argued that a duty to provide life-saving drugs need not be seen as requiring any change in the nature of corporate purpose (Hsieh 2006).[26]

Rather than focus on corporate representatives, an altogether different approach is to consider the responsibilities of the beneficiaries of the activities of MNCs. Young (2004), for example, argues that consumers in developed economies have responsibilities towards workers in

developing economies who manufacture the goods they purchase. This, in turn, invites exploration of the extent to which the responsibilities of consumers not to benefit in certain ways place
restrictions on the kinds of activities that are permissible for MNCs to pursue in generating those
benefits. Shareholders of MNCs represent another group of beneficiaries of corporate activity.
In their case, it has been argued that there are conditions under which MNCs may be best placed
to discharge more general duties of assistance that members of developed economies owe to
members of poor countries (Hsieh 2004). Under these conditions, the duties of shareholders may
require MNCs to undertake activities that benefit members of poor communities in ways they
otherwise would not from the course of normal economic activity.

Notes

1 Foreign direct investment (FDI) is a category of investment that "reflects the objective of establishing a
lasting interest by a resident enterprise in one economy (*direct investor*) in an enterprise (*direct investment
enterprise*) that is resident in an economy other than that of the direct investor" (OECD 2008a: 234). A
foreign direct investment enterprise is one in which the direct investor owns 10% or more of its voting
power (*ibid.*). To create, expand or acquire a foreign subsidiary, MNCs undertake FDI, but not all FDI
involves MNCs given the requirement of control for MNCs.
2 Consider, for example, three of the ten largest MNCs as ranked by revenues (Fortune 2013). In 2012,
Walmart, the retail corporation headquartered in the United States, had 2.2 million employees, revenues
of $446 billion, 10,800 retail units in 27 countries, and 245 million customers (Walmart 2013). Royal
Dutch Shell, the energy company headquartered in the Netherlands, had revenues of $467 billion, over
87,000 employees and operations in more than 70 countries (Shell 2013). Toyota, the automobile
manufacturer headquartered in Japan, had revenues of $235 billion, 52 overseas manufacturing companies
in 27 countries, and sales in160 countries and regions (Toyota 2013). In contrast, SABAF is an Italian
SME that produces components for gas cookers and domestic gas cooking appliances with operations in
Brazil, China, Poland and Turkey. In 2012, they employed around 700 people (SABAF 2013).
3 In the case of countries, GDP is taken as the measure of their economic size. If the revenue of MNCs is
used as a measure of their size, then MNCs comprise roughly half of the one hundred largest economic
entities in the world. However, as De Grauwe and Camerman (2003) point out, GDP is the sum of the
value added by each producer, which is not the same as the sum of the revenue of these producers.
Aggregating the revenue of producers is likely to involve counting more than once the value added by
producers. Accordingly, the authors argue that counting the revenue of MNCs overstates their relative
size. Following the authors' method of calculating the value added by MNCs, one estimate places
twenty-nine MNCs within the top one hundred economic entities in the world (UNCTAD 2002).
4 Developed economies are defined by UNCTAD to include Bermuda, Canada, USA, Israel, Japan,
Australia, New Zealand, Austria, Belgium, Bulgaria, Cyprus, Czech Republic, Denmark, Estonia,
Finland, France, Germany, Greece, Hungary, Iceland, Ireland, Italy, Latvia, Lithuania, Luxembourg,
the Netherlands, Norway, Poland, Portugal, Romania, Slovakia, Slovenia, Spain, Sweden and the
United Kingdom (UNCTAD 2009: xiv).
5 The Universal Declaration of Human Rights (United Nations 1948) specifies over two dozen rights
that apply to all person. These include *security rights* (e.g. freedom from torture and a right to bodily
integrity); *due process rights* (e.g. a right to a fair and public hearing); *liberty rights* (e.g. freedom of
movement and freedom of thought, conscience and religion); *political rights* (e.g. a right to vote);
equality rights (e.g. protection against discrimination); and *welfare rights* (e.g. rights to education, to work,
and to an adequate standard of living) (Nickel 2010).
6 For example, in the area of the environment, SustainAbility (2013) inventoried over 100 ratings systems. For a helpful completion and categorization of many of the major codes, see Leipziger (2010).
7 For an overview, see Rasche and Kell (2010).
8 In 2003, the United Nations Human Rights Commission's Sub-Commission on the Promotion and
Protection of Human Rights adopted the Norms on the Responsibilities of Transnational Corporations and other Business Enterprises with Regard to Human Rights (United Nations 2003).
The Norms proposed assigning to MNCs the same human rights duties as states under international
law. Specifically, the Norms state that "within their respective spheres of activity and influence,
transnational corporations and other business enterprises have the obligation to promote, secure the

fulfillment of, respect, ensure respect of and protect human rights recognized in international as well as national law, including the rights and interests of indigenous peoples and other vulnerable groups". The Norms engendered a great deal of debate, with both strong support and opposition, and the Human Rights Commission declined to act upon them (Ruggie 2013: xvii). John Ruggie was then appointed Special Representative of the United Nations Secretary-General to clarify the relation of the human rights regime to MNCs. For some discussions of the issues relating to human rights and business, see Campbell and Miller (2004), Cragg (2000) and Voiceulescu and Yanacopulos (2011).

9 The Clean Clothes Campaign (1998) defines living wages as "wages and benefits paid for a standard working week shall meet at least legal or industry minimum standards and always be sufficient to meet basic needs of workers and their families and to provide some discretionary income".

10 These principles have been superseded by the Ceres Roadmap for Sustainability (Ceres n.d.).

11 "Each State Party shall adopt such legislative and other measures as may be necessary to establish as criminal offences, when committed intentionally: (a) The promise, offering or giving, to a public official, directly or indirectly, of an undue advantage, for the official himself or herself or another person or entity, in order that the official act or refrain from acting in the exercise of his or her official duties" (Convention, Chapter III, Article 15). The Convention also includes the solicitation or acceptance of bribes by public officials.

12 The ISO 26000 standard on social responsibility has many of the features of a process-oriented initiative, but it is explicit in that ISO 26000 "is intended to assist organizations in contributing to sustainable development" and to "encourage them to go beyond legal compliance" (ISO 2010: 3).

13 One of most well-known set of arguments is found in the work of Michael Porter and Mark Kramer (2002, 2006, 2011). For an overview of the evidence for what has been called the "business case" for CSR, see Margolis and Walsh (2003) and Vogel (2005). For an economic treatment of the potential benefits of CSR, see Kitzmueller and Shimshack (2012).

14 Those companies which perceived it as their ethical duty to actively disregard the discriminatory employment laws of apartheid South Africa and thus to engage in active civil disobedience are a classic example of such a constellation where compliance with existing laws results in injustice, ethically (see e.g. De George 2010: 417–21).

15 For a collection of articles that engage in this debate, see the special issue of *Business Ethics Quarterly* 18 (1): (2008).

16 There is an extensive literature on ISCT. For one helpful overview, see Dunfee (2006).

17 In the frequently quoted *New York Times Magazine* article, Friedman provides a slightly different formulation of managerial responsibility. He writes (1970: 32): "In a free enterprise, a private property system, a corporate executive is an employee of the owners of the business. He has a direct responsibility to his employers. That responsibility is to conduct the business in accordance with their desires, which generally will be to make as much money as possible while conforming to the basic rules of the society, both those embodied in law and those embodied in ethical custom. Strictly speaking, this formulation opens two avenues for managers to follow standards above and beyond what is required by the law: the desires of shareholders and ethical custom. However, most commentators interpret Friedman's view as consistent with the weak constraints view.

18 For critical discussion see Hussain (2012).

19 Because of the emphasis on the practical need for attributing some form of moral responsibility to corporations, Dubbink and Smith label this second approach "pragmatic".

20 There is a voluminous literature on stakeholder theory. For one summary, see Freeman *et al.* (2010).

21 "MNEs rely on the rule of law to ensure the protection of their own interests. Without the rule of law, MNEs would cease to exist. Therefore it is inconsistent for an MNE to permit the violation of the legal rights of workers while at the same time it demands that its own rights be protected" (Arnold & Bowie 2003: 228).

22 "An entity that has, amongst its key purposes, the possession and accumulation of wealth must thus have duties to ameliorate the harms caused by the very system of property rights that enables it to achieve this purpose. The very economic purpose of corporations and their success in accumulating wealth thus highlights their crucial role in the property system and provides the basis for recognising an obligation upon them to make a contribution to alleviating at least the worst effects of such a system: the exclusion of individuals from having the resources necessary to realise their fundamental rights" (Bilchitz 2010: 15–16).

23 Margolis and Walsh (2003) too suggest a pragmatic stance toward the role of business in society. Based on the belief that corporations can play a positive role in ameliorating social misery, they propose to

focus research on the impact that corporate activity actually has in this regard. In other words: "Do corporations really make a concrete difference in curing social ills when they act as though they can do so?" (*ibid.*: 283). The focus thus lies on the question of how this belief that companies can play important roles in alleviating social grievances can be realized, that is, on how actual improvement can be achieved on the ground.

24 Connected to but distinct from this question is the more general debate on whether sweatshops can be morally justified. While proponents (see e.g. Bhagwati 2004, Maitland 2004, Powell 2006) advance economic arguments in favour of sweatshops as vehicles for development, opponents (see e.g. Arnold 2003, Santoro 2003, Radin & Calkins 2006) argue that such arguments cannot override the exploitation and humiliation inherent to such working conditions. See also Hartman *et al.* (2003), Snyder (2010) and Zwolinksi and Powell (2011).

25 For critical discussions, see Michaelson (2010) and Wettstein (2010).

26 T. M. Scanlon (1998: 224) provides one formulation of the principle: "if you are presented with a situation in which you can prevent something very bad from happening, or alleviate someone's dire plight, by making only a slight (or even moderate) sacrifice, then it would be wrong not to do so". He notes that the "cases in which it would most clearly be wrong not to give aid ... are cases in which those in need of aid are in dire straits: their lives are immediately threatened, for example" (*ibid.*).

20

CONSUMPTION AND NON-CONSUMPTION

Nicole Hassoun

Two facts about global consumption are particularly striking: the rich consume so much and the poor so little. So some suggest that those of us in the developed world must change the way that we consume. These people often believe that poverty and environmental problems are (at least partly) due to the fact that rich people are consuming a disproportionate share of the earth's resources (Daly 2005, Wenar 2008). Are they right? What should we say about consumption practices that might harm the environment or violate rights? How can we figure out what to consume? This chapter focuses on these questions. It has two aims. The first is to summarize, and critically discuss, some of the important literature on consumption and global justice. The second aim is to contribute to the debate on this important topic and suggest a possible direction for further research by defending the following claim: the moral virtues of creativity and resolve require us to try to find alternatives to what seem to be tragic choices about (for instance) what to consume. The following section sketches some of the literature on consumption and global justice and argues that we lack a general philosophical theory that can tell us what kinds of consumption are im/permissible or required. The second section considers whether we can say more about a particular case where, it seems, consumption has some negative impacts. The third section argues that we can arrive at some conclusions about what to consume (and refrain from consuming) even in the absence of a complete account of what kinds of consumption are im/permissible or required. The final section concludes.

Review of the literature

Perhaps the most pressing consumption problem is that some people cannot consume enough (Crocker 1998). Some consumption is necessary for survival. Many argue that people have a human right to this much. James Nickel suggests, for instance, that people have a right against the kind of severe poverty that afflicts the majority of the world's population (Nickel 2006). Almost a billion people lack food adequate for normal functioning. About two billion cannot secure the vitamins and minerals they need (Goodland 1998). Relatively affluent members of the world's population may have to constrain their consumption. As Robert Goodland reports, it would only be possible to feed seven billion people if everyone ate a vegetarian diet, and food was well distributed (*ibid.*).[1]

More controversially, some suggest that the extent of global inequality in individuals' ability to consume is radically unfair (Caney 2001, Moellendorf 2009). Some claim that poverty is exacerbated by international organizations and rich countries that sanction some poor countries' corrupt leaders' consumption of resources that do not rightly belong to them (Pogge 2002). Others suggest that rich people are responsible for prohibiting the poor from consuming, or otherwise using, a proportionate share of the earth's resources (Sterba 1998, Wenar 2008).

Some even argue that (relatively affluent) people in developed countries should be able to consume more. Jerome Segal argues, for instance, that most people in the US have unmet economic needs for things like housing, transportation, education and economic security. He says that these needs should be satisfied by higher levels of consumption and economic growth (Segal 1998). Moreover, some note that consumption can make people happy, stimulate the global economy, allow individuals to reinvent themselves, help groups to express their cultural values, and so forth (Schudson 1998, Sen 1998, Strudlow & Curlow 1998).

Herman Daly objects to encouraging consumption because he believes it is contributing to a host of environmental problems. For Daly, consumption includes production: the total throughput of the economy (Daly 2005). He holds that the earth's ecosystem has limited ability to supply and absorb wastes; the economy is no longer small relative to the global ecosystem. Our consumption of fossil fuels, for instance, has exceeded the climate's capacity to absorb greenhouse gases and is causing climate change (Shue 2002, Gardiner 2004, Daly 2008). Daly believes that the marginal costs of further growth are greater than the marginal benefits. He claims that welfare is negatively correlated with gross national product (Daly 2008). So, he suggests, we should have a no-growth economy, staying within the ability of the planet to sustain our consumption. Though, Daly believes, we should support some qualitative development in poor countries.[2]

Other authors, like Mark Sagoff, argue that we are not straining the capacity of the earth's ecosystems or exploiting the global South. Sagoff holds that we can always find more efficient ways of using existing resources, find new ways of securing these resources, or find new alternatives. He says that if we are really concerned about helping the poor, we should stop protecting our markets. The North should buy more of what the South produces (Sagoff 1997).

Nevertheless, Sagoff maintains that some kinds of consumption are morally problematic because they do not show proper respect for nature and other things of value, such as community (Sagoff 1997, Matthews 1999, Wong & Hassoun 2011). He believes that consumption may distract us from spending time with friends and family or enjoying nature.[3]

Even some of those who do not complain about how much people consume worry about particular consumption practices. Some object, for instance, to consuming animal products because they are concerned about the environmental consequences of meat production: the land and pesticides used and wastes produced (Goodland 1998). Others are concerned about animal suffering (P. Singer 1975). Some worry about purchasing sweatshop, or child labour-made goods because they are concerned about exploitation or suffering (Arnold & Bowie 2003, Satz 2003, Snyder 2008). All of these claims are controversial. Some suggest, for instance, that children may suffer if they are not allowed to work (Schmidtz 2002, Zwolinski 2007). Nevertheless, there are good reasons to worry about at least some of our consumption practices. At least when there are good alternatives for children, child labour is presumably impermissible (Satz 2003).

Supposing, then, that at least some of our personal consumption practices are problematic,[4] is there a general philosophical theory that can tell us what kinds of consumption are im/permissible or required? David Wasserman provides what is perhaps the most systematic attempt to arrive at an answer to this question (though he focuses only on consumption's impact on people). In his brilliant article Wasserman appeals to traditional philosophical principles for what justifies property rights. This is a great idea because consumption is one of the things standard property rights allow us to do. Property is a bundle of rights and liberties, to (for example) sell, lease, use and consume goods. Moreover, Wasserman's argument links the discussion of permissible consumption to standard debates about harm in the global justice literature. So it is worth critically discussing Wasserman's argument, as questions about permissible harm are some of the most important issues to be found in the literature to date.

Wasserman considers whether there is an interpretation of Locke's proviso applied to the case of consumption that can explain what kinds of consumption are permissible or impermissible. He starts by considering, for instance, two versions of this proviso as it is cashed out by Robert Nozick. On one way of interpreting the proviso, consumption is impermissible if it precludes similar consumption of the same resource by others; on another interpretation, consumption is permitted if non-consumers are not worse off than they would have been if the consumption had not occurred. Non-consumers may be compensated for any lost resources or the opportunity to consume them (Wasserman 1998: 539).[5] Wasserman suggests that both of Nozick's interpretations of Locke's proviso embody the idea that consumption cannot permissibly harm others. He notes, however, that there are many possible accounts of harm. Harm may need to make people worse off than they would have been in the absence of consumption, than they would have been in a state of nature, or than they have a right to be, for instance. Wasserman thinks an adequate account of harm must include other harms from depletion of resources besides their unavailability for use. He believes, for instance, that a good account must include the harm of depletion or destruction itself.

There are, however, a host of difficult issues in proving that (any particular kind of) consumption has harmed anyone in these ways (Paten 2005, Risse 2005a).[6] It is hard to know how things would have been in the absence of a history of exploitative consumption, for instance. It may not even be clear whether poor people would have been better off in the state of nature (Risse 2005a).

Moreover, if we want to adapt an account of what justifies property rights to justify consumption, Wasserman recognizes that the relevant account of harm cannot be theory-neutral (Wasserman 1998, Risse 2005a). Perhaps the most promising account of harm for these purposes is one on which people are harmed if they are made worse off than they have a right to be. Any way of filling out the details of such an account will obviously be controversial, however (Risse 2005a). So Wasserman suggests considering a trustee or stewardship model of responsibility for the earth (though he does not do much to cash out an account of stewardship). So it seems that, although Wasserman explains some ways of connecting the literature on consumption with theories of global justice, there is a lot of work left to do.

Considering an illustrative example

Perhaps we can say more about a particular case where, it seems, consumption has some negative impacts. Consider, for instance, what it takes for someone who lives in the United States to get a simple tomato for dinner. Many of the tomatoes US citizens are eating come from hybrid seeds patented in the US but grown in Mexico, Holland, Belgium or Israel (US Department of Agriculture 1999). To increase the percentage of germinating seeds most are treated with chemicals like mercury. The fields where the tomatoes are grown can be hundreds of acres large and may be fumigated with chemicals like methyl bromide (US Department of Agriculture 1998). When the tomatoes are grown in Mexico, they are often farmed by labourers paid the equivalent of US$0.50 per hour. Even in Florida, where farm workers make about US$6.77 per hour, they often have terrible working conditions, are exposed to these toxic chemicals, and are sometimes subjected to violence or enslaved (Rural Migration News 1996; Estabrook 2001, 2009). Often the tomatoes are picked green and put in plastic trays before being covered with plastic wrapping and packed in a cardboard box. The plastics are made with petrochemicals and chlorine. Some of the cardboard is probably made from trees in British Columbia that can be three hundred years old (Salitan 1994). Once the tomatoes are boxed, chemicals like ethylene may be applied to turn the tomatoes red (GEO-PIE 2006). Then the tomatoes are sent in a refrigerated truck to a warehouse. Although today's coolants are usually less destructive than CFCs, many of these still negatively impact the environment (Environmental Protection Agency 2001). Hundreds of gallons of fuel are used to transport the tomatoes and to make the machines and vehicles used to produce the tomatoes. This fuel may have come from any number of countries around the world, and the refining and transport processes used to generate this fuel would also involve inputs from many countries. Finally, after the tomatoes are purchased, the wrappers are thrown into the trash. They must then be trucked to a disposal or incinerator facility. Many of the building materials used in manufacturing the vehicles and storage areas for the tomatoes also end up in landfills. This trash can languish for decades and sometimes centuries before breaking down. A single aluminium can is estimated to take between 200 and 400 years to degrade; a plastic six-pack holder might take 450 years to degrade (Bureau of Land Management 1998).

In reflecting on this case, one might conclude that there is reason to worry about the environmental and social impacts of tomato production, but it is not at all clear what individual consumers are responsible for in this case. Most people do not know the secret life of the tomato, or any of the other products, they purchase. Sometimes it is relatively easy to find out about, and pursue, alternatives. A quick web search allows one to learn where much of one's food comes from, to connect with local farmers, and to support community agriculture in most places. But must consumers do any of these things? Should they stop buying the tomatoes? More generally, how much moral responsibility do individuals bear for possible negative effects of consumption?

One challenge to the claim that consumers are responsible for the negative consequences of consumption is that changing their consumption practices will make no practical difference to what happens. If they buy local organic produce, or plant a garden, the same number of conventional tomatoes will still be produced with the same consequences.

I am not sure this is correct. When I started buying up most of the Poblano peppers at my local grocery, I noticed that they doubled their weekly supply. The check-out machines of some large corporations (like Walmart) automatically send a request to their factories for a replica of every item bought (Gallaugher 2010). Although some purchases may have no effect on supply at all, others may have more than proportional impact. It is plausible that, as individuals, we play a large enough role in bringing about environmental damage through our consumption practices that we are responsible for changing these practices, if not ameliorating this damage. One might also hold that consumers are collectively responsible for the negative impact of their (collective) consumption but distribute responsibility for changing these practices to each of us individually. Even when individuals cannot affect change alone simply by refraining from consumption, they may be able to do some things like organize boycotts. Alternatively, they might have to compensate for the negative impact of their consumption in other ways, such as by purchasing carbon offsets.

There are better challenges to the conclusion that we are responsible for the negative impacts of consumption. It may be too difficult even to determine all of the consequences of consuming all of the things we can purchase. There are so many options. Moreover, there are good reasons not to purchase many of the things available for sale and it is not reasonable to ask people to refrain from purchasing most of them. Living off the grid is not a realistic option for most people.[7]

Although these, and related, issues merit sustained attention, the rest of this chapter will simply set these worries aside in order to focus more carefully on the issue of whether an individual's choice of whether or not to consume a tomato may, on average, have some impact on tomato production and thus on farm workers and the environment. There may be other things consumers could do – like grow their own tomatoes or buy organic tomatoes – that will have different impacts. Perhaps consumers must take these consequences into account. Even if this is so, however, it is still not clear what people should do in the case above.

One remaining problem is that if people stop purchasing conventional tomatoes, poor farmers may fare worse. This may just be one example of a terrible dilemma consumers face every day. Critics of consumption have recently focused their energy on food. They suggest that we should eat less and eat differently. Slow food advocates suggest that we should buy local foods that are made in sustainable ways rather than food shipped with fossil fuels from the other side of the world. At least, those who believe that we are morally obligated to purchase local foods may have a problem. Many of the world's poorest people survive on the agricultural produce they can sell abroad. Perhaps we, generally, have to make a terrible choice between buying local food that is better for the environment and supporting desperately poor agricultural workers in developing countries.

The rest of this chapter will consider what we can say about cases like these in the absence of a complete account of how global justice should constrain our consumption.[8] It will address the question: *how* can we figure out what kinds of consumption are im/permissible or required? In reflecting on a few concrete cases like that above, the next section suggests that we should try very hard to avoid what appear to be tragic dilemmas: it defends a kind of utopianism about consumption. In doing so, it suggests a new line of enquiry that might advance the discussion in the future.

The argument for creative resolve

This section defends the following argument for creative resolve:

(a) We should not do something that (for all we know) might be wrong on the assumption that there are no good alternatives to what we are doing. For if there are good alternatives and we fail to find them, we may avoidably do wrong.
- Even if we do not do wrong, we must do due diligence. We must guard against the epistemic possibility of doing wrong.
- We should not assume, for instance, that we are facing a tragic dilemma.
- We would normally do wrong in acting on any of the options in such a dilemma: so we cannot assume that there are no good alternatives to any of our options.
- How much evidence one needs before doing something that there is some reason to believe is wrong probably depends on the moral status of the alternatives in normal circumstances.

(b) To avoid doing something wrong on the assumption that there are no good alternatives to what we are doing, we should try to find good alternatives.
- Avoiding terrible choices often requires the virtues of moral imagination and commitment.
- People often fail morally because they do not try to find alternatives to terrible dilemmas.
- Sometimes trying is necessary, and sufficient, for succeeding in avoiding a terrible choice.

(c) We should try to find good alternatives. That is, we should cultivate the virtues of creativity and resolve in the face of apparent tragedy.
- If this conclusion is correct, it may inform many other practical debates about how to achieve global justice as well.

The first premise of the argument for creative resolve

Consider a common argument against ending traditional forms of child labour:[9] we should not try to end child labour because, if we eliminate it, children will suffer.[10] A child's next-best alternative might be prostitution, and child prostitution is impermissible.[11] (This argument applies even on the assumption that if consumers refraining from purchasing child labour-made goods, that will reduce child labour.)

The problem with purchasing child labour-made goods on this basis alone is that one is assuming (without justification) that if we end child labour, the children we prohibit from working *will* suffer for our good intentions because, for example, their next best alternative *is* prostitution. Child prostitution may not be these children's next best alternative. Even if prostitution would be these children's next best alternative holding everything else fixed, that would not show that ending child labour is impermissible. Perhaps we should end child labour *and* provide better jobs for adults and schools for all the children we liberate. If we do not have the resources to do this then we may have to try to find the resources to do so or come up with other options: that may be what morality requires. Though it may be the case that child labour is necessary, this claim requires empirical support.

Recall, here, that this chapter assumes that the fact that collective action is necessary to avoid many of the problems that consumption can cause does not eliminate responsibility for these problems. A single individual cannot end child labour simply by refraining from purchasing child labour-made goods. Even Bill Gates may not be able to create better alternatives for all the children that would otherwise have to work in sweatshops. It might be impossible for most individuals to help the particular children that would otherwise have made the things that these individuals refrain from purchasing. Nevertheless, there are many things people can do to mitigate the (shared?) responsibility this chapter presumes that they have for the negative consequences of their consumption. Even when individuals cannot affect change alone simply by refraining from consumption, they may be able to do some things like organize boycotts of sweatshop-made goods or aid organizations helping children rescued from sweatshops. A division of labour here may also be perfectly appropriate. The main argument against drinking milk is structurally similar to the argument against ending child labour in that it contains an important but undefended assumption. It asserts that if people drink milk, baby calves must be separated from their mothers. These calves will, almost invariably, be raised for veal. When baby calves are raised for veal they are often deprived of essential nutrients (P. Singer 1975). Sometimes they are kept isolated in cages so small that they cannot even turn around or lie down comfortably. (In short, they suffer tremendously.) So, the argument concludes, drinking milk is morally impermissible.

Perhaps those who want to drink milk can respond similarly to this argument, questioning its implicit assumption. It starts from an important but undefended claim. It assumes that drinking milk will result in something that (suppose for the sake of argument) there is some reason to believe is impermissible: people raising calves for veal. It is not clear that if we drink milk, calves must be raised for veal: perhaps they could be raised as free range steer and then killed humanely.

More generally, perhaps we can say this: we should not do something that (for all we know) might be wrong on the assumption that there are no good alternatives. This just is the first premise of the argument for creative resolve.

This premise can cut in both directions. To better appreciate the force of the general principle that we should not do something that (for all we know) might be wrong on the assumption that there are no good alternatives, it will help to consider the preceding cases from the opposite perspective.[12] One should not refuse to buy child labour goods on the assumption that children rescued from sweatshops *will not* suffer because we can provide them with an education. It may be infeasible to provide children with an education if children lose their jobs as a result of people refusing to buy child labour-made goods. Similarly, one should not drink milk on the assumption that it *is* feasible to raise milk calves for steer. It may not be. No one should do something that (for all they know) might be wrong on the assumption that there are no good alternatives.

Even if what one is assuming would not in fact lead to incorrect moral conclusions, one should not be so presumptuous. There is reason to guard against the epistemic risk of assuming something that may lead to a morally impermissible conclusion. Suppose that it is in fact wrong to buy child labour-made goods, and one could not be wrong in asserting that there are things we can do to protect children even if we refuse to purchase child labour-made goods. Even so, one should not simply assume that ending child labour will benefit children. If one does so, one has not done due diligence.

There is an epistemic-cum-moral obligation to guard against the epistemic possibility of doing wrong. Consider an adaptation of a famous case from the literature in epistemology: suppose someone is hosting a party and can assert that an unmarked bottle of liquid is gin. The host realizes that if she does so, one of the party-goers may drink the liquid. What the host must do to know she is just offering another a glass of gin (and, hence, for it to be permissible to offer the glass) depends on the situation. If the host recognizes or believes that there is a non-negligible chance the liquid could be poison, she must take at least some precautions before saying it is gin. What precautions are appropriate will depend on what grounds she has for believing the liquid may be poison. Still, the host who recognizes, or believes, that there is a non-negligible chance the liquid could be poison must do more to know, or be justified in believing, that the liquid is gin. Moreover, the host must do more to be morally justified in saying it is.

Acting on an apparent tragic dilemma may be the clearest example of the kind of moral failure against which the first premise of the argument for creative resolve cautions: we should not do something that (for all we know) might be wrong on the assumption that there are no good alternatives. One should not presume that terrible trade-offs are necessary when they may not be.[13] For there is something *prima facie* wrong about making such trade-offs. In a genuine tragic (or terrible) dilemma, all of the options on the table would normally be unacceptable.

How much evidence one needs before doing something that there is some reason to believe is wrong probably depends on the moral status of the alternatives in normal circumstances.[14] Sticking with the examples that illustrate how the obligation not to do something that (for all we know) might be wrong on the assumption that there are no good alternatives cuts in both directions, we might say this: If the proponent of ending child labour is wrong that children rescued from sweatshops *will not* suffer, that would be very unfortunate (because children will suffer). Causing children to suffer is *prima facie* morally impermissible. So there is a rather large burden on those who refuse to purchase child labour-made goods to make sure that refraining from doing so does not cause suffering.[15] If those who say it is impermissible to drink milk because calves will suffer are wrong, however, little may be lost. There are other ways to secure calcium. So, the burden on those who accept this proposition may be less. The general idea is that the burden is heaviest on those for whom being wrong in their assumptions would cause the most moral damage.

Although it may be ridiculous to refuse to assume that some trade-offs are necessary,[16] the requisite claim is just that if *something is prima facie morally impermissible*, we should resist simply assuming that it is unavoidable. In defending the final premise of the argument for creative resolve, the next sub-section will draw out some further practical lessons from this conclusion.[17]

The second premise of the argument for creative resolve

The preceding reflections might provide some guidance about how to respond to purportedly terrible dilemmas. Suppose a strong case against drinking milk and for buying child labour-made goods *is* made. Milk drinkers ought to stop drinking milk. Rice and soy milk provide decent alternatives. But what should we do if we suppose, for illustration's sake, that child labour is at least *prima facie* wrong. If, as the above reflections suggest, we must be very careful before we assume that we have to make terrible choices, virtue may not allow us to jump to the conclusion that we are facing a terrible and unavoidable moral dilemma. We may have an obligation to try to figure out whether, all things considered, we have a moral obligation to purchase or refrain from purchasing child labour-made goods. (There is no similar burden on us to determine whether it really is acceptable to refrain from drinking milk as long as there is nothing *prima facie* wrong about refraining from doing so.)

Or consider the tomato example discussed above. Those involved in the local food movement argue that it is better to buy local. Shipping food from the other side of the world contributes to problems like climate change as it requires a lot of fossil fuel. On the other hand, many of the world's poorest people survive on the agricultural produce they can sell abroad. One might conclude that we have to make a terrible choice between buying local food that is better for the environment and supporting desperately poor agricultural workers in developing countries. If we grow our own tomatoes or purchase local organic tomatoes, for instance, many Mexican tomato farmers may lose their jobs. The above enquiry suggests, however, that we should not assume that such a terrible choice is necessary. Perhaps we can buy local and help developing countries in other ways. If we also reduce our consumption, perhaps we can give more in foreign aid. There is good evidence that some foreign aid programmes work (Skoufias & McClafferty 2001; World Bank 2004a, 2004b; Rawlings & Rubio 2005).[18] Alternatively, we might purchase food from poor farmers in developing countries and reduce our emissions in other ways, such as by driving less (Hassoun 2005). This does not mean that it will be possible to avoid making a terrible choice between buying local food that is better for the environment and supporting desperately poor agricultural workers in developing countries. Still, we should look hard for alternatives.

Avoiding terrible choices requires moral imagination and commitment. The requisite creativity and resolve is illustrated in the aforementioned response to the proponent of child labour's assertion that children will become prostitutes if they are not employed. If we assume it is *prima facie* wrong to buy child labour-made goods, it is important to consider whether we can help children avoid prostitution by educating the children we liberate.

Sometimes avoiding what seems, initially, to be a terrible dilemma, may be difficult. There will, of course, be times when the costs of looking for other alternatives exceed the costs of making a terrible choice. An alternative may not exist. Still, there is a *prima facie* obligation to do what we can to avoid making terrible choices, even if avoiding them is very difficult, very demanding.[19]

The imperative to try hard to find alternatives should be particularly compelling if people often fail morally because they do not question their assumptions. There is significant psychological evidence that we generally fail to consider enough alternatives in making decisions.[20] Alternately, people may lack moral imagination because they take much too narrow a view of feasibility, assuming narrow time frames and financial constraints. Most of us are used to thinking about everyday business and personal problems under these kinds of constraints. Some people also seem to have a very pessimistic view of human nature, politics or political philosophy (Goodin 1995: 40). For these reasons, they may not look hard enough for alternatives to what seem to be terrible dilemmas.

It is important to recognize that "the institutional structures in which groups of people live themselves shape those people's views of both the possible and of the desirable" (Stears 2005: 341). It is important to see that "political theory may be able radically to reshape currently prevailing political attitudes rather than simply to reflect and refine them" (*ibid.*: 340).

To return to the child labour case, those arguing against ending child labour might show that if we just stop purchasing these goods then children will suffer. They might even show that we cannot prevent this suffering by educating children and providing jobs for parents. But perhaps they cannot rule out all feasible ways of helping children avoid this suffering without purchasing child labour-made goods. Perhaps programmes like Mexico's Progressa/Opportunidades, which give scholarships to poor children who attend school, are in order. Conditional cash transfer programmes like Progressa/Opportunidades may prevent child labour and help parents educate their children (Skoufias & McClafferty 2001; World Bank 2004a, 2004b; Rawlings & Rubio 2005). One might object that if we support aid programmes that help children (or, for that matter, tomato farmers) in Mexico, we should purchase child labour-made goods (or tomatoes) from other countries and thereby help other children as well. But the point is a general one: perhaps we can support aid programmes in all developing countries sufficiently to alleviate the need for child labour (or working for low wages in poor conditions on Mexican tomato farms).[21]

In short, we should try to find good alternatives to any apparent terrible dilemmas. This point applies to apparent dilemmas we face in trying to decide what to consume. It also applies more broadly. The moral virtue we lack if we do not question assumptions that may lead us to incorrect moral conclusions is a kind of creativity and resolve.[22] We must commit to avoiding purportedly terrible and unavoidable dilemmas. The only acceptable thing to do if there is a terrible and unavoidable dilemma is to act only out of necessity. Otherwise we have shown a failure of the moral imagination. Morality requires a realistic utopia in theory and in practice.

Conclusion

This chapter started by reviewing some of the literature on consumption. It suggested that we lack a well-cashed-out general theory about what kinds of consumption are morally im/permissible or required. So, this chapter considered a new question that, along with enquiry into hard questions about individual responsibility for the negative consequences of consumption, might guide discussion in the future: "*How* can we figure out what kinds of consumption are im/permissible or required?" After arguing that we must not suppose we have to make hard choices about what to consume, the chapter suggested that these arguments generalize to some much more controversial conclusions about how we should act in the face of what may seem to be terrible dilemmas. It suggested that we should not assume we have to make a terrible choice. We should be careful, for instance, before consuming goods (or refusing to do so) on the assumption that consumption violates (or does not violate) rights. We should try hard to find alternatives. This chapter's conclusions about how we should deal with such apparent dilemmas may apply not only to the case of consumption; they may help us achieve global justice more broadly.

Acknowledgements

I would like to thank Darrel Moellendorf for extensive comments. I also appreciate the feedback I received on the main argument at the Yale/Penn works in progress series, and Stanford University. I would also like to thank Sarah Wright, Paul Gowder, Aaron James, Debra Satz, Matt Frank, John Farnum, Ben Jantzen, Orsolya Reich, Allegra McCloud, Keiran Oberman,

Peter Stone, Tamar Schapiro, Manuel Vargas, Eammon Callahan and Julian Culp for comments and discussion on related work.

Notes

1 To accept this conclusion, one does not need to endorse Singer's demanding conclusion that we must give up everything that is not morally significant or comparable to help the poor (P. Singer 1972).

2 Daly says that the costs of protecting ourselves from over-consumption (e.g. oil spills) will also decrease.

3 Sagoff would probably not agree with Juliet Schor, however, in arguing that there is reason for the government to restrict advertising and access to credit and to use taxes and subsidies to promote equality and protect the environment (Schor 1999). Nor is it clear that all critics of consumption would agree with Lichtenburg that we consume primarily because others consume and, though there are good reasons for this, we might not suffer if everyone consumed less (Lichtenburg 1998).

4 This does not include saving and investment practices (Crocker 1998, Crocker & Linden 1998a).

5 Wasserman suggests that "the comparative strength of the two interpretations depends on the baseline from which we assess the harm that, under the second interpretation, needs to be compensated. If we take a broad view of the harm for which compensation is owed to include such adverse effects as the loss of natural landscapes or political autonomy, the second interpretation may turn out to be more stringent than the first, because compensation may be impossible" (Wasserman 1998: 540).

6 Thus this discussion connects with other discussions in the global justice literature over different kinds of "harm" (Pogge 2002, Risse 2005a).

7 There are also hard questions about merely intending versus doing actions that do have bad consequences (or would otherwise violate rights), but this chapter will not consider them.

8 I will assume throughout that the reader is a relatively affluent member of the world's population.

9 Some view child prostitution as a form of child labour, though it is not the kind of labour traditionally protected by governments. In any case, I will not include it under the purview of labour here.

10 On this argument, see Basu and Van (1998: 423), Basu and Tzannatos (2003), Follesdal (2009). Obviously it is not enough to establish that, in some case(s), child labour has hurt children to establish that it will hurt children in general, or that it will do so in the future, or that we should ban child labour. Nor is evidence about a few (small) cases enough to establish a presumption in favour of banning child labour. For discussion of what kinds of empirical evidence are sufficient to establish claims like this see Hassoun (2010).

11 Apparently something like this argument has also had a role to play historically in debates about child labour. See Rosenberg (2013). Some philosophers even suggest something like this. One might, for instance, interpret Debra Satz's main argument regarding child labour's permissibility in this way, though I expect she intends this argument's conclusion to be conditional upon the relevant economic facts (Satz 2003).

12 Perhaps we need not (generally) do what we can to defend all of our truth-determining assumptions. Perhaps we only need to be clear about what we are assuming. At least, if we express appropriate regret, it might be acceptable for us to make such assumptions. To see why this objection is implausible, consider the child labour example again assuming, for illustration's sake, that child labour is actually impermissible. The objector would, in effect, be saying this: it is okay to advance the claim that we should support child labour without defending the (avoidable) assumption that, otherwise, more children will become prostitutes. For, then, we can say we are sorry we do not live in a world with better alternatives for children. This is patently absurd. We cannot defend the fact that our avoidable presuppositions might lead to an incorrect moral conclusion, by saying that then we can express regret for the necessity of what we are assuming. The assumptions are, by hypothesis, avoidable. If we can, but do not, reject the assumptions then we should instead regret having to make them (if there is good reason to do so). If there is no good reason to assume things that may lead us to incorrect moral conclusions, then we should not be so presumptuous.

13 Something like this principle may also underlie the idea that arguments establish a burden that must be met for one to reject them. Once something is said in favour of an option on the table, there may be some burden to remove it from the table. How great the burden will be will depend on how much the argument in its favour adds to the claim that it is *prima facie* im/permissible or obligatory to pursue or how *prima facie* wrong it is to neglect. I owe thanks to Aaron James for discussion on this point.

14 Again, I have tried to put the point in a way that is neutral between consequentialist and deontological theories. As long as theories allow a range of moral evaluations (prohibited, permissible, required) this point should go through. Note, further, that adopting a deontological theory will not necessarily help theorists avoid making unjustified recommendations that could lead to incorrect moral conclusions. Even deontologists might wrongly suppose that the only alternative to child labour is prostitution, for instance.

15 Similarly, it is quite unfortunate if those who say children rescued from sweatshops will suffer without child labour are wrong. For child labour, presumably, causes many children to suffer because it prevents them from getting an adequate education.

16 In talking about child labour, one might echo Satz's claim that "tradeoffs between different values are inevitable" (Satz 2003: 223).

17 Nevertheless, even this claim alone is important. Many people have made careers from considering how we should ration scarce resources on the assumption that this is necessary. Most of what goes on in the discipline of cost-effectiveness analysis is probably based on this assumption. People also assume undefended feasibility constraints all of the time. Granted, it would be difficult to demonstrate that the arguments assuming the unavoidability of things *prima facie* morally impermissible are as widespread as I believe. It is easy, however, to find examples of such arguments in the literature. Consider, for instance, an argument by Chris Brown who believes that even what some see as rather modest goals are too utopian. He says we must "admit the tragic dimension of human existence" (C. Brown 2007b: 5). Brown believes, "genuinely free trade clearly involves rich countries sacrificing the interests of domestic workers in the medium term while protectionism clearly damages the interests of workers in low wage countries" (*ibid.*: 9). This requires making a terrible (he says tragic) choice between fulfilling duties to humanity and fellow citizens. It is far from obvious that we cannot completely ameliorate (absolute) poverty or that we must choose between sacrificing the interests of those in developing or developed countries. Brown provides no evidence for the proposition that the rules of trade, never mind poverty relief or political action in general, require making terrible choices (in this case between fulfilling duties to humanity and fellow citizens). He does not defend the claim that free trade "involves rich countries sacrificing the interests of domestic workers in the medium term while protectionism clearly damages the interests of workers in low wage countries" (*ibid.*). Some protectionism (even in rich countries) may harm rich workers and benefit poor workers. If the US protects its cotton industry, its textile industry may suffer because textile makers cannot purchase cheaper cotton abroad. And, while poor cotton producers may be worse off, poor textile makers may do better (because there is a greater supply of cheap cotton in poor countries, prices for cotton in poor countries may fall). There is a lot of evidence to suggest that the impacts of free trade and protectionism are not as straightforward as Brown suggests. There is some evidence, for instance, that agricultural liberalization will benefit most developing countries but net-food-importers may suffer. For discussion see Hassoun (2008). Even if free trade does harm domestic workers and protectionism harms poor workers, however, Brown does not explain why free trade poses a terrible, unavoidable (never mind tragic) dilemma. As anti-globalization advocates suggest, for example, by changing the ways that we consume – purchasing Fair Trade certified goods – we can help some of the global poor (Skoufias & McClafferty 2001; World Bank 2004a, 2004b; Rawlings & Rubio 2005). It may also be possible to compensate domestic workers for their losses due to free trade, for example. After all, some of the institutions countries might use to do so are already in existence (Hassoun 2008). Trade-related adjustment assistance programmes are, for instance, one possibility. Brown simply ridicules this possibility. He says that when people point to the costs of protecting the poor for workers in rich countries "something strange happens. 'Fair trade' is suddenly about protecting jobs in both North and South; with no sense of irony, a French farmer, Jose Bove, becomes an iconic figure in the movement on the principle, apparently, that defending the Common Agriculture Policy and subsidized French farms is a way of showing that 'the world is not for sale'" (C. Brown 2007b: 11). Even if institutions to compensate losers from trade did not exist, however, Brown would have to provide reason to think we could not come up with any other ways of avoiding terrible (if not tragic) trade-offs between fulfilling obligations to domestic and foreign workers.

18 For critical discussion of the literature on aid see Easterly (2006). For my take on this literature see Hassoun (2010).

19 Perhaps this holds true only in so far as we are committed to offering public reasons for our actions. It may, of course, turn out that we have some kind of (externalist) justification for doing things that we cannot know we are justified in doing.

20 There is some evidence in behavioural economics that we fail to search long enough in looking for solutions to all kinds of problems (Bearden *et al.* 2005). We may just be used to working with what Andreas Follesdal calls a partial rather than a total or wide reflective equilibrium. A wide reflective equilibrium takes into account all of our background empirical and epistemological theories (e.g. about social psychology, human nature, biology, etc.). A partial reflective equilibrium takes into account only some of these things (Follesdal 2009: 6).

21 One interesting implication of this chapter's argument is that finding solutions to the problems our consumption practices cause may require many things that do not, at first glance, have anything to do with consumption.

22 There may be other virtues in trying to avoid terrible dilemmas too. As Tom Hill suggests, in a slightly different context, individuals' commitment to avoiding such dilemmas may "frame a way of life for them … Living in the faith that they can reconcile the things that they most cherish enables them to live with a virtually unqualified, self-defining commitment to each value. This, we can imagine, energizes their pursuits and motivates them to anticipate and forestall crises in which the values could not be reconciled. Also, importantly, it enables them to enjoy special relationships that are built upon the similar and reciprocal commitments of others" (Hill 1996: 182). One might object that if we focus only on avoiding dilemmas we will not be prepared to face them when we must. But I see no reason to think we cannot both prepare for and avoid dilemmas, if necessary. If it is impossible to do both things, we may have to make a terrible choice. It would not clearly be better, however, to spend our energy preparing for emergencies rather than preventing them.

21

PROSTITUTION AND TRAFFICKING FOR SEXUAL LABOUR

Julia O'Connell Davidson

Since the mid-1990s, "human trafficking" has come to be seen as one of the most urgent ethical issues facing an increasingly globalized world. Described as "a modern slave trade" worth billions of dollars to transnational criminal groups, it has figured prominently in policy debate on immigration (B. Anderson 2008), and has been a focal point for the activities of a wide range of international non-governmental organizations (INGOs), NGOs, charities and political lobby groups. It has also attracted extensive research and media attention, and featured in numerous television dramas, Hollywood films and best-selling novels. Trafficking is now popularly perceived as a global problem of immense proportions.

As soon as talk of trafficking emerged as an issue of public and policy concern, critical scholars and activists started to question the assumptions about gender, race, prostitution and mobility that underpinned it (Chapkis 1997, Kempadoo & Doezema 1998, Kempadoo 1999). Today, there is a substantial body of literature that critically deconstructs trafficking discourse, pointing to its role in encouraging and legitimating more restrictive immigration policies and tighter border controls; advancing extremely conservative moral agendas on prostitution, gender and sexuality; and promoting an approach to independent child migration in the developing world that penalizes rather than protects poor children (for example, Anderson & O'Connell Davidson 2003, Chapkis 2005, Kapur 2005, Weitzer 2007, Agustin 2007, Aradau 2008, Hashim & Thorsen 2011, O'Connell Davidson 2011).

Focusing on prostitution in particular, this chapter reviews the definitional, theoretical and political problems presented by the idea of trafficking. It argues that dominant discourse on trafficking serves to dis-embed the suffering it describes from its basis in what is in reality a more pressing ethical issue in the contemporary world, namely the human cost of states' efforts to control irregular migration. It is, as a number of other commentators have remarked, a discourse of depoliticization (Anderson & Andrijasevic 2008, Aradau 2008, Jacobsen & Stenvoll 2010).

From prostitution to trafficking

Though prostitution appears as a uniformly dismal, violent and oppressive institution in the literature produced by feminists campaigning for its abolition (K. Barry 1995, Raymond 2003, Jeffreys 2009), empirical research reveals immense diversity within prostitution in terms of its social organization and the power relations it involves. The degree of control that individuals who sell sexual services exercise over whether, when, how often and on what terms they work varies according to a range of factors, including their level of economic desperation; the contractual form of the sexual-economic exchanges they enter into; and the specific legal, institutional, social, political and ideological context in which they work (see, for example, O'Connell Davidson 1998, Day & Ward 2004, Sanders 2005, Kelly 2008, Zheng 2009).

Some people prostitute independently or independently approach a third party for employment in the sex industry, others depend on middle agents to broker their employment by a third party, and others still are directly forced into prostitution by a third party or parties. It would be quite wrong to assume that those who work independently are free from all risk of violence, abuse or exploitation (those prostituting independently are often very vulnerable to attack by clients and muggers, extortion, rape and battery by police, cheating by clients, etc.), but equally wrong to assume that all those who enter into some kind of direct or indirect employment relation with a third party are abused, cheated or poorly paid. However, dependence on a third party does often leave sex workers open to abuse and exploitation, especially when they work in illegal or poorly monitored workplaces.

There are some national and regional differences in terms of how prostitution is socially organized: for example, large, geographically isolated brothel districts are found in South Asian but not in European Union or North American countries (L. Brown 2000, Saeed 2002). But not all sex work in South Asian countries takes place in such districts (it is also undertaken by independent entrepreneurs, as well as by people who enter into a variety of more informal sexual-economic exchanges), so diversity is a feature of prostitution here, as much as in other regions of the world. Likewise, even in settings that are profoundly unequal in terms of gender and conservative in terms of sexuality, prostitution is not a homogeneous experience (see Mahdavi's 2011 research in Dubai). In general, then, we can say that the experience of prostitution varies, and the earnings and conditions associated with it, as well as the degree of control exercised by the worker within it, range along a continuum. Reports of women and girls forced into prostitution by violent means, and in some cases transported across borders into forced prostitution, are more common during periods of war and in post-conflict regions, however (Moon 1997, Tanaka 2001, Dewey 2008), although it is important to remember that sexual violence is not a prominent feature of all wars, and that not all those who prostitute in wartime or in post-conflict regions have been forced to do so by a third party.

For reasons that will be considered later, migrants are often among those found at the most exploited and unfree pole of the prostitution spectrum, but the mere fact of being a migrant does not have any automatic implications for an individual's position on the continuum of experience that prostitution spans. A French man working independently in London as an escort, for example, is not necessarily more vulnerable within prostitution than a British man doing the same thing, and may actually earn more and be less vulnerable than some other British nationals involved in other forms of sex work.

The rise of trafficking

In the most general of terms, trafficking is understood to involve the transportation of persons by means of coercion or deception into exploitative or slavery-like conditions, but when it emerged as an issue of intense public and policy concern in the 1990s, the focus was very much upon cases in which women and girls were forced into prostitution. More particularly, concern was initially focused on women and girls forced into prostitution against the backcloth of the immense political, economic and social upheavals taking place in former Eastern Bloc countries following the fall of the Berlin Wall, especially in the former Yugoslavia in the context of war and its aftermath. The following account from Petra, a Slovakian teenager forced into prostitution in Dubi, a town on the Czech–German border, exemplifies the kind of case that captured public and policy attention:

> I went to a disco with a girlfriend. They just grabbed me. They threw me in a car and drove me here … They were Russian. They drove me here. I didn't want to do this. They beat me – badly. They gave me injections … they brought me to the bar … I didn't want to work. I wouldn't do what I was told. They got very angry. They beat me up. They cut me with a knife. Then they took me to a hospital … I couldn't tell anyone. They threatened me. The Russians are like that. Whatever they say, they do. They had my passport and papers. I was afraid if I went home they'd come after me. [When I left the hospital] they sold me right away. They drove me back to the bar. I worked for a few hours. Then they sold me. This guy bought me.
>
> *(Siden 2002: 75–76)*

For governments of affluent Western liberal democratic states, such cases were indicative of a much wider problem of "transnational organized crime" and other perceived threats to national sovereignty that arose in the context of more porous borders in the post-Cold War era, especially immigration crime. But for feminist lobby groups like the Coalition Against Trafficking in Women (CATW) and also religious groups campaigning for the abolition of prostitution per se, stories like that of Petra underlined the inherently violent and abusive nature of prostitution, and the issue of trafficking thus represented a vehicle through which their pre-existing political agenda on prostitution could be advanced. For other human and child rights INGOs and NGOs, meanwhile, the growing political interest in trafficking appeared as an opportunity to pursue other agendas, such as drawing attention to the plight of child migrants in various sectors and regions, such as that of migrant domestic workers trapped in slavery-like conditions, that of women and girls in forced marriages, that of children abused in the context of fostering and adoption, and so on.

As more and more governmental and non-governmental organizations, agencies and researchers came to view trafficking as *the* topical and "hot" human rights issue, the term expanded to embrace a large and disparate collection of global social problems and rights violations. This both reflects and reinforces the very serious definitional, conceptual and political problems with the term "trafficking". Indeed, it is precisely because trafficking is so ill-defined that so many individuals and interest groups – often with radically different moral and political goals – are able to claim it as their own (O'Connell Davidson & Anderson 2006).

Trafficking defined?

Until 2000, there was no international agreement as to the proper legal definition of trafficking. However, in November 2000, the UN Convention Against Transnational Organized Crime was adopted by the UN General Assembly, and with it two new protocols: one on smuggling of migrants and one on trafficking in persons. Human smuggling is held to describe "an individual's crossing of a state's international border without that state's authorization and with the assistance of paid smugglers" (Kyle & Koslowski 2011: 4), and thus a situation in which the migrant gives full and informed consent to movement. Trafficking, by contrast, is defined as:

(a) The recruitment, transportation, transfer, harbouring or receipt of persons, by means of threat or use of force or other forms of coercion, of abduction, of fraud, of deception, of the abuse of power or of a position of vulnerability or of the giving or receiving of payments or benefits to achieve the consent of a person having control over another person, for the purpose of exploitation. Exploitation shall include, at a minimum, the exploitation of the prostitution of others or other forms of sexual exploitation, forced labour or services, slavery or practices similar to slavery, servitude or the removal of organs;

(b) The consent of a victim of trafficking in persons to the intended exploitation set forth in subparagraph (a) of this article shall be irrelevant where any of the means set forth in subparagraph (a) have been used.

"Trafficking" is thus presented as an umbrella term to cover a process (recruitment, transportation and control) through which people are deceived or forced into moving for purposes of exploitation, and a very loose term at that. This is a process that can be organized in a variety of different ways, involve different types and degrees of compulsion (all of which are undefined: What kind of threats? How much deception? Which types of vulnerability?), and lead to a variety of very different outcomes, linked only by a common purpose, "exploitation", which itself is undefined (Anderson & O'Connell Davidson 2003).

Providing we restrict our focus to cases like that of Petra, the Slovakian teenager mentioned above, the looseness of this definition may appear unimportant. But the term "trafficking" has come to extend well beyond those who are abducted and moved against their will. It is widely used to refer to the situation of people who actively sought or agreed to migrate for some purpose, but ended up in a situation of "exploitation", which means that trafficking necessarily stands in some kind of relation to the more general phenomenon of migration. Defining that relationship is one of the major (and unresolved) conceptual, political and practical challenges presented by the term.

Certainly, questions about the relationship between trafficking and migration undermine the easy comparisons between trafficking and the transatlantic slave trade that so often feature in "anti-trafficking" rhetoric. For though we are invited to picture "victims of trafficking" (VoTs) as the contemporary equivalents of those Africans who, between the fifteenth and nineteenth centuries, were seized, manacled, shipped across the world, sold as chattels, branded and forced to labour under threat of torture or death (in other words, people who had no pre-existing desire or ambition to move to the New World), the people who are today described as VoTs almost invariably wanted to move to another region or country, and almost invariably had excellent reasons for wishing to do so. Petra's story is the exception rather than the rule in this regard, for it is actually very rare that migrant adults or children who end up in exploitative situations have been plucked from quietly contented lives and taken against their will to a distant place by "slavers" or their agents.

Irregular migration, coercion and exploitation

The Trafficking and Smuggling Protocols are underpinned by an assumption that forced and voluntary movement can be cleanly demarcated. This assumption does not fit well with the body of research evidence on irregular migration, however. For many migrants, the decision to leave home is based on the belief that poor life chances and earning opportunities will be improved through migration. For others, the decision to migrate is made in a context of more acute forms of human insecurity. Whatever the motivation for moving, the decision to migrate is taken in a highly unequal world and international mobility is one of many privileges that are unevenly allocated. It is widely recognized that demand for mobility in conjunction with the introduction of ever more restrictive immigration policies and tighter border controls by affluent, migrant-receiving countries has led to the emergence of a growing market for clandestine migration services, including smuggling across borders, faking travel documents, and arranging marriages (Kofman *et al.* 2000, Kapur 2005, Sanghera 2005). Such services are often expensive, and the research literature shows that irregular migration can involve a number of different forms of debt to a variety of different third parties, including spouses, lovers, friends, parents or other relatives, money-lenders, smugglers, brokers/recruiting agents and sponsors (Silvey 2004, Marshall & Thatun 2005, Chu 2010, Kegan 2011). It also reveals that debtors can be subject to an array of violent, coercive and exploitative practices both in the course of travel and at the point of destination.

In dominant discourse on trafficking, debt is often represented as the mechanism by which migrants are entrapped in "modern slavery":

> In the context of trafficking in women, debt bondage usually occurs when traffickers assist women in traveling, making illegal border crossings, and finding employment, often in the form of commercial sex work, and then require the women to "work off" the debt they owe for the services provided. In situations of debt bondage, women become virtual prisoners, as they are unable to ever earn back the amount purportedly owed to the traffickers.
>
> *(Advocates for Human Rights 2005)*

It is certainly true that in a criminalized, concealed and so entirely unregulated market, migrants are open to a variety of forms of abuse and exploitation, some of which may place their lives in jeopardy or lock them into extremely violent and exploitative situations at the point of destination. And yet their experience is not *necessarily* one of violence, exploitation and abuses. Some irregular migrants are assisted by third parties who do not cheat them or harm them in any way, and this is the case for those who migrate into sex work, as much as for those who migrate to work in other sectors.

Sex work abroad can hold the promise of unparalleled earnings, and some would-be migrants wish to avail themselves of this opportunity. As it is difficult to migrate into sex work through legal channels, they often have to rely on recruiters, brokers or middle agents to arrange their passage and effect their introduction to an employer, and/or arrange their employment. In some regions, it is fairly common for such sex work migration to be arranged as a form of indenture, with the worker bound to a brothel owner at the point of destination for a period of twelve months or more. During this period, the employer controls their labour, and provides them with somewhere to sleep, food, clothing and anything else necessary to their subsistence. Sex workers are normally entitled to a salary, but payment of that salary is withheld for one year, and then paid, minus the broker's fee and deductions for food, accommodation, clothing and any medical care they have received. After the year's indenture, the woman/girl is free to leave or to stay on and work for the employer – always providing the employer is satisfied with her work (Phongpaichit 1999, O'Connell Davidson 2005).

Such arrangements imply real and serious restrictions on the indentured worker's freedoms. However, the package described above need not appear entirely unattractive to someone in need of an opportunity to work abroad. Often, indentured sex workers are able to retain any tips they are given by clients, there is the promise of a significant lump sum at the end of the period of indenture, and for those who stay on having worked out the year, the possibility of continuing on to earn good money from prostitution. Research on Thai women who have been taken to Japan as indentured sex workers found that even those who had only worked their period of indenture, and had not stayed on with the Mamasan as a non-bonded worker after their debt was paid off, were able to save what are to them considerable sums in tips from clients (Phongpaichit 1999: 85).

And yet as "illegal" migrants in a totally unprotected sector, the worker is at the mercy of the individual brothel owner. If the owner is violent, and/or provides appalling accommodation, and/or inadequate food, and/or cheats the worker of the payment promised, the worker has no means of redress. Some brothel owners have even been known to report workers to the immigration authorities at the end of the period of indenture, and the authorities obligingly do their dirty work for them, deporting the workers so that the employer does not have to pay them. But not all workers are maltreated. Those who recruit labour for, and/or employ workers in, the sex trade are not a socially, morally or politically homogeneous category of persons, and do not all adopt the same approach to their economic activity. Some of those who use systems of indenture to secure and retain a supply of labour fully honour the terms of the agreed contract. The problem is that in the absence of any form of workplace monitoring or protection, and worse still, in the presence of immigration laws that deny irregular migrants access to protection and justice, getting a "good" or a "bad" employer is simply a matter of luck for the migrant concerned.

The practices of those who recruit and transport migrants for prostitution and/or organize their labour within it span a spectrum from what is, in effect, pure and brutal thuggery, through to behaviours guided by normal rules of mainstream business practice, or even by ethical principles. The two extremes can even co-exist in the same physical place, as illustrated by the following extract from an interview with Vanja, a Bulgarian woman working in a brothel in Dubi at the same time as Petra was forced into prostitution there. She spoke of another Bulgarian girl who was in trouble in because the third party controlling her "wanted to sell her". Vanja asked the boss of the establishment that she herself worked in to buy her, in order to rescue her from the abusive situation she was in, but her boss replied that he did not "buy and sell girls". So Vanja decided to buy the girl herself:

> I paid for her and I loaned her money. [But] I can't buy the girls and then say to them, "Bye, go home!" When a girl pays me back, she can go home or stay here, she can do anything she wants. I need my money back. I don't have money for everybody … She paid quickly, in three days. After that she had to decide if she wanted to go home or continue to work. This girl wanted to earn some money.
>
> *(Siden 2002: 98)*

The real point is that in prostitution as much as in other sectors, the abuse to which migrants may be subject in the migratory process and at the point of destination varies in severity, generating a continuum of experience, rather than a simple either/or dichotomy. At what point on the continuum do we say that the abuse and/or deception is so serious and the exploitation so extreme that the individual concerned has been "trafficked" rather than "smuggled" into prostitution? There is a temporal as well as political and moral dimension to this problem, which is especially clearly illustrated by research on Nigerian migrants in sex work in Italy.

Smuggling or trafficking?

The situation of Nigerian women who work in street prostitution under the control of a "madam" to whom they are indebted is often taken to be an exemplary instance of "sex trafficking". Cole and Booth (2007: 120) describe that situation as follows:

a woman's debt obligation commences when she (or her family) enters into an agreement with a trafficker in Nigeria (called the "sponsor"), pledging to pay for safe passage to Europe from the future earnings of the job she will receive there. The enormous initial debt is augmented by occasional penalties for insubordination or late payment and by inflated deductions for room and board and other expenses. The madam berates unruly women, reminding them of the pact they have entered, and may beat them herself or call in Nigerian male "hitters".

Anti-slavery activists, who have played an important role in promulgating "trafficking as modern slavery" discourse, hold that new slavery can be distinguished from other forms of oppression and labour exploitation through reference to its three essential elements: involuntariness, in the sense that the slave cannot "walk away from the situation they're in and someone's controlling their free will" (Bales 2000); "severe economic exploitation" (Craig *et al.* 2007: 12), which Bales (2000) describes as the absence of a wage, or payment of wages in a form that either covers only the most basic necessities for daily survival, or that can be clawed back by the employer; and violence or the prospect of violence.

In the case of Nigerian migrants in sex work in Italy, there are numerous documented cases of extremely violent, sometimes murderous, acts perpetrated against migrants or their families back home by those to whom they are indebted, and if the distinction between smuggled migrants with "ordinary" debts and VoTs who are in a condition of debt bondage pivots on the question of whether coercion by means of violence or its threat is present, then it may at first seem straightforward to describe such women as "trafficked". And yet physical violence is not a consistent or universal feature of relations between debtor-migrants and their creditors. Cole and Booth (2007: 121) describe both the use of violence and intimidation by Nigerian "madams" *and* the limits to violence as a mechanism of control:

> Nigerian madams do physically punish recalcitrant women and call for the hitters. But they prefer to send difficult women to colleagues in other cities. And, in line with their strategy of maintaining a low profile, they prefer to avoid unnecessary violence ... In general, trafficked women gain more autonomy over time. While the new recruit is kept under close surveillance, the woman who has regularly paid down the debt for a time is granted more freedom. She may send (more) money to her parents and mail letters home ... She may communicate more freely with Italian clients, friends and social workers.

Furthermore, the powers that madams exercise over "trafficked" women are typically surrendered once the debt has been worked off, so that women's inability to "walk away from the situation they're in" is actually time limited:

> It usually takes victims between one and three years to repay debts to their sponsors. The debt is sometimes increased as punishment, or the duration of the pact is protracted in other ways. Nevertheless, there eventually comes a day when the debt is repaid.
>
> *(Carling 2005)*

The picture that emerges from research is one in which violence and other forms of control are used primarily (though not necessarily exclusively) as a mechanism to enforce rapid debt repayment, as opposed to a mechanism for enforcing a chattel slavery-like relationship between creditor and debtor. Indeed, time is a crucially important factor in explaining the social organization of such creditor–debtor relations. Loans advanced for unauthorized migration are risky and the creditor has an interest in recouping her or his outlay as speedily as possible. The "madams" who control migrant Nigerian sex workers in Italy facilitate their debtors' entry into street prostitution, or coerce them into it, because street prostitution is the only (or most secure) way in which to quickly earn enough to repay the loan. This need for a speedy return on loans helps to explain why, as Malucelli (2006: 227) puts it, debt becomes a "transferable property bond", so that women are sometimes "traded between smugglers and traffickers and among traffickers themselves, who want to earn on their investment as quickly as possible". It also helps to explain why violence and close surveillance figure less prominently in relations between creditors and debtors who have already gone some way to paying off the debt.

Patrizia Testai (2008) draws attention to another vitally important point, namely that although the social relations that surround migration-related debt, especially when those debts are to be repaid through sex work, are frequently described as "trafficking" and "modern slavery" in the policy, NGO and research literature, debtor-migrants themselves do not always regard them in the same light. Her interviewees expressed a mix of feelings towards those who had assisted them in their migratory projects. In the words of one Nigerian woman:

> The madam charges us too much money ... 80 million lira (€40,000). All of them charge you a lot of money. But it's good that they brought us here. They helped us in a way. They are second to Jesus Christ.
>
> *(Ibid.: 73)*

Commentators who work uncritically with the concept of trafficking struggle to make sense of the Nigerian migrant debtors' instrumental attitudes towards their own "enslavement". So, for instance, Carling (2005) ends up by concluding that, "Ironically, the strength of the Nigerian trafficking networks lies in the element of reciprocity between traffickers and victims ... The victims' commitment to the pact makes it particularly difficult to combat this form of trafficking." It is hard to see how the idea that "trafficking is modern slavery" can be reconciled with acknowledgement of any reciprocity in the relationship between "trafficker" and "victim" (or slaver and slave). And yet to describe these women as "smuggled" rather than "trafficked" would be to accept that smuggled persons can be subject to exploitation just as violent and brutal as that which is normally deemed to be the fate of "VoTs".

The Trafficking and Smuggling Protocols are framed around an assumed dichotomy between irregular migration that is coerced and irregular migration that is consensual. And yet since there are often overlaps or close parallels between the *process* described as "trafficking" and that described as "smuggling", it is unclear at what stage in the migratory passage – if at all – a person who began their journey as a "smuggled" person becomes a "VoT". Nor is it clear why, in cases where migrants are subject to forced labour or slavery-like practices at the point of destination, questions about how they were recruited and transported into this condition should determine their status and so their entitlement to protection and assistance. Indeed, some hold that forced labour is the crucial element of the Protocol, and argue that policy interventions should focus on this, "rather than (or in addition to) the mechanisms of trafficking itself" (European Commission 2004: 53).

But even if this was the focus of policy interventions (which it is not), distinguishing the deserving "VoT" from other categories of migrant would still require judgements about the severity of their situation at the point of destination. How badly exploited and how brutally treated must an individual be to count as a "VoT" rather than simply an unlucky migrant?

There is no consensus across nations or even across different economic sectors in the same nation about the point on the continuum at which poor but tolerable working conditions slip over into forced labour. Indeed, what constitutes acceptable working conditions and employment relations is the object of political struggle. Still less is there a consensus about the point at which tolerable conditions for prostitutes (or wives or fostered or adopted children) slip into "modern slavery". It follows that there is no universal, established, external referent against which cases can be measured and judged to be trafficking or not trafficking (Anderson & O'Connell Davidson 2003).

The invisible hand of the state

In constructing trafficking as a problem of transnational organized crime and a subset of "illegal immigration", dominant discourse on trafficking frames out the ways in which states, through their actions and inactions, are responsible for the conditions under which some groups of migrants are vulnerable to abuse and exploitation. The most obvious absence in policy and public debate on trafficking is the condition of the large numbers of migrant workers who find themselves exploited and abused having moved to a foreign country through perfectly legally channels. Indeed, at the very moment that trafficking was being presented as an urgent global ethics problem, migrant workers' rights organizations were reporting a "rise in the incidents of unpaid wages, confiscated passports, confinement, lack of job training and even violence" against migrant workers who are legally present in a number of countries under various work permit schemes (AMC 2000: 5; International Labour Office 2005).

Very often workers are vulnerable to such abuses precisely *because* they have migrated legally, under work permit schemes that tie them to a named employer. Such schemes make it virtually impossible for workers to change their employer or retract from the employment contract without consequence for their immigration status, even if they discover that they have been deceived as to terms and conditions of work by the recruiting agents. To retract from such employment contracts would also often lead to demands to repay recruitment and travel costs to the agents who arranged their transport, or leave the worker unable to recoup payments already made to such agents. Work permits that tie the worker to a named employer make the worker entirely dependent on the employer for her/his immigration status and subsistence and so lock the worker into what is, in effect, a legally sanctioned form of indenture (Baines & Sharma 2002). Sex workers are among those adversely affected by such work permit schemes, since some countries admit migrant women on "entertainer" work permits for periods of six to twelve months.

There are other ways in which people's immigration status can generate or exacerbate their vulnerability to economic exploitation and other abuses, within prostitution as well as other sectors. Immigration regimes produce some migrants as "illegal", and undocumented migrants are at risk of deportation if they come to the attention of the authorities (De Genova 2002). This operates as a powerful deterrent against reporting abuse and maltreatment by an employer, whether in prostitution or any other sector. Similarly, to seek assistance or redress against injustices and ill treatment within prostitution is to become vulnerable to deportation in the case of migrants whose immigration status is conditional on not entering into paid work (e.g. asylum seekers in the UK), or not working on a self-employed basis or providing services such as entertainer (e.g. those who enter the UK on student visas). The International Labour Office (2005) global report on forced labour lists many examples in which the threat of deportation has been used by employers as a form of non-economic compulsion to exact labour from undocumented migrant workers. In this way, immigration regimes strengthen the hand of unscrupulous employers, including third-party beneficiaries of prostitution, and weaken that of certain groups of migrants.

If the forcible restrictions placed on migrants' freedom of movement and choices by immigration regimes is invisible in discourse on trafficking, so too are policy-driven deaths and the violence perpetrated against migrants by state actors. For though dominant discourse on trafficking focuses on the threat of harm from mafia thugs and other hardened criminals, immigration policy and the state actors that enforce it present an equal if not greater risk to irregular migrants' health and well-being, even life itself. Between 1993 and 2011, the organization UNITED for Intercultural Action documented 15,551 deaths of refugees and migrants attributable "to border militarisation, asylum laws, detention policies, deportations and carrier sanctions" (UNITED 2011). It is also estimated that between 3,861 and 5,607 people, adult and child, died in the fifteen years up to 2009 as a result of the US Government's border security policies on the US–Mexico border (Jimenez 2009). Hundreds of thousands of undocumented migrants are held in detention centres around the world, often in appalling conditions. Some migrants, both adult and child, are also known to experience violence and/or sexual harassment in detention centres perpetrated by police, armed guards and detention centre personnel (Human Rights Watch 2002, Bloch & Schuster 2005, IRR n.d., Feteke 2007, UNITED 2011).

Cases of families being separated in detention centres have been reported, and Section 9 of the UK 2004 Immigration and Asylum Act even allows the state to refuse all social support to families who have failed in their asylum claims, which then means that children can be taken away from parents and put into care without consent on grounds that the parents are unable to provide for them. In other words, the threat of separation is used to compel parents to comply with removal directions (Cunningham & Tomlinson 2005). Deportation proceedings by definition imply forcing people to move against their will, and it is not uncommon for violence to be perpetrated against migrants during such proceedings. Even the way in which debt is constructed as "bondage" in dominant discourse on trafficking relies on a highly selective forgetting of the kind of coercive forces that the state sanctions in other contexts. Certainly, the use of violence or its threat is not enough to cleanly distinguish the experience of the Nigerian sex workers discussed above from that of all other debtors, since "ordinary" debtors can be subject to coercion and threats of violence and imprisonment, even from actors within legally sanctioned and supposedly regulated systems of debt collection (CAB 2007, McVeigh 2009).

The real point is that when state actors employ violence to prevent people from moving where they wish to move; or detain migrants against their will; or use the threat of separation from loved ones to make migrants comply with demands to move; or forcibly transport them from one territory to another, their actions are generally either applauded or accepted as necessary to defend the sovereignty of the modern liberal nation state. When unauthorized actors employ the same techniques, they are described as "traffickers". This draws attention to the socially and politically constructed nature of "freedom" and "unfreedom".

Liberal binaries: freedom/slavery, voluntary/forced, undeserving/deserving

In liberal democratic societies, consent plays a central role in the conceptual framework used to imagine and give meaning to social and economic interaction and exchange, as well as political arrangements. It is used to mark a moral boundary between democracy and dictatorship, between rightful exchanges of property and theft, between employment and enslavement, and so on. However, the idea that "free wage labour" and slavery historically existed as entirely distinct and oppositional categories is questionable (Steinfeld 1991, 2001; Lott 1998; Brace 2004). Elements of freedom historically existed within the juridical category of slavery that sometimes matched the freedoms enjoyed by non-slaves, and it is also the case that very real legal restraints have historically been placed on the freedoms of formally "free" workers. Certainly, it has never been possible to mark a clean boundary between free and coerced labour through reference to notions of choice and consent. As Steinfeld (2001: 14–15) observes:

> When we speak about most forms of labor compulsion, we are talking about situations in which the compelled party is offered a choice between disagreeable alternatives and chooses the lesser evil ... In slavery, for example, labor is not normally elicited by directly imparting motion to a slave's limbs through overpowering physical force. It is compelled by forcing slaves to choose between very unpleasant alternatives, such as death, torture, and endless confinement, on the one hand, or back-breaking physical labor on the other. The labor of free wage workers is normally elicited by offering workers a choice, for example, between life on an inadequate welfare stipend or, in the extreme, starvation, on the one hand, and performing more or less unpleasant work for wages on the other ... In the cases of both the slave and the free wage worker, the parties may be said to have been coerced into performing the labor or to have freely chosen the lesser evil.

Although free and unfree labour are popularly imagined as clearly separable, the line between the two is a matter of convention in liberal democratic societies. It is drawn through reference to conventions and judgements about the kinds of coercive pressures that "are legitimate and illegitimate in labor relations" (*ibid.*: 16). Such judgements have varied historically, but today are generally informed by a belief that economic pressures are less coercive than physical force or the threat of imprisonment, even though "the threat of starvation may certainly operate more powerfully than a short term of confinement" (*ibid.*: 25). The same holds good in relation to judgements about the line between forced and voluntary migration. Thus, just as politicians in Europe make a distinction between "economic migrants" and "genuine" asylum seekers, so also we find that dull economic compulsion does not feature in the list of forces in the Trafficking Protocol that are deemed to nullify a person's consent to exploitation, even though being unable to feed one's self or one's children, or to pay for medical treatment for sick dependants, may be experienced as just as irresistible a force as the threat of physical violence.

So far as prostitution is concerned, one reading of these arguments would lead to the conclusion that all prostitution is forced, that even those women who apparently choose to sell sex are in fact present in prostitution because they are "vulnerable to the only means of economic existence available to them because they are women, and because they are women they are homeless, and poor" (K. Barry 1995: 196), and that governments ought thus to do everything in their power to suppress the market for prostitution. This is the position adopted by feminist abolitionist groups such as CATW. But I would argue for a different reading, one that starts from an understanding of those who trade sex as active, purposive actors who, like other social actors, always make choices, though rarely between options that are of their own choosing. This allows us to recognize that coercive pressures operate along a continuum, such that at one pole, people are faced with desperately bleak and violent alternatives (including that between death or agreeing to a form of prostitution within which they exercise no control or discretion), while at the other end of the continuum, the alternatives can hardly be described as calamitous (for example, the choice between earning a great deal of money as a dominatrix or earning a comfortable income as an academic or an estate agent). Between the two poles lies a spectrum of options.

This approach not only allows us to recognize all those who prostitute as subjects and agents (rather than regarding them as objects and eternal victims), but also focuses attention on questions about who or what determines the "background conditions that constitute the options available to individuals" (Steinfeld 2001: 22), as opposed to the individual morality of those who take advantage of their plight. As Steinfeld (*ibid*.: 23–24) argues, "Law pervasively conditions the universe of possibilities that determine the degree of economic compulsion individuals confront in all market societies," societies where, indeed, "an extensive set of background legal rules establishes to a significant degree the real alternatives working people have available, as they decide whether to enter or to remain at a job". Around the world, welfare and immigration regimes in particular serve to severely limit the alternatives open to poor women and to undocumented migrants and migrants whose immigration status denies them the right to enter paid work.[1] In this context, there are people for whom even highly exploitative and risky forms of prostitution will appear as a lesser evil than their alternatives.

In feminist abolitionist discourse, female prostitution is always forced, either in the sense that prostitutes are "victims of trafficking" or lack the capacity to consent to prostitution contracts, or in the sense that patriarchal power structures leave them with no alternative but to prostitute. Furthermore, the overwhelming majority are said to be routinely subject to the most appalling violence by clients and pimps. In this way, the complex and overlapping continuums of unfreedom and exploitation that can accompany prostitution are reduced to one crude image of brute force and bodily confinement being used to dominate helpless, choiceless, passive victims. Feminist abolitionists appear to have enjoyed some success in popularizing a view of prostitution as peopled almost entirely by "sex slaves", children, and desperate, despairing drug addicts. But they have not proselytized so effectively in terms of converting policy-makers and the public to the belief that economic pressures can exert a degree of compulsion commensurate with that exerted by physical violence and bodily confinement.

For policy-makers and for those charged with enforcing policy, the orthodox liberal distinction between coercion and consent remains real and important, and it is only those women and girls who conform to the stereotype of helpless, choiceless, non-consenting, passive victim that are deemed worthy of protection and assistance. Those who appear to exercise agency, to make choices, to consent to work in prostitution are not imagined as "innocent" and "deserving" victims and can therefore be summarily deported if they are irregular migrants or their immigration status makes it illegal for them to earn from prostitution (Doezema 2002, N. Adams 2003, C. Harrington 2005, O'Connell Davidson 2006).

Conclusion

The transatlantic slave trade transported people into societies where slavery was one of the established and recognized statuses used to define employment relations. A "slave" was thus readily identifiable in the sense that s/he was legally defined as such, and it is therefore possible to speak of and study slaves in the Americas as a specific, bounded group. Today, however, people are not being moved into societies where slavery is legally recognized and regulated as a judicial category. "VoTs" are not people who have been formally assigned the legal status of slave, and because today, as in the past, the experience of unfreedom and exploitation ranges along a continuum, this generates real confusion around who, precisely, we mean when we speak of "trafficked" persons, and how they are to be distinguished from "smuggled" persons and other categories of migrant, both regular and irregular.

Indeed, "trafficked persons" do not actually exist as some kind of prior, objective or legal category of persons that can form the object of research or policy. To be sure, "Victim of

Trafficking" exists as an administrative category in a number of states. It is a status assigned to those migrants who are considered deserving of protection and assistance on grounds that they have experienced the particular constellation of coercive and exploitative practices during the migratory process and at the point of destination that the relevant authorities understand as trafficking. But if anti-trafficking campaigners were to focus on those who are actually afforded this status, the numbers involved would be so small as to make any comparison with the transatlantic slave trade appear quite ludicrous. In the United States, for example, between 2000 and 2007 the authorities managed to identify just 1,362 victims of human trafficking brought into the United States (Weitzer 2007).

The definitional and methodological problems associated with the term "trafficking" make it impossible to accurately measure or even reliably estimate the numbers affected by it (Feingold 2010, Warren 2010).[2] And though many groups of migrants in the contemporary world are subject to a variety of forms of exploitation, abuse, violence and other forms of coercion, the concept of trafficking has proved worse than useless in terms of facilitating measures to address their condition. This is because it has been used in such a way as to detach the unfreedom and economic exploitation experienced by some groups of migrants from its basis in the global political and economic inequalities that simultaneously generate migratory pressures and set in place barriers to migration, and from the immigration regimes that make some legal as well as some irregular migrants vulnerable to abuse and exploitation.

State-sponsored violence against migrants, policy-driven migrant deaths, and the forcible restrictions placed on migrants' freedom of movement and choices by immigration regimes are invisible in dominant discourse on trafficking, even though these are undoubtedly more pressing human rights issues in terms of scale and human cost, and even though the forms of abuse and exploitation that are generally covered by the term "trafficking" are inextricably linked to them. Instead, our attention is focused on the individual morality of traffickers. Trafficking discourse has thus individualized and depoliticized what is actually a highly political global ethics issue. For many critical scholars and activists, it is time to stop talking about trafficking and to change the terms of academic and public debate on immigration, human rights and global ethics.

Notes

1 And in relation to domestic prostitution, we should note that inadequately resourced support services for drug users, the homeless, victims of domestic violence and so on restrict the real options open to those who are affected by such problems.

2 Indeed, though widely cited and hugely influential on international policy, US government estimates have even been criticized by the US Government Accountability Office, which noted, among other things, the fact that these estimates were developed by one person who did not document all his work, the huge discrepancy between the numbers of observed and estimated VoTs, and the absence of an effective mechanism for estimating the number of VoTs (Morehouse 2009).

22

DISTRIBUTIVE INSTITUTIONS

Chris Armstrong

We live in a world which contains profound inequalities along a number of key dimensions. Whereas some learn quickly to take luxury for granted – and even not to recognize it as such – many more people are faced with far inferior life chances, apparently because of the simple fact of the country they have been born into. Notwithstanding the high-profile economic growth of some Asian countries, these inequalities have shown little sign of abating over recent decades and may very well be intensifying. Some theories of global justice will object to those inequalities in their own right. But even if, at a moral level, we are untroubled by the stubborn facts of global inequality, we may find it harder to reconcile ourselves to a world which has as a constant feature deep and enduring poverty. Millions regularly go without access to clean water, or basic medicines or education. Though political theorists and economists disagree about the extent to which poverty is caused by national or global factors, there can be no doubt that many children are born into societies which offer them desperately few opportunities. Such a fact is hard to justify in any sense. Even those highly resistant to "cosmopolitan" projects of global justice are prepared to pronounce, with solemn understatement, that "We do not live in a just world" (Nagel 2005: 113).

For many people the more pressing question will be what, if anything, can be done. The lone individual, faced with a world of injustice, is likely to feel despair about the prospects for making even the smallest dent in that injustice by him- or herself. Although many will be persuaded of an individual obligation to do *something* to alleviate global injustice – by giving money to charity, for example – they may at the same time quite reasonably believe such measures to be insufficient. To be effective, our responses to injustice will need to be both more coordinated, and more likely to be accompanied by compliance on the part of others who may be less committed. This in turn gives rise to an interest in *institutions* as tools for discharging our duties of distributive justice, and bringing a more just world closer into reach.

This chapter examines the role that institutions might play in securing (more) global justice. We begin, in the first section, by identifying some of the different reasons why institutions might be thought important from a normative point of view. For our purposes the least controversial reason for emphasizing the importance of institutions is that they might be necessary or highly desirable in order to *achieve* global justice, and we briefly unpack why that might be. We then shift our focus to the *kinds* of institutions which scholars of global justice have suggested might be vested with the task of securing global justice. The second section examines arguments for using *existing* institutions to pursue global justice. Assuming that these will be useful but not sufficient to deliver on many accounts of global justice, the third section then moves on to examine some prominent arguments for establishing *new* distributive institutions, and attempts a comparison of their various merits and drawbacks.

The normative significance of institutions

Institutions can be defined narrowly, as a category of more or less formal organizations governed by (usually written) rules, and which are reasonably enduring and stable over time. Examples would include parliaments, schools, political parties or corporations. Or they might be defined more broadly, as comprising not only such organizations but also less formal phenomena such as regular practices governed (loosely or firmly) by identifiable norms, rules and conventions. Here examples could include the family, the nation or the labour market. Even if we are defining them broadly, institutions and their rules can be regularly and consciously followed by many people, and can have a great impact on the life chances of the people who do participate in them.

At first sight, we might expect institutions to be of little importance to many accounts of global justice. After all, the most prominent theories of global justice are ethically individualist, in the sense that they attribute at least primary moral significance to individuals alone. Other entities – such as corporations, nations or families – will then have derivative moral significance at best: they will be significant, if at all, only in so far as we care about their effects on their individual members (Pogge 2002: 169). We would accordingly expect individuals to be both the principal rights-bearers, and the principal bearers of moral duties to secure global justice. All of this could therefore be presumed to mean that institutions were also of limited moral significance. Nevertheless, for advocates of global distributive justice there are actually a variety of ways in which such institutions might be significant.

First, and most controversially, we might think that it is *because* there are global institutions that we need an account of global distributive justice in the first place. That view would be a *relationist* one, if we understand relationism here as a family of views each holding that it is the emergence of some kind of social or political relation which makes principles of justice applicable at the global level. That is a contentious set of views, and is challenged by the competing family of *non-relationist* views which emphasize instead factors such as our shared humanity, and suggest that whereas the emergence of global institutions may have transformed the political landscape, it has not transformed the normative landscape and made principles of global justice relevant where they were not before (see Sangiovanni 2007). Still, the view that it is the emergence of global institutions (narrowly or broadly construed) which creates the need for principles of global justice is a common one.

Second, we might think that institutions are what principles of justice ought to be *applied to*. Perhaps the primary goal of principles of justice is to evaluate institutions and their distributive effects (Rawls 1971). This view will, obviously, tend to appeal to people who embrace the first claim (that it is the emergence of global institutions which has made global justice necessary). But strictly speaking the two views are separate. One could think, for example, that principles of global justice have always been valid, but that it is only with the emergence of global institutions that such principles have found an obvious target; this view is suggested by Beitz (1999a: 204). Alternatively, we might say that we have always had certain duties – such as negative duties not to harm each other or impose injustice on one another – but that it is with the emergence of (global) institutions that such duties find their (global) application, since it is typically through institutions that we violate these negative duties (Pogge 2000).

A third reason for thinking institutions are significant focuses on their *usefulness* in implementing global justice. We might think, for instance, that whereas we have always had duties of global justice, it is only with the emergence of global institutions – or the potential emergence of global institutions – that we are able to *act* on those duties for the first time. Institutions, then, provide an efficient means of discharging duties which may themselves be pre-institutional (see Murphy 1998). In this regard their emergence can be extremely helpful. We might even want to say that whereas there are many potential ways of discharging our pre-institutional duties – and whereas many people discharging them in an uncoordinated fashion may be very chaotic and ineffective – once a reasonably just institution has emerged we are then provided with a powerful reason to comply with *its* rules in coordinating the way in which we each discharge our duties (Miklos 2006).

These various reasons for emphasizing the significance of institutions are distinct, and subscribing to one does not commit us to accepting the others. Most importantly, for the purposes of this chapter we can remain neutral on the first two views. The third view is likely to command very broad agreement, even among theorists who disagree strongly about the first two. If we agree that global justice is desirable – for whatever reason, and whether the emergence of global institutions provides a reason for thinking so or not – we are also likely to believe that global institutions are either necessary or, at least, highly desirable, in order for us to bring it about. Does this commit us to the view that in their absence global justice is somehow disqualified as an ideal? The short answer to that question is no. It has certainly been argued that principles of global justice are not "proper" principles of justice at all if an agent cannot be specified which would be capable of putting them into practice (see e.g. Meckled-Garcia 2008; see also Freeman 2007). But that argument is not entailed by our third view; it would be coherent and intelligible to claim that global justice is a valid and desirable endeavour, but that the conditions for achieving it are not yet in place. In the final section, I suggest that whereas some theorists have put their faith in the capacity of existing global institutions to serve justice, others have (in some cases also) put their faith in the creation of new institutions. But even if such new institutions could not be created in the foreseeable future, that in itself would not be enough to disqualify principles of global justice. It would merely make their (full) pursuit a very difficult and possibly forlorn enterprise.

Just why, then, might institutions be necessary or highly desirable in order for global distributive justice to be achieved? What is it that global institutions would allow us to do which is much more difficult in their absence? Writing in the context of debates about human rights, Henry Shue has suggested two central reasons why institutions are useful in trying to deliver on our moral duties. The first can be called "efficiency". If individuals were to try to fulfil their duties *as* separate individuals, the results would be highly inefficient. Individuals simply lack the relevant information and expertise about how best to serve global justice, and the result is likely to be a great deal of wasted time, effort and money (Dave Eggers's first novel satirizes just such a pair of well-intentioned but ill-informed individuals, who travel the world in an attempt to give their money away to those who deserve it more than they do; Eggers 2002). Alternatively, dedicated institutions could act on our behalf, and deliver great savings in time and money, at the same time as acting in a more coordinated and consistent way to address injustice. As a result, as Shue (1988: 696) puts it, "It will often be the case that resources are best employed not in direct action but in maintaining and enhancing institutions … or, where no effective institutions exist, in creating and building them." A second reason, "respite", refers to the corresponding savings that can be made in the demands made on individual duty-holders. Whereas individuals acting alone may feel desperately ineffective in confronting global injustice, and consumed by the enormity of the task of tackling it, institutions lift some of that burden off their shoulders and leave them free to pursue the other legitimate projects they may have in their lives. Although global justice matters, it may not be the only thing that matters: and if the economies provided by institutions can help free up time for the other things that matter, then they are to be welcomed.

Shue's suggestion, then, is that, in allowing us to discharge our duties effectively, institutions are invaluable; but he does not claim that all of the institutions in question must be global ones. Individual nation states, for example, might be very useful in delivering on our duties (and it is notable that individual nation states have *tended* to be the primary targets for arguments allocating duties to fulfil human rights in particular). Nevertheless, there may be good reasons for believing that global institutions are an important part of the picture whether our view of global justice is broadly egalitarian in nature or more modest in its goals. This need not mean that theorists of global justice are committed to very powerful global institutions, or even to a world state (see Beitz 1999b). But it may well mean that their distributive goals require institutional reform and innovation, and in many cases the creation of new, dedicated institutional structures to deal with global issues and problems. To sum up, the arguments of this section suggest that institutions are likely to be significant even if we do not believe that they create the need for global justice in the first place. They can deliver advances in efficiency and in respite for individuals, which promise to bring the goals of global justice much closer than would otherwise be the case. Not surprisingly, there have therefore been many suggestions for the kinds of global institutions which might help us to deliver on global justice. These will be discussed in the remaining sections of this chapter.

Global justice and existing global institutions

If we wanted to secure a distributively just world – or at least a *more* just world – a first step would be to enlist the help of existing institutions. Whereas it has been suggested that global justice requires global institutions which we have no reason to expect to see emerging in the near future (e.g. Nagel 2005, Freeman 2007), even *if* we are persuaded by this view, it should not blind us to the possibility of demanding that *existing* global institutions are more fair in their distributive effects. Here, most of the attention has focused on institutions such as the International Monetary Fund (IMF), World Bank, International Labour Organization (ILO) and, especially, the World Trade Organization (WTO).

For instance, Charles Beitz (1979) early on suggested that we could make the IMF a more effective agency of development, by making greater amounts of credit more readily available to developing countries. This proposal was presented as a possible application of a "global difference principle", which suggests that we ought to advance the position of the poorest as far as we can, and only accept inequalities compatible with that goal. One way to bring this goal closer would be to make funds for development available in greater volume and with fewer strings attached. More recently, there has also been emphasis on the idea that the IMF, World Bank and other lenders ought to cancel or "forgive" the debts held by developing countries (see, e.g., Caney 2006c: 123). If those debts have been incurred in the past by leaders of dubious legitimacy, and if their repayment is holding back development in the present, there may be a strong case for cancelling them (see Barry *et al.* 2007).

The WTO, though, has probably been the key focus for advocates of global justice. There are several reasons for this (Armstrong 2012). First, it is one of the most powerful institutions governing the global economy, and its influence is steadily expanding into new areas. Second, the decisions that it takes, and the rules that it formulates and defends, have obvious distributive effects. Every time a round of WTO negotiations concludes with a new agreement there will be countries which consider themselves winners, and others which consider themselves to have been hard done by. Third and finally, WTO rules – and negotiations – explicitly invoke considerations of fairness. Negotiations are supposed to be (and are often publicly claimed to be) motivated by considerations such as reciprocity and non-discrimination, which are hard-wired into the rules of the WTO itself (Brown & Stern 2007). As a result the fairness of trade rules, the protectionist policies of many countries, and the fairness of the decision-making processes of the WTO itself have come under considerable scrutiny.

Beitz, for instance, suggested that the rules of international trade could be redesigned so that they promoted redistribution towards developing countries (Beitz 1979: 174). Specifically, he asked whether we might rearrange the tariff system so that developing countries could establish lucrative industries without competition from developed countries, but still gain access to the markets of the latter. Such a suggestion has received further support more recently (see e.g. Kapstein 1999, G. Brock 2009, Moellendorf 2009). The idea behind "sequencing" the obligation to open up markets is that poorer countries ought to be able to liberalize in a gradual manner, opening up different parts of their economies one by one and with careful forethought. That way the human costs might be managed rather better than if they fully liberalized immediately, under pressure from organizations such as the WTO or IMF. This does mean allowing them to maintain tariff barriers which other countries are not allowed to operate, but that might be necessary for them to "catch up" in their development. As Moellendorf (2009: 96) puts it, "there are good reasons to believe that a trade regime should sequence the requirement to eliminate protectionism so as to provide countries in the developing and underdeveloped world with more time to develop their infant industries".

These are not the only suggestions for how we could use existing institutions to further the goals of global justice, but they are perhaps the most prominent. Other recommendations include a defence of greater cooperation between nation states on tax collection. Many corporations are able to move between tax jurisdictions in pursuit of the lowest tax rates available, and to exploit various other loopholes. But Gillian Brock has pointed out that if countries cooperated more on tax rules, and moved to close some of the more important tax loopholes, their coffers could swell by hundreds of billions of dollars annually. As Brock (2008: 162) puts it, "Even modest changes in global tax policy will mobilize revenue that is badly needed in developing countries." Another possibility centres on labour standards. Here it has been suggested that institutions such as the WTO or International Labour Organization could be used to monitor and enforce basic labour standards, preventing employers in developing countries abusing the human rights of their employees and presenting them with working conditions which are unsafe, oppressive or discriminatory (see e.g. Barry & Reddy 2008). Taken together, these steps might themselves go some way towards advancing some of the most pressing goals of global justice.

A final, albeit somewhat more controversial route we could take towards greater global justice within the parameters of existing institutions would be to make national borders more porous to migrants. As has often been pointed out, in a world of substantial inequalities the relative difficulty of moving from the poorest countries of the world to the wealthiest helps to perpetuate those inequalities. Equality of opportunity, for instance, is thwarted when individuals seeking to improve their prospects by moving to find better work abroad are prevented from doing so by restrictive immigration policies operated by most Western states (see e.g. Carens 1987, Shachar 2009). Most of the suggested reforms discussed in this section refer to reforming institutions construed narrowly – that is, they apply to formal organizations such as the WTO or IMF. But, construing institutions more broadly, we could identify the institution of the nation state – or, more precisely, a global regime of many separate nation states – as an institution which itself has hugely significant distributive effects. As such the question of how we might reform that institution to make those distributive effects more palatable is a plausible one.

Notably, many of the reforms suggested in the next section suggest that we ought to establish international organizations capable of taxing, for instance, the natural resource wealth of different countries. By moving some of the resources of the wealthy in the direction of the poor we could make a regime of relatively closed borders less likely to give rise to massively unequal opportunities. But perhaps we could bring a world of equal opportunities somewhat closer simply by allowing larger numbers of citizens of poorer countries to enter richer states. In so doing we would spread the benefits typically enjoyed by their own inhabitants – high wages, often generous health and welfare provision, free and effective education – to a larger number of people.

There is controversy, however, over whether making borders more porous would be a sensible step to take towards a more just world. One reason for this controversy is that some theorists believe that nation states have good moral reasons for maintaining relatively closed borders. Perhaps maintaining relatively closed borders is necessary to defend freedom of association, or to preserve national public cultures (see e.g. Altman & Wellman 2009 and D. Miller 2005b respectively). Another reason for scepticism is that it is far from clear that opening borders to more immigrants would be the most effective means for richer states to tackle global injustice. Such a measure would, perhaps, help just a portion of the poor of the world, and perhaps help the very poorest very little. Accordingly it has often been argued that states should be able to maintain relatively closed borders provided they redistribute an appropriate quantity of resources abroad (see e.g. Kymlicka 2001, Tan 2004, D. Miller 2005b).

Although there are some reasons for hesitation about the effectiveness of the last example – increasing immigration into richer countries – the recommendations discussed in this section suggest that we can make worthwhile progress towards global distributive justice purely by employing existing institutions more effectively. Thus, in rejoinder to the claim that principles of global justice are "unrealistic" or somehow neutered because there exists no agent to apply them, the advocate of global justice can argue that we could make substantial progress simply by requiring existing institutions to act in a more just way – and specifically to act in such as a way as to ameliorate the great degree of poverty and inequality that characterizes the contemporary world. But such progress, though worthwhile, might not be sufficient. In the next section, therefore, we will examine arguments for new distributive institutions.

Proposals for new distributive institutions

Sometimes existing institutions are inadequate to the task of securing justice, and in those circumstances we might be morally obliged to modify them or even to establish new institutions. Although we may have a duty to comply with any reasonably just institutions that do exist, there is no guarantee that those institutions will be adequate in the face of changing circumstances, or well designed to meet the many challenges of sharing a world together. John Rawls suggested that (one part of) a "natural duty of justice" was a requirement to "further just arrangements not yet established" (Rawls 1971: 115). Although Rawls himself gave a rather modest account of the institutions which would be required to secure justice at the international level (Rawls 1999c), many advocates of global justice have been much more ambitious in their recommendations for institutional innovation.

Much of the focus, here, has been on establishing institutions which would be capable of levying global taxes – which might then in turn be spent either to reduce poverty or to tackle inequality. There is disagreement, though, on just what should be taxed to provide the desired revenue. Suggestions have included carbon emissions, air flights and world trade (see G. Brock 2008 for a discussion), as well as income (Milanovic 2005). But in this section we will focus on some of the more well-known proposals, which suggest that we ought to establish institutions capable of levying taxes on the extraction or ownership of natural resources, on financial transactions, and on the transmission of citizenship itself.

In doing so, we will also evaluate the proposals one by one. A successful argument for a form of global taxation will need to perform well against several criteria, and doing so is no easy task. For one thing, there is the question of feasibility (is there a plausible legal or political path towards achieving the reform in question? Is there likely to be a degree of popular and elite support?). This is not to say that reforms should be ruled out on the basis of feasibility. But it may be that, other things being equal, we want to concentrate our efforts on those reforms which are more feasible, if we believe that global injustice is an urgent issue. A second criterion is impact (will the reform in question make a major contribution to injustice, conceived in terms of either poverty, inequality or both?). We could usefully divide impact into two varieties. A reform might have an impact by tackling the effects of poverty and inequality, for instance by redistributing income (we might also want to say that a successful reform ought to target, or prioritize, just the *right* people). Or, it might have an impact by tackling the causes of poverty and inequality, for instance by directly targeting the injustice of the international trading system. Other things being equal, we ought to favour reforms which, alongside tackling poverty and inequality directly, promise to cut them off at their source (Caney 2006c: 134). A third criterion relates to the "fit" between the costs of a particular reform and any normative responsibility for global injustice. For instance, if party x is responsible for the continuation of global poverty, then a reform taxing the income or wealth of party x and using the proceeds to ameliorate poverty would be preferable. We ought, that is, to endeavour not only to help the right people, but to place the costs in the right place, in a way that is normatively compelling (see Moellendorf 2009: 145).

The Global Resources Dividend

The Global Resources Dividend (GRD) is a tax which would be placed on the extraction of natural resources across the world. Every time a barrel-worth of oil, for example, was produced, some of the proceeds would be taxed in order to reduce global poverty. The tax would not need to be very high to achieve significant results: the champion of the Dividend, Thomas Pogge, calculates that a one per cent tax on resource extraction would raise around $300 billion every year. This is potentially enough to significantly reduce severe poverty as the World Bank currently defines it (Pogge 2002: 205). A global fund would then administer the resulting revenue, and in collaboration with international lawyers and economists it would disburse money to any developing countries which satisfied the fund that they would use the money in a relatively efficient and non-corrupt way.

Why might we embrace a GRD? Pogge provides a series of overlapping reasons which might persuade people with different substantive views about justice. We might see the Dividend as compensating the poor for the fact that richer countries have imposed an unjust institutional order on them – an order, that is, which avoidably leads to serious deficits in human rights. Or, we might see it as rectifying a brutal history of conquest, imperialism and dispossession. Alternatively, we might see it as compensating the poor for the fact that they have been deprived of a proportionate share of natural resources, as happens when Western corporations or countries buy resources from undemocratic regimes in developing countries, who sell those resources without either benefit to, or consent from the bulk of their citizens (Pogge 2002).

Pogge's proposal has attracted a number of objections. One striking point is that whichever of the three reasons we accept for adopting it, the GRD will be insufficient to rectify the injustice involved. We might, of course, still want to embrace the GRD as a first step at least towards justice. But here it has been claimed that there are other measures which ought to be given priority if we are concerned, as Pogge is, with the injustice of the contemporary world. For instance, if we believe that an unjust global institutional order is being imposed on people, then perhaps from the point of view of impact we ought to focus first and foremost on reforming that order (by changing the rules of international trade, for example) rather than on partially compensating people for its injustice. Alternatively, if we believe that poorer citizens are being unjustly dispossessed when corporations from the developed world buy natural resources from illegitimate regimes in their home countries, then perhaps we ought to focus on outlawing that illegitimate sale, rather than on merely taxing resource extraction (Wenar 2010). That said, the idea that we ought to tax resource sale or extraction has proven an attractive idea to many, especially given that countries may have relatively weak claims over the natural resources in their territories. The GRD would, on Pogge's admission, be difficult to achieve in practice, but it would represent at least a first step in tackling the injustice of resource ownership and distribution. If the GRD were difficult to achieve, it might still be possible to tax the use of specific resources which are key to human existence. Water might provide a good example, where we could divert funds from a "water levy" to secure everyone's human right to clean drinking water (Armstrong 2012).

Other global resources taxes

Although Pogge's Dividend is the most well-known example, the idea of a tax on natural resources has gained broader currency in debates about global justice. Charles Beitz (1979) has defended a resource redistribution principle which would seek to make sure that each country has sufficient resources to be able to run decent and effective institutions, and meet its members' basic rights. Proposals for redistributing either resources, or the value of those resources, have also been put forward by Brian Barry (1982), Will Kymlicka (2001) and Hillel Steiner (2005). In Steiner's case the proposal is much more challenging than Pogge's. Whereas Pogge's Dividend would redistribute one per cent of the value of resources as they are extracted, Steiner's proposal would apply to *all* natural resources (whether extracted or not), and aim to redistribute *all* of their latent value. This would be achieved by taxing the real estate values of land across the world. The proceeds would again be administered through a global fund, in this case disbursing sufficient amounts of money to guarantee either a substantial universal capital grant, or a basic income for all (Steiner 2005). The global resource tax would, in effect, require states to pay "rent" on the resources within their territories. The effect would be strongly redistributive, and would almost certainly produce a "substantial reduction in international (as well as national) economic inequalities" (*ibid.*: 36).

The main challenges levelled at Steiner's account revolve around the justice of taxing real estate values at their full economic value. One objection would be that if what we want to address is the unequal distribution of natural resources, then a tax on real estate is a rather poor proxy for that goal – given that there are countries (such as Japan) where natural resources are not available in any great abundance, but where real estate values are very high (and vice versa). This suggests, in effect, that Steiner's scheme does not distribute the costs of tackling inequality in a wholly compelling way. A related objection suggests that we ought not in any case attempt to tax *all* of the value of natural resources. Whereas their latent value may in a sense be unearned by anyone in particular, the actual value of resources is influenced by the way in which people interact with those resources, and protect or improve them. As such, perhaps local or national communities are entitled to some share of actual resource values (D. Miller 2011). Note though that whereas this argument attempts to defeat Steiner's claim that we should tax the entire value of resources, it probably could not defeat arguments, such as Pogge's, that we ought to redistribute some of that value. Even if communities are partially responsible for the actual value of resources, they are presumably not responsible for their entire value.

The Tobin Tax

The idea of a "Tobin Tax" (sometimes more broadly referred to as a Financial Transactions Tax) was originally suggested by the Nobel Prize-winning economist James Tobin, who in 1972 argued that one way to calm international currency markets would be to place a small tax on foreign exchange transactions. A tax on foreign exchange transactions would dissuade speculators looking for very short-term gains on currency markets. At present that kind of speculation can have disastrous consequences for some national economies (notably, the idea of a Tobin Tax came to gain much greater interest after the Asian Financial Crisis of 1997, in which currency speculation played a role).

The Tobin Tax, then, appears likely to smooth international currency markets, and reduce the vulnerability of poorer countries in particular to rapidly fluctuating currency markets. But although the emphasis was originally on increasing financial stability Tobin, along with various other supporters of a Tobin Tax, soon came to realize the potential of the scheme to raise funds for poverty relief. A relatively small tax – levied at some fraction of one per cent of any given currency transaction – could produce around $150–300 billion annually. Notably – and unlike many of the other proposals discussed here – the idea has gained some support from governments and non-governmental organizations. In 1999 the Canadian House of Commons, for instance, passed a motion declaring that the government should enact a tax on financial transactions, in concert with the international community. The last clause is crucial, since the tax would be ineffective if levied by one or even a few countries. Although in the UK a number of celebrities have supported this idea (under the title of a "Robin Hood tax"), international agreement has not yet been forthcoming.

Although it has not been achieved in practice, the Tobin Tax performs well in terms of feasibility, in at least one respect: it seems to be the reform most likely to attract popular and elite support. One reason for this, as Moellendorf (2009: 150) points out, may be that the Tobin Tax is directed at an activity that is widely seen as having "little social value" – and indeed which regularly produces negative consequences for many of the most vulnerable people. As such it appears an appropriate target for redistributive policies. It would also perform well on impact, at least from one point of view: at one and the same time it would reduce those negative consequences attendant on currency speculation, and help many of the people who stand to suffer from them. Nevertheless, the proposal does have some drawbacks. For one thing, the funds would, on most proposals, be used to support not the victims of currency speculation in particular but the poor in general. In this respect, admirable though the proposal may be in a number of ways, the connection between those who are to be taxed and those who are to be helped is rather a weak one, and the reform could be said to distribute the costs of tackling poverty in a rather arbitrary way. Second, there is the question of whether the reform would tackle the roots of global poverty and inequality in a suitably profound way. Although it would directly tackle one source of poverty, inasmuch as currency speculation can exacerbate the poverty of those in weakly positioned economies, it would do nothing to tackle other causes of injustice such as the nature of the international trading system. In that sense the scope of its impact is limited, and it might best be seen as a part of a broader package of measures designed to secure greater global justice.

The Birthright Levy

Ayelet Shachar has suggested that many of the key global inequalities which ought to trouble us are perpetuated by the intergenerational transmission of citizenship. After all, we tend to inherit citizenship on the basis of our parentage or our place of birth, and although these are not factors that we can claim any credit for, they tend to present us with radically different opportunities. The lives of some are blighted by the poor hand which luck deals them, whereas others can grow up, as citizens of wealthy liberal democracies, in the secure knowledge that their basic material needs will (usually) be met throughout their lives. Rather than arguing, as some have done, that wealthy countries ought to open their borders to the poor of the world in order to spread those opportunities a little more widely, Shachar (2009) suggests that rich countries ought to pay a tax or "levy" on the inheritance of "birthright" citizenship.

The levy Shachar has in mind could take the form of a resource transfer from individuals in richer to individuals in poorer countries, and could itself be fine-tuned to reflect the disparities in wealth *within* richer countries themselves (*ibid.*: 103). She also suggests, however, that it might in principle be replaced or supplemented by the performance of some form of public service by citizens of wealthy countries (such as volunteering to work overseas on development projects). Any revenue – and effort – accrued under the scheme would be used to bolster "infrastructure programs directed at enhancing the situation of children in the recipient countries (for example, eradicating malnutrition, providing clean water, investing in health, education and so forth)" (*ibid.*: 102).

It is not easy to discern how well Shachar's proposal performs on the criterion of impact. On the one hand we have the question of the extent of improvement it could produce for those dealt a "bad" hand in the birthright lottery. Here, it is striking that although Shachar explicitly criticizes the *inequality* produced by the regime of national citizenship, her reforms suggest a fairly modest contribution to tackling serious *poverty*. On the other hand we have the question of whether her reforms directly tackle the causes of poverty and inequality, as opposed to their effects. Here the picture is complex. Shachar claims that her proposal *is* radical, in the sense that it directly targets the transmission of inequality across generations. However, she does not pay attention to the broader structural causes of global injustice (such as institutions and practices governing international trade, resource sales, borrowing and lending, and so on), and her reform would do little to tackle those causes. Shachar's scheme also contains little detail about the precise nature of the citizenship levy: How much money is to be collected? To precisely whom will it be given, and who will decide how to disburse it? Will there be mechanisms in place, as in the case of Pogge's Dividend, to use the levy to incentivize good governance in developing countries? Nevertheless, in focusing on citizenship itself her proposal presents an intriguing alternative to the other schemes discussed here.

PART V
Bioethics and health justice

Introduction

The bioethics section of this handbook addresses a group of issues that are crucial to global ethics. Too often bioethical issues are treated separately from global ethical issues – as if they are somehow a separate field of study (variations of this possible field are bioethics, medical ethics, or even public health ethics). While it certainly is the case that many of those who work in these fields would not consider themselves global ethicists at all and, more problematically, fail to recognize the global implications of the ethics they do, many issues in bioethics are properly issues of global ethics as well. Fundamental standards of health and access to healthcare, for example, are basic rights necessary for achieving other rights. Without health other rights – such as freedom of movement, employment rights, relational rights and, at the most extreme, the right to life – are not attainable. And this is the case irrespective of which ethical framework one uses: health capabilities or opportunities or needs, for instance, are effectively (and in most instances) broadly interchangeable with rights. Moreover, failure to protect health has implications for other concerns of global ethics – indeed, arguably one of the strengths of global ethics is that it recognizes the connections between instances of oppression and injustice, and that these cannot adequately be addressed separately. For instance, poor health exacerbates poverty and poverty leads to poor health (through an inability to afford good housing and nutrition and drugs to address illness), and climate change increases health risks (those who have healthcare can better survive adverse weather events and prevent these turning into epidemics and other crises). A few figures will help demonstrate this claim. According to the WHO, malaria is one of the most serious health threats to communities in developing countries, and affects nearly half of the world's population. Malaria kills a child every forty-five seconds and over 90 per cent of deaths from malaria are in Africa (United Nations Department of Public Information 2010, World Health Organization 2014). The figures for death from preventable and treatable diseases, including malaria, TB (including drug-resistant TB) and HIV (particularly damaging as it strikes the traditionally most vulnerable), are particularly shocking. There have been so many deaths of parents in many parts of Africa that a new norm of grandparents raising children has emerged. Furthermore, as noted in the introduction to Part III on poverty, access to essential drugs and the failure of the current system to create drugs that address the diseases of the poor contribute profoundly to extreme poverty, morbidity and mortality. These connections mean that issues of health, access to drugs and the allocation of healthcare resources are issues that profoundly connect to other issues of global ethics.

In addition to being able to maintain reasonable health and access to basic healthcare, there are other issues which at first glance might seem to be less relevant to global ethics, but which global ethicists should not ignore. For instance, there are many "high-tech issues" connected to new scientific and technological developments, issues such as cloning, genetically modified food, new possibilities of reproductive technologies, new genetic treatments and ways and methodologies of research. Such issues obviously raise concerns about the allocation of scarce resources (is it really justified to invest in new and expensive treatments for cancer or for conception when the majority of the world's population still are not able to access basic drugs), but they also raise issues about what human life is and should be. Bioethical issues, therefore, are fundamental to concerns about the nature of human beings and to expectations about how human beings should relate to each other. For instance, issues of reproductive rights, for example in the abortion debate, are areas of longstanding controversy in ethics. Abortion raises fundamental philosophical questions about the nature of personhood, what constitutes a human being and what the good life is. Such questions are the core concerns of bioethics and they re-emerge in current controversial debates about genetic enhancement and the sale of body parts. When we ask whether a certain type of genetic enhancement is permissible the question takes us to a deeper one about the nature of human beings. If we do engage in genetic enhancement are we changing what it is to be human? Are we violating what one human may do to another?

Questions of what human life should be, and what humans should be entitled to and able to choose are not issues that should be ignored by global ethicists. If they are, then the debates will be impoverished. Global ethicists need to focus on human nature, if justice is to be done; otherwise there is a danger that the focus will only be on the mechanisms for the distribution of goods which may ignore the needs and differences of the people whom they are trying to help. Indeed, a worry about a mechanistic view of social justice is one of the drivers of the capability approach. Conversely, bioethicists should pay attention to global ethics and to the global scope of their issues, if they are to avoid promoting policies and practices that are unjust when the global consequences and implications are considered. The focus of much of bioethics is that of a professional ethics, which is concerned with the duties of the doctors, or with the permissibility of practices or research. These concerns focus almost exclusively on issues of consent. Whether or not something is deemed ethical depends on whether it is chosen under the right conditions. Although consent is important in good clinical practice and research, a narrow focus on consent ignores issues of exploitation, of oppression and of justice, including many policies and practices that have indirect effects on others – issues at the core of global ethics.

Global ethics complements the concerns of bioethics in a variety areas. Public health ethics or population ethics is concerned with communities' health and thus addresses considerations of justice that arise in global ethics, but its scope is not necessarily the globe, even though a global scope is often necessary to public health. In addition, the public health approach does not necessarily worry about injustice as such, or connect to other issues related to health justice. A justice-orientated approach is often characteristic of theorists who take a global ethics approach to bioethics.

This section contains four chapters on core issues in bioethics that are particularly relevant to global ethics. The first is on research ethics and clinical trials; the second concerns the global trade in body parts; the third discusses reproductive rights; and the fourth is devoted to intellectual property rights.

In Chapter 23 Udo Schüklenk and Ricardo Smalling address the controversial and timely issue of the ethics of research. Much of the global ethical concern about pharmaceutical research is connected with the use of people in developing countries for large-scale trials. Profit-led Western companies run research trials in the developing world at a much lower cost and arguably with less concern for safety than would be required in their home countries. Some Western research carried out in developing countries can of course benefit people in those countries, for example research into curing tropical diseases. But a key ethical question of international research is whether people in poorer countries are used effectively as the "guinea pigs" in research that will only benefit people in rich countries.

Schüklenk and Smalling begin by noting that there is unethical behaviour not only in the practices of research but in the reporting of research in academic journals. The same questions about whether it is moral to benefit from unethical research apply here as they do when considering the now familiar question of whether one should benefit from Nazi experiments (crucial to much contemporary genetic advances). Schüklenk and Smalling move from this discussion to a substantial discussion about whether or not one should be able to benefit from traditional knowledge: a topic which is currently pressing and which should be read in conjunction with Chapter 30 on biodiversity. Schüklenk and Smalling also address some of the most controversial discussions in research ethics, including benefit sharing, global standards of care, duties to harmed participants and questions about the utility of research. In the final section Schüklenk and Smalling reflect on the future of the topic.

Chapter 24 by Teck Chuan Voo and Alastair V. Campbell discusses trade in human body parts. Like Schüklenk and Smalling's chapter, this one addresses issues of whether this growing area of trade is simply another particularly ghoulish way for the rich to exploit the poor since organs (in the case of donation as well as sale) flow from the poor to the rich along the usual lines of power. The trade in body parts is one aspect of what is sometimes termed "medical tourism," a term that refers to the movement of people from one legislative area to another to obtain treatment and procedures not available (or less easily available) within the country or state of their origin. Clearly, global justice and governance are important to discussions of these matters. Chuan and Campbell begin their exploration of the topic by mapping international governance. The rest of the chapter is then divided into the following four sections: reasons for trade, reasons against, the body as property and, finally, what this debate might mean for our understandings of human beings and their bodies.

In Chapter 25 about reproductive rights and reproductive technologies, Hille Haker considers the questions these raise from a global perspective. As we have discussed, one of the strengths of global ethics is that it connects issues together, and seeks to recognize the way that injustices compound each other. This is particularly important in relation to reproductive rights, which, from abortion to access to new reproductive technologies, raise strong emotional responses. The global approach connects issues of abortion to issues of basic health rights and rights of bodily integrity, questioning whether rights to such services are necessary precursors to exercising all other civil, political, economic and social rights, and what needs to be put into place for women to be able to access these rights in this context. The global ethics approach does not permit us to consider these issues in isolation, as if these individual cases were unconnected to wider issues. For instance, issues about whether contraception is widely available are issues linked to development and women's rights.

Haker begins with this, noting that often when considering reproductive rights globally one might be tempted to divide the globe into, broadly, the developing world, where there is a debate about the number of children being born (see Chapter 31 on population ethics), and the developed world, where reproductive technologies are more the focus of discussion, as couples seek to have genetically related children or children of certain types or children with certain traits. In the first section Haker outlines reproductive technologies: from so called "low tech" interventions, such as birth control, with regard to individuals and populations, to "high-tech" interventions, of genetic testing and artificial reproductive technologies (ART). In the rest of the chapter she considers the ethics of such technologies, with a particular focus on reproductive autonomy and freedom: a topic that includes the rights and/or interests of women, children and embryos and the compatibility of such views with justice. She finishes by suggesting that work is needed to ensure that "reproductive justice is attuned to the overall struggle for global justice".

Chapter 26 is by Roger Brownsword, and concerns patents and intellectual property rights. It is hard to underestimate just how important this topic is for global ethics. The structure of the patent system and the global governance system of property rights plays a primary role in further expanding the gap between rich and poor by denying access to drugs at an affordable price, by reducing incentives to produce drugs for the diseases of the poor and by preventing low- and middle-income countries from establishing and developing pharmaceutical industries and capacities. The importance of this issue for global ethics is shown by the interest that prominent global ethicists have taken to critique it, particularly the TRIPS agreement, and to suggest alternatives (such as the Health Impact Fund).

Brownsword maps this debate, taking the reader through the complexity of the patent system and the governance of intellectual property rights, and the ethical debate that surrounds them. He begins with an introduction to the topic and the debate, and then outlines the particular concerns that surround the patenting of biotechnology. Brownsword then proceeds to consider systematically the ethical arguments for rejecting patents and for reforming patents. Here he discusses the patent system, the nature and extent of patents and what is patentable. He then considers new institutions that could replace or complement the current system, with particular attention to benefit sharing. In his conclusion Brownsword pulls together the recurrent themes to be addressed: first, patents should not be freestanding; second, serving the public interest must be a fundamental goal; third, views about patenting depend on starting premises; fourth, patents must be compatible with human rights; and fifth, when patents are part of a global trading system, human rights are weakened.

23

RESEARCH ETHICS

Udo Schüklenk and Ricardo Smalling

The modern conception of research ethics as an ongoing academic and regulatory concern gained traction following the revelations of the Nuremberg trials. Knowledge of the gruesome experiments undertaken by Nazi doctors like Dr Josef Mengele led to the first international guidelines stipulating basic ethics standards for research involving human participants (the Nuremberg Code: *Trials of War Criminals before the Nuremberg Military Tribunals under Control Council Law No. 10* [1949]). Subsequent scandals – including, for instance, the Tuskegee syphilis study in the US – led to further, and improved, ethics guidelines such as the World Medical Association's Declaration of Helsinki (World Medical Association 2008) as well as national regulatory documents such as the landmark Belmont Report in the US (National Commission for the Protection of Human Subjects of Biomedical and Behavioral Research 1979).

Academic and policy analyses in research ethics are marked by reasonably clear dividing lines between clinical and non-clinical investigations, as well as between research conducted in developed countries and research in developing countries. A few issues cut across these dividing lines, such as concerns about academic misconduct like the falsification of data, arguments about legitimate claims to authorship of a scientific publication, and plagiarism (ICMJE 2013). Most of the latter concerns have been successfully addressed in international guidance documents. The former have led to decades of continuing productive research undertaken by many academics working in the field of research ethics, itself an area of specialization within the field of bioethics. The bulk of this chapter will address concerns to do with the ethics of clinical research, but let us begin by looking briefly at authorship-related issues.

Authorship matters

The significant resources that have been invested in scientific research support the view that the results should be published in order to increase the societal utility. Academic publishing today is a multi-billion-dollar business involving multiple players. Authors, usually academics, expend public and/or other (private or multilateral) resources to investigate particular scientific questions. The findings of these research ventures are published in academic journals. These journals are produced in myriad ways, including traditional print, open access and online-only models or some hybrid of the previous models. With few exceptions, the publication of academic research results is generally organized by for-profit publishers, who generate profits from subscriber fees, author fees and/or paid advertisements. Organizations such as the World Association of Medical Editors, the International Council of Medical Journal Editors (ICMJE) and the Committee on Publication Ethics have produced ethical guidelines pertaining to such matters as research misconduct (including plagiarism, falsification of data and such matters), guidelines on authorship and conflict of interest declarations. Despite these guidelines, a major ethics debate continues with regard to the concept of ghost authorship.

In broad terms, a ghost author is usually a professional writer. They are employed by academics or pharmaceutical companies to write up research results in a manner that will make them publishable in academic journals. There is nothing problematic with this, in principle, provided the ghost author is clearly mentioned and the research is described in a fair and balanced manner. Ethical problems will arise where pharmaceutical companies pay senior academics for adding their names to scientific research outputs and publications that they had no hand in producing (Sismondo & Doucet 2009, Lacasse & Jonathan 2010). This practice is in violation of international standards that define what criteria have to be met by a scientific researcher in order to legitimately claim authorship of a publication (ICMJE 2013). One of the reasons why the authorship issue is important has to do with the need to be able to hold researchers accountable for the work they do. In this regard, ghost authors are unaccountable. However, it is worth noting that the standards prescribed by the ICMJE, which require, among other stipulations, that each author take full responsibility for every part of a manuscript, have inherent flaws. In light of the multidisciplinary nature of research today, relying on discipline specific knowledge that is not necessarily shared among all authors, the current system is unrealistic. For that reason, it has been suggested that we should move away from the concept of authorship, towards the concept of contributorship, where the individual contributions of each person on a research team are described in documents accompanying a research paper. This proposition is eminently sensible; alas, until research funding agencies take cognizance of such a change, the concept of authorship will continue to reign supreme.

Benefiting from evil

When is it justifiable to use (or benefit from) the results of clearly unethical research? This has been a significant concern in the history of research ethics. A good example of this is the previously alluded to, often gruesome medical research that Nazi scientists carried out on inmates in German concentration camps. Nazi doctors conducted extensive medical experiments in German concentration camps during the Third Reich. Josef Mengele, for instance, killed Gypsy twin teenagers because he was interested in the fact that they had differently coloured eyes. Their eyes and other organs were removed after they were killed and shipped to a laboratory for further analysis. Unfortunately, in human history, unethical research is not confined to the actions of Nazi doctors. Lasagna reports that the ancient Persian kings and the Egyptian pharaohs treated prisoners "as expendable experimental material, much as modern laboratory researchers might order a supply of rats or rabbits" (Lasagna 1972: 262). As was the case in the Mengele experiments, these also resulted in mutilation, disability and death. Some have argued that Nazi research was scientifically unsound, but it is doubtful that this holds true for all of the research conducted during this period. As Proctor notes, "Nazi inspired research was often idiotic, but not always" (Proctor 1999). The ethical issues, as they pertain to the use of research results garnered in this manner – not unlike the impact of the crimes committed on the concentration camp prisoners – are to some extent straightforward. The research was evidently unethical as the inmates were not volunteers. They did not give informed consent, and the risk–benefit ratio was unacceptable. Often, those who survived the torturous experiments were murdered after the investigation had been concluded. Even though there were no ethical review committees, in retrospect the verdict of unethical is undoubtedly correct. The Nuremberg Code, one of the most important historical documents aimed at providing ethical guidelines for the regulation of research involving human participants, as previously mentioned, emanated from the Nuremberg trials prosecuting Nazi Germany's war criminals. One of the reasons this Code was eventually eclipsed by the Declaration of Helsinki, a document developed by the World Medical Association, an umbrella grouping of national medical associations, is that it considered first-person voluntary informed consent a *conditio sine qua non* for any ethical research. This obviously would make vital research involving incompetent patient groups (patients with intellectual deficiencies, minors and many others) impossible. The Declaration of Helsinki addressed this problem.

What is more controversial is whether and to what extent we should be permitted to benefit from the suffering of others, for instance the Nazi concentration camp inmates. Researchers in Canada and the US faced the problem of wanting to use data from the Nazi hypothermia experiments in order to develop new rewarming techniques for victims of hypothermia or to design new survival suits to protect sailors. Ethical views differ as to whether researchers such as these should be permitted to use these data (Moe 1984). It has been argued, for example, that utilizing such research results would inspire copycat criminals keen on gaining notoriety at all cost, and that this would be a sufficient reason to discard such research results. Others have argued that using such data would make researchers complicit in crimes such as those committed by the Nazi researchers. It is worth noting, however, that many Jewish scholars and even some survivors of such experiments take a different stance on this. They believe that discarding usable information gathered under such criminal circumstances does an injustice to the victims of such crimes, because their suffering then would have been completely in vain.

Today, the consensus in guidance documents published by medical associations and medical journals is that such research results should be utilized like any other information that is capable of improving the human condition. However, academic papers about the research in question should either omit the name of the unethical researchers, to reduce the risk of copycats, or they should be accompanied by an editorial decrying the means by which these results were achieved. The American Medical Association (AMA) offers this policy recommendation:

> Based on both scientific and moral grounds, data obtained from cruel and inhumane experiments, such as data collected from the Nazi experiments and data collected from the Tuskegee Study, should virtually never be published or cited. In the extremely rare case when no other data exist and human lives would certainly be lost without the knowledge obtained from use of such data, publication or citation is permissible. In such a case the disclosure should cite the specific reasons and clearly justify the necessity for citation.
>
> *(American Medical Association 1998: 5)*

There have been mixed results with regard to this. Some editors of leading biomedical journals have declared that they would cease to publish the results of unethical research, while others publish unethical research while denouncing the method deployed by the researchers, in line with recommendations in the above-mentioned AMA policy guidance. In practice, however, most biomedical journals tend to continue publishing the results of unethical research.

Benefiting from traditional knowledge

In the continuing quest for new medicines or food products that offer health benefits, one source of knowledge that is being exploited is the traditional knowledge of various populations.

Traditional knowledge in this context refers to information about the medicinal properties of certain naturally occurring agents (e.g. plants, fluids) that is typically passed on from generation to generation (for example through traditional healers or community elders). Such information has proven to be a valuable indicator to pharmaceutical companies of where to focus their resources in the worldwide search for natural agents with potentially healing properties. The agents in question are usually removed from the originating country and analysed to identify the biochemical substance producing the reported health benefits; the identified substance is eventually tested in professionally designed clinical trials. The pharmaceutical company will then proceed to patenting of the product (in some jurisdictions the process may also be patented) and they will begin to market it. Inevitably, as is the case in clinical research generally, many such attempts fail and the very substantial research investment by a pharmaceutical company is ultimately a write-off.

The exploitation of traditional knowledge gives rise to several ethical questions: Is it ethical for a pharmaceutical company to remove a biological specimen from a country where it exists uniquely on Earth? Who owns the organism in question: the company, or the country in whose territory it was found? As a corollary, who is competent to give permission to the pharmaceutical company to take the specimens? What sort of authority should those who purport to speak on behalf on the traditional community have: should they be democratically chosen or should we respect traditional routes to leadership? Given that traditional knowledge contributed to the discovery of the biochemically active healing agent, should the traditional owners of that knowledge benefit financially or otherwise from the discovery? If traditional owners should benefit, how should the process be governed when the originator of the knowledge has disappeared in the mist of time? This is just a sample of the ethical questions that will have to be answered as researchers move to exploit traditional knowledge.

The impetus for these discussions seems to be the urgent need to increase access to healthcare for impoverished patients in many developing countries. Among the responses to the problem of providing the world's poor with guaranteed access to at least essential medicines has been the idea of benefit sharing. This part of the chapter will consider this idea initially in the context of bio-prospecting and will revisit it in the context of multi-centre and multi-country clinical trials involving impoverished trial participants without reliable access to life-preserving healthcare.

The prevailing idea internationally is that if you use people in developing countries for clinical research purposes, there must be some appreciable benefit flowing back to them (Lie 2010). The United Nations (UN) Convention on Biological Diversity (CBD) requires that the benefits of non-human genetic resources be shared. The Secretariat of the CBD explains the ethical rationale behind this:

> An important part of the biodiversity debate involves access to and sharing of the benefits arising out of the commercial and other utilization of genetic material, such as pharmaceutical products. Most of the world's biodiversity is found in developing countries, which consider it a resource for fueling their economic and social development. Historically, plant genetic resources were collected for commercial use outside their region of origin or as inputs in plant breeding. Foreign bio-prospectors have searched for natural substances to develop new commercial products, such as drugs. Often, the products would be sold and protected by patents or other intellectual property rights, without fair benefits to the source countries. The treaty recognizes national sovereignty over all genetic resources, and provides that access to valuable biological resources be carried out on "mutually agreed terms", and subject to "prior informed consent" of the country of origin.
>
> *(Convention on Biological Diversity 2000: 14)*

The CBD is an international instrument that is founded upon the recognition of the importance of biodiversity and measures to halt biodiversity erosion. It recognizes "the desirability of sharing equitably benefits arising from the use of traditional knowledge, innovations and practices relevant to the conservation of biological diversity and the sustainable use of its components" (Convention on Biological Diversity 1992: 2).

The rationale here is that benefit sharing should bring financial returns to the communities that enabled or facilitated these financial returns. These benefits should, at least partially, finance conservation of biodiversity and would therefore act as an incentive to its sustainable use. Article 19 deals specifically with benefits distribution. It enjoins states to provide for effective participation in the research on genetic material that originates from that state. Downes justifiably criticizes the CBD for failing to ensure that the countries or communities of origin will be compensated for the material now being held in international gene-banks (Downes 2002). These resources have been extracted, usually without the permission of the countries hosting the biological material, from locations in the developing world over many years.

Article 8(j) of the CBD (Convention on Biological Diversity 1992: 6) is the foundation of the 2002 Bonn Guidelines of the CBD (Convention on Biological Diversity 2002). It mandates that contracting parties shall:

> respect, preserve and maintain knowledge, innovations and practices of indigenous and local communities embodying traditional lifestyles relevant for the conservation and sustainable use of biological diversity and promote their wider application with the approval and involvement of the holders of such knowledge, innovations and practices and encourage the equitable sharing of the benefits arising from the utilization of such knowledge, innovations and practices.

What is relevant for this chapter's purposes are the requirements that benefits are shared equitably and that indigenous communities are asked for their approval and involvement in the process. The idea that such involvement should result in prior informed consent has gained widespread acceptance in recent years.

It has been argued by the pharmaceutical companies that while traditional knowledge assisted them in finding the relevant raw products, what really mattered for the ultimate success of the investigation was their investment in research and development. The example that follows might illustrate the conflicting views and a possible solution. What was at stake were potentially multi-billion-dollar profits derived from the marketing of an appetite suppressant. The product in question was derived from a plant that was researched by a state-backed pharmaceutical research organization, following the disclosure of relevant traditional knowledge by the indigenous San people of southern Africa.

The San are indigenous to the Kalahari Desert, an area encompassing parts of South Africa, Botswana and Namibia. The San were originally nomadic hunters well known for their ability to survive in the inhospitable desert conditions of their range for long periods. Their ancestors are thought to have arrived in the area some 150,000 years ago. The San currently live in isolated settlements, their communities afflicted by many of the same social conditions that affect indigenous populations the world over: high levels of poverty, with the associated negative consequences for quality of life, life expectancy and child mortality. For centuries the San have utilized the hoodia plant as an appetite suppressant, which enabled them to go for extended period without any food or water intake, while hunting. The South African Council for Scientific and Industrial Research (CSIR), a government research institute, learned of the plant through a 1937 publication by a Dutch ethnobiologist and also from San individuals who worked as trackers for the South African military.

In the 1980s researchers at the CSIR managed to isolate the active ingredient in the plant and patented it. The commercial potential of such a compound is clear, in light of the multi-billion-dollar worldwide weight loss industry. The compound, called P57, was licensed by CSIR to Phytopharm, a biotech company in the United Kingdom. Clinical trials followed, which confirmed the appetite-suppressing capacities of P57. The compound was later licensed to Pfizer, a US-based multinational pharmaceutical corporation, for US\$2 million. Pfizer subsequently withdrew from the license contract and Phytopharm sublicensed P57 to Unilever Plc, an Anglo–Dutch multinational consumer product giant, which developed an appetite-reducing snack bar.

Though at the time the CBD was not in existence, there was no prior informed consent from the San. More importantly, since there was no prior informed consent, no agreement on benefit sharing was initially negotiated. However, following intense lobbying from a San non-governmental organization, Phytopharm and the CSIR admitted that there had been a "mistake" (the "mistake" being their assumption that the San as a people no longer existed in southern Africa). Eventually an agreement was reached that some form of compensation should be provided to the San for the exploitation of their traditional knowledge. The interesting thing about this particular case was that this indigenous community agreed that its traditional knowledge should not be declared public knowledge, because this would have deprived them of any benefits from the commercial development process. To this end they worked towards ensuring that the patent itself was not contested, and, through their lawyer, demanded that compensation be provided to them. An agreement was reached after three years of negotiations, by which CSIR undertook to pay 6 per cent of all milestone payments (estimated to be US \$0.9–1.4 million) it receives from Phytopharm, and 8 per cent of all royalties from products developed from P57. Though this agreement was based on compromise, it was clearly much better that the equally arbitrary figure of 1–3 per cent of net profits that the Human Genome Organization's Bioethics Committee considers appropriate in such cases. The San have since set up a trust fund that is required to use the anticipated inflow of funds for local development projects. The first payments into the trust fund were received in 2005.

There is no dispute that the initial discovery of the appetite-suppressing properties of something in the hoodia plant was made by members of the San people. In the past they shared this information freely with many other parties, undoubtedly unaware of modern patent regimes and its commercial potential.

Those critical of this conception of traditional knowledge often note that much of what we think of as traditional medical knowledge is grounded on the same – baseless – scientific foundations as, say, homeopathy. In the case of the hoodia plant, for instance, they would contend that without the pharmaceutical research industry investing significantly in a scientific investigation of traditional claims, no new product would ever have resulted. If this line of reasoning is followed, the logical conclusion is that the pharmaceutical companies legitimately hold patents obtained in such circumstances, and they should be compensated for their investments through the sale of the products that were derived from their research.

Many ethicists and legal scholars have reached the opposite conclusion. They argue that without the exploitation of the special traditional knowledge shared by indigenous communities with the researchers, no new product would ever have been created because the pharmaceutical industry would not have known which organism to target. This, they insist, is the basis for indigenous groups having a legitimate claim to some kind of compensation as the traditional owners of the knowledge that eventually led to profitable products (Wynberg *et al.* 2009). The benefits derived from this knowledge should be shared between the traditional owners and the pharmaceutical companies' shareholders. When considering such benefit-sharing claims, serious questions may arise as to the modes of representation of some indigenous communities. For instance, what happens when researchers are faced with traditional groups of no fixed geographical community or where community leadership may no longer exist? How does one achieve meaningful benefit-sharing arrangements in such circumstances? It is also possible that a leadership exists in a given community, but it may not meet the standards of modern democracies, or may not be accountable. The question is: if we continue with the benefit-sharing strategy, what should be required to meet the basic standards of legitimate representation before companies pursue negotiations, if at all? This may be characterized by indigenous rights activists as Western imperialism: dictating how indigenous peoples should organize their internal affairs. Another important question is how to identify members of an indigenous community, and therefore who should be a beneficiary from the proceeds of any benefit-sharing scheme. Many indigenous communities, such as the San people, have over time reproduced with other groups that have entered their traditional territory. An equally complicated issue occurs where tribal communities' geographical distribution might not conform to modern geopolitical boundaries. After all, community can legitimately be defined through culture, language, custom, or even genetically.

It has been suggested instead that the countries or regions where such traditional knowledge is found, or from where plant or other biological materials have been extracted for research and development, should be seen as holding a legitimate benefit-sharing claim grounded in the ownership of the source material (Schüklenk & Kleinsmidt 2006).

There is a broader ethical question to be asked: what is the overarching motive driving the benefit-sharing agenda? The interest the benefit-sharing agenda has generated seems to be based on the hope that such a strategy has the potential to assist indigenous, impoverished communities to improve their quality of life. Indigenous peoples' access to decent healthcare, and whether or not someone's primary needs should be provided for, should arguably not be made contingent on "benefit-sharing" schemes of the sort discussed in above (Lowry & Schüklenk 2009). This, however, appears to be the driving motivating force behind such arrangements.

Benefit sharing

As with the case of benefit sharing in the context of bio-prospecting and the use of traditional knowledge for biomedical research purposes, ongoing debates in research ethics about the fair sharing of benefits resulting from trials undertaken in developing countries can only be understood in the context of the poverty that exists in these locations. Drugs developed as a result of trials undertaken in developed countries will eventually be made available to patients in those countries. The same does not always hold true for trial participants in developing countries. There is a danger that trial participants in developing countries may not reasonably share in the benefits accruing from their risk-taking in the same ways that their developed world counterparts would. Patients in developed countries might therefore become free-riders on developing world patients' risk-taking. Ensuring post-trial access to drugs developed during clinical research is today required by most international research ethics guidelines. The following questions have been the source of much debate: How should we determine what levels and what kinds of benefits should reasonably be provided? What procedure should be followed with a view to determining reasonable benefits? Is it the responsibility of clinical researchers to find the resources to guarantee those benefits? Is it the responsibility of trial sponsors to provide such benefits? Should benefits be provided at the individual level or the community level? Should we draw a distinction between for-profit research and non-profit investigations?

An influential procedural approach to benefit sharing states that though there may be an international consensus that requires that impoverished trial participants in the developing world to derive some benefit from their risk-taking, it is much less clear that the benefits should be in the form of medicines. Giving full effect to the concept of fair collaboration, local communities and international trial sponsors should negotiate what is considered fair benefits to the communities (Participants in the 2001 Conference on Ethical Aspects of Research in Developing Countries 2004). These benefits need not be medical benefits and may include a school, health centre or water well. Most of the ethical criticism of this approach centred on its potential to precipitate a proverbial "race to the bottom". In our current globalized research context, where free market forces may be at work, well-resourced trial sponsors could potentially search the globe for the best possible deal, and in the negotiating process required by this procedural approach, treat desperate impoverished communities unfairly by playing them off against each other in protracted benefits negotiations (London & Zollman 2010). Although what constitutes "exploitation" in an international research context is hotly debated, the potential "race to the bottom" described above would probably be considered exploitative regardless of whether one uses a traditional Kantian conception or one of the more modern conceptions of exploitation, such as that proposed by Alan Wertheimer (2008). The originator of this proposal – the above-mentioned procedural approach – eventually declared that it "suffers from a fatal flaw" (Lie 2010). Given this acknowledged failure of the predominant procedural approach, what remains unresolved and subject to ongoing intense ethical debate is whether it is possible at all to arrive at a defensible substantive consensus on what levels, and what types, of benefits are owed to trial participants in the developing world (Ballantyne 2010).

Standards of care

Like the debate on benefit sharing, the background of the ethics debates pertaining to research of ethical issues in the developing world is inextricably linked to the continuing existence of individually and societally devastating poverty in large parts of the global South. If most people in less-developed parts of the world were able to afford access to existing life-preserving medicines most discussions that exercise research ethicists today would arguably become superfluous. Standards of care in clinical trials, post-trial access to newly discovered drugs, access to life-preserving medicine for those who became infected during preventative HIV vaccine trials, and any number of other issues would cease to be problems. The concern about background justice constitutes a significant ethical insight. If ethical arguments put forward in the context of debates about global health ethics and corresponding obligations were heeded and acted upon, arguably the issues discussed below would not command a great deal of attention (Lowry & Schüklenk 2009).

One continuously debated question is whether it is ethical to provide patients in developing-world based-clinical trials that are sponsored by developed-world agencies or by pharmaceutical multinationals with lower levels of care than what would be the standard of clinical care provided in the home countries of those sponsoring agencies or corporate entities. At issue is whether or not it is acceptable to knowingly use a placebo control, or another lower than gold standard of care, when there exists a gold standard of clinical care for a particular ailment. When a gold standard has been established, any clinical investigation offering a control arm not featuring the gold standard of care does not begin with genuine clinical equipoise between the trial arms. Predictably, patients randomized into the placebo arm will be worse off, and so arguably will be harmed. The concept of clinical equipoise poses its own methodological and ethical challenges, but the ethical rationale underlying it is broadly sound (Freedman 1987). If clinical equipoise at the outset of a clinical investigation is guaranteed, no patient will be knowingly provided with care that is substandard. Clinical equipoise as such does not exclude the possibility of placebo controls, but placebo controls are ethically acceptable only under certain circumstances. For example, the use of a placebo control might be acceptable if there is no established standard of care, or if study participants who receive the placebo will not be subject to any risk of serious or irreversible harm (World Medical Association 2008).

The following is an example of just such a controversial trial. In 1994 officials of the World Health Organization (WHO), the Joint United Nations Programme on HIV/AIDS (UNAIDS), the US National Institutes of Health (NIH) and US Centers for Disease Control and Prevention (CDC) designed placebo-controlled studies to answer the question of whether a course of the drug zidovudine, when given to HIV-infected pregnant women, is more effective in preventing HIV infections of the newborns than doing nothing. In that same year another collaborative trial, undertaken only in developed countries, discovered that 25 per cent of HIV-positive pregnant women who did not use zidovudine gave birth to an infected baby, while less than 8 per cent of those using zidovudine did. This trial protocol, known as ACTG 076, led, in developed countries, to the provision of zidovudine as a matter of course to HIV-infected pregnant women. It became at the time the standard of care in the developed world. However, the implementation of the ACTG 076 protocol at 1998 prices cost approximately US$800 per pregnancy. That was far more than the per capita healthcare allocation in many developing nations.

The placebo-controlled trial was sharply criticized in a high-profile article by Peter Lurie and Sidney Wolfe in the *New England Journal of Medicine* (Lurie & Wolfe 1997). The trial sought to test whether it is possible to develop a drug regimen that is substantially cheaper but yet remains efficient with regard to the prevention of mother-to-child transmission of HIV (*ibid.*). This objective meets a demand set out in guidelines published by the Council for International Organizations of Medical Sciences (CIOMS) that it should be "responsive to the health needs and the priorities of the community in which it is carried out" (CIOMS 1993: 51). This is designed to ensure that studies are done for the sake of the participants in the host community, rather than merely to benefit future patients elsewhere. Research in developing country X should be designed for the benefit the people of country X and their specific health needs, rather than future citizens of rich country Y. The study under consideration required that all research subjects give first-person informed consent. The HIV-infected pregnant women were informed that they would be randomly assigned to receive either a placebo or zidovudine. This was intended to meet an important standard ethical requirement of any clinical trial involving competent participants, that is, that the trial participants give first-person voluntary informed consent.

Critics of the trial, such as Lurie and Wolfe, charged that the trial design was unethical, as it involved a placebo control where historical controls would have sufficed, consequently reducing the number of participants subjected knowingly to an inferior form of treatment. Lurie and Wolfe argued that the results of ACTG 076 should have led to a research design asking the question of whether a shorter (and therefore cheaper) regimen of zidovudine is just as effective as the ACTG 076 regimen, and not whether the trial regime is more effective than a placebo. They argued for the implementation of equivalency studies rather than placebo-controlled studies. The individuals who designed the trial countered that the placebo controls led more quickly to statistically predictive results, and just as important, none of the women participating in this study was in a worse position than she would have been had she not participated.

The rationale here was that the standard of care that was available to these women locally was such that they would not have been able to afford zidovudine in any case. Therefore, those in the placebo arm were not worse off, while those in the zidovudine arm were better off. Concerns have been raised about this local standard of care concept. The most obvious question is whether one can readily identify a particular local standard of care anywhere in the world. Arguably, the local standard of care in any developing world locale is a standard of care as determined by the prices of pharmaceuticals set by Western multinationals. Even within a given society multi-tier healthcare systems would give rise to different standards of care based on the patients' ability to pay. No one would accept the idea that different standards of care in a clinical trial could legitimately be applied to Americans participating in clinical research in the US, depending on whether they are poor or wealthy.

Some have questioned whether the ethical guidelines that applied to this trial and which were also used by its critics, as they govern research across the world, should be applied to developing countries given that the context in which research is undertaken is so dramatically different to that in more developed countries. Several counter-arguments have been advanced to justify the use of placebo controls in poorer parts of the world, even when a gold standard of care has been established. It has been argued, with some justification, that where the gold standard of clinical care is unavailable to the vast majority of patients, it is reasonable for researchers to explore alternative, more affordable means of medical care in a trial design involving placebo controls (Levine 1998). After all, researchers are unlikely to be able to change the economic circumstances in developing countries, but they may be able to alleviate some of the other problems by means of developing locally appropriate solutions. According to this view, the research should aim to establish whether or not a new treatment regime would leave local patients in a better situation than they would have been otherwise, rather than trying to establish that a new treatment regime is better than a locally unaffordable treatment regime that is the gold standard in wealthier parts of the world. This ethical rationale takes a classic consequentialist view.

Not surprisingly this line of reasoning has drawn its critics. These critics argue that the relatively high cost of patented medicines is the main reason for impoverished patients not being able to access even essential, life-preserving medication. The fundamental question then appears to be whether economic reasons rather than clinical rationales provide a good ethical justification for the continuation of drug trials in the developing world (Schüklenk 2004). After all, pharmaceutical companies can and have reduced drug prices, and patents can be and have been set aside in the interest of preserving human lives. The main implication of the economic rationale is this: pharmaceutical companies, by exercising their control over patented drug prices, can essentially limit the access of impoverished patients in developing countries to affordable therapies and therefore sustain their justification for the continuation of placebo controlled drug trials in these jurisdictions.

Depending on the philosophical lenses through which one views the world it is possible both to be critical of this trial and also to find it ethically justifiable. It is possible to consistently hold a view such as that of casuist philosophers Crouch and Arras, who are not entirely convinced that "even taking past injustices (people in developed nations committed against people developing nations) into account [this] would yield a moral entitlement to expensive antiretroviral treatment" (Crouch & Arras 1998: 28). From this position, clinical trials that have as their objective the development of an affordable drug could be legitimate. This is so because this line of reasoning ignores the economic context that gives rise to the need to find cheaper drugs for people living in developing countries.

Those with a consequentialist bent may conclude that the maximization of human well-being requires the availability of essential, life-preserving medicines. They may also conclude that trials such as the zidovudine trial are unethical, because a working treatment regime already existed and should be made available to those who need it. Since pharmaceutical companies generate only a small fraction of their profits in poorer communities such as the one participating in the trial discussed in this part of the chapter, it could be argued that rather than reducing standards of care provided to trial participants in such communities, greater emphasis should be placed on making existing essential medicines affordable to such patients rather using their existence as the basis for pursuing scientifically unnecessary clinical research.

Trial-related injuries

Prevention trials present their own set of ethical challenges. A classic example is whether people who become infected during HIV prevention trials can claim that their infection is a trial-related injury, entitling them to some kind of compensation, or whether the infection they acquired during the trial is a case of harm to self. At the beginning of HIV prevention trials – as with other prevention trials – the participants are not infected. The aim of such trials is to determine if a candidate agent (such as a vaccine or anti-viral gel) is better than doing nothing. At the time of writing no preventative HIV vaccine exists, therefore, since there is no gold standard vaccine, these trials can be, and are legitimately, placebo controlled. For trial participants to acquire HIV they must be engaging in certain risk-taking behaviour such as unprotected sex or sharing unsafe injecting equipment.

In developed countries if participants in such prevention trials seroconvert, they would receive access to life-preserving anti-retroviral medications. This is not the case for their developing world counterparts. The ethical implications of this inequitable situation give rise to the question: should such infections be considered trial-related injuries necessitating compensation in the form of access to life-preserving anti-retroviral drugs (Schüklenk & Ashcroft 2000)? Some insist that the voluntary risk-taking of trial participants means that there is no ethical obligation to provide post-trial care to them that can be grounded in any trial-related injury rationale. This they would argue is a classic case of *volenti non fit injuria*. Those opposed point to the "therapeutic misconception", an empirical phenomenon affecting a large proportion of trial participants in any given trial. The therapeutic misconception in the case of prevention trials is perhaps more aptly described as a preventive misconception. It involves trial participants who mistakenly think they are (more) protected because they are participating in the trial. As the argument goes, if the sponsors and investigators knowingly keep a large number of trial participants in the trial who have mistaken beliefs about the efficacy of the trial medication and the trial design, there arises an ethical duty on the part of these investigators and sponsors to provide care to infected participants. This argument has been countered by Weijer and LeBlanc (2006) via the use of a meta-analysis of studies investigating the comprehension of vaccine trials among (actual and prospective) trial participants. According to Weijer and LeBlanc, the meta-analysis demonstrated that risk-taking behaviour among trial participants decreased in comparison to the general populations from which the participants were recruited. This rightly led them to conclude that this establishes a sound basis for conducting such trials. There is a caveat however. They have suggested also that since we have no way of knowing who got infected as a result of voluntary informed risk-taking as opposed to preventive misconception, access to life-preserving medication is not therefore owed to them based on the rationale suggested earlier (*ibid.*). It is difficult to see why this view should be more persuasive than the view that under such circumstances infected trial participants should be provided with life-preserving medicines. The latter would be more in line with otherwise accepted standard practices in clinical research, requiring trial sponsors and investigators to reduce the worsening of trial participants' baselines as much as is feasible.

Most researchers, ethicists, activists and policy-makers now subscribe to the view that ensuring access to HIV treatment and care should be one of the benefits offered to prevention trial participants (e.g. Macklin 2006, Lo *et al.* 2007). Therefore, regardless of where in the world a trial is taking place, there ought to be a requirement that infected trial participants are given access to life-preserving anti-retroviral medicines while they can derive a clinical benefit from doing so. This would be the outcome in developed countries (notwithstanding that it would be provided as part of the healthcare regime provided by those countries' healthcare systems) and things should be no different in developing countries. The open question remains: why should this burden fall on the trial sponsors and investigators?

Utility of research question

The utility of particular research questions and the ethical justification for research that is considered to be of little or no social utility give rise to a whole different set of questions. The criterion of locally appropriate research serving local health needs has already been mentioned earlier in this chapter. The problem with this criterion is that ethical review committees would no longer be looking purely at the scientific soundness of a research proposal, on its risk–benefit ratio and the informed consent procedures. Ethical review committees (ERCs) would be required to take an ethical stance on the question of whether the research is locally desirable. This is arguably a qualitatively different proposition altogether. Different positions have evolved on this question. Some scholars have expressed the view that whether or not a research proposal is ethical depends exclusively on matters such as the risk–benefit ratio, the voluntariness of the participants' informed consent, and other, mostly process-related, questions that are intrinsic to a given trial. Any research project that is only of value to those asking the question would be considered ethically irrelevant on this account.

The opposing view is that whether or not a particular research project is ethical requires ethical review committees to also take a stance on the research question itself. It would not be ethical, according to this logic, to undertake a trial that satisfies all procedural conditions an ethical trial would have to meet but which aims to develop a procedure that would not benefit either the trial participants or people belonging to the same social grouping as the trial participants. Equally, a trial the results of which might put specific individuals or sections of society at a disadvantage or in harm's way would be unacceptable. The voluntariness of the well-informed trial participants' enrolment in and of itself would not make a trial ethical. The difficulty with this position is that ethical review committees would be tasked with the much more difficult question of ascribing value to a proposed research project. This opens the door to ERCs having to address questions such as whether or not it is ethical to undertake genetic research on sexual orientation in a world that is often homophobic (Schüklenk *et al.* 1997), or whether research into the biology of intelligence is acceptable in a world where ethnicity-specific answers might give rise to racist abuse of such investigations. Traditionally these types of ethical questions have been taken to be beyond the purview of ethics review.

Future challenges

In recent years, the scope of research ethics has expanded significantly beyond its traditional medical ethics-type staple issues of informed consent and other related matters. Today the focus is on background conditions of justice in international research. This also marks an important, and arguably long overdue, shift from straightforwardly ethical analysis to a more multi-faceted approach including, for instance, the critical tools political philosophy and economics can bring to bear on these problems. Significant work on matters of global justice has been undertaken by political philosophers such as Thomas Pogge (2008), Norman Daniels (2008) and Thomas Nagel (2005), and increasingly their and others' analyses are taken into consideration (e.g. Lowry & Schüklenk 2009, Ballantyne 2010, London & Zollman 2010), if not to say put centre-stage, in critical works on research ethics. We suspect that we will be seeing more of this in the years to come. It will not suffice any longer for writers in research ethics to focus on ethical issues in clinical research in the developing world as if the wider socio-economic context that gives rise to these ethical problems is irrelevant to a fair resolution of the problems at hand. These writers hope that fewer approaches to standards of care in clinical research will accept the socio-economic context in a given impoverished society as an acceptable status that does not require critical questioning. Among the issues that remain hotly contested is the question of whether or not the economic context should influence clinical research agendas, particularly in the developing world. Another hot button issue is whether or not clinical researchers should be burdened with negotiating fair benefits with prospective trial participants in developing countries. It has been justifiably pointed out that similar questions would not arise in the developed world research context, and as such, clinical researchers should stick to what they do best – research – and leave the socio-economics to those who are better equipped to deal with them.

It is beyond reasonable doubt at the time of writing that corporate sponsorship of pharmaceutical research has systemic corrupting effects on research integrity. Worse, it also corrupts academic institutions that become increasingly dependent on such research funding (e.g. Schafer 2004). Indeed, their very prestige, such as high ranking in international research quality rankings, depends to a significant extent on their capacity to attract huge amounts of external research dollars. Given that public and philanthropic funding for clinical research is on the decrease, pharmaceutical companies' money is increasingly sought by researchers and institutions alike. At least one pharmaceutical company and one of the world's largest for-profit science publishers have gone so far as to create a fake new medical journal as a vehicle of marketing (B. Grant 2009). Clinical research is often designed to answer questions that have primarily marketing purposes in mind. Research participants' time is wasted and prescribing doctors are manipulated with such corrupted research results. Academic institutions are known to protect those who arguably did wrong while at the same time persecuting whistleblowers (e.g. Basken 2012). While these problems are all too well known, research ethicists have only in recent years begun to address this issue, albeit with very limited success. Too powerful are the entrenched interests of pharmaceutical companies and the academic institutions dependent on their money, much like addicts are dependent on drugs (C. Elliott 2010). Indeed, academic bioethics centres found themselves in the firing line, in so far as they and their research depend on industry funding (C. Elliott 2001, Schüklenk & Lott 2004). There is significant need to investigate the ethical challenges that arise in this context with regard to research sponsors, grantees, the institutions that employ researchers and, last but not least, the biomedical (and possibly bioethics) journals that publish the results of industry-funded research. Conflicts of interest, of course, arise in other areas too, including in the peer review process where peer reviewers, editors or authors might encounter intellectual conflicts of interests. These and other vital areas of the real-world research industry face little to no scrutiny by research ethicists. Arguably, this constitutes a significant omission in need of future rectification.

Alex-John London has proposed the following future-oriented agenda in research ethics. It sums up nicely what has been said in this chapter with regard to ethical issues in clinical research. To his mind we need to develop an ethical "regulatory and oversight structure that (a) limits the influence of parochial interests of stakeholders in the research enterprise, (b) that avoids unnecessary cost and delay, (c) promotes high-quality, socially relevant research and (d) protects the interests of research participants" (London 2012, personal communication). One way to limit the damage that is done by mechanisms such as those described in the foregoing paragraph is to ensure that the raw data of any given trial be made available to qualified statisticians or other scientists who wish to reprocess the data (Hrynaszkiewicz & Altman 2009). This also raises questions about intellectual property rights, informed consent, patient privacy and other ethical issues.

Quite different questions arise in the context of research on human genetic enhancement. They are bound to become more pressing in the years ahead, as we move closer towards researching and realizing some of the opportunities that lie in genetic alterations of some kind or another. Take just one example: human prenatal genetic enhancement. Much like research on reproductive human cloning, research on human genetic enhancement is currently illegal across the globe, yet there can be little doubt that clandestine operations quietly continue towards producing the first cloned human. There is in principle no reason why such research should remain unsuccessful forever, given that other higher mammals have already been successfully cloned. However, a high price was paid in terms of disabled non-human animals that were created during the previous cloning research. That is one of the more serious reasons why reproductive human cloning research is officially not undertaken anywhere in the world. Most other reasons brought forward against research on reproductive human cloning are not terribly persuasive (Pence 1998). As it turns out, the same ethical problem arises in the context of prenatal human genetic enhancement, too. In order to research genetic human enhancement technologies, research on human embryos and foetuses is unavoidable. Humanity is once again faced with the ethical question of what kinds of burdens individual embryos can reasonably be subjected to if their parents wish to carry them to term. This question arises independently of other concerns that have been expressed about the liberal eugenics that seems to be driving the enhancement debate (Agar 2004). Unlike in the case of destructive embryo experimentation that took place to enable *in vitro* fertilization, in the case of prenatal genetic enhancement research many of the potential benefits as well as harms resulting from such enhancement research would only eventuate postnatally. That is, abortion would only be an option in some cases of seriously malformed embryos: other potential genetic damages might only be discovered years down the track. Potentially adult humans could be affected by long-term harmful consequences of human genetic enhancement research. Over time such problems would naturally decrease in frequency, as research progresses, and eventually a virtually infinite number of future humans could benefit from the sacrifices of the comparably few that participated (involuntarily, as a result of their parents' consent) in this kind of research. The kinds of ethical questions we face in this context are novel to a significant extent. What kinds of moral responsibilities would such prospective parents have *qua* prospective parents versus the moral responsibilities they could be said to have as citizens *qua* citizens? Is this even a sensible distinction to draw? Should such research only proceed in cases where there is a serious genetic illness affecting the embryos that the research aims to ameliorate, or would it be acceptable to proceed with prenatal genetic enhancement research that aims to truly *improve* the future human, even though in the latter case the human could live a satisfactory unenhanced life?

We will almost certainly continue to grapple with the problem of whether or not we should begin to pay trial participants. At present, payments going beyond cost-recovery are expressly prohibited in most jurisdictions, often with vague references to "undue incentives". Notwithstanding these admonitions, it is questionable whether this approach is defensible, in light of payments to all other players in the research endeavour, from lab technicians to nurses to administrators and investigators (Grady 2005). An emerging research ethics concern will also be whether biochemical warfare research of either the offensive or defensive kinds should be considered ethical, how biomedical journals should approach research papers in these areas, and whether scientists should be sanctioned (or promoted) for undertaking such research (Miller & Selgelid 2008). The justification or lack thereof for the use of higher non-human mammals in clinical research will undoubtedly also be back on the research ethics agenda in light of a decision by the US NIH to stop funding any further invasive research on chimpanzees (Gorman 2011).

No doubt other issues will arise that are less predictable than those mentioned above. They will most likely result from cutting-edge biomedical research in the neurosciences and genetics, and probably in the area of infectious disease research. One thing is certain: there will not be a lack of problems for research ethicists to address. Indeed, the priorities they set with regard to the issues they choose to address might itself be subject to ethical critiques.

24

TRADE IN HUMAN BODY PARTS

Teck Chuan Voo and Alastair V. Campbell

This chapter will examine trade in human body parts. By this we refer to the issue of whether and the extent to which people should be free to exchange their body parts (such as organs, tissues and cells) as materials for transplant treatments or biomedical research for monetary or material benefits, directly or indirectly. In the first section we begin by outlining current laws and international material regulating trade in human body parts. We then turn to issues that give reasons to advocate trade in the second section. In the third section we examine in some detail the moral opposition against trade in body parts and some proposed trading systems, before discussing the principle of self-sufficiency for regulating organ donation globally. In the fourth section we consider the legal rule of property, and alternative arrangements to address the issues raised in the second section. Finally, we raise some possibilities for how the debate on trade in human body parts might develop.

Laws and international documents

Transplant treatments

The laws of most countries permit only the donation, but not the sale, of human body parts for transplantation. For example, Section 301 the US National Organ Transplant Act (NOTA; 42 USC 274e) of 1984 states: "It shall be unlawful for any person to knowingly acquire, receive, or otherwise transfer any human organ for valuable consideration for use in human transplantation if the transfer affects interstate commerce."[1] According to Crespi, "valuable consideration" "is universally understood to cover noncash compensation, deferred compensation, and payment of compensation as directed to third parties" (Crespi 1994: 57).

European law and conventions also uphold a donation model for body parts for transplantation and other medical treatments. To protect human rights and fundamental freedoms in the application of biology and medicine, Article 21 of the European Convention on Human Rights and Biomedicine (Council of Europe 1997) states that "The human body and its parts shall not, as such, give rise to financial gain."

This principle is affirmed in the World Health Organization (WHO) Guiding Principles on Human Cell, Tissue and Organ Transplantation (World Health Organization 2010) and the Declaration of Istanbul (Participants in the International Summit on Transplant Tourism and

Organ Trafficking 2008), which was created during a summit in Istanbul convened by The Transplantation Society and the International Society of Nephrology. The documents aim to provide universal ethical guidelines for donation and transplantation practices, and call for international cooperation to deal with organ trafficking and transplant tourism that involves transplant commercialism, defined by the Declaration of Istanbul (henceforth the Declaration) as "a policy or practice in which an organ is treated as a commodity, including by being bought or sold or used for material gain" (*ibid.*: 3376). The documents are in agreement that organ trading does not include reimbursement of expenses or costs related to the donation event, including lost income, incurred by living donors, a practice which has taken root in some resource-rich healthcare systems to remove or reduce economic disincentives to donation. As the Participants in the International Summit on Transplant Tourism and Organ Trafficking state in justification, "Comprehensive reimbursement of the actual, documented costs of donating an organ does not constitute a payment for an organ, but is rather part of the legitimate costs of treating the recipient" (*ibid.*: 3377).

Biomedical research and development

Currently, no legislation explicitly addresses the issue of whether any person can charge, receive or contract for payment for use of his tissue in biomedical research and development. No court has also considered the enforceability of such arrangements, which would depend on their consistency with public interests (Gitter 2004: 263). In practice, however, tissue for use in research is usually collected from research participants, from patients' surplus diagnostic samples, or from "unwanted" parts excised during operations. Occasionally, donated deceased bodies and parts become material for research.

Issues and reasons for advocating trade

Organ shortage

Human organ transplantation is the current standard of care for patients with irreversible end-stage organ diseases. Alternative treatments exist for kidney, pancreas and heart failures. Compared to transplantation, these treatment options are less cost-effective and lead to a lower quality of life and lifespan for patients. There are no alternatives for lung and liver failures. Advances in transplant technology have made it viable for more and more people to become recipients and donors; the advent of cyclosporine therapy to prevent transplant rejection transformed the medico-social boundaries of donation by turning genetically non-related persons into potential organ sources. As the most common organ transplanted from live donation, live kidneys offer better clinical outcomes (patient and graft survival) than deceased kidneys (Ponticelli 2003). Because of acceptable risk–benefit ratios, and factors like media influence and public education, more and more people are stepping up to donate a live kidney or part of their liver. Organizational improvements in identifying potential organ donors and discussion of the donation process with families have also increased deceased donation in a number of countries.

Nevertheless, there remains a shortage of transplant organs worldwide. For example, around 1.5 million people in China are waiting for an organ transplant but only ten thousand receive them annually because of low donation numbers (Huang 2007). Demand around the world is driven by ageing populations and rising incidence of obesity and diseases such as diabetes, which provoke organ failure. The consequences of the shortage are dire. Within the European Union (EU), "more than 4000 patients died … while waiting for a kidney, liver, heart or lung during

2007, which means that 12 EU citizens died every day while waiting to be transplanted" (Council of Europe 2009: 21). This mortality rate does not include those not placed on waiting lists or those removed because of deterioration in their medical condition. Because of the shortage, many countries have to implement strict criteria, both clinical and geographical, for inclusion in waiting lists, with increasing focus on maximizing utility or transplant outcomes.

"[T]he incapacity of national health care systems to meet the needs of patients with the lack of appropriate regulatory frameworks or implementation elsewhere" (Yosuke 2007: 959) have fuelled an international organ trade. Risk of infection, graft failure, mortality and morbidity is higher in cross-border transplantations involving organ trafficking or paid organs. The WHO claims that organ trafficking accounts for 5–10 per cent of kidney transplants performed worldwide (cited in Budiani-Saberi & Delmonico 2008). Syndicates typically attract buyers from the developed world and target sellers in poor and developing countries such as China, Egypt, Pakistan, Colombia and former Soviet-bloc nations. Once in a while, cases of coercion, abduction, fraud, abuse of sellers and their death from negligent care surface in the media. Those prosecuted for illegal organ trading do not just include traffickers and brokers. In 2008, a Singapore court charged a then dying Singaporean renal patient and his prospective kidney seller (a financially desperate Indonesian man) for organ trading (Ritter 2008).

Commercialization

Organs for transplantation

Illegal forms of transplant tourism often advertise all-inclusive "transplant packages" to attract foreign patients (Yosuke 2007). Sellers are usually paid a low sum. Some forms of transplant tourism are legal, as in the case of patients travelling abroad to seek higher-quality transplant services with legally procured, donated organs. As Yosuke (*ibid.*: 956–57) points out, "Under the General Agreement of Trade in Service ... governments may choose to trade health services to achieve their national health objectives. Health service exports, through the treatment of foreign patients entering their territory ... are used by some countries as an instrument of economic development." In the US, for example, each transplant centre can reserve 5 per cent of its waiting list for foreign patients, who typically have substantial financial resources and can pay in cash (Caplan 2008).

Tissue products

Human tissue graft material is usually recovered from deceased donors. Tissue such as skin can be used "fresh", or fragmented and processed into an assortment of medical and non-medical products, and stored for long use. Many non-profit, hospital-based tissue banks that serve the local community have been replaced by, or gone into partnership with, corporate tissue banks that sell the products internationally (Schulz-Baldes *et al.* 2007). Such a shift occurred because of the need to meet burgeoning global demand and increasing quality and safety requirements for these products (*ibid.*).

Some tissue banks or companies clearly violate ethical and legal boundaries. In the case of *Commonwealth of Pennsylvania v Michael Mastromarino* (2010, No. 3443 EDA 2008), a former dentist and president of the now defunct Biomedical Tissue Services (a procurement company) was convicted for conspiring with funeral directors to harvest tissue, particularly bones for dental implants, from over two hundred bodies awaiting cremation. Many of the bodies were restructured with materials like pipes to conceal what had been done from the relatives. The tissue products, a significant portion of which violated safety standards for transplantation, were sold to medical practices in several US states, and exported to other countries.

Most human tissue companies do not engage in such "bio-piracy". Nevertheless, their commercial practices raise ethical concerns. The laws of many countries permit payment or reimbursement for costs of services or operations that might be involved in body part transplantation. NOTA, for example, permits "reasonable payments" for the services of "removal, transportation, implantation, processing, preservation, quality control, and storage" of human tissue. While some countries impose a fixed price for tissue products, pricing is virtually unrestricted in others such as the US. Skin of one donor, processed into dermal matrix for plastic surgery, is fixed at €6300 in Belgium; in the US, it can fetch about US$120,000 (Pirnay *et al.* 2010). The ambiguity of what constitutes "reasonable payments", and the lack of regulation on their limits, allow tissue banks in the US to generate "super-normal profits", creating a billion-dollar industry (Katz 2006). Although countries in general do not experience a shortage of tissue (as opposed to solid organs) for transplantation, or are able to mitigate any shortage through import, there are concerns over distribution for tissue like skin. The human tissue industry has been criticized for prioritizing sale of skin for cosmetic procedures over life-saving surgeries for burn victims because of the former's higher market value (Heisel *et al.* 2000).

In view of these issues, Pirnay *et al.* (2010: 871) suggest an ethical framework to regulate the industry, which should: define and limit "reasonable payment"; implement allocation rules and also exportation rules with an emphasis on self-sufficiency; inform donors the potential uses of the donated human tissues and cells, including non-medical and commercial use; require scientific proof of efficacy for tissue products; and enforce the rules through civil penalties.

Tissue for research

The year 1980 saw two important developments – *Diamond v Chakrabarty* (1980, US SCR 65 L Ed 2d 144) and the Bayh–Dole Act (1980, 35 USC 200–212) – in the legal background of biotechnology. In Charkabarty, the Supreme Court ruled that genetically modified bacteria were patentable. The Bayh–Dole Act provided the means for US universities (and also non-profit institutions and small businesses) to retain ownership of inventions arising from federally funded research. In return, universities are expected to file for patent protection and to commercialize the inventions, preferably through academia–industry ventures. The combination of Chakarabarty and Bayh–Dole paved the way for a whole new global industry profiting from novel human cell lines, genetically modified organisms and gene sequences.

Under this intellectual-corporate culture, sale of donated or collected human tissue from medical schools and hospitals to companies as research material became a common practice; still, this practice has, when reported, drawn public ire and criticism.[2] More controversial is the denial of patients' rights to their own biological material owing to intellectual property rights held by researchers, universities or companies. A landmark case is *Moore v Regents of the University of California* (1990, 51 Cal.3d 120; 1988, 215 Cal.App3d 709) in which a doctor and a research associate discovered that the spleen cells of a patient, John Moore, had the unusual quality of overproducing a protein which might be valuable in the development of cancer-fighting drugs and for conducting genetic research. Without Moore's consent or knowledge, they cultured a cell line using his diseased spleen tissue excised during his treatment, which was then patented by the University. In the spirit of Bayh–Dole, the doctor, assisted by the University Regents, licensed the commercial development of the immortal cell line and derivable products to two biotech firms, which brought in substantial revenue for the university and made the doctor US$15 million.

When Moore found out about the defendants' activities, he sued for a share in their proceeds as compensation for the conversion of his property in his excised cells, among other claims. The

California Supreme Court affirmed that doctors have a fiduciary duty to disclose any personal interest, whether research or financial, which they have in a patient's biological/genetic material, thus recognizing Moore's right to seek redress for injuries, *if any*, for breach of informed consent requirements. Moore's conversion claim was undermined when the court held that his excised cells were not his property because of the lack of precedent supporting such an interest and also because of the factual and legal distinction between patented cell lines and excised cells. As to whether conversion law – a strict liability tort that would apply to every party in possession of the "property" – should be extended to this case, the court declined to do so as it would "hinder research by restricting access to the necessary raw materials ... exchange of scientific materials, which still is relatively free and efficient, will surely be compromised if each cell sample becomes the potential subject matter of a lawsuit" (*Moore v Regents of the University of California* 1990: 15). Although the Moore decision is legally binding only in California, it is influential in shaping public policy debate on patients' ownership rights in their excised tissue. Cases such as *Greenberg v Miami Children's Hospital Research Institute, Inc.* (2003, 264 F. Supp. 2d 1064, S.D. Fla.) and *Washington University v Catalona* (2006, 437 F. Supp. 2d 985, E.D. Mo.) also stimulate the debate.

In the context of international research, ethical concerns and outcries have been also expressed at the conduct of those in the developed world who obtain patents on products derived from the bodily "raw material" of people in the developing world, particularly indigenous communities, or collect and export the material and corresponding data back to their countries.[3] As the body becomes even bigger business with the expansion of biotech interests in new therapeutic strategies (e.g. pharmacogenomics) and new markets, the economics of the conflicts have intensified. For example, Indian scientists objected to the export of tissue samples by foreign researchers because of potential patents and other commercial applications derivable from the biological material of "India's large and diverse population" (Upshur *et al.* 2007: 2).

To empower themselves, patients in the developed world have formed advocacy groups to negotiate their interests directly with the research community. A notable example is PXE International, a non-profit corporation started by one such group representing the interests of patients with the genetic disorder pseudoxanthoma elasticum (PXE).[4] The group set up a repository of their tissue and blood samples, and used contract law to enable the group to gain ownership rights over those samples: before accessing the repository, researchers must sign a contract stating that they agree to share ownership rights with PXE International in those samples. The gene associated for PXE was eventually isolated by some university researchers and the patent issued lists PXE International as co-owner. As part of its agreement with the university, PXE International is entitled to control licensing and to collect royalties (to be shared with the university) from any diagnostics or drugs developed, including those non-related to PXE, from studies involving the patented gene sequence.

Reasons for trade

Gift versus commodity

The "gift" is a conventional trope for framing the meaning of body parts donation, be it for the purpose of treatment, research or education. To our knowledge it was first used by Titmuss (1970) to signify a "social" policy of encouraging voluntary unpaid, anonymous donation of blood into a common pool. Proponents of trade typically interpret support for the gift framework, with its "Titmussian" lineage of thought, as claiming that individual generosity or charity represents the only morally acceptable way to transfer body parts (see e.g. Sykora 2009).

Commoditization of body parts, understood as allowing donors to benefit in some significant way, should therefore be rejected wholesale.

The continuing, overarching use of the gift to frame the donation of body parts, both regenerative and non-regenerative, and its dichotomous opposition to commoditization in the above sense has been heavily criticized for many reasons (see e.g. Arrow 1972, Lomasky 1983). One reason, as summed up by Williams and Zelizer (2005: 364), is that "This conventional bifurcated vision obscures our understanding of how economic life – the production, distribution and consumption of valuable goods and services – actually operates." Certainly, it has become common and legal in some countries to pay people to donate plasma (usually converted into products to treat diseases like haemophilia) and oocytes (for reproduction /research purposes), which are then circulated by international companies within the global marketplace. Payment is acknowledged as necessary to achieve a sufficient supply of these resources, and as justified compensation for personal risks or services.

Furthermore, the blood gift signifies a unilateral act of beneficence by one stranger for another, in which the donor relinquishes control over whom to benefit (the non-directed rule). This moral narrative does not reflect complex interests surrounding other body parts and their uses, let alone conflicts pertaining to the donation event or other forms of procurement in the health industry,[5] some of which are described earlier. This is especially so in research when (a) it is not the corporeal material per se but the information reaped that is (potentially) beneficial, and (b) the information may benefit countless present and future individuals worldwide. And when the information and associated applications are derived significantly from the tissue of a specific individual or group owing to rare genetic and cellular qualities, the issue of ownership and control over the information and its use is likely to *matter* to that individual or group.

Equity and efficiency

The perceived unfairness perpetuated by the gift framework – the "socialist" appeal to voluntarism in providing biological materials and their "capitalist" utilization by those in the health industry – leads many to argue for a shift from what amounts to its ideological adherence in health policy and law. As Mason and Laurie (2010: 455) write in their evaluation of the *Moore* decision, "It is *not* reasonable to exclude completely from the [profit-sharing] equation the one person who can make everything possible." Some level the additional charge of "hypocrisy about the ethics of buying and selling organs and indeed other body products and services" (Erin & Harris 2003, original emphasis): it is hypocritical to allow transplant surgeons and coordinators, tissue allograft manufacturers and marketers, researchers, and so on, to be paid while denying donors of body parts the right to do so.[6] Ensuring payment to donors would rectify the unequal treatment of individuals who contribute differently to the production of goods and services. Donors provide an essential "bio-capital": personal body parts necessary for the performance of transplant services and some forms of biomedical research. As Gitter (2004: 341) argues, payment would also motivate those who might otherwise decline to act altruistically while others profit from donating their body parts for the above uses.

For sure, critics of the prohibition on organ trading argue that altruism as a motive has been and would remain drastically inefficient in matching supply with demand. Markets are more efficient because they are driven by the pursuit of mutual benefits. Removing the price cap of zero for organs will induce more donations, and ultimately save or improve more lives. To provide empirical support, proponents of organ trading cite the alleged outcomes of Iran's regulated living unrelated kidney market (the only legalized organ market in the world): elimination of the kidney waiting list and removal of emotional/coercive pressure on relatives to become living donors (Daar 2006, Ghods & Savaj 2006). Moreover, it is claimed that transplant tourism involving foreign paid donors no longer takes place in Iran itself, and fewer Iranian patients are participating in illegal transplantations abroad (Ghods & Savaj 2006). So proponents of trade contend that organ markets "affect the location of demand functions by redistributing ... demand from the black market to the legal sector" (Becker & Elias 2007).

Thus some writers advocate free trade in human body parts on the ground that it is the most efficient arrangement. For example, the economist Becker (2006) argues for a free market in live and deceased transplant organs because it will optimally equilibrate supply and demand through price competition. One may also argue that economic equity between providers and users of body parts will be promoted through freely negotiated contracts that would over time generate fair agreements or price ranges for use of some body part for transplantation or research, as a matter of expectations based on historical transactions in a given society, whether viewed locally or globally. Free trade is an arrangement for exchange as strategic bargaining, empowered by the treatment of body parts as private property.

Moral opposition to trade

Human flourishing

Co-opting people into traders of their body parts may be opposed to the teleological viewpoint that it undermines human flourishing or the good life, which assumes the necessity of a plurality of values from which personhood as it relates to choice-making and relations involving the human body can be properly shaped. Such opposition is often embedded within a larger programme of resistance against free market rationalism and rhetoric: the promotion of negative liberty or non-interference with one's actions; the assimilation of use to exchange for a price; and the emphasis on the notion of property to identify or determine personhood. Laypersons tend to see property as tangible things. In law and jurisprudence, property is commonly understood instead as a "bundle of rights" or a set of legal relations between persons.[7] Nonetheless, it remains a conceptual criterion for property law to be about governing objects or things: those rights or relations between persons obtain with respect to things. Penner (1996: 802) argues that the defining attribute of "thinghood" in relation to property law is not tangibility but contingency in connection to personhood, that is, a thing could just very well be someone else's.

As we can draw from Radin's work (1987, 1996), the pervasion of free market rationalism into the domain of body parts use may degrade the human experience by diminishing or distorting human valuing and values. For example, if live organs are allowed to be freely traded as private properties, then people may come to treat their bodies and others in fungible and commensurable ways, much like how they treat external, contingent, market alienable material possessions like cars. Commensurability refers to the alignment and comparison of different things using a common scale, in this case a price metric. Fungibility refers to the interchangeability of things in a market with no effect on value to the holder. Alienation of live organs for transplantation may also be regarded as a matter of personal choice or taste, rather than a choice of human or moral significance, to be respected by forbearance from interference so long as others are not harmed. Overall, free trade and the rationalism it engenders towards bodily values and valuations would undermine our self-realization as human persons.

Metaphysical notions like the "lived body" have also been advanced to support the last claim. As presented by Leder (1999), the lived body directs us to appreciate the integral connection between personhood and body. This stands in contrast to the view of the body as a thing-machine, which (arguably) may be inferred from Cartesian thinking on mind–body dualism, and which "resonates with and supports the sort of body appropriate to capitalism" (*ibid.*: 243). According to Leder (*ibid.*: 261), "the body was from the start a gift [as a natural endowment] of which one was but a recipient, and over which one can never claim full ownership ... it is a gift renewed [i.e. through interactions with the physical and social world] from moment to moment". The Cartesian/capitalist paradigm thus conceals or obscures the phenomenology of human experiences "which emphasizes continuity between the self and body, world and other people" (*ibid.*: 255). Voluntary donation, which expresses the "rich moral and affective resonances of the gift [as intentional acts]" (*ibid.*: 258), affirms our interdependence. The lived body, and the cultural script of the gift, offers a moral psychology in the tradition of virtue ethics thinking that orients individuals towards the good life, which gives us reasons to prohibit trade in human body parts.

Some counterpoints can be raised. First is the familiar objection that price is not the same as value, nor does it sum up the total value of a thing. Importantly, "market prices are the result of our differences in how we value goods" (Gaus 2009: 89). Hannah may sell a live kidney to build a better life for her family, while recognizing the disvalue of loss of bodily integrity. Jack may buy a kidney for transplant into a dying friend, with the friend being grateful for what Jack has done. Non-use and market-inalienable values such as life, health, moral character and friendship remain part of the range of human values that drive exchange. Personal choice is respected so that individuals can act on their values in the order they prefer.

In addition, while our natural/physical and socio-historical interdependence should be duly appreciated, normatively speaking, market interaction and reciprocity may still be the better way to promote human flourishing. According to the "doux commerce" thesis, free trade is morally civilizing because it drives us to be responsive and adjust to each other's wants (R. Gordon 2000). In mutual use and free exchange, we engage each other as agents and subjects and learn that respect for the worth of other persons and their bodies is central to the personal satisfaction of each and all. It is this sort of respect that brings us to cooperate with one another and allows us to form communities of our choosing. As Schmidtz (2006: 151) writes, "The liberal ideal is free association, not atomic isolation." Free trade does not mean that people cannot continue to donate their body parts as gifts. What may and would probably happen in a free market is a proliferation of arrangements which allow people to engage in bilateral or unilateral transfers of their body parts based on their own interests, which need not be self-interested. One may therefore maintain that our engagement with self, body, others and human values would better be realized by allowing free trade in human body parts.

Reasoning that human degradation necessarily follows from free trade in body parts is surely contestable. Nevertheless, empirically speaking, people might come to treat their bodies or treat others' bodies in morally problematic objectifying ways through a market in body parts. This is especially so when buyers and sellers are strangers and market interactions are non-repeated and non-direct. Consider Scheper-Hughes's account of an organ buyer in the international black market:

> As [he] explained his frantic and dangerous search for a living kidney donor: "I chose the better way. I was able to see my donor [in a small town in Eastern Europe]. My doctor pointed him out to me. He was young, strong, healthy – everything that I was hoping for!" Here, the symbolic equations between kidney market, slave market and brothel come to the surface.
>
> *(Scheper-Hughes 2003: 214)*

There are of course competing accounts of transactions in the black market. An American kidney buyer was reported to correspond regularly with her South African seller, and "though hardly wealthy herself, says she intends to send cash gifts each Christmas and on his birthday" (Rohter 2006: 182).

As Radin (1996: 40) admits, there is no "bright line" between personhood and objectification – a pluralistic idea itself with notions like instrumentality, subjectivity, and so on – nor between market alienability and market inalienability. The patients who founded or helped to found PXE have been described as "subjects who took charge of their own destiny … they flouted the norms of property doctrine to self-consciously construct a distinct form of property in the human body by means of contract" (Rao 2007: 378). The proper scope and form of the market is always contestable, and can only be decided on a case-by-case basis by assessing its effects, including the consequences of market rhetoric such as price and property, on its varied participants (buyers, sellers and intermediaries) and also non-participants. The bottom line is whether a market promotes flourishing personalities. Those who follow Radin's pragmatic stance may argue for the "incomplete commodification" of body parts which permit market alienation in controlled ways.

Human dignity

The normative presupposition of the European Convention on Human Rights and Biomedicine is that the use of the human body and parts for financial gain or "a comparable advantage" in the context of transplantation (Council of Europe 2002) violates human dignity. Despite being propounded as a universal norm, human dignity is often criticized for being confused and imprecise as to what common value(s) it protects other than personal autonomy, which "evokes the image of a person in charge of his life, not just following his desires but choosing which of his desires to follow" (Waldron 2005a: 307) and which can be protected by "voluntary, informed consent … and the need to avoid discrimination and abusive practices" (Macklin 2003: 1419). Such requirements would not be absent in or incompatible with systems for people to trade their body parts should it be legalized. Trade in human body parts, even in a free and internationally open market, is still governed by the criminal, property, contract and regulatory laws of a given jurisdiction.

Human dignity need not be just about personal autonomy. Within Western philosophical discourse, it is often related to Kantian thinking which regards dignity as "an unconditional and incomparable worth" (Kant [1785] 1964, Hill 1980). According to Kant, human beings or persons have this worth because of a rational capacity to set values and ends, which in turn forms the basis of their moral autonomy: that is, the will as both legislator and subject of moral law. Moral autonomy endows persons with dignity, and makes them categorically different from things valued only instrumentally, obtainable or controllable for a price.

Although Kant ([1797] 1996: 177) did object to sale of body parts (even hair) because of probable conflict between motivation for sale and ethical duties to oneself, it is contentious what juridical laws Kantian dignity would prescribe for the treatment of body parts in their different states (separated, non-separated, healthy, diseased, etc.), in light of their utility in saving or improving human lives, and when their originators are dead and devoid of autonomy, moral and personal. With the claim that Kant's central concern is with the alienation of body parts integral to the normal functioning of persons as embodied rational-moral agents, Munzer (1994) argues that the sale of a body part offends Kantian dignity when done for a reason that is not proportionate to the nature of the part sold, as a person who sells a live kidney to buy an iPad may be morally charged;[8] Kantian dignity can provide only a qualified and "uneasy" case rather than a categorical objection against trade in human body parts.

Human dignity may also denote "embodied personhood" which emphasizes respect as a different mode of response to the human body than promoting its values (although at times respect requires us to promote its values). Unlike other material things or resources, the human body, in signalling or being constitutive of human personality itself, has a distinctive moral status or value such that, to quote Pettit (1993: 303), "institutions should be shaped to honour the value even if this means, as a result of various side-effects, that there is less of the value overall". The notion of the embodied person thus differs from the lived body in pointing out reasons for action involving the body that are non-teleological, that is, independent of promoting or maximizing the good.[9]

Consider this example. Dickenson (2005, 2007) discusses the case of an Australian bio-technology firm, Autogen, which announced an agreement with the Tongan Ministry of Health to collect human tissue samples from its population for the purpose of genomic research into the causes of diabetes, which is high in incidence among the Tongans. Autogen promised a range of lucrative benefits, such as royalties to the Tongan government from any drugs developed and their free provision to the Tongan people. The Tongan community objected to the agreement because consent procedures failed to reflect familial sensibilities towards the material, and most of the promised benefits were in no way secure.

However, even if these two issues were resolved, it seems that the Tongan community would ultimately reject participation. Dickenson (2007: 167) quotes the Director of the Tonga Human Rights and Democracy Movement:

> The Tongan people in general still find it inconceivable that some person or Company or Government can own property rights over a human person's body or parts thereof ... the human person should not be treated as a commodity, as something that can be exchanged for another, but always as a gift from the Creator.

Dickenson (*ibid.*) argues that "to dismiss [their objections] as incorrect – because no individual human being is owned or exchanged as a commodity by a DNA bank – is to miss the point". As she points out, the Tongans regard human tissues, even when separated from the body or converted into a bodily product, as *tapu* (sacrosanct) because they retain elements of the human person. For the Tongans, to accept the offer would be to violate "'ngeia o te tangata' ... 'the dignity of the human being' derived from the Creator" (*ibid.*).

Social justice

Opposition against commoditizing body parts as health resources may be based on the conviction of the importance of the liberal social justice perspective for shaping the basic structures of society to ensure human welfare. This objection is targeted at the organizational effects of the commodity form: the channelling of productive activities towards profit maximization and the transformation of "previously or potentially common resources (raw materials and final products) into private resources" in which economic criteria such as consumption power become the norm in determining their allocation (Frow 1995: 137). The "total" effects of the commodity form on every sphere of human life and cooperation threatens the principal concern of social justice: equality in distribution of positive freedom understood as effective power to pursue one's ends by having access to essential goods, in this case critical health resources. Titmuss's arguments for a social policy for blood, which he labelled as "the gift relationship" (Titmuss 1970), are aligned with such a concern; his defence of voluntary unpaid blood donation is at the same time a defence of British universal healthcare in his time (Tutton 2009: 53).

The gift relationship points to the idea of community to maintain health goods as a collective resource. Community-building looks to positive morality: moral beliefs, values and attitudes actually held in a given society. For the system to have moral authority and support, its rationale needs to build from and connect to existing ways of life which individuals appropriate or may appropriate for personal identity and agency. Deeply rooted beliefs in the human significance of some biological material, attitudes against body parts sale as a "taboo trade-off",[10] valued expressions of a "true, free will" in charitable acts to benefit others, and so on, count against reliance on responsiveness to market price to achieve sufficiency in supply. Instead they are elements for integrating individuals as a community that encourages voluntary donation. For Titmuss, the measure of success for social policy is not the extent to which it effects qualitative changes to human relations that are valuable per se but "by the degree to which individuals are persuaded to make unilateral transfers in the interests of some larger group or community" (cited in Plant 1977).

The effectiveness of such persuasion depends on rules (organizing the gift relationship) that individuals in general can endorse as just in constraining their private pursuits. Regulated in certain ways, a community of donors, in Titmuss's view, is at the same time a political representation of a civic fellowship between "free and equal individuals" (Titmuss 1970: 242–43). Structured by the rules of anonymity and non-directed transfer, the institution of voluntary community donation, for blood or for deceased organs, allows these resources to be redistributed according to need as a principle of justice rather than on private interests or affinities as in the market or certain charity causes. In this way, the system protects a host of negative freedoms, such as freedom from contracts of exchange to receive organs, which promotes positive freedom. Altruism (in individual choices of beneficence) and social justice (embedded in equitable rules of allocation that reasonably benefit all, including the economically disadvantaged) are therefore interlinked in the choice and justification of community donation over a private market.

That the gift framework tracks positive morality and the value order of social justice liberalism will give ammunition to some against the universalization of its principles or rules across societies to achieve policy goals like adequate supply of organs. Furthermore, ability to pay (including by foreign patients), and to some extent patients' socio-economic status, are determinants of allocation of "pooled" organs and tissues in some transplant services, their non-profit-driven operation notwithstanding. Nevertheless, Titmuss's moral criticism of the commodity form, at least as regards the transfer of therapeutic bodily material, remains illuminating. Driven by competitive private exchange, the market inevitably limits social inclusiveness in participation in giving and distribution.

Indeed, those who look to the Iranian market as a beacon of good policy should be aware of its workings and qualifications to the claim of eliminating the waiting list (A. Griffin 2007). Living unrelated kidney donors are mainly the impoverished or unemployed attracted to the fixed compensation amount and one-year free healthcare provided by the government, on top of the additional payment which they can negotiate with patients in meetings arranged by a non-profit agency. Bargaining between citizens is thus part of the Iranian regulated market. Naturally, patients who can pay the market price and beyond have an advantage in obtaining a kidney. Despite government subsidies and help from charities with costs, many patients are placed on the waiting list for *deceased* kidneys because they cannot compete in the live market, which has reportedly undermined participation in deceased and unpaid related live donation. The poorest in the country, particularly those from rural areas, are not included in any list because they lack access to diagnosis and treatment including dialysis.

Organ donation: self-sufficiency and exploitation

Social justice rationalism underpins the Declaration's exhortation of the principle of self-sufficiency, which was endorsed in the Madrid Resolution on Organ Donation and

Transplantation in a global consultation guided by the principles of the World Health Organization (2011b). The Declaration states:

> Jurisdictions, countries and regions should strive to achieve self-sufficiency in organ donation by providing a sufficient number of organs for residents in need from within the country or regional cooperation.
>
> (a) Collaboration between countries is not inconsistent with national self-sufficiency as long as the collaboration protects the vulnerable, promotes equality between donor and recipient populations, and does not violate these principles;
>
> (b) treatment of patients from outside the country or jurisdiction is only acceptable if it does not undermine a country's ability to provide transplant services for its own population.
>
> *(Participants in the International Summit on Transplant Tourism and Organ Trafficking 2008: 3376)*

The central strategy to achieve self-sufficiency is to maximize deceased donor transplantation, complemented by measures such as primary health interventions to prevent diseases that contribute to the need for transplantation, thus managing demand. The aim of promoting self-sufficiency is to minimize reliance on living donors (however small their risks, probability-wise) and, importantly, to combat exploitation of the poor and the vulnerable. Evaluation of the wrongness of exploitation here goes beyond the specifics of a transaction judged by some metric of fairness on the terms of exchange between parties A and B to a concern with national social structures and the global order that bring the parties to the transaction.[11] So while an organ market may be Pareto-efficient, that is, it results in both A and B being better off without making anyone worse off, its dependence on socially unjust resource distribution and structural deprivation of options to B to attain a baseline of welfare for transactions to continue provide sufficient moral force, from this evaluative standpoint, for blocking the market. Certainly, there is concerted effort by countries around the world, including "hotspots" for organ trafficking and transplant tourism, to abide by the principle of self-sufficiency and to eradicate the international trade in organs and tissues (World Health Organization 2011c).

Radcliffe-Richards (2010: 300) suggests, however, that opposition to live organ markets is just a visceral response, rooted in repulsion at the thought that it is probably "a desperate, last-ditch attempt [for sellers] to find the essentials of life".[12] However, prohibition of such markets can be rationally justified as ethically "strategic": certain extra-transactional circumstances such as inability to satisfy basic needs are regarded as not just exploitative but coercive (in the sense of effecting unjust compulsion of the will) so that society maintains a responsibility to foster socio-economic conditions that rectify those inabilities (Holm 2010). The WHO Guiding Principles and the Declaration's stance on the provision of care and insurance for live donors seem to follow such a view. Taking into account the reality that countries in which organ trading thrives are those lacking universal healthcare, the documents state that the provision must be related to the donation event, otherwise resources basic to health and well-being might be used as exchange items for the body parts of people unable to afford those resources otherwise. According to the World Health Organization (2010: 5), "access to the highest attainable standard of health is a fundamental right", and is therefore a good prior to and independent of exchange offers.

There are various counterviews, which can be combined into a systematic rebuttal. The first is based on scepticism of political commitment to address unjust social arrangements. As

Veatch (2003: 32) writes, "If we are a society that deliberately and systematically turns its back on the poor, we must confess our indifference to the poor and lift the prohibition on the one means [i.e. organ trading] they have to address their problems themselves." In short, permission for individual exchange should be unlocked by collective moral neglect. The second appeals to existing practices: people are allowed to participate in (globalized) markets for risky labour such as construction work.[13] While there may be significant differences in the risks and nature of the act between selling labour and body parts (especially non-regenerative parts like a live kidney), what matters to individuals under systemic, unjust social conditions is whether a choice of transaction would improve their lives. The third takes a comparative approach towards justice, the point of which is to elevate human welfare, and asks whether a given policy would realize the positive freedom of the disadvantaged more so than current policies and life options.[14] The option of a one-off sale of an organ may provide a better opportunity range than mere (poor paying) labour options for a substantial part of one's life. Building on this point, the fourth counterview turns to the power of human design. Combined with existing systems like universal healthcare, a market can be designed so as mitigate or eliminate objectionable aspects of the commodity form for body parts. Consider Erin and Harris's (2003) proposal for a strictly regulated market in live organs and tissue which operates only on the supply side:

- Limit the location of the market to a self-governing geopolitical area, such as a state or the EU, in which only citizens residing in that area can become sellers.
- Establish a central purchasing agency (such as the NHS) which would (a) set a reasonably high price to attract enough people to participate voluntarily, and (b) allocate organs fairly on the basis of relevant medical criteria.
- Impose strict rules and penalties to prevent abuse.

The authors describe their market as ethical because it would maximize supply while meeting standard objections to organ trading by incorporating the above controls. Although the majority of donors are expected to be the poor or the financially desperate, this trading proposal may be further justified by a "maximim" principle of distribution: the benefits of the market are distributed in a way that is to the greatest advantage of the worst off in society.[15] Besides receiving a high price for their organs, donors would also be "rewarded" with increased chances for themselves or relatives to receive transplantation if in need. Thus a regulated organ market may "equalize" up rather than down for society as a whole when compared to existing social structures and foreseeable developments, including for patients lacking access to the essential good of an organ for transplantation.

One wonders whether this proposed market, with its focus on maximizing supply, would in actual practice be confined to a jurisdiction (note that the authors do not suggest any controls on managing the rate and site of demand), and whether rules to prevent abuse would be efficiently enforced: the stricter the controls on donation geographical-, rule- and price-wise, the lesser the supply. The lesser or the more relaxed the controls, the higher we can expect supply but also the greater the risk for harmful outcomes. Implementation issues aside, the Nuffield Council on Bioethics report *Human Bodies: Donation for Medicine and Research* provides another reason to resist the market: "any encouragement of people to come forward as organ donors for essentially financial reasons … could undermine other countries' attempts to put a stop to unregulated and illegal organ sales", which would negatively affect the welfare of donors and patients in those countries (2011b: 173).

Property and liability rules

The rule of private property

As a legal and social institution, property refers to rules for governing control of things as resources, which arranges for their allocation and distribution at the same time. As market systems and thinking permeate economies and societies around the globe, jurisprudential analyses of property ownership have focused on the issue of the justification of private property (Waldron 2012). Private property arranges for particular agents to be the decisional authority over some resource; they have the final say on what to do with it in open-ended ways that are not necessarily sensitive to the public good (*ibid*.). As a standard "full" owner, one has the rights to possess, use, manage, alienate and derive income from the resource. The rights are often transferred to others, or fragmented among various agents (persons, groups, corporations) in complex ways to enable the pursuit of private goals. According to Gaus (2012), "property is so important to the rights of the moderns because it allows each a jurisdiction in which his values and ends hold sway and so minimizes appeal to collective choices among those who disagree on the ends of life" (*ibid*.: 107), and that the "fragmentation of property [is] a fact about the modern world … [as] an inevitable result of a system in which people are free to form bundles according to their own choosing" (*ibid*.: 100).

Body parts as private property

The legal status of the human body and parts in property terms has been described as "unsettled and reflects no consistent philosophy or approach" (Rao 2000: 415). Such ascriptions reflect the piecemeal approach of judge-made or common law in resolving contesting claims to separated body parts or cadavers using the rule of property ownership. Owing to the uncertainty of judge-made law, and in light of the controversies like *Moore v Regents of the University of California* and the UK-retained organs scandal,[16] legal theorists have argued for the implementation of a property regime to regulate separated body parts (from the living or the dead) that would better protect the rights and interests of their originators than a mere consent regime. For example, it would entitle patients to seek compensation for non-consensual use of their tissue samples in research without having to prove that harm has been caused by negligence in informed consent, which may be a difficult task. Accordingly, property and consent rules "should operate in tandem to ensure full and proper respect for individual rights" (Mason & Laurie 2001: 727).

Such arguments assume that an appropriate bundle of property rights that balance public and private interests can be constructed for different types of body parts as material resources, but do not make the stronger claim that the bundles should contain fairly unqualified rights R1 to the capital, that is, the power to alienate by sale, to license use, and so on, and R2 to the income. To justify why persons should have these rights for every part of their body, including those still within, some commentators such as Steiner (2002) argue that bodily freedom is or can be similar to decisional control over external material resources that is marked out and enforceable by the rule of private property. The notion of self-ownership has been invoked as support; in so far as the body is self-owned, bodily freedom and rights presuppose R1 and R2.[17] The self-ownership argument has been criticized for conflating body ownership (what is "naturally mine" as an essential attribute of being a person) with private property ownership as a specific arrangement socially preferred over other cooperative rules (e.g. common property) for governing control over what could be scarce and essential resources (J. W. Harris 1996).

Others argue that bodily rights can be mapped on to all the rights or "incidents" of full liberal property ownership,[18] and that some of these incidents are already recognized in law (e.g. possession and exclusion of others to use), and therefore the social construction of the human body and its parts as private tradable property (henceforth, property) is philosophically and legally coherent and practicable (Quigley 2007). According to Alexandra George (2004), such arguments for the body as property seem misplaced or unnecessary. They seem misplaced because property is the *consequence* and not the cause of law to conclude that individual ownership entitlements over some body part include R1 and R2. The designation of a body part as property follows rather than precedes an analysis of the implications of permitting or recognizing those rights to that body part in a given social context. Consider a social environment in which many people are saddled with debts (such as university students) and they have no assets of great value. If live kidneys are properties, then creditors would have right of execution over a person's live kidney for non-payment of debt and to sell it off for transplantation use. Thus, as Rao (2000: 455–56) writes, "Separate ownership of a body part within a living human being is at odds with the principle of personal autonomy because it affords one individual pervasive power over the body of another, while divided ownership of a person undermines individual equality."

Property seems unnecessary because other legal rules can be implemented to protect individuals' entitlement to benefits from others' use of their body parts that do not have or limit the socially unhealthy implications of "propertizing" the body, and in a way that is economically fair and reasonable. Harrison (2002) suggests the implementation of a liability rule in which tissue contributors (not necessarily donors) are entitled to receive compensation determined by some objective, non-market mechanism *if* significant commercial profits have been derived from research using their tissue. According to Harrison (*ibid.*: 99), this rule "could be applied uniformly to … the full range of tissues collected in hospitals anywhere in the world". A liability rule differs from a property rule in that the holder's entitlement to compensation is not based on his subjective valuation and ability to bargain.[19] A private, commercial market in human tissue between individual tissue contributors, researchers and companies or universities would therefore not develop under a liability rule for use of human tissue in research.

Among its advantages, a liability rule avoids "a tragedy of anti-commons" that may be created if human tissue is treated as property: the enduring underuse of tissue in research when compared with a social optimum.[20] The "tragedy" might occur for various reasons such as high transaction costs for all parties; diverse and conflicting individual interests in use of a tissue collection among different tissue owners, and between the tissue owners and companies and universities which seek to be patent owners; and rejection of reasonable offers for their tissue by their sources which may be based on a cognitive bias of overvaluing their property: most people do not have valuable "rare" genes or disorders like John Moore. The medical stakes are high when one considers the potential public good of biobanks: large-scale collections of samples from a patient cohort and/or public donors linking genotypic and phenotypic information to facilitate a population-based approach for investigating common human diseases such as cancer and the effectiveness of current interventions, among other functions. A property rule for human tissue may undermine the development of biobanks, particularly the establishment of *de novo* ones, and the progress of biomedical research in general (Bovenberg 2004).

Sceptical that a property rule for human tissue would result in their suboptimal transfer and use, and taking account of the increasing emergence of arrangements between tissue sources and the research community akin to PXE International's, Gitter (2004) proposes a hybrid property/liability model. Under the property component, tissue donors would be entitled to invoke R1, R2 and other property rights in their tissue samples when they negotiate in advance mutually beneficial agreements with researchers on use of their tissue. For those who had not negotiated in advance, they can bring an action for conversion against anyone who conducted research with their samples without their consent, with compensation conditional on and proportionate to the value of commercial products developed or to the revenue generated. Gitter (*ibid.*: 340) claims that her hybrid approach would "create an incentive for individuals to participate in research, compensate them equitably for their contribution, and also enable them to make decisions that will foster the availability and affordability of diagnostic and therapeutic biomedical products to other consumers".

Alternative models for donation of tissue for research

Based on a qualitative study with families of children with cancer to find out their views on donating their child's diseased tissue samples for research, Dixon-Woods *et al.* (2008: 144) state that their findings "argue for caution in introducing property rights for individuals as a means for securing 'fairness', since those in our study seemed to feel that their participation in tissue banking (whether seeking or giving consent) was founded in the 'fairness' of the community". Thus they warn of "the dangers in treating examples of litigation (which often concerns unusual and extreme cases, and are few and far between) as evidence of more general attitudes and of introducing 'solutions' [property rights] that are ill-suited to the problems that they aim to solve" (*ibid.*: 135). And on these cases, Dickenson (2007: 139) argues that "when tissue donors file legal actions for the right to capital or income, it is often because they have no other option. What Moore really wanted was acknowledgment that his tissue had been taken fraudulently; his action in conversion was merely the most plausible legal means to that end".

There are of course many individuals in the world who would want control over their biological material and information such that they can prevent or claim compensation for what they regard as mismanagement (e.g. their use in personally morally objectionable research), and to gain some private benefits from their donation while desiring that the utility of their biological material and information be optimized for the good of others. The charitable trust, as proposed by Winickoff and Winickoff (2003),[21] presents a cooperative arrangement that accommodates and governs such plural interests. Compared with the vague notion of "stewardship", the charitable trust is a more accountable and transparent model with rights legally divided between tissue donors and biobanks to benefit a designated class of persons (Dickenson 2007: 138). In a charitable trust, individuals would formally transfer their property interest in their tissue samples to the trust. A trustee would be collectively appointed by the donors, which have legal fiduciary duties to use and manage the property to benefit a designated third party, which could well be the public at large. Applications for permission to do research on the collection would be evaluated by the trustees to ensure that the production and circulation of benefits align with the charitable purpose. The terms of the trust agreement could be set to allow donors to enjoy a share in resultant profits, or to appoint representatives on the board of trustees or a donor advisory committee that would assess the public value of research proposals. "Democratic control" is thus part of the benefits in participating in charitable trusts.

The view that the human genome – and by extension human tissue and cells – constitute mankind's common heritage or resource has been used to support the case for benefiting people whose tissue is used in genetic research even when there is no legal obligation or general ethical obligation to provide these benefits. "Benefits", however, are to circulate in a community-oriented way, rather than directly to tissue contributors in the form of personal profit. Models such as benefits-sharing or "tissue-tax" (as suggested by Bovenberg 2009) are premised on such views. In line with the advancement of the "fair benefits framework" in international research involving resource-poor countries (Participants in the 2001 Conference on Ethical Aspects of Research in Developing Countries 2004), the benefits-sharing model directs researchers, institutions and companies to initiate the provision of benefits, such as access to medical care or capacity-building, to the community or society from which the tissue samples are collected.[22] The tissue tax model proposes that a special tax should be levied on profits made on patents and products developed from tissue and cell research, which could be designated to subsidize or provide healthcare insurance for those in society who cannot otherwise afford it, among its possible social uses.

Each model has its challenges and criticisms.[23] For example, funding for a charitable trust may be an issue and while partnerships with the private sector can be made to sustain the trust, conflicts over use of the tissue collection may occur. Nevertheless, charitable trust, benefit sharing and tissue tax are applicable at the transnational level, and can work alongside each other. Taking into account "the history of 'scientific-imperialism' and 'biocolonialism'" between developed and developing countries, Emerson *et al.* (2011: 4) propose a tissue trust/benefits-sharing model to facilitate access to human tissues for advancing global health whereby "the trust becomes an investment tool used to build up local capacity [in the developing country], so that eventually research may be conducted locally and exportation of tissues can be reduced".

Body futures?

We have discussed both the ethical and the legal aspects of the debate over trade in human body parts. We hope to have shown that the issues are extremely complex, and that simplistic solutions to the dilemmas and uncertainties, whether in terms of advocacy for a free market or for a pure gift relationship, are unlikely to be adequate. We predict that the debate over trade in human body parts will intensify, as demand for organs, tissues and cells continues to grow exponentially. Some well-travelled grounds will be retrodden. Titmuss (1970) compared the British system of collective blood provision to the then US mixed system to argue for the superiority of the former on both economic and ethical grounds. Similarly, as regards the use of human tissue and related information in biomedical research, sides have been and will be continue to be taken on why "biocommons" like the UK Biobank should or should not be preferred over commercializable property arrangements developing in the US, such as PXE International. The reality is that we live in an era when "tissue economies" have become global and ever more profitable. Waldby and Mitchell (2006: 7) spell out the stakes: the "proliferation of tissue fragments, and of medical and social technologies for their sourcing, storage and distribution, has profound implications for health and embodiment, for civil identity and social order, and for delineating relations between the global and the local".

As medicine becomes ever more globalized and seen as a tradeable asset to gain leverage in the world economy, the moral contours of organ transplantation will become blurred, or maybe wholly obscured. Already, transplant ethics committees face the unenviable task of judging facts and information about potential donors and recipients, and stories presented by them, with an understanding that the cost of non-approval would be (significant) financial loss to the hospital and in likelihood a human life. As health providers from different countries join together to create transplantation hubs that attract patients (who bring their own donors) from over the world, the claim that altruistic-directed living unrelated organ donation is a legal fiction (Epstein & Danovitch 2009) will certainly gain greater force. For example, should an employer and employee donor-recipient pair from another country ever be approved?

In the more distant future, the controversies stirred by organ transplantation may well be abated and perhaps become largely a matter of historical interest. Breakthroughs in regenerative medicine, tissue engineering and synthetic biology therapies will greatly ease the pressure on the supply side. Implantation of synthetic windpipes and corneas has taken place, and researchers are working on the development of synthetic organs with more complex structures and functions like kidneys (Gravitz 2010). This renal product is expected to deliver most of the health benefits of its human biological analogue, with an advantage of freeing patients from a lifelong regimen of taking immunosuppressive drugs.[24] Should it become affordable to the mass public (within developed countries at least), then the choice between a synthetic kidney and a human kidney for transplantation might be likened to a choice between processed food and organic food for consumption. With the qualities of replaceability and potential customizability and upgradability, synthetic organs might even be promoted as the superior choice as life is pursued as what Scheper-Hughes (2003: 206) calls the "ultimate commodity fetish". With the ascendancy of transhumanism, cyborg and enhancement philosophies, such a view would find its adherents and advocates. Opponents of trade in human organs and other body parts would have to revise or strengthen their position accordingly.

Yet, even if such technological solutions are found to the current dilemmas over trade in body parts, the fundamental issues will remain unresolved. Deeper moral questions have been raised by the controversies over organ trading and the rapid escalation of the tissue economy. Is the human body yet another "natural resource" to be exploited for maximum profit, with safeguards of some kind to prevent the excesses of the logic of markets? Or should we see our bodies as so closely allied to our identity as persons that all intrusions by the market ideology are inherently hazardous morally? Is medicine really just another form of business, albeit gaining respectability by making strong claims to be ethical (Freidson 1970)? Or do we see medicine and health care as essential aspects of our commitment to human solidarity, our willingness to help others irrespective of personal advantage? As worldwide resistance to the more ruthless forms of capitalism appears to be growing, perhaps we might expect a future in which medicine rediscovers its moral purpose. Time alone will tell.

Notes

1 The term "human organ" as defined by NOTA covers human tissue including foetal tissue and bone marrow.
2 One such incident occurred in Germany. See Lenk and Beier (2012).
3 Some cases involved the Human Genome Diversity Project and the Hagahai people of Papua New Guinea. See Halbert (2005) and Hirsch and Strathern (2006).
4 For a sociological account of PXE International, see Waldby and Mitchell (2006: 153–59).
5 Conflicts between relatives of potential deceased donors and those working in organ procurement are not uncommon.
6 For a criticism of the hypocrisy charge, see A. V. Campbell (2009: 44–45).
7 For an in-depth discussion of law's treatment of property, see Clarke and Kohler (2005).
8 A teenager in China sold a kidney to buy Apple products. See Patience (2011).
9 Such an approach would be based on deontological reasoning. See Gaus (2001).
10 Tetlock (2003) has shown experimentally that a significant percentage of people who regard organ trading as taboo and morally objectionable would qualify their opposition when convinced that such transactions are the only way to save lives that would otherwise been lost through organ shortages, and that the poor and vulnerable would be adequately protected.
11 Wertheimer (2007) argues that exploitation is different from justice and should be seen as "transaction-specific".
12 In an earlier paper with other authors, Radcliffe-Richards make a similar claim that arguments against organ trading are typically driven by "feelings of repugnance among the rich and healthy". See Radcliffe-Richards et al. (1998).
13 A proponent of such an argument is Savulescu (2003).
14 This point is inspired by Amartya Sen's views on justice. See Sen (2009).

15 Ballantyne (2010) argues for the application of the maximim principle in the context of international research.

16 The controversy concerned the non-consensual removal and retention of organs and tissue, including children's, following post-mortem examination in various hospitals and medical schools across England from 1988 to 1995.

17 For a concise discussion on the self-ownership argument, see Gaus (2009: 79–80).

18 For an enumeration and discussion of each of the incidents in the notion of full liberal ownership, see Honoré (1961).

19 The distinction between liability and property rules was made by Calabresi and Melamed (1972).

20 To read more about the anti-commons theory, see Heller (1998).

21 For further discussion on the application of the charitable trust model, see Winickoff and Neumann (2005).

22 The HUGO Ethics Committee (2000) recommends that entities that profit from genetic research should dedicate a percentage of their annual net profit to healthcare infrastructure or humanitarian efforts.

23 For a good summary of the criticisms, see Bovenberg (2009).

24 Because of their genetic make-up, some transplant recipients can stop taking immunosuppressive drugs after a while. In the latest transplantation tolerance research, clinical trials are taking place to create chimeric immune systems (which combine both donor and recipient cells) in recipients so that the majority of such patients can eventually be weaned off these drugs even if they receive mismatched and unrelated organs. See Leventhal *et al.* (2012).

25

REPRODUCTIVE RIGHTS AND REPRODUCTIVE TECHNOLOGIES

Hille Haker

From the twentieth century up to the present, questions concerning human reproduction emerged as one of the major battlefields of moral reasoning. Reproductive technologies (RT) are usually considered to embrace the "modern" technologies concerning reproduction emerging since the second half of the twentieth century, particularly assisted reproductive technologies (ART) and genetic tests applied to early forms of human life (pre-implantation and prenatal diagnosis). I will, however, start the discussion of RT as emerging from the context of birth control based on the assumption that, first, the "quantitative" control of reproduction is one important historical context of RT, and second, the ethical claim of reproductive autonomy embraces both birth control and RT. It might now be tempting to divide the global landscape into those parts of the world where couples – or states – try to establish efficient systems of birth control, and other parts of the world where individuals or couples, sometimes funded by their national healthcare systems, are medically assisted in procreating; while in this picture one part of the world is eager to control the *quantity* of children who are born, the other part is eager to assist couples who wish for a child of their own and at the same time to control the *quality* of the offspring. The concepts of "developing" and "developed" world could then serve as the dividing line between the quantitative and qualitative approach, and both would be addressed in the claim of reproductive rights. But this division conceals the fact that even if "development" is still a category of international politics,[1] it is not constrained to geographical or political borders; rather, birth control and ART exist alongside each other in almost any country, and individuals may find themselves invested in both avoidance and assistance of reproduction over the course of their lives.

Evidently, poverty, lack of education, poor healthcare and gender inequality are increased by lack of access to birth control, and the major changes of adults' biographies in those milieus where a decent standard of life, education, access to healthcare, and gender equality are available may serve as indications for the higher demand of ART. Technologies play a crucial role in both scenarios: the introduction of chemical contraceptives has or may have a major impact on the reproductive freedom of billions of people, and the introduction of assisted reproductive technologies as well as the development of genetic tests applicable in early stages of human development address infertility and/or inherited diseases. From a technological perspective, the newer developments of reproductive technologies are just one further step of scientific progress, helping couples and, moreover, women either to avoid pregnancies or to establish them at a time of their life that they themselves may choose. Science and technologies are thereby considered as instrumental to *individual and social values*, reflecting and increasing the freedom of individuals and at the same time serving the public good.[2] For political ethics, access to contraceptives is considered one of the central means of national or global policies to control population growth. Access to birth control can be considered as one field in which *social* policies aimed at raising especially women's standard of living, and *ecological* policies aimed at reducing population growth while securing energy sources that at the same time decrease the effects of climate change, intersect. In the emerging debate on the interrelation of population control and social as well as climate policies, the perspective of the "public good" may easily result in trumping the individual reproductive freedom rights of those women who are most vulnerable to such policies.

In bioethics, however, human reproduction has so far predominantly been presented as a question of women's reproductive freedom and autonomy, claiming the right not to be hindered in one's own choices, whether to avoid or to seek procreation: a right that must be granted by the social and political institutions dealing with human reproduction and family policies. The negative formulation of this right is commonly shared by most ethicists. The positive formulation – the right to medical and/or social *assistance* in matters of reproduction – is contested; it requires justifying the scope and limit of the right.[3] Apart from the normative question of reproductive rights, both birth control and RT must be seen in the context of the personal and social *value* of human procreation. Questions of (individual and social) values are primarily examined in anthropological and sociological studies, but they also need to be reflected in a hermeneutical ethics.[4] Although the globally diverse contexts of social and cultural interpretations certainly shape the *empirical* discourse of RT, the relation between empirical studies, hermeneutical ethics, and normative ethics is far from clear.[5] Studies in cultural anthropology show, for example, that the conceptual understandings of kinship, the family, parenthood or personhood are "embedded" in diverse traditions of *interpretation*; that these interpretations and traditions need to be addressed in ethical analyses, too, together with their implicit or explicit normative claims, is not contested; what is contested is the status of social values and social norms with respect to moral norms.

In the Western context, the two major hermeneutical frameworks which are relevant for an ethics of reproductive rights and reproductive technologies are, first, parenthood as a "gift of love" and second, parenthood as a "choice of a life-form".[6] Rather than resting with the descriptive analysis of these interpretations that emerge in social practices, hermeneutical ethics examines the ethical implications of the conceptual understandings and relates them to the normative argumentation of ethics; here, the validity of the claims will be scrutinized in view of established normative standards, such as the human rights framework.

Looking at concepts of reproduction from the point of view of kinship relationships only may easily result in indifference towards socio-economic frameworks underlying the understanding of reproduction: for many families who have no financial or other "life" insurance, having children is the only way to ensure they will be looked after in phases of dependence, either through illness or through age. Rather than emphasizing individual freedom rights, reproductive rights concern the socio-economic rights to a "decent" life, sustained by family planning rather than by political–legal institutions. If reproduction is constrained without replacing the social security of families by appropriate state systems, the results are catastrophic for the most vulnerable population: not (only) because an abstract freedom right is violated but (also) because the normative constraints of families are overlooked.

Even though bioethics did not address global justice issues for a long time, reproduction is one of the most important practices in which individual rights, social values and norms, and socio-political frameworks are negotiated. In the following, I will take a closer look at different practices of reproductive technologies, and end with some thoughts about the future of reproductive rights and global ethics.

The emergence of reproductive technologies

Birth control as context of reproductive technologies

The development of chemical contraceptives in the 1950s and 1960s paved the way to major social changes in reproduction: for the first time in history, heterosexuality could be practised without immediate concerns about pregnancy. With this change, family planning became part of almost every (heterosexual) adult's biographical planning (see Giddens 1992, Beck-Gernsheim 2002). Access to contraceptives is a condition for the reproductive freedom of men and women alike: birth control enables women and men to live the life they choose with respect to procreation, and this freedom right may well be the main factor for their own flourishing. Although some religions or denominations (such as the Catholic Church) link sexuality and reproduction on *moral* grounds, interpreting the conception of a child as the ultimate expression of the love bond between a married couple (Congregation of the Doctrine of Faith 2008), the separation of sexuality and reproduction was broadly welcomed by the end of the twentieth century, first as sexual liberation in Western societies and then as part of international policies aimed at improving life and health conditions of women. In countries, regions or social communities with patriarchal social structures, denial of reproductive rights is often the result of a lack of overall social rights for women, such as access to healthcare and education; in these contexts, women are therefore often caught in structures of lifelong dependence on their families (Nussbaum 2000, World Bank 2012). By the end of the twentieth century, international efforts like the United Nations Millennium Development Goals had therefore identified these social structures, together with poverty and lack of access to healthcare, as main factors that block or inhibit the realization of women's rights, which clearly go beyond freedom rights, also addressing the overall social and economic rights (R. T. Cook 1993). In sum, birth control is considered an *individual's* right that must not be denied by states.

But even in countries where women have access to contraceptives, there is still a vast number of unintentional pregnancies (Santelli *et al.* 2003).[7] In the newer human/women's rights tradition, *abortion* is therefore considered as part of women's reproductive rights. Abortions require medical facilities in order to be performed without major health risks for women, and medication abortions can be performed at a very early stage of pregnancy or before a pregnancy is established without doubt. However, since abortion in its different kinds is not provided for in all countries *and* is also contested by several groups on moral grounds, it has stirred an ongoing debate that has not left the struggle for reproductive rights unaffected. As a result, birth control framed the ethical debate on RT long before it was introduced as a measure of assisted reproduction. First, it has started the debate on the concept of reproductive autonomy and freedom, particularly as part of women's rights, now including the social and economic rights to well-being. Second, especially with the turn to abortion as part of the reproductive rights of women, it has reinforced the debate on the moral status of human embryos.

While these debates focus, above all, on individuals' rights and responsibilities, birth control has also led to a re-interpretation of population control since the second half of the twentieth century (Mosher 2008, Connelly 2010). International policies of population control, too, emerge as quantitative and as qualitative measures: the quantitative approach is certainly on the agenda of numerous states, and until recently it was also an explicit goal of global development policies; today, it is a legal practice, for example, in the Chinese state's so-called one-child policy. Population-based birth control is echoed in some *qualitative* approaches to birth control

that apply RT, and they are tightly connected to the new social norm of "responsible reproduction", which I will address below: in several countries, mandatory genetic tests are required
before marriage by either state or religious authorities – this is the case in some Arab countries,
Iran, and Cyprus, who has established genetic carrier screening programmes – or couples are
encouraged to participate in voluntary programmes to diagnose, for example, monogenetic
disorders such as sickle cell anaemia, beta thalassemia or Tay–Sachs disease (Zlotogora 2009).
These programmes combine the modern measures of (individual) birth control with the availability
of genetic tests. Furthermore, in some countries, such as India and China, abortion is also subject to
social norms rather than the object of individual autonomy: sex-selective abortions are carried out
for social or economic reasons, with legal institutions passively accepting these practices or actively
supporting them. Interpreting these practices only as the result of *individual* reproductive autonomy
and choice ignores these contexts and the force of social norms that shape and potentially constrain
the freedom they declare to promote. Hence, individualistic theories of human action have little to
say about the interrelation of social contexts and individual actions. Complementing the normative,
universalistic dimension of ethics, hermeneutical ethics interprets exactly this interaction of social
norms and imageries and individual values and life concepts.[8] I will show at the end of the chapter
why this metaethical debate matters for a global ethics.

Assisted reproductive technology and pre-implantation genetic diagnosis

Like birth control, ART increase the scope of action for those individuals or couples who wish to
have a child but need medical services in order to realize their wishes. Traditionally, couples who
could not reproduce sought to raise a child via adoption. Since the second half of the twentieth
century, international adoption has become more and more regulated in order to protect children's rights, but when there is a the tendency to provide individuals or couples with a child
rather than to provide children with a social family, this becomes a problem, because parental
interests and children's rights may clash.[9] Since the introduction of ART in the late 1970s,
reproductive technology has become an alternative service for those who cannot procreate via
sexual intercourse. In cases where hormonal therapy or insemination is not successful, couples are
offered *in vitro* fertilization (IVF): the fertilization of ova and *in vitro* development of embryos,
before transferring some or all of these to a woman's womb. It is estimated that in the first forty
years of assisted reproduction, five million children were born via IVF (European Society of
Human Reproduction 2012). Couples often need more than one treatment over the period of
several years before a pregnancy is established and before they can "take home" a child;
furthermore, it is estimated that on average about thirty embryos are created for every child born
(Bergart 2000).[10] Many factors add to the success rate, which is usually stated as 25–30 per cent
per cycle, depending on several factors such as the number of transferred embryos, maternal age or
medical history. As a second standard procedure, intra-cystoplasmatic sperm injection (ICSI), was
developed and first introduced in the early 1990s in cases of male infertility. In addition to these,
treatments that involve sperm and/or oocyte donation are an option in cases where infertility
renders the use of a couple's own gametes impossible; although sperm donation is widely
accepted at least under certain conditions, oocyte donation is more contested because of the
related health risks for the donors, such as ovarian hyperstimulation syndrome (see Joint Society of
Obstetricians and Gynaecologists of Canada–Canadian Fertility and Andrology Society Clinical
Practice Guidelines Committee 2011). Mainly because of these risks, oocyte donation is either
prohibited or strictly regulated in several countries, while in other countries financial incentives
have created an oocyte donation market that transforms the "donation" of human tissue into a
commercialized good (see Dickenson 2002).[11] In case a woman cannot become pregnant herself,

surrogate motherhood is possible in some countries, using the gametes of the future parents or, if this is not possible, donor gametes. The result of these different techniques of reproduction is a multiplied or "split parenthood": in addition to its social parents, a child may have different kinds of biological parents: (a) a genetic father and genetic mother who are identical with the social parents, (b) a sperm donor as genetic father plus the genetic/social mother, (c) an egg donor as genetic mother plus the biological/social father, (d) a gestational "surrogate" mother plus the genetic/biological mother and father, (e) both male and female donors as genetic father and genetic mother who are not identical with the social parents; and (f) male and female donors plus surrogate mothers plus heterosexual or homosexual couples, or single parents.

From the beginning of the development of ART, questions concerning the future children's health were raised. Embryos are, for example, examined morphologically before being transferred to the woman's womb, and usually, pregnant women are monitored closely. With the development of genetic diagnosis and genetic tests, however, the possibility to detect health risks before birth led to the introduction of prenatal diagnosis as a measure of pregnancy monitoring: since IVF clients were offered prenatal diagnosis, too, it became a question of time before genetic testing of embryos before implantation was offered to this group. By the turn of the century, pre-implantation genetic diagnosis (PGD) was introduced as part of ART, but then broadened to those couples who can conceive sexually but carry the risk of transmitting monogenetic diseases identifiable via genetic tests.[12] In the next step, PGD for individuals was broadened to pre-implantation genetic screenings (PGS), aimed at the detection of chromosomal disorders that often result in early miscarriages.[13] With the combination PGD or PGS, assisted reproduction goes beyond a treatment of infertility or involuntary childlessness; rather, it has become a method to select from a number of embryos one or two embryos for transferral to a woman's womb. In recent decades, the application of PGD has been steadily broadened, although each step has been followed by public debates: while in the beginning the future health of an embryo was used as the criterion for PGD, it is now performed as carrier screening to identify children who will not be affected by a particular disease themselves but carry the risk of transmitting the genetic trait to their own offspring; PGD is performed to select embryos whose DNA match with a sibling who needs it for his/her own medical treatment; PGD is performed to select the sex of an embryo for "social" reasons (in other words, to accord with parental wishes – or economic needs – to either have a girl or a boy); and, although controversially, it is performed to choose a particular genetic profile, such as deafness. The twenty-first century's discourse on reproduction will most certainly embrace yet another step in the technological evolution, namely the question of pre-implantation genetic modification or so-called "germ line therapies" to eradicate particular genetic traits. Furthermore, enhancement is promoted by some bioethicists as part of reproductive autonomy; also, reproductive cloning is not objected to by all bioethicists (see J. Harris 2007). All these applications are feasible as future technological possibilities but are banned internationally on moral grounds. Considering this development it is evident that the parental and medical concern for a child's future health as justification for PGD has – to say the least – been complemented, if not replaced by the paradigm of a medically assisted parental choice of the kind of child they want to have. Therefore, the ethical analysis cannot only address the implications of the technologies step by step, but rather, it needs to attend to both the hermeneutical framework and the normative questions.

The ethics of RT

Assisted reproduction and genetic diagnosis or screening of embryos raise multiple ethical questions which have been studied in myriad books and articles. The re-interpretation of parenthood as reproductive autonomy and choice serves, however, as a hermeneutical-ethical framework, which also shapes the way in which normative questions are addressed.

The re-interpretation of parenthood: reproductive autonomy and the concept of choice

It is hard to underestimate the new freedom that has accompanied the technological development in the area of reproduction, especially for those couples who otherwise could not or did not dare to have children of their own; that some of the new constellations of parenthood applying RT are closer to the traditional concept of adoption than to the traditional concept of biological parenthood, is, however, striking because ART was introduced as a means to have *biologically* related offspring. Given the variety of family constellations that I have indicated above, the new forms of bio-social parenthood seem to resonate, however, with studies from cultural anthropology that have recently re-interpreted the overall concept of kinship relations.[14] The new concepts made possible by ART are especially visible (and contested) in the case of same-sex parenthood where donation and, in the case of male parents, surrogacy is required. While many (Western) societies still debate whether same-sex marriage should be legalized and same sex-adoption is (still) controversial, ART has become a rather common practice for same-sex couples who wish to procreate. And indeed: if reproductive freedom is a right and kinship is a bio-social concept anyway, it is hard to see why same-sex couples should be denied a technology that is offered to others under otherwise equal conditions.

The social changes have been analysed descriptively and/or empirically but they also need to be critically examined in their normative implications (see Franklin 1997, D. S. Davis 2001, Beck-Gernsheim 2002). RT are particularly critiqued in the name of (the Foucauldian concept of) "biopower", assuming that in an age of biotechnology and "biopolitics", power does not function as domination but rather as a self-disciplining force constituting the social institutions or practices via bodily and embodied practices of (self-)surveillance, constraining freedom rather than increasing it (Foucault 1978, Inhorn 2007). Other approaches, mostly from a "liberal" philosophical perspective, emphasize, however, that the freedom of "choice" is the central concept underlying reproductive autonomy. In their by now famous book *From Chance to Choice* (2000), Buchanan and colleagues emphasize that from a liberal ethics perspective, the meaning of parent–child relations should rather be framed according to the framework of "chosen relationships" than according to a framework of "chance" or "givenness".[15] While the "traditional" IVF of ICSI treatment may not be a problem in this respect, the parental choice to pass on a *multiplied* biological heritage to the child is, however, not unproblematic if considered from the child's perspective (see O. O'Neill 2000a).[16] An ethics of parenthood must attend to these questions, because family constellations following ART demand a more reflective approach.

Reproductive freedom and/or rights are inevitably entwined with *social* expectations and norms, as with moral responsibilities – the question is how these can be identified and ultimately justified. New social and ethical expectations arise, for example, when infertile couples are advised by their families, friends or doctors to seek ART; after all, in many countries, women's biographies are socially shaped by the ideal of motherhood.[17] *Responsibility*, however, becomes the key *social* concept with respect to genetic diagnosis as part of the parental care for their child: as prenatal genetic diagnosis and pre-implantation genetic diagnosis enable couples (or individuals) to avoid giving birth to children with particular genetic traits or chromosomal disorders, future parents are expected to seek the necessary (genetic) information about their future child in order to make "responsible" *qualitative* reproductive choices based upon information and knowledge.[18] From the perspective of a critical ethics, the shift from the emphasis on (and celebration of) the newly gained reproductive freedom to new social norms of repro-ductive responsibilities is a particular concern, not the least because it is hard to see how a newly defined "voluntary eugenics" can be avoided. Apart from the complex history of eugenics that rarely only functioned as coercive eugenics but rather implemented exactly the same language of parental responsibility that liberal and utilitarian bioethics does, the choices of genetic traits, based on judgements of quality of life, may violate future children's rights to an "open future", as Jürgen Habermas argues; evidently, they are also prone to discriminatory judgements of disabilities (Habermas 2001b, Landsman 2008, Haker 2011). It is therefore necessary to clarify what the paradigm of choice means with respect to RT.

Normative ethics of RT: the limits of reproductive freedom

The debate on the scope and limits of parental freedom and responsibilities, that is, their right (or duties) to determine what kind of kinship relations should be allowed and on what conditions embryos may be tested and selected, over against the protection of human embryos and future children, has become a major field of ethical analysis and debate. Medical ethicists have argued that in applying ART and PGD or PGS, they act in accordance with traditional ethical principles, namely the physician's obligation to care for the patient (*neminem laedere*), the obligation not to harm the patient (*primum non nocere*), or to seek a patient's health as primary concern of their actions (*salus aegroti suprema lex*). These traditional principles are complemented by the modern ethical principle to respect the freedom right of their patient, and the political–ethical principle of justice[19] – but it is not exactly clear *whose* rights must be protected and/or respected in ART and PGD, and what exactly a reproductive justice framework must entail.

In claiming moral rights to be respected by others, a person must have reasons other than "mere" interests or desires, and she must reciprocally respect the rights of others. The Human Rights Declarations state the right of any human being to be protected against violent and/or discriminatory actions; they condemn practices that restrict the individual's freedom without justification, and the justification must not override a person's integrity and autonomy, which is sometimes expressed in the concept of human dignity and freedom. In the case of RT, several specific human rights treaties have been ratified or are in the process of being ratified, and they shape the normative framework of the political–ethical deliberation; the most prominent treaties are the Universal Declaration on the Human Genome and Human Rights and the Council of Europe's Convention of Human Rights and Biomedicine. From this perspective, I will shortly address three areas of concern: (a) women's health risk through RT, (b) the protection of human embryos, and (c) future children's health. A fourth area addresses (d) the difficulties of establishing a coherent framework of reproductive justice in an age of a reproductive consumer market.

Women's health risks

For women, several health risks associated with RT need to be considered: ovarian hyper-stimulation syndrome occurs in a minority of cases, while minor side-effects of hormone sti-mulation are more common but seem to have no long-term effects (Joint Society of Obstetricians and Gynaecologists of Canada–Canadian Fertility and Andrology Society Clinical Practice Guidelines Committee 2011); severe physical and psychological health risks may occur during pregnancy, mainly caused by multiples pregnancies, caesareans, premature births, or childbirth complications; additional psychological risks concern so-called foetus reduction, that is, abortions in multiple pregnancies. In contrast to the expectations raised in the early phases of IVF, the success rate of the so-called baby-take-home per cycle does not extend beyond 25–30 per cent, so the process of assisted reproduction may take several years, resulting in considerable lifestyle monitoring and psychological stress for the persons involved. In bioethics, the psychological effects on couples who fail to give birth has not gained much attention. With respect to male infertility or subfertility, IVF raises another ethical question, namely whether a woman's health and well-being may be put at risk in order to treat the reproductive condition of another person, usually her partner or husband. The same question needs to be answered with respect to oocyte donors and surrogate mothers whose health risks are often ignored in advertisements; in both cases, liberal ethics considers consent as a sufficient condition, but from a human rights perspective, the normative relation of autonomy (consent by contract) and the physician's obligation to care for the well-being of the patient is far from clear. The global RT market applies the rhetoric of choice and altruistic donation; however, this conceals the fact that in the vast majority of cases, donors exchange their sperms and eggs for money, or IVF couples respond to incentives to donate "spare" eggs or embryos, in order to reduce the costs of their ART treatment (see Widdows 2009). In order to protect the female donors' health and ban exploitative practices in the field of RT, international legislation and better control strategies for trafficking are still needed.[20]

The moral protection right of human embryos

With the possibility of IVF, human embryos are not only accessible outside a woman's womb but "pro-created" independent of sexual intercourse. As was already the case in the moral debate on abortion rights, the moral status of human embryos *in vitro* needs to be determined. Often, more embryos are fertilized than needed for one cycle. Depending on the legal regulations, some are selected and others discarded, many are frozen for future cycles, and so-called "surplus" embryos may be handed over to other couples or used for embryo research. Practically, human embryos are therefore treated radically differently from any other human being. Nevertheless, the human rights' treaties demand the protection of embryos' dignity, and hence include them as subjects of moral rights. In the ethical debate, several arguments have been brought forward to determine the moral status both in line with the human rights frameworks and the scientific knowledge of embryology: hence, the moral status has been linked to the Aristotelian concept of *potentiality* of the embryo to develop as (or into) a moral agent, to be distinguished from the mere *possibility* that in the process of fertilization a new human being may come to existence;[21] potentiality is linked to the individual *identity* that is established with a new genome, and to the *continuity* of a human being's life starting with fertilization. A more process-oriented argument refers to the *gradual* development of the fertilized egg into a human being, with different "qualitative leaps" in this development: some argue that nidation is more decisive than fertilization, others argue that a limited self-perception is the condition for moral protection, and still others argue that the decisive point for moral and legal protection is the day of birth, when the *public* legal and moral *recognition and right* of a person is established (Appiah 2010b, Joas 2011).[22]

Up to the present, there is no philosophical consensus on this central question of the starting point of moral protection. Yet, two apparently extreme claims seem to be weakly argued: on the one hand, the *personhood claim* does not distinguish the moral status of an embryo from the status of any "other" person, thereby ignoring the process of human development; and on the other hand, the *neutrality claim* does not distinguish an embryo from "other" somatic cells, thereby ignoring that human embryos are not only possible but potential future children. It may therefore be helpful to remember that human embryos are not entities or "beings" that exist without a context; even an embryo's existential right is relative to a woman's *capability* to respond to it, and, particularly under the conditions of ART, also relative to her *decision* to become pregnant at all. Hence, embryo protection must not be isolated from this relational, ultimately procreative context; quite to the contrary, the (prospective) gestational mother carries the weight to respond to the existential needs of an embryo, which under the human rights framework are generally translated into specific rights.[23] This view may render several of the practices of ART – especially surrogacy, but also the fertilization of oocytes outside of the context of procreation – ethically problematic; but I cannot see how human embryo protection, as it is claimed in the bioethical normative frameworks, can be otherwise maintained. Considered as a relational right, it also respects the particular position of the "mother" as first addressee of a claim that an embryo cannot yet articulate for him/herself.[24]

Rights of children

With respect to reproductive technologies, *children's rights* concern, first of all, their well-being, second, their freedom, and third, their right to know their genetic heritage (United Nations 1990, Fuchs 2007). Though bioethical studies rarely address children's rights as such, medical studies consider the children's well-being as part of the quality control of ART. By now, several long-term studies have been published which show that children born after IVF or ICSI indeed show some developmental difficulties, but in most cases, these seem to be compensated around puberty (Hansen *et al.* 2005). Especially children born prematurely, however, mostly because of multiples pregnancies caused by ART, face more and considerable health and development risks. Surprisingly, the cases of so-called "wrongful life" have been much more debated within bioethics than health issues caused by assisted reproduction: wrongful life cases seem to prove that the quality of life may decrease below a threshold of a "good" life owing to genetic conditions, as argued by some children themselves (see Nussbaum 2006); these cases have been used to argue in favour of prospective parents' responsibility to determine their future child's genetic health status (or even "enhance" it genetically). Hence, a or couple may not only have the *freedom* but also the *duty* to refrain from having a *particular* child, and women may be at least strongly advised to terminate a pregnancy (see Buchanan *et al.* 2000). This claim, however, runs contra to *all* existing normative treaties concerning reproductive rights; in fact, it is a violation of women's freedom rights, embryos' basic protection rights, future children's welfare rights, and potentially even their future freedom rights (in the case of "enhancement"). In contrast to this conclusion about parental responsibilities, assisted reproduction practices carrying a greater risk for the future child's health themselves need to be studied more closely and communicated to the prospective parents. In particular, multiples pregnancies and births resulting from multiple embryo transfers should be avoided even if this will reduce the overall success rate of IVF. As mentioned above, another problem concerns a child's right to know their genetic and/or biological heritage: anonymous sperm or oocyte donations obviously violate this right. Donors, for example, often demand anonymity, or clinics do not want to store the data for several decades. Central databases are rarely established, with the effect that children who wish to claim their right to know their genetic parents fail to find the necessary data. In sum, from the ethical perspective of children's rights, RT does not yet provide a satisfying framework that grants children the rights they are guaranteed under the international ethical and legal frameworks, and in many countries throughout the globe, national legislation needs to be reframed in order to catch up with the more and more advanced reproductive technologies.

Reproductive justice

In recent years, reproductive justice has become an issue within bioethics, and it has even been argued that a radically new framework of reproductive justice is needed (see Galpern 2007). In bioethics debates, this is predominantly discussed as distributive justice, addressing access rights and the equal treatment of individuals or couples who seek ART. Different countries handle financial costs differently: some countries leave it to the private market, others consider ART as part of the healthcare service that is covered by insurances, and yet others have constrained IVF to an infertility treatment. Independent of national legislation, however, RT and reproductive services are offered on the global market, enabling those individuals or couples who can afford it to buy the treatment they want.[25] If, however, reproductive autonomy is not only a negative right but rather also a positive right to have access to RT, the addressee of this right needs to be determined. Bioethics therefore enters into yet another discussion, namely the debate on (global and national) healthcare justice and public healthcare. It is unclear how medical services for social reasons (as is the case with ART for same-sex couples but also for healthy couples risking passing on particular genetic traits) rather than infertility treatment can be solved without creating new injustices in other fields of public healthcare. Bioethicists therefore seem to be hesitant to claim reproductive rights as positive rights and rather accept the injustice of a private market solution.

However, the questions about justice do not only concern "access" and "compensation" rights. Rather, a reproductive justice theory needs to embrace the socio-economic impact of the "reproduction industry": by the beginning of the twenty-first century, reproductive services have developed into a consumer market, and the image of a physician helping couples or individuals in their desperate struggle to overcome childlessness conceals the fact that reproductive services contribute at least in part to a competitive market: reproductive services are offered in almost any country independent of their public basic healthcare services; genetic tests are developed and marketed at an ever-earlier stage of human development suggesting that the genetic make-up is the decisive factor for the future child's health; for the purpose of oocyte or sperm trading, concealed as "donation", gametes can be ordered via the internet and chosen from catalogues according to one's preferences; advertisements in US college students' magazines regularly look especially for young women whom they offer large sums as "compensation" for their services; surrogate mothers are paid to intentionally give birth to children they will never parent. Agencies systematically ignore the physical and psychological risks of these surrogates with the argument that consent to a contract justifies the exploitation of a person's body for the reproductive interests of another person. Reproductive services, including medication, clinical services and gamete trade, have an estimated annual value between $3 billion and $5 billion in the US alone; this market seeks its consumers who welcome the commercial offers addressing their alleged reproductive fears or desires.[26] Furthermore, RT companies advertise the quality of the genetic "material" they are selling, implying that their clients will want oocytes or sperms of "high genetic quality", but in fact the criteria for "good quality" are prone to genetic discrimination or even racism (D. Roberts 1997).[27]

All these practices are not private in the sense of the privacy of personal relations; rather they are private in the sense of the economic cooperation with interacting partners who exchange goods in the global market; neither the contribution of medical professionals who participate in these exchanges nor the ethical self-regulation of agencies can conceal the role of this consumer market for the shaping of the new concepts of parenthood.[28] Ultimately, societies need to discuss whether "chosen" kinship relations are to be interpreted in light of choices that favour instrumental relations, or in light of relations of recognition, in which parents choose to approve – and "adopt" – the children they create as moral subjects. *Moral* autonomy entails that we respect any human being as a subject of rights and therefore demands that we opt for the latter model – but it is not at all clear whether this view is shared in societies which seem to favour a concept of choice that was framed in the context of the early market capitalism and which today is applied to the global RT market.

Conclusion

RT have changed the overall possible constellations of parenthood and thereby increased the reproductive freedom for millions of people. A new concept of kinship relations as chosen relations emerged, resulting in a re-interpreted concept of parental responsibility. In one interpretation, it is claimed that prospective parents are responsible for the health risks of their offspring; in this view, "good" parenthood entails the use of ART and PGD. Others argue that the concept of reproductive rights needs to be interpreted in relation to other human rights and an overall framework of reproductive justice. In the view that I have taken here, first, reproductive rights concern women's health rights; second, they need to embrace the relational rights of *future children* (related to the gestational mothers and relative to their decision to become pregnant); and third, they need to embrace rights of children *in their future*, especially the right to well-being and freedom. Reproductive rights that attend to these other rights are one important element of a framework of reproductive justice, striving to provide any person a decent standard of living and the freedom to live, together with others, the life he or she chooses.

Looking at reproductive technologies in the broad understanding I have adopted in this essay, the tension between the two main concepts cannot be overlooked: while on the one hand the public, if not even the global, interest of population control becomes once more prominent in view of the necessary requirements of food, water and energy security, threatening the accomplishments of the twentieth-century struggle for reproductive rights; the global RT market, on the other hand, has contributed massively to an over-individualized interpretation of reproductive claim rights. Not only biomedicine but also bioethics has mainly been complicit in this interpretation of human reproduction, and has closed its eyes for a long time to the reality of a market-economy-driven over-determination of the practices. Translating desires into needs, needs into consumer choices, and choices into rights that cannot be denied, ART mirror exactly the dynamics of any consumer good, thereby obliterating the distinction between a good that may indeed be exchanged and also substituted, and a human person for whom this is exactly not the case. Individuals who have undergone ART treatment see the tension between their (certainly "authentic") desires[29] and the reductionist treatment inherent to ART. Given the positive response to the late-twentieth-century turn to "quality control" of offspring, it may well be the case that the coming decades will show new measures of genetic interventions, including germ line modifications, which are banned up to the present.

For an ethics that aims to function globally, reproductive rights are one, if not the most important means in the struggle against poverty. After a period of opposition, stirred and supported by several religious groups, birth control will most certainly reappear on the agenda of any international institution in the coming years. It remains to be seen whether the intersection of the social and ecological impasse will, for example, increase the pressure on the Catholic Church to change its powerful anti-birth control position. Still, ethicists will insist that reproductive rights are ultimately always individual rights, and even though one may disagree with particular decisions on moral grounds, the negative right must be maintained over against any political, religious or social argument. Unless women defend their negative reproductive freedom right globally, I expect these rights to come under new fire: it would not be the first time that political goals conceived as public goods have been used to trump the rights of individuals.

For women and families living in socially and economically insecure conditions, having multiple children is a "desperate" choice resulting from their social conditions rather than a "happy" and free choice; access to birth control without changing the social conditions not only will not suffice, it would be unethical. Likewise, practices of selective abortions, egg selling or surrogate pregnancies must be seen in the light of background structures creating exactly the atmosphere of indirect coercion that nineteenth-century critics of an exploitative market economy identified to contradict the moral vision of the public good. To respond to these challenges globally in order to secure individual rights, together with ameliorating structural injustice, will involve, among other thing, the re-interpretation of those social values that make women hostage to (reproductive) choices that others, men and women alike, make for them, disregarding their status as moral agents who must not become, in Kant's words, merely the means to someone else's ends.

The aforementioned dialectic between hermeneutical and normative ethics is crucial for overall ethical reflection sensitive to global affairs: human reproduction is not just a biological or medical fact; it is also the site for individual, social, cultural and ethical interpretation, and interpretations are as diverse as the contexts in which reproductive practices occur. For the majority of people, especially women who are denied a decent standard of living, children do not have the same function as for those who have the means to realize their desire for a child with the help of ART. For those who are dependent on bearing and raising children in order to survive poverty, both quantity (the number of children) and quality (children's health) matter; but both the number and the health of their offspring play a decisive role in their own basic well-being and are therefore interpreted differently than the wishes of the well-off consumers the RT market targets. For ethics, both contexts must be distinguished and, yet, they both must be addressed in a manner that does not simply play off the desires and rights of some against those of others.

One could certainly argue that the human rights framework that has been the normative premise of this essay has a "Western" touch in spite of its institutionalization in the United Nations to which almost all nation states belong as voting members. But even if one accepts the human rights framework, it cannot be denied that on practical terms it is mostly used rhetorically, leaving human rights violations the rule rather than the exception. The often raised suspicion around the appeal to human rights in the global ethics discourse is therefore understandable, even though a bad practice is never a sufficient reason for a wrong theory. Criticism of human rights is also prominent, however, within the discipline of bioethics; but as I have shown, in the discourse of reproductive ethics, rights are often spelled out as freedom rights, and freedom rights as rights to choose. Reproductive rights as human rights are, however, not to be defined in this overly reductionist interpretation; rather human rights are enabling rights to live a "good life, together with others, in just institutions", to repeat the famous phrase by Paul Ricoeur (1992: 172). Furthermore, the new emphasis on the "common good" or "public good", associated with a new emphasis on population control in recent years, is prone to override individual rights in the name of greater interests unless it takes individual rights as the limit of (political) intervention.

In sum, reproductive rights need, first, to be defended against social value traditions that have a long history of discriminating against women; second, they will need to be defended against policies indifferent to women's (and families') socio-economic status. And third, reproductive rights must be defended against a market model that interprets moral rights as consumer choices, and transforms human reproduction into one commodity among others. Since none of these three areas can be addressed locally or nationally, a global ethics needs to be further developed. Since reproductive technologies are one important site in which to spell out how this could be done, it remains to be seen whether the human rights framework is a strong enough normative foundation that is still sensitive enough to the ever-changing understandings of reproduction and kinship relationships.

Notes

1 Escobar (2012), but also the post-development approach (Rahnema & Bawtree 1997), criticize the concept of development as part of a colonial approach to countries that do not fit into the conceptual understanding of human flourishing and the "Western" normative order dividing the world into the "North" and "South".

2 Axel Honneth (2011) has recently presented a thorough analysis of freedom as the core value of (Western) modern societies.

3 Dan Brock (2005) gives a good survey of the discussion. For a thorough analysis of the moral dimensions of reproductive freedom see Buchanan *et al.* (2000).

4 I coin the "evaluative" tier of ethics as hermeneutical ethics because I believe that the *interpretation* of the ethical *meaning* of a practice is at stake here. However, different terms are used depending on the traditions one refers to; the methodological implications of the two tiers, i.e. hermeneutical and normative ethics, are thoroughly analysed, for example, by Krämer (1992), Ricoeur (1992) and Habermas (1994).

5 For a discussion of empirical, contextual or experiential ethics cf., for example: Musschenga (2005), De Vries and Gordijn (2009), M. Parker (2009), Appiah (2010a, 2010b), De Vries and van Leuen (2010).

6 Elsewhere, I have identified other hermeneutical concepts of parenthood, still based, however, upon "Western" contexts and philosophical concepts, namely the "natural law" concept that considers reproduction as the telos of sexuality; the "romantic" concept that is linked to reproductive autonomy as "authenticity"; the social freedom concept that links reproductive autonomy to a relational and social understanding of freedom; and the economic concept that links reproductive autonomy to market exchange relations. Hence, the concept of "gift" is closely linked to a teleology of sexuality represented in the natural law tradition while the concept of "choice" can be understood in line with either the romantic and/or authenticity concept, the social freedom concept or the economic-exchange concept. Cf. Haker (2013). Below, I will focus on the framing of parenthood in the context of reproductive autonomy, i.e. different interpretations of parental choices.

7 According to the US Centers for Disease Control and Prevention, for example, it is estimated that in 2006 roughly 50% of all pregnancies were unintentional, with higher figures in teens and other subgroups, especially low income and cohabitant. Cf. Santelli *et al.* (2003) for a thorough discussion.

8 Joas (2000), Mackenzie Stoljar (2000) and C. Taylor (2008) provide a critique of an individualistic interpretation of autonomy – this was also the object of the debate on liberalism and communitarianism of the 1990s.

9 Historically, however, the rise of children's rights is only a recent accomplishment, echoed in the Convention on the Rights of the Child of 1990 (United Nations 1990).

10 Only an estimated 50% of couples seeking ART succeed in having a child through ART. Cf. Bergant (2000), with more literature.

11 For example, oocyte donation is prohibited in Germany and Austria, whereas the European Union Tissue Directive prohibits only the trading of oocytes and sperms; in the US, oocyte "donation" is unregulated at the federal level but subject to state regulation and self-regulation via the medical association. Cf. from a feminist perspective Dickenson (2002).

12 Nevertheless, PGD is prohibited by law in several countries, or permitted only under strict conditions.

13 When PGS was introduced in the 1990s, there was hope to raise the success rate of IVF: but this was, to the surprise of many, not the case.

14 Analysing all major studies on kinship relations, beginning in the early twentieth century, Carsten shows convincingly that kinship always integrated social and biological ties, and even though blood relations are of primary concern in many countries, they do not make up for all kinship relations: cf. Carsten (2004). This finding is particularly interesting in view of the new developments in RT, which show an overall tendency to re-interpret the concept of the family. Cf. among many others Almond (2006), Austin (2009).

15 For a critical discussion cf. Habermas (2001b), Haker (2008).

16 O'Neill (2000a) raises these questions with view to the Kantian terms of perfect and imperfect obligations; comparing the (assumed) adopted children's and IVF children's perspective she states: "Children

can often look on their adoption as a result of the unforeseen or even unforeseeable misfortunes of their birth parents, and their adoptive parents may be seen as rescuing them from intolerable situations. It may be harder for children to see a *plan* to bring them into the world with a confused and ambiguous heritage and without contact with their genetic parents or gestational mother as amounting even to 'good enough' parenting" (*ibid.*: 43). This reaction is echoed in blogs by IVF children who demand to know their genetic and/or gestational parents.

17 Several studies have shown that the relationship between the ideal of individual choices and socially mediated standard biographies is more complicated than bioethical studies sometimes reflect; women especially may struggle with the social expectation to become mothers, and their desires may be complex even though they seek ART (Fränznick & Wieners 1996). The (social) imagery of the "natural" female desire for a child is contrasted by the growing number of women who deliberately choose not to have children. This does not question, of course, that many women (and men) suffer tremendously because they cannot conceive other than via ART.

18 This case is made by Buchanan *et al.* (2000), but also by utilitarian bioethics, such as John Harris or Julian Savulescu (Harris 2007, Savulescu & Kahane 2009). For a critical analysis cf. Andrew (2001).

19 For a "classical" argument for the combination of traditional medical ethical principles complemented by autonomy and justice cf. Beauchamp and Childress (2009).

20 Trafficking and commodification is banned by several UN conventions, as well as by the UN and EU bioethics treaties and EU Directives.

21 The view of possible personhood is held, in contrast to the human rights treaties, by John Harris or Julian Savulescu.

22 The UN Convention on the Rights of the Child (United Nations 1990) proves that changes in the social recognition of particular groups are ultimately echoed in the (international) rights systems; how these changes occur is more difficult to describe. For an interesting study on changes in moral attitudes towards "moral agency" and human rights cf. Appiah (2010b); for the idea of the "sacredness" of human beings as one important historical, albeit non-religious foundation of human rights cf. Joas (2011).

23 Philosophically, it is possible, of course, to contest either the human rights framework as relevant for moral reasoning, or the applicability of human rights to human embryos, or both. But as I said above, several human rights declarations relevant to reproductive technologies are already in place, and they are the result of international debates and negotiations. In addition to the specific declarations I quoted above, others also need to be considered: in the context of reproductive – namely women's – rights, children's rights, and rights of persons with disabilities serve *de facto* as the normative human rights framework.

24 Therefore, reproductive freedom turns into an ethical concept of reproductive autonomy that first and foremost needs to address the parents' responsible response to the *existential* right claim, which has priority over the health right. Even if an embryo may not be considered to have a right, parents are still *somehow* responsible for an embryo (or a number of embryos) who without their intervention would not have come to existence. This is why "split" parenthood is not only difficult socially but also ethically: morality requires that we identify moral agents as the subjects of responsibility.

25 Oocyte trafficking and surrogacy are especially of ethical concern and cannot be addressed by distributive justice only.

26 This highly naïve approach to capitalist economy is criticized by Donna Dickenson who shows how desires (and fears) are created for the consumers' market; cf. Dickenson (2009), Honneth (2011).

27 I have not addressed the discriminative potential of genetic testing with respect to disability. Cf. for a defence that individual eugenics is not discriminatory, Buchanan *et al.* (2000).

28 Axel Honneth shows how the social concept of family relations, constituted as emotional bonds over time, is thereby likely to be overridden by the socio-economic concept of market cooperation, constituted by reciprocal, yet instrumental relations. Cf. Honneth (2011).

29 Authentic desires are desires stemming from a person's self-conscious question about her choices regarding how to live, and live well. I put the term in quotation marks to underline that one does not need to question the agents' authenticity while acknowledging that it may have been influenced by multiple factors, not least of those the social value of a family, ideal biographies, and the social status of a parent. That this idealized imagery is often not upheld in the practice also does not change the authenticity of the desire.

26

PATENTS AND INTELLECTUAL PROPERTY RIGHTS

Roger Brownsword

Intellectual property rights (IPRs) operate across a broad spectrum of protected subject matter, including innovative products and processes, literary, creative and artistic works, trade secrets, trade marks, designs and images, and so on. The particular interest at issue might be one of being recognized as the originator of a work (in civilian legal systems, the so-called *droit d'auteur* is seen as an important moral right); however, in the Anglo-American tradition, the principal driver is the interest in controlling access to and use of the property so that its commercial value can be realized. In the marketplace, IPRs typically represent an asset having some cash value; and whether the claimant is a multinational pharmaceutical company or a celebrity in the music or film industry, IPRs matter.

Within the range of IPRs, it is patents and copyright that tend to be most frequently in the spotlight; and, not surprisingly, it is the breadth and depth of these particular IPRs that has attracted most discussion. Globally, the existing regime of copyright protection has been called into question by the serial violations of file-sharers. In the leading US Supreme Court case of *MGM Studios Inc v Grokster Ltd* (2005, 125 S.Ct 2764, (2005) 545 US 913), the evidence collected by MGM (the copyright holders) indicated that some 90 per cent of the files shared by using Grokster's software involved copyright-infringing material. As Justice Souter, delivering the Opinion of the Court, remarked, "[in view of the fact that] well over 100 million copies of the software in question are known to have been downloaded, and billions of files are shared across the … networks each month, the probable scope of copyright infringement is staggering" (545 US 913 (2005) at 923). In the face of such large-scale non-compliance, one of the regulatory challenges is to find ways of making the law more effective, that is to say, more fit for purpose. However, it is clear that, for many – particularly for those who are involved in such movements as the Open Source Initiative, the Creative Commons and copyleft – it is not so much the (in)effectiveness but the (il)legitimacy of copyright law that is the real issue (see e.g. Lessig 2001). Although much could be written about the global ethics of copyright, in this chapter, the focus will be on patents.

The chapter is in eight sections. I start with a thumbnail sketch of the way that patent law defines and then protects an "invention". In the next section, I outline the mainstream debate about patents, where views are polarized to the point that one is pressed to declare that one is either for or against patents. In recent years, the patentability of inventive work in biotechnology has been at the centre of this storm and this vexed question is the focus of the third section. In the following three sections, I try to disentangle the claim that patents are unethical *tout court* from the more nuanced claims that there should be more ethical regulation of (a) what is treated as patentable and (b) the scope and duration of patents. In the seventh section, a number of proposals for better and more equitable strategies to promote innovation are reviewed. Finally, in some short concluding remarks, the thread of the chapter is summarized. Broadly speaking, the thrust of it is that the shape and substance of IPRs, particularly patents, should track the public interest; that the public interest comprises both economic and ethical interests; and that, although there are many competing ethical views, there is a general commitment to respect for human rights. From this, it follows that, for patents to pass muster from a global ethical perspective, they must at least be compatible with the protection, preservation and promotion of human rights.

Patents: a thumbnail sketch

In general, patent law is designed to incentivize the development of (useful) innovative products and processes, and then to protect the interests of those who disclose the working of their inventions. So, for example, in the UK, section 1(1) of the Patents Act 1977 provides as follows:

> 1.(1) A patent may be granted only for an invention in respect of which the following conditions are satisfied, that is to say –
>   (a) the invention is new;
>   (b) it involves an inventive step;
>   (c) it is capable of industrial application;
>   (d) the grant of a patent for it is not excluded by subsections (2) and (3) or section 4A below; and references in this Act to a patentable invention shall be construed accordingly.

Briefly, the nature of the exclusions to which section 1(1)(d) refers is as follows. The exclusions in subsection (2) relate to: "(a) a discovery, scientific theory or mathematical method; (b) a literary, dramatic, musical or artistic work or any other aesthetic creation whatsoever; (c) a scheme, rule or method for performing a mental act, playing a game or doing business, or a program for a computer; [or] (d) the presentation of information"; and those in section 4A relate to the invention of "(a) a method of treatment of the human or animal body by surgery or therapy, or (b) a method of diagnosis practised on the human or animal body".

For present purposes, it is the exclusion in subsection (3) that is most significant. In this subsection, the Act provides that, even if the process or product is an invention (in the sense defined by section 1(1)), it will not be patentable where its commercial exploitation "would be contrary to public policy or morality". If we think that the grant of a patent might give rise to ethical concerns, this looks like the legal peg on which to hang such objections.

Once granted, the patent protects the commercial interests of its proprietor for (usually) a period of twenty years. In effect, the patent proprietor is put in the position of a monopolist for this period, during which time others will infringe the patent if they exploit the invention without an appropriate licence (and without due payment of royalties).

Patents: polarized views

On the face of it, regimes of patent law (if not of intellectual property law more generally)[1] are well intended, for the regulatory purpose of such regimes is to encourage both investment in the research and development of innovative processes and products as well as, crucially, the disclosure of the methods underlying the invention. If the inventor is to become a patent proprietor (and, concomitantly, a monopolist for a limited period), the nature of the invention must be taught.

Immediately, three points should be emphasized. First, as a particular (incentivizing) element of the regulatory environment, it surely cannot be right to view patent law (in the way that patent practitioners sometimes seem to see it) as an autonomous and largely technical body of rules (Brownsword 2008, Schneider 2009). Like any other regulatory intervention, patent law needs to be assessed for both the legitimacy and coherence of its purposes and its effectiveness in delivering them. Second, it is necessarily implicit in any patent regime that patents will be granted only where this is consistent with the public interest: it makes no regulatory sense to incentivize innovation that is contrary to the public interest. When patent lawyers say, as they frequently do, that the purpose of the patent system is to grant patents, this has to be interpreted as subject to the caveat that the grant is compatible with the public interest. Third, we need to be careful with remarks along the lines that patents are to compensate for investment in innovation. It bears labouring that disclosure is a necessary part of the deal: without putting the innovative knowledge into the public domain, there will be no patent; once patented, an invention can no longer be protected as a trade secret.

Despite these good intentions, patents attract, to put it mildly, mixed reviews. While some defend patents, arguing that without the monopoly incentive and protection against infringement there would be significantly less investment in innovation, others accuse patents of being counterproductive (hindering rather than supporting innovation) and, most seriously, denying millions of people in the developing world access to essential drugs. This is a familiar exchange which, if it were not so tragic, might seem almost tired: for example, how many times have we heard the accusation that "patents bar the way to essential drugs" being met with the response that "the vast majority of drugs on the WHO *Essential Medicines List*[2] are out of patent protection", or that, "when the infrastructure for health care is poor, patents on drugs make no difference one way or the other"? There is a sense that the debate is stuck, that there will be some pragmatic concessions to vulnerable agents in the developing world but that it is difficult to achieve more clarity on the merits of the rival arguments. Yet, for global ethicists, with access to healthcare as a matter of urgent concern (compare A. L. Taylor 2007), it is important to understand whether patents are part of the problem (whether patents and property are, without good moral reason, being put ahead of people: see e.g. Sterckx 2005) or whether they are the key to making technological progress in general and to improving therapeutic resources in particular (whether, without patents, the pharmaceutical companies would return to manufacturing dyes or, instead, focus on the cosmetics market).

When views about patents are so polarized, it is tempting to reduce the issue to the blunt question of whether one is for or against patents. However, this hardly does justice to the many questions that are implicated in the proposition that patents are unethical (for a helpful overview, see Helfer & Austin 2011: 90–170). In order to bring some of the issues and arguments more clearly into focus, we need to distinguish the following four claims: first, that patenting is unethical *tout court*; second, that patenting is not unethical in itself but there needs to be a more ethically sensitive control over what is treated as patentable; third, that patenting is not unethical in itself but there needs to be more ethically sensitive control over the scope and duration of patents; and, fourth, that the regulatory objectives of patent regimes could be more effectively (and ethically) realized if their monopolistic features were replaced by new institutional forms that incentivized innovation and benefit sharing (see e.g. Pogge 2005a).

It is also tempting, when debates about the global impact of patents are so familiar and well formed, to take our ethics (and our empirical findings) deep into those debates. Succumbing to that temptation, in the next section, we will consider a proposal made by Mary Warnock

(Warnock 1993) that looks as though it might resolve the ethical disputes that have erupted with the patenting of modern biotechnologies. However, we will find that there is no short cut. In the end, we need to go back to first principles. We need to determine whether our baseline principle is that agents (individual agents, agents within corporations, agents in government, *all agents*) do or do not have a root ethical responsibility to assist others. If they do have such a responsibility, then the patent regime should be designed to assist agents to discharge that responsibility; by contrast, if they do not have such a responsibility, if the only responsibility is not to harm others, then the incentives of the patent system are laid over what is morally optional: and this, of course, impacts on any assessment of the ethics of patents. Accordingly, as we respond to the four claims, we need to tease out how we might judge the root responsibilities of agents.

However, before we tackle these four claims, we can introduce the general question of whether it is ethically permissible to treat the products and processes of modern biotechnology as patentable subject matter. As we have said, it was in this context that Mary Warnock suggested a way of ordering our ethical criteria.

The ethics of patenting modern biotechnology

In the 1980s, applications to patent the processes and products associated with modern bio-technology began to present new questions for patent offices. The focal question was whether such inventions were patentable (that is, whether they were the kind of subject matter that might, in principle, be patented). In the United States, following the seminal Supreme Court decision in *Diamond v Chakrabarty* (1980), the US Patent Office (USPO) indicated that it would take a fairly liberal approach: mere discoveries were not patentable but pretty much any process or product that was inventive was eligible. Adopting this standard, by the end of the 1980s, the USPO had signalled that it was ready to grant a patent on a genetically engineered mouse, the famous Harvard Onco-mouse (an animal model for cancer research).

In Europe, the Harvard Onco-mouse application was seen as far more problematic. According to Article 53(a) of the European Patent Convention, patents were not to be granted on inventions where the commercial exploitation of the invention would be contrary to ordre public or morality. However, in the absence of a jurisprudence relating to this Article, it was unclear whose or which morality should be taken as guiding. In the early 1990s, speaking at a symposium at the European Patent Office, Mary Warnock offered the following advice:

> Technology has made all kinds of things possible that were impossible, or unimagin-able in an earlier age. Ought all these things to be carried into practice? This is the most general ethical question to be asked about genetic engineering, whether of plants, animals or humans. The question may itself take two forms: in the first place, we may ask whether the benefits promised by the practice are outweighed by its possible harms. This is an ethical question posed in strictly utilitarian form … It entails looking into the future, calculating probabilities, and of course evaluating outcomes. "Benefits" and "harm" are not self-evidently identifiable values. Secondly we may ask whether, even if the benefits of the practice seem to outweigh the dangers, it never-theless so outrages our sense of justice or of rights or of human decency that it should be prohibited whatever the advantages.
>
> *(Warnock 1993: 67)*

If we were to follow Warnock's advice (or proposal), we would start with a calculation of, on the one side, the prospective benefits and, on the other side, the possible harms (very much in line with a standard utilitarian approach). In the event that the harms outweigh the benefits, if the technology is simply too risky, then we should not proceed. If, by contrast, the calculation indicates a net benefit, then we ought to proceed provided that there is not some overriding consideration of justice, rights or human decency, or the like.

Arguably, Warnock's advice was followed in the examiners' handling of the Harvard Onco-mouse application, for they applied their understanding of a utilitarian calculation to conclude that there was no reason to categorically exclude the claims on moral grounds (for extended analysis, see Beyleveld & Brownsword 1993).[3] However, in the absence of any overriding considerations of justice, human rights, human decency, or the like, we do not know whether, or when, the examiners might have been prepared to set aside their utilitarian judgement that the mouse was patentable subject matter.

Irrespective of whether the examiners did or did not apply Warnock's approach, we might see this as a way of settling the differences between the rival camps that, on the one side, advocate and, on the other, oppose patents on modern biotechnology. Quite simply, adopting this kind of strategy, we would say that the advocates are right in pointing to the *general* utility of patent incentives but that the opponents are also right in highlighting the *particular* cases where our sense of justice, rights and decency is outraged. When the shoe pinches, we simply have to loosen it.

However, such a short way with the debate surely is too quick. If we are to apply Warnock's advice to the various patent questions that we have identified, it becomes critical to know quite how the proposed two-tier ethic works. For example, if we start with a utilitarian argument (as is the wont of those who defend the patent system) to offer a general justification for patenting, then we need to know whether the override applies only in extremis (only most exceptionally) or whether it has greater scope than this: not everyone's senses will be outraged at the same point. More fundamentally, not everyone will accept that this two-tier ethic is either coherent or appropriate. We need not grapple with the question of coherence (in general, on split-level ethics of this kind, see Frey 1985). Rather, suffice it to say that we cannot assume its general acceptance. Whereas some who start with utilitarian reasoning will stick with it, others will start with, say, human rights or human dignity (or human decency) and at no stage will they countenance utilitarianism (see e.g. Brownsword 2008: 31–69).

This suggests that, having replaced the question "patents, for or against?" with a series of more focused questions, we are probably going to find that the answers vary depending upon the particular ethical criteria that we employ. Moreover, as intimated in our earlier remarks, it is the ethical criteria that we employ in relation to the root responsibilities of agents that set the rival arguments off in a particular direction.

Is patenting unethical *tout court*?

Let us imagine a world without patents in which I invent the first sewing machine. My family uses the sewing machine at home and we give a few away as presents to friends. However, we have no intention to exploit the machine commercially and we do not do so. When we die, there has been no wider beneficial use of the sewing machine (let alone cross-border transfer of the technology) and the secret of the machine is buried with our bodies.

Now, let us contrast this with a scenario in which there is a patent regime, in which I again invent a sewing machine, but in which I now patent the machine and exploit it commercially. In this scenario, I die a wealthy man and the patented sewing machine is found in almost every home. If patenting is unethical *tout court*, there has to be something unethical about this latter scenario. But, to work out what we think about that, we need to focus on the former (no patent) scenario to assess whether there is anything unethical in my keeping the sewing machine largely to myself.

In the patentless scenario, there are three possible characterizations of my actions: namely, I act as ethically required, or as ethically permitted (but without also being required), or as ethically prohibited. Which is the correct characterization? From a number of ethical standpoints – for example, from a standpoint that is guided by utilitarian principles, or by the duty of beneficence,[4] or by a strong theory of positive rights[5] – it seems that I have not acted in accordance with ethical requirements, I have not done the right thing. On any of these views, I am ethically required to tell others about the sewing machine and to disclose its mechanism. However, there is at least one ethical standpoint that insists that I do no wrong by keeping the sewing machine to myself, my family and a few friends. This is a libertarian or negative rights view, according to which the critical point is that I have not directly harmed anyone else, or made anyone else worse off. The complaint of others is that I have not taken steps to make them better off; and we can grant that it would not have been burdensome to broadcast the existence of the sewing machine. Nevertheless, from a negative rights perspective, this cuts no ice. The question remains: provided that I do not harm others, why am I ethically required to do more? Even if my invention would be a life-saver for others, I am not required to disclose its existence or its mechanism (compare Nozick 1974: 181). To be sure, on the negative rights view, it is perfectly permissible to assist others. If I choose to tell others about the sewing machine, I do no wrong. However, this is merely a permission, an option, not a requirement.

If we could strike out the negative rights view, the analysis would be easier; but, without a full-scale defence of one of the rival positions we cannot reject it out of hand (for such a defence, see Brownsword 2010). Moreover, even if we could dismiss the negative rights ethic, the implications of the other views might not be identical when we consider what they entail for the adoption of a patent regime (as in the second scenario). To simplify the discussion somewhat, let us suppose that we are dealing with three classes of ethics as follows:

Class 1: the emphasis of ethics in this class is on assisting and benefiting others, particularly those who are most in need and who are unable to help themselves;
Class 2: this is the family of utilitarian ethics; and
Class 3: this is the class of ethics, epitomized by a libertarian or minimalist negative rights view, that holds that the only responsibility to others is not to harm them (not to make them worse off).

Given these three classes of ethics, let us suppose that we regard a patent regime as offering merely *prudential* reasons for innovation and disclosure (which is all that the reasons could be for class 3 ethics); the patent regime appeals to the self-interest of prospective and actual innovators, the incentive being that a limited monopoly is conferred in return for disclosure. In so far as patent regimes fit this description, the question is how such a prudentially geared institution looks relative to the ethical standpoints that we have already identified in relation to the first scenario.

Consider, first, those class 1 views, based either on the duty of beneficence or positive rights, that hold that there is a moral obligation to share the sewing machine with others. In an ideal world, agents should simply disclose their useful inventions, in the way that the European team that was working on the sequencing of the human genome put its research findings into the public domain at the earliest opportunity (thereby, *inter alia*, barring the way to prospective patent applicants). However, in a non-ideal world, the adoption of a patent regime might be a necessary stimulus. If those who invent useful objects fail in their moral responsibilities to others, the moral signal needs to be stronger (there needs to be some moral education); and, if this fails to change conduct, then something like the patent regime, with its appeal to prudential reason, might be a useful back-up. However, given this kind of ethics, it needs to be understood that there is some loss when agents do the right thing only because it advances their self-interest. Think, for example, about the analogous case of giving blood, in one case altruistically, and in the other case for financial reward (seminally, compare Titmuss 1970, Nuffield Council on Bioethics 2011b). Moreover, patent regimes are clearly becoming dysfunctional if "instead of being a reward for inventors who place private information into the public domain, [they] become a means of recycling public information as private monopolies" (Drahos & Braithwaite 2002: 165).

For class 2 ethicists, for utilitarians, the first of the sewing machine scenarios is a truly shocking case, a dreadful failure to maximize utility. There definitely needs to be a correction for this utility-failure. Whether a patent regime is the best option, it is hard to say. The fact that patent systems can allow massive utility to be captured by groups of large corporate interests at the expense of small businesses and starving millions is not necessarily an objection; for aggregating purposes, this might be the optimal arrangement. On the other hand, there might be alternatives that would generate even more net utility, but not necessarily involving any more equitable distribution of the benefits. Still, if it is a simple choice between scenario one and two, the utilitarian will argue for the latter.

This leaves class 3 ethics, according to which there is no ethical failure in the first scenario. If regulators wish to incentivize innovation and benefit sharing, the patent regime is one way of giving regulatees prudential reasons for acting this way – and this is fine. However, the proponents of negative rights will insist that we should never forget that, whatever consequences and costs are incurred by the patent regime, those who seek patent protection and who stand on their rights have no baseline ethical responsibility to be innovative or to disclose the workings of their inventions. If regulators want to encourage innovation and benefit sharing, that is all well and good, provided that they do not slip into thinking that they are giving agents reasons for acting on their *moral* responsibilities, and provided of course that the patent regime does not impinge on the negative rights of agents.

Before we proceed, two other matters call for short comment. First, in the patentless scenario, might it be argued that it would be ethically *prohibited* for me to tell others about my sewing machine? If this seems unlikely, what would we say if what I had invented was not a sewing machine but a letter bomb? On any of the ethical views canvassed so far, it is arguable that (barring some special context) broadcasting the existence and workings of the letter bomb would be unethical. Accordingly, a patent regime that incentivized disclosure of such inventions would be compounding the wrong. Or, to put this more generally, whatever the features of a patent regime, it would compromise its regulatory purpose if it encouraged invention and disclosure of processes and products that are clearly contrary to the public interest. We will return to this point in the next section. The second matter is whether, in the same patentless scenario, anyone would argue that, as the original inventor of the sewing machine, I have a right to be recognized as the originator or to prevent others (who find out about my invention) from copying it. While recognition of me as the originator might attract broad support, a preventive right – at any rate, in the one-off and localized context of the sewing machine – seems to be antithetical to most positions other than that of negative rights. However, even for a proponent of negative rights, it is not clear that exploitation of the invention by others necessarily harms me (compare Hollis & Pogge 2008: 64–66).

What does this analysis mean for the question of whether patenting is unethical *tout court*? Whereas, on one set of views, the *prudential* features of patent regimes operate to correct for *moral* failure, on another they try to steer agents towards a particular morally *optional* course of action. On none of these views does it seem to be the case that patents are categorically ethically offensive. Indeed, the worst that we can say, thus far, is that, from some ethical standpoints, it is a matter of regret that we need to have the prudential incentives of patenting to push innovators into doing the right thing. But, then, absent a community of saints, it is characteristic of the criminal law that there needs to be a repertoire of prudential signals to reinforce its moral signals; and, if we do not condemn the criminal code for the way in which it compensates for weakness of moral will, we should surely exercise the same restraint in relation to patent law.

Should there be a more ethically sensitive control over what is treated as patentable?

In the previous section, we noted that patent regimes should differentiate between sewing machines and letter bombs: that they should be sensitive to the public interest in determining what is and what is not patentable subject matter. As a matter of principle, we would expect the patent regime to be designed in such a way that (a) it excludes inventions that are contrary to the public interest, (b) it incentivizes inventions that are consistent with the public interest and, quite possibly, (c) it gives incentives-plus for inventions that meet urgent public needs.

In practice, patent regimes do not seem to exclude and incentivize in quite this way. Nevertheless, they have at their disposal a variety of controlling mechanisms. For example, control can be exercised to a certain extent through the interpretation and application of the standard requirements of novelty, inventiveness, utility, and so on, and use can be made of bespoke exclusions.[6] Controls can also be exercised through general exclusions of the kind contemplated by Article 27(2) of TRIPS, according to which:

> Members may exclude from patentability inventions, the prevention within their territory of the commercial exploitation of which is necessary to protect *ordre public* or morality, including to protect human, animal or plant life or health or to avoid serious prejudice to the environment, provided that such exclusion is not made merely because the exploitation is prohibited by their law.

The drafting of the main part of the Article is a bit gauche, but the intention is clear. By contrast, the proviso is clearly drafted but its intent is puzzling: or, at any rate, this is so if we follow the analysis in the text. To explain: if some kind of research and development (say, synthetic biology or nanofoods) is judged to be highly dangerous and of no utility, then it makes sense for regulators to prohibit such activity (including a prohibition on its downstream exploitation). Where there is such a prohibition, it would be irrational for regulators to encourage the activity by treating inventive work in the field as patentable. In other words, where there is a regulatory prohibition against such exploitation (where, as Article 27(2) puts it, "exploitation is prohibited by … law"), then this is at least a sufficient condition for exclusion from patentability. In a single jurisdiction, it makes no regulatory sense to prohibit x but, at the same time, to encourage x. In a more complex regional scheme, the position needs more analysis; we will turn to this shortly. However, the proviso in Article 27(2), by detaching the exclusions against patentability from background regulatory prohibitions, seems to perpetuate the idea that patent law has some freestanding role in the regulatory environment.

In Europe, there are two overlapping patent regimes, one pursuant to the European Patent Convention 1973 (the EPC), the other within the European Community (pursuant to

Directive 98/44/EC on the Legal Protection of Biotechnological Inventions). These regimes are unusual in embracing quite explicitly the TRIPS Article 27(2) option. So, in Article 6(1) of Directive 98/44/EC (and similarly in Article 53(a) of the EPC) we have a provision to the effect that "Inventions shall be considered unpatentable where their commercial exploitation would be contrary to *ordre public* or morality; however, exploitation shall not be deemed to be so contrary merely because it is prohibited by law or regulation."

In the Directive, Article 6(2) embellishes this by specifically excluding the following:

(a) processes for cloning human beings;
(b) processes for modifying the germ line genetic identity of human beings;
(c) uses of human embryos for industrial or commercial purposes;
(d) processes for modifying the genetic identity of animals which are likely to cause them suffering without any substantial medical benefit to man or animal, and also animals resulting from such processes.

In the wake of the Harvard Onco-mouse decision, the European Patent Office applied the moral exclusion with the lightest of touches;[7] at the same time, the European Court of Justice signalled in the *Netherlands* case[8] that it took a rather similar approach. However, in two recent decisions, much to the consternation of many patent practitioners, the world of European patenting has been turned on its head (see Plomer & Torremans 2009).

First, in the *Wisconsin Alumni Research Foundation* (the WARF) case,[9] the Enlarged Board of Appeal at the EPO was asked by the Technical Board of Appeal[10] to rule, *inter alia*, on the question of whether Article 6(2)(c), as incorporated in the EPC Rules, forbids the patenting of a human embryonic stem cell culture which, at the time of filing, could be prepared only by a method that necessarily involved the destruction of human embryos (even though the method in question is not part of the claim). The EBA held that this was precisely the exclusionary effect of Article 6(2)(c). Rejecting the argument that human embryos were not actually being used for commercial or industrial purposes, the EBA held that, where the method of producing the claimed product necessarily involved the destruction of human embryos, then such destruction was "an integral and essential part of the industrial or commercial exploitation of the claimed invention"[11] and, thus, the prohibition applied and precluded the patent.

Second, in a parallel development, the European Court of Justice has held, in *Brüstle v Greenpeace eV*,[12] that Article 6(2)(c) of the Directive excludes the patenting of inventions that involve the destruction of human embryos. In so ruling, the Court followed, without much elaboration, the much fuller (and equally controversial) Opinion written by Advocate General Bot.[13] In this Opinion, the Advocate General made it perfectly clear that he was all too aware of the many different views as to both the meaning of a human embryo and the degree to which ethics demands that such embryos should be protected. Nevertheless, he insisted that the legal position as settled by the Directive is plain. Within the terms of the Directive, the concept of a human embryo must be taken as applying from "the fertilisation stage to the initial toti-potent cells and to the entire ensuing process of the development and formation of the human body".[14] *In themselves*, isolated pluripotent stem cells would not fall within this definition of a human embryo (because they could not go on to form a whole human body). So, did it follow that the use of such cells in the inventive work in question (which involved the development of precursor cells for neural disorders such as Parkinson's disease) was unproblematic? The Advocate General held that it did not. Crucially, the history of these particular cells was tainted: they were isolated only at the cost of destroying the original human embryo, or, to put this another way, the research and invention amounted to "using human embryos as a simple base material".[15] In the light of the Court's adoption of the position staked out by the Advocate General, the European patent courts have expressed a very clear view that, at the regional level, they do not wish to give any encouragement to research (having commercial or industrial purposes) that involves the destruction of human embryos.

For present purposes, there is one particular section of Advocate General Bot's Opinion that merits special attention. One of the arguments pleaded for the claimants was that there was clear water between the destruction of the human embryos and the isolated stem cells used by the researchers; indeed, in Germany, where Brüstle conducted his research, local regulators had tried famously to make sure that there was a clear separation between the destruction of human embryos and the derived materials used by researchers. Even if the prior act was unethical, should this earlier wrongdoing count against the patent application? Some patent regimes[16] frame the moral exclusion in rather forward-looking terms and many European patent practitioners understood the revised version of the regional exclusion to preclude such rear-window moral considerations (see Beyleveld *et al.* 2000). However, the Advocate General was having none of this, posing the following question:

> The current judicial activity of the International Criminal Tribunal for the former Yugoslavia shows us, obviously subject to the presumption of innocence, that in the course of those events prisoners were killed in order to remove organs for trafficking. If, rather than trafficking, there were experiments which resulted in "inventions" within the meaning of the term in patent law, would they have had to have been recognised as patentable on the ground that the way in which they were obtained was outside the scope of the technical claim in the patent?[17]

For the Advocate General, the answer to the question was clear. Quite simply, such prior wrongdoing should not be ignored. Inventions tainted in this way should be excluded from patentability. Without doubt, if patents are to have an integrity within the overall regulatory environment, the Advocate General must be correct. It makes no sense to encourage innovation that is contrary to the public interest, and it makes no sense to reward innovation that is the outcome of practices that are contrary to the public interest.

It is worth pausing to emphasize that, in principle, the Advocate General's Opinion has enormous implications for global ethics. It is not just that European patent law excludes innovation that involves the destruction of human embryos. The logic of the rear-window approach is that Europe should also exclude patents where there have been acts of bio-piracy, exploitation of research subjects, defective informed consent procedures, and so on (compare Pottage 1998).

Earlier, we noted that the proviso in Article 27(2) of TRIPS, and comparably in the European patent regimes, is strange where the context is that of a single jurisdiction. In regional patent regimes, where some members might prohibit exploitation and others permit it, the position is less straightforward. What the proviso means in such a mixed context is that the patent should not be excluded on moral grounds simply because one or more of the members have prohibitions in their national law. Where the majority of members do not have such prohibitions, this might make some sense, preventing the minority from dictating to the majority; but, in Europe, it co-exists with the pre-WARF light-touch view that the moral exclusion should not be applied unless there is an overwhelming consensus that it would be immoral to exploit the invention.

How, then, should we answer the question of whether patent law regimes should internalize more sensitive ethical controls over what is treated as patentable subject matter? Taking

European patent law as our model, we can say that, although there has been a clear tendency to default to a light-touch application of the moral exclusion, the recent indications in WARF and *Brüstle* are that this aspect of the jurisdiction is being taken far more seriously.

Should there be a more ethically sensitive control over the scope and duration of patents?

When the Nuffield Council on Bioethics (2002) reported on the ethics of the patenting of DNA, it concluded that patents asserting rights over human DNA sequences were being granted too readily (the Council recommended that, in future, such grants should be the exception rather than the rule) and that patent offices were granting patents on claims that were too broad. Although the consequence of such patents being exploited was that it was becoming difficult for smaller bioentrepreneurs to carry out innovative work (arguably, with much larger ethical consequences), the Council did not recommend that examiners should make more use of their moral jurisdiction. Rather, the Council argued that the usual criteria of novelty, inventive step and the like should be applied more stringently.

Where patents seem to be counterproductive because of a liberal approach to granting (creating patent thickets) or overbroad claims (creating blockages), one option is to try to trim the breadth and duration of patent protection. However, these are not the only options. For example, the thickets and blockages might be eased by compulsory licensing or by widening the so-called research exemption.[18] However, for at least two reasons, this is a tricky calculation. First, to some extent, regulators see themselves as being in competition with one another and they will not want to take such a restrictive approach that key businesses move their research operations to regulatory environments that they find more supportive of their business activities: witness, for example, the concerns expressed in the UK about the possible relocation of the European biotechnology industry following the European Court of Justice's decision in *Brüstle*. Second, if certain kinds of research cannot be protected by patents, then commercial researchers might resort to reliance on trade secret protection. As an impediment to innovative research, this might be even more of a problem, for patented innovations, unlike trade secrets, are at least in the public domain and, while some researchers might be prepared to take their chances in infringing complex patent thickets (by proceeding without a licence), they cannot so easily access vital information that is locked up as a trade secret (see Engelbrekt 2009). In a global regulatory marketplace, local regulators hope to stimulate innovation but they also need to give researchers an incentive for putting their inventive work in the public domain.

That said, there might be some contexts in which there is a distinct national advantage in taking a more restrictive approach to the focus and length of patent protection: indeed, in India, the domestic manufacturers of generic drugs were supported for some years by just such a regulatory strategy (which, of course, operated against the business interests of big pharma elsewhere).

So much for the real world of regulation and regulatory arbitrage; but what would our leading ethical approaches make of a policy that aims to restrict the breadth and duration of patent protection? For class 1 ethicists, the imperative is to assist those who really need help. The patent regime is supposed to facilitate this. If, in practice, the patent regime incentivizes research into developed-world rather than developing-country diseases – as it does – and if, in practice, patents push up prices so that basic goods become unaffordable in the developing world – as they do – then trimming the breadth and length of patents seems like the least one should be doing. For class 2 ethicists, such fine-tuning of the patent regime involves quite difficult calculations because the knock-on effects are hard to predict in a context of differential pricing, compulsory licensing, generic drugs and hard bargaining. The question is not whether such adjustments will better serve the spirit of the patent regime, or whether they will address the needs of the worst off, or anything of that kind; it is simply whether they will increase overall utility. Finally, for class 3 ethicists, there is little to say about such adjustments. The patent regime is an enterprise that has particular regulatory objectives. So long as the regime respects the negative rights of agents, the only question is whether such adjustments will assist the regulators' purposes. Whether they do or do not succeed in doing so is of no ethical significance.

Do we need new institutional forms to incentivize innovation and benefit sharing?

In the twenty-first century, innovation is rarely the work of isolated individuals; the sewing machine scenario is anachronistic – indeed, patentable subject matter has moved on from machines (see Pottage & Sherman 2011), and the creators and innovators rarely hold the intellectual property rights. If most of the patents are held by corporations in the developed world, most of the global problems are experienced by individuals in the developing world. Drahos and Braithwaite (2002: 16) give readers a reality check:

> Attempts by corporate owners to give legitimacy to their intellectual property empires through appeals to romantic notions of individual authorship and inventorship look less and less morally persuasive in a world where intellectual property rights, and TRIPS especially, are being linked to bigger themes and issues – widening income inequalities such as those between developed and developing countries, excessive profits, the power and influence of big business on government, the loss of national sovereignty, globalization, moral issues about the use and direction of biotechnology, food security, biodiversity … sustainable development, the self-determination of indigenous people, access to health services and the rights of citizens to cultural goods.

This suggests that patents, as corporate assets that are utilized in global trade, have little moral traction and that regulators need to think again about the most effective way to support beneficial innovation but without granting monopoly rights.

Within nation states, regulators have responsibilities that the states have freely adopted. No matter which of the root ethics we apply, if the state has freely undertaken to respect and promote human rights, these commitments are binding. For example, Article 25(1) of the Universal Declaration of Human Rights (UDHR) recognizes an entitlement to a broad range of goods and services, including food, clothing, housing and medical care, which are essential for human health and well-being. More pointedly, perhaps, Article 27 of the UDHR provides:

(1) Everyone has the right freely to participate in the cultural life of the community, to enjoy the arts and to share in scientific advancement and its benefits.
(2) Everyone has the right to the protection of the moral and material interests resulting from any scientific, literary or artistic production of which he is the author.

Even if we take a class 3 (negative rights) starting point, these commitments cannot be ignored. But, how are we to do justice to both limbs of Article 27 (see e.g. Helfer 2007)? With the best regulatory will, how can the interests of innovators be protected (as human rights) when the benefits of inventions are to be freely available (also as a matter of human rights)?

One imaginative proposal is for a Health Impact Fund (HIF) (Pogge 2005a, Hollis & Pogge 2008). Stated simply, the idea is that pharmaceutical companies would have the option of registering a new drug with the HIF. The drug would then be sold at cost price (way below the premium monopoly price) and, in return, the company would be compensated by reference to the actual impact of the drug. Rather than targeting innovative products and processes at smaller profitable markets, the HIF would encourage companies to aim for volume sales. There are obviously questions about both how the HIF would be funded and how attractive it would be relative to the co-existing unreconstructed patent regime as well as about the generalizability of the model, but it opens up new ideas about how to reward inventors who put their work into the public domain.

There are several other ideas in circulation (see Hollis & Pogge 2008: 97–108); for example, patent pools;[19] priority review vouchers (which aim to incentivize the development of drugs for neglected diseases); prizes (Love & Hubbard 2007);[20] "advanced purchase commitments" and "advanced marketing commitments"; and a proposed Medical Research and Development Treaty (Love 2005). However, in so far as such suggestions are premised on private innovative enterprise, there might seem to be a tension, because (unless private enterprise is to act philanthropically) it obviously needs a viable business model – and this means that the private sector will naturally default to those (optional) incentive schemes, products and markets that show most profit. There is also the thought that a huge amount of basic research is carried out in universities at public expense and that, rather as with the banking sector, the public ends up paying several times over for the profitability of the private sector. Without this degenerating into a polemic against the private sector, it is hard to escape the thought that, if nation states are to honour their human rights commitments, the obvious thing is for them to become more proactive and more focused by continuing to fund public sector research and development as well as the mechanisms for transferring the benefits to those who are most needy.

Conclusion

There are several recurrent themes in this chapter. The first is that, even though patent practitioners tend to treat the patent regime as freestanding (their script says that examination of claims is simply to establish that the process or product is inventive; it does not guarantee that the invention can be exploited), this makes no regulatory sense. Patent offices are much more than private clubs, patents are publicly enforced, and this all needs to be in line with the public interest. Second, though the nature of the public interest is contestable, it is a place holder for both economic and cultural (including ethical) considerations. Third, what we make of patenting ethically depends on our root ethical premises, and there is much to contest at this level. Fourth, no matter what our particular ethical premises, where nation states have committed themselves to respecting human rights, they cannot treat patenting as exempt from these commitments. It follows that, at all points, patenting must be compatible with the commitments to human rights that have been undertaken. Finally, by connecting patenting to global trade, there is a real danger that the commitments to human rights are seriously weakened, or "collateralized" (Leader 2004). Some serious correction is required, arguably by removing patents altogether from those processes and products that are part of the essential infrastructure for human health and well-being.

Notes

1 For an excellent critical conspectus, see Boyle (2008).
2 The WHO Model Lists of Essential Medicines have been updated regularly since 1977. The current versions are the eighteenth WHO Essential Medicines List and the fourth WHO Essential Medicines List for Children (updated in April 2013). See www.who.int/medicines/publications/essentialmedicines/en (accessed May 2014).

3 Decision Onco-mouse/Harvard, 14 July 1989 (OJ EPO 11/1989, 451; [1990] 1 EPOR 4). Initially, the examiners did not see the application as raising an issue under Article 53(a). Rather, they rejected the application on the grounds: (a) that there had not been sufficient disclosure of the working of the invention (as required by Article 83 of the European Patent Convention); and (b) that Article 53(b) excluded the patenting of "animal varieties". It was only when the case was referred to the Board of Appeal that the centrality of Article 53(a) was recognized: see EPO Decision T 19/90 (OJ EPO 12/1990, 476; [1990] 7 EPOR 501).

4 Compare the Presidential Commission for the Study of Bioethical Issues (2010: 119–22) where, under the guiding principle of public beneficence, the mission of intellectual property (especially patent) regimes is considered.

5 Particular theories of positive rights might take more or less restrictive views about the circumstances in which I am required to assist others. This will hinge on such factors as the level of need of others (for example, only where there are imminent threats to their life or physical well-being), on the level of sacrifice that I must make, and on the ability of others to assist themselves (Brownsword 2007). With regard to the opportunities for developing countries to help themselves in serving their own pharmaceutical needs, see Kuanpoth (2010).

6 See "Patents: a thumbnail sketch" (p. 355 above) for the bespoke exclusions in UK patent law. Globally, Article 27(3) TRIPS copies many national patent regimes by providing that members may exclude from patentability "diagnostic, therapeutic and surgical methods for the treatment of humans or animals". Following the analysis in the text, this is just the kind of innovation that should be encouraged and supported rather than being excluded. Clearly, whatever the reasons for exclusion, they are to do with very different considerations: possibly that clinicians and vets will do the right thing by disclosing and the exclusion closes a door to prudential distortion of their reasoning.

7 See, e.g., PLANT GENETIC SYSTEMS/Glutamine Synthetase Inhibitors [1995] EPOR 357; HOWARD FLOREY INSTITUTE/Relaxin Hormone [1995] EPOR 541; and LELAND STANFORD/Modified Animal [2002] EPOR 2.

8 *Kingdom of the Netherlands v European Parliament and Council of the European Union* Case C-377/98. On which, see Beyleveld and Brownsword (2002).

9 Case G 0002/06, 25 November 2008.

10 T 1374/04 (OJ EPO 2007, 313).

11 Case G 0002/06, 25 November 2008, at para 25.

12 Case C 34–10, judgment given 18 October 2011.

13 The full text of the Advocate General's Opinion is available at: http://curia.europa.eu/juris/liste.jsf?language=en&jur=C,T,F&num=C-34/10&td=ALL (accessed May 2014).

14 Advocate General's Opinion, para. 115.

15 Advocate General's Opinion, para. 110.

16 For example, section 13(3) of the Singapore Patents Act 1995 provides: "An invention the publication or exploitation of which would be generally expected to encourage offensive, immoral or anti-social behavior is not a patentable invention."

17 Advocate General's Opinion, para. 106.

18 On the current understanding of this exemption for researchers, see Hellstadius (2009).

19 However, it is important to distinguish between virtuous and vicious forms of pooling. If a small group of corporate patent holders cross-license their patents, this can develop into a cartel-like arrangement. What is needed is a pool that puts into the public domain a set of key patents that otherwise stand in the way of meeting the needs of the most vulnerable.

20 Why shift from prices to prizes? Quite simply, as Love and Hubbard (2007: 1551) argue: "Tying the incentive for R&D to the price of products ... has led to appalling disparities of access to medicines, well-known pricing abuses in both high- and low-income countries, massive waste in terms of excessive marketing of products and investments in medically unimportant products, and under-investment in products that have the greatest medical benefits."

PART VI
Environmental and climate ethics

Introduction

Environmental and climate ethics are increasingly prominent in global ethics. In previous introductions we have suggested that global poverty is considered by some to be *the* issue of global ethics; the issue that inspired key thinkers – such as Singer and O'Neill – to begin writing about specifically global duties, and for many, such as Thomas Pogge, it is still the most important issue to address. However, for others the threat of climate change is such that addressing the environmental crisis is at least equally important. Indeed, there are controversial arguments which suggest that addressing poverty will exacerbate climate change; for instance, through increased consumption of scare resources and increased emissions, which follow development. For example, a recent study from Oregon State University (2009) concluded that on average a child in the US has a long-term effect on raising carbon emissions that is 160 times higher than a child in Bangladesh (consumption is addressed in Chapter 20, as well as in Chapters 29 and 31 in this section).

Part of what makes climate change a prominent topic in global ethics is the magnitude of the threat – a threat to the survival of the human species. Addressing environmental catastrophe requires a global response as local responses will be manifestly inadequate. It cannot be addressed, as arguably poverty can, step by step in piecemeal measures which may be partially and locally successful. Rather, it has to be addressed collectively, as a shared response, where everyone takes the actions necessary. Only globally coordinated action will be sufficient to deal with the problem. Other current challenges might also be said to require a global response; for instance, the need to protect the efficacy of antibiotics could constitute a global health threat of the type which might threaten human survival. But while pandemics of previously treatable diseases (a very real possibility if antibiotic resistance continues its current trajectory) would be devastating, they might not have quite the potential as an uninhabitable planet to wipe out the whole human race.

Simon Caney addresses climate change in Chapter 27, where he discusses six fundamental ethical issues. The first concerns the evaluative criteria to apply to climate change. In short, is climate change bad because it reduces overall welfare or because it threatens human rights? The second concerns the proper response to risk and uncertainty. Is a risk–benefit analysis adequate for assessing climate change and responses to it? Or, in light of uncertainty, is a version of the precautionary principle warranted? The third concerns the long-term impact of climate change.

Because a substantial fraction of the CO_2 that humans emit remains in the atmosphere for hundreds, even thousands of years, our actions have an intergenerational impact. But which costs must the present generation assume in the form of climate change mitigation in order to do justice to future generations? The fourth issue is about responsibility for climate change mitigation, adaptation and compensation. How should the costs of these programmes be distributed? The fifth issue is about the distribution of entitlements to emit greenhouse gasses. Which distributive principal would be the fairest? The sixth and final issue that Caney discusses concerns the governance of climate change policy. Who should decide which climate change policy to adopt and what would count as procedural fairness within climate change negotiations? These are, of course, not the only ethical questions relevant to climate change, but the chapter provides a comprehensive survey of several of the most important issues in the ethics of climate change policy.

In Chapter 28 Benjamin S. Hale addresses the topic of pollution using three different frameworks and approaches: those of harm, trespass and vice. Hale considers each of these in turn. Which view one has, Hale argues, determines how pollution should be tackled. If pollution is an economic harm then it is remedied by taxation; if a vice, then it is remedied by education; and, if a trespass, then prosecution for a rights violation. The harm view is the dominant in policy discussions. It is enshrined in legislation and is applied to all types of pollution, from noise to environmental. But some harms are such that they cannot be tolerated, such as the harms caused by asbestos, whereas others can be mitigated using taxes. Objections to the harm view arise mostly from the requirement that people need to be harmed in order for a wrong to be recognized. In environmental terms this is problematic because the harms of pollutions often come to pass in the future and sometimes affect people who are not yet born. The vice view takes the usual virtue ethics approach by considering the character of those who degrade the environment. While including some things that the harm view ignores, this view takes the whole wrong as a character wrong, making it difficult to account for the damages to the environment as such. The final view, trespass, focuses on pollution as the violation of rights and as the thwarting of interests. Towards the end of the chapter Hale focuses on emerging areas of concern, most importantly the need for more attention to non-human animals and on climate altering pollutants.

Chapter 29 by John O'Neill addresses the concept of sustainability, used both with regard to preserving specific resources, such as fish stocks, and more broadly in phrases like "sustainable development". He suggests that local understandings of the sustainability of some particular thing (such as a particular fish stock), and the more general account stand in some tension. O'Neill employs a welfarist account of sustainability, while recognizing that this account could be challenged and broadened, for instance, to be less anthropocentric. He interrogates understandings of sustainability by considering how well-being should be understood and maintained over time. To this end he considers how well-being has traditionally been understood in the economics tradition, where well-being is expected to constantly improve over time and depends upon the existence of capital, which is understood as something to be preserved and grown. Sustaining capital requires that it be measured and that there be substitutes for objects of value. Hence, O'Neill considers notions of substitution. Accounts of the substitutability of capital depend on conceptions of well-being. For instance, standard economic accounts of well-being adopt a preference satisfaction conception of well-being, which allows the substitution of the satisfaction of one preference for another. In contrast, according to objective conceptions of well-being, substitutability is more problematic. The goods that satisfy one need cannot be replaced with others that satisfy a different need, in so far as each is a component of minimum well-being. O'Neill also discusses what all this means for our understanding of environmental preservation.

The discussion about why the environment matters, and what it means for environments to be sustainable leads directly to the next on biodiversity. For the protection of biodiversity is one prominent goal of sustainability. In Chapter 30 Andrew Brennan and Norva Lo explore global biodiversity. This chapter sets out the fundamental issues of the debate. These include problems of conceptualizing and measuring biodiversity, questions about how biodiversity relates to the stability of the wider ecosystem and the protection of individual species, and the tensions between anthropocentrism, biocentrism and ecological holism. After discussing how biodiversity can be understood, Brennan and Lo consider whether or not it is intrinsically valuable, rather than simply instrumentally valuable for human purposes. They suggest that the answer to this depends on two further questions: "first, whether all living things – irrespective of species – are intrinsically valuable; and second, whether a world with diversity in intrinsic values is better than a world homogeneous in intrinsic values". The rest of the chapter is devoted to answering these two questions.

In Chapter 31 Tim Mulgan considers population ethics. The chapter begins with is a discussion about why justice to future generations has only recently emerged as a central problem in moral and political philosophy. Subsequent sections address core philosophical concerns of population ethics. The first is the difficulty of balancing the rights of obligations to future and current people, an issue which is particularly pressing in climate change where a "popular argument is that the *future* benefit of preventing climate change is not worth the *present* cost." The justification for "discounting" future happiness or well-being just because it lies in the future is often simply that this is how people do behave. Such discounting is standard in economic terms, but ethically problematic. Second, Mulgan discusses Parfit's non-identity problem. Third, Mulgan addresses utilitarianism, the tradition of much population ethics. Utilitarianism in virtue of its commitment to impartiality, including temporal impartiality, offers an account of why we have obligations to future people. The advantages and disadvantages of this position are outlined. Fourth, Mulgan considers non–utilitarian arguments for intergenerational obligations, in the form of an extension of social contract theory. The final three sections address additional problems in population ethics. The first is over-population and reproductive freedom, and the controversial question about whether coercive fertility policies are ethically permitted, or even required. Mulgan discusses the claims of Amartya Sen who argues that empowering women and providing reproductive freedom is likely to be more effective than coercive policies. The second is the relationship of food aid, and other aid, to population. Here Mulgan argues for an approach that connects issues of aid to environmental and sustainability concerns. Finally, he discusses directly the way that environmental ethics has an impact on and changes population policy. His final word is bleak, namely that the question we may realistically have to answer, given the threat of climate catastrophe, is not one about the flourishing and sustainability of the environment for future generations, but rather how much worse off we should leave future people.

27

CLIMATE CHANGE

Simon Caney

The prospect of anthropogenic climate change raises many ethical issues. In particular, as the United Nations Framework Convention on Climate Change emphasizes, it raises questions of justice and equity (UNFCCC Article 3.1). My aim in this chapter is to give an overview of some of the ethical issues at stake and to indicate some of the main arguments made concerning these issues.[1] I shall begin by identifying six ethical issues that are thrown up by the occurrence of climate change, and then turn to examine each in turn. I should make clear at the start that it is not possible to examine *all* the ethical questions posed by climate change, so I have chosen to focus on some of the most fundamental ones.[2]

One question raised by the onset of global climate change is the following:

> *Question 1: evaluative criteria.* What criterion (or criteria) should be employed to evaluate the impacts of climate change?

To put it bluntly: What is wrong with climate change? Why is it bad? Is it, as utilitarians argue, its impact on welfare? Or should we consider its impact on human rights? Or something else?

The effects of climate change are not known with certainty. There is considerable unclarity both about the magnitude of the effects of greenhouses gases on the climate system and also on the effects that changes in the climate system will have on the quality of people's lives. In light of this, we face a second ethical question:

> *Question 2: risk and uncertainty.* How should policy-makers respond to the risks and uncertainties surrounding some of the impacts of climate change?

Does a cost–benefit analysis provide the best way of responding to risk and uncertainty? Or would it be misconceived to adopt such a perspective?

A further ethical question arises because some greenhouse gases last for an extremely long time in the atmosphere. The distinguished climate modeller David Archer writes in *The Long Thaw* that when a ton of coal is burned "[t]he CO_2 coming from a quarter of that ton will still be affecting the climate one thousand years from now" (Archer 2009: 1). He adds that "[a]bout 10% of the CO_2 from coal will still be affecting the climate in one hundred thousand years" (*ibid.*).

Our actions now thus cast a shadow for an extraordinarily long time. Given this, climate change raises questions of intergenerational justice. A third question, then, is:

> *Question 3: intergenerational equity and impact assessment.* What, if anything, do members of one generation owe to future generations?

May current generations discount the interests of future generations and employ a positive pure time discount rate? Or is such discounting unethical?

Suppose that we have answers to the first three questions, we also need to know who ought to make the sacrifices needed to combat climate change. One can distinguish between three kinds of action that are required to address climate change: mitigation, adaptation and compensation. The terms "mitigation" and "adaptation" are part of the technical vocabulary used by climate scientists and social scientists. The Intergovernmental Panel on Climate Change (IPCC) provides useful definitions of both. It defines mitigation as follows: "[a]n *anthropogenic* intervention to reduce the anthropogenic forcing of the *climate system*; it includes strategies to reduce *greenhouse gas sources* and emissions and enhancing *greenhouse gas sinks*" (Parry *et al.* 2007: 878). It defines adaptation as an "[a]djustment in natural or *human systems* in response to actual or expected climatic stimuli or their effects, which moderates harm or exploits beneficial opportunities" (*ibid.*: 869). To put it in broad terms: mitigation minimizes changes in the climate system, whereas adaptation implements social and economic policies that minimize the harms to humans that result from a changing climate system. Suppose that – as seems likely – people engage in insufficient mitigation (so there continues to be serious changes to the climate system) and they provide insufficient adaptation (so people are unable to adapt to the changing climate system). Then there is a case for compensation: compensation is appropriate when someone's entitlements have been violated. Some might argue, for example, that those who are forcibly displaced from small island states and coastal settlements are owed compensation for the wrong done to them.

In the light of this we then face a fourth ethical question, namely:

> *Question 4: responsibility.* Who should bear the burdens of climate change? That is, who should pay for the necessary mitigation, adaptation and compensation?

Article 3.1 of the UNFCCC refers to "common but differentiated responsibilities", but on what basis might we *differentiate* responsibilities among actors? Various different principles have been proposed – including the polluter pays principle (costs should be borne by those who caused the problem) and the ability to pay principle (costs should be borne by those with the ability to pay). What are the strengths and weaknesses of these principles?

One sacrifice required is to limit the emission of greenhouse gases. This then prompts a further question:

> *Question 5: the equitable distribution of greenhouse gas emissions.* How should the ability to emit greenhouse gases be distributed?

The total volume of greenhouse gas emissions needs to be lowered but, given this, there is a need for a distributive principle to specify the fairest distribution of greenhouse gas emissions. Some, for example, have defended the concept of *subsistence emissions* (Shue 1993) and others have argued for the view that there should be *equal per capita* emissions (A. Meyer 2000). Others have defended a *grandfathering* approach, arguing that people's share of emissions should correspond to the use of emissions in the past (Bovens 2011). Which, of any of these, is fair?

So far the focus has been on what ought to be done, but another key question is:

Question 6: just governance. Who should decide what mitigation and adaptation policies should be selected?

Climate change has effects which are both global and intergenerational. In light of this, what would be a procedurally fair decision-making process? Who is entitled to take part in climate negotiations? How do we evaluate the importance of procedural legitimacy and effectiveness?

Criteria

Having identified some key questions, let us turn now to consider the first identified above. Climate scientists maintain that human activities are having, and will continue to have, profound effects. How should one assess these impacts?

These questions may seem unnecessary, or even in questionable taste. A critic might ask: is it not obvious that climate change is disadvantageous and should we therefore not focus our attention on the other more pressing issues? Such a dismissal would, however, be too hasty. One answer is that (irrespective of any practical benefits of such an account) having an accurate understanding of what is at stake is valuable in itself, and that it is important to know *why* action to address climate change is required. Without such an account we are living without full knowledge and understanding: we are, in a sense, blind or even possibly deluded. Second, however, there are a number of practical reasons why we need such a criterion (or set of criteria).

First, following Article 2 of the UNFCCC, many institutions state their target as "stabilization of greenhouse gas concentrations in the atmosphere at a level that would prevent *dangerous* anthropogenic interference with the climate system" (UNFCCC, Article 2, emphasis added). Given this, however, a criterion is needed to specify what constitutes "dangerous" anthropogenic interference. In addition to this, we need to know what climatic goal (defined, say, in terms of the concentration of greenhouse gases in the atmosphere or in terms of upper limits on permissible increases in temperature or sea levels) we should aim at. These two questions are related, but they are distinct: it seems natural to suggest that the goal should be to prevent dangerous climatic changes. However, in very non-ideal circumstances (and those seem quite likely at the moment) they may come apart. For example, someone may think that an increase of 1.0°C in global mean temperatures over pre-industrial times is dangerous in a morally relevant sense, but they might also argue that given the situation that we are in, and given the refusal of people to reduce emissions in the last twenty years, the cost involved in meeting a 1.0°C target would be so great that seeking to meet it would come at too high a price. In this case they might reconcile themselves to a dangerous climatic system on the basis that it is less bad than the policies that would be employed (or even ought to be employed) to avoid it. Or – to choose another scenario – their criterion of what constitutes "dangerous" climate change might commit them to thinking that we have already gone past that level. So, although climate policy should be very much focused on preventing "dangerous" changes it does not *necessarily* follow that our criterion of dangerous climate change is the only relevant consideration, or that it alone should dictate climate policy.

Second, the criterion employed for assessing the impacts of climate change is very relevant for determining what kind of "adaptation" is employed. As we have seen above, one component of climate policy is adaptation: social and economic policies need to be put in place so that those living in an environmentally degraded world are able to lead the kinds of lives that they are entitled to. Adaptation is thus defined in terms of a moral baseline. Given this, adaptation policies require criteria to inform us which changes are undesirable (and hence adaptation is required) and which ones do not affect some morally relevant interest (and hence adaptation is not required). They also need criteria that give us a sense of which harms should be prioritized.

A third reason why we need to have criteria to assess the impacts of climate change stems from the fact that political authorities have a number of competing objectives. They therefore need some criteria by which to evaluate and compare each of these objectives. An analysis of the impacts of climate change is therefore needed in order to make such a comparison.

So how should we evaluate the effects of climate change?[3]

Many economists employ subjective tests like a willingness to pay criterion. On this approach one determines how bad an outcome is by asking people how much they would be willing to pay not to experience this loss. These approaches have, however, been notoriously problematic. We can see why – and also why this first issue is so morally important – if we consider the IPCC's Second Assessment Report and the response to it. This report used a willingness to pay criterion. Now, how much people are willing to pay to prevent some undesirable outcome is a function of how wealthy they are. One consequence, therefore, of the IPCC's use of this method was that the value of the lives of members of developing countries was accorded much less value than that of affluent members of the world. This application of the willingness to pay criterion understandably led to a vehement denunciation from the Indian Environment Minister, Kamal Nath, among many others.[4] The core point here is this: criteria of climatic impacts rest on moral assumptions and which moral assumptions are employed will have an effect on the assessment of the badness of climate change.

An alternative view – one that treats all persons as having the same moral value – holds that climate change should be evaluated (at least in part) by examining its impact on fundamental human rights. One can identify at least three well-established human rights that are threatened by anthropogenic climate change. First, it is arguable that anthropogenic climate change violates "*the human right to life*", where this is defined as the right not to be arbitrarily deprived of one's life. The storm surges and heatwaves associated with climate change will lead to direct loss of life and, as such, violate this right. Second, climate change violates "*the human right to health*". This human right can be interpreted in different ways. For example, the International Covenant on Economic, Social and Cultural Rights (ICESCR) (1966) affirms "the right of everyone to the enjoyment of the highest attainable standard of physical and mental health" (Article 12.1). One does not, however, need to rely on this potentially controversial conception in order to make the claim that climate change violates the human right to health. One might hold, for example, that there is a human right to health in the sense that each person is entitled that others do not act in such a way as to create dangerous threats to their health. Persons, on this account, have a human right not to be exposed to serious threats to their health. Working with this conception of the human right to health, it is clear that climate change violates this right. Climate change is projected to result in an increased incidence of dengue, cardio-respiratory problems and diarrhoea. Consider now a third human right: *the human right to subsistence*. Again, this might be interpreted in a number of different ways. The International Covenant on Economic, Social and Cultural Rights (ICESCR) and the Universal Declaration of Human Rights (1948) affirms "the right of everyone to an adequate standard of living for himself and his family, including adequate food" (ICESCR Article 11.1) and asserts "the fundamental right of everyone to be free from hunger" (ICESCR Article 11.2). Article 25.1 of the Universal Declaration of Human Rights asserts that:

> Everyone has the right to a standard of living adequate for the health and well-being of himself and of his family, including food, clothing, housing and medical care and necessary social services, and the right to security in the event of unemployment,

sickness, disability, widowhood, old age or other lack of livelihood in circumstances beyond his control.

These formulations appear to assert a positive right to receive assistance and some may fault them for this. Though I endorse such a positive conception, it is worth again noting that one can formulate a less contentious version of the human right to subsistence, namely that all persons have a human right that other people do not act so as to deprive them of the means of subsistence. Conceived of in this way, it is clear that climate change jeopardizes this right as well. The projected increase in temperatures will lead to crop failure and drought in some areas and the rise in sea levels will also involve loss of agricultural land to the sea (see Caney 2005b, 2006b, 2008a, 2009a, 2010b). Utilizing a human rights framework we may say that anthropogenic climate change involves the violations of several key human rights.

The three rights listed above (and the interests they protect) are quite minimal. What about other rights and interests? Some, for example, argue that persons have vital interests in the protection of their culture and their traditional ways of life. These will be severely compromised by rising sea levels which threaten those living in low-lying areas by seas and oceans and the inhabitants of small island states. And they may also be forced to leave previously fertile lands because of temperature increases. For these reasons some argue that climate change constitutes a case of cultural injustice (Heyward forthcoming, de-Shalit 2011).

We might, of course, also go one step further and argue that a full account of what is wrong with anthropogenic climate change should go beyond considering its impact on human beings and should also attribute fundamental importance to its impact on (a) non-human animals and (b) the natural world (Palmer 2011; Cripps 2013: chapter 4) (where by "fundamental importance" is meant importance that does not derive from its impact on human beings).

Risk and uncertainty

The preceding section has discussed the impacts of climate change, but predicting what changes will occur, and to what extent, is fraught with difficulty. Although the overwhelming majority of climate scientists affirm that there is climate change and that it is anthropogenic, there is, however, unclarity about just how much sea levels and temperatures will increase (both globally and at regional levels) and where severe weather events will occur. In addition to this lack of knowledge about the effects on the climate system there is a lack of knowledge about how socio-economic systems will be affected by these climatic changes. So there are two areas – one concerning climate science and a second concerning social science – where our knowledge is incomplete. In light of this, any adequate analysis of how to respond to climate change must include an account of how to respond to *risk* (where this refers to outcomes with a known probability) and *uncertainty* (where this refers to an outcome where one cannot assign a probability).[5]

One can distinguish between two different approaches. The first employs the tools of cost–benefit analysis and combines the probability of an event (where that is known) with the value of that event, thereby producing an estimate of its expected value. A second approach rejects this kind of probabilistic assessment and affirms a "precautionary" principle. The precautionary principle has been formulated in a number of very different ways. The key idea is that under certain conditions (e.g. when there is a possibility of a dire outcome), and where there are other reasonable options, then an actor should engage in precautionary behaviour (where that might involve moderating their behaviour or abstaining altogether from the action) (Manson 2002). Action thus must be taken even if it is not certain that there will be severe harm.

Consider, first, a cost–benefit approach to risk. This is criticized by many political philosophers. The central objection is that it is not an appropriate method for determining when *some* people expose *other* people to risk when there is a risk of calamitous outcomes. It might be appropriate for someone to use this method when she is considering a course of action that affects only herself. Suppose she is considering two options – to choose a safe option but one which has low value attached to it or to choose an option which has a much higher probability of death but which has high value to it. In such a circumstance it may be appropriate for her to calculate the expected value of both options and, on this basis, plump for the high-risk strategy. *She* makes the decision; *she* will gain the benefit if it works out; and *she* will suffer the bad consequences if the danger is realized. However, the situation is completely different when *some* persons are taking the risks and *other* persons are the likely victims of the risky behaviour. Given this fundamental difference it is wrong to apply a method that may be appropriate in one context (intrapersonal context) and export it to another one which is fundamentally different (the interpersonal context) (Caney 2009b: 176–77). This argument draws on a more general problem with certain consequentialist moral and political theories. As John Rawls famously argued in *A Theory of Justice*, utilitarianism "does not take seriously the distinction between persons" (1999b: 24). The complaint here is the same, a cost–benefit analysis of risk and uncertainty ignores the separateness of persons: it treats a case where one person exposes herself to risk in exactly the same way as it treats a case where one person exposes another to risk.

In light of this, we should consider now approaches which might be said to instantiate the precautionary principle: a principle which is affirmed in Principle 15 of the (1992) Rio Declaration on Environment and Development (Principle 15) and Article 3.3 of the United Nations Framework Convention on Climate Change. This principle can be formulated in a number of different ways. Given this variety it is inappropriate to specify a particular interpretation and stipulate that this is how it should be interpreted. A more plausible way forward is to consider different arguments for precaution and see which particular variant(s), if any, they justify.

Why should one adopt a precautionary approach to climate change? One answer is given by Stephen Gardiner in his article "A Core Precautionary Principle" (2006). Gardiner draws on Rawls's maximin principle to defend what he calls the "Rawlsian Core Precautionary Principle" (*ibid.*: 48). This maintains that precaution is required when three conditions are met: (a) there is uncertainty; (b) people do not particularly value increases above the kind of minimum guaranteed by the maximin principle; and (c) people strongly object to falling below the minimum standard guaranteed by maximin (*ibid.*: 47). Drawing on this, he concludes that it is appropriate to adopt a precautionary principle for global climate change (*ibid.*: 55).

Henry Shue advances a similar argument. He argues that states are under a duty to take precautionary action when: (a) there is a possibility of "massive loss", (b) the possibility of this occurring is above a certain threshold: "the likelihood of the losses is significant, even if no precise probability can be specified", and (c) "the costs of prevention are not excessive" (2010: 148). Shue's and Gardiner's arguments both, then, make reference to the high potential costs of "business as usual" and the lowness of the costs of avoiding the risk. One difference concerns Gardiner's first condition and Shue's second condition: whereas Gardiner grounds his conclusion that the major industrialized countries should adopt a precautionary approach on the assumption that there is *uncertainty* about dangerous climate change, Shue grounds the same conclusion on the assumption that there is a *significant probability* that there will be dangerous climate change and that we have a good understanding of the mechanisms that bring about the changes. So Gardiner's argument appeals to the lack of a known probability whereas Shue argues that although we cannot specify the precise probability we can say that it is above the relevant threshold level.

Note that both the formulations require us to specify critria which can be used to determine both (a) what outcomes trigger the precautionary approach (what counts as the serious harm that needs to be averted?) and also (b) what kinds of alternative policies are deemed reasonable to require of people.

Answering these questions takes us back to the issues discussed in the first section. Suppose, for example, that one draws on the ideal of human rights (Caney 2009b). One might then argue that it is wrong for some to act in such a way that they run the risk of violating others' fundamental *human rights* if they can eschew such risky behaviour without loss of their own *human rights*. Spelt out more fully, one might argue as follows:

(R1) The changes to the climate involve both (a) a high probability of severe threats to large numbers of persons' fundamental human rights and (b) a possibility of even more catastrophic threats to fundamental human rights.

This, however, is insufficient to ground a precautionary approach, because the cost of precaution may be excessive. The second necessary step in the argument then is thus:

(R2) Affluent members of the world can abstain from emitting high levels of greenhouse gases, and thereby exposing others to risk, without loss of their own *human rights*. (*Ibid.*)

Before concluding our discussion of risk and uncertainty it is worth noting one further consideration, namely that the benefits that arise when the affluent of the world emit high levels of greenhouse gases fall almost entirely to them, and not to those most at risk from climate change, and the harms will probably fall most severely on the disadvantaged. So there is a misalignment between those imposing these risks and those vulnerable to these risks. This matters because there might be cases where imposing risks is justified because the potential benefits and the potential costs are shared equitably. This, though, is not currently the case (though this will change as developing countries continue to industrialize).

One corollary of this is that major industrialized countries should adopt the precautionary principle (because they can comply with it without loss of their human rights) but it does not impose exactly the same responsibilities on developing countries (because it is not necessarily true of them that they can practise a precautionary approach without undermining their ability to uphold the basic economic human rights of their citizens). So humanity *as a whole* should adopt a precautionary approach, but this duty should fall only on those who can mitigate and fund adaptation without jeopardizing their own rights.

Intergenerational equity

The analysis so far has focused on the impacts of climate change and in particular what criteria to employ and how to factor in the uncertain/risky nature of climate change. A further ethical question concerns what obligations one generation has to future generations. This is of considerable importance to the issue of global climate change because, as was noted in the introduction, some greenhouse gases can last for extremely long periods of time. The emissions of the contemporary generation thus can have an effect on both currently alive people later on in their lives and on people who have not yet been born.

This raises two questions. First, do members of one generation have any moral obligations to future generations? One view, for example, might be that current people owe nothing to future generations. Suppose, however, that this view is incorrect. A second question then arises, namely, how much weight should current generations accord to future generations. May they "discount" the interests of future generations?

It is notable that almost everyone holds that current generations have *some* obligations to future generations. There is disagreement about what grounds this. Some, for example, place their emphasis on duties and hold simply that persons have a duty to respect their interests (Beckerman & Pasek 2001: 2, 28). This view would also be held by consequentialist moral and political theories such as utilitarianism. Others argue that principles of intergenerational equity should be grounded in the rights of future people (Feinberg 1980, Elliot 1989, L. H. Meyer 2003, Caney 2009b).[6] Despite their different starting points, then, many orthodox ethical theories converge in their conclusion that current generations have duties of justice to future generations.[7]

Let us turn now from the first question (do current generations have duties to future generations?) to the second (can current generations employ a positive discount rate?). It is important to begin by clarifying what is meant by discounting. As it is conventionally defined, the social discount rate refers to the extent to which current generations should devote resources to contemporaries in priority to future generations. With this in mind, let us now note that one can identify at least two separate reasons for devoting resources to the present rather than to the future.[8] First, one might simply accord lesser weight to some future interest just because it is in the future. People, for example, often prefer a pleasure now to an even greater pleasure later on. This phenomenon is referred to as *pure time discounting*. Second, even if one weights the interests of people equally through time one might wish to devote resources to the present in preference to the future on the grounds that people will be wealthier in the future and hence the resources will achieve greater benefit if they are devoted to the present. William Nordhaus refers to this as "growth discounting" (Nordhaus 1997: 317).

Consider pure time discounting first. Should we do this? The central argument for a zero pure time discount rate maintains that to employ a positive (or negative) pure time discount rate is wrong because it penalizes people for morally arbitrary reasons. Impartiality, this argument contends, requires us to treat each equally and not prioritize some over others for morally irrelevant reasons such as their ethnicity or class. By analogy, it argues, we should also not privilege some over others because of an irrelevant feature.

Some, though, dispute this argument. Perhaps the most common objection is that to apply a zero pure time discount rate would result in extremely demanding policies. Each generation would have to sacrifice an immense amount for its successors. To see why, consider a situation in which a current generation could spend x on itself which would yield a benefit of y to itself, or it could spend x on a policy that would benefit many generations to come by an amount much greater than y (Arrow 1999). If we apply a zero pure time discount rate here, it is argued, it will call for enormous demands on the current generation.

Although this argument against zero pure time discounting is often advanced, it too is subject to a powerful objection, for whether this argument succeeds depends on what other assumptions we make. For example, proponents of this argument regularly assume that political policies should maximize well-being. It is true that a theory of intergenerational justice that is both committed to maximization and to zero pure time discounting is demanding. However, it does not follow from this that one should reject zero pure time discounting. One could, instead, reject a commitment to maximization (Parfit 1984: 484–85; Broome 1992: 106; Rawls 1999b: 262). For example, a theory that demands the protection of human rights (including rights jeopardized by climate change) is not vulnerable to this objection (Caney 2008a, 2009b).

What about growth discounting? It is sometimes suggested that it would be better not to devote resources to mitigating climate change now but rather allow the economy to grow on the assumption that since future generations will be wealthier than current generations are they should pay (Nordhaus 1997: 317; Lomborg 2001). This raises both empirical and normative issues. Two empirical points are worth noting. First, even if there is continued economic growth it is risky to assume that this will necessarily result in protection from climatic harms. Economic growth is compatible, for example, with dramatic inequalities which would leave the disadvantaged vulnerable to severe climatic harms. Furthermore, some, such as Stern (2007), argue that it would be much cheaper to mitigate climate change now, rather than allow climate change and then try to adapt to it.[9]

Responsibility

Much of the preceding discussion has focused on the effects of climate change and on its victims. Any adequate ethical analysis of climate change must also address the question of who should bear the burden of combating climate change. What would be a fair way of sharing the burden?

Prior to examining several proposed distributive criteria, it is important to clarify the nature of the burden. As was noted above, addressing climate change requires *mitigation* (reducing greenhouse gases and maintaining greenhouse gas sinks), *adaptation* (enabling people to live in a changing climate system) and *compensation* (compensating those who have been harmed). Others might add that it calls for *geoengineering*.

With this in mind, let us now turn to the question of how such responsibilities should be apportioned. One leading approach argues that the responsibility for addressing a problem lies with those who caused the problem. Henry Shue subscribes to a version of this approach, arguing that:

> When a party has in the past taken an unfair advantage of others by imposing costs upon them without their consent, those who have been unilaterally put at a disadvantage are entitled to demand that in the future the offending party shoulder burdens that are unequal at least to the extent of the unfair advantage previously taken in order to restore equality.
>
> *(Shue 1999: 534–37)*

This view allocates responsibilities in accordance with agents' "contribution to the problem" (*ibid.*: 533). Many invoke this principle and conclude that members of affluent industrialized societies should bear the greatest burden for dealing with climate change.

A number of objections to this principle have, however, been made.

Objection 1: excusable ignorance

First, some argue that this principle cannot be applied to all those who have emitted high levels of greenhouse gases because some agents were excusably ignorant of their actions. According to this objection, it is unfair to hold people accountable for the ill effects of their actions if they could not reasonably have been expected to know that their actions would have had such ill effects. It is then pointed out that our knowledge of the links between the emission of greenhouse gases and changes to the climate is fairly recent.

A number of different responses have been made to this argument. First, the link between the emission of greenhouse gases and climate change has been well established for several decades. It is, of course, hard to specify exactly at what point ignorance of climate change is inexcusable. However, it is clear that one cannot apply it now, and it is arguable that it cannot be invoked for any emissions occurring after 1990.

Second, one might argue that people should be held culpable for the ill effects of their actions even when the link between those actions and certain harmful outcomes is not fully established if there are good grounds for thinking that there is a possible connection. One might argue, that is, that even where there is not certain knowledge there is still a duty to adopt a precautionary approach (see section above), and hence that if one fails to do so and thereby produces harmful outcomes one is liable. Put another way: if the argument for a precautionary principle is persuasive then there is a duty to comply with it. And it would seem odd to affirm this duty while at the same time denying that failure to comply with this duty does not generate liabilities.

A third response to the "excusable ignorance" argument argues that there are some circumstances in which it is appropriate to apply a strict liability approach and hold people responsible even if they were excusably ignorant of the effects of their actions. The thought underlying the argument from excusable ignorance is that a strict liability approach is unfair on the would-be duty-bearer. It contends that it is unfair to burden them given that they could not have been expected to know the effects of their action. Suppose, however, that the person who unwittingly causes harm also benefits considerably from the harmful activity. In such circumstances it no longer seems unfair to burden them for the harmful actions of their policy. It is true that they could not be expected to know the consequences of their action. However, since they have profited from this activity one can ascribe responsibilities to them without leaving them, for example, worse off than they were prior to the commission of the harmful actions (Caney 2010a: cf also P. Singer 2002: 34; Gosseries 2004: 40–41; Baer 2006: 136).

Objection 2: past generations

Having considered one objection to the application of the "contribution to the problem" principle to climate change, we may now consider a second. Some argue that the contribution to the problem principle cannot give a complete account of who should bear the burdens of dealing with climate change. The problem arises because humans have been contributing to the problem for over 150 years. Since the industrial revolution, members of European and North American societies have been emitting ever-increasing amounts of greenhouse gases. Many of these have, however, now died. It appears, therefore, that the contribution to the problem principle cannot fully answer the question of who should deal with global climate change.

One response to this line of reasoning maintains that members of industrialized countries should pay for the emissions of earlier generations on the grounds that they have all inherited benefits that stem from excessive use of the earth's atmosphere and that if they enjoy the benefits they should cover some of the costs (Shue 1999: 536–37; Neumayer 2000: 189; Gosseries 2004: 42ff; Caney 2006a, 2009a, 2010a).

Objection 3: poverty

A third problem with a pure contribution to the problem principle should also be noted. One concern with making people pay strictly in accordance with their emissions is that this would be unfair on those living at a very low standard of living. It is unreasonable, according to this objection, to make the poor pay for their emissions when those emissions are needed for achieving a minimal standard of living and when making them pay would push them beneath a decent minimum threshold. This objection contends that people have a right to a minimal standard of living and that a contribution to the problem principle is unfair to the extent that it violates this right and makes unreasonable requests of the poor and vulnerable. This objection is, of course, of considerable practical importance given the emissions of countries like India and China.

If this objection is correct then we need to modify the contribution to the problem principle to specify that the poor are exempt from it (Caney 2010a). This does not require us, however, to abandon the contribution to the problem principle but rather to qualify it and to locate in a more general account of people's entitlements.

Let us turn now to a second commonly invoked ethical principle – namely the principle that people should pay in accordance with their ability to pay. The ability to pay principle ascribes responsibility to agents *not* by examining who caused a problem but by considering who is most able to afford the cost of combating the problem (Shue 1999: 537–40; Caney 2005a, 2009a, 2010a).

What is the normative rationale for endorsing an ability to pay principle? One might appeal directly to our intuitions and argue simply that the ability to pay principle has great intuitive appeal. Some thinkers, however, argue that it can be grounded in a more basic principle. For example, David Miller defends it by appealing to an ideal of "equality of sacrifice" (D. Miller 2008: 125, 146ff).

Others might go yet further and appeal to an egalitarian conception of (global) justice. For if one thinks that justice requires broadly equal shares then it follows that those who currently have less than their fair (equal) share should pay less and those who currently have more than their fair (equal) share should pay more. From a global egalitarian viewpoint, agents should (in line with the polluter pays principle) be held accountable for their choices but, as noted above, this applies only when they have their fair share of opportunities and holdings. And if the background theory of justice is an egalitarian one then we have reason – in our very unequal world – to ascribe greater burdens to the more advantaged and less to the disadvantaged.

The equitable distribution of greenhouse gas emissions

Having considered who should bear the burdens of combating global climate change, let us now turn to the question of how greenhouse gases should be distributed. Since the emission of greenhouse gases causes dangerous climate change, there needs to be a cap on the total volume of emissions. But if there is to be a restriction on the amount of greenhouse gas emissions there must also be a principle of distributive justice specifying how emission rights are to be shared. Note that this question is related, but is not identical, to the question of how the burden should be shared (Shue 1993: 49). The two questions differ for several reasons. First, lowering emissions is only one aspect of combating dangerous climate change. There is currently a need for lowering total emissions, maintaining greenhouse gas sinks, fostering technological innovation and transfer, funding adaptation, and compensating those who have been harmed by dangerous climate change. Restricting the emission of greenhouse gases is thus only one component in the tasks to be performed and, hence, the question of how to distribute the right to emit greenhouse gases is not the same as the question of how to distribute the burden of combating climate change. A second reason why the two questions differ arises because of the existence of "flexibility mechanisms" (such as emissions trading schemes or the Clean Development Mechanism). These have proved problematic in practice. However, *if they could be applied successfully* (which some query) they would enable some to discharge their responsibility in part by paying more money and investing in clean technology and not just through the amount of emissions they produced.

In what follows I shall consider three different ethical principles that have been proposed.

Grandfathering

First, several environmental markets have adopted a principle of grandfathering. That is, they have allocated emission rights in proportion to the distribution of emission rights at a point in recent history. The EU Emissions Trading Scheme inaugurated on 1 January 2005 began by using grandfathering, although it is now moving away from such a scheme to an upstream auction.

Grandfathering has been much criticized (though cf. Bovens 2011). One concern is that it is unfair on the poorest and most vulnerable, who have historically had very low emissions. Grandfathering, it is argued, is indifferent to people's basic needs and if imposed it would lock the poor and vulnerable into a permanent state of underdevelopment. (The extent to which this applies or not would, though, depend on whether the disadvantaged have other non-fossil-fuel-based sources of energy, a point explored below.)

Subsistence emissions

Given this, some may be attracted to Henry Shue's proposal in a pioneering article (1993) that everyone is entitled to meet their "subsistence emissions". A similar idea also underlies the recent proposal for "Greenhouse Development Rights" (Baer *et al.* 2007). On this approach emissions should be allocated to the disadvantaged in the world to enable them to develop. Prior to evaluating this account, however, it is also worth considering an alternative proposal.

Equality

This is the idea that emission rights should be shared *equally* among all. This approach differs from the preceding one in that it is concerned not with everyone having *enough* emissions (a suffi-cientarian ideal), but it insists that people should have the *same* emission rights (an egalitarian ideal). This principle was famously proposed by Anil Agarwal and Sunita Narain (1991) and has been supported by a number of political philosophers (Jamieson 2005a: 231). The equal per capita view is also at the heart of the model of contraction and convergence as developed by Aubrey Meyer (2000) and the Global Commons Institute.[10]

Prior to evaluating this approach we might note that it comes in different versions. One difference concerns the rights bearers: some, for example, apply the equal per capita view to countries (holding that each country should be allocated emission rights in proportion to its population size), whereas others apply it to individuals (holding that each person should have a right to equal emissions).

A second issue on which proponents of the equal per capita approach may diverge concerns the attitude to the past. One view is that people's fair share of emissions should be determined by an egalitarian principle, but that we should then subtract earlier emissions from that egalitarian baseline (Neumayer 2000); a second group thinks that we should ignore the past and allocate the remaining shares on an equal basis; and a third possibility is that we should treat equality as the target and move towards it over time, thus tolerating some inequality during that process (A. Meyer 2000).

A third issue is whether one should adopt a purist egalitarian approach and not combine it with other principles, or whether one should instead combine the equal per capita approach with other principles. Steven Vanderheiden, for example, adopts the second approach. He does so in response to the concern that an equal per capita emissions approach is unfair on those with greater needs. Someone might ask: why should we give people the same amount of greenhouse gases when some have much greater (energy and other) needs than others? In response to this he argues that people's subsistence emissions should be met and then the remainder (if there is any) should be shared equally (Vanderheiden 2008: 226–27, 249).

Let us turn now to an evaluation of the equal per capita principle. Although it has intuitive appeal, it is vulnerable to several objections. First, as several have pointed out, it is odd to fix on one resource (greenhouse gas emissions) and seek to equalize that (Bell 2008: 250; D. Miller 2008: 142–43; Caney 2009c, 2012: 265–82). Normally theories of justice focus on people's overall package of resources and call for a fair distribution of each person's overall set of resources. Given this, it is not clear why we should construct a specific distributive principle for one particular resource considered in isolation.

Second, and more radically, some argue that it is wrong to focus on emissions *per se*. They argue that we care about greenhouse gas emissions because they contribute to goods (like food or health). Hence they – not emissions – should be our focus (Hayward 2007; Caney 2009c, 2012). Consider, for example, emissions associated with the use of fossil fuels for energy. Energy can often be provided for in other ways (solar, geothermal, wave, tidal, hydroelectric, wind, biomass, nuclear – and possibly in other ways). Given this it seems inappropriate to fix on distributing emissions rather than ensuring that energy sources are available to meet interests (Caney 2012: 285ff). This challenge, if correct, undermines not simply the equal per capita view but also any view that applies principles of justice to emissions when considered in isolation from any other goods (including other energy sources). As such it has force against proposals for "grandfathering emissions" or "subsistence emissions" or for "greenhouse development rights".[11]

Who decides?

The preceding sections have drawn attention to questions of *distributive* justice: that is, how should the burdens associated with combating climate change be distributed? Another important question, however, is: who should decide? What would be a fair decision-making process?

There are at least two kinds of relevant considerations here – one procedural in nature and the other more outcome-oriented. Consider the procedural first. This holds, roughly, that those whose interests are greatly and involuntarily affected by a phenomenon are entitled to have a say in the political process (Pogge 2008: 84; for a seminal discussion see Whelan 1983). David Held, for example, writes that "those whose life expectancy and life chances are significantly affected by social forces and processes ought to have a stake in the determination of the conditions and regulation of these, either directly or indirectly through political representatives" (2004: 100, 98–102, 174). Note that a full account of this must specify (a) what interests should be included in this account, (b) how great the extent of affectedness must be to generate the right, and (c) what kind of "say" is envisaged (the right to vote, the right to representation?). Expressed like this, it is clear that there are a number of different formulations of the principle at stake, depending on how one defines (a), (b) and (c). However, they have in common the core idea that those in thrall to powerful social economic or environmental forces are entitled to have some kind of input into the political process regulating these forces.

When applied to climate change, two further features need to be factored in. First, given the global nature of climate change there is a strong argument that there must be a democratic and accountable global decision-making process. The decision-making process (one which will govern major emitters) must include the potential victims of climate change in their discussions. Otherwise some are being subject to political decisions but are denied an input into the process and there would be a democratic deficit. Second, as was stressed above, climate change is an intertemporal problem and this raises the question of how we represent the interests of future generations (Dobson 1996b, O. O'Neill 2001, Ekeli 2005, D. Thompson 2005).

Once we have a notion of procedural fairness on hand, we then face a second question, namely: how do we evaluate the importance of procedural legitimacy if, and when, it conflicts with other criteria for institutional design? This takes us to the outcome-oriented perspective mentioned above. Many, for example, would argue that it is of paramount importance to have an institutional framework that produces good outcomes, or, at the least, avoids terrible outcomes. Drawing on the preceding sections, some might then argue that we should favour whichever decision-making process is most likely to (a) prevent dangerous climate change and (b) allocate the burdens involved in dealing with climate change fairly. This takes an essentially consequentialist, or results-oriented, approach to institutional design.

Such a consequentialist approach, however, clearly differs in principle from a proceduralist approach to institutional design. The latter, by contrast with the former, focuses solely on the intrinsic fairness of the process and not the quality of the outcomes produced. Of course, it might be argued that in practice the two criteria converge, but this is not necessarily the case. For example, it is arguable that including all affected parties (which is what the proceduralist approach would counsel) might include so many participants that it makes an agreement less likely and as such would not produce the best outcome. In such a case we face a conflict between a purely procedural approach and a purely consequentialist one. Such a possibility gives us powerful reasons to try to design a global institutional framework that combines the virtues of both approaches. One interesting example of this kind of approach has been developed by Robyn Eckersley, who proposes what she terms "inclusive minilateralism" (Eckersley 2012: 25). This involves a small "Climate Council" which is enabled to take decisive action (the "minilateral" component), but which, unlike in other minilateral proposals, is accountable to all members of the UNFCCC (the "inclusive" element) (Eckersley 2012).

Concluding remarks

Climate change raises very many ethical concerns. In this chapter I have focused on six of the key challenges. Namely: (a) How do we evaluate climatic impacts, define "dangerous" climate change and identify the target of climate policy? (b) How should we think about risk and uncertainty? (c) What do we owe to future generations? (d) Who should bear the burden of tackling climate change? (e) How should emissions should be distributed? And (f) how should we design the decision-making process of the climate governance regime? These are both practically important but also normatively complex. They raise deep challenges for the way that we, as individuals, live, and they pose fundamental questions for the socio-economic and political constitution of our societies.

Acknowledgement

This chapter draws from a longer paper which I wrote while holding an ESRC Climate Change Leadership Research Fellowship (2008–12). I am extremely grateful to the ESRC for its support.

Notes

1 For an important and useful review of the ethical implications of climate change see Gardiner (2004).
2 I shall not discuss, for example, the ethical issues surrounding some of the policies that might be adopted to respond to climate change including: (a) geoengineering the climate (Gardiner 2011, chapter 10), (b) using other energy sources (such as nuclear energy or biofuels (Nuffield Council on Bioethics 2011a) or hydroelectric energy or gas resulting from hydraulic fracturing), (c) demographic policy, or (d) the ethical issues surrounding emissions trading schemes (Caney & Hepburn 2011). All of these raise important ethical issues.
3 For a useful survey of the adequacy of some of these criteria and their implications for the assessment of climate change see Edward Page (2006, chapter 3).
4 For instructive overviews of the controversy surrounding the Second Assessment Report of the IPCC, to which I am indebted, see Grubb (1995: 471–72); Grubb *et al.* (1999, appendix 2: 306); and Spash (2002: 190–91).

5 See Frank Knight's seminal discussion in *Risk, Uncertainty, and Profit* (1921: especially 19–20, 197–232).

6 For criticism of the last claim see Beckerman and Pasek (2001: 11–28, especially 15–16 & 19).

7 For useful overviews of the debate see L. H. Meyer (2008) and Page (2006).

8 The "at least" is important. There are other kinds of discounting such as "opportunity cost" discounting (Parfit 1984: 482–84) that are also relevant. For an excellent discussion of discounting more generally see *ibid.*: 480–86.

9 Given this last point it is worth exploring the option (canvassed by John Broome 2012: chapter 3 and Matthew Rendall 2011) that current generations should *mitigate* now but may pass on some of the costs of that mitigation to future generations. For discussion see Caney (2014, forthcoming).

10 See www.gci.org.uk.

11 Interestingly, Henry Shue emphasizes in his paper "Avoidable Necessity" that persons have a right to subsistence emissions *given the existing energy regime* (1995, esp. 251, 254, 256–57, 259). See also Hayward (2007: 432, 440–41).

28

POLLUTION

Benjamin S. Hale

For many people the wrong of pollution is self-evident. Take any natural and pristine environment, introduce a deleterious additive, and this additive, by dint of the harm that it does to this natural and pristine environment, is rightly considered a pollutant. Call this the "harms view" of pollution.

Roughly speaking, the harms view proposes that the wrong of pollution consists in the harm or damage caused by the pollution. Pollution is wrong because it damages the environment. For instance, water with high dioxin levels, say, is said to be polluted by virtue of the damage done to the water, whereas water that otherwise may carry pathogens but that has been "treated" with chlorine (an otherwise toxic chemical) is said not to be polluted. It is the disutility of the water, in this case, that accounts for the wrong of pollution. By contrast, water with ostensibly healthy levels of fluoride is generally not thought to be polluted. Fluoride, for instance, is an additive conferring health benefits, though it does not "treat" the water *per se*. Fluoride improves upon water. In other words, it is the *utility* of the water, and the purpose to which the water is being put, that will establish whether the additive is harmful or beneficial, and thus pollution or not. At its base, the harms view is a deeply consequentialist position, mostly utilitarian in origin, locating the wrong of the polluting action fundamentally in the bad consequences brought about from the action.

On one hand, the problem with polluting seems obvious and uncontroversial: polluting degrades the environment. Closer examination, however, reveals that there are several possible views in play. At least three familiar alternatives present themselves:

- *The harms view:* pollution devalues the environment, either intrinsically or extrinsically.
- *The trespass view:* pollution disrespects and/or trespasses on the rights of others.
- *The vice view:* pollution is a vice and not the sort of thing that a person of upstanding or virtuous moral character would do.

The harms view is but one of many variant positions on pollution, though it is arguably the dominant position. It is reflected throughout US environmental legislation, including the National Environmental Policy Act (NEPA), the Clean Air Act (CAA), the Clean Water Act (CWA), Superfund (CERCLA), the Pollution Prevention Act of 1990 (PPA),[1] among many other federal and state laws. Each of these laws specifies the degree and extent to which a polluter is responsible for damage resulting from her actions. NEPA, for instance, is in place "to promote efforts which will prevent or eliminate damage to the environment" (42 USC §4321). Through this charge, NEPA aims at "pollution prevention".[2] The CAA specifically seeks out "harmful pollution". Each of the other acts, similarly, aim to prevent pollution damage to the environment.

The harms view is probably the dominant view because of its extreme versatility. It works well to describe the wrong of almost any form of pollution: air pollution (as air is damaged through the addition of deleterious substances), soil contamination (as soil loses its capacity to support life), litter (as the aesthetic properties of the landscape become degraded), noise pollution (as the aural environment becomes congested), light pollution, thermal pollution, visual pollution, polluting one's body, and so on.

In what follows, I will introduce some of the core literature on the various positions, with an eye towards articulating a somewhat more robust defence of the vice and the trespass views. I believe the harms view to be the dominant position, and thus in need of critical counterbalancing. It is my position that a more satisfying view can be had by appealing to the idea of trespass and I will offer a short argument for this at the end of this chapter. I will suggest specifically that the wrong of pollution consists in the unjustifiability of the polluting act. In many circumstances, unjustifiability will track either the degradation of value or, more closely, disrespect and trespass on rights, thus contributing to the confusion. The position I advocate nevertheless falls within the purview of the rights tradition. For reasons of space, I will only briefly outline each of the three views in the following few sections. I will not address them in great depth.

A case

If Dodgson owns a swimming pool and Duckworth dumps a five-gallon bucket of ammonia into Dodgson's swimming pool, many would rightly charge Duckworth with polluting Dodgson's pool. Depending on the facts of the case, many would further charge that, in polluting Dodgson's pool, Duckworth has wronged Dodgson. That is, Duckworth's pollution of Dodgson's pool is wrong. This sentiment stems, presumably, from the simple fact that ammonia is damaging to pools and pool water, and that by dumping the bucket of ammonia in the pool, Duckworth has thereby injured Dodgson.

The degree of wrongness of Duckworth's action may well be mitigated by external factors, of course. Duckworth's pollution of Dodgson's pool may be a case of malicious vandalism, or it easily may have been an accident. Depending on the facts, Dodgson may have more reason to forgive Duckworth in one case than in another. This much seems clear enough. It is also possible that Dodgson may have asked Duckworth to put the ammonia in the water, perhaps if Dodgson were a pool manager and Duckworth his assistant, or if Dodgson were filming a movie and Duckworth were in place to create a toxic fog on the surface of the pool. So it is not clear, from the mere fact that Duckworth has dumped ammonia in Dodgson's pool, thereby polluting the pool with ammonia, that he has therefore wronged Dodgson. Most readers will probably accept these explanations as well.

Nevertheless, many people think that pollution is wrong, and that everything else being equal, dumping ammonia in a person's pool is wrong. Many people further believe that what makes pollution wrong, or what makes dumping ammonia wrong, is that it is harmful. The question discussed in this chapter relates to the wrong of pollution, or by extension, the wrong of environmental damage. Does the wrong of pollution consist fundamentally in the harm-causing effects of sullying some environment? Or is there something more?

In our opening case, it is easy to find great fault with Duckworth's actions. Many would like to believe that what Duckworth has done wrong is that he has harmed Dodgson. He has cost Dodgson money: money that he otherwise might have spent on a new yacht or a new car. He has also, conceivably, put Dodgson at risk, from chlorine gas inhalation – ammonia and chlorine combine to form chlorine gas – or he has damaged the filters in Dodgson's pool, or he has shortened the lifespan of the paint on the pool walls.[3] Of course, for our purposes, the pool need not be a pool at all. It can be a pond, or a lake, or quadrant of air, or anything. So long as anything can be sullied, it is pollutable. What, ultimately, is wrong with what Duckworth has done to Dodgson?

Plainly, harm is not the only factor that goes into a determination of wrongdoing. There are other factors as well, including a consideration of the reasons why damages subtract value or utility, or also why a person may be polluting in the first place. In most, but not all, cases of pollution, the wrongness of harm-causing appears to rest also on the property rights of the injured party, as with Duckworth and Dodgson: what makes Duckworth's action wrong seems to be that he has damaged *Dodgson's* pool. Dodgson has been injured as his property has been valued. Following this line of reasoning, many people have sought to characterize pollution of common pool resources, or community property, but this raises serious questions about the extent to which one can be said to do wrong by introducing deleterious additives into unowned spaces. Further, most people will accept the influence of extraneous factors like motive and bad luck, just as they may have accepted Duckworth's excuses for unintentionally or accidentally poisoning Dodgson's pool. We tend to treat these as "mitigating factors", but I think that ignoring these factors can lead to big problems, some of which I will explain in the next section.

Harm, vice and trespass

The above discussion may smack of hairsplitting triviality, but how we conceive of the wrong of pollution has far-reaching practical implications. It impacts how we address pollution. If, for instance, we view the problem of pollution fundamentally as a problem of harm, then we may be inclined to approach pollution in a distinctively economic fashion: as a "negative externality". That is, we may claim that the harms caused by pollution are unaccounted-for negative costs, external to a producer's and a consumer's expense figuration. If by contrast we view it as a vice, then we may believe that what is wrong is a problem of character formation or moral education. If, alternatively, we view it as trespass, then we may think of the problem as primarily a violation of rights or the denial of consent.

Assuming such views about pollution then invites a prescription, depending on which view is endorsed. One simple way of dealing with pollution, if it is aptly understood as a harm, is to alter the incentives of the polluter: perhaps with a Pigouvian tax, with the threat of regulation, or with a cap-and-trade regime. These approaches are put into place in order to "internalize the externality" by forcing the polluting producer to account for overlooked costs. A tax, for instance, may shift the purchase price of the product, thereby reducing demand and shifting supply, in which case a more optimum outcome can be achieved. Similarly, regulation may shift the production cost of a product, or ensure that the externality is only produced to an acceptable degree, once again ensuring a more optimal outcome. If, by contrast, we subscribe to the vice view, our solution may be to introduce upstanding exemplars into the environmental community. Finally, if we assume that it is a case of trespass, then our solution may be to impose constraints on the movement of others.

Naturally, there are cases in which the harms from pollution are too grave to countenance: say, a pollutant is found to cause mesothelioma. If this is the case, then a different prescription for the harms problem arises. Instead of taxing, regulating, or capping the pollutant, we may place strict side-constraints on the behaviour of the producer: restricting pollution altogether, thereby forcing the producer to develop new technologies that rely on substitute resources, to choose an alternative supply path, or to develop new industries entirely. This is essentially the history of asbestos. As its carcoginicity became more evident, the harms from asbestos were deemed too extreme, and industries reliant upon it were forced to adjust. Some industries fell away and alternative industries emerged in their place. In fact, a whole new market for asbestos clean-up was created.

Taxes and side-constraints are two exceptionally common, albeit politically controversial, responses to pollution. The underlying idea is the same: to shore up – or bootstrap – the inefficiencies or failures in the market by introducing top-down fixatives that force the market to right itself.

It is important to note, however, that these top-down prescriptions are objectionable to many. The famous economist Ronald Coase, for instance, claimed that in some instances they can be inefficient. He proposed that we should assign property rights to producers and polluters in order to more optimally internalize external costs. Assigning property rights, he reasoned, would allow producers to achieve equilibrium between one another without bearing the inefficient bureaucratic costs associated with collective action problems (Coase 1960). Coase's solution argues for the expansion, not the constriction, of property rights, insisting that a more optimal outcome can be achieved by way of putting control in the hands of those with a vested interest. Of course, the extent of this efficiency is an empirical matter, and Coase was speaking only theoretically. Even still, his position represents the core reasoning of a view that frowns upon top-down responses to negative externalities.

The "Coase theorem" demonstrates this important position by appealing to the case of a railroad operator and several farmers. Imagine, Coase proposes, that a locomotive has to get from one destination to another. Lining the railroad, however, are several farms that are periodically set aflame by sparks emitted from the passing coal engine. On one hand, it seems obvious that a railroad operator who sets fire to farms adjoining his railroad is responsible for having damaged the farmers. But Coase points out that, at least from the standpoint of economics, it is just as reasonable to suggest that the farmers who abut their farms against railroads cause damage to the railroad operator. That may seem counterintuitive until you consider that the situation is describable in terms of a net loss of value. Coase wants us to see that in circumstances of such conflict, both actors have an incentive to bargain with one another to reach a mutually agreeable resolution.

Among other things, what Coase demonstrates is that while regulatory intervention may seem like the most direct method of stopping one actor from harming another, the market may in fact also be an efficient method for arriving at a resolution between the parties. Where the standard view has been to hold one or the other party *liable* for causing damage to the other party – suggesting, for instance, that the railroad operator is responsible for causing damages to the farmer, and therefore further that owing to this liability the railroad must pay the farmers for damages to their crops – the Coasian position is to harness the efficiency of the market by assigning and securing property rights.

But the Coasian solution to the pollution problem calls attention to another oft-overlooked feature of pollution. That is, pollution is not neatly characterized as a straight harm/benefit problem. Whether an additive is rightly considered deleterious will depend on who is doing the accounting. A farmer keeping his hay near a railroad may consider the sparks emitted from a passing railcar to be a negative externality, a pollutant. But in the same arrangement, the railroad operator considers not the sparks, but the hay, to be the negative externality. Coase's observation is vital here: damages are reciprocal. What is a negative externality to the farmer is a positive externality to the locomotive operator, and vice versa. As a consequence, the liability and resolution is not clearly established simply by the fact of damage.

Coase too operates on the presupposition that the wrong of pollution consists in the harms of pollution, though his unique observation is that the harm itself is relative to the baseline arrangement.

From the standpoint of moral wrongdoing (as opposed to mere economic efficiency), theorists have tended to presume the harms view and then bootstrap from there. Henry Shue, for instance, has stipulated a distinction between necessary emissions and luxury emissions (Shue 1993) in an attempt to accept the harms view but also to call attention to the varieties of activities that give rise to pollution. His point is tied up in the justice discussion: some emissions are easier (more acceptable) to reduce than others. Shue does not elaborate much on how one might distinguish between a luxury and a subsistence emission, but at least one handy metric may be to cut the distinction according to elasticity of demand.

Price elasticity of demand is a measurement of how much the demand for a good changes in the face of marginal increases or decreases in price. Goods that are very elastic, like yachts and high-definition televisions (HDTVs), demonstrate a precipitous drop-off as they get more expensive. These "luxury goods" stand in sharp contrast, economically speaking, to goods that are less elastic, like pasta, rice and potatoes. If the price of these goods were suddenly to sky-rocket, assuming that there were no other backstop resources, consumers would continue to purchase them and make adjustments to their budgets elsewhere.[4]

Emissions that have a low elasticity of demand can thereby be said to be subsistence emissions, where those with higher elasticity of demand fall in the luxury category. For instance, fossil fuel emissions from daily trips to the grocery store may be considerably less elastic than fossil fuel emissions for heating one's house, which can be offset by other technologies. Or, conversely, fossil fuel emissions from daily trips to the grocery store may be more elastic than the use of wood for a cookstove. Many factors can go into the determination of whether a good is a luxury or a necessity/subsistence good.

On the other end of the spectrum, William Baxter points out that some pollution is necessary for us to do the sorts of things that we want to do, even if it is sometimes harmful (Baxter 1974). Need dinner? You will have to cook it, which will take energy, and will involve some sort of degradation of the environment. Need shelter? You will have to build it, which will take space, and involve some degradation of the environment. Baxter cartoons the pollution challenge when he asks whether we should privilege people or penguins, and he was much maligned by many in the environmental community for his stance. But his point is an important one, inasmuch as it points to a wide failing of the harms view. That is, the harms view cannot easily accommodate prevalent intuitions that many of us have about pollution.

More recently, Kevin Elliott has advanced a slightly modified version of this thesis, raising the question of whether a little pollution might be good for a person (Elliott 2011). He relies on a curious phenomenon called "hormesis" in which some otherwise toxic substances exhibit beneficial effects on individuals at low levels. Certainly some minerals are like this. Many of us take daily vitamins that are supplemented with iron. At low doses the iron is understood to promote health; but at much higher doses, it can be fatal. Indeed, iron toxicity is a major cause of poisoning death in children under six years old (Tenenbein 2005). Some carcinogens are like this as well.

The harms view, however, admits of several complications. For one, it implies that wrongs require victims. This point inspired Derek Parfit's famous argument against the "person-affecting principle" and his non-identity problem. Parfit explains that, if true, the person-affecting principle can indeed pose serious problems for concerns about pollution with regard to future generations whose existence is contingent on our actions (Parfit 1986b). If future persons would not exist except for our energy policy, which through pollution presumably leaves one set of persons worse off than a different set of persons, assuming the persons born into the polluted world still have "lives worth living" it seems strange to claim that we have somehow harmed them by pursuing the policy. On the basis of his non-identity problem, Parfit thinks that we can dispense with the person-affecting principle, but others are less persuaded. Several have sought to save the classical version of the harms view from concerns about the person-affecting principle. Within the environmental literature, Dale Jamieson has extended Peter Singer's argument of duties to the distant to apply also to future generations (Singer 1972, Jamieson 2005b). Alan Carter as well has argued that we can harm future generations by engaging in environmentally damaging activities (Carter 2001). More than this, however, he demonstrates that even if we are unsuccessful at harming these future people through pollution, this alone does not entail that pollution is permissible.

This points to a different implication of the harms view. It comes ready-made with a pre-scription for violations: fix the harm. We are left to wonder: if the harm can be repaired, is the wrong also undone? The very idea seems odd to many people. Repairing a harm no more undoes a wrong than fixing a window undoes a break-in. Thus, there is merit considering alternatives to the harms view.

Of vice and virtue

The harms view, intuitive though it seems to modern English speakers, is in fact relatively new. Etymologically speaking, the term "pollution" as related specifically to the environment can only be traced back to 1828, where it is used for the first recorded time, ostensibly metaphorically, to mean "contamination of the environment". The term more historically conjures "defilement" or "desecration of that which is sacred" and dates as far back as 1390, where it was used to mean, bizarrely, "ejaculation of semen without sexual intercourse".[5] This more archaic use of the term carries not the harms view, but instead the vice view: that pollution is a blemish, or a mar, on a person's character.

Though obtuse, etymological entanglement between pollution and defilement cannot be overlooked if one hopes to gain a grip on environmental virtues (R. Parker 1983). In fact, both ancient and contemporary ethicists have sought to characterize pollution as the sort of thing that a person of strong moral character would not do (Van Wensveen 1999). In an extraordinary work that explores the notion of contagion and taboo in Leviticus, Mary Douglas suggests that talk of ritual uncleanness pervades ancient and pre-literary custom (Douglas 2003). Such talk was mirrored in secular thought too. In the *Euthyphro*, Plato discusses pollution as μίασμα (pron. "miasma"), meaning, roughly, pollution or defilement (McPherran 2002).

The past twenty years have seen an explosion of work clearly articulating the vice position, mostly generally, but at times related specifically to pollution. Indeed, when Geoffrey Frasz proposed in 1993 that environmental ethics look closely at the virtues, he was actually follow-ing up on the rich tradition in moral theory mentioned above (Frasz 1993). In *Dirty Virtues*, Louke van Wensveen argues that acts of pollution can be characterized by a range of familiar vices, including greed, contempt, exploitation and gluttony (Van Wensveen 1999). Thomas Hill Jr famously also argues that environmental preservation is much more than a matter of infringed rights or degraded utilities (Hill 1983). Instead, he proposes, we can get at the ques-tion by asking "what sort of person would destroy the natural environment?" Ronald Sandler has argued forcefully against consequentialist accounts of environmental wrongdoing (Sandler

2007, 2010). Phil Cafaro has argued in favour of the virtues of simplicity and localization (Cafaro & Sandler 2005, Gambrel & Cafaro 2010). Allen Thompson has argued that climate change may result in significant changes in our consumer vices (Thompson 2010). And of course, many others have argued for virtues of environmental citizenship (de-Shalit 1995, Dobson & Bell 2005). Some of the virtue and vice language has even been picked up in the ecofeminist literature. Val Plumwood, for instance, accesses the problem of pollution through the language of care (Plumwood 1991, 1993).

Far from a conceptual concern limited to the salons of philosophers, the vice view predominates to this day throughout the environmental discourse. It is reflected in a variety of anti-pollution advertisements that characterize the early environmental movement. The famous "Crying Indian" advertisement of the 1970s, in which a Native American lands his canoe on a trash-strewn riverbank and sheds a tear for the loss of natural beauty, offers an instance of this. The voiceover in the ad says it all: "Some people have a deep abiding respect for the natural beauty that was once this country. Some people don't. People start pollution. People can stop it." Or, memorably, from roughly the same era, the Woodsy Owl commercials admonishing children never to be a dirty bird, with the catchy slogan "Give a hoot; don't pollute," serve the same end.

As with the harms view, the vice view also strikes some as odd. Is it possible to say that wrongdoing consists primarily and solely in traits of character? What of damages? Surely these must be considered. Is pollution best understood as the sort of thing that can be remedied only when the polluter becomes repentant (Basl 2010)? If one changes how one is, or who one is, does this then undo the wrong? Is an apology enough to repair a wrong? Clearly there is something missing here. Thus, we should consider other views as well.

More on trespass

As with the other views, the variety of threads within the trespass position are too numerous to recount in great detail. Some theorists approach the problem as one related to the encroachment and accumulation of harms (Feinberg 1984b); others as one primarily concerning rights and consent (Lercher 2007); still others by identifying disproportionate burdens and thus respect or justice (Sagoff 2003, Shrader-Frechette 2007, Hale & Grundy 2009).

Perhaps the most sophisticated version of what I am calling the trespass view has been articulated by Joel Feinberg, where he characterizes trespass in terms of the harm principle. Feinberg claims that a person harms another "by invading, and thereby thwarting or setting back, his interest" (Feinberg 1984b). What distinguishes Feinberg's position from the standard harms view is that for Feinberg harm is done not by causing a loss in a victim, but rather through the violation of a right or a principle. By characterizing harm in terms of an invasion and thwarting of interests, Feinberg epitomizes the trespass view. At points he suggests that some forms of pollution are better understood as "accumulative harms" against the public, reasoning that such pollutants are more aptly understood as the consequence of individual contributions that approach a threshold of harm, though each contribution itself may be "harmless" (Feinberg 1984a). As such, Feinberg proposes that the legislative challenge is to try to keep pollution levels below this specific threshold. It is therefore the crossing of the threshold, not the harm itself, that constitutes the violation. Accordingly, pollutants can be divided out into non-toxic pollutants, like carbon dioxide; exposure-limited pollutants which are increasingly and accumulatively dangerous, like iron supplements; and pollutants for which there is no safe level of exposure, like ground-level ozone or carbon monoxide (Hancock 2007).

The trespass view is not limited to the mere trespassing on rights or principle however. It can also turn on consent. Samuel Scheffler, for instance, discusses three familiar and influential views on the importance of consent as it relates to risk (Scheffler 1985). According to the first view, consent is primarily instrumental. On the second view, consent is an important component of a good life, and so therefore has intrinsic value. On the third view, consent is derivative of individual rights. Following in this tradition, Aaron Lercher (2007) proposes that there is an environmental moral right against pollution and that this is a right against negligent, reckless or intentional risk imposition. A fair bit of the risk/consent variation within the trespass discussion turns in part on epistemic limitations related to how our lives are affected by pollution. Some, like Andreas Teuber, aim to specify the conditions under which risk impositions can be justified, and thus the circumstances in which harm and consent intermingle (Teuber 1990). Carrie Hull points out that there are essentially two schools of thought on the question of how reliable reports of the damage from pollution are. Many seek to identify a clear causal connection, whereas others seek to show that actual damage is underestimated by lab studies (Hull 1999). Hull's argument can explain how, in some instances, causal responsibility for harm done is not necessary to establish moral responsibility. In a somewhat different vein, Carl Cranor has claimed that if too high an evidentiary burden is required for the use of toxic substances, this may leave the public at risk (Cranor 1993).

Lockean logic emerges rapidly as one of the most pervasive positions from which to defend the trespass view, though it needs some shoring up. Says Narveson: "Redressing the effects of, say, pollution is a tricky matter, but it is not one that is denied by the market philosophy – precisely the reverse. What's wrong with pollution is, precisely, that it invades persons and their property" (Narveson 2003a). Peter Railton, disagreeing somewhat with positions such as Narveson's, argues that even though Lockean natural rights theories are commonly associated with laissez-faire policies, when the question of pollution enters the picture, Lockean theories actually end up requiring far stronger restrictions on individual freedom (Railton 2003). Where Narveson finds the resources within Lockean theory to explain the wrong of pollution, Railton suggests that Lockeanism cannot easily answer questions with regard to pollution and risk. There is a difficult line to toe with this view since property rights are on one hand exceptionally permissive, in that they permit the property holder to do with her property as she sees fit, but also exceptionally restrictive in that they restrict others from trespassing on the property of others. Emissions and pollution complicate this picture considerably.

Finally, efforts to understand trespass in terms of obligations to respect have been advanced by Kantians such as Onora O'Neill, for instance, who has suggested in an important but somewhat overlooked article that obligation-based reasoning may better serve our environmental goals (O'Neill 1997). Kristin Shrader-Frechette has also advanced an important obligation-oriented view by arguing on democratic grounds that everyone has a responsibility to prevent environmental fatalities and to become informed and engaged in environmental health (Shrader-Frechette 2007, 2011).

So which view is correct? It is not easy to say. The harms view seems too limited and to overlook questions of reparation. The vice view raises questions about what sorts of behaviours actually qualify as behaviours that a morally upstanding member of society would not do. And the trespass view seems to invite questions about permissible and impermissible trespass, threatening to collapse back into a risk-harms position. Understanding the nuances of each view can assist in approaching pollution more delicately. My thought is that though the temptation to understand pollution from a consequentialist vantage is strong, we crowd out vice and trespass positions if we place too much emphasis on harms. I shall seek to elaborate on the obligation-oriented "respect" thread below (see also Hale & Grundy 2009, Hale 2012).

Polluter pays principle: or undoing the damage

The polluter pays principle is a principle of environmental law and ethics that requires parties responsible for polluting the natural environment also to pay to clean up the natural environment. It is a reasonable principle, all things considered, inasmuch as damage to the environment is precisely the sort of thing that appears to be the core concern of pollution.

The principle is supported by a range of legal entities, including the United Nations (UN), the European Community (EC), the United States (US) in many of the aforementioned laws, and the Organisation for Economic Co-operation and Development (OECD). In the Rio Declaration on Environment and Development, it is codified as principle 16:

> National authorities should endeavour to promote the internalization of environmental costs and the use of economic instruments, taking into account the approach that the polluter should, in principle, bear the cost of pollution, with due regard to the public interest and without distorting international trade and investment.[6]

The Comprehensive Environmental Response, Compensation, and Liability Act of 1980 (CERCLA), which goes by the more portentous heading of "Superfund", authorizes the federal government to clean up spills that place the environment or public health in danger. Though Superfund is thought by many people – indeed, as the nickname implies – to be a fund established by the United States government to clean up spills, more than 75 per cent of the funding for the clean-up actually comes from the polluters themselves.[7] Thus, polluter pays. The United States Corporate Average Fuel Economy (CAFE) standards impose a fine on those who sell cars below a set fuel economy standard, essentially requiring them to pay for polluting.

The polluter pays principle is essentially a guiding presupposition of "corrective justice", which proposes that in order to rectify a wrong, the injurer must repair what injury he is responsible for (Shrader-Frechette 2011). Corrective justice stands in sharp contrast to "retributive justice", which proposes not only that the injurer must pay damages for harm done, but that the injurer must also pay an extra penalty and/or must be made to suffer, over and above the corrective cost, for wrongdoing.

Take this first by examining a simple case of damage or harm. Consider first a case introduced by environmental ethicist Robert Elliot, who wrote in 1982 an article called "Faking Nature", which he later expanded to become a book (Elliot 1982, 1997). Elliot proposes that destroying a valuable artwork and replacing it with a passable fake invariably leaves an ineffable remainder: the intrinsic value of the artwork. His objective is to argue on behalf of the intrinsic value of nature. The "causal genesis of forests, rivers, lakes and so on is important to establishing their value" (Elliot 1982: 85). Elliot uses the case of artworks to illustrate his point. Just as Elliot does, I will give cases of non-environmental harm and trespass in hopes of priming your intuitions to see that there is quite a bit more to pollution than environmental harm. Suppose:

> *Malicious vandal:* You have very expensive, original John Tenniel woodcut print hanging in your hall. A notorious art vandal breaks into your house and cuts the print to pieces, irrevocably destroying it.

Malicious vandal is a case in which there are at least two sorts of wrongings going on. For one, the vandal has damaged a valuable artwork, causing harm either extrinsically or intrinsically. Second, the vandal has broken into your house, trespassing on your person. The problem with the polluter pays principle and the harms view can here be made clear. Simply replacing the woodcut, or paying for damages, does not undo the wrong. Consider the following comparison case:

> *Clever vandal:* You have a very expensive, original Tenniel woodcut print hanging as before. A clever vandal – a detractor of important illustration art – deeply desires to destroy this original Tenniel. He breaks into your house and does so. To cover his tracks, and to avoid penalty, he replaces your Tenniel print with a cheap but perfect fake; a replica so good that not even the best expert can tell the difference between the two prints. By assumption the print is so good that it would sell at market for the same price as the original. You are none the wiser.

It seems to me that despite the fact that, from the standpoint of the monetary value of the prints, you are not harmed in any way by the clever vandal's act, you have still been wronged. This is akin to Elliot's classic "faking nature" case, and it would appear that what is wrong here is that the intrinsically valuable artwork, the Tenniel, is destroyed. Something inimitable has been lost. Elliot would have us observe that in light of this loss we can understand intrinsic value. But notice:

> *Impulsive vandal:* Again you have the expensive Tenniel. An impulsive vandal sneaks into your house while you are away. So incensed that you would have a Tenniel print on your wall, he proceeds to destroy it. Immediately feeling release after destroying your artwork, he grows worried about the legal implications of his impulsive act. To make amends, he digs deep into his bank account, and though it pains him to do so, purchases another identical woodcut to hang on your wall. He does so before you return home. You are neither better nor worse off. You simply have a different original and expensive Tenniel.

This is a classic case of trespass, and the wrong here consists solely in the breaking and entering, as well as in the destruction of the art. The two are, essentially, the same act. The destruction of the art is a violation of your will, a wronging of you, and it is very much this wronging of you that qualifies the act as wrong. Had you invited the vandal into your home and asked him to destroy your artwork, the circumstances would be different indeed. So too if you had invited him into your home, thereby removing considerations about trespass into your home, and he had impulsively destroyed your art, or accidentally destroyed your art. We should reject such vandalism as a violation, despite the fact that you may never learn of the home invasion. Now consider this case:

> *Benevolent vandal:* As a longtime aficionado of children's literature, you have a cheap replica of a famous Tenniel print hanging on your wall. Suppose that a notorious vandal and detractor of cheap kitsch breaks into your house and destroys this print on your wall. Ugh! Gross. He cannot stand such garbage! Courteously, he replaces the replica with an original and authentic Tenniel print.

You may think this quite nice of the benevolent vandal. He has given you a precious artwork. But there is still the minor matter of the breaking and entering, as well as the kitschy fake that had previously adorned your wall. Without any information about you, or about your commitment to that kitschy fake, it seems to me that the benevolent vandal has still wronged you in some way, even though, in retrospect, his actions may have benefited you in perhaps such a way that you are grateful to the vandal. I want to hold that there is still an important violation of your person, and that you would be correct to criticize the vandal for doing as he has. This, at least, is what I shall claim about pollution. But let us examine a bit more closely.

This discussion sheds light on the manner in which the harms view of pollution is too narrow. In the remainder of this chapter I discuss undoing harm and/or correcting a wrong.

A mad tea party; or, the hatter's riddle

There are several cases in which environmental remediation technologies point to an oft-overlooked aspect of environmental damage: that respect for others, or what I am here calling "trespass", is also in play (Hale & Grundy 2009). Consider:

> *Poison*: The Mad Hatter develops a poison that has the potential to kill Alice, but for which he has the antidote. Once the antidote is administered, Alice will suffer no ill effects.

Suppose the Hatter puts this poison in Alice's tea while they are chatting, fully intending to administer the antidote immediately once Alice has ingested the tea. It seems plausible that the Hatter will be wronging Alice by adding the poison to her tea, even though Alice will not be harmed by the poison.

You may have your doubts. Perhaps you think that the problem here is that the Hatter has put Alice at *risk*. But consider other examples to address such concerns:

> *Inert additive*: Before putting the poison in Alice's tea, the Mad Hatter mixes the poison with the antidote, thus making the poison an inert additive.

Even with this knowledge, it would appear that the Mad Hatter is wronging Alice by adding an inert additive to her tea. Even adding a substance so inert and harmless to Alice's tea as water without her consent is, on its face, a kind of wronging of Alice.

To see the conflict here, it may help to parallel this case with that of the benevolent vandal.

> *Health potion*: The Hatter has discovered an additive that will add years to a person's life. He and Alice are having tea.

Where in the vandal cases there was a clear two-step violation – first an incidence of trespass and then an incident of vandalism or harm – the two-step process has been collapsed in the mad tea party cases. It appears at first that the problem lies clearly with the harm or risk to Alice, but removing the harm or risk suggests that even here there is a sort of trespass, or disrespect of the person. Further, it would seem not incorrect to suggest that the health potion serves as a kind of pollutant. It is plausible, then, that the wrong of pollution lies in the trespass, or the disrespect, of Alice's will. Plainly, there are circumstances that would make the Hatter's actions permissible: if, for instance, he acquires her consent first, or if, through a bizarre twist, the Hatter finds Alice unresponsive but understands that, had she her druthers, she would have willed herself into health. In these cases, the unauthorized addition of a health potion can be understood not as a breach of respect, but a considered and respectful action. The critical consideration is not whether Alice is benefited, but whether the Hatter has taken the full suite of facts about Alice, including her interests, her desires and her autonomy, into account.

This is all very abstract, I confess, but the upshot of my argument will begin to take on a more plausible ring if we consider a real case. In the next section, I would like to drill deeper.

Directions for further research

There are at least three emerging areas for further research. First, and arguably most importantly, much more must be said on pollution and non-human animals and non-rational nature. One ostensible strength of the harms view is that it elides any deeply embedded anthropocentrism that the trespass view may engender. Trespass seems limited to entities that can be trespassed upon, which is more or less limited to rights holders. One need not specify what rights are violated here – they may be property rights or rights to self-ownership or even rights to privacy – only that some right of some sort is violated. Without an account clearly spelling out the rights of non-human animals, the trespassed upon are mostly humans. This would appear to be a strike against the trespass view. But perhaps this need not necessarily be so. One could cast this just as easily in terms of duties to respect others and not in terms of rights. The wrongs associated with pollution could be construed as stemming from a failure of the duty of justification, where this duty is understood fundamentally in terms of what can be justified (Habermas 1991, Hale & Grundy 2009, Hale & Dilling 2011, Hale 2012). Harms and benefits matter, of course, but what will matter as well is whether such trespass could be agreed by all affected parties.

Second, there is a fair bit of work to be done on climate-altering pollutants. Most recently in the policy community there has been concerted effort to focus on carbon emissions as a form of pollution. The US Environmental Protection Agency (EPA), for instance, recently sought to characterize carbon as a pollutant, which it did by framing carbon as a harmful pollutant.[8] This finding, known as the "Endangerment Finding" under the US Clean Air Act, asserted that concentrations of six critical greenhouse gases – carbon dioxide (CO_2), methane (CH_4), nitrous oxide (N_2O), hydrofluorocarbons (HFCs), perfluorocarbons (PFCs) and sulphur hexafluoride (SF_6) could accumulatively "threaten public health and welfare of current and future generations". Immediately the EPA's Endangerment Finding was seized upon by political opponents on grounds that challenge the nature of the harms associated with these emissions. Some particularly bombastic political actors argued that carbon dioxide ought not to be considered a pollutant, since it is essential to life and, under most circumstances, a harmless gas.[9] To many this was little more than political theatre, but, more critically, the Endangerment Finding relies on the harms view of pollution to make its case.

Finally, Kevin Elliott and Daniel McKaughan have gone some distance already in exploring the influence of the above-mentioned non-epistemic values on research protocols (Elliott & McKaughan 2009). These directions could be explored by appealing to some of the more recent work in experimental philosophy, particularly the work related to ordinary language and disgust (Knobe 2003, McGinn 2011). Such work may illuminate the underpinnings of the vice view.

Final thoughts on trespass

Return for a moment to Duckworth and Dodgson's pool. What Duckworth is doing by dumping ammonia in Dodgson's pool is trespassing on Dodgson's morally established jurisdiction: his rights. If Duckworth adds ammonia and then immediately neutralizes the ammonia, he will still be trespassing on Dodgson's jurisdiction, much like the clever vandal. If Duckworth is making a product and accidentally spills ammonia in Dodgson's pool, he will certainly be required, among other things, to clean up his mess, but he will nevertheless be trespassing on Dodgson's jurisdiction. Whether Dodgson forgives him for the accident, it is plain enough to see, will depend not entirely on the damage done, but on the reason that Duckworth can give for having caused the problem in the first place.

It is interesting to note that on the harms view a pond of water equivalent in volume to Dodgson's pool but absent of chlorine does not form the same toxic chloramines that may lead us to evaluate Duckworth's ammonia dumping harshly. In other words, Duckworth's addition of ammonia to a swimming pool is made that much worse by the fact that Dodgson has already added chlorine to the pool; and though both Dodgson and Duckworth have engaged in roughly the same act – one the addition of chlorine, the other the addition of ammonia – it is the act of adding ammonia and not the act of adding chlorine that we evaluate as contaminating the pool.

The nature of Duckworth's wrongdoing is contingent largely on the reasons that Duckworth has for doing what he is doing. Far from hairsplitting, these reasons lie at the heart of moral action; and yet, they are crowded out by attempts to internalize the externalities, by attempts to characterize environmental problems in terms of benefits and costs.

What these examples suggest is that the environmental wrong of pollution amounts to a unique sort of trespass. This is a trespass on the rights of other persons: again, which specific rights here is immaterial. It is, in essence, the disrespecting of others; but more fundamentally it is the failure of the agent to adequately justify her actions, to fulfil the requirement that actions be justified.

I have explored three rough categories of positions related to pollution: the harms view, the trespass view, and the vice view. There are reasons to think that the harms view holds the presumptive crown in this triumvirate, and that this dominance is reflected throughout environmental law. In the second section, I discussed the potential implications of the harms view, vice view and the trespass view, respectively. In the next section, I discussed the polluter pays principle and suggested that it is self-undermining. In the fourth section, I introduced the case of Alice and the Hatter to help crystallize the trespass view. And in the final section, I proposed some directions for further research.

In a big, shared environment, we often do not have discrete property boundaries like those that enable Dodgson to claim that he has been trespassed upon. As a consequence, the moral idea of trespass faces into the dominance of concern over harms. But theorists like Ronald Coase (1960), J. J. Thomson (1980,1992), Joel Feinberg (1990) and Mark Sagoff (2004), among others, remind us that much more than harms are already in play. The circumstances in which the addition of ammonia to a swimming pool, and the conditions under which such an act might be deemed wrong, are contingent in large part on the full suite of reasons that best explains, and either does or does not justify, the action. To deny this is to reduce the question of wrongdoing from pollution to simplified caricature; and more distressingly, to defang the bite of the environmentalist's claim against the polluter.

Acknowledgement

Portions of this chapter appear in Michael Boylan's *Environmental Ethics*, 2nd edn (2013). The original piece offered an argument for a non-consequentialist account of pollution. This chapter has been revised substantially to suit the specifications of this volume.

Notes

1 See www.epa.gov/p2/pubs/p2policy/act1990.htm.

2 See http://ceq.hss.doe.gov/nepa/regs/poll/ppguidnc.htm.

3 Please note: this reaction is extremely volatile and dangerous. Do not, under any circumstances, try to create this chemical reaction. Doing so could result in serious injury or death.

4 For instance, at the time of writing, a decent 48″ HDTV sells for about $1000 (£592). Some are more expensive, some less expensive, but roughly speaking, they sell for $1000. Suppose that there is a sale on these televisions, say, offering them for $100 (£59) each. One assumes naturally that such a sale would result in a rush of buyers for the televisions. At a low price, demand is very high for the televisions. Suppose, instead, that there is a sudden scarcity in these televisions, raising the price to $10,000 (£5,920) for a television. One would assume naturally that such a price would yield a significant drop in demand. At a high price, demand is quite a bit lower. This is the price elasticity of demand. Whether a good is more or less elastic is an empirical matter. It is also, however, a question of luxury.

5 pollution, n. *Oxford English Dictionary*, third edn, September 2006; online version June 2011, www.oed.com/view/Entry/146992 (accessed 27 July 2011). An entry for this word was first included in the *New English Dictionary* in 1907.

6 See http://en.wikisource.org/wiki/Administrative_Instruction_ST/AI/189 (accessed May 2014).

7 See www.epa.gov/superfund/community/today/pdfs/whopays.pdf (accessed August 2011).

8 See http://epa.gov/climatechange/endangerment.

9 See www.humanevents.com/2010/05/10/lord-monckton-scolds-house-democrats-at-climategate-hearing (accessed May 2014).

29

SUSTAINABILITY

John O'Neill

The concept of "sustainability"

"Sustainability" has become a key normative concept in environmental policy-making and politics. It has also become a standard observation that the concept is used in a variety of different ways. Sustaining something is in its core sense about maintaining something over a period of time. The concept of sustainability originated in resource management in areas such as agriculture, forestry and fisheries. In these contexts it was used in a specific sense to describe a sustainable yield for the resource in question. What rates of extraction from the stock of resources could be maintained over a particular period of time without diminishing the stock? A fishing policy that leads to the depletion of stocks in particular fishing grounds, or agricultural practices that lead to irreversible losses of topsoil in a particular area, are said to be unsustainable. Reference to such specific goods remains typical in the use of the concept of sustainability in the natural sciences and resource management.

These specific uses of the concept of sustainability need to be distinguished from a more general use that the concept has enjoyed at least since the introduction of the concept of "sustainable development" in the Brundtland Report. The "Brundtland" formulation is the following: "Sustainable development is development that meets the needs of the present without compromising the ability of future generations to meet their own needs" (World Commission on Environment and Development 1987). The report goes on to say that overriding priority should be given to the essential needs of the world's poor. In subsequent economic literature the concept of sustainability has been used to characterize an obligation to maintain human well-being over time. This general use is not tied to the use of any specific stock of resources. Indeed, one influential characterization has gone so far as to deny that sustainability should be concerned with any specific object or resource: "Sustainability as a moral obligation is a general obligation not a specific one. It is not an obligation to preserve this or preserve that" (Solow 1993a: 86). This general use involves important changes in the use of the concept. First, it describes the conditions that national or global social and economic arrangements must meet rather than some particular practices or policies about the employment of a specific stock of resources. Second, it is conjoined to the concept of "development". Thus conjoined it can be understood in one of two ways, either as marking a constraint on development or as marking the idea that what is being maintained is not a given state but an improvement in some conditions over time.

How should sustainability in this general sense be characterized? One useful starting point is through an answer to three questions: The sustainability of what? For whom? And why? In the economic literature that informs much public policy on sustainability following the Brundtland Report, the answer to these questions runs roughly as follows. What is to be sustained is a certain level of human welfare or well-being. In the original Brundtland formulation welfare is characterized objectively in terms of needs. In standard welfare economics it is understood in terms of preference satisfaction. For whom it is to be sustained are present and future generations of humans. The question why it should be sustained is normally given either a broadly utilitarian answer – to maximize welfare over time – or an answer that appeals to intergenerational justice – to meet the demands of distributional justice between generations. Sustainable *development* is then defined as economic and social development that at least maintains and if possible improves levels of human welfare. Typically it is argued that what is required to maintain or improve levels of human welfare over generations is for each generation to leave its successor a stock of capital assets no less than it receives. The term "sustainable" is applied to entire social and economic arrangements to capture what classically would have been called changes to "the wealth of nations".

There are clearly large normative and conceptual questions that might be raised about this characterization of sustainability. The account is welfarist: it assumes that what matters for sustainability is maintaining or improving welfare. It also assumes that only human welfare matters. One set of debates around this concept of sustainability centres on the defensibility of these assumptions. One might reject the second assumption, that only human welfare matters. The welfare of sentient beings, or more generally the good of living things, might be argued to matter independently of the welfare of human beings. The first assumption might also be rejected. Welfare is not the only value. For example, one might hold that there are impersonal values, that is, that there are certain things or states, for example biodiversity or beauty, that are valuable in themselves but not of value for the life of any being. Something close to this position about beauty was, for example, held by G. E. Moore who thought that beauty was of value even though there was no agent conscious of that beauty (Moore 1903: 85–87). Many might similarly think that the accelerated loss of species is bad even if it is not bad for any particular being. If either of these objections is telling then one might still defend a wider conception of environmental sustainability, for example, as the maintenance or improvement of levels of human and non-human welfare over time or levels of total value, including impersonal value, over time. These arguments raise important issues that deserve detailed consideration. However, they will not be my central concern in this chapter. For the remainder of this chapter I will focus on the narrower definition of sustainability in terms of the maintenance and improvement of human well-being. I will argue that even so understood there are some major problems with the way it has been characterized in the economic literature.

The paradox of sustainability

A useful starting point to the discussion is with an apparent paradox in current discussions of sustainability. Sustainability is used both specifically to characterize what is required to maintain yields of some specific resource and generally to characterize the condition to maintain and improve levels of human well-being. Sustainability in the use of some specific local goods and the general sustainability of human welfare in an economy can depart from each other without inconsistency. The unsustainable uses of specific resources can exist within a globally sustainable economy. Globally unsustainable economies can include uses of specific goods that are sustainable. However, there is a paradox that descriptions of uses of specific resources and economic characterizations of the state of economies appear to depart from each other not occasionally but systematically. Descriptions by natural scientists of the sustainability of specific resources appear to show that in a series of key resources current uses are unsustainable. When economists typically tell their story of economic development, the impact of those local failures of sustainability seems to disappear from view. As Dasgupta notes, there is "a puzzle created by conflicting intuitions that have been derived from two different empirical perspectives concerning the question of whether the character of contemporary economic development is sustainable":

> On the one hand, if we look at specific resources and services (e.g. fresh water, eco-system services, and the atmosphere as a carbon sink), there is convincing evidence that the current rates of utilization are unsustainable. On the other hand, if we look at historical trends in the prices of marketed resources or the recorded growth in GNP per capita in countries that are currently rich, resource scarcities would not appear yet to have bitten.
>
> *(Dasgupta 2001: 87–88)*

How should this conflict of perspectives be resolved? One response is to question the accounts of sustainability and sustainable development that underpin some influential versions of the economic characterization of the concepts. Changes in the monetary prices of market goods and market transactions need not be good indicators either of how far levels of human well-being are maintained or improved or of how far the conditions exist for their continued maintenance in the future. Hence, the continuing growth in GDP is not a good measure of sustainability: "GDP is an inadequate metric to gauge well-being over time particularly in its economic, environmental, and social dimensions, some aspects of which are often referred to as *sustainability*" (Stiglitz *et al.* 2009: 8, emphasis original). Thus stated the objection raises important questions about how well-being should be understood and what is required to maintain human well-being over time. It is those questions that form the main focus of this chapter.

Sustainability, well-being and capital

Sustainability in the mainstream economic tradition is understood to be about maintaining levels of well-being over time:

> "Sustainability" therefore implies something about maintaining the level of human well-being so that it might improve but at least never decline (or, not more than temporarily, anyway). Interpreted this way, sustainable development becomes equivalent to some requirement that well-being does not decline through time.
>
> *(Pearce 1993: 48)*

Thus understood the specification of sustainability involves answering at least two prior questions:

- How is well-being to be understood?
- What are the conditions for maintaining well-being over time?

There are standard responses to these questions in the literature. To the first question, the mainstream economics approach specifies well-being in terms of preference satisfaction. Well-being consists in the satisfaction of preferences: the stronger the preference satisfied, the greater the improvement in well-being. For the economist a virtue of this account is that it brings changes in well-being directly under the "measuring rod of money". A person's willingness to pay at the margin for some good is taken to reveal the strength of the preference for the good. The view has its critics, not just among philosophers, but within economics itself, from the revived hedonic account on the one side and from the more objective perspective represented by the capabilities approach on the other. For reasons I outline below, which perspective is taken on well-being makes a difference to an answer to the second question about what is required to maintain well-being over time. The standard answer to this second question runs something as follows: what is required is that "we leave to the future the option or the capacity to be as well off as we are" (Solow 1993a: 181). What is required to leave those in the future this option or capacity is not any particular good or goods but stocks of capital. "Whether these levels of well-being can be sustained over time depends on whether stocks of capital that matter for our lives (natural, physical, human, social) are passed on to future generations" (Stiglitz *et al.* 2009: 11). The levels of capital required for human well-being should not decline over time, and if possible, they should improve.

On this account, natural environments, resources and beings should be understood as "capital". What is involved in the use of a concept that has its core meaning as commercial assets in this environmental context? At least part of the answer is that it involves an understanding of parts of the natural world as assets that are valued in terms of the services and benefits they provide, either directly for the welfare of those who use them or indirectly as inputs into production and as the background conditions for human life and production. Ayres and Kneese's influential characterization of resources provides a useful starting point:

> Almost all of standard economic theory is in reality concerned with services. Material objects are merely the vehicles which carry some of these services, and they are exchanged because of consumer preferences for the services associated with their use or because they can help to add value in the manufacturing process.
>
> *(Ayres & Kneese 1969: 284)*

Given this view much of the value of the natural world is in terms of the ecosystem services they provide: "the links between nature and the economy are … described using the concept of *ecosystem services*, or flows of value to human societies as a result of the state and quantity of natural capital" (TEEB 2010: 7). The assets are understood as capacities to "provide humankind with the services of resource provision, waste assimilation, amenity and life support" (Jacobs 1995: 62).

Given this account of sustainability as providing stocks of capital required to maintain and improve human well-being, debates have largely focused on the degree to which different kinds of capital are substitutable for each other. The question of substitutability in recent environmental discussion is Janus-faced. On the one hand, a condition of sustainability is the possibility of widespread substitutability of one set of resources by others with lower environmental impacts: for example of substituting sources of energy with high greenhouse gas emissions, such as coal and oil, with sources that have lower emissions, such as wind power. On the other hand, those concerned with sustaining natural environments and biodiversity want to insist on the limits of substitutability, in particular limits in the degree to which "natural" capital has substitutes in "human-made" capital.

The degree of substitutability of natural and human-made capital is the object of the debates between proponents of "weak" and "strong" sustainability. "Natural capital" is distinguished from human-made capital. Human-made capital is construed widely to include not just particular physical items such as machines, roads and buildings, but also other forms of "capital" such as knowledge, skills, capabilities and social networks. Natural capital is also typically construed widely to include not just particular organic and inorganic physical items, but also other forms such as genetic information and biodiversity. Both human capital and natural capital are understood in terms of the services they provide. The question then becomes one of how far the services provided by natural capital can be substituted by forms of human capital. Proponents of "weak sustainability" are normally taken to claim that a wide degree of substitutability of goods at the margin is possible, so that all that matters for sustainability is that the total level of capital, human-made and natural, does not decline. Proponents of "strong sustainability" are normally taken to claim that there are limits to the substitutability of natural and human-made capital and hence that sustainability requires that there is some level of "natural capital" that does not decline.[1]

Thus outlined it might look as if debate is largely an empirical argument about how far services provided for by one kind of capital do in fact have substitutes of another kind (Ayres 2007). However, the debate does presuppose some resolution of a number of prior conceptual and normative questions that are more philosophical. One concerns how the distinction between "natural" and "human-made" capital is being drawn in the first place. One way that the distinction might be drawn is terms of the contrast between the natural and artificial (Hume [1739–40] 2000: III.i.ii). One useful starting point for this sense of "natural" is that offered by J. S. Mill as that which "takes place without the agency, or without the voluntary and intentional agency, of man" (Mill 1874: 8).[2] However, as it is used in the literature, the term "natural" is often used in a much looser sense to include many living resources such as managed forests which are not obviously "natural" in this sense. I return to this point later. Before doing so I want to consider two different questions. The first concerns what is meant by saying that one thing is a substitute for another. The second concerns the adequacy of understanding our relation to the natural world in terms of capital that is valued for its services.

The concept of substitutability

What is it for one thing to be a substitute for another?[3] What is it for one thing to be an adequate substitute for another? To answer those questions two concepts of substitutability that are central to this debate need to be distinguished (O'Neill *et al.* 2008: 189).

Technical substitute

One thing is a technical substitute for another if it realizes the same purpose or goal. For example we might say that saccharine substitutes for sugar as a sweetener. Wind power might substitute for coal power as a source of energy. In this sense a particular object serves a substitute if it can perform a similar function in achieving some particular end.

Economic substitute

Welfare economists also, however, use the concept of a substitute in a wider sense with respect to maintaining a particular level of welfare. For any agent, one good, A, is a substitute for another good, B, if replacing B by A does not change the overall level of welfare of that agent. Goods in this sense are not substitutes for another in the sense that they do the same job or perform the same function. Rather, goods are substitutes in the sense that, as Hillel Steiner puts it, "although they each do a different job, those two jobs are *just as good* as one another" (Steiner 1994: 171, original emphasis). The concept of economic substitutability allows for a much greater degree of substitutability than does the technical concept. Beer may not be a technical substitute for sugar as a sweetener in tea. It can be an economic substitute if the beer improves the welfare of the drinker at least as much as the sweetened tea would have done.

Both senses of the term matter for the debates. Much of the empirical debate is concerned with the possibilities for human technologies substituting for natural capital in the sense of being able to provide the same service or perform the same function. For example, faced with a development of a wetland one might ask questions such as: "Are there human technologies that could perform the same waste assimilation functions as this wetland?" or "Are there human-made substitutes that will allow the breeding of this particular species of birds to continue?" where the birds themselves will provide some service, say in terms of agricultural pest control or as objects of delight for bird-watchers. Or at a more global scale, faced with greenhouse gas emissions, the geoengineer might ask if there are human technologies for regulating climate either through the removal of green-house gases from the ambient atmosphere or increasing the earth's albedo which could compensate for the damage to the natural systems that provide the service of climate regulation. These services are understood to matter only instrumentally. Technical substitutes are not required if there are economic substitutes. For example, if the loss of birds for the bird-watcher can be substituted for by some other good, say increasing entertainment on television, so that the bird-watcher's overall welfare stays the same, then while technically televisions are not substitutes for the birds provided by wetlands, they might be economic substitutes.

The question of the degree to which goods are substitutable for each other on this account turns on questions both of technical and economic substitutability. However, different accounts of economic substitutability allow for very different levels of substitution. Two things are substitutes for each other in the economic sense if replacing one by the other leaves a person's level of well-being unchanged. What is it to leave a person's level of well-being unchanged? The answer to that question depends on the account of well-being one assumes. Standard neo-classical economics assumes a preference-satisfaction account of well-being. Well-being consists in the satisfaction of preferences: the stronger the preference satisfied the greater the improvement in well-being. If one assumes this view then two alternative goods or bundles of goods x and y are substitutable for each other if they are equally preferred: if x is at least as preferred as y and y is at least as preferred as x. The person is said to be indifferent between them. Given additional assumptions about the structure of preferences – in particular that preferences are transitive (if x is preferred to y and y is preferred to z, then x is preferred to z), complete (for any two bundles of goods x and y a person either prefers x to y or prefers y to x or is indifferent between them) and continuous (if one bundle of goods x is preferred to another bundle of goods y, then either bundle can be fractionally altered without changing this preference ordering) – then one can draw the continuous indifference curves of economic textbooks which join all the points at which goods are equally preferred. At any point on that curve, its slope indicates the marginal rate of substitution between goods, that is, how much of one good a person is willing to give up in order to gain an improvement in the other.

This account of well-being allows for a wide substitutability of goods for each other. If the bird-watcher comes to prefer watching television to watching birds, then wetlands are replaceable with televisions with respect to that specific function. If consumers come to prefer plastic furniture to wood furniture then some of the "natural capital" embodied in forests can be replaced by human oil-based technologies. Given preferences are mutable enough, the realm of non-substitutable natural capital could, on this account of well-being, turn out to be very small indeed.

If one moves from a preference satisfaction account of well-being to a more objective account, then the extent of substitutability is much more limited. Contrast for example a preference satisfaction account of well-being with a needs-based account. There are standard differences in the logical properties of the concepts of "preference" and "need". First, the concept of need is extensional, whereas the concept of preference is intensional. From "Joseph needs glucose" and "glucose is $C_6H_{12}O_6$", we can infer "Joseph needs $C_6H_{12}O_6$". From "Oedipus prefers to marry Jocasta to any other woman in Thebes" and "Jocasta is Oedipus's mother", one cannot infer "Oedipus prefers to marry his mother to any other woman in Thebes". Whether or not a person needs an object depends on the objective condition of the person and the nature of the object. Specifically, it depends on the capacities of the object to contribute to the flourishing of a person. Whether a person prefers one object to another depends not on the properties of the object as such but rather upon the nature of the person's beliefs about the objects. Second, the concept of a categorical need is a threshold concept, where the concept of a preference is not. Categorical needs are those conditions that are necessary for a flourishing life, such that their absence would harm the person (Wiggins 1998). A person needs a certain amount of water, food and shelter, and also certain social relations, if they are to flourish at all. Categorical needs have lower and upper bounds, thresholds such that if a person goes below or above them her well-being will suffer. The concept of a preference is not a threshold concept in this sense. It is true that if some preferences for essential goods are not met, a person is harmed, but this is because the preference tracks an essential need. For many preferences, say for first edition postage stamps or bottles of pink champagne, there are no lower bounds such that a person is harmed if they fall below those lower bounds, or for the dedicated collector, for example, upper bounds at which they are satiated.

These differences between needs and preferences have clear implications for how wide economic substitutability is possible. The goods that satisfy one categorical need cannot be replaced by goods that satisfy another need. If a person is dehydrated then she needs water. Good books that satisfy her needs for education or vitamin C that satisfies other nutritional needs are not substitutes. She needs goods that take her above the minimal threshold. More generally any objective state account of well-being which is pluralist in the different dimensions of well-being will involve limits in substitutability across the dimensions of well-being. Consider any standard objective list account of well-being. To live well is to have or realize particular objective goods or states of affairs: particular forms of personal relation, physical health, autonomy, knowledge of the world, aesthetic experience, accomplishment and achievement, sensual pleasures, a well-constituted relation with the non-human world, and so on.[4] There is no reason to assume that goods are substitutable across different dimensions of well-being. It is not the case that for a loss of goods under one heading, say bodily health, there is a gain under some other, say personal relations, that leaves the person's well-being unchanged. A loss in one dimension that takes a person below a minimal threshold can only be properly addressed by the provision of goods in that dimension. A person who suffers from malnutrition requires specific objects of nutrition: more entertainment or better housing and education will not do.

Given this objective account, there are limits to economic substitutability of goods across different dimensions of well-being. The question of whether there are substitutes for a good within any dimension becomes a matter of technical substitutability. If a wetland provides a service of waste assimilation that is necessary for the satisfaction of categorical needs, then it only has a substitute if there is a technical substitute for the wetland that provides that service. One cannot replace the services offered by the wetland by another which satisfies another need, say for better education.

In the debates between proponents of weak and strong sustainability, there are then two distinct issues at stake. The first is a conceptual question of how well-being should be characterized and hence how far economic substitution is possible across different dimensions of well-being so that overall levels of well-being are maintained. The second is an empirical question about how far technical substitutes exist for the services provided by one good for another in some dimension of well-being. Proponents of weaker versions of sustainability tend to assume a preference satisfaction account of well-being that allows for a wider degree of economic substitutability and a form of technological optimism that allows for high levels of technical substitutability. Proponents of strong sustainability tend to assume a more objective account of well-being which is more restrictive on the possibility of economic substitutes and are more sceptical about the possibilities for technological substitutes within particular dimensions of well-being.

One thing that should be noted about this dispute is that it is a particular version of a more general debate and is thus not confined to natural capital. If sustainability is understood in terms of maintaining or improving human welfare over generations the dispute can arise across a variety of different dimensions of well-being. Given a pluralist objective account of well-being, sustainability requires each generation to pass on a bundle of goods that maintain welfare across the different dimensions of human life. Sustainability requires the maintenance of the specific conditions and bundles of goods required for livelihood and good health, for social affiliation, for the development of capacities for practical reason, for engaging with the wider natural world and so on. Each dimension will have goods that are specific to that dimension which do not have substitutes in goods that satisfy other dimensions. The capacities of reason require particular formal and informal institutions and goods for their development. The goods of social affiliation require cultural and physical conditions, including particular environments and physical places that are constitutive of good community. The limited economic substitutability of natural and human-made capital becomes a special case of more general limits to economic substitutability.

The concept of "natural capital"

A feature of standard accounts of strong sustainability is that they are concerned only with the limits of substitutability between "natural" and "human-made" capital, and not with limits of substitutability *within* these domains. In particular they still allow for considerable substitutability within natural capital itself. A distinction is sometimes drawn between two kinds of natural capital: "constant natural capital" includes those elements of natural capital which admit of substitution by other elements of natural capital; "critical natural capital" includes elements which cannot be substituted by other elements of natural capital. Thus, for example, English Nature draws the following distinction between different kinds of biodiversity as follows:

> Those aspects of native biodiversity which cannot be readily replaced, such as ancient woodlands, we call *critical natural capital*. Others, which should not be allowed, in total, to fall below minimum levels, but which could be created elsewhere within the same Natural Area, such as other types of woodland, we refer to as *constant natural assets*.
>
> *(English Nature 1993, emphasis original)*

Strong sustainability on this account involves two distinct tasks: protecting critical natural capital and ensuring that as parts of constant capital are lost to development they are replaced with equivalent parts of natural capital elsewhere. Both kinds of natural capital are still understood as forms of capital – as bundles of assets that provide services. The distinction between the two kinds of capital is an issue of technique. We have a variety of different assets: habitat types, woodlands, heathlands, lowland grasslands, peatlands and species assemblages. Where it is technically and economically possible to re-create this asset within a specified time period it belongs to constant natural capital. Where it is not, the asset belongs to critical natural capital. On this account, if the domain of constant natural capital is large enough, then there is considerable scope of substitution between different components of natural capital.

The possibility for such widespread substitutability within the domain of natural capital underpins a number of recent market-based policies on sustainability. The use of market-based approaches to sustainability has become central to recent global sustainability policy (UNEP 2011). Their defensibility is increasingly a central area of normative disagreement. Consider, for example, the development of biodiversity offsetting as a strategy for achieving sustainability. Biodiversity offsetting introduces into policy for sustaining levels of biodiversity mechanisms that are similar to the carbon-offsetting used in carbon markets. Credits are assigned to landowners who create, restore or enhance a site of biodiversity. Those credits can then be sold to developers to offset losses to biodiversity caused by a development. As a result of these market transactions, the arguments runs, there is no net loss of biodiversity. Constant natural capital is maintained. Different versions of biodiversity offsetting exist, for example, in New South Wales, Australia and, in the form of wetland mitigation banking, in the United States, and it is becoming increasingly prevalent elsewhere (Kiesecker *et al.* 2009, Madsen *et al.* 2011, UNEP 2011).

How plausible is the account of substitutability within the domain of natural capital that underpins these market-based approaches to sustainability? One question here is again an empirical one about how far different sites of biodiversity do deliver the same services. An answer to that question will require some account of what those services are. There is a prior question, however, as to whether the value of biodiversity and other aspects of the natural and indeed social world are appropriately understood as "capital". As noted above, at least one implication of the characterization of parts of the natural world as "capital" is that they should be valued as a source of services: "Material objects are merely the vehicles which carry some of these services" (Ayres & Kneese 1969: 284). What are valued are services. Any object as such is valued simply as a "vehicle" for these services. What assumptions are being made in making ecosystem *services* the central object of valuation and denying that objects themselves are the object of value?

An important distinction to be drawn here is between two modes of valuation, *de dicto* and *de re*. Hare offers the following mildly funny joke about Zsa Zsa Gabor to illustrate the distinction:

> Zsa Zsa: "Ah! People misunderstand me! They think that I am just a creature of leisure, that I do nothing useful, but they are wrong. I am constantly finding new ways to do good for people."
> Interviewer: "Like what?"
> Zsa Zsa: "I have found a way of keeping my husband young and healthy, almost forever."
> Interviewer: "Eternal youth ... that is quite a discovery! How do you do it?"
> Zsa Zsa: "I get a new one every five years!"
>
> *(C. Hare 2007: 514)*

The joke turns on an ambiguity. In saying she does good, we expect Zsa Zsa to have found a way of keeping the particular person who is her husband young and healthy. It turns out that Zsa Zsa is simply concerned that whoever turns out to fit the description of being her husband, this person be young and healthy. One initial way of capturing the difference is in terms of the scope of the quantifier in value claims. We expect her to be valuing *de re*, to be valuing a particular object:

$$\exists x \ (x \text{ is the husband of ZZG and ZZG values the health of } x).$$

It turns out that she is valuing *de dicto*: she values whoever happens to fall under the description of being her husband:

ZZG values $\exists x$ (x is the husband of ZZG and x is healthy).

The distinction allows us to answer the question as to what assumptions are made in taking ecosystem services to be the object of value. To value something only as a vehicle for services presupposes that it should be valued only *de dicto* and not *de re*. It is this assumption that underpins the practice of biodiversity markets and offsets. The practice assumes that policy-makers should only value sites of biodiversity *de dicto*:

P values $\exists x$ (x is a site of high biodiversity).

At least part of the reason for opposition to this understanding of sustainability as natural capital is that individuals value sites of biodiversity *de re*:

$\exists x$ (x is a site of high biodiversity and P values x).

One way of capturing the question about the degree to which substitutability is possible, not just between "natural capital" and "human made capital", but within the sphere of natural capital itself, is in terms of different answers to the question about the extension of the class of objects for which a purely *de dicto* valuation is appropriate. Both sides of the debate between weak and strong sustainability, in using the language of capital and services, assume purely *de dicto* valuations. Objects are valued *de dicto* as vehicles for the provision of services and are substitutable by whatever other object provides similar services. One reason for assuming stronger limits to substitutability lies in the fact that the class of objects to which a *de re* valuation is owed and which are not thus substitutable is wider than either side assumes.

What is the extension of the class of objects for which *de re* valuation is required? What is the class of objects for which *de dicto* valuations are permissible? The answer to those questions turns on whether the object in question is properly valued as a particular, in particular where its history and distinctiveness matters to the valuation. *De re* valuation is most notably required with respect to human persons. Zsa Zsa Gabor isn't finding a "way of doing good for people" by substituting a new person with the required qualities for an old one. Neither do actual wives have Stepford substitutes that perform the same services. We properly value persons as particulars. There are other classes of objects which are similarly valued as particulars. Works of art are valued as particulars with their own history. To value whatever objects have the same properties regardless of history is to value fakes. On the other hand many ordinary fungible objects are appropriately valued in a purely *de dicto* sense. I may, on occasion, value a particular apple *de re* – the first apple picked by my daughter from a tree that we planted together when she was younger. However, most apples are replaceable. I value that there is an apple that satisfies nutritional and gustatory needs, not any particular apple. An apple might be replaceable in turn by some other fruit that satisfies the same needs. One question that underpins debates about sustainability is about the class of objects to which *de re* valuation is required.

Some of the issues involved were raised in the debates on sustainability by one of the main proponents of weak sustainability, Robert Solow:

It makes perfectly good sense to insist that certain unique and irreplaceable assets should be preserved for their own sake; nearly everyone would feel that way about

Yosemite or, for that matter, about the Lincoln Memorial, I imagine. But that sort of situation cannot be universalized: it would be neither possible nor desirable to "leave the world as we found it" in every particular. Most routine natural resources are desirable for what they do, not for what they are. It is their capacity to provide usable goods and services that we value. Once that principle is accepted, we are in the everyday world of substitutions and trade-offs.

(Solow 1993b: 168)

Solow allows that where "environmental assets have a claim to intrinsic value", such as Yosemite or the Grand Canyon, then "the calculus of trade-offs does not apply" (*ibid.*: 171). However, he clearly assumes that this class of objects is small, a rare exception:

The duty imposed by sustainability is to bequeath to posterity not any particular thing – with the sort of rare exception I have mentioned – but rather to endow them with whatever it takes to achieve a standard of living at least as good as our own and to look after their next generation similarly.

(Ibid.: 168)

It is the value of objects as vehicles for services – "for what they do, not for what they are" – that matters for most debates on sustainability. Despite the fact that the concept of sustainability began in discussions of specific resources, and is still so used in many contexts, on this account this is a mistake. Sustainability is not concerned with the conservation of any specific thing.

[G]oods and services can be substituted for one another. If you don't eat one species of fish you can eat another species of fish. Resources are, to use a favourite word of economists, fungible in a certain sense. They can take the place of each other. That is extremely important because it suggests that we do not owe to the future any particular thing. There is no specific object that the goal of sustainability, the obligation of sustainability, requires us to leave untouched.

(Solow 1993a: 181)

While proponents of strong sustainability deny that the services offered by natural capital can be substituted by those provided by human-made capital, both sides in the subsequent debate between weak and strong sustainability follow him in treating "environmental assets" as capital valued for the services they provide and not as particulars. However, there is a prior question as to whether this account is defensible: whether the class of objects valued *de re* is wider than this framing of the debate assumes.

One useful starting point for a case for a much wider extension to the class of objects to which *de re* valuation is owed is to return to a question I left unanswered earlier on, as to how the distinction between "natural" and "human-made capital" is drawn. As I noted then, the concept that looks like it should do the work here is the "natural" as contrasted with the "artificial". The distinction is one that is owed detailed examination, but for the purposes of the argument here I will assume the following provisional characterization of the concept of the artificial: "Something is artificial if and only if it is what it is at least partly as the result of a deliberate or intentional act, usually involving the application of some art or skill" (O'Neill *et al.* 2008: 129). In contrast, something is natural if it is not what it is as the result of a deliberate or intentional act. This characterization captures an important feature of the use of the term "natural" in this context, that is, that it is a concept that is concerned with the history of an object, with the processes that made it what it is. The point is made well by Goodin:

> According to the distinctively [green theory of value] … what it is that makes natural resources valuable is their very naturalness. That is to say, what imparts value to them is not any physical attributes or properties that they might display. Rather, it is the history and process of their creation. What is crucial in making things valuable, on the green theory of value, is the fact they were created by natural processes rather than by artificial human ones. By focusing in this way on the history and process of its creation as the special feature of a naturally occurring property that imparts value, the green theory of value shows itself to be an instantiation of yet another pair of more general theories of value – a *process* based theory of value, on the one hand, and a *history* based theory of value, on the other.
>
> (Goodin 1992: 26–27)

An important distinction being drawn here is between end-state accounts of the value of particular environments and historical or process-based accounts of the value of those environments. One way one might value a particular habitat or ecosystem might be simply as an end state, in terms of the assemblage of species it contains. Its historical origins are irrelevant (Attfield 1994: 49). If that is the case, naturalness as such is not a relevant value. This view informs the account of "natural capital" that underpins the distinction between critical and constant natural capital and the forms of substitutability that underpin biodiversity offsetting. If the same assemblages of species variety can be maintained, then the replacement of a natural habitat by a human-created artificial habitat is permissible: overall levels of natural capital are maintained. The term "natural" in the phrase "natural capital" is being used in a loose sense to include any assemblage of living organisms, be this artificial or not. If, on the other hand, the historical processes that created a place matter, then it is that particular that is the object of value. Particular environments will be valued *de re* and not only *de dicto*. As such they will not be replaceable. It is this thought that underpins the defensible kernel of the claim that it is not possible to "fake nature" through human restoration or recreation of a natural environment that has been marred or destroyed: "nature is not replaceable without depreciation of one aspect of its value which has to do with its genesis, its history" (Elliot 1982: 87).

This historical account of the value of environments is not however confined to "natural" environments. Similar points apply to the human history that is embodied in particular places. Place-based values are similarly normally *de re* values of particulars that are rooted in the history that makes a place what it is. The point is indeed implicit in Solow's own examples of monuments such the Lincoln memorial. However, it has much wider application in ordinary places that are valued by those who live within them. Consider the following passage from a person facing eviction to make way for the development of the Narmada dam:

> You tell us to take compensation. What is the state compensating us for? For our land, for our fields, for the trees along our fields. But we don't live only by this. Are you going to compensate us for our forest? … Or are you going to compensate us for our great river – for her fish, her water, for vegetables that grow along her banks, for the joy of living beside her? What is the price of this? … How are you compensating us for fields either – we didn't buy this land; our forefathers cleared it and settled here. What price this land? Our gods, the support of those who are our kin – what price do you have for these? Our adivasi life – what price do you put on it?
>
> (Bava Mahalia 1994)

There are some services provided by the river which are invoked here: the provision of water and fish, and the watering of soil for growing vegetables. However, what pervades the response are not just services that a river provides, but the loss of a particular place in which the past of a community is embodied and which is constitutive of particular social relations in the present. It is the disintegration of a community and way of life as homes are flooded and people dispersed that matters here. It involves a loss in a basic dimension of human well-being – that of human affiliation and community – which cannot be compensated for by a gain in other dimensions of well-being. Moreover, it is a dimension of well-being that is rooted in a particular place. It is a particular place in which the life of a community is embodied that matters here. The place is valued as a particular and not as a mere vehicle for services.

Similar points apply to more mundane habitats and landscapes which are valued as places. People's relationships are to particular environments that embody their histories, personal and collective. An item that at the level of species assemblage might be easy to replace – a pond or copse of woodland – might have a significance as a particular that no end-state account of its value is able to capture. It is valued as the village pond in which livestock have long been watered and where as a child I caught newts in a net with my father. Livestock might be watered elsewhere and newts, if they are to be caught at all, can be netted in other ponds. However, it is this particular place with its history and distinctiveness that a person values. Correspondingly, the role that time plays in conservation policy is not simply as a technical constraint on what can be re-created to replace what is lost. Rather, the particular history of a place enters as one source of its value.

In the background here are arguments about the nature of human well-being and the role of environmental goods as conditions for human well-being. The picture offered by standard economic approaches to environmental goods is to conceive of them as bundles of fungible resources that are valued for the provision of services. Sustainability is a matter of maintaining a bundle of goods into the future that sustains the options for future generations to realize levels of well-being at least as good as our own. There are two assumptions underlying this picture that should be questioned.

The first assumption, which Solow articulates so clearly, is that particular things and places matter only marginally to human well-being. This claim is false. Relationships to particular persons and places are central components of human well-being. They do not all matter equally. Some things that I value *de re*, say the autographed shirt of some second-rate footballer, may be of marginal value to my well-being. However, many environmental goods that are valued *de re* matter centrally to the well-being of individuals. This is true of the ordinary and everyday places people inhabit and not just of the spectacular or culturally iconic landscapes and monuments. It is why environmental concern with local places is central to so much environmental conflict. It is attachment to particulars that matters to people. Particular places often embody social relations of a community, as in the case of the Narmada, over time. They matter not just as resources that are an external causal condition for the realization of some good, but as conditions for making sense of the life of a person or community. Goodin make a similar point about natural environments: they provide a context in which people can make "some sense and patterns to their lives" (Goodin 1992: 37).

The second assumption is that what we need to pass on to future generations to maintain well-being are simply options or opportunities to satisfy preferences. Some particulars we do not pass on simply as options that will be exercised or not in the satisfaction of whatever set of preferences future people happen to have. It does not make sense, for example, of policies to preserve particular cultural goods such as artworks or books that they are simply providing options for future generations which they may exercise by pulping them for some other ends.

The goods are passed on to form preferences and not just as options to satisfy whatever preferences they might have. Similarly it does not make sense of what moves environmentalists to preserve an old-growth forest that they do so that the next generation has the option to chop it down for expensive chopsticks instead. If one rejects a crude preference satisfaction account of well-being, then improving well-being is about creating the conditions through which preferences for the goods of human life are informed and shaped. Preserving certain particulars, be this in the form of particular parts of nature or particular cultural objects, is often an important part of creating those conditions.

There is an objection to this view that deserves consideration. Brian Barry, after criticizing a purely preference-based account of well-being as a basis for understanding sustainability, considers the alternative "that what should be maintained for future generations is their chance to lead a good life as we conceive it" (B. Barry 1999: 103). He rejects this proposal for the following reason:

> [O]ne of the defining characteristics of human beings is their ability to form their own conceptions of the good life. It would be presumptuous – and unfair – of us to pre-empt their choices in the future … What this suggests is that the requirement is to provide future generations with the opportunity to live good lives according to their conception of what constitutes a good life. This should surely include their being able to live good lives according to our conception but should leave other options open to them.
>
> (Ibid.: 103–4)

The upshot of Barry's proposal is that we still leave future generations options or opportunities, but these are understood as conditions for a choice of good life rather than simply as the means for preferences. There is something clearly right about what Barry says here. We do not expect any generation to impose only one conception of the good life on all successor generations even if it were possible. However, the alternative Barry suggests is too open. It does not rule out any conception of the good life, and as such looks to be at least as open as the preference-satisfaction model he rejects. It may turn out that their conception of the good life is one in which most trees are plastic.

The alternative to imposing a conception of the good is not to simply leave a set of options. It is rather to understand the relationship between generations to be one of deliberation rather than coercion. There is an ongoing dialogue about the nature of the good life that crosses generations. One expression of these different voices is to be found in the particular goods they aim to pass to the future. The persons who pass on an old-growth forest do it with the aim of creating the conditions through which the voice of a particular conception of the good life is maintained (cf. Norton 2003a: 439–42) – as do those who pass on particular forms of art or a particular literature. They do so as an expression of a viewpoint in the dialogue, not as the final word. For that reason we pass on not just options but specific goods. To say this is not to say that our understandings of the nature of human well-being will not change or that any conception is final. They will and they should, but they should so as part of a dialogue across and within generations, and not simply through happenstance changes of preferences or through some open menu of possible conceptions of the good life.

None of this is to claim an extreme conservatism, that it is possible and desirable to "leave the world as we found it". It is not possible: the social and natural worlds are always changing in ways beyond human control. It is not desirable: there are often some strong reasons for change. What it does entail is that it is false to claim that replacements are always possible that leave levels of well-being unaltered. There are some losses for which there exist no compensations.

Since they are valued as particulars they are irreplaceable without loss. While loss is sometimes unavoidable, it is an occasion for sorrow that cannot be consoled with a compensatory gain elsewhere. If responses owed to such losses are to be appropriate they need to be recognized as such and not as something that can be incorporated into the "calculus of trades and losses". What I hope to have shown in this chapter is that the class of objects for which this is true is much larger than standard economic approaches to sustainability policy assume.

Acknowledgements

The arguments of this chapter owe a great deal to conversations with Alan Holland, Paul Knights, Andrew Light, Tyler DesRoches and Michael Scott. Earlier versions of the arguments were read to seminars in Oxford, Manchester, Nijmegen and Turku. I would like to thank the participants at those seminars for their helpful comments. Particular thanks are owed to Ada Wossink and Graham Stevens. Finally I would like to thank the editors of this volume for their helpful comments on an earlier version of the chapter.

Notes

1 For discussions see Beckerman (1994, 1999, 2000), Daly (1995), Jacobs (1995), Dobson (1996a), Holland (1997).
2 For a discussion of different senses of nature see O'Neill *et al.* (2008: 125–50).
3 For a related discussion of this issue see Holland (1997) and J. O'Neill (2007: 32–35).
4 See for example the list in Nussbaum (2000: 78–80).

30

BIODIVERSITY

Andrew Brennan and Norva Y. S. Lo

Biodiversity, conservation and ecological civilization

Twenty-five years ago, biodiversity was not a central concern of biologists or ecosystems theorists (Tilman 2000). Nonetheless, a significant number of books and papers by biologists and philo-sophers were sounding a warning about the loss of species, the possible impact of such losses on ecosystem functions and the reduction in value – both moral and economic – that was likely as a consequence of the reduction in natural variety (Norton 1986, 1987; E. O. Wilson 1992). These writers emphasized that biodiversity encompassed a number of different levels. In E. O. Wilson's view, there were at least three different levels of natural variety that were worth preserving: first, the variety of alleles (gene variants within individuals); second, the variety of species themselves; and finally, the range of varied ecosystems found across the surface of the planet and within its caverns, rivers, lakes and oceans. In his 1987 book, Bryan G. Norton emphasized a number of features that have since come to prominence in writing on biodiversity. First, a case – but not necessarily a strong one – for preserving the current variety of species can be built on the utility they have – whether actually or potentially – for human beings, rather than because of any deeper value they may have in their own right. If the value of systems, plants and animals is viewed solely in terms of what economists call "demand values" – those features for which we have preferences in light of the pleasure, utility and other benefits and services they provide to us – then the value of biodiversity is in theory measurable by various techniques (such as surveys of consumer preferences, willingness to pay to protect areas of diversity, estimating the expenditures people make to visit areas of biodiversity, and so on). Given our limited knowledge, such attributed economic values may well underestimate the full economic value of many species, and any non-economic values they may have (Sagoff 1988, O'Neill *et al.* 2008).

Second, Norton argued that the best way to preserve natural variety was through preserva-tion of habitats. Unlike this relatively uncontroversial point, a third component of his argument was, and remains, more controversial. Norton claimed that by leaving wild nature alone and encouraging humans to have appropriate interactions with natural species, there was a prospect for a transformation of values: "experiences of wild species have value because they play a positive role in transforming less acceptable into more acceptable values" (Norton 1987: 237). Such transformation would affect not only the individual preferences a person has, but even the person's ordering among such preferences. Some might argue that in the twenty-five years since the publication of Norton's work, values have already undergone some level of transformation, as evidenced by the fact that concern for biodiversity, wilderness places, and for ecosystem health, flourishing and prosperity is now much more widespread than it was and is, at least nominally, a central plank of much government and corporate planning and policy worldwide. Further, the rising popularity of rewilding movements testifies to the idea that experiences of wild nature may be able to transform values and develop our characters in a multitude of ways (C. Fraser 2009, Monbiot 2013).

One factor in the emergence of the greater interest in biodiversity was probably the consilience between the work of scientists and philosophers just mentioned, and the publication in 1992 of the United Nations Convention on Biological Diversity. This document was finalized in May 1992, in time to be launched at the Rio Summit in June of that year, and finally brought into force in December 1993 (Convention on Biological Diversity 1992). The preamble to the document refers explicitly both to the utility of nature, and also to its intrinsic value. The contracting parties, it explains, are conscious "of the intrinsic value of biological diversity and of the ecological, genetic, social, economic, scientific, educational, cultural, recreational and aesthetic values of biological diversity and its components". They are also "conscious of the importance of biological diversity for evolution and for maintaining life sustaining systems of the biosphere" (*ibid.*: 1).

The convention has set the context for a range of initiatives associated both with protecting biodiversity for its own sake, and also seeking to ensure that the components of biodiversity are used in a sustainable way. The involvement of biological scientists with national and international policy-making has been aided by the emergence of conservation biology as an academic field of study focusing on the preservation of biodiversity. As a result, reports on the state of the planet's biodiversity are now a central feature of science inputs to policy at high levels and of reporting in the leading science journals (see for example Butchart *et al.* 2010).

A further central ambition of the convention was that the benefits arising from use of the planet's genetic resources should be shared equitably and fairly across the globe. Such initiatives and ambitions are also endorsed by the independently sponsored Earth Charter, launched in June 2000, the first principle of which calls for respect for life in all its diversity. Like the convention, the charter also calls for social justice to be combined with care for biodiversity and natural processes, thus aiming simultaneously to protect the intrinsic values of nature and diversity, and also ensure that environmental goods and services are made available to all without bias or discrimination (Earth Charter Commission 2000). As a civil society initiative, the charter has been endorsed by thousands of individuals and organizations, including UNESCO. By contrast, the biodiversity convention is for ratification by states and federations of states, such as the European Union. Two notable abstentions from ratification of the convention to date are the USA and the Holy See.

Some have seen both the convention and the charter as documents whose aspirations and demands are best located within a universal or global ethic, hence providing philosophers and other ethical theorists the opportunity to explore the prospects for global ethics. Since both documents recognize the value of human cultural, linguistic and social diversity, their appeal to a universal convergence of values is not meant to suggest that one ethic will be appropriate for everyone everywhere (Dower 2005). Rather, the documents can be seen as embodying values that are shared by different individuals, groups and nation states, independent of the variety of different social, ethical and religious perspectives that characterize their underlying worldviews. But what shared values might these be? There are clearly many goods derived from nature ranging from the pleasure and excitement derived from studies of various parts of nature and communicated through nature documentaries all the way through to the extraction and conversion of natural resources for human benefit. One key idea that can unite different per-spectives on natural values is based on an appeal to preserving future opportunities for the enjoyment of such goods. As Norton has put it, very different human groups, with widely varying perspectives, can perhaps "accept responsibility to maintain a non-declining set of opportunities based on possible uses of the environment". The preservation of options for the future can be readily linked to notions of equity in the way we approach sustainability so that "the future ought not to face, as a result of our actions today, a seriously reduced range of options and choices, as they try to adapt to the environment that they face" (Norton 2002: 419).

A further reason for thinking of biodiversity in global rather than national or regional terms is that species loss is often caused by, and will in turn affect, different groups of people and dif-ferent nations in a multitude of different but interconnected ways. Both the causes and the results of species loss are dispersed in space and in time. Climate change that leads to species loss is a good example of such dispersal. Once greenhouse gases are released into the atmosphere, they can have effects geographically far away from their source. Since the gases persist for many hundreds of years in the atmosphere, they also have effects remote in time from when they were produced (Gardiner 2011). Moreover, since rich people, with the highest consumption patterns, are themselves dispersed over many different countries, per capita responsibility for CO_2 emissions is not evenly correlated with the relative affluence of particular countries. In nation states with high levels of social and economic inequality and low levels of social welfare, the effects of ecosystem degradation and species loss caused by climate change are likely to have the highest impact on those who are less well off. In consequence, just as the preservation of nature and natural systems poses a global problem, so do questions about mitigation and justice for individuals and communities affected by environmental decline (Jamieson 2010).

Biodiversity, conceptual issues and human–centredness

How is biodiversity to be measured? Can measuring the biodiversity of an area reveal something about its "natural" value? Debates over these questions go to the heart of contemporary dis-cussions on biodiversity. First, the ethics of conservation need not have a specific focus on preservation of wilderness as such. Likewise, biodiversity should not be taken as a surrogate for "natural" value in general. For high biodiversity can be associated with human use and occu-pation, as when adding a farming system to a desert raises local diversity. Hence, not all "natural" systems maximize biodiversity when left undisturbed (see Brennan & Lo 2010, 113–37, for discussion on what is "natural"). In some temperate forest systems, it is disturbance to the forest – including human land clearing activities – that provokes an increase in diversity in tree species (Brennan 2014: 92–108). On the other hand, many highly prized wild places are not particularly rich in natural variety (Sarkar 2005: 21–44). In some places, wilderness and biodiversity are indeed closely related, as in those set-aside wild areas that are also hotspots of biodiversity. There is no doubt that management and preservation of natural variety is easier in the presence of low human population density (Mittermeier *et al.* 2003). Nonetheless the protection of biodiversity is quite a different issue from the preservation of wilderness.

Second, there continues to be no single agreed measure of biodiversity (Maier 2012: 115–20). In fact, the concept of species itself is one that is capable of being defined in a variety of different ways. This is a complicating factor in any discussion about policies dealing with species numbers and diversity. The everyday understanding of the concept is the *biological species concept*: that for sexually reproducing plants and animals, a species is a population of organisms that closely resemble each other genetically and are capable of interbreeding so as to produce fertile offspring. An alternative account of species takes them as determined by patterns of historical evolution.

According to certain genealogical or *phylogenetic species concepts*, two individuals are members of the same species if they both belong to the smallest group of individuals that share a common ancestor. Consider two individual salamanders, for example, that look very much alike. Whether they belong to the same species under this phylogenetic concept is not a question of capacity to produce fertile hybrid offspring, but rather a question of whether they belong to a population of salamanders that have a single common and unique ancestor species.

The two concepts mentioned above are just two of many different species concepts in circulation among biologists, economists, policy analysts and conservationists (Mayden 1997). Those who adopt the phylogenetic species concept will count species numbers differently from those who adopt the biological species concept. For example, one study claims that adopting the phylogenetic concept rather than one of the others would lead to large increases in the numbers of species to be found in various places. Looking at eighty-nine published studies on species populations, the study found that adopting the phylogenetic concept led to nearly a 50 per cent increase in the number of species identified in the various studies. Using the same concept resulted in a nearly 260 per cent increase in the number of lichen species identified and an 87 per cent increase in the number of mammal species (Agapow *et al.* 2004). If species are the fundamental units both of evolution and of biodiversity, then it is important to get the species concept sorted out. "If our species counts are problematic, so will be our assessments of biodiversity" (Richards 2010: 10). Furthermore, this is not just a matter of theory. Since conservation and restoration attempts at preserving species and biodiversity break down to decisions on which and what individual plants or animals or colonies of them to protect or reintroduce, the adoption of one species concept rather than another has immediate practical implications.

Many biologists have also investigated relations among three features: biodiversity, ecosystem stability and biological productivity. The already mentioned problem of measuring biodiversity has been compounded by ones involved in measuring both stability and productivity, leading to extended controversy among theorists in the 1990s (described in Sarkar 2005: 106–44). While some authorities regarded high levels of biodiversity as correlated with high systemic productivity and high stability, this view was at odds with the observation that many of the world's most highly productive systems are not very species-rich. Within the last decade, however, some consensus has emerged that moderately diverse systems have high productivity and that extra diversity within such systems may yield insurance against external perturbations that might lead to a reduction in productivity. The arguments here are highly technical (for summary, see deLaplante & Picasso 2011). They point to the view that conservation and rehabilitation efforts are best focused not on defending or restoring individual species, but rather on clusters of species making up landscape, forest or river systems.

The protection of biodiversity is often cited as a reason for preserving endangered species. If the idea is that biodiversity is important for the proper functioning of ecosystems upon which human life and well-being depend so that efforts should be made to maintain biodiversity by protecting threatened species, then critics would point out that many rare species are already functionally marginal to the systems in which they are found (Maier 2012: 173–74). Biodiversity is patchily present over the globe, high in some places, but relatively low in others. Some studies show that 70 per cent of terrestrial biodiversity is concentrated in countries whose area in total constitutes less than 10 per cent of the earth's land area (Australian Bureau of Statistics 2010). By contrast, grazing and farmland constitute more than 30 per cent of land area. For the most part, the ecosystem services which satisfy a large number of human preferences are supplied by relatively simple, non-diverse systems, such as salt marshes (useful for water filtration), and the low-diversity agricultural systems in which food is produced. These facts are consistent with and indeed support Norton's original claim that the strongest arguments for the preservation of biodiversity may actually not be based on its utility for human beings. From a purely human-centred utilitarian point of view, it appears that the importance of biodiversity is contestable. But perhaps human-centred utility is not the only important thing to consider, and there may be other values in nature – besides the ones that contribute to human economy and satisfactions – on which stronger arguments for protecting biodiversity can be based.

A number of educational and policy initiatives over the past twenty years seem to have drawn on a less human-centred utilitarian approach to the environment and to natural things in general. An increased public perception of the importance of preserving nature has been evinced in schemes such as "reconciliation ecology", whereby a certain amount of wild diversity is introduced into human habitats (Rosenzweig 2003; cf. Grove-Fanning 2010). Increasing diversity of birds, for example, can be encouraged in cities by the construction of ponds and lakes that attract a variety of animals, and "green rooftops" on city buildings not only host a variety of plants, but also attract invertebrates and birds as well. Children can also benefit, so some argue, from adventures in areas of undeveloped and less heavily managed land in urban areas, hence overcoming what one author has called the "experiential impoverishment" that can result from the reduction of fauna and flora in contemporary cities (Pyle 2002).

Is the introduction of wild lives into urban areas for the purpose of entertaining humans not itself another case of human-centred utility? Some would reply that if a programme to bring city dwellers closer to nature can help people to see value in non-human wild lives – a value that is independent of human purposes – then the benefit is not merely that people will derive pleasure from appreciating nature but also that their evaluative and moral outlook will be transformed and enhanced. This change, of appreciating wild lives for their own sakes, may be one that brings about better protection for such lives in the future (Sarkar 2005). The approach here is arguably parallel to the Aristotelian take on friendship: while a friend may be of tremendous instrumental value to oneself, recognizing a friend or friendship as *intrinsically* valuable (that is, a valuable *end-in-itself*), instead of a mere means to benefit oneself, is a morally good state for one to be in. The ability and willingness to respect, love and support one's friends for their own sake will also make one's own life as a whole more worthwhile. Such a recognition, or moral reckoning, affirms the inherent worth of others and also, at the same time, the worth of oneself as a moral being precisely because one is capable of taking such a perspective and acting upon it. Many environmental philosophers have argued that anthropocentrism or human-centredness, with its valuation of nature and the non-human beings and entities within it in purely instrumental terms, is human egoism at the species level (see for example Plumwood 1993: 141–64). If Aristotle was not too optimistic in thinking that an ordinary person's selfishness could be transformed into "true self-love" via the path of virtuous pursuit of "things that are noblest and best", of which friendship is one (Aristotle 1954: 1165^{b}35–1166^{b}27), then an environmental virtue ethic that attributes intrinsic value to both humans and non-human nature might be practicable (J. O'Neill 1992; cf. Lo 2006, Hursthouse 2007). As will be seen later, the adoption of the stance that values natural things for their own sakes is compatible with a high-level theory of value that regards values themselves as things of human origin.

Biodiversity, individual organisms and systems

Some writers have suggested that conservation biology should be regarded not as a separate branch of empirical science, and not simply an extension of resource economics, but instead should be seen as a value-laden enterprise to which philosophy and the social sciences are also able to make contributions (Norton 2002, 2003b; Sarkar 2005). Developments in environmental ethics and philosophy since the mid-twentieth century have helped spread the non-anthropocentric idea that natural objects, systems and processes are things of intrinsic value independent of their usefulness to humans (see Guha 1999 for a critical discussion of non-anthropocentrism). Various forms of non-anthropocentric theories have been proposed within the field. For example, it has been proposed that all individual living things, plants and animals alike, can be regarded as owed moral respect in their own right (P. W. Taylor 1981, 1986; Varner 1998), and that all natural collective entities, such as species and ecosystems, are also worthy of moral respect as holders of intrinsic value (Callicott 1989, 1999; Rolston 1989, 2012). Alongside with core concepts like "intrinsic value" (or "inherent worth") and "moral respect" is the notion of *moral standing*. To say that something has moral standing is to say that its interests, well-being or continued existence ought to be given direct consideration when we make decisions that are likely to affect it. These concepts are commonly used in discussions about what moral obligations we owe to other things in the environment.

The *biocentric* idea that all living things have moral standing is often founded on the proposition that all living things have *interests* or goods of their own (despite the fact that the ones that lack awareness will not be conscious of what is or is not good for them). For a thing to have interests or goods of its own in this sense is simply for it to be able to fare better or worse. A plant, for example, has an interest in getting an appropriate amount of water, sunlight and nutrients. When it does, it fares better. The life of a plant can flourish or deteriorate, just as the life of an animal can go better or worse. If the plant is a weed in a garden, clearly what is in the plant's interest may not be in the gardener's interest. The point here, however, is that plants – and indeed all living things, for that matter – are beings that have interests and goods of their own independently of whether they benefit the gardener or any other creature.

Some critics are sceptical of the idea that entities that lack awareness can be said to have interests in any morally relevant sense. They argue that even if we grant that all living things have interests in the biological sense, it does not automatically follow that any biological interest is worth protecting or respecting in its own right (J. O'Neill 1992, P. Singer 1993, Rowlands 2000). Biocentrists, who propose that moral respect is owed to all individual living things, are in turn critical of the even more onerous proposition of ecological *holism*, which says that holistic or collective entities, such as species and ecosystems, are themselves things of moral standing because these entities also possess interests or goods of their own which should be directly taken into account. The core objection to the metaphysics of ecological holism is the biocentric view that only individual living things can be meaningfully said to have interests, and that the notion of collective interest is ultimately to be explained in terms of, and therefore reducible to, the interests of the individuals that make up the collective in question (P. W. Taylor 1986: 99–168; cf. Varner 1998: 10–18).

To make more sense of the holistic approach towards the environment, however, some theorists proposed early on that the entire population of a single species is akin to a large scattered organism or "superorganism" (D. L. Hull 1978). The justification for such an idea may be drawn from comparing the collective role played by groups of individuals to the role individuals themselves play as units of selection in evolutionary theory. It is individuals who compete against each other most fiercely for the resources that enable them to reproduce and pass on their genetic material. But a group of individuals – for example a colony of ants – seems to be able to collectively act like a unified entity, struggling against other entities of the same kind in the battle for continued collective existence. If a colony of ants can be viewed as a superorganism – similar to an individual organism in terms of its mode of operations in enhancing its chance of passing on genetic material – then perhaps it also makes sense to think of a whole species population, an even larger collective, as a superorganism (Hamilton *et al.* 2009). Furthermore, if individual organisms are, as the biocentrists have argued, things having moral standing and deserving moral respect because they have interests and goods of their own, then if collective entities like species and ecosystems are superorganisms capable of faring better or worse, it may not be unreasonable to grant them a similar kind of respect and standing (cf. Brennan & Lo 2010: 87–112).

The idea that natural collective entities have moral standing can be taken even further. The concept of moral standing is often compared to that of legal standing. Individual human persons are the paradigm case of entities that have both moral and legal standings. While entities with moral standing deserve consideration and respect by moral agents (that is, those who are capable of making moral choices and acting upon them), entities with legal standing are furthermore entitled to consideration and protection by law. Many people have long accepted the attribution of legal standing to collective entities in the human world, such as corporations, church organizations and nation states, whose interests can be represented and defended before the law. Christopher D. Stone argued that it is neither unthinkable nor unreasonable for non-human objects in the natural world also to be granted legal standing. Not only individual natural entities, such as plants and animals, but also collective natural entities, such as species populations, ecosystems, forests, rivers, oceans, and indeed the natural environment as a whole, should be able to have their interests legally represented, defended and protected (Stone 1972, 1987).

The puzzle about the moral status of ecological wholes also raises a question about how best to understand some of the terminology employed in conservation circles. With the focus on the preservation of diversity at the genetic, species and ecosystem levels, it is not surprising that concepts such as *health, flourishing* and *integrity*, whose primary application is to individuals, are employed: see for example the widespread use of metaphors such as "ecosystem health" or "biological integrity" (deLaPlante & Picasso 2011). As the world's two orangutan species get closer to extinction, it seems natural to say they – the species themselves, not just the individual specimens that make up the species – are not doing well, and to say that the one closer to extinction is in a less healthy condition than the other. It remains a matter of contention, however, whether the health metaphor used in this way is well founded in any scientifically or philosophically plausible conception of species as entities that can be healthy or unhealthy.

In environmental ethics and philosophy, there are also continuing debates over the *degree* of intrinsic value that different things in the environment may possess. Most people regard human beings and their projects as having greater intrinsic value than animals or plants and their projects. The *hierarchical* biocentrists would agree, for they maintain that while all individual living things are valuable, those belonging to certain species – for example, the human species – are even more valuable (Attfield 1987, Varner 1998). The *egalitarian* biocentrists, however, take all individual living things to have equal intrinsic value regardless of species, and therefore reject the notion of the superiority of humans (or any species, for that matter) over other species (P. W. Taylor 1981, 1986). By contrast, holistic thinkers have emphasized that nature's systems provide something more enduring and valuable than the individual lives within and supported by it. In Aldo Leopold's "land ethic", for example, an action "is right when it tends to preserve the integrity, stability, and beauty of the biotic community. It is wrong when it tends otherwise" (Leopold 1949: 224–25). Whether an ecosystem as a whole is seen as a superorganism or a "biotic community", modern followers of Leopold, particularly those who focus on the holism aspect of the land ethic, have championed the thesis that the whole is more than the sum of its parts. From this perspective, a species as a whole is seen as more valuable than, and indeed having some special value on top of the value possessed by, the individual specimens that make up the species. An ecosystem is something of greater value still: again a value irreducible to that of its individual constituent parts (Callicott 1989, 1999). The anti-reductionist thesis of value holism may find support in the fact that nature's systems provide a context, a set of constraints, opportunities and challenges within which particular human, animal and plant lives have evolved and flourished, and the idea (quite a debatable one) that if life is valuable then the very foundation that has made life possible is also valuable (Rolston 1989; and see discussion in Brennan & Lo 2010: 87–112).

The proposition that an ecosystem is something of intrinsic value, which may not be entirely reducible to that of its parts, may not seem too radical an idea. But many critics find it unacceptable that the moral rightness or wrongness of any action should be solely determined by its impact on the well-being of the ecosystem or biotic community in which it is carried out – as Leopold's land ethic apparently suggests. For example, some animal welfare theorists have labelled actions such as the culling of over-sized animal populations for the sake of protecting ecosystem integrity as "environmental fascism", not dissimilar to a totalitarian regime suppressing and sacrificing the interests of individual citizens for the benefit of the state (Regan 1983: 362). Furthermore, if the land-ethical logic seeking to justify sacrificing individual interest for the protection of holistic environmental goods is to be applied to the most over-populated species on the planet, namely the human species, then the land ethic will seem to be as misanthropic as it is holistic (see discussions in Lo 2001a). Theorists writing on environmental ethics are usually vocal about the value of biodiversity. When it comes to analysing the causes of biodiversity reduction in recent decades and finding solutions to the problem, however, the issue of human over-population is relatively less discussed (for exceptions, see Rolston 1996, Brennan 1998, Carter 1999).

Is biodiversity intrinsically valuable?

The typical anthropocentric argument for protecting biodiversity has already been outlined: human beings ought to protect biodiversity because human prosperity depends on the health and productivity of nature's systems, and moderately diverse ecosystems with extra biodiversity are likely to be more resilient to environmental stresses and perturbations, whether naturally occurring or caused by human exploitations. Recall Norton's early observation that cost–benefit analysis in terms of human interests alone is unlikely to provide the strongest argument for protecting biodiversity. The idea may be compared to the view that the strongest reason for governments to protect the welfare of their citizens should come from the moral notion of human dignity: an inherent worth possessed by each person whom is to be respected regardless of the person's circumstances and relations, including the person's cost-and-benefit relations to others (cf. Brennan & Lo 2007). For if the government of a state has no intrinsic moral concern for the dignity and well-being of its citizens, and its reason for raising or enforcing standards of health and security, for example, is merely that a healthier population and safer streets will generate more GDP, more revenues for the state and more money and power for those running it, then it is unlikely that such a government will be motivated to protect those citizens who are considered too weak, too aged, or otherwise unfit to be productive in economic or other instrumental terms. In a parallel fashion, many endangered species have already become functionally marginal to the ecosystem in which they are found. Someone who takes a purely cost–benefit perspective could argue that the negative impacts of the further demise of those species on the system's productivity might well be negligible or otherwise acceptable in anthropocentric terms, since the resources that would be required to preserve or restore the populations of those species could be used to promote human benefits in other ways. Cost–benefit anthropocentrism towards nature does not seem to provide sufficiently compelling reason for protecting many of the endangered species.

So, what would a stronger argument look like? First, notice that while the instrumental value of biodiversity is to be investigated by empirical science, philosophical and ethical questions over the *intrinsic* value, if any, of biodiversity are to be explored from entirely different angles, the answers to which are no less important in their implications for how humans should relate to nature and the other species on Earth. The question whether biodiversity considered in itself is something intrinsically valuable, independently of its potential benefits for human or other creatures, can be reflected upon more clearly if the value of diversity *per se* is first questioned.

There seems to be no *prima facie* reason for thinking that diversity is a value considered in itself. For example, a world containing certain good things would be less diverse than a world containing all and exactly those good things but in addition also certain bad things. But the former does not seem less good a world than the latter. The crucial question to ask here is: diversity of *what*? Many people appreciate cultural diversity within a society, as displayed in the different art and musical traditions, languages and cuisines inherited and practised by various parts of the society. Consider music for example: it is perhaps because each musical tradition is itself seen as a good thing that the diversity in musical traditions is also seen as a good thing. The diversity in musical traditions may of course be valued on instrumental grounds, since such diversity can be useful to individuals or society in general, for example in generating more employment opportunities in and revenues for the entertainment and education industries, or as a means to promoting cross-cultural understandings, social harmony and thus a more secured society. But diversity in musical traditions may also be considered as a worthwhile end-in-itself. The fact that something is instrumentally valuable does not rule out the possibility that it is also intrinsically valuable. The dual aspect of the value of friendship is one example seen earlier. Many people would also consider honesty, courage, generosity, beauty and truth to be among the things that are not only instrumentally valuable (at least some, if not most or all, of the time) but also intrinsically good regardless.

What is perceived or considered as good may not be genuinely good: people can and do make mistakes in their evaluative or moral judgements. One hallmark of genuine value is that it is something significantly more enduring than mere liking or preference. Nevertheless, many philosophers and ethicists since the Enlightenment have argued that there is a close connection between something's value on the one hand and the human capacity and disposition, on the other, to appreciate it under certain conditions, such as having relevant knowledge about it (see for example, Mackie 1990; Lewis 1989; M. Smith 1994; Korsgaard 1996; Hume [1739–40] 2000; Lo 2006, 2009). The term "universal values", for example, could be reserved to designate only those human desires and preferences that can survive sustained reflection and scrutiny by people across time and culture. Likewise, if allowance is made for less encompassing notions, such as "cultural values", "group values" or, in the extreme case, "individual personal values", then the terms could be used to refer to only those desires and preferences that can survive reflection and scrutiny by people belonging to the culture or group in question, or by the individual person in question, as the case may be (see discussion in Brennan & Lo 2010: 138–62). The central idea behind the kind of value theory described above can be summarized as follows:

> Something is intrinsically valuable (either universally or at least for some group) if and only if (either all or at least some group of) people would find it appealing as an end in itself after sustained reflection on, and scrutiny of, it.

Values understood in this way are clearly anthropo*genic* in character, for whether something is valuable has an essential connection to human emotions and reflections. However, values need not be anthropo*centric*: that is, it need not be the case that only human beings and their projects are intrinsically worthy. For human beings seem capable of a very wide range of emotions that can survive repeated and continuing reflections: including cross-species altruistic feelings, such as care and respect for various non-human inhabitants of the earth's environment, for inanimate objects like waterfalls and landscapes, and even for the planet itself (Lo 2006; cf. Callicott 1982, Lo 2001b).

So, is biodiversity an intrinsic good worth protecting as an end-in-itself regardless of the instrumental values that it may or may not have for humans? The answer seems to depend on answers to at least two further questions: first, whether all living things, irrespective of species, are intrinsically valuable; and second, whether a world with diversity in intrinsic values is better than a world homogeneous in intrinsic values. Take the second question first. In terms of mere preference or liking, people often prefer having a variety of things they like to just having more of the same thing they like. The same pattern of appraisal may actually be true of values as well. Suppose people generally prefer an assembly of good things of different kinds to a bigger collection of good things of the same kind, and suppose this preference for diversity in good things can survive sustained reflection and scrutiny by people across time and culture, then, under the value theory introduced above, diversity in good things is of itself also a good thing. Thus, if one starts with the moral biocentric outlook that each and every life form is intrinsically valuable, then it will be natural as well as correct for one to accept the further proposition that biodiversity – that is, the diversity in biological forms of life – is also something intrinsically valuable. In short, if life is a good thing, and if a world containing good things of more different kinds is better than a world containing good things of fewer kinds, then higher biodiversity is better than lower biodiversity.

What is critical, then, is the first question: Is *each and every* living thing – irrespective of species – really valuable in itself? The argument from biocentrism for its core thesis has already been reviewed: every living organism is intrinsically valuable because each has interests and goods of its own and each is capable of flourishing. The underlying idea is that if something is able to fare better or worse, it is *prima facie* morally better if it fares better rather than worse. But there is a sceptical challenge which calls into question the moral relevance of biological interests. What *reasons* could there be really for us to respect or give moral weight to the biological interests of the HIV virus (J. O'Neill 1992: 131–32) or, to take a more fanciful example, the lethal creatures in sci-fi movies like the *Alien* series? To this request for reasons, the biocentrist may reply with the more fundamental question: what good reasons do we have for thinking that members of the human species are more worthy than members of other species on Earth?

Many traditional arguments for attributing intrinsic value in a significantly higher degree, if not exclusively, to human beings have a common structure: they appeal to the fact that humans have certain traits, such as self-consciousness, rationality, the capacities for language, for moral decision, for aesthetic creation and appreciation, and many other abilities and skills that are considered as meritorious or otherwise worthy, traits which no other life form on Earth has, or has to nearly such a great extent that humans have them. The underlying idea is that since these traits are the most valuable and morally relevant, creatures who possess them to a greater extent are more worthy than creatures who possess them to a lesser extent or lack them altogether. As many critics have pointed out, however, these arguments setting out to compare the moral worth of different species do not actually start off from neutral ground. Instead, the set of traits identified and assumed by the arguments to be the most morally relevant and worthy are, conveniently, exactly those traits characteristically and typically possessed by members of our own species (P. W. Taylor 1986, Plumwood 1993).

If a group of composers are arguing over whose compositions are superior, for example, it would hardly be fair or cogent for one of them to argue that his are superior to all the rest just because his ones carry to the greatest extent exactly those characteristics typifying his work. The issue would be whether some further argument might be given to explain why the characteristics in question are important and superior to the other characteristics displayed in the works of other composers. Likewise, in questioning the commonly assumed human superiority over other species (which is endorsed not just by anthropocentrists who see no inherent worth in anything other than humans, but also endorsed by hierarchical biocentrists who attribute more intrinsic value to members of the human species than to members of other species), P. W. Taylor (1981: 211–13) asks:

> In what sense are humans alleged to be superior to other animals? We are different from them in having certain capacities that they lack. But why should these capacities be a mark of superiority? ... After all, various nonhuman species have capacities that humans lack. ... Why should not these be taken as signs of their superiority over humans? ... It is not difficult here to recognize a begging of the question. Humans are claiming human superiority from ... a point of view in which the good of humans is taken as the standard of judgment. All we need to do is to look at the capacities of nonhuman animals (or plants, for that matter) from the standpoint of *their* good to find a contrary judgment of superiority. The speed of the cheetah, for example, is a sign of its superiority to humans when considered from the standpoint of the good of its species. If it were as slow a runner as a human, it would not be able to survive. And so for all the other abilities of nonhumans which further their good but which are lacking in humans. In each case the claim to human superiority would be rejected from a nonhuman standpoint. ... If all living things have a good of their own, it at least makes sense to judge the merits of nonhumans by standards derived from *their* good. To use only standards based on human values [or the good of humans] is already to commit oneself to holding that humans are superior to nonhumans, which is the point in question.

Each member of a species has certain biological interests or goods of its own which are similar to those of the other members of the same species. These species-specific interests and goods can be studied and identified by the biological and life sciences. Arguably objective comparisons can be made of different individuals of the same species regarding their species-specific merits (that is, those capacities and skills required for living a good life relative to the species): for example, over whether a certain antelope is better in detecting and escaping from dangers than another antelope, or whether a certain bear has better skills in catching fish than another bear. But there is no one single standard of the good life that is applicable across all species. Hence, going further than Taylor, it would be possible to argue that it would not even be conceptually coherent or sensible to compare the merits of individuals belonging to different species. For example, it would not make sense to ask whether an antelope who has the capacities and skills to live a good antelope life is "better" than a bear who has the capacities and skills to live a good bear life. If this is right, then the same logic should apparently apply when evaluating those arguments that seek to attribute superiority to humans over other living things: it would likewise not make sense to say that a human being who has the capacities and skills (e.g. self-consciousness, rationality, language, moral freedom, aesthetic creativity) to live a good human life is "better" than a living thing of another species who has the capacities and skills to live a good life relative to its species.

Logic and reason appear not to provide cogent grounds for thinking that humans are "better" or superior to other animals and living things. Suppose they are not better, suppose they are not more entitled, then how should humans relate to members of the other species in the earth's biosphere? In asking this question, it would seem important to bear in mind that the survival of other species has become increasingly threatened – many actually pushed beyond the point of recovery – by the activities of the human species in pursuit of its better living and profits. It is noteworthy that demonstrating the problems with – and even failure of arguments for – human superiority does not amount to positively establishing the general biocentric thesis that all living things are intrinsically valuable, let alone the more specific egalitarian biocentric proposition that all living things are equal in intrinsic value. Nevertheless, on the supposition that the appeal to human superiority is the only line of defence that humans have in attempting morally to justify their exploitation of the earth's environment and its other inhabitants, then, given that humans have already benefited disproportionately at the great expense of members of many other species, the onus appears to be on the humans to demonstrate that they are indeed "greater" than the rest. There is a paradox in such a conclusion. If the greatness of humanity is not mere human self-aggrandisement, then such greatness may consist at its core in a moral capacity to look beyond the interests of oneself and one's close associates, and to show a willingness to care for and share with those who are less able to fend for themselves.

31

POPULATION

Tim Mulgan

Population ethics – also known as intergenerational justice or obligations to future people – brings together abstract value theory, practical ethics, economics and public policy. Population ethics is a fast-moving field, and any summary of empirical or policy-oriented literature would date quickly. Accordingly, this chapter focuses not on practical policy debates, but on the philosophical issues behind them. Many of these underlying issues have implications elsewhere in global ethics – and in moral philosophy more broadly.

This chapter is in eight sections. The first asks why philosophers have been so slow to focus their attention on intergenerational issues. The next four sections deal with broad philosophical issues: the social discount rate, Parfit's non-identity problem, utilitarian aggregation and the possibility of an intergenerational social contract. The final three sections cover the connections between population policy and other issues in global ethics, namely reproductive freedom, development aid and environmental ethics.

The side-lining of future people

Until the late twentieth century, moral philosophy concentrated on interactions between contemporaries. Future generations were only ever an afterthought. This was largely because philosophers assumed, often implicitly, that future people will be better off than present people. We need only look after ourselves, do what is best for present people, and then bequeath our stable liberal democratic institutions, thriving economy and scientific advances to future people. What is good for us, is also good for them. There is no conflict between present and future. One classic example is the American philosopher John Rawls. Rawls's magnum opus *A Theory of Justice* (Rawls 1971) devotes just ten pages to justice between generations, and his only intergenerational ethical question is the just savings problem: how much better off should we leave our descendants?

One longstanding exception to this general optimism has been the worry, made famous by Robert Malthus, that over-population might reduce average welfare (Malthus [1798] 2008). As a result, over-population has long been a prominent issue in philosophical discussion of famine in the developing world, especially in Africa.

Since the 1970s, a variety of developments – including oil shocks, financial crises, ozone depletion and climate change – have led philosophers to question their optimism. Even if it is not already too late to prevent future generations from being worse off than present people, it seems certain that any serious attempt to minimize the future harm of economic recession or climate change will impact very severely on the welfare of present people in both developed and developing countries. Moral philosophers have thus had to grapple, for the first time, with the real possibility of serious conflicts of interest between present and future people.

The social discount rate

Once conflicts of interest arise between generations, one key ethical question is how to balance our obligations to future people against our obligations to our contemporaries. Academic debate centres on the controversial practice of *discounting* future harms or benefits. Even a modest discount of 5 per cent per annum makes it "uneconomic" to spend even one dollar today to avert a global catastrophe in five hundred years' time. (To be worth a dollar today, the catastrophe has to cost $39,323,267,827) This issue comes to the fore in policy debates regarding climate change, where one popular argument is that the *future* benefit of preventing climate change is not worth the *present* cost.

Discounting is relatively uncontroversial as a proxy for uncertainty, and to accommodate the remote possibility that there will be no future people. (Humanity might be wiped out by an asteroid strike, of instance.) It also makes sense to discount if you are confident that future people will be richer than present people. In terms of its contribution to *well-being*, a dollar is worth more to a poor person than to a rich one. (But, of course, this argument must be reversed if we expect future people to be worse off.)

The controversial ethical question is whether we should, as many economists do, go further and apply a *pure time preference* – where future happiness counts for less simply *because* it lies in the future. One common justification is that this is how people actually behave. We do discount future benefits both to ourselves and to others.

Pure discounting is a common practice among *economists*. Even with a modest discount rate, we can effectively ignore distant future people. However, most *ethicists* reject pure discounting. This rejection is especially strong among utilitarians, who typically embrace temporal impartiality. Human beings are equally valuable, no matter when they live. Present happiness is not intrinsically more valuable than future happiness. Given the vast number of future people, this principled refusal to discount *at all* means that population ethics is arguably the most important area of ethics. Indeed, our obligations to future people now threaten to overwhelm all other moral concerns. (An influential early discussion is Cowen & Parfit 1992. For economic discussion, especially in relation to climate change, see Stern 2006 and Nordhaus 2007.)

Parfit's non–identity problem

The publication of Derek Parfit's *Reasons and Persons* (Parfit 1984) was a landmark in population ethics. Parfit introduces several theoretical puzzles that have influenced subsequent debate. His first puzzle is often illustrated by two simple tales.

> *Mary's choice:* Mary is deciding whether to have a child in summer or winter. Mary suffers from a rare medical condition. Any child she has in winter will suffer serious ailments, while a summer child will be perfectly healthy. On a whim, Mary opts for a winter birth. Despite his ailments, her child has a life worth living (*ibid.*: 358).

Mary's behaviour seems morally wrong. But why? Intuitively, Mary acts wrongly because she harms her child. But the winter child has a life worth living – and would not otherwise have existed at all. (A child born in summer, made from different genetic materials, would be a different person.) How can someone be harmed if they would otherwise not have existed at all?

(It would be even odder to say that Mary harms the child she would have had in summer. How can you harm someone who *never* exists?)

> *Risky policy:* We must choose between two energy policies. The first is completely safe. The second is cheaper, but riskier. (Perhaps burying nuclear waste where there is no earthquake risk for several centuries, but a significant risk in the distant future.) Suppose we choose the risky policy. Many centuries later, an earthquake releases radiation, killing thousands of people (*ibid.*: 371–72).

Again, our choice seems clearly wrong. But suppose the two energy policies would lead to radically different patterns of migration and social interaction. Now take any particular individual killed by the catastrophe. If we had chosen differently, her parents would never have met, and she would never have existed. We have not harmed *her*, any more than Mary has harmed her winter child. But if we harm no one, how can our choice be wrong?

Parfit distinguishes two kinds of moral choice. In a *same people choice*, our actions affect what will happen in the future, but not who will exist. When our actions affect who exists, we are making a *different people choice*. (Parfit further divides different people choices into *same number* – when our choice does not affect how many people exist – and *different number* when it does. We discuss different number choices below.)

These two tales demonstrate that different people choices are very common. Parfit called this the *non-identity problem*. It is a problem because many moral principles are *person-affecting*: an action can *only* be wrong if some particular person is adversely affected. In a different people choice, where no one is ever worse off, it appears that nothing can be wrong (M. Roberts 2009, Roberts & Wasserman 2009).

Some philosophers conclude that we can only compare possible futures from the point of view of those who exist *now* (Heyd 1992). But this would give the present generation free rein to despoil the environment in pursuit of their own happiness.

Others reply that we *can* compare different possible futures from the point of view of those who will exist *even if* different futures contain different people. Phrases such as "the British people of the twenty-second century" can be used to refer to whoever is alive then and there. We can then say that a future with clear air and drinkable water is better *for those people* than one without (Kumar 2003).

Utilitarians respond by rejecting person-affecting principles. They evaluate different possible futures in terms of aggregate happiness, without asking whether the same people exist in different possible futures. We return to utilitarianism below.

The non-identity problem has implications in many areas of practical ethics. In medical ethics, it arises whenever any individual reproductive choice or medical procedure affects the identity of the resulting child. For instance, many people object to new reproductive technologies on the grounds that they harm the resulting children. But if they affect a child's genetic make-up, and if genetic identity is a component of individual identity, then such technologies generate different people choices – and the resulting children would not otherwise have existed. If their lives are worth living, how can they be said to be harmed? The non-identity problem also arises in discussions of reparations for historical injustice. Should present people be compensated for some past wrong if they would not have existed in an alternative future where the injustice did not occur? Can the descendants of those who suffered from slavery or colonization consistently complain about injustices without which they themselves would not exist? Or do they need to make their claims on behalf of groups that would otherwise have existed? As these practical issues often arise in a global context, this seemingly abstruse metaphysical puzzle thus has a deep impact on global ethics.

Utilitarianism and aggregation

Since the late twentieth century, most discussion of population ethics has taken place within the utilitarian ethical tradition. Utilitarians base morality on the promotion of human well-being. Utilitarians judge everything – actions, moral codes, political and legal institutions, and even beliefs – by its impact on human flourishing (Mulgan 2007, 2011a).

Utilitarianism places population ethics centre-stage. Utilitarianism has always been character-ized by a commitment to *impartiality* – and especially *temporal impartiality*. This is commonly summed up in the slogan: "Each is to count for one, and none for more than one." Human well-being is equally valuable, no matter whose it is *or when they live*. Utilitarianism thus offers a natural and compelling account of why we have obligations to people in the future. If there will be future people, and if our actions can impact on their quality of life, then we have obligations regarding them. Those obligations are no different to those we have regarding present people. Utilitarianism thus side-steps Parfit's non-identity problem (see above), as well as the other difficulties faced by its rivals (see below).

Because they base morality on the maximization of happiness, utilitarians obviously need to know what counts as "the greatest happiness of the greatest number". Utilitarians need a *theory of aggregation*: taking us from the values of individual lives to the value of a population as a whole. Suppose you could create any possible world, with any possible population. Which should you choose? The hope is that the answer to this abstract question can then be combined with practical information to generate policy advice. (It is not only utilitarians who need a theory of aggrega-tion. Any ethical theory – and any policy-maker choosing between different possible populations for her society – must have some way to choose between different possible futures.)

The utilitarian tradition offers two contrasting accounts of aggregation. On the *total view*, one outcome is better than another if and only if it contains a greater total amount of happiness. On the *average view*, one outcome is better than another if and only if it contains a higher average level of happiness. Prior to the twentieth century, the two views were not always clearly distinguished. This is understandable. In any choice where numbers are not at stake, the two views must coin-cide, as whatever maximizes the total also maximizes the average. But the two views can come apart. Suppose a society must decide between two population policies. One would yield a large population where each person has a moderate level of happiness, while the other would produce a smaller population who are all very happy. Suppose the former policy offers greater total happiness, and the latter offers higher average happiness. Which outcome is better *in terms of human happiness*?

The total view is the simplest theory of aggregation. It has been the most popular account of value in the utilitarian tradition. (At least among philosophers. Economists often favour the average view.) The basic argument for the total view is simple. If we value happiness, then presumably we should aim to produce as much happiness as possible.

Unfortunately, the total view has problems. The most famous of these is highlighted by Derek Parfit, who argues that the total view implies the following (Parfit 1984: 388):

> *The repugnant conclusion*: For any possible population of at least ten billion people, all with a very high quality of life, there must be some much larger imaginable popula-tion whose existence, if other things are equal, would be better, even though its members have lives that are barely worth living.

To see why the total view implies the repugnant conclusion, begin with a world where ten billion people all have extremely good lives. Call it A. Imagine a second world, with twice as many people, each slightly more than half as happy as the people in A. Call this new world B.

Total happiness in B is higher than in A. Now repeat this process until we reach a world where a vast population each have a life barely worth living. Call this world Z. As each step increases total happiness, Z must be better than A.

Parfit finds this conclusion "intrinsically repugnant" (*ibid.*: 390). If this is a consequence of the total view, then the total view is unacceptable. The repugnant conclusion is a classic case of a thought experiment that allegedly provides a decisive counter-example to a philosophical view. This puzzle is one of the organizing problems of contemporary philosophical population ethics. Philosophers either reject Parfit's intuition that A is better than Z (in those cases where the total view prefers Z to A), or they reject the total view (Ryberg & Tannsjo 2004; Mulgan 2006: 55–81, 2011a; Arrhenius *et al.* 2010).

It is tempting to reject intuitions altogether. Surely what counts is whether a conclusion follows from well-established premises, not whether it has intuitive appeal. But then we must ask what grounds ethical premises if it is *not* a moral intuition of some kind. (When a philosopher says that they reject intuitions, this usually means that they reject some intuitions in favour of others.) Some non-utilitarians reject all intuitions about the comparative value of possible futures (Foot 1985). But utilitarians do not have this option. Without a theory of aggregation, their moral theory lacks foundation. And even non-utilitarian population ethics presumably needs *some* comparative judgements about the value of possible futures.

One more modest approach rejects all intuitions regarding very large numbers. John Broome says: "We have no reason to trust anyone's intuitions about very large numbers, however excellent their philosophy. Even the best philosophers cannot get an intuitive grasp of, say, tens of billions of people" (Broome 2004: 57–58). Broome does not think we should abandon population ethics – or give up on moral intuitions altogether. Instead, we should rely on a *theory* built on our everyday intuitions. And Broome argues that that theory is the total view.

Other proponents of the total view object that Parfit's abstract characterization of A and Z invites us to mis-imagine the two worlds. They defend the repugnant conclusion by examining the Z-world more closely. Yew-Kwan Ng objects that, when we consider the repugnant conclusion, we privilege our own perspective and are guilty of "misplaced partiality" (Ng 1989). We picture the A-lives as similar to our own, and imagine the A-people choosing between A and Z. If we were more impartial, we might see that Z contains more total value than A, and is thus better.

The total view says that we should create an extra life *only* when this would raise the total happiness. If we create a new person, then – setting aside the impact on already existing people – we raise total happiness if and only if the extra life itself is worth living. If we imagine a numerical scale of well-being, then the lives in Z must be above zero. If the zero level is higher than Parfit thinks, then the Z-lives may be better than his discussion suggests.

What does it means to say that a life is "barely worth living" – as the Z-lives are meant to be? This phrase can evoke a life of frustration and pain – one that we would rather not live at all. Parfit himself describes the Z-lives as consisting of "nothing but muzak and potatoes" (Parfit 1986a: 148). If they are *human* lives, then it is natural to suppose that such lives also contain negative elements – such as boredom, frustration, or lack of accomplishment and friendship. These features reduce the value of a life. A friendless under-achieving human is badly off in a way that a friendless slug is not. We may well feel that a muzak and potatoes life is well *below* zero. But, if the Z-lives are like *that*, then the total view does not conclude that Z is better than A. Rather, Z (as pictured by Parfit) will be much *worse* than A. So the *real* Z-lives must be much better than Parfit's bleak description suggests.

Some philosophers distinguish two values of a life: its *general* value and its *personal* value. Personal value is the value that a life has for the person who lives it, whereas general value is that amount by which the presence of an extra life raises the value of the total population. The general zero level may be higher than the personal zero. A person's life could then be worth living from her point of view, but not good enough to ensure that adding her life increases the value of the world. The repugnant conclusion concerns the general zero level. So the lives in Z must be very good in personal terms. In Z, each person's life is well worth living *for her*. This distinction is useful in practical population ethics, as we can now argue that it is desirable to limit population growth without implying that, if growth does occur, the resulting lives are not worth living.

For instance, Partha Dasgupta draws a sharp distinction between the notions of "a life worth living" and "a life above the zero level" (Dasgupta 1994: 116). These correspond to the personal and general zero levels respectively. Dasgupta then explicitly links his discussion of the repugnant conclusion to the plight of the global poor. He suggests that hundreds of millions of people currently live well below the (general) zero level:

> A person whose life is barely worth living has a *very low, negative* living standard. She is one of the wretched of the earth, and there are hundreds of millions of such people today, disenfranchised, malnourished, and prone to illness, but surviving, and tenaciously displaying that their lives are worth living by the persistence with which they continue to wish to live.
>
> *(Ibid.)*

On this view, if Parfit's Z-world is accurately imagined, it will include lives above the (general) zero level. Z would then be much better than the actual developing world, and the repugnant conclusion is thus not repugnant.

Some utilitarians do defend the total view. But others agree with Parfit's intuition, and seek alternatives. The most popular has been the average view. This easily avoids the repugnant conclusion, as A has a higher average happiness than Z. To evaluate the average view, we must first dissolve an obvious objection. If we average over everyone *alive in the future*, then the average view tells us to kill anyone whose happiness is below average. We should then kill anyone below the new average and so on – until two people remain and the happier one should kill the other. To avoid this absurd consequence, we must average over *all those who will ever live*. Killing someone merely makes their life go worse; it does not make it the case that they never existed. Killing *lowers* the average – unless it improves the welfare of the person killed.

Unfortunately, the average view faces real problems of its own. One of the most discussed is the following.

> *The hermit problem*: Everyone in the cosmos is extremely happy. On a distant uninhabited planet, we create a new person. His life, while very good, is slightly below the cosmic average.

The average view says that we have made things worse; and that what we ought to do depends on the happiness of people in distant corners of the cosmos with whom our hermit will never interact. Both claims seem intuitively implausible. As Parfit puts it, the *mere addition* of lives worth living cannot make things worse, and present moral decisions should not depend on how happy the ancient Egyptians were (Parfit 1984: 420).

The hermit problem plays a similar dialectical role to the repugnant conclusion. Defenders of the average view have the same broad options. They can reject the intuition or deny that this result follows from their theory. One popular response is to focus on the average happiness of those affected by our actions, thus removing the need to take account of the welfare of people in the distant past or on distant planets.

Both the total and average views concentrate on aggregate features of a population, without regard to how equally happiness is distributed. By contrast, many approaches to global ethics focus not on total or average measures of well-being, but on the obligation to ensure that *everyone* reaches some threshold of well-being. This brings us to a third theory of aggregation, based on the notion of *lexicality*. Suppose you enjoy both Mozart and muzak. Someone offers you a choice between one day of Mozart and as much muzak as you like. You opt for the former, because *no amount* of muzak could match the smallest amount of Mozart. Philosophers would say you believe that Mozart is *lexically superior* to muzak.

We can use lexicality to avoid the repugnant conclusion (J. Griffin 1986: 85–89, 338–40; Parfit 1986a; Mulgan 2006: 64–80). Suppose the creatures in A and Z belong to different species. Perhaps A contains flourishing human beings while Z is full of slugs. Lexicality seems plausible here, as its says that ten billion human lives are more valuable than any number of slug lives. A is better, because ten billion human lives are more valuable than any number of slug lives. A lexical divide within view of human well-being would imply that ten billion flourishing human lives trump any number of human lives that are barely worth living. A is better than Z.

On a lexical view, the task of raising everyone above the lexical threshold has absolute priority over any possible benefits above that threshold. Lexicality thus offers a more egalitarian and individualist account of aggregation than either the total or average views.

The most worrying problem for any lexical account is Parfit's *continuum objection*:

> Mozart and Muzak ... seem to be in quite different categories. But there is a fairly smooth continuum between these two. Though Haydn is not as good as Mozart, he is very good. And there is other music which is not far below Haydn's, other music not far below this, and so on. Similar claims apply to the ... other things which give most to the value of life. ... Since this is so, it may be hard to defend the view that what is best has more value than any amount of what is nearly as good.
>
> *(Parfit 1986a: 164)*

The challenge for the lexical view is to tell us where to draw the line – and why. How do we decide that some possible lives are lexically more important than others?

The philosophical literature contains many other theories of aggregation (Hurka 1983, Blackorby *et al.* 1997). However, these all raise the same broad issues as the three theories we have discussed. Some philosophers conclude that it is impossible to construct an intuitively plausible theory, because our intuitions themselves are inconsistent. One focus of debate is Parfit's *mere addition paradox*, which shows that we cannot avoid the repugnant conclusion and at the same time claim that the mere addition of happy lives never makes things worse (Parfit 1984: 419–41; Arrhenius 2000).

All these problems arise because we seek to rank all possible worlds on a single objective scale of betterness. Some philosophers propose relativized models of value, where we evaluate different possible worlds relative to the interests of the people who live in them. This can yield the result that A is better than B from the perspective of those who live in A, while B is better than A from the perspective of those who live in B (Dasgupta 1994, M. Roberts 2002). Others attempt to side-step the standard debates by construing puzzles such as Parfit's repugnant conclusion as pertaining to obligations, rather than the comparative values of possible futures (Mulgan 2006).

Utilitarian aggregation is exclusively about human well-being. This may seem unacceptably parochial, speciesist or anthropocentric. What about ecological values or the welfare of animals? However, utilitarian values can be combined with non-human values. If we believe that human well-being is *one* value, then we still need an account of aggregation – which we can then supplement with other ecological values. The question of how to balance these different values is a key issue in environmental ethics. (We return to the connection between population ethics and environmental ethics below.)

An intergenerational social contract

In light of the problems faced by utilitarian population ethics, it is natural to seek alternative foundations for intergenerational obligations. One popular alternative – both in philosophy and in public discourse – is the notion of a social contract. Social contract theory models both morality and justice as a contract between rational individuals – a bargain to govern our reciprocal interactions to our mutual advantage. This tradition goes back to Thomas Hobbes and John Locke in the seventeenth century, and has been very influential ever since. The traditional social contract concerns a single generation. We are asked to imagine that all the people who are alive at a particular time gather together to agree on basic moral rules.

Any attempt to extend a social contract across generations must address the problem of *power imbalance*. The lives of future people depend on our decisions. By contrast, our lives are unaffected by their decisions. We can do a great deal to (or for) posterity but posterity cannot do anything to (or for) us. Where there is no reciprocal interaction for mutual advantage, there can be no meaningful talk of a *contract*. If morality depends on a contract for mutual advantage, then it seems there can be no intergenerational obligations.

Some philosophers are prepared to bite the bullet. We may choose to take future people into account. And, if some of our contemporaries happen to care about future people (perhaps their own distant descendants), then we owe it to those contemporaries to consider the interests of those future people. But we have no obligations to future people (Heyd 1992).

However, while some may embrace this conclusion in theory, virtually no practitioner of global ethics defends it. The classic philosopher's thought experiment here involves a *time bomb*: an action today that devastates people in the distant future but has no direct impact until then. Suppose the people who will be affected are so far in the future that no one alive today cares for them. Is it wrong to plant a time bomb? If so, is this as wrong as planting a bomb that would cause the same devastation today (Gosseries 2001)?

Utilitarians, who advocate strict temporal neutrality, would say that planting a time bomb is just as wrong as planting a bomb that explodes today. Anyone who feels there is something wrong with planting a time bomb needs some account of intergenerational obligation.

Suppose we want to construct an intergenerational social contract. We might first note that overlapping generations *do* interact and bargain. We can then extend our contract indefinitely into the future, using what Gosseries (*ibid.*) dubs the *zipper argument*. Suppose we have only three generations: G1, G2 and G3. G1 and G3 do not interact, but G2 interacts with both G1 and G3. G2 know that they will have to bargain with G3. So G2 will take G3's interests into account when bargaining with G1 – and ask G1 not to leave a bomb that will devastate G3.

Unfortunately, this ingenious argument is problematic. Standard social contracts assume self-interest. But then why will G2 object to a time bomb that will impact only on G3? On the contrary, G2 might welcome the bomb, as it strengthens G2's position against G3 ("If you don't give us what we want, we will not defuse the time bomb"). G2 would then ask G1 to plant such a bomb. This would make time bombs morally desirable – surely an implausible conclusion (Mulgan 2006: 28–32).

Many philosophers conclude that a self-interested contract is a poor foundation for morality. They prefer hypothetical or idealized contracts. Since its publication, the dominant theory has been that of Rawls (1971). Rawls asks what people would agree to under certain idealized circumstances. He seeks principles of justice everyone can recognize as a fair basis for mutual interaction. These principles are chosen in an original position, from behind a veil of ignorance. The choosers know what their society will look like if any given principle is adopted, but they do not know who they will be in that society. Imagine a very simple society with two groups: rich and poor. What principles would a rational person choose if they did not know whether they were rich or poor?

In Rawls (1971: 284–93), the parties to the original position belong to the same generation. Unless they care about future people, intergenerational justice will not feature in their principles. Nothing we do to future people – however devastating – could count as unjust. As an egalitarian, this conclusion would be unacceptable for Rawls. He must accommodate future generations. Rawls originally added a motivational assumption. Those in the original position care about their descendants, at least for the next generation or two. This solution is ad hoc. Why allow concern for descendants, when we allow no concern for contemporaries? Furthermore, any realistic motivational assumption only works for a few generations. It thus cannot remove the threat of time bombs. Rawls focuses on savings from one generation to the next, not on longer-term environmental or resource issues. This focus was controversial even at the time – and seems much more problematic now.

Rawls (1993: 273–4) abandoned this solution, and stipulated instead that those in the original position must behave in a way that they would want previous generations to have behaved. Total self-sacrifice is ruled out, as the cost of our sacrifice outweighs the benefits of the sacrifices of others. Total selfishness also fails, as the damage of earlier selfishness outweighs our own freedom to behave as we wish. We need something in between. Unfortunately for Rawls, it is very hard to say what that something will be.

A more intriguing option for Rawls is to extend the veil of ignorance, so that people do not know what generation they belong to (B. Barry 1989: 179–203). Each generation then cares for the interests of all. But now we must decide who participates in this new original position. Parfit's non-identity problem now comes to the fore. Before the present generation decides how they will live, there is no fact of the matter as to who will exist in the future. Should we thus imagine an original position containing everyone who *might* exist? Now we do not even know whether we will ever exist. Can we make sense of this imaginary choice?

Another common contractualist move is to introduce *trustees*: present people who represent the interests of future people in the bargain between contemporaries. This develops a device commonly used to bring children, animals and the non-sentient environment within the scope of a social contract theory (Scanlon 1998). At this point, opponents wonder whether the device of the contract still does any meaningful work. Utilitarians, for instance, argue that we should replace the artificiality of a contract between trustees with an insistence that all present people have a direct obligation to care for future people. (For more on intergenerational social contracts, see Gosseries & Meyer 2009).

Like utilitarianism, the social contract seems to need radical revision if it is to ground intergenerational ethics. It is thus no surprise that philosophers seek alternatives to both utilitarianism and social contract. They seek to ground intergenerational ethics in something other than the welfare of individual human beings, or the interactions of contemporaries. Perhaps our obligations are owed, not to future people, but to past people, who sacrificed so that we could thrive, and would expect us to do the same for those who will come after. Our obligations regarding future people would then actually be debts owed to our ancestors. Or perhaps our moral obligation is to a community that persists through the generations – or perhaps even to humanity as a whole. One early exploration of the various resources available to communitarian intergenerational ethics is de-Shalit (1995). These solutions remove the distinctiveness of population ethics, by focusing on features it shares with relations between contemporaries.

Over-population and reproductive freedom

According to the 2012 revision of the official United Nations (United Nations 2012b) population estimates and projections, world population is projected to surpass 9.6 billion by 2050 and 10.9 billion by 2100, up from 6.8 billion in 2009. (These were the most recent figures available as of May 2014.) Most of the additional people will live in the developing world, where population growth is already often correlated with poverty, social unrest and environmental degradation. Population growth may also exacerbate the impact of climate change, as countries with growing populations are also often those most likely to suffer from aridity, crop failure, water shortage or rising sea levels. Limiting population growth is thus a major issue for population ethics. (Perhaps it is the fear that population growth will overwhelm the planet's ability to feed humanity, rather than any abstract intuition about the comparative value of possible futures, that lies behind many people's negative reaction to Parfit's repugnant conclusion.)

One central question in population ethics is whether coercive fertility policies are necessary to avoid over-population. The most prominent actual example has been the Chinese government's one-child-family policy. Opponents of coercion offer many counter-arguments (Sen 1999: 161–96; Mulgan 2006: 204–26). Technological optimists deny the link between population *growth* and *over*-population. They argue that population rises have always been accompanied by advances in food technology and agricultural efficiency, and that there is no reason to expect human beings to be less inventive in the future. One obvious empirical question is whether this optimistic extrapolation from historical trends still holds true in light of the threat of climate change (see Chapter 27).

Defenders of liberal or libertarian political principles, by contrast, would argue that reproductive freedom is a basic human right that governments cannot legitimately infringe, even in pursuit of desirable population goals. Aside from raising general issues about the scope of human rights – and the tension between individual freedom and public policy (see Chapter 6) – this liberal response also brings to the fore the tension between the freedoms of present people and the needs of future people – a tension that liberal and libertarian thinkers have only recently begun to explore (Mulgan 2011b).

These two responses rest on controversial empirical or philosophical claims. Most defenders of reproductive freedom seek a more robust reply. They aim to bypass the theoretical possibility of a conflict between reproductive freedom and population policy by arguing that, in practice, the best way to limit population growth is via the education and empowerment of women. If we want to achieve a sustainable population, we should aim to enhance reproductive freedom rather than limiting it.

The most influential work in this area is by the Nobel Prize-winning economist Amartya Sen, whose *Development as Freedom* is the classic summary of the case against coercion (Sen 1999). Subsequent literature has added many details, but the basic outlines of Sen's case remain largely unchallenged (see Chapter 25). Opponents of coercion argue that, while it may *seem* more reliable than individual choice, coercion is actually less reliable. Because it largely leaves people's underlying inclinations unchanged, a coercive policy must continually be enforced to defeat people's determined efforts to subvert it. For instance, Sen quotes the architects of China's family policy as admitting that "the birth concept of the broad masses has not changed fundamentally" (*ibid*.: 220). Opponents of coercion also question whether coercion works. They note that correlation is not causation. Although the implementation of the one-child policy may have coincided with a reduction in average fertility in China, those changes also followed significant improvements in education, healthcare and female job opportunities. To separate out the different causal factors, we must compare changing fertility patterns across different countries with divergent population policies. Sen introduced into the popular debate a now-standard comparision between China and the Indian state of Kerala. General development policy in China shares many of the features of the socialist government in Kerala. Yet Kerala's fertility rate has declined even faster than China's, despite the fact that coercive policies are not followed in Kerala (*ibid.*: 219–26).

A general presumption in favour of empowerment and freedom – and against centralized coercion – has become something of an orthodoxy in development circles. As a result, attention has moved away from national-level population policy and towards more localized initiatives designed to increase women's access to education, employment opportunities, and lifestyle choices more broadly. Population ethics thus complements other development goals rather than being in conflict with them (see Chapters 13, 16 and 25).

Population ethics and aid

A central question in global ethics is what affluent people owe to those in less fortunate lands (see Chapter 13). One influential argument suggests that policies relating to over-population undermine all charitable obligations. This *Malthusian argument* (pioneered by the nineteenth-century economist Robert Malthus) grants the (controversial) empirical premise that we are able to improve and safeguard the lives of those who are currently starving, but concludes that this would be an undesirable result. If we aid those who are starving, then more of them will live to maturity. As the birth rate in poor countries is often very high, this will lead to a population explosion. The result is an unsustainably high population in the future, with more people starving. Unpleasant as it may seem, a high rate of infant mortality is necessary in the long term.

The Malthusian argument remains very influential in popular discussion of development aid. If it were sound, this argument would have radical implications for the ethics of aid. As with the alleged conflict between population policy and reproductive freedom, most defenders of aid respond by denying Malthus's empirical claims. Increases in the standard of living tend to be followed by *decreases* in the birth rate, so that population growth declines. This suggests that *if* aid can succeed in raising living standards, then it will also complement a sustainable population policy. (Of course, if aid will not succeed, then there is presumably no obligation to provide it.) Population ethics and development ethics are thus supporters, not rivals.

Even if Malthus's original argument does not succeed, however, it does highlight the fact that development aid cannot be isolated from population policy. Any evaluation of current aid must take account of its likely impact on the number and welfare of future people. Climate change, and other environmental issues, raise new concerns about the future sustainability of present aid (see Chapter 27).

Population ethics and the environment

Environmental issues impact on population policy in many complex practical ways. They also give population policy a new urgency. Though some environmental problems affect us now, many of the most worrying problems arise only in the distant future. Climate change, environmental degradation, and pollution all impact primarily on future people (see Chapters 27–30).

More fundamentally, environmental problems also undermine two assumptions that are shared by almost all traditional approaches to population policy. The first is the assumption that the present population level is sustainable. Economists, philosophers and policy-makers often ask whether *increases* in population would be good for society or the economy. The aim is to limit population *growth*. Although we are familiar with the idea that rapid population increase may be undesirable, it is usually taken for granted that there is no harm in maintaining the population at its present level indefinitely. However, if climate change is as bad as some estimates suggest, then perhaps we should focus instead on the question of how large a reduction in population is required, and how quickly. Even if education and reproductive freedom are the best way to limit population growth, are they reliable ways to bring about a population reduction? Or must we reconsider coercion?

One sense in which the present population may not be sustainable is that it may not be possible to maintain six billion people at the present global average standard of living. This brings us to the second implicit assumption that environmental issues call into question. Traditional political philosophy often asks whether, and to what extent, we are obliged to enable future generations to be better off than ourselves. We take it for granted that, at the very least, we can leave our descendants no worse off than ourselves – and that we can do so at relatively little cost to ourselves. The threat of environmental catastrophe raises serious doubts about this assumption. It may turn out that the question before us is much bleaker. How much worse off should we leave future people, and at what cost to ourselves (Mulgan 2011b)?

BIBLIOGRAPHY

Abizadeh, A. 2007. "Cooperation, Pervasive Impact and Coercion: On the Scope (not Site) of Distributive Justice". *Philosophy and Public Affairs* 35(2): 318–58.

——forthcoming. "The Special-Obligations Challenge to More Open Borders". In *Migration in Political Theory: The Ethics of Movement and Membership*, S. Fine & Lea Ypi (eds). Oxford: Oxford University Press.

Abrahamsen, R. 2000. *Disciplining Democracy: Development Discourse and Good Governance in Africa*. London: Zed Books.

Abu-Laban, Y. 2012. "A World of Strangers or a World of Relationships? The Value of Care Ethics in Migration Research and Policy". In *Rooted Cosmopolitanism: Canada and the World*, W. Kymlicka & K. Walker (eds), 156–77. Vancouver: University of British Columbia Press.

AccountAbility 2008. *AA1000 Assurance Standard 2008*. London: AccountAbility UK.

Ackerman, P. & J. DuVall 2000. *A Force More Powerful*. New York: St Martin's Press.

Adams, J. 1984. *The Unnatural Alliance*. London: Quartet Books.

Adams, N. 2003. "Anti-trafficking Legislation: Protection or Deportation?" *Feminist Review* 73: 135–38.

Advocates for Human Rights 2005. "Debt Bondage and Trafficking in Women". www.stopvaw.org/debt_bondage_and_trafficking_in_women.html (accessed April 2014).

African Development Bank Group n.d. "Japan". www.afdb.org/en/topics-and-sectors/topics/partnerships/non-regional-member-countries/japan/ (accessed March 2013).

Agapow, P. M., O. R. P. Bininda-Emonds, K. A. Crandall, J. L. Gittleman, G. M. Mac, J. C. Marshall & A. Purvis 2004. "The Impact of Species Concept on Biodiversity Studies". *Quarterly Review of Biology* 79: 161–79.

Agar, N. 2004. *Liberal Eugenics: In Defence of Human Enhancement*. Oxford: Blackwell.

Agarwal, A. & S. Narain 1991. *Global Warming in an Unequal World: A Case of Environmental Colonialism*. New Delhi: Centre for Science and Environment.

Aguilera, R. V., D. Rupp, C. Williams & J. Ganapathi 2007. "Putting the S Back in CSR: A Multi-level Theory of Social Change in Organizations". *Academy of Management Review* 32(3): 836–63.

Agustín, L. 2007. *Sex at the Margins*. London: Zed.

Aiken, W. 1996. "The 'Carrying Capacity' Equivocation". See Aiken & LaFollette (1996), 16–25.

Aiken, W. & H. LaFollette (eds) 1996. *World Hunger and Morality*. Engelwood Cliffs, NJ: Prentice Hall.

Alcock, P. 1993. *Understanding Poverty*. Basingstoke: Palgrave Macmillan.

Alexander, M. & J. R. Bruning 2008. *How to Break A Terrorist: The US Interrogators Who Used Brains, not Brutality, to Take Down the Deadliest Man in Iraq*. New York: Free Press.

Ali, T. (ed.) 2000. *Masters of the Universe? NATO's Balkan Crusade*. London: Verso.

Alkire, S. 2005. *Valuing Freedoms*. Oxford: Oxford University Press.

Alkire, S. & A. Sumner 2013. *Multidimensional Poverty and the Post-2015 MDGs*. Oxford: Oxford Poverty & Human Development Initiative (OPHI).

Allen, B. 1996. *Rape Warfare*. Minneapolis, MN: University of Minnesota Press.

Almond, B. 2006. *The Fragmenting Family*. Oxford: Oxford University Press.

Altman, A. & C. H. Wellman 2009. *A Liberal Theory of International Justice*. Oxford: Oxford University Press.

AMC 2000. *Asian Migrant Yearbook 2000: Migration Facts, Analysis and Issues in 1999*. Hong Kong: Asian Migrant Centre.

American Medical Association 1998. "CEJA Report 5 – A-98: Information from Unethical Experiments". www.ama-assn.org//ama/pub/physician-resources/medical-ethics/code-medical-ethics/opinion230. page (accessed April 2014).

Améry, J. [1966] 1980. *At the Mind's Limits: Contemplations by a Survivor on Auschwitz and its Realities*, S. Rosenfeld & S. P. Rosenfeld (trans.). Bloomington, IN: Indiana University Press.

Amin, S. 1976. *Unequal Development*. New York: Monthly Review.

Anderson, B. 2008. "'Illegal immigrant': Victim or Villain?" COMPAS Working Paper WP-08-64. Oxford: COMPAS.

Anderson, B. & R. Andrijasevic (2008). "Sex, Slaves and Citizens: The Politics of Anti-trafficking", *Soundings* 40: 135–45.

Anderson, B. & J. O'Connell Davidson 2003. *Is Trafficking in Human Beings Demand Driven? A Multi-Country Pilot Study*, IOM Migration Research Series No. 15. Geneva: IOM.

Anderson, E. S. 1999. "What is the Point of Equality?" *Ethics* 109: 287–337.

Andrew, L. 2001. *Future Perfect: Confronting Decisions about Genetics*. New York: Columbia University Press.

Appiah, K. A. 2010a. *Experiments in Ethics*. Cambridge, MA: Harvard University Press

——2010b. *The Honor Code: How Moral Revolutions Happen*. New York: Norton.

Aradau, C. 2008. *Rethinking Trafficking in Women*. Basingstoke: Palgrave Macmillan.

Archer, D. 2009. *The Long Thaw: How Humans are Changing the Next 100,000 Years of Earth's Climate*. Princeton, NJ: Princeton University Press.

Arendt, H. 1979. *The Origins of Totalitarianism*. San Diego: HBJ.

Aristotle 1954. *Nicomachean Ethics*, W. D. Ross (trans.). London: Oxford University Press.

Armstrong, C. 2012. *Global Distributive Justice*. Cambridge: Cambridge University Press.

Arndt, H. 1981. "Economic Development: A Semantic History". *Economic Development and Cultural Change* 29(3): 457–66.

Arneson, R. J. 2005. "Do Patriotic Ties Limit Global Justice Duties?" *Journal of Ethics* 9(1/2): 127–50.

Arnold, D. G. 2003. "Human Rights and Business: An Ethical Analysis". In *Business and Human Rights: Dilemmas and Solutions*, R. Sullivan (ed.), 69–81. Sheffield: Greenleaf Publishing.

——2006. "Corporate Moral Agency". In *Midwest Studies in Philosophy, Volume XXX: Shared Intentions and Collective Responsibility*, P. French & H. Wettstein (eds), 279–91. Malden, MA: Blackwell.

——2010. "Transnational Corporations and the Duty to Respect Basic Human Rights". *Business Ethics Quarterly* 20(3): 371–99.

Arnold, D. G. & N. E. Bowie 2003. "Sweatshops and Respect for Persons". *Business Ethics Quarterly* 13(2): 221–42.

Arrhenius, G. 2000. "An Impossibility Theorem for Welfarist Axiologies". *Economics and Philosophy* 16: 247–66.

Arrhenius, G., J. Ryberg & T. Tännsjö 2010. "The Repugnant Conclusion". In *Stanford Encyclopedia of Philosophy*, Edward N. Zalta (ed.). http://plato.stanford.edu/archives/fall2010/entries/repugnant-conclusion (accessed April 2014).

Arrighi, G. 2007. *Adam Smith in Beijing: Lineages of the Twenty-First century*. London: Verso.

Arrow, K. 1972. "Gifts and Exchanges". *Philosophy and Public Affairs* 1(4): 343–62.

——1999. "Discounting, Morality, and Gaming". In *Discounting and Intergenerational Equity*, P. R. Portney & J. P. Weyant (eds), 13–21. Washington, DC: Resources for the Future.

Attfield, R. 1987. *A Theory of Value and Obligation*. London: Croom Helm.

——1990. "The Global Distribution of Health Care Resources". *Journal of Medical Ethics* 16(3): 153–56.

——1994. "Rehabilitating Nature and Making Nature Habitable". In *Philosophy and the Natural Environment*, R. Attfield & A. Belsey (eds), 45–58. Cambridge: Cambridge University Press.

——1999. *The Ethics of Global Environment*. Edinburgh: Edinburgh University Press.

Austin, M. W. 2009. *Conceptions of Parenthood: Ethics and the Family*. Aldershot: Ashgate.

Australian Bureau of Statistics 2010. "Year Book Australia, 2009–10", www.abs.gov.au/AUSSTATS/abs@.nsf/Lookup/1301.0Chapter3022009–10 (accessed April 2013).

Autesserre, S. 2010. *The Trouble with the Congo: Local Violence and the Failure of International Peacebuilding*. Cambridge: Cambridge University Press.

Ayres, R. U. 2007. "On the Practical Limits to Substitution". *Ecological Economics* 61: 115–28.

Ayres, R. U. & A. V. Kneese 1969. "Production, Consumption, and Externalities". *American Economic Review* 59: 282–97.

Baer, P. 2006. "Adaptation: Who Pays Whom?" In *Fairness in Adaptation to Climate Change*, W. N. Adger, J. Paavola, S. Huq & M. J. Mace (eds), 131–53. Cambridge, MA: MIT Press.

Baer, P., T. Athanasiou & S. Kartha 2007. *The Right to Development in a Climate Constrained World: The Greenhouse Development Rights Framework*. Berlin: Heinrich Böll Foundation.

Baghramian, M. 2004. *Relativism*. London: Routledge.

Baines, D. & N. Sharma 2002. "Is Citizenship a Useful Concept in Social Policy Work? Non-Citizens: The Case of Migrant Workers in Canada". *Studies in Political Economy* 69: 75–107.

Balakrishnan, R. & U. Narayan 1996. "Combining Justice with Development: Rethinking Rights and Responsibilities in the Context of World Hunger and Poverty". See Aiken & LaFollette (1996), 231–47.

Bales, K. 2000. *Disposable People: New Slavery in the Global Economy*. Berkeley, CA: University of California Press.

Ballantyne, A. J. 2010. "How to Do Research Fairly in an Unjust World?" *American Journal of Bioethics* 10 (6): 26–35.

Banerjee, A. V. & E. Duflo 2011. *Poor Economics: A Radical Rethinking of the Way to Fight Global Poverty*. New York: Public Affairs.

Baran, P. 1957. *The Political Economy of Growth*. New York: Monthly Review.

Barber, B. 2007. *Consumed: How Markets Corrupt Children, Infantilize Adults and Swallow Citizens Whole*. New York: W. W. Norton.

Barfield, T. 2009. *Afghanistan*. Princeton, NJ: Princeton University Press.

Barnett, M. & T. G. Weiss (eds) 2008. *Humanitarianism in Question: Politics, Power, Ethics*. Ithaca, NY: Cornell University Press.

Baron, D. P. 2001. "Private Politics, Corporate Social Responsibility and Integrated Strategy". *Journal of Economics and Management Strategy* 10(1): 7–45.

Barry, B. 1982. "Humanity and Justice in Global Perspective". In *Nomos XXIV: Ethics, Economics and the Law*, J. Pennock & J. Chapman (eds), 219–52. New York: New York University Press.

——1989. *Theories of Justice*. Berkeley, CA: University of California Press.

——1997. "Sustainability and Intergenerational Justice". *Theoria* 45(89): 43–65.

——1999. "Sustainability and Intergenerational Justice". In *Fairness and Futurity: Essays on Environmental Sustainability and Social Justice*, A. Dobson (ed.), 93–117. Oxford: Oxford University Press.

——2001. *Culture and Equality*. Cambridge: Polity.

Barry, C. 2011. "Human Rights Conditionality in Sovereign Debt Relief." *Journal of Political Philosophy* 19 (3): 282–305.

Barry, C. & G. Øverland 2012. "The Feasible Alternatives Thesis: Kicking Away the Livelihoods of the Global Poor". *Politics, Philosophy and Economics* 11(1): 97–119.

Barry, C. & S. Reddy 2008. *International Trade and Labor Standards: A Proposal for Linkage*. New York: Columbia University Press.

Barry, C., B. Herman & L. Tomitova (eds) 2007. *Dealing Fairly with Developing Country Debt*. Oxford: Blackwell.

Barry, K. 1995. *The Prostitution of Sexuality*. New York: New York University Press.

Barry, S. & S. Wisor 2013. "World Trade Organization". In *International Encyclopedia of Ethics*, Hugh Lafollette (ed.), 5541–46. Chichester: Wiley-Blackwell.

Basken, P. 2012. "Penn Whistle-Blower Says University Side-Stepped Ghostwriting Complaint". *Chronicle of Higher Education* (26 June). http://chronicle.com/article/Penn–Whistle–Blower–Says/132609/ (accessed April 2014).

Basl, J. 2010. "Restitutive Restoration: New Motivations for Ecological Restoration". *Environmental Ethics* 32(2): 135–47.

Basu, K. & Z. Tzannatos 2003. "The Global Child Labor Problem: What Do We Know and What Can We Do?". *World Bank Economic Review* 17(2): 147–73.

Basu, K. & P. H. Van 1998. "The Economics of Child Labor". *American Economic Review*, 88(3): 412–27.

Bauer, J. R. & D. A. Bell (eds) 1999. *The East Asian Challenge for Human Rights*. Cambridge: Cambridge University Press.

Bauer, P. T. 1984. *Reality and Rhetoric*. Cambridge, MA: Harvard University Press.

Bava Mahalia 1994. "Letter from a Tribal Village". *Lokayan Bulletin* 11(2/3): 157–58.

Baxter, W. F. 1974. *People or Penguins: The Case for Optimal Pollution*. New York: Columbia University Press.

Bayart, J. F. 2007. *Global Subjects: A Political Critique of Globalization*. Cambridge: Polity Press.

Bearden, J. N., R. O. Murphy & A. Rapoport 2005. "A Multi-Attribute Extension of the Secretary Problem: Theory and Experiments". *Journal of Mathematical Psychology* 49: 410–25.

Beauchamp, T. L. & J. F. Childress 2009. *Principles of Biomedical Ethics*. Oxford: Oxford University Press.

Beck, U. & N. Sznaider 2006. "Unpacking Cosmopolitanism for the Social Sciences: A Research Agenda". *British Journal of Sociology* 57(1): 1–23.

Beck-Gernsheim, E. 2002. *Reinventing the Family: In Search of New Lifestyles*. Malden, MA: Polity Press.

Becker, G. 2006. "Should the Purchase and Sale of Organs for Transplant Surgery be permitted?" *Becker-Posner Blog* (1 January). www.becker-posner-blog.com/2006/01/should-the-purchase-and-sale-of-organs-for-transplant-surgery-be-permitted-becker.html (accessed April 2014).

Becker, G. S. & J. J. Elías 2007. "Introducing Incentives in the Market for Live and Cadaveric Organ Donations". *Journal of Economic Perspectives* 21(3): 3–24.

Beckerman, W. 1994. "'Sustainable Development': Is it a Useful Concept?" *Environmental Values* 3: 191–209.

——1999. "Sustainable Development and Our Obligations to Future Generations". In *Fairness and Futurity: Essays on Environmental Sustainability and Social Justice*, A. Dobson (ed.), 71–92. Oxford: Oxford University Press.

——2000. "Review of J. Foster ed. *Valuing Nature? Ethics, Economics and the Environment*". *Environmental Values* 9: 122–24.

Beckerman, W. & J. Pasek 2001. *Justice, Posterity, and the Environment*. Oxford: Oxford University Press.

Beitz, C. R. 1979. *Political Theory and International Relations*. Princeton, NJ: Princeton University Press.

——1999a. *Political Theory and International Relations*, 2nd edn. Princeton, NJ: Princeton University Press.

——1999b. "International Liberalism and Distributive Justice: A Survey of Recent Thought". *World Politics* 51(2): 269–96.

——2004. "Human Rights and the Law of Peoples". See Chatterjee (2004), 193–214.

——2009. *The Idea of Human Rights*. Oxford: Oxford University Press.

Bell, D. 2008. "Carbon Justice? The Case Against a Universal Right to Equal Carbon Emissions". In *Seeking Environmental Justice*, S. Wilks (ed.), 239–57. Amsterdam: Rodolphi.

Bellamy, A. J. 2010a. "Military Intervention". In *The Oxford Handbook of Genocide Studies*, D. Bloxham & A. D. Moses (eds), 59–82. Oxford: Oxford University Press.

——2010b. "The Responsibility to Protect – Five Years On". *Ethics and International Affairs* 24(2): 143–69.

——2010c. *Responsibility to Protect: The Global Effort to End Mass Atrocities*. Cambridge: Polity Press.

Bellamy, A. J. & P. D. Williams 2011. "The New Politics of Protection? Libya, Cote d'Ivoire and the Responsibility to Protect". *International Affairs* 87(4): 825–50.

Bello, W. 2004. *Deglobalization: Ideas for a New World Economy*. New York: Palgrave Macmillan.

Benhabib, S. 2004. *The Rights of Others*. Cambridge: Cambridge University Press.

——2011. *Dignity in Adversity: Human Rights in Troubled Times*. Cambridge: Polity Press.

——2013. "Reason-Giving and Rights-Bearing: Constructing the Subject of Rights". *Constellations* 20: 38–50.

Bergart, A. M. 2000. "The Experience of Women in Unsuccessful Infertility Treatment." *Social Work in Health Care* 30(4): 45–69.

Berman, P. 2003. *Terror and Liberalism*. New York: W. W. Norton.

Best, G. 1994. *War and Law Since 1945*. Oxford: Clarendon Press.

Beyleveld, D. & R. Brownsword 1993. *Mice, Morality and Patents*. London: Common Law Institute of Intellectual Property.

——2002. "Is Patent Law Part of the EC Legal Order? A Critical Commentary on the Interpretation of Article 6(1) of Directive 98/44/EC in Case C-377/98". *Intellectual Property Quarterly* 4: 97–110.

Beyleveld, D., R. Brownsword & M. Llewelyn 2000. "The Morality Clauses of the Directive on the Legal Protection of Biotechnological Inventions: Conflict, Compromise, and the Patent Community". In *Pharmaceutical Medicine, Biotechnology and European Law*, R. Goldberg & J. Lonbay (eds), 157–81. Cambridge: Cambridge University Press.

Bhagwati, J. 1998. *A Stream of Windows: Unsettling Reflections on Trade, Immigration, and Democracy*. Cambridge, MA: MIT Press.

——2004. *In Defence of Globalization*. Oxford: Oxford University Press.

——2008. *Termites in the Trading System: How Preferential Agreements Undermine Free Trade*. New York: Oxford University Press.

Bilchitz, D. 2010. "Do Corporations Have Positive Fundamental Rights Obligations?" *Theoria* 57(125): 1–35.

Birdsall, N., D. Rodrik & A. Subramaniam 2005. "If Rich Governments Really Cared about Development", www.acp-eu-trade.org/library/files/RODRIK-BRIDSA-SUBRAMANIAN_EN_what-rich-can-do_0405_ICTSD_If-rich-governments-really-cared-about-development.pdf (accessed February 2013).

Blackorby, C., W. Bossert & D. Donaldson 1997. "Critical-Level Utilitarianism and the Population-Ethics Dilemma". *Economics and Philosophy* 13: 197–230.

Blake, M. 2001. "Distributive Justice, State Coercion, and Autonomy". *Philosophy and Public Affairs* 30(3): 257–96.

Blake, M. & M. Risse 2009. "Immigration and Original Ownership of the Earth". *Notre Dame Journal of Law, Ethics & Public Policy* 23: 133–65.

Bloch, A. & L. Schuster 2005. "At the Extremes of Exclusion: Deportation, Detention and Dispersal". *Ethnic and Racial Studies* 28(3): 491–512.

Bloxham, D. 2007. "Genocide: Can We Learn from History?" *BBC History Magazine* (January): 33–48.

Bohman, J. F. 2007. *Democracy Across Borders: From Demos to Demoi.* Cambridge, MA: MIT.

Boli, J. & G. Thomas 1999. *Constructing World Culture: International Nongovernmental Organizations Since 1875.* Stanford, CA: Stanford University Press.

Booth, K. 1991. "Security in Anarchy: Utopian Realism in Theory and Practice". *International Affairs* 67 (3): 527–45.

Boughton, J. 2003. "Who's in Charge: Ownership and Conditionality in IMF Supported Programs". IMF Working Paper 3/191: 1–24.

Bovenberg, J. 2004. "Inalienably Yours? The New Case for an Inalienable Property Right in Human Biological Material: Empowerment of Sample Donors or a Recipe for a Tragic Anti-Commons?". *Script–ed* 4, www2.law.ed.ac.uk/ahrc/script-ed/issue4/bovenberg.asp (accessed May 2014).

——2009. "Moore's Law and the Taxman. Some Theses on the Regulation of Property in Human Tissue". See Steinman *et al.* (2009), 161–68.

Bovens, L. 2011. "A Lockean Defense of Grandfathering Emission Rights". In *The Ethics of Global Climate Change*, D. G. Arnold (ed.), 124–44. Cambridge: Cambridge University Press.

Bowden, P. 1997. *Caring: Gender-Sensitive Ethics.* London: Routledge.

Boylan, M. (ed.) 2013. *Environmental Ethics*, 2nd edn. Chichester: John Wiley.

Boyle, J. 2008. *The Public Domain.* New Haven, CT: Yale University Press.

Brace, L. 2004. *The Politics of Property: Freedom and Belonging.* Edinburgh: Edinburgh University Press.

Brecher, B. 2007. *Torture and the Ticking Bomb.* Malden, MA: Blackwell Publishing.

Brenkert, G. G. 2009. "Google, Human Rights, and Moral Compromise". *Journal of Business Ethics* 85(4): 453–78.

Brennan, A. 1998. "Poverty, Puritanism and Environmental Conflict". *Environmental Values* 7: 305–31.

——2014. *Thinking About Nature: An Investigation of Nature, Value and Ecology.* London: Routledge.

Brennan, A. & Y. S. Lo 2007. "Two Conceptions of Dignity: Honour and Self-determination". In *Perspectives on Human Dignity*, N. Lickiss and J. Malpas (eds.), 43–58. Dordrecht: Springer.

——2010. *Understanding Environmental Philosophy.* London: Acumen.

Brighouse, H. & I. Robeyns 2010. *Measuring Justice: Primary Goods and Capabilities.* Cambridge: Cambridge University Press.

Brilmayer, L. 1989. "Consent, Contract and Territory". *Minnesota Law Review* 74: 1–35.

Brock, D. W. 2005. "Shaping Future Children: Parental Rights and Societal Interests." *Journal of Political Philosophy* 13: 377–98.

Brock, G. 2005. "Egalitarianism, Ideals, and Cosmopolitan Justice". *Philosophical Forum* 36: 1–30.

——2008. "Taxation and Global Justice: Closing the Gap Between Theory and Practice". *Journal of Social Philosophy* 39(2): 161–84.

——2009. *Global Justice: A Cosmopolitan Account.* Oxford: Oxford University Press.

——(ed.) 2013. *Cosmopolitanism Versus Non-Cosmopolitanism.* Oxford: Oxford University Press.

Brock, G. & H. Brighouse (eds) 2005. *The Political Philosophy of Cosmopolitanism.* Cambridge: Cambridge University Press.

Brodie, B. 1946. *The Absolute Weapon: Atomic Power and World Order.* New York: Harcourt Brace.

Broome, J. 1992. *Counting the Cost of Global Warming.* Cambridge: White Horse Press.

——2004. *Weighing Lives.* Oxford: Oxford University Press.

——2012. *Climate Matters: Ethics in a Warming World.* New York: W. W. Norton.

Brown, A. & R. Stern 2007. "Concepts of Fairness in the Global Trading System". *Pacific Economic Review* 12(3): 293–318.

Brown, C. 2007a. "Reimagining International Society and Global Community". In *Globalization Theory: Approaches and Controversies. Global Transformations*, 4th edn, D. Held & A. McGrew (eds.), 172–83. Cambridge: Polity.

——2007b. "Tragedy, 'Tragic Choices' and Contemporary International Political Theory". *International Relations* 2(1): 5–13.

Brown, L. 2000. *Sex Slaves: The Trafficking of Women in Asia*. London: Virago.

Brownlie, I. 1963. *International Law and the Use of Force by States*. Oxford: Clarendon Press.

Brownlie, I. & G. S. Goodwin-Gill, eds 2010. *Brownlie's Documents on Human Rights*, 6th edn. Oxford: Oxford University Press.

Brownsword, R. 2007. "The Ancillary Care Responsibilities of Researchers: Reasonable but Not Great Expectations". *Journal of Law, Medicine and Ethics* 35: 679–91.

——2008. *Rights, Regulation and the Technological Revolution*. Oxford: Oxford University Press.

——2010. "Regulatory Cosmopolitanism: Clubs, Commons, and Questions of Coherence". TILT Law and Technology Working Paper 018/2010, Tilburg University.

Bubeck, D. 1995. *Care, Gender, and Justice*. Oxford: Oxford University Press.

Buchanan, A. E. 2000. "Rawls's Law of Peoples: Rules for a Vanished Westphalian World". *Ethics* 110: 697–721.

——2004. *Justice, Legitimacy, and Self-Determination: Moral Foundations for International Law*. Oxford: Oxford University Press.

——2010a. *Human Rights, Legitimacy and the Use of Force*. Oxford: Oxford University Press.

——2010b. "The Egalitarianism of Human Rights". *Ethics* 120: 679–710.

Buchanan, A. E., D. Brock, N. Daniels & D. Wikler (eds) 2000. *From Chance to Choice: Genetics and Justice*. Cambridge: Cambridge University Press.

Budiani-Saberi, D. A. & F. L. Delmonico 2008. "Organ Trafficking and Transplant Tourism: A Commentary on the Global Realities". *American Journal of Transplantation* 8(5): 925–29.

Bufacchi, V. & J. M. Arrigo 2006. "Torture, Terrorism and the State: A Refutation of the Ticking-Bomb Argument". *Journal of Applied Philosophy* 23: 355–73.

Bureau of Land Management 1998. Environmental Education Homepage. www.blm.gov/education/lnt/background/packing.htm (accessed December 2008).

Butchart, S. H. M., M. Walpole, B. Collen, A. van Strien, J. P. Scharlemann, R. E. Almond, J. E. Baillie *et al.* 2010. "Global Biodiversity: Indicators of Recent Declines". *Science* 328: 1164–68.

CAB 2007. "Abuse of Powers by Bailiffs Set to Get Much Worse, Citizens Advice Warns". www.citizensadvice.org.uk/press_20070305.

Cafaro, P. & R. Sandler 2005. *Environmental Virtue Ethics*. Lanham, MD: Rowman & Littlefield.

Calabresi, G. & A. D. Melamed 1972. "Property Rules, Liability Rules, and Inalienability: One View of the Cathedral". *Harvard Law Review* 85(6): 1089–1128.

Callicott, J. B. 1982. "Hume's Is/Ought Dichotomy and the Relation of Ecology to Leopold's Land Ethic". In *In Defense of the Land Ethic: Essays in Environmental Philosophy*, J. B. Callicott (ed.), 117–27, 286–88. Albany, NY: SUNY Press.

——1989. *In Defense of the Land Ethic: Essays in Environmental Philosophy*. Albany, NY: SUNY Press.

——1999. *Beyond the Land Ethic: More Essays in Environmental Philosophy*. Albany, NY: SUNY Press.

Callinicos, A. 2010. *The Bonfire of Ilusions: The Twin Crises of the Liberal World*. Cambridge: Polity Press.

Campbell, A. V. 2009. *The Body in Bioethics*. London: Routledge.

Campbell, T. 2006. *Rights: A Critical Introduction*. New York: Routledge.

Campbell, T. & S. Miller (eds) 2004. *Human Rights and the Moral Responsibilities of Corporate and Public Sector Organizations*. Dordrecht: Kluwer Academic Publishers.

Caney, S. 1997. "Human Rights and the Rights of States: Terry Nardin on Non-Intervention". *International Political Science Review* 18(1): 27–37.

——2001. "Cosmopolitan Justice and Equalizing Opportunities". *Metaphilosophy* 32(1/2): 113–34.

——2005a. "Cosmopolitan Justice, Responsibility and Global Climate Change". *Leiden Journal of International Law* 18(4): 747–75.

——2005b. *Justice Beyond Borders: A Global Political Theory*. Oxford: Oxford University Press.

——2006a. "Environmental Degradation, Reparations and the Moral Significance of History". *Journal of Social Philosophy* 73(3): 464–82.

——2006b. "Global Justice, Rights and Climate Change". *Canadian Journal of Law and Jurisprudence* 19(2): 255–78.

——2006c. "Global Justice: From Theory to Practice". *Globalizations* 3(2): 121–37.

——2008a. "Climate Change, Human Rights and Discounting". *Environmental Politics* 17(4): 536–55.

——2008b. "Global Distributive Justice and the State". *Political Studies* 57: 487–518.

——2009a. "Human Rights, Responsibilities and Climate Change". In *Global Basic Rights*, C. Beitz & R. Goodin (eds), 227–47. Oxford: Oxford University Press.

——2009b. "Climate Change and the Future: Time, Wealth and Risk". *Journal of Social Philosophy* 40(2): 163–86.

——2009c. "Justice and the Distribution of Greenhouse Gas Emissions". *Journal of Global Ethics* 52: 125–46.

——2010a. "Climate Change and the Duties of the Advantaged". *Critical Review of International Social and Political Philosophy* 13(1): 203–28.

——2010b. "Climate Change, Human Rights and Moral Thresholds". In *Human Rights and Climate Change*, S. Humphreys (ed.), 69–90. Cambridge: Cambridge University Press.

——2012. "Just Emissions". *Philosophy and Public Affairs* 40(4): 255–300.

——2014. "Two Kinds of Climate Justice". *Journal of Political Philosophy* 22(2).

——forthcoming. "Climate Change, Intergenerational Equity and the Social Discount Rate". *Politics, Philosophy & Economics*.

Caney, S. & C. Hepburn 2011. "Emissions Trading: Unethical, Ineffective and Unjust?" *Royal Institute of Philosophy Supplement* 69: 201–34.

Canovan, M. 2000. "Patriotism is Not Enough". *British Journal of Political Science* 30(3): 413–32.

Caplan, A. 2008. "Organ Transplantation". In *From Birth to Death and Bench to Clinic: The Hastings Center Bioethics Briefing Book for Journalists, Policymakers, and Campaigns*, M. Crowley (ed.), 129–32. Garrison, NY: The Hastings Center.

Cardoso, F. & E. Faletto 1979. *Dependency and Development in Latin America*. Berkeley, CA: University of California Press.

Carens, J. H. 1987. "Aliens and Citizens: The Case for Open Borders". *Review of Politics* 49(2): 251–73.

——2013. *The Ethics of Immigration*. New York: Oxford University Press.

Carling, J. 2005. "Trafficking in Women from Nigeria to Europe". Migration Information Source, www.migrationinformation.org/Feature/display.cfm?ID=318 (accessed April 2013).

Carr, E. H. 1939. *The Twenty Year's Crisis 1919–1939*. London: Macmillan.

Carroll, A. B. 1979. "A Three-Dimensional Conceptual Model of Corporate Performance". *Academy of Management Review* 4(4): 497–505.

——1999. "Corporate Social Responsibility: Evolution of a Definitional Construct". *Business and Society* 38(3): 268–95.

——2008. "A History of Corporate Social Responsibility: Concepts and Practices". See Crane *et al.* (2008), 19–46.

Carsten, J. 2004. *After Kinship*. Cambridge: Cambridge University Press.

Carter, A. 1999. "Moral Theory and Global Population". *Proceedings of the Aristotelian Society* 99: 289–313.

——2001. "Can We Harm Future People?" *Environmental Values* 10(4): 429–54.

Caselli, M. 2012. *Measuring Globalization*. Milan: Springer.

Castells, M. 1991. *The Informational City*. Oxford: Blackwell.

——[1996] 2000. *The Rise of the Network Society, The Information Age: Economy, Society and Culture Vol. I*. Malden, MA: Blackwell.

——[1998] 2000. *End of Millennium, The Information Age: Economy, Society and Culture Vol. III*. Malden, MA: Blackwell.

——[1997] 2004. *The Power of Identity, The Information Age: Economy, Society and Culture Vol. II*. Malden, MA: Blackwell.

Center for Global Prosperity 2013. "Index of Global Philanthropy and Remittances". www.hudson.org/content/researchattachments/attachment/1229/2013_indexof_global_philanthropyand_remittances.pdf (accessed May 2014).

Central Intelligence Agency 1963. *Kubark Counterintelligence Interrogation*. File: Kubark, Box 1: CIA Training Manuals. Washington, DC: National Security Archive.

Ceres n.d. "History and Impact". www.ceres.org/roadmap-assessment/about (accessed May 2014).

Chadwick, R. 2011. "The Communitarian Turn: Myth or Reality?" *Cambridge Quarterly of Healthcare Ethics* 20(4): 546–53.

——(ed.) 2012. *Encyclopedia of Applied Ethics*, 4 vols. Boston, MA: Elsevier.

Chadwick, R. & H. Strange 2009. "Harmonisation and Standardisation in Ethics and Governance: Conceptual and Practical Challenges". In *The Governance of Genetic Information: Who Decides?*, H. Widdows & C. Mullen (eds), 201–13. Cambridge: Cambridge University Press.

Chambers, R. 1997. *Whose Reality Counts? Putting the Last First*. London: Intermediate Technology Publications.

Chandler, A. & B. Mazlish (eds) 2005. *Leviathans: Multinational Corporations and the New Global History*. Cambridge: Cambridge University Press.

Chapkis, W. 1997. *Live Sex Acts*. London: Cassell.

———2005. "Soft Glove, Punishing Fist: The Trafficking Victims Protection Act of 2000". In *Regulating Sex*, E. Bernstein & L. Schaffner (eds), 51–66. London: Routledge.

Chatterjee, D. K. (ed.) 2004. *The Ethics of Assistance: Morality and the Distant Needy*. Cambridge: Cambridge University Press.

Chen, S. & M. Ravallion 2012. *An Update to the World Bank's Estimates of Consumption Poverty in the Developing World*. Washington, DC: World Bank. http://siteresources.worldbank.org/INTPOVCALNET/Resources/Global_Poverty_Update_2012_02-29-12.pdf (accessed May 2014).

Chesterman, S. 2001. *Just War or Just Peace? Humanitarian Intervention and International Law*. Oxford: Oxford University Press.

Chomsky, N. 1999. *The New Military Humanism: Lessons from Kosovo*. London: Pluto Press.

Chowla, P., J. Oatham & C. Wren 2007. "Bridging the Democratic Deficit", www.brettonwoodsproject.org/2007/02/art-549743/ (accessed May 2014).

Christiano, T. 2006. "Democracy". In *Stanford Encyclopedia of Philosophy*, Edward N. Zalta (ed.). http://plato.stanford.edu/archives/fall2006/entries/democracy/ (accessed February 2013).

Chu, J. 2010. *Cosmologies of Credit*. London: Duke University Press.

CIOMS 1993. *International Ethical Guidelines for Biomedical Research Involving Human Subjects*. Geneva: WHO. www.cioms.ch/publications/layout_guide2002.pdf (accessed June 2012).

Clark, W. 2002. *Waging Modern War*. New York: Public Affairs.

Clarke, A. & P. Kohler 2005. *Property Law: Commentary and Materials*. Cambridge: Cambridge University Press.

Clausewitz, C. von 1995. *On War*, A. Rapaport (trans.). Harmondsworth: Penguin.

Clean Clothes Campaign 1998. "Code of Labour Practices for the Apparel Industry Including Sportswear". www.cleanclothes.org/resources/publications/clean-clothes-campaign-model-code-of-conduct/view (accessed August 2013).

Clifford, J. 1988. *The Predicament of Culture: Twentieth Century Ethnography, Literature and Art*. Cambridge, MA: Harvard University Press.

Cloud, D. 2007. "Corporate Social Responsibility as Oxymoron: Universalization and Exploitation at Boeing". See May *et al.* (2007), 219–31.

Coase, R. 1960. "The Problem of Social Cost". *Journal of Law and Economics* 3: 1–44.

Cohen, A. & C. Wellman (eds) 2005. *Contemporary Debates in Applied Ethics*. Oxford: Blackwell.

Cohen, Jean L. 2012. *Globalization and Sovereignty: Rethinking Legality, Legitimacy, and Constitutionalism*. Cambridge: Cambridge University Press.

Cohen, Joshua 2004. "Minimalism About Human Rights". *Journal of Political Philosophy* 12: 190–213.

———2006. "Is there a Human Right to Democracy?" In *The Egalitarian Conscience: Essays in Honour of G. A. Cohen*, C. Sypnowich (ed.), 226–48. Oxford: Oxford University Press.

Cohen, Joshua & C. Sabel 2006. "Extra Republicam Nulla Justitia?" *Philosophy and Public Affairs* 34: 147–75.

Cole, J. & S. Booth 2007. *Dirty Work: Immigrants in Domestic Service, Agriculture and Prostitution in Sicily*. New York: Lexington.

Cole, P. 2000. *Philosophies of Exclusion: Liberal Political Theory and Immigration*. Edinburgh: Edinburgh University Press.

Collier, P. 2008. *The Bottom Billion: Why the Poorest Countries are Failing and What Can be Done About It*. Oxford: Oxford University Press.

———2013. *Exodus: How Migration Is Changing Our World*. Oxford: Oxford University Press.

Congregation of the Doctrine of Faith 2008. "Instruction Dignitas Personae: On Certain Bioethical Questions". www.vatican.va/roman_curia/congregations/cfaith/documents/rc_con_cfaith_doc_20081208_dignitas-personae_en.html (accessed April 2014).

Connelly, M. 2010. *Fatal Misconception: The Struggle to Control World Population*. Cambridge, MA: Harvard University Press.

Constitution Project 2013. *Detainee Treatment: The Report of the Constitution Project's Task Force*. Washington, DC: The Constitution Project.

Convention on Biological Diversity (CBD) 1992. *Convention on Biological Diversity*, 5 June 1992. Montreal: UNEP/CBD. www.cbd.int/doc/legal/cbd-en.pdf (accessed June 2012).

———2000. *Sustaining Life on Earth: How the Convention on Biological Diversity Promotes Nature and Human Well-being*. Montreal: UNEP/CBD. www.cbd.int/doc/publications/cbd-sustain-en.pdf (accessed June 2012).

———2002. *Bonn Guidelines on Access to Genetic Resources and the Fair and Equitable Sharing of the Benefits Arising out of their Utilization*. Montreal: UNEP/CBD. www.cbd.int/doc/publications/cbd-bonn-gdls-en.pdf (accessed June 2012).

Cook, J. W. 1999. *Morality and Cultural Differences*. Oxford: Oxford University Press.

Cook, R. T. 1993. "International Human Rights and Women's Reproductive Health." *Studies in Family Planning* 24(2): 73–86.

Corbin, J. 2002. *Al-Qaeda*. New York: Nation.

Cottey, A. 2008. "Beyond Humanitarian Intervention: The New Politics of Peacekeeping and Intervention". *Contemporary Politics* 14(4): 429–46.

Council of Europe 1997. "Convention for the Protection of Human Rights and Dignity of the Human Being with Regard to the Application of Biology and Medicine: Convention on Human Rights and Biomedicine". 4 April, Oviedo. European Treaty Series No. 164.

——2002. "Additional Protocol to the Convention on Human Rights and Biomedicine, on Transplantation of Organs and Tissues of Human Origin". 24 January, Strasbourg. European Treaty Series No.186.

——2009. "Trafficking in Organs, Tissues and Cells and Trafficking in Human Beings for the Purpose of the Removal of Organs". Joint Council of Europe/United Nations study. www.coe.int/t/dghl/monitoring/trafficking/docs/news/OrganTrafficking_study.pdf (accessed April 2012).

Cowen, T. & D. Parfit 1992. "Against the Social Discount Rate". In *Justice Between Age Groups and Generations*, P. Laslett & J. Fishkin (eds.), 144–61. New Haven, CT: Yale University Press.

Cox, R. 1981. "Social Forces, States and World Orders: Beyond International Relations Theory". *Millennium: Journal of International Studies* 10(2): 126–55.

Cragg, W. 2000. "Human Rights and Business Ethics: Fashioning a New Social Contract". *Journal of Business Ethics* 27(1–2): 205–14.

——2012. "Ethics, Enlightened Self-Interest and the Corporate Responsibility to Respect Human Rights". *Business Ethics Quarterly* 22(1): 9–36.

Craig, G., A. Gaus, M. Wilkinson, K. Skrivankova, & A. McQuade, (2007). *Contemporary Slavery in the UK: Overview and key issues*. York: Joseph Rowntree Foundation.

Crane, A., A. McWilliams, D. Matten, J. Moon & D. Siegel (eds) 2008. *The Oxford Handbook of Corporate Social Responsibility*. Oxford: Oxford University Press.

Cranor, C. F. 1993. *Regulating Toxic Substances: A Philosophy of Science and Law*. New York: Oxford University Press.

Crespi, G. S. 1994. "Overcoming the Legal Obstacles to the Creation of a Futures Market in Bodily Organs". *Ohio State Law Journal* 55(1): 1–77.

Cripps, E. 2013. *Climate Change and the Moral Agent: Individual Duties in an Interdependent World*. Oxford: Oxford University Press.

Crocker, D. 1998. "Consumption, Well-being, and Capability". See Crocker & Linden (1998b), 366–90.

——2008. *Ethics of Global Development: Agency, Capability, and Deliberative Democracy*. Cambridge: Cambridge University Press.

Crocker, D. & T. Linden 1998a. "Introduction". See Crocker & Linden (1998b), 1–18.

——(eds) 1998b. *Ethics of Consumption: The Good Life, Justice, and Global Stewardship*. Lanham, MD: Rowman and Littlefield.

Crouch, R. A. & J. D. Arras 1998. "AZT Trials and Tribulations". *Hastings Center Report* 28(6): 26–34.

Cullity, G. 2004. *The Moral Demands of Affluence*. Oxford: Oxford University Press.

Cunningham, S. & J. Tomlinson 2005. "'Starve Them Out': Does Every Child Really Matter? A Commentary on Section 9 of the Asylum and Immigration (Treatment of Claimants, etc.) Act, 2004". *Critical Social Policy* 25(2): 253–75.

Daar, A. S. 2006. "The Case for a Regulated System of Living Kidney Sales". *Nature Clinical Practice Nephrology* 2(11): 600–601.

Daly, H. E. 1995. "On Wilfred Beckerman's Critique of Sustainable Development". *Environmental Values* 4(1): 49–55.

——2005. "Economics in a Full World". *Scientific American* 293(3): 100–107.

——2008. "Climate Policy: From 'Know How' to 'Do Now'". Keynote address to AMS's workshop on Federal Climate Policy, 4 September. www.climatepolicy.org/?p=65 (accessed April 2014).

Dancy, J. 1993. *Moral Reasons*. Oxford: Blackwell.

——2004. *Ethics Without Principles*. Oxford: Clarendon Press.

Daniels, N. 2008. *Just Health: Meeting Health Needs Fairly*. Cambridge: Cambridge University Press.

Danner, M. 2004. *Torture and Truth: America, Abu-Ghraib and The War on Terror*. New York: HarperCollins.

Dasgupta, P. 1994. "Savings and Fertility: Ethical Issues". *Philosophy and Public Affairs* 23: 99–127.

——2001. *Human Well-Being and the Natural Environment*. Oxford: Oxford University Press.

Davis, D. S. 2001. *Genetic Dilemmas: Reproductive Technology, Parental Choices, and Children's Futures*. New York: Routledge.

Davis, K. 1960. "Can Business Afford to Ignore Social Responsibilities?" *California Management Review* 2: 70–76.

Day, S. & H. Ward (eds) 2004. *Sex Work, Mobility and Health in Europe*. London: Kegan Paul.

Deane, H. A. 1963. *The Political and Social Ideas of St Augustine*. New York: Columbia University Press.

Deaton, A. 2011. "What Does the Empirical Evidence Tell Us About the Injustice of Health Inequalities?" *SSRN eLibrary*, http://papers.ssrn.com/sol3/papers.cfm?abstract_id=1746951 (accessed July 2012).

De Genova, N. 2002. "Migrant 'Illegality' and Deportability in Everyday Life". *Annual Review of Anthropology* 31: 419–47.

De George, R. T. 1993. *Competing with Integrity in International Business*. New York: Oxford University Press.

——2010. *Business Ethics*, 7th edn. Upper Saddle River, NJ: Prentice Hall.

De Grauwe, P. & F. Camerman 2003. "Are Multinationals Really Bigger Than Nations?" *World Economics* 4(2): 23–37.

deLaplante, K. & V. Picasso 2011. "The Biodiversity–Ecosystem Function Debate in Ecology". In *Philosophy of Ecology: Handbook of the Philosophy of Science*, K. deLaplante, B. Brown & K. A. Peacock (eds), 169–200. Amsterdam: Elsevier.

Dempsey, J. 2013. "Corporations and Non-Agential Moral Responsibility". *Journal of Applied Philosophy* 30 (4): 334–50.

Der Spiegel 2002. *Inside 9–11*. New York: St Martin's Press.

De-Shalit, A. 1995. *Why Posterity Matters: Environmental Policies and Future Generations*. London: Routledge.

——2011. "Climate Change Refugees, Compensation, and Rectification". *Monist* 94(3): 310–28.

Deva, S. 2006. "Global Compact: A Critique of UN's 'Public-Private' Partnership for Promoting Corporate Citizenship". *Syracuse Journal of International Law and Commerce* 34(1): 107–51.

De Vries, M. C. & E. van Leuen 2010. "Reflective Equilibrium and Empirical Data: Third Person Moral Experiences in Empirical Medical Ethics". *Bioethics* 24(9): 490–98.

De Vries, R. & B. Gordijn 2009. "Empirical Ethics and its Alleged Meta-Ethical Fallacies". *Bioethics* 23(4): 193–201.

Dewey, S. 2008. *Hollow Bodies: Institutional Responses to Sex Trafficking in Armenia, Bosnia and India*. Sterling, VA: Kumarian Press.

Diamond, L. 2008. "The Democratic Rollback: The Resurgence of the Predatory State". *Foreign Affairs* 87 (2): 247–63.

Dicken, P., P. F. Kelly, K. Olds & H. Wai-Chung Yeung 2001. "Chains and Networks, Territories and Scales: Towards a Relational Framework for Analysing the Global Economy". *Global Networks* 1(2): 89–112.

Dickenson, D. 2002. "Commodification of Human Tissue: Implications for Feminist and Development Ethics". *Developing World Bioethics* 2(1): 55–63.

——2005. "Human Tissue and Global Ethics". *Genomics, Society and Policy* 1(1): 41–53.

——2007. *Property in the Body: Feminist Perspectives*. Cambridge: Cambridge University Press.

——2009. *Body Shopping: The Economy Fuelled by Flesh and Blood*. London: Oneworld.

Dieterlen, P. 2005. *Poverty: A Philosophical Approach*. New York: Rodopi.

Dine, J. 2005. *Companies, International Trade and Human Rights*. Cambridge: Cambridge University Press.

Dixon-Woods, M., D. Cavers, C. J. Jackson, B. Young, J. Forster, D. Heney & K. Pritchard-Jones 2008. "Tissue Samples as 'Gifts' for Research: A Qualitative Study of Families and Professionals". *Medical Law International* 9(2): 131–50.

Doane, D. 2005. "The Myth of CSR". *Stanford Social Innovation Review* 3(4): 22–29.

Dobson, A. 1996a. "Environmental Sustainabilities: An Analysis and a Typology". *Environmental Politics* 5: 401–28.

——1996b. "Representative Democracy and the Environment". In *Democracy and the Environment: Problems and Prospects*, W. M. Lafferty & J. Meadowcroft (eds), 124–39. Cheltenham: Edward Elgar.

——2006. "Thick Cosmopolitanism". *Political Studies* 54: 165–84.

Dobson, A. & D. Bell (eds) 2005. *Environmental Citizenship*. Cambridge, MA: MIT Press.

Dockery, K. 2007. *Future Weapons*. New York: Berkley.

Doezema, J. 2002. "Who Gets to Choose? Coercion, Consent, and the UN Trafficking Protocol". In *Gender, Trafficking and Slavery*, R. Masika (ed.), 20–27. Oxford: Oxfam.

Donaldson, T. 1982. *Corporations and Morality*. Englewood Cliffs, NJ: Prentice Hall.

——1989. *The Ethics of International Business*. New York: Oxford University Press.

——1996. "Values in Tension: Ethics Away From Home". *Harvard Business Review* 74(5): 48–56.

Donaldson, T. & T. Dunfee 1999. *Ties that Bind*. Boston, MA: Harvard Business School Press.

Donnelly, J. 2003. *Universal Human Rights in Theory and Practice*, 2nd edn. Ithaca, NY: Cornell University Press.

Dorsey, D. 2008. "Toward a Theory of the Basic Minimum". *Politics, Philosophy and Economics* 7 (4): 423–45.

Douglas, M. 2003. *Purity and Danger: An Analysis of Concept of Pollution and Taboo*. New York: Routledge.

Dowding, K. 2006. "Can Capabilities Reconcile Freedom and Equality?" *Journal of Political Philosophy* 14 (3): 323–36.

Dower, N. 2000. "Human Development – Friend or Foe to Environmental Ethics?" *Environmental Values* 9(1): 39–54.

——2005. "The Nature and Scope of Global Ethics, and the Relevance of the Earth Charter". *Journal of Global Ethics* 1: 25–43.

——2009. *The Ethics of War and Peace*. Cambridge: Polity Press.

——2012. "Global Ethics, Approaches". See Chadwick (2012), vol. 2, 504–13.

Downes, D. 2002. "New Diplomacy for Biodiversity Trade: Biodiversity, Biotechnology & Intellectual Property in the Convention on Biological Diversity". In *International Environmental Law and Policy*, 2nd edn, D. Hunter, J. Salzman & D. Zaelke (eds), 945–49. New York: Foundation Press.

Doyle, M. W. & N. Sambanis 2006. *Making War and Building Peace*. Princeton, NJ: Princeton University Press.

Drahos, P. & J. Braithwaite 2002. *Information Feudalism*. London: Earthscan.

Dreher, A. 2006. "IMF and Economic Growth: The Effects of Programs, Loans, and Compliance with Conditionality.". *World Development* 34(5): 769–88.

Dubbink, W. & J. Smith 2011. "A Political Account of the Corporation as a Morally Responsible Actor". *Ethical Theory and Moral Practice* 14(2): 223–46.

Dunfee, T. 2005. "Do Firms with Unique Competencies for Rescuing Victims of Human Catastrophes Have Special Obligations? Corporate Responsibility and the AIDS Catastrophe in Sub-Saharan Africa". *Business Ethics Quarterly* 16(2): 185–210.

——2006. "A Critical Perspective of Integrative Social Contracts Theory: Recurring Criticisms and Next Generation Research Topics". *Journal of Business Ethics* 68(3): 303–28.

——2008. "Stakeholder Theory: Managing Corporate Social Responsibility in a Multiple Actor Context". See Crane *et al.* (2008), 346–63.

Dunfee, T. & D. Warren 2001. "Is Guanxi Ethical? A Normative Analysis of Doing Business in China". *Journal of Business Ethics* 32(3): 191–204.

Dworkin, R. 1986. *Law's Empire*. Cambridge, MA: Harvard University Press.

Earth Charter Commission 2000. "The Earth Charter". www.earthcharterinaction.org/content/pages/read-the-charter.html (accessed April 2013).

Easterly, W. 2006. *The White Man's Burden: Why the West's Efforts to Aid the Rest Have Done So Much Ill and So Little Good*. New York: Oxford University Press.

Eckersley, R. 2012. "Moving Forward in the Climate Negotiations: Multilateralism or Minilateralism?" *Global Environmental Politics* 12(2): 24–42.

Economist Intelligence Unit (EIU) 2011. *Democracy Index 2011: Democracy Under Stress*. London: Economist Newspapers.

Eggers, D. 2002. *And You Shall Know our Velocity*. New York: McSweeney's Books.

Ehrenreich, B. & A. Hochschild (eds) 2003. *Global Woman: Nannies, Maids, and Sex Workers in the New Economy*. New York: Metropolitan Books.

Eide, A. 1998. "The Historical Significance of the Universal Declaration". *International Social Science Journal* 158: 475–98.

Ekeli, K. 2005. "Giving a Voice to Posterity – Deliberative Democracy and Representation of Future People". *Journal of Agricultural and Environmental Ethics* 18(5): 429–50.

Elliot, R. 1982. "Faking Nature". *Inquiry* 25: 81–93.

——1989. "The Rights of Future People". *Journal of Applied Philosophy* 6(2): 159–69.

——1997. *Faking Nature*. London: Routledge.

Elliott, C. 2001. "Pharma buys a conscience." *American Prospect* 12(17): 16–20.

——2010. "The Deadly Corruption of Clinical Trials". *Mother Jones* (September/October). www.motherjones.com/environment/2010/09/dan-markingson-drug-trial-astrazeneca (accessed June 2012).

Elliott, K. C. 2011. *Is a Little Pollution Good for You? Incorporating Societal Values in Environmental Research*. Oxford: Oxford University Press.

Elliott, K. C. & D. J. McKaughan 2009. "How Values in Scientific Discovery and Pursuit Alter Theory Appraisal". *Philosophy of Science* 76(5): 598–611.

Emerson, C., P. A. Singer & R. E. G. Upshur 2011. "Access and Use of Human Tissues from the Developing World: Ethical Challenges and a Way Forward Using a Tissue Trust". *BioMed Central Medical Ethics* 12(2): 1–5.

Engelbrekt, A. B. 2009. "Stem Cell Patenting and Competition Law". In *Embryonic Stem Cell Patents: European Law and Ethics*, A. Plomer & P. Torremans (eds), 369–98. Oxford: Oxford University Press.

English Nature 1993. *Position Statement on Sustainable Development*. Peterborough: English Nature.

Engster, D. 2007. *The Heart of Justice: Care Ethics and Political Theory*. New York: Oxford University Press.

Environmental Protection Agency 2001. "Cost and Emission Reduction Analysis of the HFC Emissions from Refrigeration and Air-Conditioning in the United States". www.epa.gov/highgwp/pdfs/chap7_ac.pdf#search=%22refrigerated%20truck%20shipping%20coolants%20climate%20change%20cfc%22 (accessed April 2014).

Epstein, M. & G. Danovitch 2009. "Is Altruistic-Directed Living Unrelated Organ Donation a Legal Fiction?". *Nephrology Dialysis Transplantation* 24(2): 357–60.

Equator Principles 2013. "About the Equator Principles". www.equator-principles.com/index.php/about-ep (accessed August 2013).

Erin, C. A. & H. Harris 2003. "An Ethical Market in Human Organs". *Journal of Medical Ethics* 29(3): 137–38.

Erman, E. 2005. *Human Rights and Democracy: Discourse Theory and Human Rights Institutions*. Aldershot: Ashgate Publishing.

Escobar, A. 2012. *Encountering Development: The Making and Unmaking of the Third World*, 2nd edn. Princeton, NJ: Princeton University Press.

Eshtain, J. B. 2003. *Just War Against Terror*. New York: Basic Books.

Esposito, L. & P. J. Lambert 2011. "Poverty Measurement: Prioritarianism, Sufficiency and the 'I's of Poverty". *Economics and Philosophy* 27(2): 109–21.

Estabrook, B. 2001. *Tomatoland: How Modern Industrial Agriculture Destroyed Our Most Alluring Fruit*. Kansas City, MO: Andrew McMeel Publishing.

——2009. "Politics of the Plate: The Price of Tomatoes". *Gourmet Magazine*. www.gourmet.com/magazine/2000s/2009/03/politics-of-the-plate-the-price-of-tomatoes (accessed May 2014).

Esteva, G. [1992] 2010. "Development". In *The Development Dictionary: A Guide to Knowledge as Power*, 2nd edn, W. Sachs (ed.), 1–23. London: Zed Books.

European Commission 2004. *Report of the Experts Group on Trafficking in Human Beings*. Brussels: European Commission.

European Society of Human Reproduction 2012. "The World's Number of IVF and ICSI Babies has Now Reached a Calculated Total of 5 Million". Press Release, 2 July. www.eshre.eu/ESHRE/English/Press-Room/Press-Releases/Press-releases-2012/5-million-babies/page.aspx/1606 (accessed August 2012).

Evans, G. 2009. *The Responsibility to Protect: Ending Mass Atrocity Crimes Once and For All*. Washington, DC: Brookings Institution.

Fair Labor Association 2012. "FLA Workplace Code of Conduct". www.fairlabor.org/labor-standards (accessed August 2013).

Falk, R. 1994. "The Making of Global Citizenship". In *The Condition of Citizenship*, B. van Steenbergen (ed.), 127–40. London: Sage.

——2002. *The Great Terror War*. New York: Olive Branch Press.

Favez, J. 1999. *The Red Cross and the Holocaust*. Cambridge: Cambridge University Press.

Feinberg, J. 1980. "The Rights of Animals and Unborn Generations". In his *Rights, Justice, and the Bounds of Liberty: Essays in Social Philosophy*, 159–84. Princeton, NJ: Princeton University Press.

——1984a. "Environmental Pollution and the Threshold of Harm". *The Hastings Center Report* 14(3): 27–31.

——1984b. *The Moral Limits of the Criminal Law, Vol 1. Harm to Others*. Oxford: Oxford University Press.

——1990. *Harmless Wrongdoing*. New York: Oxford University Press.

Feingold, D. 2010. "Trafficking in Numbers: The Social Construction of Human Trafficking Data". In *Sex, Drugs and Body Counts: The Politics of Numbers in Global Crime and Conflict*, P. Andreas & K. Greenhill (eds), 46–74. Ithaca, NY: Cornell University Press.

Fekete, L. 2007. "Detained: Foreign Children in Europe". *Race and Class* 49(1): 93–104.

Fine, S. 2010. "Freedom of Association Is Not the Answer". *Ethics* 120(2): 338–56.

——forthcoming. *Immigration and the Right to Exclude*. Oxford: Oxford University Press.

Finnemore, M. 1996. *National Interests in International Society*. Ithaca, NY: Cornell University Press.

——2008. "Paradoxes in Humanitarian Intervention". In *Moral Limit and Possibility in World Politics*, R. M. Price (ed.), 197–224. Cambridge: Cambridge University Press.

Finnis, J. 1980. *Natural Law and Natural Rights*. Oxford: Oxford University Press.

Fischer, K., G. Hödl & W. Sievers 2008. *Klassiker der Entwicklungstheorie: Von Modernisierung bis Postmoderne*. Vienna: Mandelbaum.

Fleming, P. & M. T. Jones 2013. *The End of Corporate Social Responsibility: Crisis and Critique*. London: Sage.

Follesdal, A. 2009. "Methods of Philosophical Research on Human Rights". Norwegian Centre for Human Rights Working Paper, University of Oslo.

——2011. "The Distributive Justice of a Global Basic Structure: A Category Mistake?" *Politics, Philosophy and Economics* 10(1): 46–65.

Food and Agriculture Organization 2006. *Food Security Policy Brief* 2. Rome: Food and Agriculture Organization.

Food Ethics Council 2003. *Engineering Nutrition: GM Crops for Global Justice?* London: FEC.

Foot, P. 1985. "Utilitarianism and the Virtues". *Mind* 94: 196–209.

Forde, S. 1992. "Classical Realism". In *Traditions in International Ethics*, T. Nardin & D. Mapel (eds), 62–84. Cambridge: Cambridge University Press.

Forest Stewardship Council n.d. "Certification". https://us.fsc.org/certification.194.htm (accessed August 2013).

Forst, R. 1999. "The Basic Right to Justification: Toward a Constructivist Conception of Human Rights". J. M. Caver (trans.). *Constellations* 6: 35–60.

——2001. "Towards a Critical Theory of Transnational Justice". *Metaphilosophy* 32: 160–79.

——2010. "The Justification of Human Rights and the Right to Justification: A Reflexive Approach". *Ethics* 120: 711–40.

——2012. *The Right to Justification: Elements of a Constructivist Theory of Justice*, J. Flynn (trans.). New York: Columbia University Press.

Forsythe, D. P. 1977. *Humanitarian Politics: The International Committee of the Red Cross* Baltimore, MD: Johns Hopkins University Press.

——2005. *The Humanitarians*. Cambridge: Cambridge University Press.

——2011. *The Politics of Prisoner Abuse: The United States and Enemy Prisoners after 9/11*. Cambridge: Cambridge University Press.

Fortna, V. P. 2008. *Does Peacekeeping Work? Shaping Belligerents' Choices After Civil Wars*. Princeton, NJ: Princeton University Press.

Fortune 2013. "Global 500". http://money.cnn.com/magazines/fortune/global500/ (accessed August 2013).

Foucault, M. 1978. *The History of Sexuality*, vols 1–3. London: Random House.

Frank, A. 1967. *Capitalism and Underdevelopment in Latin America*. New York: Monthly Review.

Franklin, S. 1997. *Embodied Progress: A Cultural Account of Assisted Conception*. New York: Routledge.

Fränznick, M. & K. Wieners 1996. *Ungewollte Kinderlosigkeit. Psychosoziale Folgen, Bewältigungsversuche und die Dominanz der Medizin*. Weinheim: Beltz Juventa.

Fraser, C. 2009. *Rewilding the World: Dispatches from the Conservation Revolution*. New York: Metropolitan Books.

Fraser, N. 2008. *Scales of Justice: Reimagining Political Space in a Globalizing World*. New York: Columbia University Press.

Frasz, G. B. 1993. "Environmental Virtue Ethics: A New Direction for Environmental Ethics". *Environmental Ethics* 15: 259–74.

Frederick, W. 1960. "The Growing Concern over Business Responsibility". *California Management Review* 2(4): 54–61.

Freedman, B. 1987. "Equipoise and the Ethics of Clinical Research". *New England Journal of Medicine* 317: 141–45.

Freeman, R. E., J. Harrison., A. Wicks, B. Parmar & S. De Colle (eds) 2010. *Stakeholder Theory: The State of the Art*. Cambridge: Cambridge University Press.

Freeman, S. 2006. "The Law of Peoples, Social Cooperation, Human Rights, and Distributive Justice". *Social Philosophy and Policy* 23: 29–68.

——2007. *Rawls*. London: Routledge.

Freidson, E. 1970. *Profession of Medicine: A Study of the Sociology of Applied Knowledge*. New York: Harper & Row.

French, P. 1996. "Integrity, Intentions, and Corporations". *American Business Law Journal* 34: 141–55.

Frey, R. G. (ed) 1985. *Utility and Rights*. Oxford: Basil Blackwell.

Frieden, J. 2007. *Global Capitalism: Its Fall and Rise in the Twentieth Century*. New York: W. W. Norton & Company.

Friedman, M. 1970. "The Social Responsibility of Business is to Increase its Profits". *New York Times Magazine* (13 September): 32.

——2002. *Capitalism and Freedom*. Chicago, IL: University of Chicago Press.

Frost, M. 2003. "Tragedy, Ethics and International Relations". *International Relations* 17(4): 477–95.

Frow, J. 1995. "Elvis' Fame: The Commodity Form and the Form of the Person". *Cardozo Studies in Law and Literature* 7(2): 131–71.

Fuchs, E. 2007. "Children's Rights and Global Civil Society". *Comparative Education* 43(3): 393–412.

Fukuyama, F. 1992. *The End of History and the Last Man*. New York: Free Press.

Fuller, L. L. 2005. "Poverty Relief, Global Institutions, and the Problem of Compliance". *Journal of Moral Philosophy* 2(3): 285–97.

Gallaugher, J. 2010. "Data Asset in Action: Technology and the Rise of Wal–Mart". *Information Systems: A Manager's Guide To Harnessing Technology*. www.flatworldknowledge.com/pub/gallaugher/41219#ftn. fwk–gallaugher–fn11_042 (accessed April 2014).

Galpern, E. 2007. "Assisted Reproductive Technologies: Overview and Perspectives using a Reproductive Justice Framework". http://geneticsandsociety.org/downloads/ART.pdf (accessed April 2014).

Gambrel, J. & P. Cafaro 2010. "The Virtue of Simplicity". *Journal of Agricultural and Environmental Ethics* 23 (1): 85–108.

Gans, C. 2003. *The Limits of Nationalism*. Cambridge: Cambridge University Press.

Gardiner, S. M. 2004. "Ethics and Global Climate Change". *Ethics* 114(3): 550–600.

——2006. "A Core Precautionary Principle". *Journal of Political Philosophy* 14(1): 33–60.

——2011. *A Perfect Moral Storm: The Ethical Tragedy of Climate Change*. Oxford: Oxford University Press.

Gasper, D. 2004. *The Ethics of Development*. Edinburgh: Edinburgh University Press.

Gaus, G. 2001. "What is Deontology? Part Two: Reasons for Action." *Journal of Value Inquiry* 35(2): 179–93.

——2009. "The Idea and Ideal of Capitalism". In *The Oxford Handbook of Business Ethics*, G. G. Brenkert & T. L. Beauchamp (eds), 73–99. Oxford: Oxford University Press.

——2012. "Property". In *The Oxford Handbook of Political Philosophy*, D. Estlund (ed.), 93–114. Oxford: Oxford University Press.

Gbadegesin, S. 2009. "Culture and Bioethics". In *A Companion to Bioethics*, H. Kuhse & P. Singer (eds), 24–35. Malden, MA: Wiley.

GEO-PIE 2006. "Delayed Fruit Ripening". Genetically Modified Organisms Public Issues Education Project. New York: Cornell University. www.geo-pie.cornell.edu/traits/fruitrip.html (accessed April 2014).

Geoghegan, M. 2010. "From West to East." Speech to the American Chamber of Commerce in Hong Kong, 27 April. Hong Kong: HSBC. www.china-briefing.com/news/2010/04/29/from-west-to-east-hsbcs-geoghegan-on-china.html (accessed May 2014).

George, A. 2004. "Is 'Property' Necessary? On Owning the Human Body and its Parts". *Res Publica* 10(1): 15–42.

George, R. P. 1998. "Natural Law and International Order". In *International Society: Diverse Ethical Perspectives*, D. R. Mapel & T. Nardin (eds), 54–69. Princeton, NJ: Princeton University Press.

Gereffi, G., J. Humphrey & T. Sturgeon 2005. "The Governance of Global Value Chains". *Review of International Political Economy* 12(1): 78–104.

Gewirth, A. 1978. *Reason and Morality*. Chicago, IL: Chicago University Press.

——1982. *Human Rights: Essays on Justification and Applications*. Chicago, IL: Chicago University Press.

Ghods, A. J. & S. Savaj 2006. "Iranian Model of Paid and Regulated Living Unrelated Kidney Donation". *Clinical Journal of the American Society of Nephrology* 1(6): 1136–45.

Giddens, A. 1992. *The Transformation of Intimacy: Sexuality, Love, and Eroticism in Modern Societies*. Stanford, CA: Stanford University Press.

Gilabert, P. 2008. "Global Justice and Poverty Relief in Nonideal Circumstances". *Social Theory and Practice* 34(3): 411–38.

Gill, L. 2004. *The School of the Americas: Military Training and Political Violence in the Americas*. Durham, NC: Duke University Press.

Gilligan, C. 1982. *In a Different Voice: Psychological Theory and Women's Development*. Cambridge, MA: Harvard University Press.

Gills, B. (ed.) 2010. *Globalization in Crisis: Rethinking Globalizations*. London: Routledge.

Gilpin, R. 2001. *Global Political Economy: Understanding the International Economic Order*. Princeton, NJ: Princeton University Press.

——2002. "The Rise of American Hegemony". In *Two Hegemonies*, P. Karl O'Brien & A. Clesse (eds), 165–82. Aldershot: Ashgate Publishing.

Ginbar, Y. 2010. *Why Not Torture Terrorists? Moral, Practical, and Legal Aspects of the "Ticking Bomb" Justification for Torture*. Oxford: Oxford University Press.

Gitter, D. M. 2004. "Ownership of Human Tissue: A Proposal for Federal Recognition of Human Research Participants' Property Rights in their Biological Material". *Washington and Lee Law Review* 61 (1): 257–345.

Glanville, L. 2011. "The Antecedents of Sovereignty as Responsibility". *European Journal of International Relations* 17(2): 233–55.

Global Poverty Project 2013. "Introduction to the Challenges for Achieving Gender Equality". www.globalcitizen.org/Content/Content.aspx?id=058f8fee-01f4-4508-a54d-464ff22a4716 (accessed May 2014).

Goebel, J. W. *et. al.* 2009. "Legal and Ethical Consequences of International Biobanking from a National Perspective: The German BMB–EUCoop Project". *European Journal of Human Genetics* 18 (5): 522–25.

Goldstein, J. S. 2011. *Winning the War on War: The Decline of Armed Conflict Worldwide*. New York: Dutton.

Goodin, R. 1992. *Green Political Theory*. Cambridge: Polity Press.

——1995. "Political Ideals and Political Practice". *British Journal of Political Science* 25: 37–56.

Goodland, R. 1998. "The Case Against Consumption of Grain-Fed Meat". See Crocker & Linden (1998b), 95–112.

Goodpaster, K. E. 2007. *Conscience and Corporate Culture*. Malden, MA: Blackwell Publishing.

Gordon, J. S. 2011. "Global Ethics and Principlism". *Kennedy Institute of Ethics Journal* 21(3): 251–76.

Gordon, R. 2000. "Kant, Smith and Hegel: The Market and the Categorical Imperative". In *Paradoxes of Civil Society: New Perspectives on Modern German and British History*, F. Trentmann (ed.), 85–104. Oxford: Berghahn.

——2014. *Mainstreaming Torture: Ethical Approaches in the Post-9/11 United States*. New York: Oxford University Press.

Gorman, J. 2011. "US Will Not Finance New Research on Chimps". *New York Times* (15 December). www.nytimes.com/2011/12/16/science/chimps-in-medical-research.html (accessed January 2012).

Gosseries, A. 2001. "What Do we Owe the Next Generation(s)?" *Loyola of Los Angeles Law Review* 35: 293–354.

——2004. "Historical Emissions and Free-Riding". *Ethical Perspectives* 11(1): 36–60.

Gosseries, A. & L. Meyer (eds) 2009. *Intergenerational Justice*. Oxford: Oxford University Press.

Gould, C. 1988. *Rethinking Democracy: Freedom and Social Cooperation in Politics, Economics and Society*. New York: Cambridge University Press.

——2004. *Globalizing Democracy and Human Rights*. Cambridge: Cambridge University Press.

Goulet, D. 1995. *Development Ethics: A Guide to Theory and Practice*. New York: Apex Press.

Grady, C. 2005. "Payment of Clinical Research Subjects". *Journal of Clinical Investigation* 115: 1681–87.

Grant, B. 2009. "Merck Published Fake Journal". *The Scientist* (30 April). http://classic.the-scientist.com/blog/display/55671 (accessed June 2012).

Grant, R. K. 2008. *Battle*. Berlin: Dorling Kindersley.

Gravitz, L. 2010. "Building an Implantable Artificial Kidney". *MIT Technology Review* (9 September 2010). www.technologyreview.com/biomedicine/26239/page2/ (accessed April 2012).

Greig, A., D. Hulme & M. Turner 2007. *Challenging Global Inequality. Development Theory and Practice in the 21st Century*. Basingstoke: Palgrave Macmillan.

Griffin, A. 2007. "Kidneys on Demand". *British Medical Journal* 334(7592): 502–5.

Griffin, J. 1986. *Well-Being*. Oxford: Oxford University Press.

——2008. *On Human Rights*. Oxford: Oxford University Press.

Groenewold, J. 1996 (ed.). *World in Crisis: The Politics of Survival at the End of the Twentieth Century*. London: Routledge.

Grove-Fanning, W. 2010. "Biodiversity Loss, the Motivational Gap, and the Failure of Conservation Education". *Southwest Philosophy Review* 26: 119–30.

Grubb, M. 1995. "Seeking Fair Weather: Ethics and the International Debate on Climate Change". *International Affairs* 71(3): 463–96.

Grubb, M., C. Vrolijk & D. Brack 1999. *The Kyoto Protocol: A Guide and Assessment*. London: Royal Institute of International Affairs.

Guha, R. 1999. "Radical American Environmentalism Revisited". In *Philosophical Dialogues: Arne Næss and the Progress of Eco-Philosophy*, N. Witoszek & A. Brennan (eds), 437–39. Lanham, MD: Roman & Littlefield.

Günther, K. 1992. "Die Freiheit der Stellungnahme als politisches Grundrecht". In *Theoretische Grundlagen der Rechtspolitik*, P. Koller, C. Varga & O. Weinberger (eds), 58–73. Stuttgart: Steiner Verlag.

——2011. "Von der gubernativen zur deliberativen Menschenrechtspolitik". In *Menschenrechte und Volkssouveränität in Europa*, G. Haller, K. Günther & U. Neumann (eds), 45–60. Frankfurt: Campus.

Gutmann, A. 1998. "Freedom of Association: An Introductory Essay". In *Freedom of Association*, A. Gutmann (ed.), 3–32. Princeton, NJ: Princeton University Press.

Habermas, J. 1991. *Discourse Ethics: Moral Consciousness and Communicative Action*. Cambridge, MA: MIT Press.

——1994. *Justification and Application: Remarks on Discourse Ethics*. Cambridge, MA: MIT Press.

——1996. *Between Facts and Norms: Contributions to a Discourse Theory of Law and Democracy*, W. Rehg (trans.). Cambridge, MA: MIT Press.

——2001a. "Remarks on Legitimation through Human Rights". In *The Postnational Constellation*, M. Pensky (trans.), 113–30. Cambridge, MA: MIT Press.

——2001b. *Die Zukunft der menschlichen Natur: Auf dem Weg zu einer liberalen Eugenik?* Frankfurt: Suhrkamp.

Hadas, M. 1943. "From Nationalism to Cosmopolitanism in the Greco-Roman World". *Journal of the History of Ideas* 4(1): 105–11.

Haker, H. 2008. "On the Limits of Liberal Bioethics". In *The Contingent Nature of Life*, M. Düwell, C. Rehmann-Sutter & D. Mieth (eds), 191–208. Berlin: Springer.

——2011. *Hauptsache gesund? Ethische Fragen der Pränatal-und Präimplantationsdiagnostik*. Munich: Kösel.

——2013. "Eine Ethik der Elternschaft". In *Kinderwunsch und Reproduktionsmedizin*, Eichinger, T. & G. Maio (eds), 267–90. Munich: Alber.

Halbert, D. 2005. *Resisting Intellectual Property*. New York: Routledge.

Hale, B. 2012. "Getting the Bad Out: Remediation Technologies and Respect for Others". In *The Environment: Philosophy, Science, and Ethics*, Topics in Contemporary Philosophy, J. K. Cambell, M. O'Rourke & M. Slater (eds), 223–43. Cambridge, MA: MIT Press.

Hale, B. & L. Dilling 2011. "Geoengineering, Ocean Fertilization, and the Problem of Permissible Pollution". *Science, Technology, and Human Values* 36(2): 190–212.

Hale, B. & W. Grundy 2009. "Remediation and Respect: Do Remediation Technologies Alter Our Responsibilities?" *Environmental Values* 18(4): 397–415.

Halliday, F. 1996. "The Future of International Relations: Fears and Hopes". In *International Theory: Positivism and Beyond*, S. Smith, K. Booth & M. Zalewski (eds), 318–27. Cambridge: Cambridge University Press.

Hamilton, A., N. R. Smith & M. H. Haber 2009. "Social Insects and the Individuality Thesis: Cohesion and the Colony as a Selectable Individual". In *Organization of Insect Societies*, J. Gadau & J. Fewell (eds), 572–89. Cambridge, MA: Harvard University Press.

Hampton, J. 1993. "Selflessness and the Loss of Self". *Social Philosophy and Policy* 10(1): 135–65.

Hancock, J. 2007. "Toxic Pollution as a Right to Harm Others: Contradictions in Feinberg's Formulation of the Harm Principle". *Capitalism Nature Socialism* 18(2): 91–108.

Hanlon, J., A. Barrientos & D. Hulme 2010. *Just Give Money to the Poor: The Deveopment Revolution from the Global South*. Sterling: Kumarian Press.

Hansen, M., C. Bower, E. Milne, N. de Klerk & J. J. Kurinczuk 2005. "Assisted Reproductive Technologies and the Risk of Birth Defects – A Systematic Review". *Human Reproduction* 20(2): 328–38.

Haq, M. 1995. *Reflections on Human Development*. New York: Oxford University Press.

Hardin, G. 1974. "Lifeboat Ethics – A Case Against Helping the Poor". *Bioscience* 24(10): 561–68.

Hardt, M. & A. Negri 2000. *Empire*. Cambridge, MA: Harvard University Press.

Hare, C. 2007. "Voices from Another World: Must We Respect the Interests of People Who Do Not, and Will Never, Exist?" *Ethics* 117: 498–523.

Hare, R. M. 1981. *Moral Thinking: Its Level, Method and Point*. Oxford: Oxford University Press.

Harmon, S. 2006. "Solidarity: A (New) Ethic for Global Health Policy". *Health Care Analysis* 14(4): 215–36.

Harrington, C. 2005. "The Politics of Rescue: Peacekeeping and Anti-Trafficking Programs in Bosnia-Herzegovina and Kosovo". *International Feminist Journal of Politics* 7(2): 175–206.

Harrington, M. 1999. *Care and Equality: Inventing a New Family Politics*. New York: Knopf.

Harris, J. 2007. *Enhancing Evolution: The Ethical Case for Making Better People*. Princeton, NJ: Princeton University Press.

Harris, J. W. 1996. "Who Owns my Body?" *Oxford Journal of Legal Studies* 16(1): 55–84.

Harrison, C. H. 2002. "Neither Moore Nor the Market: Alternative Models for Compensating Contributors of Human Tissue". *American Journal of Law and Medicine* 28(1): 77–105.

Harrison, M. & Wolf, N. 2009. "The Frequency of Wars". www2.warwick.ac.uk/fac/soc/economics/staff/academic/wolf/war_frequency.pdf (accessed May 2014).

Hart, H. 1961. *The Concept of Law*. Oxford: Clarendon Press.

Hartigan, R. S. 1983. *Lieber's Code and the Law of War*. Chicago, IL: Precedent.

Hartman, L., D. Arnold & R. Wokutch 2003. *Rising Above Sweatshops: Innovative Approaches to Global Labor Challenges*. Westport, CT: Praeger.

Harvey, D. 1989. *The Condition of Postmodernity*. Oxford: Basil Blackwell.

Hashim, I. & D. Thorsen 2011. *Child Migration in Africa*. London: Zed.

Hassoun, N. 2005. "The Case for Renewable Energy and a New Energy Plan". *International Journal of Environmental, Cultural, Economic and Social Sustainability* 1(5): 197–208.

——2008. "Free Trade, Poverty, and the Environment". *Public Affairs Quarterly* 22(4): 353–80.

——2010. "Empirical Evidence and the Case for Foreign Aid". *Public Affairs Quarterly* 24(1): 1–21.

——2011. "Free Trade, Poverty, and Inequality". *Journal of Moral Philosophy* 8(1): 5–44.

Haynes, W. J. II 2002. "Action Memo for Secretary of Defense from General Counsel: Counter-Resistance Techniques". In *The Torture Papers: The Road to Abu Ghraib*, K. J. Greenberg & J. L. Dratel (eds), 236–37. Cambridge: Cambridge University Press.

Hayward, T. 2007. "Human Rights Versus Emissions Rights: Climate Justice and the Equitable Distribution of Ecological Space". *Ethics and International Affairs* 21(4): 431–50.

Heckscher, E. [1919] 1991. "The Effects of Foreign Trade on the Distribution of Income". In *Heckscher–Ohlin Trade Theory*, H. Flam & M. June Flanders (eds), 39–69. Cambridge, MA: MIT Press.

Hehir, J. B. 1995. "Intervention: From Theories to Cases". *Ethics and International Affairs* 9: 1–13.

Heisel, W., M. Katches & L. Kowalczyk 2000. "The Body Brokers – Part 2: Skin Merchants". *Lifeissues.net*, www.lifeissues.net/writers/kat/org_01bodybrokerspart2.html (accessed April 2012).

Held, D. 1995. *Democracy and the Global Order: From the Modern State to Cosmopolitan Governance*. Stanford, CA: Stanford University Press.

——2004. *Global Covenant: The Social Democratic Alternative to the Washington Consensus*. Cambridge: Polity Press.

Held, D., A. McGrew & J. Perraton 1999. *Global Transformations: Politics, Economics and Culture*. Cambridge: Polity.

Held, V. 1993. *Feminist Morality: Transforming Culture, Society, and Politics*. Chicago, IL: University of Chicago Press.

——2006. *The Ethics of Care: Personal, Political, and Global*. New York: Oxford University Press.

——2008. *How Terrorism is Wrong: Morality and Political Violence*. New York: Oxford University Press.

——2010. "Can the Ethics of Care Handle Violence?" *Ethics and Social Welfare* 4(6): 115–29.

——2011. "Morality, Care, and International Law". *Ethics and Global Politics* 4(3): 173–94.

Helfer, L. R. 2007. "Towards a Human Rights Framework for Intellectual Property". *UC Davis Law Review* 40: 971–1020.

Helfer, L. R. & G. W. Austin 2011. *Human Rights and Intellectual Property*. Cambridge: Cambridge University Press.

Heller, M. A. 1998. "The Tragedy of the Anticommons: Property in the Transition from Marx to Markets". *Harvard Law Review* 111(3): 621–88.

Hellstadius, Å. 2009. "The Research Exemption in Patent Law and its Application to hESC Research". In *Embryonic Stem Cell Patents: European Law and Ethics*, A. Plomer & P. Torremans (eds), 323–42. Oxford: Oxford University Press.

Henkin, L. 1979. *How Nations Behave: Law and Foreign Policy*, 2nd edn. New York: Columbia University Press.

Hessler, P. 2007. *Oracle Bones: A Journey Between China's Past and Present*. New York: HarperCollins.

Heyd, D. 1992. *Genethics: Moral Issues in the Creation of People*. Berkeley, CA: University of California Press.

Heyward, C. forthcoming. *The Cultural Dimension of Climate Justice*. Cheltenham: Edward Elgar.

Hill, T. E, Jr. 1980. "Humanity as an End in Itself". *Ethics* 91(1): 84–99.

——1983. "Ideals of Human Excellence and Preserving Natural Environments". *Environmental Ethics* 5(3): 211–24.

——1996. "Moral Dilemmas, Gaps, and Residues". In his *Human Welfare and Moral Worth: Kantian Perspectives*, 362–402. Oxford: Oxford University Press.

Hinsch, W. 2001. "Global Distributive Justice". *Metaphilosophy* 32: 58–78.

Hirsch, E. & M. Strathern 2006. *Transactions and Creations: Property Debates and the Stimulus of Melanesia*. New York: Berghahn Books.

Hirst, P., G. Thompson & S. Bromley 2009. *Globalization in Question: The International Economy and the Possibilities*, 3rd edn. Cambridge: Polity.

Hobbes, T. [1651] 1971. *Leviathan*, C. B. Macpherson (ed.). Harmondsworth: Penguin.

Hochschild, A. R. 2003. "Love and Gold". In *Global Woman: Nannies, Maids, and Sex Workers in the New Economy*, B. Ehrenreich & A. Hochschild (eds), 15–30. New York: Metropolitan Books.

Hoffman, W. M. & R. E. McNulty 2009. "International Business, Human Rights, and Moral Complicity: A Call for a Declaration on the Universal Rights and Duties of Business". *Business and Society Review* 114(4): 541–70.

Holland, A. 1997. "Substitutability: or, Why Strong Sustainability is Weak and Absurdly Strong Sustainability is not Absurd". In *Valuing Nature*, J. Foster (ed.), 119–34. London: Routledge.

Hollis, A. & T. Pogge 2008. *The Health Impact Fund: Making New Medicines Accessible for All*. New Haven, CT: Incentives for Global Health.

Holm, S. 1995. "Not Just Autonomy – The Principles of American Biomedical Ethics". *Journal of Medical Ethics* 21(6): 332–38.

——2010. "Is Bioethics Only For the Rich and Powerful?" In *Argument and Analysis in Bioethics*, M. Häyry, T. Takala & P. Herissone-Kelly (eds), 23–36. Amsterdam: Rodopi.

Holmes, R. 1989. *On War and Morality*. Princeton, NJ: Princeton University Press.

Holt, V. K. & T. C. Berkman 2006. *The Impossible Mandate? Military Preparedness, the Responsibility to Protect and Modern Peace Operations*. Washington, DC: The Henry L. Stimson Center.

Holton, R. 2005. *Making Globalization*. London: Palgrave.

Holzgrefe, J. L. 2003. "The Humanitarian Intervention Debate". In *Humanitarian Intervention: Ethical, Legal and Political Dilemmas*, J. L. Holzgrefe & R. O. Keohane (eds.), 15–52. Cambridge: Cambridge University Press.

Honneth, A. 2011. *Das Recht der Freiheit. Grundriss einer demokratischen Sittlichkeit*. Frankfurt: Suhrkamp.

Honoré, T. 1961. "Ownership". In *Oxford Essays in Jurisprudence: A Collaborative Work*, A. G. Guest (ed.), 107–47. London: Oxford University Press.

Hooker, B. 2000. "Moral Particularism: Wrong and Bad". In *Moral Particularism*, B. Hooker & M. Little (eds), 1–22. Oxford: Oxford University Press.

Hopper, P. 2012. *Understanding Development*. Cambridge: Polity Press.

Hrynaszkiewicz, I. & D. G. Altman 2009. "Towards Agreement on Best Practice for Publishing Raw and Clinical Trial Data". *Trials* 10(17): 1–5.

Hsieh, N. 2004. "The Obligations of Transnational Corporations: Rawlsian Justice and the Duty of Assistance". *Business Ethics Quarterly* 14(4): 643–61.

——2006. "Voluntary Codes of Conduct for Multinational Corporations: Coordinating Duties of Rescue and Justice". *Business Ethics Quarterly* 16(2): 119–35.

——2009. "Does Global Business Have a Responsibility to Promote Just Institutions?". *Business Ethics Quarterly* 19(2): 251–73.

——2013. "Multinational Enterprises and Incomplete Institutions: The Demandingness of Minimum Moral Standards". In *Business Ethics*, 2nd edn, M. Boylan (ed.), 409–22. Hoboken, NJ: John Wiley & Sons.

Huang, J. F. 2007. "Ethical and Legislative Perspectives on Liver Transplantation in The People's Republic of China". *Liver Transplantation* 13(2): 193–96.

HUGO Ethics Committee 2000. "Statement on Benefit-Sharing, April 9 2000". www.hugo-international. org/img/benefit_sharing_2000.pdf (accessed April 2012).

——2007. "HUGO Statement on Pharmacogenomics (PGx): Solidarity, Equity and Governance". *Genomics, Society and Policy* 3(1): 44–47.

Hull, C. L. 1999. "When Something is to be Done: Proof of Environmental Harm and the Philosophical Tradition". *Environmental Values* 8(1): 3–25.

Hull, D. L. 1978. "A Matter of Individuality". *Philosophy of Science* 45: 335–60.

Human Rights Watch 2002. "Nowhere to Turn: State Abuses of Unaccompanied Migrant Children by Spain and Morocco". www.hrw.org/reports/2002/spain-morocco (accessed April 2014).

Hume, D. [1752] 1957. *An Inquiry Concerning the Principles of Morals*. New York: Liberal Arts.

——[1739–40] 2000. *A Treatise of Human Nature*, D. F. Norton & M. J. Norton (eds). Oxford: Oxford University Press.

Hunt, L. 2007. *Inventing Human Rights: A History*. New York: Norton.

Hurka, T. 1983. "Value and Population Size". *Ethics* 93: 496–507.

——1997. "The Justification of National Partiality". In *The Morality of Nationalism*, R. McKim & J. McMahan (eds), 139–57. Oxford: Oxford University Press.

Hurrell, A. 2001. "Global Inequality and International Institutions". *Metaphilosophy* 32: 34–57.

Hursthouse, R. 2007. "Environmental Virtue Ethics". In *Working Virtue: Virtue Ethics and Contemporary Moral Problems*, R. L. Walker & P. J. Ivanhoe (eds), 156–71. Oxford: Clarendon Press.

Hussain, W. 2012. "Corporations, Profit Maximization and the Personal Sphere". *Economics and Philosophy* 28(3): 311–31.

Husted, B. & J. Salazar 2006. "Taking Friedman Seriously: Maximizing Profits and Social Performance". *Journal of Management Studies* 43(1): 75–91.

ICMJE (International Council of Medical Journal Editors) 2013. "Recommendations for the Conduct, Reporting, Editing, and Publication of Scholarly Work in Medical Journals". http://icmje.org/icmje-recommendations.pdf (accessed May 2014).

Ignatieff, M. 2001a. *Human Rights as Politics and Idolatry*. Princeton, NJ: Princeton University Press.

——2001b. *Virtual War: Kosovo and Beyond*. London: Picador.

Ikenberry, J. 2010. "The Liberal International Order and its Discontents". *Millennium* 38(3): 1–13.

Independent Panel to Review Department of Defense Detention Operations 2004. "Final Report ['The Schlesinger Report']". In *The Torture Papers: The Road to Abu Ghraib*, K. J. Greenberg & J. L. Dratel (eds), 908–75. Cambridge: Cambridge University Press.

Inglehart, R. & P. Norris 2009. *Cosmopolitan Communications: Cultural Diversity in a Globalized World*. New York: Cambridge University Press.

Inhorn, M. 2007. *Reproductive Disruptions. Gender, Technology, and Biopolitics in the New Millennium*. Oxford: Berghahn.

Inkeles, A. 1966. "The Modernization of Man". In *Modernization: The Dynamics of Growth*, M. Weiner (ed.), 151–66. New York: Basic Books.

International Atomic Energy Agency (IAEA) 1970. "Treaty on the Non-proliferation of Nuclear Weapons". www.iaea.org/Publications/Documents/Infcircs/Others/infcirc140.pdf (accessed May 2014).

International Council of Mining and Metals 2013. "Our Members". www.icmm.com/members (accessed August 2013).

International Labour Office 2005. *A Global Alliance Against Forced Labour*. Geneva: International Labour Office.

——2012. *Global Employment Trends 2012*. Rome: United Nations.

International Labour Organization 2010. "ILO Declaration on Fundamental Principles and Rights at Work". www.ilo.org/declaration/thedeclaration/textdeclaration/lang – en/index.htm (accessed August 2013).

International Monetary Fund 2012a. "IMF Conditionality". www.imf.org/external/np/exr/facts/conditio.htm (accessed February 2013).

——2012b. "IMF Quotas". www.imf.org/external/np/exr/facts/quotas.htm (accessed February 2013).

——2013a. "Debt Relief Under the Heavily Indebted Poor Countries (HIPC) Initiative". www.imf.org/external/np/exr/facts/hipc.htm (accessed February 2013).

——2013b. "IMF Members' Quotas and Voting Power, and IMF Board of Governors". www.imf.org/external/np/sec/memdir/members.aspx (accessed February 2013).

——n.d. a. "Cooperation and Reconstruction". www.imf.org/external/about/histcoop.htm (accessed February 2013).

——n.d. b. "Our Work". www.imf.org/external/about/ourwork.htm (accessed February 2013).

IRR n.d. "Roll Call of Deaths of Asylum Seekers and Undocumented Migrants". www.irr.org.uk/news/roll-call-of-deaths-of-asylum-seekers-and-undocumented-migrants-2005-onwards.

Irwin, D. 1996. *Against the Tide: An Intellectual History of Free Trade*. Princeton, NJ: Princeton University Press.

ISO 2010. "Discovering ISO 26000". Geneva: International Organization for Standardization.

——n.d. "ISO 14000 – Environmental Management". www.iso.org/iso/home/standards/management-standards/iso14000.htm (accessed August 2013).

Jackson, R. 2000. *The Global Covenant: Human Conduct in a World of States*. Oxford: Oxford University Press.

Jacobs, M. 1995. "Sustainable Development, Capital Substitution and Economic Humility: A Response to Beckerman". *Environmental Values* 4(1): 57–68.

Jacobsen, C. & D. Stenvoll 2010. "Muslim Women and Foreign Prostitutes: Victim Discourse, Subjectivity and Governance". *Social Politics* 17(3): 270–94.

Jaggar, A. M. 2006. "Reasoning about Well-Being: Nussbaum's Methods of Justifying the Capabilities". *Journal of Political Philosophy* 14(3): 301–22.

——(ed.) 2009. *Global Gender Justice. Philosophical Topics* 37(2).

James, A. 2012. *Fairness in Practice: A Social Contract for a Global Economy*. Oxford: Oxford University Press.

James, H. 2002. *The End of Globalization: Lessons from the Great Depression*. Cambridge, MA: Harvard University Press.

Jamieson, D. 2005a. "Adaptation, Mitigation, and Justice". In *Perspectives on Climate Change: Science, Economics, Politics, Ethics*, W. Sinnott-Armstrong & R. B. Howarth (eds), 217–48. Amsterdam: Elsevier.

——2005b. "Duties to the Distant: Aid, Assistance, and Intervention in the Developing World". *Journal of Ethics* 9(1/2): 151–70.

——2010. "Climate Change, Responsibility and Justice". *Science and Engineering Ethics* 16: 431–45.

Jeffreys, S. 2009. *The Industrial Vagina*. London: Routledge.

Jensen, M. 2002. "Value Maximization, Stakeholder Theory, and the Corporate Objective Function". *Business Ethics Quarterly* 12(2): 235–56.

Jimenez, M. 2009. "Humanitarian Crisis: Migrant Deaths at the US–Mexico Border". ACLU, Mexico's National Commission of Human Rights. www.aclu.org/pdfs/immigrants/humanitariancrisisreport.pdf (accessed April 2014).

Joas, H. 2000. *The Genesis of Values*. Chicago, IL: Chicago University Press.

——2011. *Die Sakralität der Person. Eine neue Genealogie der Menschenrechte*. Frankfurt am Main: Suhrkamp.

Johnson, J. T. & G. Weigel (eds) 1991. *Just War and Gulf War*. Washington, DC: University Press of America.

Johnson, O. 2005. "Country Ownership of Reform Programs and the Implications for Conditionality". G24 Discussion Papers No. 35. www.g24.org/TGM/TGM/ojohnson.pdf (accessed February 2013).

Joint Society of Obstetricians and Gynaecologists of Canada–Canadian Fertility and Andrology Society Clinical Practice Guidelines Committee 2011. "The Diagnosis and Management of Ovarian Hyper-stimulation Syndrome". *International Journal of Gynaecology and Obstetrics* 116(3): 268–73.

Jones, A. 2010. *Globalization: Key Thinkers*. Cambridge: Polity Press.

Jones, C. 1999. *Global Justice*. Oxford: Oxford University Press.

Jones, G. 2005a. *Multinationals and Global Capitalism*. New York: Oxford University Press.

——2005b. "Multinationals from the 1930s to the 1960s". See Chandler & Mazlish (2005), 81–104.

Jones, J. D. 1990. *Poverty and the Human Condition: A Philosophical Inquiry*. Lewiston, NY: Edwin Mellen Press.

Jones, T. 1980. "Corporate Social Responsibility, Revisited, Redefined". *California Management Review* 22(3): 59–67.

Jubilee Debt Campaign n.d. a. "Drop the Debt!". http://old.jubileedebtcampaign.org.uk/?lid=99 (accessed May 2014).

——n.d. b. "Why Should We Drop the Debt?". http://jubileedebt.org.uk/faqs-2/why-should-we-drop-the-debt (accessed April 2014).

Julius, A. J. 2006. "Nagel's Atlas". *Philosophy and Public Affairs* 34(2): 176–92.

Kamm, F. 2004. "The New Problem of Distance in Morality". See Chatterjee (2004), 59–74.

Kant, I. [1795] 1903. *Perpetual Peace: A Philosophical Essay*, M. C. Smith (trans.). London: Simon Sonnenschein & Co.

——[1785] 1964. *Groundwork of the Metaphysics of Morals*, H. J. Paton (trans.). New York: Harper & Row.

——[1795] 1983. *Perpetual Peace and Other Essays*, T. Humphrey (trans.). Indianapolis, IN: Hackett.

——[1781]1991. *Practical Philosophy*, M. Gregor (ed.). Cambridge: Cambridge University Press.

——[1797] 1996. *The Metaphysics of Morals*, R. Sullivan (ed.), M. J. Gregor (trans.). Cambridge: Cambridge University Press.

Kapstein, E. 1999. "Distributive Justice and International Trade". *Ethics and International Affairs* 13(1): 175–204.

Kapur, R. 2005. "Cross-Border Movements and the Law: Renegotiating the Boundaries of Difference". In *Trafficking and Prostitution Reconsidered*, K. Kempadoo, J. Sanghera & B. Pattanaik (eds), 25–41. London: Paradigm.

Karl, T. L. 1997. *The Paradox of Plenty: Oil Booms and Petro-States*. Berkeley, CA: University of California Press.

Katz, R. A. 2006. "The Re-Gift of Life: Who Should Capture the Value of Transplanted Human Tissue?" *Health Lawyer* 18(14): 14–43.

Keegan, J. 1994. *A History of Warfare*. New York: Vintage.

Kegan, C. 2011. *Experiences of Forced Labour Among Chinese Migrant Workers*. London: Joseph Rowntree Foundation.

Kelly, P. 2008. *Lydia's Open Door*. Berkeley, CA: University of California Press.

Kempadoo, K. 1999. "Slavery or Work? Reconceptualising Third World Prostitution". *Positions* 7(1): 225–37.

Kempadoo, K. & J. Doezema 1998. *Global Sex Workers: Rights, Resistance and Redefinition*. New York: Routledge.

Khan, M. & S. Sharma 2001. *IMF Conditionality and Country Ownership of Programs*. IMF Working Paper No. 1/142. www.imf.org/external/pubs/ft/wp/2001/wp01142.pdf (accessed February 2013).

Kiesecker, J., H. Copeland, A. Pocewicz, N. Nibbelink, B. Mckenney, J. Dahlke, M. Holloran & D. Stroud 2009. "A Framework for Implementing Biodiversity Offsets". *Bioscience* 59: 77–84.

Kindleberger, C. 1973. *The World in Depression 1929–1939*. London: Penguin Press.

Kissinger, H. 1992. "Humanitarian Intervention has its Hazards". *International Herald Tribune* (14 December): 5.

——1995. *Diplomacy*. New York: HarperCollins.

Kittay, E. F. 1999. *Love's Labor: Essays on Women, Equality, and Dependency*. New York: Routledge.

Kitzmueller, M. & J. Shimshack 2012. "Economic Perspectives on Corporate Social Responsibility". *Journal of Economic Literature* 50(1): 51–84.

Klasen, S. 2009. "Levels and Trends in Absolute Poverty in the World: What We Know and What We Don't". See Mack *et al.* (2009), 21–36.

Kleinman, S. 2006. "KUBARK Counterintelligence Interrogation Review: Observations of an Interrogator. Lessons Learned and Avenues for Further Research". In *Educing Information: Interrogation: Science and Art*, Intelligence Science Board (ed.), 95–140. Washington, DC: National Defense Intelligence College Press.

Klingebiel, S. 2012. *Entwicklungszusammenarbeit: Auslaufmodell oder Entwicklungsmotor in Sub-Sahara Afrika?* Analysen und Stellungnahmen 3/2012. Bonn: Deutsches Institut für Entwicklungspolitik. www.die-gdi.de/uploads/media/AuS_3.2012.pdf (accessed April 2014).

Knight, F. 1921. *Risk, Uncertainty, and Profit*. Boston, MA: Houghton Mifflin Company.

Knobe, J. 2003. "Intentional Action and Side Effects in Ordinary Language". *Analysis* 63(3): 190–94.

Knorr-Cetina, K. 2007. "Microglobalization". In *Frontiers of Globalization Research: Theoretical and Methodological Approaches*, I. Rossi (ed.), 65–93. New York: Springer.

KOF Swiss Economic Institute 2011. "KOF Index of Globalization 2011". Press Release. Zurich: KOF Swiss Economic Institute. http://globalization.kof.ethz.ch/media/filer_public/2013/03/25/press_release_2011_en.pdf (accessed May 2014).

Kofman, E., A. Phizacklea, P. Raghuram & R. Sales 2000. *Gender and International Migration in Europe*. London: Routledge.

Kolodny, N. 2010. "Which Relationships Justify Partiality? The Case of Parents and Children". *Philosophy and Public Affairs* 38(1): 37–75.

Kordon, D., L. Edelman, D. Lagos, E. Nicoletti, D. Kersner & M. Groshaus [1992] 2007. "Torture in Argentina". In *Torture and its Consequences: Current Treatment Approaches*, Metin Başoğlu (ed.), 433–51. Cambridge: Cambridge University Press.

Korsgaard, C. M. 1996. *The Sources of Normativity*. Cambridge: Cambridge University Press.

Kotler, P. & N. Lee 2005. *Corporate Social Responsibility: Doing the Most Good for Your Company and Your Cause*. Hoboken, NJ: John Wiley & Sons.

Krämer, H. 1992. *Integrative Ethik*. Frankfurt: Suhrkamp.

Kreimer, S. F. 2003–4. "Too Close to the Rack and the Screw: Constitutional Constraints on Torture in the War on Terror". *University of Pennsylvania Journal of Constitutional Law* 6: 278–325.

Krishnamurthy, M. 2012. "Reconceiving Rawls's Arguments for Equal Political Liberty and its Fair Value: On our Higher-Order Interests". *Social Theory and Practice* 38(2): 258–78.

——forthcoming. "Completing Rawls's Arguments for Equal Political Liberty and its Fair Value: The Argument from Self-Respect". *Canadian Journal of Philosophy*.

——n.d. a. "Economic Policy Conditionality: Theory and Practice". Unpublished manuscript.

——n.d. b. "Against Weighted Voting in the IMF and Bank". Unpublished manuscript.

Kristof, N. 2002. "Farm Subsidies That Kill". *New York Times* (5 July). www.nytimes.com/2002/07/05/opinion/farm-subsidies-that-kill.html (accessed December 2012).

Krugman, P. 1998. "Ricardo's Difficult Idea: Why Intellectuals Can't Understand Comparative Advantage". In *Freedom and Trade: The Economics and Politics of International Trade*, vol. 2, G. Cook (ed.), 22–36. New York: Routledge.

Kuanpoth, J. 2010. *Patent Rights in Pharmaceuticals in Developing Countries*. Cheltenham: Edward Elgar.

Kukathas, C. 2006. "The Mirage of Global Justice". In *Justice and Global Politics*, E. Paul, F. Miller & J. Paul (eds), 1–28. Cambridge: Cambridge University Press.

Kumar, R. 2003. "Who Can be Wronged?" *Philosophy and Public Affairs* 31: 99–118.

Kuper, A. 2000. "Rawlsian Global Justice: Beyond the *Law of Peoples* to a Cosmopolitan Law of Persons". *Political Theory* 28: 640–74.

Kurjanska, M. & M. Risse 2008. "Fairness in Trade II: Export Subsidies and the Fair Trade Movement". *Philosophy, Politics, and Economics* 7(34): 29–56.

Kurucz, E., B. Colbert & D. Wheeler 2008. "The Business Case for Corporate Social Responsibility". See Crane *et al.* (2008), 83–112.

Kyle, R. & R. Koslowski (eds) 2011. *Global Human Smuggling: Comparative Perspectives*. Baltimore, MD: Johns Hopkins University Press.

Kymlicka, W. 1989. *Liberalism, Community and Culture*. Oxford: Clarendon Press.

——1995. *Multicultural Citizenship: A Liberal Theory of Minority Rights*. Oxford: Oxford University Press.

——2001. "Territorial Boundaries: A Liberal Egalitarian Perspective". In *Boundaries and Justice: Diverse Ethical Perspectives*, D. Miller & S. Hashmi (eds), 249–75. Princeton, NJ: Princeton University Press.

——2002. *Contemporary Political Philosophy: An Introduction*. Oxford: Oxford University Press.

Laberge, P. 1995. "Humanitarian Intervention: Three Ethical Positions". *Ethics and International Affairs* 9: 15–35.

Lacasse, J. R. & L. Jonathan 2010. "Ghostwriting at Elite Academic Medical Centers in the United States". *PLoS Medicine* 7(2): 1–4.

Lackey, D. 1984. *Moral Principles and Nuclear Weapons*. Totowa, NJ: Rowman & Littlefield.

Laclau, E. & C. Mouffe 2001. *Hegemony and Socialist Strategy: Towards a Radical Democratic Politics*. London: Verso.

LaFollette, H. 2003. "World Hunger". In *A Companion to Applied Ethics*, E. Frey & W. C. Heath (eds), 238–53. Oxford: Blackwell Publishing.

Landsman, G. 2008. *Reconstructing Motherhood and Disability in the Age of Perfect Babies*. Oxford: Routledge.

Lane, M. 2005. "The Moral Dimension of Corporate Responsibility". In *Global Responsibilities*, A. Kuper (ed.), 229–50. New York: Routledge.

Laqueur, W. 1987. *The Age of Terrorism*. Boston, MA: Little Brown.

——1999. *New Terrorism*. New York: Oxford University Press.

Larmore, C. E. 1996. *The Morals of Modernity*. Cambridge: Cambridge University Press.

Lasagna, L. 1972. "Special Subjects in Human Experimentation". In *Experimentation with Human Subjects*, P. A. Freund (ed.), 262–75. London: George Allen & Unwin.

Leader, S. 2004. "Collateralism". In *Human Rights*, R. Brownsword (ed.), 53–67. Oxford: Hart.

Lebow, R. N. 2003. *The Tragic Vision of Politics: Ethics, Interests and Orders*. Cambridge: Cambridge University Press.

Lebret, L. 1960. Editorial. *Développement et Civilisations* 1 (March): 1.

Leder, D. 1999. "Whose Body? What Body? The Metaphysics of Organ Transplantation". In *Persons and Their Bodies: Rights, Responsibilities, Relationships*, M. J. Cherry (ed.), 233–64. Dordrecht: Kluwer Academic.

Lee, K., A. Holland & D. McNeill (eds) 2000. *Global Sustainable Development in the 21st Century*. Edinburgh: Edinburgh University Press.

Leipziger, D. 2010. *Corporate Responsibility Code Handbook*, 2nd edn. Sheffield: Greenleaf Publishing.

Lenk, C. & K. Beier 2012. "Is the Commercialisation of Human Tissue and Body Material Forbidden in the Countries of the European Union?" *Journal of Medical Ethics* 38(6): 342–46.

Leopold, A. 1949. *A Sand County Almanac*. Oxford: Oxford University Press.

Lepard, B. 2002. *Rethinking Humanitarian Intervention: A Fresh Legal Approach Based on Fundamental Ethical Principles in International Law and World Religions*. University Park, PA: Pennsylvania State University Press.

Lepenies, P. 2009. "Lernen vom Besserwisser: Wissenstransfer in der Entwicklungshilfe aus historischer Perspektive". In *Entwicklungswelten. Globalgeschichte der Entwicklung*, H. Büschel & D. Speich (eds), 33–59. Frankfurt: Campus.

Lercher, A. 2007. "Are There Any Environmental Rights?" *Environmental Values* 16(3): 355–68.

Lessig, L. 2001. *The Future of Ideas*. New York: Random House.

Levene, M. 2004. "A Dissenting Voice: Or, How Current Assumptions of Deterring and Preventing Genocide May be Looking at the Problem Through the Wrong End of the Telescope: Part I". *Journal of Genocide Research* 6(2): 153–66.

Leventhal, J. *et al.* 2012. "Chimerism and Tolerance Without GVHD or Engraftment Syndrome in HLA-Mismatched Combined Kidney and Hematopoietic Stem Cell Transplantation". *Science Translational Medicine* 4(124): 124–28.

Levine, R. J. 1998. "The 'Best Proven Therapeutic Method' Standard in Clinical Trials in Technologically Developing Countries." *IRB: A Review of Human Subjects Research* 20(1): 5–9.

Levy, N. 2002. *Moral Relativism*. Oxford: Oneworld.

Lewis, D. K. 1989. "Dispositional Theories of Value". *Proceedings of Aristotelian Society* Suppl. 63: 113–37.

Lichtenburg, J. 1998. "Consuming Because Others Consume". See Crocker & Linden (1998b), 155–75.

——2010. "Negative Duties, Positive Duties, and the 'New Harms'". *Ethics* 120(3): 557–78.

Lie, R. K. 2010. "The Fair Benefit Approach Revisited". *Hastings Center Report* 40(4): 3.

Lin, J. 2012. *New Structural Economics*. Washington, DC: The World Bank. https://openknowledge.worldbank.org/bitstream/handle/10986/2232/663930PUB0EPI00nomics09780821389553.pdf?sequence=1 (accessed May 2014).

Linklater, A. 1998. *The Transformation of Political Community*. Cambridge: Polity.

List, F. 1841. *The National System of Political Economy*. Cornell Digital Library Digital Collections Edition. Philadelphia, PA: J. B. Lippincott and Company.

Lo, B., N. Padian & M. Barnes 2007. "The Obligation to Provide Antiretroviral Treatment in HIV Prevention Trials". *AIDS* 21(10): 1229–31.

Lo, Y. S. 2001a. "The Land Ethic and Callicott's Ethical System (1980–2001): An Overview and Critique". *Inquiry* 44: 331–58.

——2001b. "A Humean Argument for the Land Ethic?" *Environmental Values* 11: 523–39.

——2006. "Making and Finding Values in Nature". *Inquiry* 49: 123–47.

——2009. "Is Hume Inconsistent? – Motivation and Morals". In *Hume on Motivation and Virtue*, C. Pigden (ed.), 57–79. Basingstoke: Palgrave Macmillan.

Lodge, G. & C. Wilson 2006. *A Corporate Solution to Global Poverty*. Princeton, NJ: Princeton University Press.

Lomasky, L. 1983. "Gift Relations, Sexual Relations and Freedom". *Philosophical Quarterly* 33(132): 250–58.

Lomborg, B. 2001. *The Skeptical Environmentalist: Measuring the Real State of the World*. Cambridge: Cambridge University Press.

London, A. J. & K. J. S. Zollman 2010. "Research at the Auction Block: Problems for the Fair Benefits Approach to International Research". *Hastings Center Report* 40(4): 34–45.

Long, G. 2004. *Relativism and the Foundations of Liberalism*. Exeter: Imprint Academic.

Lott, T. 1998. "Early Enlightenment Conceptions of the Rights of Slaves". In *Subjugation and Bondage*, T. Lott (ed.), 99–129. Lanham, MD: Rowman & Littlefield.

Lötter, H. 2008. *When I Needed a Neighbour Were You There? Christians and the Challenge of Poverty*. Wellington, South Africa: Lux Verbi.

——2011. *Poverty, Ethics, and Justice*. Cardiff: University of Wales Press.

Love, J. 2005. "Medical Research and Development Treaty". www.cptech.org/workingdrafts/rndtreaty4.pdf (accessed April 2014).

Love, J. & T. Hubbard 2007. "The Big Idea: Prizes to Stimulate R&D for New Medicines". *Chicago-Kent Law Review* 82:1520–54.

Lowry, C. & U. Schüklenk 2009. "Two Models in Global Health Ethics". *Public Health Ethics* 2: 276–84.

Luban, D. 2005. "Liberalism, Torture, and the Ticking Bomb". *Virginia Law Review* 91: 1425–61.

——2006. "Liberalism, Torture, and the Ticking Bomb". In *The Torture Debate in America*, K. J. Greenberg (ed.) 35–83. Cambridge: Cambridge University Press. Reprinted in Luban (2014), 43–73.

——2009. "Unthinking the Ticking Bomb". In *Global Basic Rights*, C. R. Beitz & R. E. Goodin (eds), 181–206. Oxford: Oxford University Press. Reprinted in Luban (2014), 74–108.

——2014. *Torture, Power and Law*. Cambridge: Cambridge University Press.

Luban, D. & H. Shue 2012. "Mental Torture: A Critique of Erasures in US Law". *Georgetown Law Journal* 100: 823–63. Reprinted in Luban (2014), 153–94.

Lukes, S. 2008. *Moral Relativism*. London: Profile Books.

Lurie, P. & S. M. Wolfe 1997. "Unethical Trials of Interventions to Reduce Perinatal Transmission of the Human Immunodeficiency Virus in Developing Countries". *New England Journal of Medicine* 337: 853–56.

Macedo, S. 2007. "The Moral Dilemma of US Immigration Policy". In *Debating Immigration*, C. Swain (ed.), 63–81. Cambridge: Cambridge University Press.

Machiavelli, N. 1998. *The Prince*. New York: Penguin Classics.

Mack, E., M. Schramm, S. Klasen & T. Pogge (eds) 2009. *Absolute Poverty and Global Justice: Empirical Data – Moral Theories – Initiatives*. Farnham: Ashgate.

Mackenzie, C. & N. Stoljar (eds) 2000. *Relational Autonomy: Feminist Perspectives on Automony, Agency, and the Social Self*. New York: Oxford University Press.

Mackie, J. L. 1990. *Ethics: Inventing Right and Wrong*. London: Penguin.

Macklin, R. 2003. "Dignity is a Useless Concept". *British Medical Journal* 327 (7429): 1419–20.

——2006. "Changing the Presumption: Providing ART to Vaccine Research Participants". *American Journal of Bioethics* 6(1): W1–W5.

Madsen, B., N. Carroll, D. Kandy & G. Bennett 2011. *State of Biodiversity Markets*. Washington, DC: Forest Trends.

Mahdavi, P. 2011. *Gridlock: Labor, Migration and Human Trafficking in Dubai*. Stanford, CA: Stanford University Press.

Mahon, R. & F. Robinson (eds) 2011. *Feminist Ethics and Social Policy: Towards a New Global Political Economy of Care*. Vancouver: University of British Columbia Press.

Maier, D. S. 2012. *What's So Good About Biodiversity? A Call For Better Reasoning About Nature's Value*. Dordrecht: Springer.

Maitland, I. 2004. "The Great Non-Debate Over International Sweatshops". In *Ethical Theory and Business*, 7th edn, T. L. Beauchamp & N. Bowie (eds), 597–607. Englewood Cliffs, NJ: Prentice Hall.

Malthus, T. [1798] 2008. *On the Principle of Population*. Oxford: Oxford University Press.

Malucelli, L. 2006. "Gendered Transitions: Made to Prostitute, Prostitute to Maid". In *Post-Conflict Cultures: Rituals of Representation*, C. Demaria & C. Wright (eds), 222–239. London: Zoilus.

Mamdani, M. 2011. "Libya: Politics of Humanitarian Intervention". *Al-Jazeera* (31 March). www.aljazeera.com/indepth/opinion/2011/03/201133111277476962.html.

Maneschi, A. 1998. *Comparative Advantage in International Trade: A Historical Perspective*. Cheltenham: Edward Elgar.

Manson, N. A. 2002. "Formulating the Precautionary Principle". *Environmental Ethics* 24 (3): 263–74.

Mapel, D. 1996. "Realism and the Ethics of War and Peace". In *The Ethics of War and Peace: Religious and Secular Perspectives*, T. Nardin (ed.), 180–200. Princeton, NJ: Princeton University Press.

Margalit, A. & J. Raz 1990. "National Self–Determination". *Journal of Philosophy* 87(9): 439–61.

Margolis, J. D. & J. P. Walsh 2003. "Misery Loves Companies: Rethinking Social Initiatives by Business". *Administrative Science Quarterly* 48(2): 268–305.

Marshall, P. & S. Thatun 2005. "Miles Away: The Trouble with Prevention in the Greater Mekong Sub-Region". In *Trafficking and Prostitution Reconsidered*, K. Kempadoo, J. Sanghera & B. Pattanaik (eds.), 43–64. London: Paradigm.

Martin, R. & D. Reidy 2006. *Rawls's Law of Peoples: A Realistic Utopia?* Malden, MA: Blackwell.

Mason, A. & N. J. Wheeler 1996. "Realist Objections to Humanitarian Intervention". In *The Ethical Dimensions of Global Change*, Barry Holden (ed.), 94–110. Basingstoke: Macmillan.

Mason, J. K. & G. Laurie 2010. "Should There Be Property in Human Material?" In their *Mason and McCall Smith's Law and Medical Ethics*, 8th edn 447–74. Oxford: Oxford University Press.

Mason, K. & G. Laurie 2001. "Consent or Property? Dealing with the Body and its Parts in the Shadow of Bristol and Alder Hey". *Modern Law Review* 64(5): 710–29.

Matten, D. & A. Crane 2005. "Corporate Citizenship: Toward an Extended Theoretical Conceptualization". *Academy of Management Review* 30(1): 166–79.

Matthews, F. 1999. "Letting the World Grow Old: An Ethos of Countermodernity". *Worldviews* 3: 119–37.

Mattoo, A. & A. Subramanian, 2004. "The WTO and the Poorest Countries: the Stark Reality". *World Trade Review* 3(3): 385–407.

May, S., G. Cheney & J. Roper (eds) 2007. *The Debate Over Corporate Social Responsibility*. Oxford: Oxford University Press.

Mayden, R. L. 1997. "A Hierarchy of Species Concept: The Denouement in the Saga of the Species Problem". In *Species: The Units of Biodiversity*, M. F. Claridge, H. A. Dawah & M. R. Wilson (eds), 381–424. London: Chapman & Hall.

Mayer, J. 2008. *The Dark Side: The Inside Story of How the War on Terror Turned into a War on American Ideals*. New York: Doubleday.

McCoy, A. W. 2006. *A Question of Torture: CIA Interrogation, from the Cold War to the War on Terror*. New York: Henry Holt and Co.

McGinn, C. 2011. *The Meaning of Disgust*. New York: Oxford University Press.

McGoldlick, D. 2004. *The Congressional Commission Report on the Attacks of 9/11*. Washington, DC: US Congress.

McKeown, R. 2009. "Norm Regress: US Revisionism and the Slow Death of the Torture Norm". *International Relations* 23(1): 5–25.

McMahan, J. 1996. "Realism, Morality and War". In *The Ethics of War and Peace: Religious and Secular Perspectives*, T. Nardin (ed.), 78–92. Princeton, NJ: Princeton University Press.

——2011. *Killing in War*, 2nd edn. Oxford: Oxford University Press.

McNamara, R. 1973. "Address to the Board of Governors". Washington, DC: The World Bank. http://siteresources.worldbank.org/EXTARCHIVES/Resources/Robert_McNamara_Address_Nairobi_1973.pdf (accessed May 2012).

McPherran, M. L. 2002. "Justice and Pollution in the 'Euthyphro'". *Apeiron: A Journal for Ancient Philosophy and Science* 35(2): 105–29.

McVeigh, T. 2009. "Debt Chasers Accused of Bullying Calls and Threats". *Observer* (28 June). www.theguardian.com/money/2009/jun/28/debt-chasers-bullying-credit-cards (accessed June 2014).

MDG Gap Task Force 2012. *The Global Partnership for Development: Making Rhetoric a Reality*. New York: United Nations.

Meckled-Garcia, S. 2008. "On the Very Idea of Cosmopolitan Justice: Constructivism and International Agency". *Journal of Political Philosophy* 16(3): 245–71.

Meisels, T. 2005. *Territorial Rights*. Dordrecht: Springer.

Meyer, A. 2000. *Contraction and Convergence: The Global Solution to Climate Change*. Foxhole: Green Books.

Meyer, J. W. 2010. "World Society, Institutional Theories, and the Actor". *Annual Review of Sociology* 36: 1–20.

Meyer, L. H. 2003. "Past and Future: The Case for a Threshold Notion of Harm". In *Rights, Culture, and the Law: Themes from the Legal and Political Philosophy of Joseph Raz*, L. H. Meyer, S. L. Paulson & T. Pogge (eds), 143–59. Oxford: Oxford University Press.

——2008. "Intergenerational Justice". In *Stanford Encyclopedia of Philosophy*, Edward N. Zalta (ed.). http://plato.stanford.edu/archives/spr2010/entries/justice-intergenerational (accessed April 2014).

Meyer, W. H. 1996. "Human Rights and MNCs: Theory Versus Quantitative Analysis". *Human Rights Quarterly* 18(2): 368–97.

Michaelson, C. 2010. "Revisiting the Global Business Ethics Question". *Business Ethics Quarterly* 20(2): 237–51.

Miklos, A. 2006. "Institutions in Cosmopolitan Justice". *Global Society* 20(3): 239–50.

Milanovic, B. 2005. *Worlds Apart: Measuring International and Global Inequality*. Princeton, NJ: Princeton University Press.

——2012. "Global Inequality Recalculated and Updated: The Effect of New PPP Estimates on Global Inequality and 2005 Estimates". *Journal of Economic Inequality* 10(1): 1–18.

Milgram, S. 1974. *Obedience to Authority: An Experimental View*. New York: Harper & Row.

Mill, J. S. 1874. "Nature". In *Three Essays on Religion*, 3–65. New York: Henry Holt.

——2003. *Utilitarianism and On Liberty*, M. Warnock (ed.). Oxford: Blackwell.

——[1848] 2004. *Principles of Political Economy*. Indianapolis, IN: Hackett.

Miller, D. 1995. *On Nationality*. Oxford: Clarendon Press.

——2000. *Citizenship and National Identity*. Cambridge: Polity Press.

——2005a. "Distributing Responsibilities". In *Global Responsibilities*, A. Kuper (ed.), 95–115. New York: Routledge.

——2005b. "Immigration: The Case for Limits". See Cohen & Wellman (2005), 193–206.

——2005c. "Reasonable Partiality Towards Compatriots". *Ethical Theory and Moral Practice* 8(1–2): 63–81.

——2007. *National Responsibility and Global Justice*. Oxford: Oxford University Press.

——2008. "Global Justice and Climate Change: How Should Responsibilities Be Distributed?" Tanner Lectures on Human Values, 24–25 March, Tsinghua University, Beijing. http://tannerlectures.utah.edu/_documents/a-to-z/m/Miller_08.pdf (accessed April 2014).

——2011. "Property and Territory: Locke, Kant and Steiner". *Journal of Political Philosophy* 19(1): 90–109.

——forthcoming. "Is There a Human Right to Immigrate?" In *Migration in Political Theory: The Ethics of Movement and Membership*, S. Fine & Lea Ypi (eds.). Oxford: Oxford University Press.

Miller, R. W. 1998. "Cosmopolitan Respect and Patriotic Concern". *Philosophy and Public Affairs* 27(3): 202–24.

——2004. "Beneficence, Duty, and Distance". *Philosophy and Public Affairs* 32(4): 357–83.

——2006. "Global Institutional Reform and Global Social Movements: From False Promise to Realistic Hope". *Cornell International Law Journal* 39: 501–14.

——2010. *Globalizing Justice: The Ethics of Poverty and Power*. Oxford: Oxford University Press.

Miller, S. & M. Selgelid 2008. *Ethical and Philosophical Consideration of the Dual-Use Dilemma in the Biological Sciences*. Dordrecht: Springer.

Mittermeier, R. A., C. G. Mittermeier, T. M. Brooks, J. D. Pilgrim, W. R. Konstant, G. A. B. da Fonseca & C. Kormos 2003. "Wilderness and Biodiversity Conservation". *Proceedings of the National Academy of Sciences* 100: 10,309–13.

Modelski, G., T. C. Devezas & W. R. Thompson (eds) 2008. *Globalization as Evolutionary Process: Modeling Global Change*. Abingdon: Routledge.

Moe, K. 1984. "Should the Nazi Research Data be Cited?" *Hastings Center Report* 14(6): 5–7.

Moellendorf, D. 2002. *Cosmopolitan Justice*. Boulder, CO: Westview Press.

——2005. "The World Trade Organization and Egalitarian Justice". *Metaphilosophy* 36(1/2): 145–62.

——2009. *Global Inequality Matters*. Basingstoke: Palgrave Macmillan.

Monbiot, G. 2013. *Feral: Searching for Enchantment on the Frontiers of Rewilding*. London: Allen Lane.

Monge, R. 2013. "Business Practice and Dirty Hands: Managerial Action in the Face of Moral Conflict". Doctoral thesis, Department of Legal Studies and Business Ethics, The Wharton School, University of Pennsylvania.

Monist 2011. 94(4): special issue on cosmopolitanism.

Moon, K. 1997. *Sex Among Allies: Military Prostitution in US–Korea Relations*. New York: Columbia University Press.

Moore, G. E. 1903. *Principia Ethica*. Cambridge: Cambridge University Press.

Moore, K. & D. Lewis 1999. *Birth of the Multinational: 2000 Years of Ancient Business History – From Ashur to Augustus*. Copenhagen: Copenhagen Business School Press.

Moore, M. 2001. *The Ethics of Nationalism*. Oxford: Oxford University Press.

Moorhead, C. 1998. *Dunant's Dream: War, Switzerland and the History of the Red Cross*. New York: Carroll and Graf Publishers.

Morehouse, C. (2009). *Combating Human Trafficking: Policy Gaps and Hidden Agendas in the USA and Germany*. Wiesbaden: VS Verlag.

Morgenthau, H. J. 1970. *Politics Among Nations*, 5th edn. New York: Knopf.

Morrow, P. 2010. "Ricardian–Heckscher–Ohlin Comparative Advantage: Theory and Evidence". *Journal of International Economics* 82(2): 137–51.

Mosher, S. W. 2008. *Population Control: Real Costs, Illusory Benefits*. Somerset, NJ: Transaction Publishers.

Moyn, S. 2010. *The Last Utopia: Human Rights in History*. Cambridge, MA: The Belknap Press/Harvard University Press.

Moyo, D. 2009. *Dead Aid: Why Aid is Not Working and How There is Another Way for Africa*. London: Penguin Press.

Mukherjee, A. 2004. *Hunger: Theory, Perspectives and Reality. Assessment Through Particpatory Methods*. Aldershot: Ashgate.

Mulgan, T. 2006. *Future People*. Oxford: Oxford University Press.

——2007. *Understanding Utilitarianism*. Stocksfield: Acumen.

——2011a. "Ethical Consequentialism". In *Oxford Bibliographies Online: Philosophy*. http://oxfordbibliographiesonline.com/view/document/obo-9780195396577/obo-9780195396577-0026.xml (accessed September 2011).

——2011b. *Ethics for a Broken World*. Stocksfield: Acumen.

Munzer, S. 1994. "An Uneasy Case Against Property Rights in Body Parts". *Social Philosophy and Policy* 11(2): 259–86.

Murphy, L. 1993. "The Demands of Beneficence". *Philosophy and Public Affairs* 22(4): 267–92.

——1998. "Institutions and the Demands of Justice". *Philosophy and Public Affairs* 27(4): 251–91.

Murray, W. & R. Scales 2003. *The Iraq War*. Cambridge, MA: Harvard University Press.

Musschenga, A. 2005. "Empirical Ethics, Context-Sensitivity, and Contextualism". *Journal of Medicine and Philosophy* 30(5): 467–90.

Muthu, S. 2003. *Enlightenment Against Empire*. Princeton, NJ: Princeton University Press.

Myrdal, G. 1957. *Economic Theory and Under-Developed Regions*. London: Duckworth.

Nagel, T. 2005. "The Problem of Global Justice". *Philosophy and Public Affairs* 33(2):113–47.

Narayan, D. & P. Petesch 2002. *Voices of the Poor: From Many Lands*. New York: Oxford University Press and the World Bank.

Narayan, D., R. Chambers, M. K. Shah & P. Petesch 2000a. *Voices of the Poor: Crying Out for Change*. Oxford: Oxford University Press and the World Bank.

Narayan, D., R. Patel, K. Schafft, A. Rademacher & S. Koch-Schulte 2000b. *Voices of the Poor: Can Anyone Hear Us?* Oxford: Oxford University Press and the World Bank.

Narayan, U. 1997. "Contesting Cultures: 'Westernization', Respect for Cultures, and Third-World Feminists". In *The Second Wave: A Reader in Feminist Theory*, L. Nicholson (ed.), 396–418. New York: Routledge.

——2000. "Essence of Culture and a Sense of History: A Feminist Critique of Cultural Essentialism". In her *Decentering the Center: Philosophy for a Multicultural, Postcolonial and Feminist World*, S. Harding (eds), 80–100. Bloomington, IN: Indiana University Press.

Nardin, T. 2002. "The Moral Basis of Humanitarian Intervention". *Ethics and International Affairs* 16: 57–70.

Narveson, J. 2003a. "The 'Invisible Hand'". *Journal of Business Ethics* 46(3): 201–12.

——2003b. "We Don't Owe Them a Thing! A Tough-Minded But Soft-Hearted View of Aid to the Faraway Needy". *Monist* 86(3): 419–33.

National Commission for the Protection of Human Subjects of Biomedical and Behavioral Research 1979. "The Belmont Report: Ethical Principles and Guidelines for the Protection of Human Subjects of Research". http://ohsr.od.nih.gov/guidelines/belmont.html (accessed January 2012).

Navaretti, G. & A. Venables 2004. "Facts and Issues". In their *Multinational Firms in the World Economy*, 1–22. Princeton, NJ: Princeton University Press.

Neumayer, E. 2000. "In Defence of Historical Accountability for Greenhouse Gas Emissions". *Ecological Economics* 33(2): 185–92.

Ng, Y.-K. 1989. "What Should we Do about Future Generations? Impossibility of Parfit's Theory X". *Economics and Philosophy* 5: 235–53.

Nickel, J. 2006. *Making Sense of Human Rights*, 2nd edn. Oxford: Blackwell.

——2010. "Human Rights". In *Stanford Encyclopedia of Philosophy*, E. Zalta (ed.). http://plato.stanford.edu/archives/fall2010/entries/rights-human (accessed April 2014).

Niebuhr, R. 1938. *Beyond Tragedy: Essays on the Christian Interpretation of History*. London: Nisbet & Co.

Nine, C. 2008. "A Lockean Theory of Territory". *Political Studies* 56: 148–65.

Noddings, N. 1986. *Caring: A Feminine Approach to Ethics and Moral Education*. Berkeley, CA: University of California Press.

——2002. *Starting at Home: Caring and Social Policy*. Berkeley, CA: University of California Press.

Nordhaus, W. 1997. "Discounting in Economics and Climate Change". *Climatic Change* 37(2): 315–28.

——2007. "A Review of the Stern Review on the Economics of Climate Change". *Journal of Economic Literature* 45: 686–702.

Norman, R. 1995. *Ethics, Killing and War*. Cambridge: Cambridge University Press.

Norton, B. G. (ed.) 1986. *The Preservation of Species*. Princeton, NJ: Princeton University Press.

——1987. *Why Preserve Natural Variety?* Princeton, NJ: Princeton University Press.

——2002. "Can There be a Universal Earth Ethic? A Reflection on Values for the Proposed Earth Charter". In his *Searching for Sustainability: Interdisciplinary Essays on the Philosophy of Conservation Biology*, 396–419. Cambridge: Cambridge University Press.

——2003a. *Searching for Sustainability*. Cambridge: Cambridge University Press.

——2003b. "Conservation: Moral Crusade or Environmental Public Policy?" In *Reconstructing Conservation: Finding Common Ground*, B. A. Minteer & R. E. Manning (eds), 187–206. Washington, DC: Island Press.

Norwegian Nobel Committee 2012. "The Nobel Peace Prize for 2012". www.nobelprize.org/nobel_prizes/peace/laureates/2012/press.html (accessed May 2014).

Noueihad, L. & A. Warren 2012. *The Battle for the Arab Spring*. New Haven, CT: Yale University Press.

Nozick, R.1974. *Anarchy, State, and Utopia*. New York: Basic Books.

Nuffield Council on Bioethics 2002. *The Ethics of Patenting DNA*. London: Nuffield Council on Bioethics.

——2003. *The Use of Genetically Modified Crops in Developing Countries*. London: Nuffield Council on Bioethics.

——2011a. *Biofuels: Ethical Issues*. London: Nuffield Council on Bioethics.

——2011b. *Human Bodies: Donation for Medicine and Research*. London: Nuffield Council on Bioethics.

Nurkse, R. 1953. *Problems of Capital Formation in Underdeveloped Countries*. New York: Oxford University Press.

Nuscheler, F. 2006. *Entwicklungspolitik*. Bonn: Bundeszentrale für politische Bildung.

Nussbaum, M. 1996. "Patriotism and Cosmopolitanism". In *For Love of Country: Debating The Limits of Patriotism*, J. Cohen (ed.), 3–20. Boston, MA: Beacon Press.

——1997. "Capabilities and Human Rights". *Fordham Law Review* 66: 273–300.

——2000. *Women and Human Development: The Capabilities Approach*. Cambridge: Cambridge University Press.

——2002. "Capabilities and Social Justice". *International Studies Review* 4(2): 123–35.

——2003. "Capabilities as Fundamental Entitlements: Sen and Social Justice". *Feminist Economics* 9(2–3): 33–59.

——2006. *Frontiers of Justice: Disability, Nationality, and Species Membership*. Cambridge, MA: Harvard University Press.

——2011a. *Creating Capabilities: The Human Development Approach*. Cambridge, MA: Harvard University Press.

——2011b. "Perfectionist Liberalism and Political Liberalism". *Philosophy and Public Affairs* 39(1): 3–45.

Oberman, K. forthcoming. "Migration and Development". In *Migration in Political Theory: The Ethics of Movement and Membership*, S. Fine & L. Ypi (eds.). Oxford: Oxford University Press.

O'Connell Davidson, J. 1998. *Prostitution, Power and Freedom*. Cambridge: Polity Press.

——2005. *Children in the Global Sex Trade*. Cambridge: Polity Press.

——2006. "Will the Real Sex Slave Please Stand Up?" *Feminist Review* 83: 4–22.

——2011. "Moving Children: Child Trafficking, Child Migration, and Child Rights". *Critical Social Policy* 31: 454–77.

O'Connell Davidson, J. & B. Anderson 2006. "The Trouble with Trafficking". In *Trafficking and Women's Rights*, C. Van den Anker & J. Doomernik (eds), 11–26. London: Palgrave Macmillian.

OECD 2008a. *OECD Benchmark Definition of Foreign Direct Investment*, 4th edn. Paris: OECD Publishing.

——2008b. *Development Aid at a Glance 2008: Statistics by Region*. Paris: OECD Publishing.

——2008c. *The Paris Declaration on Aid Effectiveness and the Accra Agenda for Action*. Paris: OECD Publishing.

——2009a. *Civil Society and Aid Effectiveness: Findings, Recommendations, and Good Practice*. Paris: OECD Publishing.

——2009b. *Managing Aid: Practices of DAC Member Countries*. Paris: OECD Publishing.

——2011a. *How's Life? Measuring Well-Being*. Paris: OECD Publishing.

——2011b. *OECD Guidelines for Multinational Enterprises*. Paris: OECD Publishing. http://dx.doi.org/10.1787/9789264115415-en (accessed April 2014).

——2011c. "Official Development Assistance: Definition and Coverage". www.oecd.org/document/4/0,3746,en_2649_34447_46181892_1_1_1_1,00.html (accessed December 2011).

——2011d. "DAC List of ODA Recipients". www.oecd.org/dataoecd/32/40/43540882.pdf (accessed December 2011).

——2012a. *Aid Effectiveness 2011: Progress in Implementing the Paris Declaration*. Paris: Better Aid, OECD.

——2012b. "Development Co-operation Report 2012", www.oecd.org/dac/dcr2012.htm (accessed April 2014).

——2013a. "What Do We Know About Multilateral Aid?" www.oecd.org/dac/aid-architecture/13_03_18%20Policy%20Briefing%20on%20Multilateral%20Aid.pdf (accessed April 2014).

——2013b. "OECD StatExtracts". http://stats.oecd.org (accessed November 2013).

OECD Insights 2012. *From Aid to Development: The Global Fight Against Poverty*. Paris: OECD Publishing.

Ohlin, B. 1933. *Interregional and International Trade*. Cambridge, MA: Harvard University Press.

O'Neill, J. 1992. "The Varieties of Intrinsic Value". *Monist* 75: 119–37.

——2007. *Markets, Deliberation and Environment*. London: Routledge.

O'Neill, J., A. Holland & A. Light 2008. *Environmental Values*. London: Routledge.

O'Neill, O. 1986. *Faces of Hunger: An Essay on Poverty, Justice and Development*. London: Allen & Unwin.

——1990. "Justice, Gender and International Boundaries". *British Journal of Political Science* 20(4): 439–59.

——1996. *Towards Justice and Virtue: A Constructive Account of Practical Reasoning*. Cambridge: Cambridge University Press.

——1997. "Environmental Values, Anthropocentrism and Speciesism". *Environmental Values* 6: 127–42.

——2000a. "The 'Good Enough Parent' in the Age of the New Reproductive Technologies". In *The Ethics of Genetics in Human Procreation*, H. Haker & D. Beyleveld (eds), 33–48. Aldershot: Ashgate.

——2000b. *Bounds of Justice*. Cambridge: Cambridge University Press.

——2001. "Agents of Justice". In *Global Justice*, T. Pogge (ed.), 188–203. Oxford: Blackwell.

——2008. "Rights, Obligations and World Hunger". In *Global Ethics: Seminal Essays*, T. Pogge & K. Horton (eds), 139–55. St Paul, MN: Paragon House.

Oregon State University 2009. "Family Planning: A Major Environmental Emphasis". http://oregonstate. edu/ua/ncs/archives/2009/jul/family-planning-major-environmental-emphasis (accessed May 2011).

Orend, B. 2000. *War and International Justice: A Kantian Perspective*. Waterloo: Wilfrid Laurier University Press.

——2002a. "Justice After War". *Ethics and International Affairs* 16(1): 43–56.

——2002b. *Human Rights: Concept and Context*. Peterborough: Broadview Press.

——2006. *The Morality of War*. Peterborough: Broadview Press.

——2012. *Introduction to International Studies*. Oxford: Oxford University Press.

——2013. *The Morality of War*, 2nd edn. Peterborough: Broadview Press.

Orford, A. 2003. *Reading Humanitarian Intervention: Human Rights and the Use of Force in International Law*. Cambridge: Cambridge University Press.

Ormrod, D. 2003. *The Rise of Commercial Empires: England and the Netherlands in the Age of Mercantilism, 1650–1770*. Cambridge: Cambridge University Press.

Orts, E. W. & A. Strudler 2009. "Putting a Stake in Stakeholder Theory". *Journal of Business Ethics* 88(4): 605–15.

Page, E. 2006. *Climate Change, Justice and Future Generations*. Cheltenham: Edward Elgar.

Paine, L. S. 1994. "Managing for Organizational Integrity". *Harvard Business Review* 72(2): 106–17.

——2000. "Does Ethics Pay?" *Business Ethics Quarterly* 10(1): 319–30.

Palazzo, G. & U. Richter 2005. "CSR Business as Usual? The Case of the Tobacco Industry". *Journal of Business Ethics* 61(4): 387–401.

Palmer, C. 2011. "Does Nature Matter? The Place of the Nonhuman in the Ethics of Climate Change". In *The Ethics of Global Climate Change*, D. G. Arnold (ed.), 272–91. Cambridge: Cambridge University Press.

Pandey, M., A. Abizadeh & S. Abizadeh forthcoming. "Wage Competition and the Special-Obligations Challenge".

Parekh, B. 1997. "Rethinking Humanitarian Intervention". *International Political Science Review* 18(1): 55–74.

——2006. *Rethinking Multiculturalism*, 2nd edn. Basingstoke: Macmillan.

Parfit, D.1984. *Reasons and Persons*. Oxford: Oxford University Press.

——1986a. "Overpopulation and the Quality of Life". In *Applied Ethics*, P. Singer (ed.), 145–64. Oxford: Oxford University Press.

——1986b. *Reasons and Persons*. Oxford: Oxford University Press.

——2011. *On What Matters*, vol. 1. Oxford: Oxford University Press.

Parker, M. 2009. "Two Concepts of Empirical Ethics". *Bioethics* 23(4): 202–13.

Parker, R. 1983. *Miasma: Pollution and Purification in Early Greek Religion*. Oxford: Clarendon Press.

Parry, M., O. Canziani, J. Palutikof, P. van der Linden & C. Hanson (eds) 2007. *Climate Change 2007. Impacts, Adaptation and Vulnerability. Contribution of Working Group II to the Fourth Assessment Report of the Intergovernmental Panel on Climate Change*. Cambridge: Cambridge University Press.

Participants in the 2001 Conference on Ethical Aspects of Research in Developing Countries 2004. "Moral Standards for Research in Developing Countries: From 'Reasonable Availability' to 'Fair Benefits'". *Hastings Center Report* 34(3): 17–27.

Participants in the International Summit on Transplant Tourism and Organ Trafficking (convened by The Transplantation Society and International Society of Nephrology) 2008. "The Declaration of Istanbul on Organ Trafficking and Transplant Tourism". *Nephrology Dialysis Transplantation* 23(11): 3375–80.

Paten, A. 2005. "Should We Stop Thinking about Poverty in Terms of Helping the Poor?" *Ethics and International Affairs* 19: 19–27.

Patience, M. 2011. "China: Teenager 'Sells Kidney for iPad'". *BBC News Asia-Pacific*, www.bbc.co.uk/news/world-asia-pacific-13639934 (accessed April 2012).

Pearce, D. 1993. *Economic Values and the Natural World*. London: Earthscan.

Peet, R. 2009. *Unholy Trinity: the IMF, World Bank and WTO*, 2nd edn. New York: Zed Books.

Pence, G. 1998. *Who's Afraid of Human Cloning?* Lanham, MD: Rowman & Littlefield.

Penner, J. E. 1996. "The 'Bundle of Rights' Picture of Property". *UCLA Law Review* 43(3): 711–820.

Perrini, F. 2005. "Book Review of *Corporate Social Responsibility: Doing the Most Good for Your Company and Your Cause*". *Academy of Management Perspectives* 19(2): 90–93.

Peterson, V. S. & A. S. Runyon (eds) 1993. *Global Gender Issues*. Boulder, CO: Westview Press.

——2010. *Global Gender Issues in the New Millennium*, 3rd edn. Boulder, CO: Westview Press.

Pettit, P. 1993. *The Common Mind*. Oxford: Oxford University Press.

Pevnick, R. 2011. *Immigration and the Constraints of Justice: Between Open Borders and Absolute Sovereignty*. New York: Cambridge University Press.

Phillips, J. E. S. 2010. *None of Us Were Like This Before: American Soldiers and Torture*. New York: Verso.

Phongpaichit, P. 1999. "Trafficking in People in Thailand". In *Illegal Immigration and Commercial Sex: The New Slave Trade*, P. Williams (ed.), 74–104. London: Frank Cass.

Pieterse, J. N. 2000. "After Post-Development". *Third World Quarterly* 21(2): 175–91.

Pigou, A. C. 1946. *The Economics of Welfare*, 4th edn. London: Macmillan.

Pinker, S. 2011. *The Better Angels of Our Nature: The Decline of Violence in History and its Causes*. London: Allen Lane.

Pirnay, J.-P. *et al.* 2010. "Human Cells and Tissues: The Need for a Global Ethical Framework". *Bulletin of the World Health Organization* 88(11): 870–72.

Plant, R. 1977. "Gifts, Exchanges and the Political Economy of Health Care". *Journal of Medical Ethics* 3(4): 166–73.

Plomer, A. & P. Torremans (eds) 2009. *Embryonic Stem Cell Patents: European Law and Ethics*. Oxford: Oxford University Press.

Plumwood, V. 1991. "Nature, Self, and Gender: Feminism, Environmental Philosophy, and the Critique of Rationalism". *Hypatia* 6(1): 3–37.

Plumwood, V. 1993. *Feminism and the Mastery of Nature*. London: Routledge.

Pogge, T. 1989. *Realizing Rawls*. Ithaca, NY: Cornell University Press.

——1992. "Cosmopolitanism and Sovereignty". *Ethics* 103: 48–75.

——1994. "An Egalitarian Law of Peoples". *Philosophy and Public Affairs* 23(3): 195–224.

——2000. "On the Site of Distributive Justice: Reflections on Cohen and Murphy". *Philosophy and Public Affairs* 29(2): 137–69.

——2001. "Priorities of Global Justice". *Metaphilosophy* 32(1/2): 6–24.

——2002. *World Poverty and Human Rights: Cosmopolitan Responsibilities and Reforms*. Cambridge: Polity Press.

——2004. "'Assisting' the Global Poor". See Chatterjee (2004), 260–79.

——2005a. "Human Rights and Global Health: A Research Program". *Metaphilosophy* 36(1): 182–209.

——2005b. "Introduction: International Institutions and Responsibilities". *Metaphilosophy* 36(1): 1–2.

——2008. *World Poverty and Human Rights: Cosmopolitan Responsibilities and Reforms*, 2nd edn. Cambridge: Polity Press.

——2009. "How World Poverty is Measured and Tracked". See Mack *et al.* (2009), 51–65.

——2010. *Politics as Usual: What Lies Behind the Pro-Poor Rhetoric*. Cambridge: Polity Press.

——2011. "The Health Impact Fund". In *Global Health and Global Health Ethics*, S. Benatar & G. Brock (eds), 241–50. Cambridge: Cambridge University Press.

——2012. "Poverty and Human Rights". www2.ohchr.org/english/issues/poverty/expert/docs/Thomas_Pogge_Summary.pdf (accessed October 2013).

Pogge, T. & K. Horton (eds) 2008. *Global Ethics: Seminal Essays*. St Paul, MN: Paragon House.

Pogge, T. & D. Moellendorf (eds) 2008. *Global Justice: Seminal Essays*. St Paul, MN: Paragon House.

Polman, L. 2010. *War Games: The Story of Aid and War in Modern Times*, L. Waters (trans.). London: Viking/Penguin Books.

Ponticelli, C. 2003. "Altruistic Living Renal Transplantation". *Journal of Nephrology* 16 (suppl. 7): S6–S9.

Porter, M. E. & M. R. Kramer 2002. "The Competitive Advantage of Corporate Philanthropy". *Harvard Business Review* 80(12): 56–69.

——2006. "Strategy & Society: The Link Between Competitive Advantage and Corporate Social Responsibility". *Harvard Business Review* 84(12): 76–92.

——2011. "Creating Shared Value". *Harvard Business Review* 89(1/2): 62–77.

Post, J. 2002. "Global Corporate Citizenship: Principles to Live and Work By". *Business Ethics Quarterly* 12 (2): 143–53.

Pottage, A. 1998. "The Inscription of Life in Law: Genes, Patents, and Biopolitics". In *Law and Human Genetics: Regulating a Revolution*, R. Brownsword, W. R. Cornish & M. Llewelyn (eds), 148–73. Oxford: Hart.

Pottage, A. & B. Sherman 2011. *Figures of Invention: A History of Modern Patent Law*. New York: Oxford University Press.

Powell, B. 2006. "In Reply to Sweatshop Sophistries". *Human Rights Quarterly* 28(4): 1031–42.

Prahalad, C. K. 2006. *The Fortune at the Bottom of the Pyramid*. Prentice Hall: Pearson.

Prainsack, B. & A. Buyx 2011. *Solidarity: Reflections on an Emerging Concept in Bioethics*. London: Nuffield Council on Bioethics.

Prebisch, R. 1950. *The Economic Development of Latin America and its Principal Problems*. New York: United Nations.

Presidential Commission for the Study of Bioethical Issues 2010. *New Directions: The Ethics of Synthetic Biology and Emerging Technologies*. Washington, DC: Presidential Commission for the Study of Bioethical Issues.

Proctor, R. N. 1999. *The Nazi War on Cancer*. Princeton, NJ: Princeton University Press.

Przeworski, A. & J. Vreeland 2000. "The Effect of IMF Programs on Economic Growth". *Journal of Development Economics* 62: 385–421.

Pyle, R. M. 2002. "Eden in a Vacant Lot: Special Places, Species and Kids in the Neighbourhood of Life". In *Children and Nature: Psychological, Sociocultural and Evolutionary Investigations*, P. H. Kahn & S. R. Kellert (eds), 305–28. Cambridge, MA: MIT Press.

Qiu, R.-Z. 2011. "A Chinese Perspective". Paper presented at the twentieth anniversary symposium of the Nuffield Council on Bioethics on "Global Health: Responsibility, Ethics and Policy", 22 June, London.

Quan-Haase, A. & B. Wellman 2004. "How Does the Internet Affect Social Capital?" In *Social Capital and Information Technology*, M. Huysman & V. Wolf (eds), 113–31. Cambridge, MA: MIT Press.

Quigley, M. 2007. "Property and the Body: Applying Honoré". *Journal of Medical Ethics* 32(11): 631–34.

Quong, J. 2006. "Cultural Exemptions, Expensive Tastes, and Equal Opportunities". *Journal of Applied Philosophy* 23: 55–73.

Radcliffe-Richards, J. 2010. "Consent with Inducements: The Case of Body Parts and Services". In *The Ethics of Consent: Theory and Practice*, F. G. Miller & A. Wertheimer (eds), 281–303. New York: Oxford University Press.

Radcliffe-Richards, J. *et al.* 1998. "The Case for Allowing Kidney Sales. International Forum for Transplant Ethics". *Lancet* 351(9120): 1950–52.

Radin, M. J. 1987. "Market-Inalienability". *Harvard Law Review* 100(8): 1849–1937.

——1996. *Contested Commodities: The Trouble with Trade in Sex, Children, Body Parts, and Other Things*. Cambridge, MA: Harvard University Press.

Radin, T. J. & M. Calkins 2006. "The Struggle against Sweatshops: Moving Toward Responsible Global Business". *Journal of Business Ethics* 66(2–3): 261–72.

Rahnema, M. 1991. "Global Poverty: A Pauperizing Myth". *Interculture* 24(2): 4–51.

——[1992] 2010. "Poverty". In *The Development Dictionary*, 2nd edn, W. Sachs (ed.), 158–76. London: Zed Books.

Rahnema, M. & V. Bawtree (eds) 1997. *The Post-Development Reader*. London: Zed Books.

Railton, P. 2003. "Locke, Stock, and Peril: Natural Property Rights, Pollution, and Risk". In his *Facts, Values and Norms*, 187–225. New York: Cambridge University Press.

Ramsey, P. 2002. *The Just War: Force and Political Responsibility*. Lanham, MD: Rowman & Littlefield.

Rao, R. 2000. "Property, Privacy and the Human Body". *Boston University Law Review* 80(2): 359–460.

——2007. "Genes and Spleens: Property, Contract, or Privacy Rights in the Human Body?" *Journal of Law, Medicine and Ethics* 35(3): 371–82.

Rapkin, D. & J. Strand 2006. "Reforming the IMF's Weighted Voting System". *The World Economy* 29(3): 305–24.

Rapley, J. 2007. *Understanding Development*, 2nd edn. Boulder, CO: Lynne Rienner.

Rasche, A. & G. Kell (eds) 2010. *The United Nations Global Compact: Achievements, Trends and Challenges*. Cambridge: Cambridge University Press.

Rawlings, L. & G. Rubio 2005. "Evaluating the Impact of Conditional Cash Transfer Programs". *The World Bank Observer* 20: 29–55.

Rawls, J. 1971. *A Theory of Justice*. Cambridge, MA: Harvard University Press.

——1993. *Political Liberalism*. New York: Columbia University Press.

——1998. *A Theory of Justice*, rev. edn. Cambridge, MA: Harvard University Press.

——1999a. *A Theory of Justice*, 2nd edn. Cambridge, MA: Belknap Press of Harvard University Press.

——1999b. *A Theory of Justice*, rev. edn. Oxford: Oxford University Press.

——1999c. *The Law of Peoples with "The Idea of Public Reason Revisited"*. Cambridge, MA: Harvard University Press.

——2001. *Justice as Fairness: A Restatement*, E. Kelly (ed.). Cambridge, MA: The Belknap Press of Harvard University Press.

——2002. *The Law of Peoples*. Cambridge, MA: Harvard University Press.

——2005. *Political Liberalism*, expanded edn. New York: Columbia University Press.

Raymond, J. 2003. "10 reasons for not legalizing prostitution". Prostitution Research & Education. www. prostitutionresearch.com/laws/000022.html.

Raz, J. 2010. "Human Rights without Foundations". In *The Philosophy of International Law*, S. Besson & J. Tasioulas (eds), 321–38. Oxford: Oxford University Press.

Regan, R. 1996. *Just War: Principles and Cases*. Washington, DC: Catholic University Press of America.

Regan, T. 1983. *The Case for Animal Rights*. London: Routledge & Kegan Paul.

Reidy, D. 2006. "Political Authority and Human Rights". In *Rawls's Law of Peoples: A Realistic Utopia?*, R. Martin & D. Reidy (eds), 169–88. Malden, MA: Blackwell.

Reisman, W. & C. Antoniou (eds) 1994. *The Laws of War*. New York: Vintage.

Reitberger, M. 2008. "Poverty, Negative Duties, and the Global Institutional Order". *Politics, Philosophy and Economics* 7(4): 379–402.

Rejali, D. 2007. *Torture and Democracy*. Princeton, NJ: Princeton University Press.

Rendall, M. 2011. "Climate Change and the Threat of Disaster: The Moral Case for Taking Out Insurance at Our Grandchildren's Expense". *Political Studies* 59(4): 884–99.

Rengger, N. J. 2000. *International Relations, Political Theory and the Problem of Order: Beyond International Relations Theory?* London: Routledge.

Ricardo, D. [1817] 1821. *On the Principles of Political Economy and Taxation*, 3rd edn. London: John Murray. www.econlib.org/library/Ricardo/ricP.html (accessed May 2014).

Richards, R. 2010. *The Species Problem: A Philosophical Analysis*. Cambridge: Cambridge University Press.

Ricoeur, P. 1992. *Oneself as Another*. Chicago, IL: University of Chicago Press.

Riddell, R. 2008. *Does Foreign Aid Really Work?* Oxford: Oxford University Press.

Riley, J. 2010. "Mill's Extraordinary Utilitarian Moral Theory". *Politics, Philosophy, and Economics* 9: 67–116.

Risse, M. 2005a. "How Does the Global Order Harm the Poor?" *Philosophy and Public Affairs* 33(4): 349–76.

——2005b. "What We Owe to the Global Poor". *Journal of Ethics* 9(1/2): 81–117.

——2006. "What to Say About the State". *Social Theory and Practice* 32: 671–98.

——2012. *On Global Justice*. Princeton, NJ: Princeton University Press.

Rist, G. 2008. *The History of Development: From Western Origins to Global Faith*. London: Zed Books.

Ritter, P. 2008. "Legalizing the Organ Trade?" *Time* (19 August). www.time.com/time/world/article/0,8599,1833858,00.html (accessed April 2012).

Ritzer, G. 2004. *The Globalization of Nothing*. Thousand Oaks, CA: Sage.

——[1993] 2008. *The McDonaldization of Society*, 5th edn. Thousand Oaks, CA: Sage.

——2010. *Globalization: A Basic Text*. Oxford: Basil Blackwell.

Robb, J. 2008. *Brave New War: The Next Stage of Terrorism and the End of Globalization*. New York: John Wiley & Sons.

Roberts, A. & R. Guelff (eds) 1999. *Documents on the Laws of War*. Oxford: Oxford University Press.

Roberts, D. 1997. *Killing the Black Body. Race, Reproduction, and the Meaning of Liberty*. New York: Random House.

Roberts, M. 2002. "A New Way of Doing the Best We Can: Person-Based Consequentialism and the Equality Problem". *Ethics* 112: 315–50.

——2009. "The Non-Identity Problem". In *Stanford Encyclopedia of Philosophy*, Edward N. Zalta (ed.). http://plato.stanford.edu/archives/fall2009/entries/nonidentity-problem (accessed April 2014).

Roberts, M. & D. Wasserman (eds) 2009. *Harming Future Persons: Ethics, Genetics and the Nonidentity Problem*. Dordrecht: Springer.

Robertson, R. 1992. *Globalization: Social Theory and Global Culture*. London: Sage Publications.

Robeyns, I. 2005. "Assessing Global Poverty and Inequality: Income, Resources, and Capabilities". *Metaphilosophy* 36(1/2): 30–49.

——2006. "The Capability Approach in Practice". *Journal of Political Philosophy* 14(3): 351–76.

Robinson, F. 1999. *Globalizing Care: Ethics, Feminist Theory, and International Affairs*. Boulder, CO: Westview Press.

——2006. "Care, Gender and Global Social Justice: Rethinking 'Ethical Globalization'". *Journal of Global Ethics* 2(1): 5–25.

——2011a. *The Ethics of Care: A Feminist Approach to Human Security*. Philadelphia, PA: Temple University Press.

——2011b. "Care, Gender and Global Social Justice". In *Feminist Ethics and Social Policy: Towards a New Global Political Economy of Care*, R. Mahon & F. Robinson (eds), 127–44. Vancouver: University of British Columbia Press.

Rodin, D. 2005. *War and Self-Defence*. Oxford: Oxford University Press.

——forthcoming. "Explaining the Absolute Prohibition of Torture".

Rodrik, D. 2001. "The Global Governance of Trade: As if Development Really Mattered". United Nations Development Programme Background Paper. http://files.wcfia.harvard.edu/529 – Rodrik5.pdf (accessed April 2014).

——2011. *The Globalization Paradox: Democracy and the Future of the World Economy*. New York: W.W. Norton.

Roemer, J. 1996. *Theories of Distributive Justice*. Cambridge, MA: Harvard University Press.

Rohter, L. 2006. "The Organ Seller". In *Men of the Global South: A Reader*, A. Jones (ed.), 179–82. New York: Zed Books.

Rolston, III, H. 1989. *Philosophy Gone Wild*. New York: Prometheus Books.

——1996. "Feeding People versus Saving Nature?" See Aiken & LaFollette (1996), 248–67.

——2012. *A New Environmental Ethics: The Next Millenium for Life on Earth*. London: Routledge.

Rorty, R. 1993. "Human Rights, Rationality and Sentimentality". In *On Human Rights: Oxford Amnesty Lectures*, S. Shute & S. Hurley (eds), 111–34. New York: Basic Books.

Rosenberg, C. M. 2013. *Child Labor in America*. Jefferson, NC: McFarland.

Rosenzweig, M. 2003. *Win–Win Ecology: How the Earth's Species Can Survive in the Midst of Human Enterprise*. Oxford: Oxford University Press.

Ross, M. 1999. "The Political Economy of the Resource Curse". *World Politics* 51: 297–322.

——2012. *The Oil Curse: How Petroleum Wealth Shapes the Development of Nations*. Princeton, NJ: Princeton University Press.

Ross, W. D. 1930. *The Right and the Good*. Oxford: Clarendon Press.

Rostow, W. 1960. *The Stages of Economic Growth: A Non-communist Manifesto*. Cambridge: Cambridge University Press.

Rowlands, M. 2000. Review of G. E. Varner, *In Nature's Interests: Interests, Animal Rights, and Environmental Ethics*. *Philosophical Review* 109: 598–601.

Ruddick, S. 1980. "Maternal Thinking". *Feminist Studies* 6: 342–67.

——1989. *Maternal Thinking: Toward a Politics of Peace*. Boston, MA: Beacon Press.

——2009. "On *Maternal Thinking*". *Women's Studies Quarterly* 37(3–4): 305–8.

Ruggie, J. 2013. *Just Business. Multinational Corporations and Human Rights*. New York: W. W. Norton.

Rural Migration News (RMN) 1996. "Mexican Tomatoes and Avocados". *Rural Migration News* 2(4) (October). http://migration.ucdavis.edu/rmn/more.php?id=159_0_5_0 (accessed April 2014).

Ryan, M. P. 1998. *Knowledge Diplomacy: Global Competition and the Politics of Intellectual Property*. Washington, DC: Brookings Institution Press.

Ryberg, J. & T. Tannsjo (eds) 2004. *The Repugnant Conclusion: Essays on Population Ethics*. Dordrecht: Kluwer.

Ryder, G. 2010. "The Promise of the Global Compact: A Trade Union Perspective on the Labour Principles". In *The United Nations Global Compact: Achievements, Trends and Challenges*, A. Rasche & G. Kell (eds), 44–58. Cambridge: Cambridge University Press.

SABAF 2013. "Annual Report 2012". http://rapportoannualesabaf.com/2012/en (accessed August 2013).

Sachs, J. D. 2005. *The End of Poverty: How We Can Make it Happen in Our Lifetime*. London: Penguin Books.

Sachs, W. (ed.) [1992] 2010. *The Development Dictionary*, 2nd edn. London: Zed Books.

Saeed, F. 2002. *Taboo: The Hidden Culture of a Red Light Area*. Oxford: Oxford University Press.

Sagoff, M. 1988. *The Economy of the Earth: Philosophy, Law, and the Environment*. Cambridge: Cambridge University Press.

——1997. "Do We Consume Too Much?" *Atlantic Monthly* 279(6): 80.

——2003. "Cows are Better than Condos, or How Economists Help Solve Environmental Problems". *Environmental Values* 12(4): 449–70.

——2004. *The Philosophical Common Sense of Pollution: Price, Principle, and the Environment*. New York: Cambridge University Press.

Salitan, L. 1994. "The Tomato as Economic Metaphor". *Human Economy* 14(2): 10.

Sandel, M. 2012. *What Money Can't Buy: The Moral Limits of Markets*. New York: Farrar Straus & Giroux.

Sanders, T. 2005. *Sex Work: A Risky Business*. Cullompton: Willan.

Sandler, R. 2007. *Character and Environment: A Virtue-Oriented Approach to Environmental Ethics*. New York: Columbia University Press.

——2010. "Ethical Theory and the Problem of Inconsequentialism: Why Environmental Ethicists Should be Virtue-Oriented Ethicists". *Journal of Agricultural and Environmental Ethics* 23: 167–83.

Sands, P. 2008. *Torture Team: Deception, Cruelty and the Compromise of Law*. London: Allen Lane.

Sanghera, J. 2005. "Unpacking the Trafficking Discourse". In *Trafficking and Prostitution Reconsidered*, K. Kempadoo, J. Sanghera & B. Pattanaik (eds), 3–24. London: Paradigm.

Sangiovanni, A. 2007. "Global Justice, Reciprocity and the State". *Philosophy and Public Affairs* 35(1): 3–39.

Santelli, J. *et al.* 2003. "The Measurement and Meaning of Unintended Pregnancy". *Perspectives on Reproductive and Sexual Health* 35(2): 94–101.

Santoro, M. A. 2000. *Profits and Principles: Global Capitalism and Human Rights in China*. Ithaca, NY: Cornell University Press.

——2003. "Beyond Codes of Conduct and Monitoring: An Organizational Integrity Approach to Global Labor Practices". *Human Rights Quarterly* 25(2): 407–24.

——2009. *China 2020: How Western Business Can – and Should – Influence Social and Political Change in the Coming Decade*. Ithaca, NY: Cornell University Press.

——2010. "Post-Westphalia and its Discontents: Business, Globalization, and Human Rights in Political and Moral Perspective". *Business Ethics Quarterly* 20(2): 285–97.

Sarkar, S. 2005. *Biodiversity and Environmental Philosophy: An Introduction*. Cambridge: Cambridge University Press.

Sassen, S. [2005] 2008. *Territory, Authority, Rights: From Medieval to Global Assemblages*, 2nd edn. Princeton, NJ: Princeton University Press.

Satz, D. 2003. "Child Labor: A Normative Perspective". *World Bank Economic Review* 17(2): 297–309.

——2011. *Why Some Things Should Not be for Sale: The Moral Limits of Markets*. New York: Oxford University Press.

Savulescu, J. 2003. "Is the Sale of Body Parts Wrong?" *Journal of Medical Ethics* 29(3): 138–39.

Savulescu, J. & G. Kahane 2009. "The Moral Obligation to Create Children with the Best Chance of the Best Life." *Bioethics* 23(5): 274–90.

Scanlon, T. 1998. *What We Owe to Each Other*. Cambridge, MA: Harvard University Press.

Schachter, O. 1984. "The Legality of Pro-Democratic Invasion". *American Journal of International Law* 78(3): 645–49.

Schafer, A. 2004. "Biomedical Conflicts of Interest: A Defense of the Sequestration Thesis – Learning from the Cases of Nancy Oliviery and David Healy". *Journal of Medical Ethics* 30: 8–24.

Scheffler, S. 1985. *The Role of Consent in the Legitimation of Risky Activity. To Breathe Freely: Risk, Consent, and Air*, M. Gibson (ed.). Totowa, NJ: Rowman & Allenheld.

——2001. *Boundaries and Allegiances: Problems of Justice and Responsibility in Liberal Thought*. Oxford: Oxford University Press.

——2010. *Equality and Tradition: Questions of Value in Moral and Political Theory*. New York: Oxford University Press.

Schell, J. (ed.) 1984. *The Abolition*. New York: Knopf.

Scheper-Hughes, N. 2003. "Rotten Trade: Millennial Capitalism, Human Values and Global Justice in Organs Trafficking". *Journal of Human Rights* 2(2): 197–226.

Scherer, A. G. & G. Palazzo 2007. "Toward a Political Conception of Corporate Responsibility: Business and Society Seen from a Habermasian Perspective". *Academy of Management Review* 32(4): 1096–1120.

——2011. "A New Political Role of Business in a Globalized World: A Review and Research Agenda". *Journal of Management Studies* 48(4): 899–931.

Schmidtz, D. 2002. "Are All Animals Equal?" In *Environmental Ethics: What Really Matters, What Really Works*, D. Schmidtz & E. Willott (eds), 96–103. Oxford: Oxford University Press.

——2006. *Elements of Justice*. Cambridge: Cambridge University Press.

Schneider, I. 2009. "Can Patent Legislation Make a Difference? Bringing Parliaments and Civil Society into Patent Governance". In *Politics of Intellectual Property*, S. Haunss & K. C. Shadlen (eds), 129–57. Cheltenham: Edward Elgar.

Scholte, J. A. 2005. *Globalization: A Critical Introduction*, 2nd edn. Basingstoke: Palgrave Macmillan.

Schor, J. 1999. "The New Politics of Consumption: Why Americans Want So Much More Than They Need". *Boston Review* (Summer). http://pages.ucsd.edu/~aronatas/Schor%20et%20al%20New%20Politics%20of%20Consumption%201999.pdf (accessed May 2014).

Schudson, M. 1998. "Delectable Materialism: Second Thoughts on Consumer Culture". See Crocker & Linden (1998b), 249–68.

Schüklenk, U. 2004. "The Standard of Care Debate: Against the Myth of an International Consensus Opinion". *Journal of Medical Ethics* 30: 194–97.

Schüklenk, U. & R. E. Ashcroft 2000. "International Research Ethics". *Bioethics* 14: 158–72.

Schüklenk, U. & A. Kleinsmidt 2006. "North–South Benefit-Sharing Arrangements in Bioprospecting and Genetic Research: A Critical Ethical and Legal Analysis". *Developing World Bioethics* 6: 122–34.

Schüklenk, U. & J. Lott 2004. "Bioethics and Public Policy". In *Bioethics in a Small World*, F. Thiele (ed.), 129–38. Berlin: Springer.

Schüklenk, U., E. Stein, J. Kerin & W. Byne 1997. "The Ethics of Genetic Research on Sexual Orientation". *Hastings Center Report* 27(4): 6–13.

Schulz-Baldes, A., N. Biller-Andorno & A. M. Capron 2007. "International Perspectives on the Ethics and Regulation of Human Cell and Tissue Transplantation". *WHO Bulletin* 85(12): 941–48.

Schumacher, E. F. 1974. *Small is Beautiful*. London: Abacus.

Schwartz, M. S. 2011. *Corporate Social Responsibility: An Ethical Approach*. Peterborough, ON: Broadview Press.

Schwartz, M. S. & A. B. Carroll 2003. "Corporate Social Responsibility: A Three-Domain Approach". *Business Ethics Quarterly* 13(4): 503–30.

Segal, J. 1998. "Consumer Expenditures and the Growth of NRI". See Crocker & Linden (1998b), 176–97.

Seglow, J. 2005. "The Ethics of Immigration". *Political Studies Review* 3(3): 317–34.

Sen, A. 1983. "Poor, Relatively Speaking". *Oxford Economic Papers* 35(2): 153–69.

——1984. "Goods and People". In *Resources, Values and Development*, A. Sen (ed.), 509–32. Oxford: Basil Blackwell.

——1992. *Inequality Reexamined*. Cambridge, MA: Harvard University Press.

——[1980] 1997. "Equality of What?" In *Choice, Welfare and Measurement*, A. Sen (ed.), 353–72. Cambridge, MA: Harvard University Press.

——1998. "The Living Standard". See Crocker & Linden (1998b), 277–311.

——1999. *Development as Freedom*. Oxford: Oxford University Press.

——2004. "Elements of a Theory of Human Rights". *Philosophy and Public Affairs* 32(4): 315–56.

——[1988] 2008. "The Concept of Development". In *Global Ethics: Seminal Ethics*, T. Pogge & K. Horton (eds), 157–80. St Paul, MN: Paragon House.

——2009. *The Idea of Justice*. Cambridge, MA: Harvard University Press.

Sevenhuijsen, S. 1998. *Citizenship and the Ethics of Care: Feminist Considerations on Justice, Morality and Politics*. London: Routledge.

Shachar, A. 2009. *The Birthright Lottery: Citizenship and Global Inequality*. Cambridge, MA: Harvard University Press.

Sharp, G. 2005. "The Technique of Nonviolent Action". In *Nonviolence in Theory and Practice*, 2nd edn, R. Holmes & B. Gan (eds), 253–56. Long Grove, IL: Waveland.

Shell 2013. "Shell at a Glance". www.shell.com/global/aboutshell/at-a-glance.html (accessed August 2013).

Shrader-Frechette, K. 2007. "Human Rights and Duties to Alleviate Environmental Injustice: The Domestic Case". *Journal of Human Rights* 6: 107–30.

——2011. *Taking Action, Saving Lives: Our Duties to Protect Environmental and Public Health*. Oxford: Oxford University Press.

Shue, H. 1978. "Torture". *Philosophy and Public Affairs* 7(2): 124–43.

——1988. "Mediating Duties". *Ethics* 98: 687–704.

——1993. "Subsistence Emissions and Luxury Emissions". *Law and Policy* 15(1): 39–59.

——1995. "Avoidable Necessity: Global Warming, International Fairness, and Alternative Energy". In *Nomos XXXVII: Theory and Practice*, I. Shapiro & J. Wagner (eds), 239–64. New York: New York University Press.

——1996a. "Solidarity Among Strangers and the Right to Food". See Aiken & LaFollette (1996), 113–32.

——[1980] 1996b. *Basic Rights: Subsistence, Affluence, and US Foreign Policy*, 2nd edn. Princeton, NJ: Princeton University Press.

——1999. "Global Environment and International Inequality". *International Affairs* 75(3): 531–45.

——2002 "Global Environment and International Inequality". In *Environmental Ethics: What Really Matters, What Really Works*, D. Schmidtz & E. Willott (eds), 531–45. Oxford: Oxford University Press.

——2003. "The Debate on Torture: Response". *Dissent* 50: 90–91.

——2004. "Thickening Convergence: Human Rights and Cultural Diversity". See Chatterjee (2004), 217–41.

——2006. "Torture in Dreamland". *Case Western Reserve Journal of International Law* 37: 231–39.

——2009. "Making Exceptions". *Journal of Applied Philosophy* 26: 307–22.

——2010. "Deadly Delays, Saving Opportunities: Creating a More Dangerous World?". In *Climate Ethics: Essential Readings*, S. M. Gardiner, S. Caney, D. Jamieson & H. Shue (eds), 146–62. New York: Oxford University Press.

Shultz, G. P., W. J. Perry, H. A. Kissinger & S. Nunn 2007. "A World Free of Nuclear Weapons". *Wall Street Journal* (January 4). http://online.wsj.com/news/articles/SB116787515251566636 (accessed May 2014).

Siden, A. 2002: *Warte Mal! Prostitution after the Velvet Revolution*. London: Hayward Gallery.

Silver, D. 2005. "A Strawsonian Defense of Corporate Moral Responsibility". *American Philosophical Quarterly* 42(4): 279–93

Silvey, R. 2004. "Transnational Domestication: Indonesian Domestic Workers in Saudi Arabia". *Political Geography*, special issue on gendering the state, 23(4): 245–64.

Simmons, A. J. 1979. *Moral Principles and Political Obligations*. Princeton, NJ: Princeton University Press.

——2000. *Justification and Legitimacy: Essays on Rights and Obligations*. Cambridge: Cambridge University Press.

Singer, H. 1950. "The Distribution of Gains Between Investing and Borrowing Countries". *American Economic Review* 40(2): 473–85.

Singer, P. 1972. "Famine, Affluence, and Morality". *Philosophy and Public Affairs* 1(3): 229–43.

——1975. *Animal Liberation: A New Ethics for our Treatment of Animals*. New York: New York Review/ Random House.

——1993. *Practical Ethics*, 2nd edn. Cambridge: Cambridge University Press.

——2002. *One World: The Ethics of Globalization*. New Haven, CT: Yale University Press.

——2004. "Outsiders: Our Obligations to Those Beyond Our Borders". See Chatterjee (2004), 11–32.

——2006. *Children at War*. Berkeley, CA: University of California Press.

——2009. *Wired for War*. New York: Penguin.

——2011a. *The Expanding Circle: Ethics, Evolution, and Moral Progress*. Princeton, NJ: Princeton University Press.

——2011b. *Practical Ethics*. Cambridge: Cambridge University Press.

Singh, A. 2013. *Globalizing Torture: CIA Secret Detention and Extraordinary Rendition*. New York: Open Society Justice Initiative.

Sismondo, S. & M. Doucet 2009. "Publication Ethics and the Ghost Management of Medical Publication". *Bioethics* 24: 273–83.

Skoufias, E. & B. McClafferty 2001. *Is PROGRESA Working? Summary of the Results of an Evaluation by IFPRI*. FCND Discussion Paper No. 118. Washington, DC: The International Food Policy Research Institute.

Slim, H. 2008. *Killing Civilians: Method, Madness and Morality in War*. New York: Columbia University Press.

Slote, M. A. 2007. *The Ethics of Care and Empathy*. London: Routledge.

Smith, A. 1776. *An Inquiry into the Nature and Causes of the Wealth of Nations*. New York: Modern Library Edition. www.econlib.org/library/Smith/smWN13.html#B.IV (accessed May 2014).

Smith, K., T. Fordelone & F. Zimmerman 2010. "Beyond the DAC: The Welcome Role of Other Providers in Development Co-operation". OECD DCD Issues Brief 2010. www.oecd.org/investment/ stats/45361474.pdf (accessed November 2013).

Smith, M. 1994. *The Moral Problem*. Oxford: Blackwell.

Snyder, J. 2008. "Needs Exploitation". *Ethical Theory and Moral Practice* 11(4): 389–405.

——2010. "Exploitation and Sweatshop Labor: Perspectives and Issues". *Business Ethics Quarterly* 20(2): 187–213.

Sobhan, R. 2010. *Challenging the Injustice of Poverty: Agendas for Inclusive Development in South Asia*. New Delhi: Sage Publications India.

Solow, R. M. 1993a. "Sustainability: An Economist's Perspective". In *Economics of the Environment: Selected Writings*, N. Dorfman & R. Dorfman (eds), 179–87. New York: Norton.

Solow, R. M. 1993b. "An Almost Practical Step toward Sustainability". *Resources Policy* 19: 162–72.

Spash, C. L. 2002. *Greenhouse Economics: Value and Ethics*. New York: Routledge.

Srinivasan, T. N. 1998. *Developing Countries and the Multilateral Trading System: From the GATT (1947) to the Uruguay Round and the Future.* Boulder, CO: Westview Press.

Stears, M. 2005. "The Vocation of Political Theory: Principles, Empirical Inquiry, and the Politics of Opportunity". *European Journal of Political Theory* 4: 325–50.

Steiner, H.1994. *An Essay on Rights.* Oxford: Blackwell.

——1999. "Just Taxation and International Redistribution". In *Nomos XLI: Global Justice*, I. Shapiro & L. Brilmayer (eds), 171–91. New York: New York University Press.

——2001. "Hard Borders, Compensation, and Classical Liberalism". In *Boundaries and Justice: Diverse Ethical Perspectives*, D. Miller & S. H. Hashmi (eds), 79–88. Princeton, NJ: Princeton University Press.

——2002. "The Right to Trade in Human Body Parts". *Critical Review of International Social and Political Philosophy* 5(4): 187–93.

——2005. "Territorial Justice and Global Redistribution". See Brock & Brighouse (2005), 28–38.

——2008. "May Lockean Doughnuts Have Holes? The Geometry of Territorial Jurisdiction: A Response to Nine". *Political Studies* 56: 949–56.

Steinfeld, R. 1991. *The Invention of Free Labor.* Chapel Hill, NC: University of North Carolina Press.

——2001. *Coercion, Contract and Free Labor in the Nineteenth Century.* Cambridge: Cambridge University Press.

Steinman, M., P. Sykora & U. Wiesing (eds) 2009. *Altruism Reconsidered: Exploring New Approaches to Property in Human Tissue.* Aldershot: Ashgate.

Sterba, J. 1998. *From Liberty to Equality: Justice for Here and Now.* Cambridge: Cambridge University Press.

——(ed.) 2003. *Terrorism and International Justice.* Oxford: Oxford University Press.

Sterckx, S. 2005. "Can Drug Patents be Morally Justified?" *Science and Engineering Ethics* 11(1): 81–92.

Stern, N. 2006. "Stern Review: The Economics of Climate Change". http://webarchive.nationalarchives. gov.uk/+/http://www.hm-treasury.gov.uk/sternreview_index.htm (accessed April 2014).

——2007. *The Economics of Climate Change: The Stern Review.* Cambridge: Cambridge University Press.

Sternberg, E. 2000. *Just Business: Business Ethics in Action*, 2nd edn. Oxford: Oxford University Press.

Stiglitz, J. 2003. *Globalization and its Discontents.* New York: W. W. Norton & Company.

——2006. *Making Globalization Work.* New York: W. W. Norton & Company.

——2012. *The Price of Inequality: How Today's Divided Society Endangers Our Future.* New York: W. W. Norton.

Stiglitz, J. & A. Charlton 2006. *Fair Trade for All: How Trade Can Promote Development.* Oxford: Oxford University Press.

Stiglitz, J., A. Sen & J. Fitoussi 2009. "Report by the Commission on the Measurement of Economic Performance and Social Progress". www.stiglitz-sen-fitoussi.fr/documents/rapport_anglais.pdf (accessed April 2014).

Stilz, A. 2011. "Nations, States, and Territory". *Ethics* 121: 572–601.

Stone, C. D. 1972. "Should Trees Have Standing? – Toward Legal Rights for Natural Objects". *Southern California Law Review* 45: 450–501.

——1987. *Earth and Other Ethics: The Case for Moral Pluralism.* New York: Harper & Row.

Stout, L. 2012. *The Shareholder Value Myth: How Putting Shareholders First Harms Investors, Corporations, and the Public.* San Francisco, CA: Berrett-Koehler Publishers.

Strudlow, A. & E. Curlow 1998. "Consumption as Culture: A Desert Example". See Crocker & Linden (1998b), 269–86.

Sumner, A. 2010. *Global Poverty and the New Bottom Billion: Three-Quarters of the World's Poor Live in Middle-Income Countries.* IDS Working Paper 349. Brighton: Institute of Development Studies.

——2012. *Where Do the World's Poor Live? A New Update.* IDS Working Paper 393. Brighton: Institute of Development Studies.

Sussman, D. 2005. "What's Wrong with Torture?" *Philosophy and Public Affairs* 33: 1–33.

SustainAbility 2013. "Rate the Raters". www.sustainability.com/projects/rate-the-raters (accessed August 2013).

Sykora, P. 2009. "Altruism in Medical Donations Reconsidered: The Reciprocity Approach". See Steinman *et al.* (2009), 13–50.

Sypnowich, C. 2005. "Cosmopolitans, Cosmopolitanisms, and Human Flourishing". See Brock & Brighouse (2005), 55–74.

Talbott, W. 2005. *Which Rights Should be Universal?* Oxford: Oxford University Press.

——2010. *Human Rights and Human Well-Being.* Oxford: Oxford University Press.

Tamir, Y. 1993. *Liberal Nationalism.* Princeton, NJ: Princeton University Press.

Tan, K. C. 2000. *Toleration, Diversity, and Global Justice*. University Park, PA: Penn State University Press.

——2004. *Justice Without Borders: Cosmopolitanism, Nationalism, and Patriotism*. Cambridge: Cambridge University Press.

——2005. "The Demands of Justice and National Allegiance". See Brock & Brighouse (2005), 164–79.

Tanaka, Y. 2001. *Japan's Comfort Women: Sexual Slavery and Prostitution During World War II and the US Occupation*. London: Routledge.

Tasioulas, J. 2007. "The Moral Reality of Human Rights". In *Freedom from Poverty as a Human Right*, T. Pogge (ed.), 75–101. Oxford: Oxford University Press.

——2010. "Taking Rights out of Human Rights". *Ethics* 120: 647–78.

Taylor, A. L. 2007. "Addressing the Global Tragedy of Needless Pain: Rethinking the United Nations Single Convention on Narcotic Drugs". *Journal of Law, Medicine and Ethics* 35: 556–70.

Taylor, C. 1999. "Conditions of an Unforced Consensus on Human Rights". In *The East Asian Challenge for Human Rights*, J. Bauer & D. Bell (eds), 124–44. Cambridge: Cambridge University Press.

——2008. *Modern Social Imaginaries*. Durham, NC: Duke University Press.

Taylor, P. W. 1981. "The Ethics of Respect for Nature". *Environmental Ethics* 3: 197–218.

——1986. *Respect for Nature*. Princeton, NJ: Princeton University Press.

TEEB 2010. *The Economics of Ecosystems and Biodiversity: Mainstreaming the Economics of Nature: A Synthesis of the Approach, Conclusions and Recommendations of TEEB*. London: Earthscan. www.teebweb.org/wp-content/uploads/Study%20and%20Reports/Reports/Synthesis%20report/TEEB%20Synthesis%20Report%202010.pdf (accessed June 2014).

Teichman, J. 1986. *Pacifism and the Just War*. Oxford: Basil Blackwell.

Tenenbein, M. 2005. "Unit-Dose Packaging of Iron Supplements and Reduction of Iron Poisoning in Young Children". *Arch Pediatr Adolesc Med* 159(6): 557–60.

Tesón, F. R. 1997. *Humanitarian Intervention: An Inquiry into Law and Morality*, 2nd edn. New York: Transnational Publishers.

——1998. *A Philosophy of International Law*. Boulder, CO: Westview Press.

——2003. "The Liberal Case for Humanitarian Intervention". In *Humanitarian Intervention: Ethical, Legal and Political Dilemmas*, J. L. Holzgrefe & R. O. Keohane (eds.), 93–129. Cambridge: Cambridge University Press.

Testai, P. 2008. "Debt as a Route to Modern Slavery in the Discourse on 'Sex Trafficking': Myth or Reality?" *Human Security Journal* 6: 68–77.

Tetlock, P. E. 2003. "Thinking the Unthinkable: Sacred Values and Taboo Cognitions". *TRENDS in Cognitive Science* 7(7): 320–24.

Teuber, A. 1990. "Justifying Risk". *Daedalus* 119(4): 235–54.

Thompson, A. 2010. "Radical Hope for Living Well in a Warmer World". *Journal of Agricultural and Environmental Ethics* 23(1): 43–59.

Thompson, D. 2005. "Democracy in Time: Popular Sovereignty and Temporal Representation". *Constellations* 12(1): 245–61.

Thomson, J. J. 1980. "Rights and Compensation". *Nous* 14(1): 3–15.

——1992. *The Realm of Rights*. Cambridge, MA: Harvard University Press.

Tickner, J. A. 1992. *Gender in International Relations*. New York: Columbia University Press.

Tilman, D. 2000. "Causes, Consequences and Ethics of Biodiversity". *Nature* 405: 208–11.

Titmuss, R. M. 1970. *The Gift Relationship: From Human Blood to Social Policy*. London: George Allen & Unwin.

Tomlinson, J. 2003. "Globalization and Cultural Analysis". In *Globalization Theory: Approaches and Controversies. Global Transformations*, 2nd edn, D. Held & A. McGrew (eds.), 269–78. Cambridge: Polity.

——2007. *The Culture of Speed: The Coming of Immediacy*. London: Sage.

Tooke, J. D. 1975. *Just War in Aquinas and Grotius*. London: SPCK.

Townsend, P. 1979. *Poverty in the United Kingdom: A Survey of Household Resources and Standards of Living*. London: Allen Lane.

Toyota 2013. "Worldwide Operations". www.toyota-global.com/company/profile/facilities/worldwide_operations.html (accessed August 2013).

Tripathi, S. 2005. "International Regulation of Multinational Corporations". *Oxford Development Studies* 33(1): 117–31.

Tronto, J. C. 1993. *Moral Boundaries: A Political Argument for an Ethic of Care*. New York: Routledge.

——2008. "Is Peace Keeping Care Work?" In *Global Feminist Ethics: Feminist Ethics and Social Theory*, R. Whisnant & P. DesAutels (eds), 179–200. Lanham, MD: Rowman & Littlefield.

Truman, H. 1949. *Inaugural Addresses of the Presidents of the United States.* Washington, DC: USGPO. www. bartleby.com/124/pres53 (accessed May 2014).

Tuck, R. 1979. *Natural Rights Theories: Their Origin and Development.* Cambridge: Cambridge University Press.

——1999. *The Rights of War and Peace.* Oxford: Oxford University Press.

Tutton, R. 2009. "Notes on Policy, Language, and Human Tissue". See Steinman *et al.* (2009), 51–64.

Ulrich, P. 2008. *Integrative Economic Ethics. Foundations of a Civilized Market Economy.* Cambridge: Cambridge University Press.

UN General Assembly 1970. "Resolution Adopted by the General Assembly: 2626 (XXV). International Development Strategy for the Second United Nations Development Decade". 24 October. www.un-documents.net/a25r2626.htm (accessed April 2014).

UNCTAD 1994. *World Investment Report.* Geneva: United Nations Conference on Trade and Development.

——2002. "Are Transnationals Bigger than Countries?" Press Release. Geneva: United Nations Conference on Trade and Development.

——2009. *World Investment Report.* Geneva: United Nations Conference on Trade and Development.

——2011. *World Investment Report: Non-Equity Modes of International Production and Development.* Geneva: United Nations Conference on Trade and Development.

——2013. "Transnational Corporations (TNC)". http://unctad.org/en/Pages/DIAE/Transnational-corporations-(TNC).aspx (accessed August 2013).

UNEP 2011. "Towards a Green Economy: Pathways to Sustainable Development and Poverty Eradication". www.unep.org/greeneconomy/greeneconomyreport/tabid/29846/default.aspx (accessed April 2014).

Unger, R. M. 2007. *Free Trade Reimagined: The World Division of Labor and the Method of Economics.* Princeton, NJ: Princeton University Press.

UNICEF 2012. *Children in an Urban World: The State of the World's Children 2012.* New York: United Nations.

UNITED 2011. "List of 15551 Documented Refugee Deaths through Fortress Europe". https://docs.google.com/file/d/0B2UTLsd792i4NzgwNTJiNGEtZDEyNi00NDUwLWFmYjMtOGM5MTM2ZDY5ZTkw/edit?pli=1 (accessed April 2014).

United Nations 1945. *Charter of the United Nations.* www.un.org/en/documents/charter/index.shtml (accessed July 2012).

——1948. *Universal Declaration of Human Rights.* www.ohchr.org/EN/UDHR/Documents/60UDHR/bookleten.pdf (accessed August 2013).

——1966. *International Covenant on Civil and Political Rights.* www.ohchr.org/en/professionalinterest/pages/ccpr.aspx (accessed May 2014).

——1990. *Convention on the Rights of the Child.* New York: United Nations. www.ohchr.org/en/professionalinterest/pages/crc.aspx (accessed May 2014).

——2003. "Norms on the Responsibilities of Transnational Corporations and other Business Enterprises with Regard to Human Rights". www1.umn.edu/humanrts/links/norms-Aug2003.html (accessed August 2013).

——2004. *United Nations Convention Against Corruption.* Vienna: United Nations Office on Drugs and Crime.

——2005. *2005 World Summit Outcome,* A/RES/60/1. New York: United Nations.

——2007. *Declaration on the Rights of Indigenous Peoples.* www.ohchr.org/en/Issues/IPeoples/Pages/Declaration.aspx (accessed May 2014).

——2012a. *The Millennium Development Goals Report.* New York: United Nations.

——2012b. "Population Trends". www.un.org/en/development/desa/population/theme/trends/index.shtml (accessed May 2014).

United Nations Conference on Environment and Development 1992. *The Rio Declaration on Environment and Development.* www.un.org/documents/ga/conf151/aconf15126–1annex1.htm (accessed May 2014).

United Nations Department of Public Information 2010. "Goal 6: Combat HIV/AIDS, Malaria and Other Diseases". Fact Sheet DP1/2650 F/Rev.1. New York: UNDPI. www.un.org/millenniumgoals/pdf/MDG_FS_6_EN.pdf (accessed May 2014).

United Nations Development Fund for Women (UNIFEM) 2008. *Progress of the World's Women 2008/2009: Who Answers to Women.* New York: UNIFEM.

United Nations Development Programme 1990. *Human Development Report*. New York: Oxford University Press.

——2003. *Millennium Development Goals: A Compact among Nations to End Human Poverty. Human Development Report 2003*. New York: Oxford University Press.

——2010. *The Real Wealth of Nations: Pathways to Human Development. Human Development Report 2010*. Twentieth Anniversary edn. New York: Palgrave Macmillan.

——2011. *Sustainability and Equity: A Better Future for All. Human Development Report 2011*. New York: Palgrave Macmillan.

——2013. *Human Development Report 2013: The Rise of the South: Human Progress in a Diverse World*. New York: The United Nations Development Programme.

United Nations Global Compact 2013. "Overview of the Global Compact". www.unglobalcompact.org/AboutTheGC/index.html (accessed August 2013).

United Nations Security Council 1999. *Resolution 1265*. New York: United Nations. www.securitycouncilreport.org/atf/cf/%7B65BFCF9B-6D27–4E9C-8CD3-CF6E4FF96FF9%7D/Civilians%20SRES1265.pdf (accessed May 2014).

Upshur, R. E. G, J. V. Lavery & P. O. Tindana 2007. "Taking Tissue Seriously Means Taking Communities Seriously". *BioMed Central Medical Ethics* 8(11): 1–6.

US Department of Agriculture 1998. "The Impact of Methyl Bromide Alternatives in Tomato on Double-Cropped Cucumber". *Agricultural Research Services* 4(4). Washington, DC: US Department of Agriculture. www.ars.usda.gov/is/np/mba/oct98/impact.htm (accessed December 2008).

——1999. "Vegetables and Specialties – Summary". ERS–VGS–277. Washington, DC: US Department of Agriculture. http://usda.mannlib.cornell.edu/usda/ers/VGS//1990s/1999/VGS–04–22–1999_Summary.asc (accessed December 2008).

Valentini, L. 2011. *Justice in a Globalized World*. Oxford: Oxford University Press.

Valentino, B. A. 2011. "The True Costs of Humanitarian Intervention". *Foreign Affairs* 90(6) (November/December): 60–73.

Vanderheiden, S. 2008. *Atmospheric Justice: A Political Theory of Climate Change*. New York: Oxford University Press.

Van Evera, S. 1991. "American Intervention in the Third World: Less would be Better". *Security Studies* 1(1): 1–24.

Van Hooft, S. 2012. "Cosmopolitanism". See Chadwick (2012), vol. 1, 674–81.

Van Oosterhout, J. &. P. Heugens 2008. "Much Ado about Nothing: A Conceptual Critique of Corporate Social Responsibility". See Crane *et al.* (2008), 197–223.

Van Wensveen, L. 1999. *Dirty Virtues: The Emergence of Ecological Virtue Ethics*. Amherst, NY: Humanity Books.

Varner, G. E. 1998. *In Nature's Interest? Animal Rights and Environmental Ethics*. Oxford: Oxford University Press.

Vaughn, S. K. 2008. *Poverty, Justice, and Western Political Thought*. Lanham, MD: Lexington Books.

Veatch, R. 2003. "Why Liberals Should Accept Financial Incentives for Organ Procurement". *Kennedy Institute of Ethics Journal* 13(1): 19–36.

Velasquez, M. 1992. "International Business, Morality, and the Common Good". *Business Ethics Quarterly* 2(1): 27–40.

——2003. "Debunking Corporate Moral Agency". *Business Ethics Quarterly* 13(4): 531–62.

Venkatapuram, S. & M. G. Marmot 2011. *Health Justice: An Argument From the Capabilities Approach*. Cambridge: Polity Press.

Vincent, R. J. 1986. *Human Rights and International Relations*. Cambridge: Cambridge University Press.

Vogel, D. 2005. *The Market for Virtue: The Potential and Limits of Corporate Social Responsibility*. Washington, DC: Brookings Institution Press.

Voiculescu, A. & H. Yanacopulos 2011. "Human Rights in Business Context: An Overview". In *The Business of Human Rights: An Evolving Agenda for Corporate Responsibility*, A. Voiculescu & H. Yanacopulos (eds), 1–9. London: Zed Books.

Vreeland, J. 2006. *The International Monetary Fund: Politics of Conditional Lending*, new edn. New York: Routledge.

Waldby, C. & R. Mitchell 2006. *Tissue Economies: Blood, Organs, and Cell Lines in Late Capitalism*. Durham, NC: Duke University Press.

Waldron, J. 1992. "Minority Rights and the Cosmopolitan Alternative". *University of Michigan Journal of Law Reform* 25: 751–93.

——2005a. "Moral Autonomy and Personal Autonomy". In *Autonomy and the Challenges to Liberalism: New Essays*, J. Christman & J. Anderson (eds), 307–29. New York: Cambridge University Press.

——2005b. "Torture and Positive Law: Jurisprudence for the White House". *Columbia Law Review* 105: 1681–1750. Reprinted with revisions in J. Waldron 2010. *Torture, Terror, and Trade-Offs: Philosophy for the White House*, 186–260. Oxford: Oxford University Press.

——2012. "Property and Ownership". In *Stanford Encyclopedia of Philosophy*, E. N. Zalt, (ed.). http://plato. stanford.edu/archives/spr2012/entries/property (accessed April 2012).

Walmart 2013. "Our Story". http://corporate.walmart.com/our-story (accessed September 2013).

Walzer, M. 1977. *Just and Unjust Wars: A Moral Argument with Historical Illustrations*. New York: Basic Books.

——1983. *Spheres of Justice: A Defence of Pluralism and Equality*. Oxford: Basil Blackwood.

——1994. *Thick and Thin: Moral Argument at Home and Abroad*. Notre Dame, IN: Notre Dame University Press.

Wantchekon, L. 2002. "Why do Resource Abundant Countries Have Authoritarian Governments?" *Journal of African Finance and Economic Development* 5(2): 57–77.

Ward, M. 2009. "Identifying Absolute Global Poverty in 2005: The Measurement Question". See Mack *et al.* (2009), 37–49.

Warnock, M. 1993. "Philosophy and Ethics". In *Genetic Engineering: The New Challenge*, C. Cookson, G. Nowak & D. Thierbach (eds), 67–72. Munich: European Patent Office.

Warren, K. 2010. "The Illusiveness of Counting 'Victims' and the Concreteness of Ranking Countries: Trafficking in Persons from Colombia to Japan". In *Sex, Drugs and Body Counts: The Politics of Numbers in Global Crime and Conflict*, P. Andreas & K. Greenhill (eds), 110–26. Ithaca, NY: Cornell University Press.

Wasserman, D. 1998. "Consumption, Appropriation and Stewardship". See Crocker & Linden (1998b), 537–51.

Weijer, C. & G. J. LeBlanc 2006. "The Balm of Gilead: Is the Provision of Treatment to Those who Seroconvert in HIV Prevention Trials a Matter of Moral Obligation or Moral Negotiation?" *Journal of Law, Medicine and Ethics* 34(4): 793–808.

Weinstock, D. 2006. "The Real World of Global Democracy". *Journal of Social Philosophy* 37(1): 6–20.

Weiss, T. G. 2005. *Military–Civilian Interactions: Humanitarian Crises and the Responsibility to Protect*, 2nd edn. Lanham, MD: Rowman & Littlefield.

Weissman, F. 2010. "Not in Our Name: Why Médecins Sans Frontières Does Not Support the Responsibility to Protect". *Criminal Justice Ethics* 29(2): 194–207.

Weitzer, R. 2007. "The Social Construction of Sex Trafficking: Ideology and Institutionalization of a Moral Crusade". *Politics and Society* 35: 447–74.

Welch, D. 1993. *Justice and The Genesis of War*. Cambridge: Cambridge University Press.

Wellman, A. 2005. "Famine Relief: the Duty we Have to Others". See Cohen & Wellman (2005).

Wellman, C. H. 1996. "Liberalism, Political Legitimacy, and Samaritanism". *Philosophy and Public Affairs* 25 (3): 211–37.

——2008. "Immigration and Freedom of Association". *Ethics* 119(1): 109–41.

Wellman, C. H. & P. Cole 2011. *Debating the Ethics of Immigration: Is there a Right to Exclude?* New York: Oxford University Press.

Wenar, L. 2001. "Contractualism and Global Economic Justice". *Metaphilosophy* 32(1/2): 79–94.

——2008. "Property Rights and the Resource Curse". *Philosophy and Public Affairs* 36(1): 2–32.

——2010. "Realistic Reform of International Trade in Resources". In *Thomas Pogge and His Critics*, A. M. Jaggar (ed.), 123–50. New York: Polity.

Wendt, A. 1999. *Social Theory of International Relations*. Cambridge: Cambridge University Press.

Werhane, P. 1985. *Persons, Rights and Corporations*. Englewood Cliffs, NJ: Prentice Hall.

——2007. "Corporate Social Responsibility/Corporate Moral Responsibility: Is there a Difference and the Difference it Makes". See May *et al.* (2007), 459–74.

Wertheimer, A. 2007. "Exploitation in Health Care". In *Principles of Health Care Ethics*, 2nd edn, R. E. Ashcrof, A. Dawson, H. Draper & J. McMillan (eds), 247–54. Chichester: John Wiley and Sons.

——2008. "Exploitation in Clinical Research". In *Exploitation and Developing Countries: The Ethics of Clinical Research*, J. Hawkins & E. Emanuel (eds.), 63–104. Princeton, NJ: Princeton University Press.

Wettstein, F. 2009. *Multinational Corporations and Global Justice: Human Rights Obligations of a Quasi-Governmental Institution*. Stanford, CA: Stanford University Press.

——2010. "For Better or Worse: Corporate Social Responsibility Beyond 'Do No Harm'". *Business Ethics Quarterly* 20(2): 275–83.

——2012a. "CSR and the Debate on Business and Human Rights: Bridging the Great Divide". *Business Ethics Quarterly* 22(4): 739–70.

——2012b. "Human Rights as a Critique of Instrumental CSR: Corporate Responsibility Beyond the Business Case". *Notizie di POLITEIA* 28(106): 18–33.

Wheeler, N. J. 2000. *Saving Strangers: Humanitarian Intervention in International Society*. Oxford: Oxford University Press.

Wheeler, N. J. & J. Morris 1996. "Humanitarian Intervention and State Practice at the End of the Cold War". In *International Society after the Cold War*, J. Larkins & R. Fawn (eds.), 135–71. London: Macmillan.

Whelan, F. 1983. "Prologue: Democratic Theory and the Boundary Problem". *NOMOS XXV: Liberal Democracy*, J. R. Pennock & J. W. Chapman (eds), 13–47. New York: New York University Press.

White, S. 1997. "Freedom of Association and the Right to Exclude". *Journal of Political Philosophy* 5(4): 373–91.

Whitworth, S. 2004. *Men, Militarism and UN Peacekeeping: A Gendered Analysis*. Boulder, CO: Lynne Rienner.

Widdows, H. 2009. "Border Disputes Across Bodies: Exploitation in Trafficking for Prostitutions and Egg Sale for Stem Cell Research". *International Journal of Feminist Approaches to Bioethics* 2(1): 5–24.

——2011. *Global Ethics: An Introduction*. Durham: Acumen.

Wiens, D. forthcoming. "Natural Resources and Government Responsiveness". *Politics, Philosophy and Economics*. http://philpapers.org/rec/WIENRA (accessed December 2012).

Wiggins, D. 1998. "Claims of Need". In his *Needs, Values, Truth*, 3rd edn, 1–58. Oxford: Blackwell.

Wilkins, M. 2005. "Multinational Enterprise to 1930: Discontinuities and Continuities". See Chandler & Mazlish (2005), 45–79.

Williams, B. 1973. "A Critique of Utilitarianism". In *Utilitarianism: For and Against*, J. J. C. Smart & B. Williams, 77–150. Cambridge: Cambridge University Press.

——2005. "Humanitarianism and the Right to Intervene". In his *In the Beginning was the Deed: Realism and Moralism in Political Argument*, G. Hawthorn (ed.), 145–53. Princeton, NJ: Princeton University Press.

Williams, F. 2011. "Towards a Transnational Analysis of the Political Economy of Care". In *Feminist Ethics and Social Policy: Towards a New Global Political Economy of Care*, R. Mahon & F. Robinson (eds), 21–38. Vancouver: University of British Columbia Press.

Williams, J. C. & V. A. Zelizer 2005. "To Commodify or Not to Commodify: That is Not the Question". In *Rethinking Commodification*, M. M. Ertman & J. C. Williams (eds), 362–82. New York: New York University Press.

Williams, O. F. 2004. "The UN Global Compact: The Challenge and the Promise". *Business Ethics Quarterly* 14(4): 755–74.

Williamson, J. 1990. "What Washington Means by Policy Reform". In *Latin American Adjustment: How Much has Happened?*, J. Williamson (ed.), 7–20. Washington, DC: Institute for International Economics.

Wills, S. 2009. *Protecting Civilians: The Obligations of Peacekeepers*. Oxford: Oxford University Press.

Wilson, E. O. 1992. *The Diversity of Life*. Cambridge, MA: Harvard University Press.

Wilson, F. & M. Ramphele 1989. *Uprooting Poverty: The South African Challenge, Report for the Second Carnegie Inquiry into Poverty and Development in Southern Africa*. Cape Town: David Philip.

Windsor, D. 2001. "The Future of Corporate Social Responsibility". *International Journal of Organizational Analysis* 9(3): 225–56.

Winickoff, D. E. & L. B. Neumann 2005. "Towards a Social Contract for Genomics: Property and the Public in the 'Biotrust' Model". *Genomics, Society and Policy* 1(3): 8–21.

Winickoff, D. E. & R. N. Winickoff 2003. "The Charitable Trust as a Model for Genomic Biobanks". *New England Journal of Medicine* 349(12): 1180–84.

Wisor, S. 2012. "Property Rights and the Resource Curse: A Reply to Wenar". *Journal of Philosophical Research* 37: 185–204.

Wolf, S. 1985. "The Legal and Moral Responsibility of Organizations". In *NOMOS XXVII: Criminal Justice*, J. R. Pennock & J. W. Chapman (eds), 267–86. New York: New York University Press.

Wolfendale, J. 2007. *Torture and the Military Profession*. Basingstoke: Palgrave Macmillan.

Wong, D. B. 1984. *Moral Relativity*. Berkeley, CA: University of California Press.

——2006. *Natural Moralities: A Defence of Pluralistic Relativism*. Oxford: Oxford University Press.

Wong, D. & N. Hassoun 2011. *Conserving Nature; Preserving Identity*. Carnegie Mellon University Working Paper. Pittsburgh, PA: Carnegie Mellon University.

Wood, S. 2012. "The Case for Leverage-Based Corporate Human Rights Responsibility". *Business Ethics Quarterly* 22(1): 63–98.

Woodward, B. 2004. *Plan of Attack*. New York: Simon & Schuster.

Woodward, P. (ed.) 2001. *The Doctrine of Double Effect*. Notre Dame, IN: University of Notre Dame Press.

World Bank 1980. *Poverty and Human Development*. New York: Oxford University Press.

——2004a. *Assessing Aid: What Works, What Doesn't and Why*. Oxford: Oxford University Press.

——2004b *The Impact of Conditional Cash Transfer Programs: A Review of Evaluation Results*. Second International Workshop on Conditional Cash Transfer Panel. Oxford: Oxford University Press.

——2011. *Global Development Horizons: Multipolarity in International Finance*. Washington, DC: World Bank.

——2012 *World Development Report 2012: Gender Equality and Development*. Washington, DC: The World Bank. http://siteresources.worldbank.org/INTWDR2012/Resources/7778105–1299699968583/7786210–1315936222006/Complete-Report.pdf (accessed August 2012).

World Bank Group 2012. "What We Do". www.worldbank.org/en/about/what-we-do (accessed February 2013).

——2013a. "Board of Governors". www.worldbank.org/en/about/leadership/governors (accessed February 2013).

——2013b. "About Us – Who We Are". http://web.worldbank.org/WBSITE/EXTERNAL/EXTABOUTUS/0,contentMDK:20046292~menuPK:1696892~pagePK:51123644~piPK:329829~theSite PK:29708,00.html (accessed February 2013).

World Commission on Environment and Development 1987. *Our Common Future*. London: Oxford University Press.

World Economic Forum (WEF) 2011. *Global Risks 2011*, 6th edn. Geneva: World Economic Forum.

World Health Organization 2010. "WHO Guiding Principles on Human Cell, Tissue and Organ Transplantation". World Health Assembly 63.22/2010. www.who.int/transplantation/Guiding_PrinciplesTransplantation_WHA63.22en.pdf (accessed April 2012).

——2011a. "World Health Day 2011: Frequently Asked Questions". www.who.int/world-health-day/2011/presskit/WHD2011-QA-EN.pdf (accessed January 2014).

——2011b. "The Madrid Resolution on Organ Donation and Transplantation". *Transplantation* 91(suppl. 11): S29–S31.

——2011c. "Report of the Madrid Consultation Part 1: European and Universal Challenges in Organ Donation and Transplantation, Searching for Global Solutions". *Transplantation* 91(suppl. 11): S39–S66.

——2014. "10 Facts on Malaria". www.who.int/features/factfiles/malaria/en/ (accessed May 2014).

World Medical Association 2008. "WMA Declaration of Helsinki – Ethical Principles for Medical Research Involving Human Subjects". www.wma.net/en/30publications/10policies/b3/index.html (accessed October 2010).

World Trade Organization 1994. "The Uruguay Round". www.wto.org/english/thewto_e/whatis_e/tif_e/fact5_e.htm (accessed May 2014).

——2011a. "The WTO in Brief: Part 2". www.wto.org/english/thewto_e/whatis_e/inbrief_e/inbr02_e.htm (accessed September 2011).

——2011b. "Members and Observers". www.wto.org/english/thewto_e/whatis_e/tif_e/org6_e.htm (accessed September 2011).

——2011c. "Principles of the Trading System". www.wto.org/english/thewto_e/whatis_e/tif_e/fact2_e.htm (accessed September 2011).

Wynberg, R., D. Schroeder & R. Chennells (eds) 2009. *Indigenous Peoples, Consent and Benefit-Sharing*. Dordrecht: Springer.

Yeates, N. 2005. "A Global Political Economy of Care". *Social Policy and Society* 4(2): 227–34.

Yosuke, S. 2007. "The State of the International Organ Trade: A Provisional Picture Based on Integration of Available Information". *Bulletin of the World Health Organization* 85(12): 955–62.

Young, I. M. 1990. *Justice and the Politics of Difference*. Princeton, NJ: Princeton University Press.

——2003. "From Guilt to Solidarity: Sweatshops and Political Responsibility". *Dissent* 50(2): 39–44.

——2004. "Responsibility and Global Labor Justice". *Journal of Political Philosophy* 12(4): 365–88.

——2006. "Responsibility and Global Justice: A Social Connection Model". *Social Philosophy and Policy* 23(1): 102–30.

——2011. *Responsibility for Justice*. New York: Oxford University Press.

Zalk, S. R. & J. Gordon-Kelter (eds) 1992. *Revolutions in Knowledge: Feminism in the Social Sciences*. Boulder, CO: Westview Press.

Zheng, T. 2009. *Red Lights: The Lives of Sex Workers in Postsocialist China*. Minneapolis, MN: University of Minnesota Press.

Ziai, A. 2004. "The Ambivalence of Post-Development: Between Reactionary Populism and Radical Democracy". *Third World Quarterly* 25(5): 1045–60.

——(ed.) 2007. *Exploring Post-Development: Theory and Practice, Problems and Perspectives*. London: Routledge.

Žižek, S. 2007. "Knight of the Living Dead". *New York Times* (24 March). www.egs.edu/faculty/slavoj-zizek/articles/knight-of-the-living-dead.

Zlotogora, J. 2009. "Population Programs for the Detection of Couples at Risk for Severe Monogenic Genetic Diseases". *Human Genetics* 126(2): 247–53.

Zorn, T. E. & E. Collins 2007. "Is Sustainability Sustainable? Corporate Social Responsibility, Sustainable Business, and Management Fashion". See May *et al.* (2007), 405–16.

Zwolinski, M. 2007. "Sweatshops, Choice, and Exploitation". *Business Ethics Quarterly* 17: 689–727.

Zwolinski, M. & B. Powell 2011. "The Ethical and Economic Case Against Sweatshop Labor: A Critical Assessment". *Journal of Business Ethics* 107(4): 449–72.

INDEX

Please note that page numbers relating to Notes will have the letter "n" following the page number.

trafficking, 50, 214; defined, 281–82, 291; or smuggling, 281, 284–87; from prostitution to trafficking, 279–80; rise of, 280–81; Trafficking and Smuggling Protocols, 282, 286; VoTs (victims of trafficking), 282, 285, 286, 290–91; *see also* prostitution, and trafficking
tragedy of the anti-commons, 335, 339n
trans-border outsourcing, 10
transnational justice, 31, 34
transnational production networks (TPNs), 10, 16n
Transplantation Society, 322
transplant treatments, 321–22; organs for transplantation, 323; packages, 323
trespass view, pollution, 387, 388, 393–94, 398–99; future research directions, 398; *Mad Tea Party* case, 397–98; *vandal* cases, 395–97
trial-related injuries, 317–18
Trials of War Criminals before the Nuremberg Military Tribunals under Control Council Law No. 10 (1949), 307
TRIPS Agreement *see* Agreement on Trade-Related Aspects of Intellectual Property Rights (TRIPS)
Truman, Harry, Four Point Speech, 171, 177
trust, 58–59
Tunisia, 13
Turkmenistan, 144
Tuskegee syphilis study, US, 307
tyranny, and torture, 120–21

Uganda, 138
Ukraine, 144
Ulrich, P., 256, 260
UN Development Fund for Women, 57
uniformization, 5
UNITED for Intercultural Action, 288
United Kingdom, 12, 13, 15; Biobank, 337; and British Empire, 101; Food Ethics Council, 30; nuclear weapons development, 143; war power, 103
United Nations (UN): Charter *see* Charter, United Nations; Convention Against Corruption, 254, 255; Convention Against Transnational Organized Crime, 281; Convention on Biological Diversity, 310, 417; Convention on the Rights of the Child (1990), 352n, 353n; creation, 171; Economic and Social Council, 212; Funds and Programmes, 172; Global Compact, 253–54; Human Rights Commission, 264n; Millennium Development Goals (MDGs), 57, 163–64, 342; Protect, Respect and Remedy Framework, 254, 262; World Commission on Environment and Development, 175–76; World Summit Outcome Document (2005), 135
United Nations Conference on Trade and Development (UNCTAD), 211, 242, 264n

United Nations Development Programme (UNDP), 30, 162, 165, 180, 182, 211; Human Development Index, 34n, 166; Human Development Reports, 162, 170, 174
United Nations Framework Convention on Climate Change (UNFCCC), 372; Article 2, 374; Article 3.1, 373
United Nations General Assembly (UNGA), 181n, 281
United Nations High Commission for Refugees (UNHCR), 212
United Nations Security Council (UNSC), 103, 131, 132, 139; Resolutions, 101, 136
United States: Bill of Rights, 136; civil rights crusade (1960s), 101; Corporate Average Fuel Economy, 395; democracy deficit, 239; full democracy, 13; and global integration, 5, 7, 8, 12, 13; Government Accountability Office, 291n; hegemony, 8; and international law, prospects for, 58; National Organ Transplant Act (1984), 321; 9/11 terrorist attacks, 104, 111; nuclear weapons development, 142, 143; School of the Americas torture techniques, 113; torture in, 96, 113–26; war power, 103
Universal Declaration of Human Rights (1948), 72, 77, 92, 182, 253, 254, 365, 375
Universal Declaration on the Human Genome and Human Rights, 346
universalism, 19, 36, 82–94; of application, 23, 83–84; conflicting moralities, 90; of content, 88–89, 93, 94; contextual, 189; and cultural contexts, 79–80; and difference, 20, 23, 91–94; global business, universal moral standards for, 257–58; humanitarian intervention, 137; and human rights, 79–80, 83, 84, 90, 92; of justification, 23, 86, 89–90; and Kantianism, 83, 84; moral, 84, 89; and relativism, 23, 85–87; of structure, 23, 87–88; universalisms and anti-universalisms, 90–91; and utilitarianism, 83–84, 87
unmanned weapons systems, 107
Unnatural Alliance, The (Adams), 151n
Uprooting Poverty: The South African Challenge (Wilson and Ramphele), 167
Uruguay Round trade negotiations, 224
utilitarianism, 20, 23, 377, 430, 435; and aggregation, 431–35; and ethical theory, 24, 25, 26, 29; and gender and care, 51, 52; intergenerational social contract, 436; and justice, 36, 48n; and universalism, 83–84, 87
Uzbekistan, 144

Valentino, B. A., 139
Van Oosterhout, J., 256
Veatch, R., 333
Versailles, Treaty of (1919), 108, 143

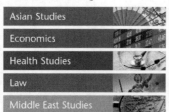